Applied Neuropsychology of Attention

The concept of attention in academic psychology has been treated with varying degrees of importance over the years. From playing a key role in the nineteenth century, it was discarded in the first half of the twentieth century, as clinical psychologists claimed it was superfluous to the essential subconscious processes of the mind, and experimental psychologists thought it was not a scientific term. *Applied Neuropsychology of Attention* aims to review the considerable developments in the field of attention over the last 20 years as it makes its comeback.

This collection of essays forms a comprehensive overview of this crucial component of human cognitive function. The book begins with an explanation of the essential theoretical concepts and definitions. Aspects of diagnosis are then discussed as the assessment and impairments of attention are reviewed in normal ageing and in specific neurological categories. Victims of brain injury and patients with cerebrovascular or neurodegenerative diseases are considered. A critical analysis of existing practices in cognitive rehabilitation is given and a review of the techniques and methodologies used for treating attentional disturbances brings the book to a conclusion.

Leclercq and Zimmermann have compiled a book of cutting-edge research which provides an effective framework to detect, analyse and understand the nature of attention deficit. The book will be invaluable to clinicians, mental health specialists and all academic psychologists in the field.

Michel Leclercq practises neuropsychology at the William Lennox Neurology Centre in Ottignies, Belgium, where he works with adult patients. **Peter Zimmermann** teaches in the Psychology Institute at Freiburg University and specialises in methodology, cognitive processes and neuropsychology.

Applied Neuropsychology of Attention

Theory, Diagnosis and Rehabilitation

Edited by Michel Leclercq and Peter Zimmermann

Routledge
Taylor & Francis Group
LONDON AND NEW YORK

First published 2002 by Psychology Press

Published 2022 by Routlege
2 Park Square, Milton Park, Abingdon, Oxon OX14 4RN
605 Third Avenue, New York, NY 10017

Routledge is an imprint of the Taylor & Francis Group, an informa business

Typeset in Garamond by RefineCatch Limited, Bungay, Suffolk
Cover design by Sandra Heath

Publisher's Note

The publisher has gone to great lengths to ensure the quality of this reprint but points out that some imperfections in the original copies may be apparent.

British Library Cataloguing in Publication Data
A catalogue record for this book is available from the British Library

Library of Congress Cataloging-in-Publication Data
Applied neuropsychology of attention: theory, diagnosis, and rehabilitation/[edited by] Michel Leclercq & Peter Zimmermann.
p. cm.
Includes bibliographical references and index.
ISBN 1–84169–188–7 (alk. paper)
1. Attention. 2. Psychology, Pathological. 3. Clinical neuropsychology. 4. Cognitive therapy. I. Leclercq, Michel, 1946– . II. Zimmermann, Peter, 1936– .
[DNLM: 1. Attention. 2. Brain Diseases—physiopathology. 3. Brain Diseases—diagnosis. 4. Brain Diseases—therapy. 5. Neuropsychological Tests. WL 348 A652 2002]
RC455.4.A85 A67 2002
616.8—dc21 2001043109

ISBN 13: 978-0-415-65356-5 (pbk)
ISBN 13: 978-1-84169-188-6 (hbk)

Contents

List of contributors

Prof. Philippe AZOUVI, MD, PhD, Professor of Physical Medicine and Rehabilitation, Department of Neurological Rehabilitation and Formation de Recherche Claude Bernard, Raymond Poincare Hospital, René Descartes University, F 92380 Garches, France.

Prof. Wiebo H. BROUWER, Professor of Clinical Neuropsychology and Gerontology at the Department of Clinical and Developmental Psychology, University of Groningen. Department of Neuropsychology AZG, P.O. Box 30001, NL 9700 RB Groningen, the Netherlands.

Anna CANTAGALLO, MD, Director of Neuropsychological Rehabilitation, Department of Rehabilitation, Hospital and University of Ferrara, Unità Operativa di Medicina Riabilitativa (UOMR), via Boschetto, 20, I 44100 Ferrara, Italy.

Barbara CARACCIOLO, Research Assistant at the Rehabilitation Center San Raffaele Pisana, 235, Via della Pisana , I 00163 Rome, Italy.

Fabienne COLLETTE, Post-doctoral Researcher at the Belgian National Fund for Scientific Research (FNRS) Neuropsychology Unit, University of Liège, Boulevard du Rectorat, B.33, B 4000 Liège, Belgium.

Nadjette CREMEL, Psychologist, Service de Neuropsychologie et de Rééducation du Langage, Clinique Neurologique, HUS, B.P. 426, F 67091 Strasbourg, France.

Prof. Gérard DELOCHE, Professor of Neuropsychology and Dean of the Faculty of Human Sciences at University of Reims, U.F.R. Lettres et Sciences Humaines, 57, rue Pierre Taitinger, F 51096 Reims, France.

Dr. Bruno FIMM, Clinical Neuropsychologist, Department of Neurology, Section of Neuropsychology, 30, Pauwelstraße, D 52074 Aachen, Germany.

Michel LECLERCQ, Clinical Neuropsychologist, Centre Neurologique William Lennox, B 1340 Ottignies, Belgium.

Dr. Pierre NORTH, Conventioned Professor at the University Louis Pasteur at Strasbourg, Coordinating Doctor of UEROS, Centre of Revalidation at Mulhouse. Contact address: 5, rue Gustave Doré, F 67000 Strasbourg, France.

Dr. Anne PASSADORI, Assistant Doctor of UEROS, Centre of Revalidation at Mulhouse, 57, rue Albert Camus, F 68093 Mulhouse, France.

Luigi PIZZAMIGLIO, Professor of Neuropsychology, University of Roma La Sapienza, Department of Psychology, Via dei Marsi, 78, I 00185 Rome, Italy.

Dr. Marc ROUSSEAUX, MD, PhD, Neurologist and specialist in Physical Medicine and Rehabilitation, Psychologist. Head of Department of Neurological Rehabilitation, Hôpital Swynghedauw, Centre Hospitalier Universitaire, F 59037 Lille, France.

Prof. Dr. Walter STURM, Head of the section 'Clinical Neuropsychology', Neurologische Klinik, 30, Pauwelstrasse, D 52057 Aachen, Germany.

Prof. Martial VAN der LINDEN, Professor of Psychopathology and Neuropsychology in the University of Geneva (Switzerland) and in the University of Liège. Service de Neuropsychologie, Boulevard du Rectorat, B.33, B 4000 Liège, Belgium.

Dr. Peter ZIMMERMANN, Associated Professor at the Psychological Institute of the University of Freiburg, Psychologische Institut, Niemenstrasse, 10, D 79085 Freiburg, Germany.

Prof. Pierluigi ZOCCOLOTTI, Professor of Psychology of Perception in the Department of Psychology of the University of Roma and Neuropsychology, consultant in the Research Center Fondazione Santa Lucia at Roma. Contact addresses: University of Rome La Sapienza, Department of Psychology, Via dei Marsi, 78, I 00185 Rome, Italy, and Research Center, Fondazione Santa Lucia, Via Ardeatina, 306, I 00179 Rome, Italy.

Foreword

When I first read the manuscript of this book, two thoughts came to my mind: that it is clearly a European enterprise, and that it has a very long historical background.

In times past, attention was a key concept in academic psychology. The introspecting psychologists of the nineteenth century ascribed a central role to attention. Even in 1908, Titchener, a British student of Wundt, wrote that 'the doctrine of attention is the nerve of the whole psychological system'. However, new schools in psychology arose and discarded this central concept. Psychoanalysis had no use for attention, as the essential processes in the mind were supposed to be unconscious. Likewise, Gestalt psychology did not embrace the concept of attention, as perception and other cognitive processes were supposed to be ruled by 'laws' that were not under the control of the subject. Behaviourism had no need for attention as the theorists of this school considered behaviour to be ruled completely by laws from learning theory: between S and R, attention seemed a superfluous concept.

Still, attention did not disappear completely: it survived in several forms in applied disciplines such as clinical neurology and clinical psychology. Neurologists with an interest in behaviour went on using bedside tests of attention, usually methods to test 'mental control' by placing a certain load on working memory. Serial Sevens, the serial subtracting of 7 from 100, is a well-known example. In this way, neurologists tested the ability of their patients to concentrate on a cognitive task. In clinical psychology and in industrial psychology, several tests were used to assess the ability of subjects to work quickly and efficiently in visual search tasks. Well-known European examples are the Bourdon dot configuration task and the Brickenkamp d2 test. Apparently, although academic psychology had dismissed the concept of attention, it could not be dismissed in practice.

More or less abruptly, attention made its comeback after World War II. It had been noted in wartime conditions that soldiers and sailors, keeping watch at radar screens or with sonar devices, lost their ability to detect signals rapidly. Also, in industry it had been observed that workers had a limited capacity in the monitoring of complex control panels. These practical problems inspired the famous research on vigilance by Mackworth as well as the 'information processing approach' in experimental psychology. In this approach, largely based on the mathematical information theory and the computer metaphor, man is seen as an information processing system. Many readers of this book will be familiar with the rapid developments and the coming and going of theoretical models in the second half of the twentieth century. This evolution was documented in the series of books 'Attention and Performance', with contributions by cognitive psychologists from various schools of thought (the opening chapter of this book presents a highly readable review of the successive models). However, this rapid growth was not without problems. In particular, numerous ill-defined concepts of attention came into being, which inspired Moray in 1969 to the gloomy statement that the terminology related to the subject of attention was 'at best confusing and at worst a mess'.

Although attention had never been completely absent from clinical neurology and clinical psychology, it can still be argued that attention made a remarkable comeback in these fields too. After 1970, when neuropsychology had developed into a discipline with its own identity and journals, the word 'attention' began to appear in titles of articles, and, at a later stage, in book titles. It seems that clinical investigators tackled the old problems of attentional impairments with a new vigour, assisted this time by experimental psychologists with a lively interest in clinical questions. However, students of attention now looked at 'attention' quite differently from the armchair psychologists of the nineteenth century. In particular, attention was operationalized in paradigms derived from sound theoretical models. Also, assessment of attention now had to meet standards of validity and reliability that had been developed in psychometric theory and in statistics. Furthermore, there was a tendency to define aspects of attention more precisely. In other words, there seemed to be a growing awareness that 'Moray's mess' should be avoided as much as possible.

The present book fits perfectly in this historical evolution. Attention is back, particularly in Europe where the concept first came into being. In this volume, attention is considered and discussed as a central concept in applied neuropsychology. The first part of the book deals with essential theoretical aspects and with definitions. Next, the book reviews assessment of attention and impairments of attention in the three largest categories of neurologic patients (i.e. those with cerebrovascular diseases, neurodegenerative diseases and brain injury). Finally, the book presents two chapters on the cognitive rehabilitation of attentional impairments – reflecting the editors' view that assessment, based on sound theory, is not the last step, but rather a basis for attempts to improve the performance of patients.

I must confess that this book contains so many clever views and new ideas that I felt an immediate urge to rewrite everything I have published on attention (after head injury) in the past. Many chapters even made me feel slightly guilty, as they made me face the question of why I had never come up with these clever ideas myself. Anyway, this feeling illustrates that the neuropsychology of attention has indeed developed rapidly.This book gives an admirable overview of the state of the art, and I hope that many readers will perceive it as a goldmine of ideas – as I did.

Adriaan H. van Zomeren
Groningen, May 2001

Preface

In the last two decades, attentional deficiencies after brain lesions, their diagnosis and their treatment, have become one of the central challenges in clinical neuropsychology. Progress has been made by the insight that the concept of attention implies a bundle of more specific functions, opening new roads for diagnosis and treatment. With this background, it seems the right moment to attempt a synopsis of the various forms of attentional deficiencies and their manifestation in different forms of brain lesions and diseases. But we attempt this with the humble insight that there is no close link between specific brain damage and circumscribed losses in attentional performance; as the clinician knows, each patient has his own pattern of losses which demands a straight differential diagnosis.

The project of this book was born in the scope of a concerted action supported by the European Communities: the Biomedical Health Research programme (BIOMED 1). The main aim of this programme was to encourage closer European collaboration and to improve the efficiency of national research efforts in selected topics. Most of the contributors to this book were members of the workshop 'Attention'. In this workshop, several years of close collaboration were devoted to the development, normalization and validation of specific tools for assessing attentional functions, on the one hand, and to a multicentric study concerning the rehabilitation of attentional disorders, on the other.

At the end of this workshop, participants agreed about the value of bringing together their views on the state of the field, concentrating on the aspects liable to be of interest more particularly to the professionals involved at a clinical level. The task was distributed according to the affinities of each participant for particular aspects of the field. The work was completed thanks to the contribution of some colleagues who did not participate in the original workshop, but who agreed to cover specific aspects.

We want to warmly thank here all the colleagues who have contributed to this work. We wish also to thank those whose help with the presentation of this book was invaluable: William Lay, John and Jacqueline Rush. Furthermore, this book would not have been possible without the support and efforts of the team at Psychology Press, especially Caroline Osborne, Rachel Brazil, Paul Dukes and Lucy Farr.

About the state of advancement of our knowledge concerning the attentional mechanisms and functioning, Cohen wrote in 1993: 'Even though progress has been made toward an understanding of the processes of attention, the neuropsychology of attention is still in its infancy' (*Neuropsychology of Attention*, New York: Plenum Press, p. 9). Today this statement remains true, but we hope that this work will contribute to show that this child is growing up and that its future is promising.

Michel Leclercq and Peter Zimmermann
May 2001

Part I

Theory

Chapter 1

Theoretical aspects of the main components and functions of attention

Michel Leclercq

Different possibilities exist in relation to the presentation of the numerous and at first sight relatively disparate data coming from research in the attention domain. We propose here a presentation organized on the basis of the main attentional components, an option that in our opinion presents several merits. First of all, and in spite of the apparent heterogeneity of currently available data, it enables both a descriptive and a comprehensive analysis of the different attentional aspects. Indeed, as we will attempt to show, most of the observations emanating from specific research on attention can be gathered and reorganized around the main concepts currently used to describe attentional phenomena. Moreover this type of presentation presents an evident practical interest: it offers those involved in this field a tool which allows them to orient both the type and the methodology of analysis, and so the interpretation of the observations collected; more specifically it allows clinicians to intervene if the case arises, in a manner which is specific, adequate and therefore efficient. Finally, this type of presentation will allow us to detail the main notions specific to each attentional component. Indeed, although an increasingly large consensus is emerging, some confusion still exists about the use of some of these concepts and their specific significance. We hope that this presentation, despite its own limitations, will help to promote this 'conceptual unity' and, consequently, will increase the recourse to a common vocabulary for everyone, whether student, researcher or clinician.

We will intentionally limit this presentation to the relatively 'elementary' attentional aspects, i.e. those implied in usually simple tasks (detection, analysis and/or selection of not very complex physical or semantic stimuli), to the detriment of the attentional aspects intervening during the resolution of complex situations and requiring highly elaborated cognitive operations such as reasoning, programming, planning, etc. For these latter aspects, we refer the reader to specific publications (among others Cohen, 1993; Shallice, 1988; van Zomeren and Brouwer, 1994).

1 Selective or focal attention

Selective attention corresponds to the most current and common use of the general term 'attention': the ability of the subject to process selectively some events to the detriment of others. This corresponds to the first attempt at definition proposed by James (1890):

> It is the taking possession of the mind, in clear and vivid form, of one out of what seem several simultaneously possible objects or trains of thought. Focalisation, concentration, of consciousness are of its essence. It implies withdrawal from some things in order to deal effectively with others.
>
> (pp. 403–404)

The multitude of information with which we are continually confronted requires from us prior selection without which we would be totally submerged by stimulations and unable to process any of these efficiently. This imperative necessity of information selection will be at the root of the first attempts at modelling in the attention field.

1.1 Auditory selective attention

The abundance of contemporary studies on visual attention tends to ignore the fact that it was auditory attention that formed the core of the first specific studies, for about fifteen years. Most authors agree in attributing to Colin Cherry (1953) the first systematic studies with a cognitive orientation in the attention field, and more specifically those dealing with selective attention. She developed the paradigm of dichotic listening: an auditory message sent to one ear must be repeated aloud by the subject ('shadowing') while a second message which he/she has to ignore is sent to the other ear. By using this technique, Cherry and others after her observed:

- The facilitation of the subject's capacities of selective attention when messages are spatially distinct (Cherry, 1953); indeed, whereas subjects show marked difficulties in separating two messages stated by the same voice and reaching the two ears simultaneously, they are, however, easily able to discriminate these messages when they are delivered simultaneously, one to the left ear and the other to the right ear.
- Very little information seems to be extracted from the non-relevant message, i.e. the message on which the subject's selective attention is *not* focused. For example, one will observe the almost complete absence of memorization of a short list of items integrated into the unattended message, despite the fact that this list was read out more than 35 times (Moray, 1959).
- On the other hand, physical changes, such as the speaker's gender

(Treisman, 1960), the use of a different language for each message (Treisman, 1964), the voice intensity or the arbitrary insertion of a pure sound, were almost systematically detected (Cherry, 1953).

These observations allow us to assert that selective auditory attention is strongly improved by being able to discriminate the physical attributes of the message to be processed; on the other hand, selective discrimination in the binaural task is very difficult when it can only be based on the meaning of messages.

Broadbent (1958) was the first author to propose a model attempting to deal with the totality of data we have just described: the early filtering model. You will find a representation of this model in Figure 1.1. The author based his model on an observation that he considered crucial: the subject repeated aloud according to the spatial origin of the messages. Thus, for example, if A-C-E is delivered in one ear of the patient and B-D-F in his/her other ear, the subject shadowed either 'A-C-E' or 'B-D-F' according to whether his/her attention was selectively oriented on one or the other message. This observation confirmed quite well the importance of physical attributes – the spatial origin of the message, i.e. the ear to which the message is delivered – to the detriment of other factors such as the sequential chronology; the subject would then have evoked 'A-B-C' and 'D-E-F', re-establishing the classical chronology. According to Broadbent, this observation proves that the information had been 'serialized' by channel. He considered that the nervous system behaves in some ways as a single communication channel which can be considered as having a limited capacity.

The functional description of this model is as follows: the simultaneously presented stimuli or messages reach parallel sensory receptors from which they are transferred into short-term memory. Up to this point, all this

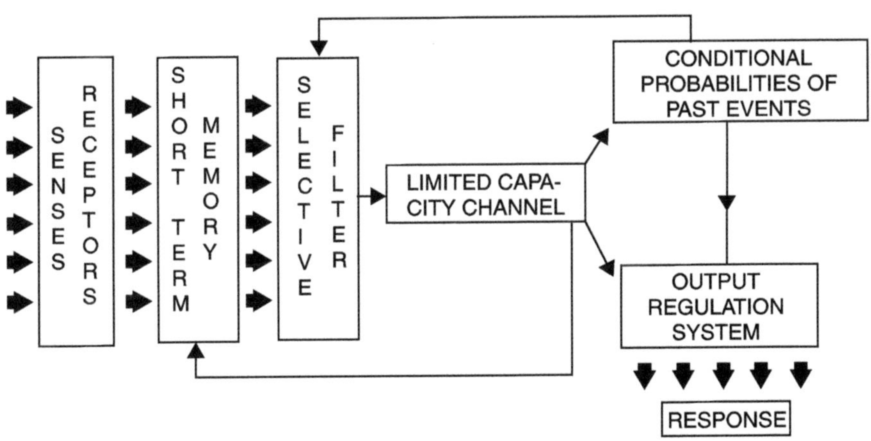

Figure 1.1 Broadbent's filter model (adapted from Broadbent, 1958)

information reaching the system is superficially processed in parallel. At this stage, the system has to select among all the stimuli those that will penetrate in the deep and serial channel of limited capacity. This selection will operate from a mechanism of filtering based upon the physical features of inputs. This filtering is adjusted by conditional probabilities of past events stored in long-term memory. The inputs that have not gone through the filter are maintained only a short time in the buffer and vanish quickly if they are not processed. However, a mental repetition loop allows the afferent information to stay in the short-term memory, and this at the expense of the transmission capacity of the serial channel. As Lecas (1992) points out:

> Since at the entry of the system the multiplicity of our sensory receptors is organized in parallel and at the exit only one single action is produced out at the time, the postulate of serialty is a logical and reasonable principle for the modellization, to which the notion of overload adds a sort of empirical confirmation.
>
> (p. 44, our translation)

This Broadbent model is qualified as 'early' or 'peripheral' filtering, as the selection is operating in the first stages of processing and is based on general physical features of the signal.

In spite of a considerable stir in the scientific community, this model was rapidly disproved. Indeed, several studies demonstrated that the selection does not depend only on elementary physical characteristics of the message.

Thus, a small modification in Broadbent's experimentation, considered as crucial by him, completely modifies the results. Indeed, Gray and Wedderburn (1960) used a task version of dichotic listening in which a message, such as 'Who 2 there', was presented to one ear, while '3 goes 9' was at the same time presented to the other. In this case the preferential order in which the data were repeated by the subjects was not ear by ear but determined by meaning, namely: 'Who goes there' followed by '3 2 9'. This observation indicates that the selection can operate from aspects other than purely physical characteristics of inputs. The same authors also presented in rapid succession and alternately to each ear some target words fragmented beforehand into syllables. They observed that subjects were able to recognize easily these words. This implies a complete (semantic) analysis of the information from the two ears and a rapid attentional switching by the subject from one channel to the other, the commutation allowing the reconstitution of the fragmented message. Selection possibly based on the meaning is incompatible with the filter theory.

In another study, Allport, Antonis and Reynolds (1972) combined text passages with the learning of words presented auditorily. The recognition performances evaluated at the end of shadowing were haphazard. This absence of memorization was expected on the basis of Broadbent's filter theory.

However, the authors demonstrated that the memorization became effective when the shadowing task was combined with the visual presentation of the written words. Moreover, when the same task was combined with the presentation of pictures, iconic memorization became excellent (90% success). This observation shows that limitations of simultaneous processing of two inputs are not as rigid as those expected from the Broadbent model. More precisely, if the two inputs are dissimilar, for example according to the sensory modality presentation, it becomes possible to process them simultaneously in a more complete manner than the filter theory predicted.

Moray (1959) carried out research in which he asked subjects not only to repeat aloud the message coming from the attended channel but also, if they heard them, to react to some orders inserted in the unattended channel. Half of these orders were preceded by strongly emotional words such as swear words, the other half being preceded by neutral words. Subjects were able to react to 51% of orders preceded by a highly emotional word, versus only 11% of orders preceded by a neutral word.

In other respects, the importance of the degree of expertise in a dichotic listening task was demonstrated by Underwood (1974) during an experiment in which subjects were asked to attempt to detect a single digit inserted either in the targeted or in the unattended message. Inexperienced subjects detected only 8.3% of the digits inserted in the unattended message, which suggests a very limited processing of this channel. When the same task was performed by Neville Moray, the researcher having submitted himself to many experiences in dichotic listening, he detected 66.7% of the digits inserted in the unattended channel.

Finally, Treisman (1960) carried out research in which the two channels were switched without warning the subjects. Thus, on several occasions, the channel targeted by the subject became the unattended channel and vice versa. The subject's attention was continuously oriented towards the same headphone, the task being to repeat aloud the delivered message to this ear. The author observed that subjects demonstrated a marked tendency to continue shadowing the unattended message for at least one or two seconds after the channel switching, for as long as the content of the unattended message could constitute semantically the logical continuation of the first one, as in the following example:

> Attended channel: leaving on her passage an impression of *grace and* / is idiotic idea of . . .
> Unattended channel: singing men and then it was jumping in the tree/ *charm and a*. . . .

Therefore, none of these observations is compatible with the idea defended by Broadbent according to which selective processing would be limited to purely physical characteristics of the information. Other aspects can be considerable determining factors at the selection level, as for example the meaning of the message.

Treisman (1960) proposed a revised version of Broadbent's model: the attenuator model (Figure 1.2). Instead of totally rejecting the filter notion, she gave it a new function, more 'nuancé'. Rather than excluding purely and simply the information that did not share some common characteristics with the attended message, she proposed a hierarchical model in which information processing could work at a double level: first, through an 'acoustical' filter analysing sensorial inputs from their physical dimensions (intensity, tonality, position, etc.), and undertaking a first sorting before their possible transmission to the recognition system in long-term memory. After this first filtering a discrimination would be operated by the more or less marked raising of the mnesic unit threshold intervening in the recognition. The attenuator works in such a way that only the unattended message elements that have a sufficiently low activation threshold could cross the whole system to be completely processed; the other elements, which did not reach a sufficient activation level, not being processed.

Thus, in the schematic representation in Figure 1.2, thresholds of words B and C will be lowered because of their high occurrence probability after the word A is processed into the target channel. Activation by means of the unattended channel increases the probability that C is heard by the subject. C could possibly be processed because it constitutes 'a unit in the word-matching system which had been made more sensitive or more available by high transition probabilities' (p. 247). Thus, in Moray's experiment (1959) described above, most of the neutral words in the unattended message will never be heard whereas swear words, even attenuated, will activate the appropriate elements and will be completely processed.

Considering that the two levels of the Treisman model are redundant, Anthony and Diana Deutsch (1963) proposed a model directly centred on recognition mechanisms in memory. These authors construct their model on

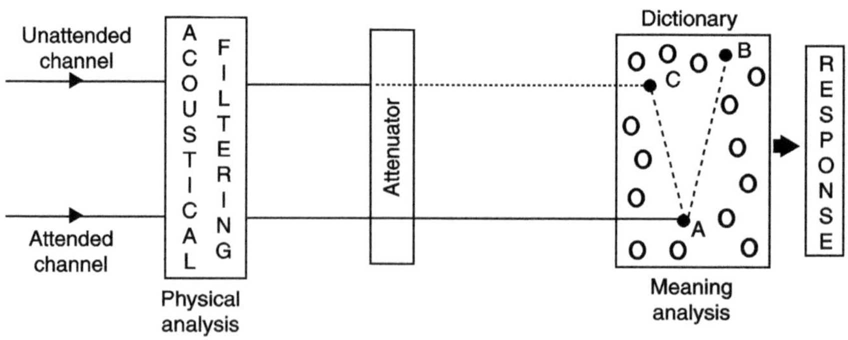

Figure 1.2 Treisman's attenuator model (adapted from Treisman, 1960)

the basis of a collection of neurophysiological data. They consider that all the inputs are completely analysed before any selection. Contrary to the Broadbent and Treisman models, the filter or bottleneck would be placed downhill from the processing system, just before the emission of response. So, it is here a 'late' filtering theory. Indeed, the selection operates only after the message has been processed up to a point which allows the subject to determine its possible relationship to the other messages. Such processing is situated beyond the stimulus level and implies some degree of semantic analysis. Selection operates not only from physical characteristics but indeed from some semantic aspects in the ultimate processing stage. It would depend on the importance or relative pertinence of concurrent messages according to the situation and the needs of the organism. Input and memory representation matching could trigger off an activity, the extent of which could depend on weighting, itself dependent on the subject's past experience. This theory is particularly expensive requiring a complete analysis of all the stimuli appearing at the system entry. Despite this it is still very popular.

Norman's model (1968) attempts to reconcile the concern to limit extensive deep processing to a limited number of stimuli with the fact that some elements of the unattended message may be fully processed. According to this author, a pertinence index would be assigned to each signal along the chain of processing. Only signals with a sufficiently high index would be processed more deeply. This pertinence index can vary according to the result of the successive stages of processing. Thus, a pertinent message at the beginning of the chain can see a gradually decreasing valence during further processing. At the end of the processing, only some elements – and perhaps none – will actually be selected. This system is then able to discard the non-relevant elements from the early processing stages (Broadbent, 1958; Treisman, 1960), just as during the late stages of processing (Deutsch and Deutsch, 1963), relieving the potential processing demands on the system.

In this model, there is no longer a bottleneck as such which would constitute a fixed, rigid structure: selection can intervene at any given time and at any point of the chain of processing according to the limitations that the system imposes on itself. The system acts continuously according to the demands and constraints that are imposed upon it. The single limit with which the organism is confronted is the available processing capacity and the imperative necessity to remain within it. The concept of limitation of processing resources will play a central role in theoretical developments aiming to explain divided attention phenomena, developments to which we shall later see that Norman has largely contributed.

But as pointed out by Hirst (1986), 'This model, however, signals the downfall of the bottleneck metaphor', in the sense that the structural aspect (filter) is replaced by a functional mechanism (processing capacity). Indeed, the author explicitly considers that there is no constitutive element of the system, no obligatory crossing point for the information where it would be submitted to some limitations imposed by the system itself. 'There is no bottleneck, then; just a limited processing capacity that the organism must constantly struggle to stay within' (Hirst, 1986, p. 113).

Finally, to the different models that we have described, one must add Neisser's model (1976). Neisser also attempted to develop a theoretical position aiming to eliminate the role of an attentional filter. In this author's conception, the subject would select information that he/she considers pertinent according to his/her current expectations, previous experiences and *schemata*. Other information will simply be ignored. Apart from some exceptions, stimuli or thoughts incompatible with the current schema would have no access to the subject's awareness. Neisser makes the distinction between, on the one hand, the existence of innate schemata which are continuously active, such as those which orient the attention towards important noises, pain or sudden environmental modifications, and, on the other hand, other schemata which develop themselves during the subject's own experiences.

The author's definition of the schema is very large: 'That portion of the entire perceptual cycle which is internal to the perceiver, modifiable by experience, and somehow specific to what is being perceived.' According to Neisser, the schema constitutes what allows the subject to sample and to select, within the environment, relevant information for the current action, from anticipation linked to his/her expectations and past experiences; with this experience, schemata will modify themselves to become progressively more efficient. This notion of schema, central in Neisser's conception, must be replaced in a dynamic view of perception, i.e. quite different from an isolated system whose main function would only consist in capturing stimuli considered as neutral.

By emphasizing some aspects ignored by filtering models, Neisser's conception resolves different problems: the importance of the subject's expectations, of past experience and thus of learning, the aimed goal and the perceptual content. What previously was considered as attention becomes now a function of the current schema. However, this top-down model does not easily explain the subject's capacity to capture immediately the meaning of new, unexpected or unpredictable stimuli. So, for instance, when changing from one TV channel to another, we are able to decode immediately the picture on the screen, even when it has absolutely no perceptual and/or semantic relationship with the preceding one.

In fact, one can consider the two types of models as complementary. In some way, filter theory describes structures triggered by schemata. In combination, these two theoretical currents lead to a more comprehensive view of the role of attention: schemata determine *why* something is selected whereas filter theories describe *how* things happen and the constraints to which is submitted the analysis of the diversity of signals composing the environment. This fundamental notion of schema is found in some further theoretical developments, including some attempts at modelling which aim to take into account the most complex attentional aspects (Norman and Shallice, 1980, 1986; Shallice, 1982, 1988; 'Script': Schank and Abelson, 1977; 'Memory Organisation Packets' (MOPs): Schank, 1982; 'Managerial Knowledge Units' (MKU): Grafman, 1989).

Although the dichotic listening paradigm was still used in a lot of research concerning the study of hemispheric specialization or dominance, the 1970s saw the progressive decline of the use of this technique in auditory selective attention studies. This decline was mainly linked to two factors. First, the ambiguity surrounding the term 'information channel', a central concept in most of the models we have described above. As is underlined by Lecas (1992):

> When a subject receives two differents messages in his/her headphones, the term 'channel' refers to an abstract entity that does not concern the physical distinction between the two receiving ears, but a *meaningful* content. It is yet intriguing that this notion of channel, which in the beginning had a general meaning (system entry, or material initially submitted to attention, or also anatomical structures of transit), has finally been specified only by the attentional *operational effect* which for comprehension's sake is at the basis of the separation of wording. Such a use of the term 'channel' has obvious aspects of circularity. The problem comes from the fact that an 'information channel' is arbitrarily defined since the word information has no precise meaning (every event is an information), while at the same time *necessarily* implying a processing mechanism. In fact, these two notions define each other mutually. . . . Confusion between information/meaning is a serious logical error that forbids any analytical approach by assimilating the initial material with the outcome of a process.
>
> (pp. 48–49, our translation)

The second factor which led to the progressive abandoning of dichotic listening in studies of auditory attention is the observation of involuntary, automatic semantic processing, operating without the subject's knowledge. Indeed, the first studies suffered from an important limitation: based on the lack of the subject's awareness of the meaning of the unattended message, they postulated the absence of processing of the meaning of this message on which the attention was not deliberately oriented. In fact, different studies have demonstrated that, under some conditions, the meaning of the unattended message can be processed in spite of the fact that the subject is not aware of it. These studies have showed that recognition operations of the spoken language are assisted by some automatic processes independent of the voluntary attention which the first models attempted to explain. These automatic processes concern the totality of the processing chain: they are situated at a subliminal level from the receptive phase up to and including response emission. Later we will come back to this differentiation between automatic and voluntary processing. At present, we will review some studies which have demonstrated in selective auditory attention the existence of involuntary automatic semantic processing, of which the subject is not aware.

Thus, for example, Lewis (1970) showed that signals inserted in the unattended channel could significantly interfere (word rate correctly repeated aloud) with those of the attended channel if the two words were semantically related. Lackner and Garrett (1972) and MacKay (1973) made similar observations for sentences.

In two famous experiments (Corteen and Wood, 1972; Corteen and Dunn, 1974), the authors presented the subjects with a list of words which included, among others, names of cities. With each city name was associated a slight electrical shock. A significant psychogalvanic response was recorded when in dichotic listening the same names were inserted in the unattended message and this despite the fact that, focalizing their attention on the attended channel, subjects were not aware of the presentation of the same names of cities in the distractor channel. Moreover, these authors can demonstrate the existence of a generalization phenomenon: the psychogalvanic response was also recorded when some city names different from the first list were inserted in the attended channel.

A similar experiment showing involuntary processing working unbeknown to the subject was carried out by Von Wright, Anderson and Stenman (1975). In a first stage, subjects were requested to pay attention to a long list of words. An electrical shock was associated with the appearance of a specific word within the list. In a second stage and in dichotic listening, subjects shadowed a list of words presented on the attended channel, while being instructed to ignore the simultaneously presented list on the distractor channel. When the word earlier associated with the electrical shock was presented in the unattended channel, a significant galvanic response was recorded. This response was also present when a word phonologically or semantically close to that with which the electrical shock had beforehand been associated was included in the unattended channel (generalization).

So, these observations indicate quite clearly that the information from the unattended message can be processed both at a physical (sound) and at a semantic (meaning) level, even if subjects are not aware of its presence. Nevertheless, it is necessary to underline that in these experiments, just as in other similar ones, galvanic responses were effective only for part of the trials. Moreover, the response amplitude was frequently attenuated comparatively to the psychogalvanic reactions following the detection in the attended channel of a word with which the electrical shock had been beforehand associated. It seems therefore that processing of stimuli coming from the channel on which the attention is not preferentially directed is neither systematic, nor always complete. Nevertheless, these observations clearly show the existence of processing of information towards which the attention is not voluntarily directed, even if this processing is only partial or limited. This involuntary processing can be deep, i.e. semantic. It can present some degree of semantic and/or phonological generalization while operating in the absence of any awareness by the subject.

These attempts at modelling of selective attention in auditory modality have the merit of circumscribing different parameters that will prove crucial for subsequent research. Indeed, whereas this research will tend to concentrate on the visual modality, it will be directly inspired by different concepts elaborated in the studies that we have described: limited processing capacity, notion of schema, voluntary versus automatic processing, etc. Apart from the fact that the question concerning early or late information processing remains now largely debated, this research will have to take into consideration the main parameters modulating the attentional efficiency that these first attempts at formalization have helped to bring to the fore, namely:

- the subject's capacity to orient preferentially his/her attention to a specific source of information;
- the physical particularities of the stimuli, their meaning and emotional load;
- the subject's expectations and his/her degree of expertise.

1.2 Visual selective attention

In the broad corpus of research and observation concerning visual selective attention, we will limit ourselves to three aspects, namely:

(a) Spatial focalization of attention within the visual field.
(b) Spatial orientation of attention within the visual field.
(c) The integrative function of attention in perception.

1.2.1 Spatial focalization of attention within the visual field

As we have seen above, whereas the filter metaphor was used to illustrate some theories of attention in the auditory modality, the use of the spotlight metaphor is classically used to illustrate the aspects specific to the visual modality. Indeed, visual attention is comparable to a light beam, i.e. a selective lighting with a certain intensity, which would correspond to the degree of attentional investment. This beam is mobile, its obvious motions being underlain by head or eye movements, and in some situations by trunk movements. The extent of the field so scanned varies from one situation to another, its adjustment being dependent on the degree of attentional focalization required by the task: the stimuli being found in a relatively narrow field will be perceived (processed) in a very precise manner (deep) to the detriment of the elements situated outside the attentional field. As underlined by van

Zomeren and Brouwer (1994): '[This metaphor is] used in a general sense in which the spotlight is a metaphor for selection enhancement possible at different levels of perceptual, cognitive and motor representation. Theories of attention specify how the movement and intensity of the spotlight are regulated and sustained' (p. 7). But is the recourse to this metaphor justified?

Convincing observations justifying this metaphor were made by LaBerge (1983). In this study, the author presented subjects with words and non-words always composed of five letters. In one experimental condition, he asked subjects to focalize their attention on the central letter of the word or non-word by asking them to determine if this letter was included in the set formed by letters A to G; in this case, subjects had to press a response key. In a second condition, the author asked subjects to categorize the word in its entirety (semantic categorization), the hypothesis being that this instruction would bring the subjects to adopt a larger attentional beam. In this condition, subjects had to press the response key when a particular word appeared and had to refrain from any reaction on the presentation of another word. What is more, from time to time a target (digit 7) requiring a rapid response was presented instead of or immediately after the word or non-word in the same position as one of the five letters. The main results are illustrated in Figure 1.3.

If attentional focalization is comparable to a luminous beam, one can reasonably suppose that the target (digit) detection time will be shorter if the target is situated inside the attentional beam, and longer if the target is outside. Results indicate clearly that there is adjustment of the attentional spotlight according to the constraints of the task. In the condition requiring the categorization of words, the attentional beam is large and therefore systematically elicits a short reaction time (RT) since attention is every time pre-oriented towards the target. On the other hand, in the condition requiring

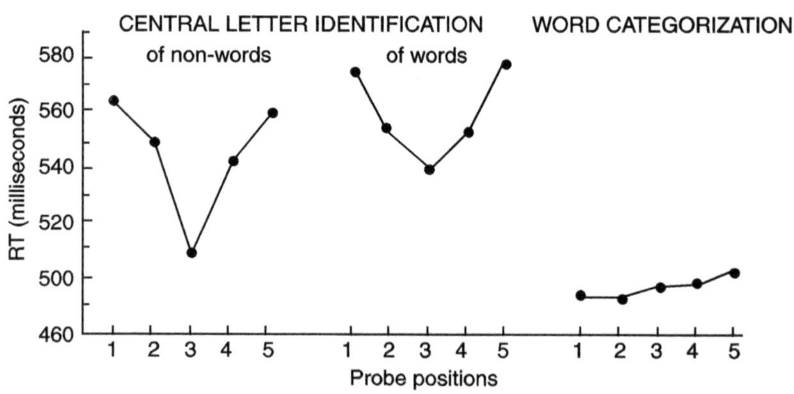

Figure 1.3 Average RTs to the target according to its occurrence location and the spatial pre-orientation of the attention (adapted from LaBerge, 1983)

the identification of the central letter, RT varies according to the location of the target: the further the target appears away from the central position on which the attention had been focalized beforehand, the more the RT increases. This observation is true for the presentation of both words and non-words, RTs for non-words being slightly shorter than those for words.

Other modulations of this experiment have allowed researchers to specify the minimal extent of the attentional spotlight. In experiments led by Humphreys (1981), the minimum width of the attentional beam was less than 0.5° when the attention was focalized on the fovea where the visual acuity is optimal; this minimum width increased by more than a degree when attentional focalization was moved by one degree from the fovea centre.

Another experiment led by Egly and Homa (1984) also studied the impact of the attentional beam 'adjustment'. These authors used a detection task in which the target may appear on the perimeter of one of three concentric circles. In one experimental condition, the subject's attention was first focalized on the intermediate circle. While the subject expected to detect the target in this region, the stimulus to which he had to react appeared on the perimeter of one of the two other circles. Referring to the spotlight analogy, one would expect that the attentional focalization on the intermediate circle would facilitate at the same time the detection of targets appearing in the region delimited by the central circle. If the RT slow-down linked to the attentional focalization depends on the whole area on which the attentional beam is focused, one can predict that the performance will be better when the target appears in the central circle rather than in the external circle. In fact, the results obtained do bear in this out. The performance is equally poor in the two cases: RTs to targets appearing in the external or central circle are comparable and significantly slower than RTs for targets presented in the intermediate circle, the area on which the subject's attention has been first focalized. Thus, the form that the attentional beam can take is variable and modelled according to the task constraints. In Egly and Homa's experiment, this beam takes the form of a ring or crown, which has brought some authors to differentiate the metaphor of the 'spotlight' from that of the 'ring' (McCalley, 1995).

This adjustment adaptability was confirmed in observations relevant to the distinction between local and global attention. Navon (1977) has indeed demonstrated that the processing of hierarchized stimuli (Figure 1.4) is carried out by grasping the stimulus first as a whole, in a global manner, and then processing its constitutive elements situated at a local level.

Thus, in our illustration, the large letter H will be processed before the small letter Es that compose it. When subjects have to identify the small letters (or digits, figures or other symbols), the identification time increases if there is no concordance between the global and local level. In our example, the identification time for the small Es forming the large H will be longer

```
EEEEEE     E       E   |       4          8
E          E       E   |      44         88
E          E       E   |     4 4        8 8
E          E       E   |    4  4       8  8
EEEEEE     EEEEEEE     |   4   4      8   8
E          E       E   |   44444444   88888888
E          E       E   |       4          8
E          E       E   |       4          8
EEEEEE     E       E   |       4          8
```

Figure 1.4 Examples of hierarchized stimuli

than the identification time for the small Es forming the large E; it will be the same case for the identification of 8s forming the large 4 (on the right) compared to the small 4s situated on the left. On the other hand, the identification at a global level is not so much influenced by the nature of elements constituting the local level: in our example, identification times for either one of the large 4s will be identical. Nevertheless, Kinchla, Solis-Macias and Hoffman (1983) have demonstrated that this priority of global processing over local processing can be inverted by a preferential orientation of the attention. Indeed, in a detection task during which targets can appear at the global or local level, one records shorter RTs for targets situated at a local level if their appearance probability at this level is higher. So, there is an attentional beam adjustment according to the task constraints. The high probability of target appearance at a local level generates in some way a narrowing of the subject's attentional window and, consequently, a performance optimization at this level, thus reversing the natural tendency to favour the global aspect.

Some studies (Sergent, 1982; Robertson and Lamb, 1991) have demonstrated the existence of a left-hemispheric dominance for local attention and a right dominance for global attention. Some data specific to pathology support this hemispheric differentiation. Indeed, patients with left visual hemineglect have a marked tendency to favour the local processing of hierarchized stimuli with which they are confronted, contrary to patients with left-hemispheric lesion (Delis *et al.*, 1986, 1988; Siéroff, 1990, 1994; Halligan and Marshall, 1994). These patients behave as if, due to their lesion, they have lost the adjustment adaptability of the attentional spotlight: they suffer from a hyperfocalization of their attentional beam, an excessive and more or less permanent narrowing of their attentional window. Thus, Siéroff (1994) wrote:

> Patients with a right parietal lesion present difficulties in directing their attention towards the global level, whereas those with a left lesion have difficulties in directing their attention towards the local level. . . . Left hemineglect after right lesion could be the consequence of a deficit of the

> global apprehension of spatial information, added to an orientation deficit: patients would prefer to process local information whereas the attentional orientation bias would be fully expressed, as patients direct their attention by contiguity. On the contrary, patients with left lesion would keep a good apprehension of the global spatial information, allowing them to compensate an attentional orientation bias: this would permit them to be aware of the information in the whole field.
>
> (p. 145, our translation)

Despite the adjustment precision of this beam or attentional 'window', the question arises as to the possible impact of the environment in which targets are processed, including elements located outside the attentional beam. Indeed, we should remember that authors studying auditory focal attention have finally abandoned their initial postulate according to which the message towards which attention was not deliberately oriented was not subject to any processing. We have seen above that, despite the fact that the subject was not aware of this, different studies have demonstrated that, under some conditions, the meaning of the unattended message could be processed. What happens in the visual modality?

The experiment conducted by Johnston and Dark (1985) contributes in some way to answer this question. These authors used a task in which subjects were asked to pay attention to some precise locations in order to detect occasional presentation of target words. The screen was subdivided into four rectangular parts arranged in a cross form. The two horizontal cells constituted the pertinent locations for half of the subjects and for the other half those vertically arranged. From time to time a prime word – facilitator word – was presented during time periods varying between 67 and 500 msec. The prime word was semantically related to the target word (semantic priming) or strictly identical to the target (morphologic priming). The prime was presented in a location situated in or outside the attentional beam and was followed by the target word presentation. The latter was initially presented in an unreadable form being then gradually clarified until it could be identified by subjects.

Results show that both semantic and morphologic prime presentation in a relevant location significantly facilitated the identification of the target word. On the other hand, semantic primes presented outside the attentional beam had no facilitator effect on the identification; morphological priming for the same non-relevant locations had an effect only for the longest presentation durations, i.e. 500 msec. So, these observations indicate the existence of a complete analysis of stimuli presented in the relevant locations, the processing of elements situated out of the attentional beam being very limited and based only on their physical characteristics.

Distractors can have some impact when they are presented simultaneously with the target within the attentional beam. In 1977, using the Stroop task

(1935), Neill had already pointed out a significant slowing down of the subject's response when the colour to name for an item corresponded to that of the distractor word presented in the preceding item; this was the case, for example, if the word 'blue' written in red followed the word 'red' written in yellow, items for which the expected responses were respectively 'red' and 'yellow'. This type of observation is attributable to the existence of residual inhibition which persists during the next item presentation and which has a repercussion on the RT specific to this item.

This paradigm was taken up and deepened by Tipper *et al.* (1991), which led them to highlight what is generally known as 'negative priming' or 'suppression effect'. For instance, one presents to the subject some visual stimuli that he/she will have to process in a categorization activity. Together with the presentation of the stimuli to be processed, there systematically appears in the background a distractor element with or without a semantical and/or morphological link with the target. Thus, for example, whereas in the foreground there appears the representation – in red – of a table, in the background and in some way becoming entangled with the target, the drawing – in green – of a guitar is presented. The subject is instructed to pay attention only to the red target in the foreground, trying as far as possible to ignore the green distractor stimulus appearing in the background.

From this paradigm, the authors have demonstrated a progressive speeding up of the target processing when targets were associated with systematically identical distractors. This observation is attributable to the gradual deployment of mechanisms of habituation. Furthermore, when a distractor specific to a trial becomes a target in the next, one records a significant RT increase, just as in Neill's experiment (1977). This response slow-down reveals the residue of inhibition associated to the stimulus when the latter had the status of distractor, and which is once again demonstrated when, suddenly, it becomes a target. This inhibition residue can be effective for several seconds (Tipper *et al.*, 1991). In our example, RT will increase significantly when the guitar distractor appearing several times in the background, becomes the target by passing to the foreground. Tipper (1985) demonstrated that this negative priming could appear also for morphologically different distractors belonging to the same semantic category. He demonstrated also (Tipper, 1991) the attenuation of these inhibitory mechanisms with age, an observation which helps to account for certain cognitive difficulties in older people which, finally, would be the consequence of a degradation of specific mechanisms of selective attention.

All of these observations confirm the dynamic aspects of attentional process and the importance not only of the spatial disposition between targets and distractors but also of relationships (morphological and semantic) that they have between themselves, as well as their frequency and chronology of presentation.

1.2.2 Spatial orientation of attention within the visual field

It is obvious that the analysis of elements from the environment depends directly on visual scanning. As already mentioned above for the spotlight metaphor, eye and head movements allow us to direct attention preferentially towards some elements to the detriment of others. The quality of this scanning will depend on factors such as the physical particularities of the stimuli to be analysed (position, size, colour, contrast, etc.) and their context (spatial proximity, continuity, similarity laws, etc., defined by the gestalt theory), visual acuteness, visual field integrity, control of ocular movements and saccades, to which one should add the importance of motivational and emotional factors governing each behaviour aiming at a goal. To the external manifestations of visual orientation, perceptible and objectivizable phenomena for the observer, are added internal displacement mechanisms of attention which are *not* accompanied by motor behaviours specific to the active research of stimuli in the environment or to the orientation reflex. Indeed, under some circumstances, attention can be oriented towards a different source from that on which sensorial organs are directed. Thus, for example, at an evening reception, a subject can continue to turn his/her glance to the person with whom he/she is talking, while deliberately orienting his/her attention to the neighbouring group where participants are debating a subject of interest to him/her. Furthermore, the attentional orientation, visual as well as other modalities, may just concern the processing of mental representations. For example, this will be the case during the description from memory of a complex journey: it will be carried out independently of head and eye orientation. Similar situations are common for other sensorial modalities: executing a complex mental calculation, remembering a melody, identifying some object by means of tactile modality in total darkness or more simply with closed eyes, etc.

This differentiation between obvious, overt orientation and internal, covert attention in visual modality has been experimentally demonstrated by Posner, Nissen and Ogden (1978). The general paradigm used by these authors to study displacements of focalized covert attention is illustrated in Figure 1.5. The subject's task consists in reacting as quickly as possible to the presentation of an easily identifiable target, i.e. a cross in our schema. Target detection is performed under three conditions: (a) in the case of valid cueing, before each trial an arrow points to the left or right corresponding to the location where the target will really appear; (b) in another case, cueing is not valid, i.e. the side pointed to by the arrow is opposite to the location where the target will really appear. The subject is warned that this cueing will sometimes be erroneous. In fact, cueing will be valid in 80% of cases; (c) finally, a neutral condition in which targets appear in the absence of any prior cueing.

Results of this experiment clearly show the 'benefit' of valid cueing and

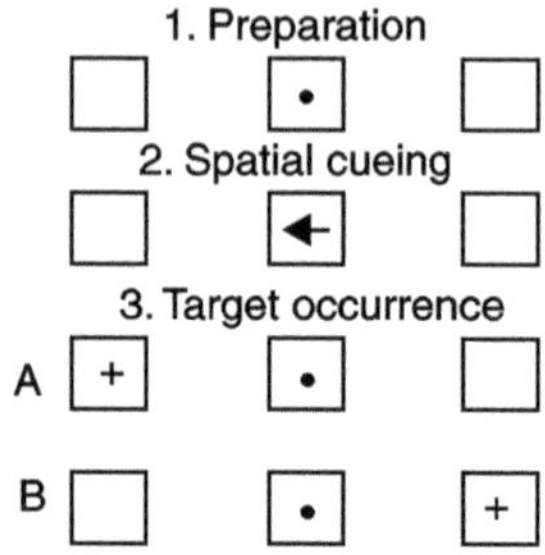

Figure 1.5 Paradigm elaborated by Posner *et al.* (1978) A = valid cueing condition; B = non-valid cueing condition

the 'cost' of an erroneous cue comparatively to the neutral condition. Indeed, RTs corresponding to items preceded by valid cueing are the shortest, followed by RTs for non-cued targets (neutral condition), with RTs corresponding to items preceded by non-valid cueing being the highest. These differences clearly show the existence of the subject's preparatory attitude, which has a favourable or, on the contrary, deleterious impact on the performance, according to the type of cueing, valid or not. The observed differences in RT according to each presentation condition confirm the covert displacements of the attentional focus: valid cueing decreases the response times given the fact that the attentional focus is already correctly pre-oriented towards the location where the target will appear. In the non-valid cueing condition, not only is the attentional focus incorrectly oriented but the cost on the RT depends on the necessary time for the subject to extract his/her attentional focus from the non-valid anchorage point, to bring it then to the actual location where the target is appearing. Response time in the neutral condition is intermediate given that, obviously, absence of pre-signalization generates neither benefit nor cost.

From this kind of paradigm, from some observations specific to the pathology and from different studies using sophisticated medical imagery techniques, it becomes classic to distinguish three types of mechanisms underlying the internal orientation of attention (Posner, 1988; Posner and Petersen, 1990):

(1) The attention disengagement from its current point of focalization. This mechanism would be specifically underlain by parietal structures (Posner *et al.*, 1984).
(2) The attentional displacement or shifting towards other spatial locations where the information is to be processed, a mechanism which would be underlain by the mesencephalic structures and more specifically the colliculus superior and neighbouring areas (Rafal *et al.*, 1988).
(3) The engagement or attentional focalization on the new point of

anchorage to which is added a mechanism allowing the maintenance of the attentional focus on this new centre of interest: 'Inhibition of return' (Posner and Cohen, 1984). These processes would depend more particularly on the thalamus and lateral pulvinar (Petersen, Robinson and Morris, 1987; Posner, 1988).

This breaking up of the internal orientation of the attention into several mechanisms does not just present a theoretical interest but allows us to explain why some processes are selectively disturbed within different pathologies. It explains, for example, the strongly marked difficulty of patients suffering from a left visual hemineglect – consecutive to a right parietal posterior lesion – to disengage their attention from the right space portion in order to process the stimuli presented in the field contralateral to the lesion (Posner *et al.*, 1984).

The princeps paradigm that we have just described (Posner *et al.*, 1978) was taken up again in several studies (Shulman, Remington and McLean, 1979; Downing and Pinker, 1985; Hughes and Zimba, 1985, 1987; Rizzolatti *et al.*, 1987). The authors introduced different modifications in order to analyse covert displacements of attention in the whole visual space. So, they controlled the target eccentricity degree, the distance separating the anticipated location from the real location of target presentation, the temporal cueing efficiency, etc. Downing and Pinker (1985) analysed the field depth factor, i.e. displacements carried out not only on a bidimensional frontal plane with respect to the subject, but also in terms of 'near' or 'far' from the subject. All of these studies have led to the elaboration of a detailed displacements cartography of the attentional spotlight or of this 'mental glance' within a tridimensional visual space (for a detailed analysis see Lecas, 1992).

1.2.3 Integrative function of attention in perception

The model elaborated by Treisman and her collaborators (Treisman, Sykes and Gelade, 1977; Treisman and Gelade, 1980; Treisman, 1992, 1995) emphasizes the active aspect of attention. At the perceptive level they differentiate a first step, considered as 'pre-attentional', in the course of which a rapid initial parallel processing of the visual features (i.e. colour, form, particular orientation of lines) of objects in the environment would be carried out. According to these authors, this processing stage would not depend on attention, strictly speaking. The latter would work only in a second stage, this time during a sequential processing, by which features are combined to finally form an object.

This model attributing mainly an integrative role to attention is supported by a series of experiments using different detection tasks. In one of these studies (Treisman and Gelade, 1980), subjects have to detect a target within

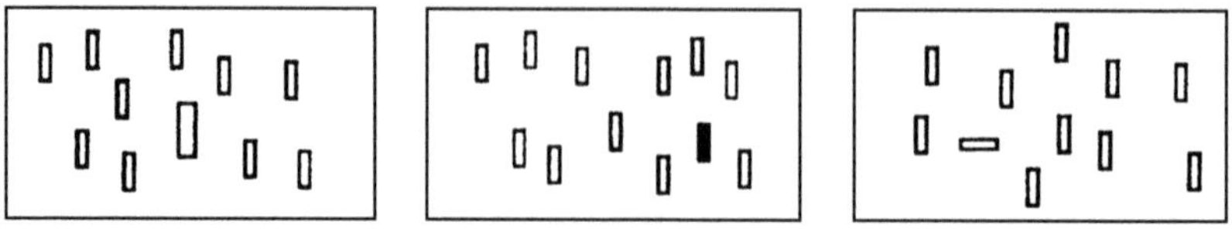

Figure 1.6 Targets differentiating from distractors by a single feature: size, colour, orientation (from Treisman, 1992, with permission)

different screens including 1 to 30 items. The target to be detected is differentiated from distractors by a single feature – size, colour or orientation (see Figure 1.6) – or, on the contrary, by several features. Thus, for example, in the single-feature condition, the target consists of a green (or large or horizontally placed) 'T' presented among a lot of Ts which are all red (or small or vertically placed). In this case, detection time is short and constant, regardless of the number of distractors and whatever the (single) feature by which the target is different from the distractors. This easiness to identify the target independently of the number of distractors is qualified as 'pop-out' because, wrote Treisman (1992), 'it is quite obvious like a single black sheep alone in a white herd' (p. 157, our translation). On the other hand, the detection time increases significantly according to the number of distractors if these share with the target one or several common features. For example, this is the case for a green T among a lot of Ts of different colours; or also for a green T among some green Xs and several brown Ts. In this case, RT increases linearly with the number of distractors, by approximately 60 milliseconds per added element (Treisman and Gelade, 1980). According to the authors, this linear increase is linked to the need for the subject to have recourse to focalized attention to select the target. This recourse is not necessary during the detection of targets differentiated from distractors by a single feature, the discrimination being carried out in a parallel and automatic manner at a pre-attentional level.

For more elaborate stimuli, the authors consider that features can be combined by attentional focalization on object location, focalized attention providing in some way the 'glue' that builds the object unity from available features. Feature combination can also be influenced by past experience (for example, a banana is generally yellow). In the absence of focalized attention or anterior knowledge, features will be combined at random, this arbitrary combination frequently producing a type of mixture called 'illusory conjunctions' (confirmed by Treisman and Schmidt, 1982).

Treisman (1992) synthesizes her model – illustrated in Figure 1.7 – as follows:

> Today I am arriving at the idea – this is still just a speculation – that vision at the first levels of parallel analysis forms cards of functional features in specialized and separated modules that give access only to the

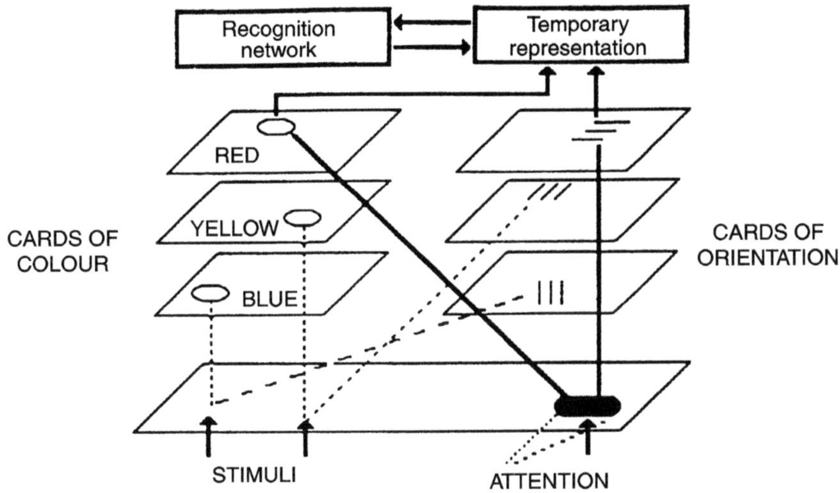

Figure 1.7 Feature integration model of Treisman *et al.* (from Treisman, 1992, with permission)

presence of features coded positively. To have access to their positions or specify their absence from a particular region, or also to link them correctly to the other features of the same object, it is necessary to focalize attention successively on each position. One therefore chooses the features that make, at a given moment, the object of this focalized attention, and one gathers them in a temporary structure which represents a particular object in the selected position. Once features are gathered, one can compare their conjunction to recollections in memory of familiar objects and make the appropriate identification. Unusual conjunctions, hairy eggs or green rabbits, are eliminated at this stage, but downward constraints have no effect on the selection of features to be registered in the object file. If the features of the object change, information in the file is updated, but perceptual unity and object continuity are preserved as long as the spatio-temporal coordinates are compatible with the presence of a single object. The frog that becomes a prince in fairy tales remains the same individual, although with a very different appearance. He has always his personal identity while changing his nominal identity. These temporary representations that we have called object files are the basis of our awareness experience. These are our subjective windows which open on to the mind!

(p. 190, our translation)

Despite the importance of empirical observations in favour of this integration theory, there is an increasing amount of data questioning this approach (for a detailed evaluation see Humphreys and Bruce, 1989). Thus, for example, LaBerge's experiment (1983) described above indicates that the subject is able to process simultaneously all the letters of a word, this observation suggesting that serial attention is not required to integrate the features of each letter before they are combined and form the word. One could have argued that this combination is linked to learning, which would facilitate perceptive processing. One has to note however that Treisman and Gelade (1980) have failed to obtain, after a long practice on subjects, a parallel processing for targets requiring the conjunction of features.

A more convincing observation demonstrating that features do not always have to be combined via serial attentional processing was made by Humphreys, Riddoch and Quinlan (1985). These authors used a similar task to that of Treisman and Gelade (1980), in which targets to be detected consisted of a reversed 'T' on a background composed of 'T's normally oriented. They observed that the time for target detection was not really affected by the number of distractors. This observation suggests that target features (in this case: a vertical and a horizontal line) could be combined without intervention of focal attention. Thus, feature combination by serial attentional processing could be required only in some particular situations of discrimination between targets and distractors.

To conclude this section, one should also note the essential role of attention at the multisensorial and therefore plurimodal integration level. Indeed, whereas we have mentioned some aspects of the integrative action of attention in visual modality, some authors (Wagensonner and Zimmermann, 1991; Sprengelmeyer *et al.*, 1993; Zimmermann and Fimm, 1994) have studied the role played by attention in integration of perceptions coming from different systems of information processing. Thus, Zimmermann, North and Fimm (1993) quote the example of a schizophrenic patient having lost this integration capacity, a case described by Jaspers:

> In the garden, a bird is twittering. I hear the bird and I know that it is twittering but that this is a bird and that it is twittering, this is so disperse. There is a gap. I am just fearing that I will not be able to bring it together, so as if the bird and the twittering have nothing in common.
>
> (Jaspers, 1973, p. 55, cited in Zimmermann *et al.*, 1993)

The authors comment on this case as follows:

> Surely, for the exposed case, the integration disorder is on a very high level of processing. However, there are much more basic levels of integration . . . some patients had great problems in identifying a critical stimulus that was defined by characteristics in two different modalities, that is to say: acoustic and visual. But also, other domains claim the continuous

integration of different stages as, for example in visuo-motor tasks, where the motoric execution must be under the constant control of vision.

(p. 5)

Although the comprehension and analysis of these mechanisms of supramodal integration are only in their infancy, given the crucial importance that they can have for the interpretation of some clinical syndromes they deserve to be studied in more depth.

2 Divided attention

According to Lane (1982): 'Situations that require divided attention are the rule, not the exception' (p. 121). Indeed, examples are legion: taking notes while phoning, conversing with a passenger while driving a vehicle, planning an action or solving a complex problem while walking, drinking, eating or smoking while watching TV, etc.

Besides the fact that it is not easy to measure the degree of difficulty of tasks when these are performed separately, the problem is still more complex when the subject is asked to perform the same tasks, but simultaneously. Indeed, as emphasized by Eysenck and Keane (1991), the attentional resources demands when two tasks are performed simultaneously are not equal to the sum of the demands for the same tasks performed separately because 'the necessity to perform two tasks together often introduces new demands of coordination and avoidance of interferences' (p. 114).

Several theoretical elaborations have endeavoured to account for the subject's ability to divide, share or allocate his/her attention to two or several tasks performed simultaneously. The two most important are the central capacity theory and the theory of multiple resources, to which, as we shall see, are added other alternative explanations.

2.1 The central or single capacity theory

The notion of capacity or resources of attentional processing plays a determinant role in the understanding of mechanisms allowing the performance of two tasks simultaneously, as well as in the way in which attention can be distributed between sensory, cognitive and motor tasks. The capacity constitutes all the available processing resources of a given subject at a given moment. These resources are limited (Norman and Bobrow, 1975). Their exploitation or consumption will be a function of the degree of investment, motivation and effort (Kahneman, 1973) deployed by the subject. These resources can be distributed, allocated differently according to the constraints of the situation or the task instructions. Task demands in terms of consumption of available resources are defined by the notion of workload.

A subject's performance in double tasks will depend on either the available resources (resources-limited) or the quality of inputs (data-limited) (Norman and Bobrow, 1975). A performance limited by the inputs' quality can be illustrated by the impossibility for a subject to decode accurately or completely an auditory message within a very noisy context, and this in spite of the optimal effort that he/she expends to catch this message.

Resources are described in two ways:

- as a 'fuel' (Hirst, 1986) or a mental energy allowing the progress, or the 'driving' of cognitive processes;
- or as the consequence of structural limitations, as, for example, the content of the short-term memory (notion of mnesic span) – limitations that cannot be exceeded independently by the effort provided by the subject.

Navon and Gopher (1979) illustrated this double conception of the notion of resource by drawing a parallel with the economic power of a region which can be linked to its dependence on either its deposits and natural riches or its industrial and/or transformation capacity.

One of the advantages of this model is that it bypasses in a way the problem of evaluating the degree of difficulty of tasks performed simultaneously. Indeed, this degree of difficulty no longer has to be defined a priori since it will vary according to the amount of resources consumed. Thus, in so far as the motivation, the effort deployed by the subject and the quantity of available resources are maintained constant, it becomes theoretically possible to assess the quantity of resources consumed by the tasks. With a constant degree of the subject's attentional investment, it also becomes possible to appreciate the manner in which he/she preferentially allocates the available resources to one task rather than to another. The illustration of this resource consumption and allocation between tasks was formalized by different authors (Norman and Bobrow, 1975; Navon and Gopher, 1979; Kinchla, 1980) in the type of schematization shown in Figure 1.8: Performance Operating Characteristics (POC) or Attention Operating Characteristics (AOC).

If a second task deteriorates the performance of the first, the experimenter may conclude that the two tasks depend on the same attentional resources: it is the concurrent cost or the cost linked to the simultaneity of the execution. If the two tasks can be performed simultaneously with the same level of efficiency as separately, either they do not depend on the same resources or they are data-limited rather than resources-limited. One will note that it can happen that the execution of one of the tasks is facilitated by the second: in this case, there is concurrent benefit or benefit linked to the simultaneous execution. For example, this is the case when a musician attempts to improve his/her performance with the help of a metronome in order to respect the rhythm of the partition that he/she is executing.

The curve form of this type of representation depends on the degree to which tasks A and B share the available resources. If tasks do not share the

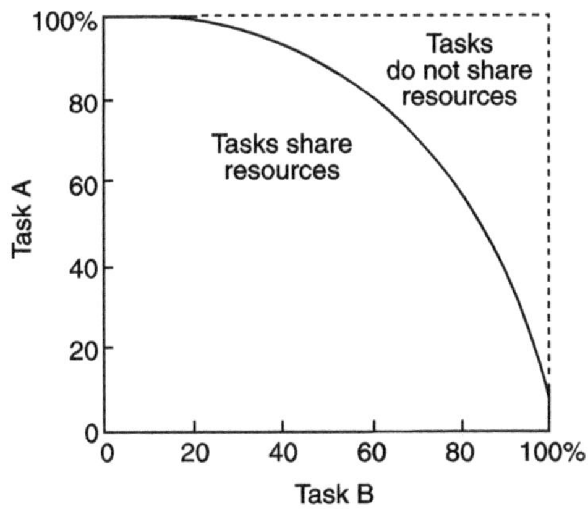

Figure 1.8 Performance Operating Characteristics (POC or AOC) for a constant effort level (from Cohen, 1993, with permission)

same resources, performance levels in double tasks will be identical to those obtained in single tasks (Figure. 1.8: broken line); on the other hand, if tasks share the resources, the performance in one of the two tasks will vary according to the performance in the other (curve). When tasks depend on the same resources, the performance level of one of the tasks can vary according to the amount of resources that the subject allocates to it, and this can be to the detriment or the advantage of the other task.

Theoretically, it would therefore be possible, based on the importance of task demands on the quantity of available resources, to predict the performance in multiple tasks. Such a predictive power would, of course, be of an evident practical interest in determining at what point one can expect someone – an airline pilot, for example – to correctly perform different tasks simultaneously. Unfortunately, this possibility of prediction exists only on a strictly theoretical level.

Despite its degree of elaboration, this type of model presents different limitations. First of all, one is forced to observe that it does not teach us anything about the mechanisms that underlie resources and the way in which they are working. It does not render any account of the manner in which these resources are allocated, shared or consumed. Furthermore, although promising on a mathematical and experimental level, it does not actually account for the diversity of observations of some specific task combinations, or for factors intervening in the interaction and the reciprocal competition between tasks performed simultaneously. So, for example, if a task A deteriorates more strongly the performance of a task C comparatively to the interaction between tasks B and C, the central capacity model will consider that task A requires more resources than B. This conclusion will lead us to predict that task A will deteriorate more strongly the performance of a task D than task B would do. In practice, this prediction is far from always being confirmed. In other words, the predictive power of this type of model has frequently been proven false. Therefore one can have some doubt about the value of being preoccupied with resources and their available capacity if parameters modulating the form of the curve can be expressed in general terms such as 'motivation' or 'effort'. Finally, doubts such as these have led to the single central capacity model being replaced by a more complex model of multiple resources.

2.2 Multiple resources theory

The upholders of this theory no longer solely base their model on the amount of resources but also on the types of available resources. Returning to Hirst's metaphor (1986), there is no longer only one but several 'fuel' tanks, each of these tanks having the function of supplying different types of specific processing, to 'drive' different specific cognitive processes. According to this model, the absence of interferences between tasks is due to the fact that each task depends on different processing resources. Indeed, several studies agree with this idea. Thus, for example, defenders of this theory consider that it is necessary to differentiate specific pools of resources processing for each sensorial modality. The experiment of Allport *et al.* (1972) described above goes in this way. In a double task combining repetition of an auditorily presented message with a memorization task, these authors demonstrated the absence of memorization if the data to memorize were also presented in auditory modality; the memorization, although partial, increased significantly when the same data were presented in the form of written words, and became excellent (90% success) if the data were presented in the form of pictures. The variation of the performance level in one of the tasks, i.e. here the memorization rate, seems therefore to depend on the inputs channel. The interpretation in terms of multiple resources consists in considering that the poverty of the memorization during the auditory presentation of words is due to the fact that the two tasks request the same pool of resources, i.e. the pool that underlies auditory encoding. On the other hand, when the data are presented in the form of written words or pictures, two pools of resources are requested simultaneously, one (verbal) for auditory encoding of the message to be repeated, and the other (visual) for the pictures encoding; visual encoding would greatly improve the performance due to the independence of the two pools of resources.

In the same study, Allport *et al.* (1972) demonstrated the capacity of musician subjects to perform with the same degree of efficiency the sight-reading of a piece of music in a single task, or in a dual task while simultaneously following texts in dichotic listening.

Another example is provided in an experiment carried out by McLeod (1977), focused on the relation between the level of performance in a double task and the response mode. The author submitted 22 subjects to a task of continuous tracking simultaneously with a task of sound identification. Half of the subjects had to react vocally to the sound whereas the others reacted with the hand not used in the tracking task. The author observed a low number of errors for the sound identification, but the performance in the tracking task was significantly poorer in the case of response similarity: subjects made to react manually to the two tasks committed a significantly more important number of errors than subjects reacting vocally to the sound identification. In a second experiment, the author submitted the subjects to the same tracking task but this time combined with a calculation task including two difficulty levels: to add 2 or to subtract 7 from numbers under 100. He observed that the calculation task had no impact on the tracking quality. These observations support the idea of the existence of independent resources pools underlying each specific task.

One of the most elaborated forms of this multiple resources model comes from Wickens (1984a, 1984b) who, in a review of literature on divided attention, suggests a model (Figure 1.9) based on the existence of different pools of resources which he differentiates according to:

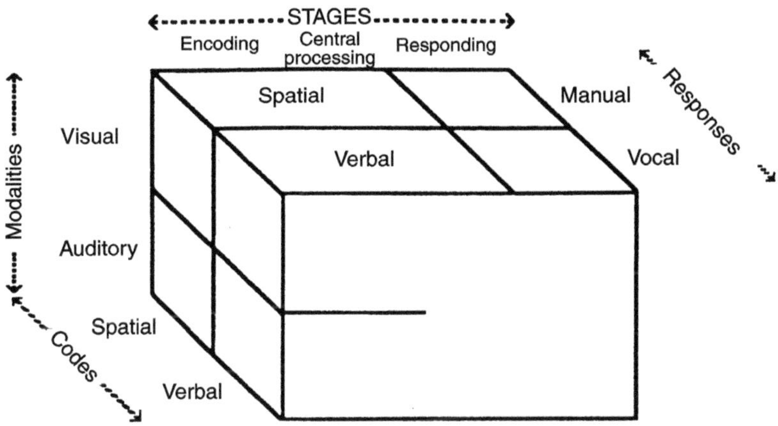

Figure 1.9 Multiple resources model proposed by Wickens (1984b)

- the encoding mode (visual vs. auditory)
- the encoding type (spatial vs. verbal)
- the different stages of processing (encoding, central and output elaboration)
- the type of response (manual vs. vocal).

This model was rapidly criticized for its few possibilities in practical applications. So, Cohen (1993) points out that, just for the resources pool categorizations proposed by Wickens, one already has to take into account 2 × 2 × 3 × 2, i.e. 24, conditions which can influence the degree of difficulty. Even if it seems justified from a theoretical point of view, this differentiation becomes impossible to manage on an experimental basis; with the added restriction that we are still not sure to have taken into consideration all the pertinent variables at work. Besides, Hirst (1986) noted:

> Wickens's model, with its four dimensions, goes a long way toward providing this description. However as Wickens himself noted, his description is incomplete. It is possible that as more research is done, the number of resources will multiply. . . . If the number of different resources becomes too large, the theory will lose much of its elegance. It will be cumbersome to predict the ease with which two tasks can be combined. Each calculation will have to consider the way the two tasks call upon, let's say, 200 different resources, an awesome and perhaps overwhelming task. Recent work in my laboratory suggests that the number 200 may be much too small.
>
> (p. 131)

2.3 Alternative explanations

Different alternatives which finally turn out to complement these two models of resources have been proposed to explain the performance decline linked to the simultaneous execution of the tasks.

From Navon's point of view (1985), two tasks can have reciprocal impacts on their respective performance levels for quite other reasons than the resources that underlie them. According to this author, tasks are difficult to perform jointly not because they have to share some common resources but because they interfere with each other. It is not their competitiveness in terms of processing resources consumption which affects the performance level but their reciprocal interferences at the processing mechanisms level. In the same perspective, Hampson (1989) points out that: 'Anything which minimizes interference between processes, or keeps them "further apart" will allow them to be dealt with more readily either selectively or together' (p. 267). This conception finds some support in works demonstrating that interferences between tasks increase all the more as the cerebral structures concerned in performing these tasks are close (Kinsbourne and Hicks, 1978; Hellige, Cox and Litvac, 1979; Kinsbourne, 1982).

Interferences between tasks would also depend on what the author describes as 'difficulty in making non-habitual transitions' (Navon 1985, p. 140). Thus, when a given event leads systematically to the same response, a preferential transit of information is forming within the central nervous system. Consequently, when a situation makes the subject consider responses other than those currently emitted, or also when he/she has to generate new responses, the link between the event and the response will require non-habitual transitions. The fact of having to consider the same event from another point of view or having to emit new responses will interfere with processes which are running in parallel and usually associated with the situation. This point of view is very close to the notion of the schema already described above (Neisser, 1976), as well as to the model developed by Shallice (1982, 1988). It implies the dissociation between automatic and controlled attentional processes, a differentiation that we are going to analyse now by describing Shiffrin and Schneider's model (1977).

This theoretical model (Shiffrin and Schneider, 1977; Schneider and Shiffrin, 1977; Shiffrin, Dumais and Schneider, 1981) has had and still has now a major impact on the analysis and the understanding of the attentional mechanisms. It was elaborated from different experimental paradigms based on the recognition of items stored in short-term memory. We will now describe the basic paradigm (Figure 1.10) used by these authors.

Subjects have to determine if an item which is part of a small set of targets (1 to 4) memorized beforehand is, or is not, included among the stimuli presented on a screen. The subject's task is to trigger the correct response key according to the presence or absence of a target. The recognition concerns two

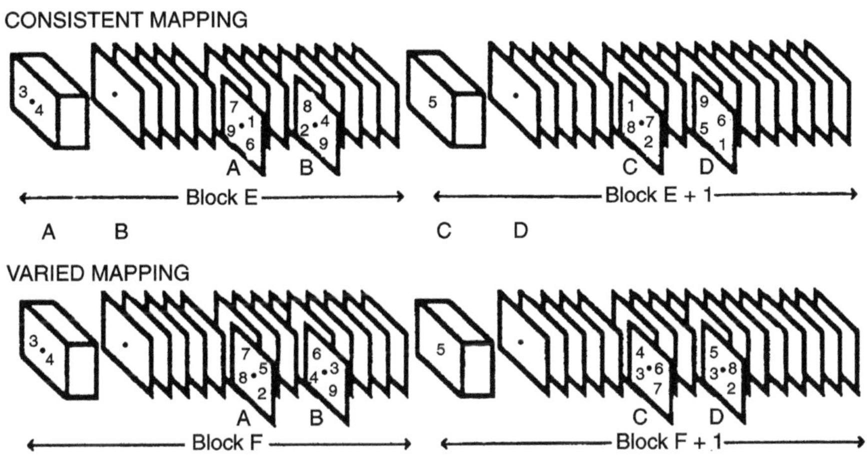

Figure 1.10 Illustration of the experimental protocol used by Shiffrin and Schneider (1977)

distinct conditions. In the condition of 'varied mapping', specific targets in a trial block can also be used as distractors in another block; on the other hand, in the condition of 'consistent mapping', targets and distractors are chosen in such a way that they are systematically different for all the trials of the task.

Thus, for example, in the consistent mapping condition illustrated in Figure 1.10, targets are always the digits 3, 4 or 5, the other digits (126789) being distractors. In block E, the first screen indicates to the subject the targets he/she has to memorize (digits 3 and 4) and which he/she will have to detect later. Screen A does not contain a target, contrary to screen B. During block E + 1, the subject has only one target to detect: the digit 5 which is only present in screen D. Both in block E and block E + 1, one notes that only targets selected for the specific test appear among the distractors. The fact that targets which are present in all blocks never have the status of distractor indicates the consistent mapping condition. This is not the case in varied mapping in which the targets are only defined for a particular block. This is shown in Figure 1.10: whereas in block F the targets to detect are the digits 3 and 4, one notes that the digit 5, the target in block F + 1, appears among the distractors. It is the same for block F + 1 in which the target is the digit 5: the targets 3 and 4, in the preceding block, appear among the distractors.

By applying this paradigm to different types of material (letters, digits or patterns of dots), Schneider and Shiffrin (1977) demonstrated that the processing underlying the consistent mapping improved spectacularly with practice, contrary to that underlying the varied mapping. The main results obtained can be summarized as follows:

- In the varied mapping condition, both the number of targets to be detected and the stimuli appearing on the screen, greatly modify the decision speed; one observes effects of similar amplitude in negative trials, i.e. when the screen includes distractors only.
- On the other hand, in the consistent mapping condition, decision speed is almost independent of the number of targets to detect or of the number of stimuli shown on the screen.
- Practice considerably reduces the detection time in the consistent mapping condition, in contrast with the varied mapping condition.

From the fact that the same factors – task complexity, intervals between targets, etc. – do not have the same effect in the consistent mapping condition compared to varied mapping, the authors consider that the mechanisms of detection are different according to the condition used. For them, controlled processing underlies varied mapping. This controlled processing implies that the subject carries out serial comparisons between each into memory item and each item presented on the screen until a 'match' is found, or until all comparisons have been carried out in order to ensure the absence of targets. On the other hand, the significant improvement of performance in consistent mapping through practice shows the progressive emergence of automatic processing, which is run in parallel and in an independent way.

The authors have also demonstrated that when automatic processing is installed, this latter is less flexible than the controlled processing, more resistant to change and liable to disturb performances consecutive to modifications in the experimental situation. Thus, if subjects are submitted to a long learning session (more than 2,000 trials) in the consistent mapping condition, with targets selected from the first part of the alphabet and distractors from the second, the authors observe that an inverted selection – targets coming from the second part of the alphabet and distractors from the first – requires almost 1,000 supplementary trials before the subjects regain the same level of performance; comparatively, the introduction of modifications in the varied mapping condition shows only minor repercussions on the level of performance.

This type of observation was confirmed by Schneider and Fisk (1982) in an experiment during which the subjects were instructed to react only to targets appearing on a specific portion of the screen while ignoring targets shown elsewhere. Subjects who had developed automatic processing following a consistent mapping training were less able to ignore this portion of the screen, compared to subjects using controlled processing after a varied mapping training. So, these observations indicate that automatic processing is much less malleable and flexible than controlled processing.

Note finally that Poltrock, Lansman and Hunt (1982) obtained results very similar to those of Shiffrin and Schneider concerning the effects of consistent and varied mapping in detection tasks, but this time in the auditory modality. (See Table 1.1.)

Table 1.1 Characteristics of the automatic and controlled processes (adapted from Schneider *et al.*, 1984)

	Automatic processes	*Controlled processes*
Type of operating	Parallel	Serial
Speed	Fast	Slow
Course control	Low	High
Resources consumption	Poor	High
Efficacy	High	Poor
Flexibility	Poor	Important
Incidence of practice	Important	Very poor
Awareness	Few or none	High

As Eysenck and Keane (1991) pointed out:

> In sum, Shiffrin and Schneider discovered that attention can be divided among several information sources with reasonable success when automatic processes are used. The position is quite different with respect to focused attention, in which some sources of information must be attended to and others ignored. Under such circumstances, controlled processes largely prevent unwanted processing from occurring, whereas automatic processes disrupt performance because of automatic responses to to-be-ignored stimuli.
>
> (p. 121)

All of the described observations can also be analysed and interpreted in terms of processing capacity and resources consumption. Indeed, whereas a task with which the subject is relatively unfamiliar requires as a first step the use of different processing resources, with practice, the subject gradually installs a mode of more economical functioning (automatic), which will finally show itself by a lower cost concerning these specific resources. Thus, practice reduces attentional demands and the demand on other central resources. This is also true for double tasks. Practice leads to a decrease in resources demand, a decrease which generates an improvement of performances which may be linked either to the automation of one of the tasks, or to the skill acquired as the result of simultaneous and repeated handling of two or several tasks.

A classic example of automation in multiple tasks and of transformation in skill is learning to drive a car. To start with the learner will need to allocate all his/her attentional resources to the numerous tasks necessary to control his/her vehicle: as well as the different manoeuvres that he/she has to carry out, he/she will have to put these together with the movement of the vehicle in traffic. At this stage, all his/her attention will be concentrated on a large number of events to be coordinated and the novelty of the task will require mainly the use of controlled processes. At this first level of familiarization with the task, the novice will probably prefer the person who accompanies him/her to speak only in case of real necessity, just leaving him/her to cope with the essentials. With practice, some aspects of driving will gradually become more automatic and will reorganize themselves to progressively lead to a new aptitude or skill. At the end of the apprenticeship, the driver will no longer experience any difficulty in talking with a passenger while controlling the vehicle; practice and therefore automatic processing in driving will in turn release some available quantity of attentional resources which the subject will then be able to allocate to other tasks, as for example talking with a passenger. Note nevertheless that even in the case of strongly automated tasks, according to the constraints imposed by the situation, recourse to controlled processes is sometimes necessary. Therefore an experienced driver in an unknown place where there are a lot of events to process – dense traffic, numerous indicator panels, etc. – will interrupt the conversation in progress so as to allocate all his/her attentional resources to the situation requirements.

This type of example brings up the question of the automation degree of the task with which the subject is confronted and the impact of this automation on divided attention. This aspect takes us back to the problem of assessing the degree of task difficulty. The degree of automation is not only linked to the requirements and constraints inherent in the task itself but also to inter- and intra-individual variations. Indeed, familiarization or competence degree for a specific task can bring about some important inter- and intra-individual variations. Intra-individual because it is evident that, for example, if one selects a reading task, the academic subject will undoubtedly have much less difficulty in combining this type of activity with another, compared to a lesser schooled subject or simply a bad reader. Similarly, a trainee typist will have a significantly lower performance if he/she has to hold a conversation while working, which will not be the case with an experienced typist. We must also take into account the intra-individual variations given that the same subject can familiarize himself gradually with a task but can also, through apprenticeship, acquire with time a high level of competence and maybe some expertise in the task in question. Note finally that the competences are specific to the tasks: so, a person able to play the piano while talking will probably be unable to do the same when typing and vice versa.

Practice impact in double tasks has been studied by Spelke, Hirst and Neisser (1976) and Hirst *et al.* (1980) who conducted different experiments during which they taught their subjects to cope simultaneously with two tasks, which apparently seemed at the time incompatible: prose reading while writing under dictation. In a famous study (Spelke *et al.*, 1976), two students, Diana and John, were trained five hours a week for four months. They were instructed to write words being dictated while reading and understanding short stories. At the end of six weeks of training, they were able to read as rapidly and with the same rate of comprehension while writing under dictation as in the single task. With time, the quality of their handwriting improved remarkably.

However, despite the quality of this performance in the dual task, the rate of memorization for dictated written words remained limited. It was true even when twenty successive words composed a sentence or were extracted from the same semantic category. In a later phase, the two subjects were able to write the names of the categories to which the dictated words belonged, and this while keeping to a normal reading speed as well as a correct understanding of the read text.

Viewing the quality of these performances, the authors ponder the well-founded notion of limitation of the processing capacity:

> They understood both the text they were reading and the words they were copying. In at least this limited sense, they achieved a true division of attention: they were able to extract meaning simultaneously from what they read and from what they heard. . . . People's ability to develop skills in specialised situations is so great that it may never be possible to define general limits on cognitive capacity.
>
> (Spelke *et al.*, 1976, p. 229)

From this type of observation and in a literature review, Hirst (1986) proposes a large model, in the sense that it has the advantage of synthesizing most of the aspects we have described in this section devoted to divided attention. His model follows various research studies and observations concerning skills or the degree of a subject's competence when submitted to multiple tasks. In fact, the author proposes to substitute the notion of skill for that of resource.

> Proponents of resource theory concentrate on the way that people allocate resources to task demands. The processes involved in doing two things at once are of secondary importance. . . . It is not that the capacity of the available commodities changes with practice, but rather the processing itself. Resource theorists try to accommodate this observation by noting that as tasks become automatic, they no longer require resources. However, this argument seems circular. If commodities cannot change with practice, then what must change is the demands the practiced task places on the commodity. You know, however, that the demand changed because there is no competition for the commodity when originally there was. It seems easier, free from fewer reified entities, to assume that at times people can do two things at once and then to devote one's energies to trying to understand both the conditions that make this possible, and the processes underlying the performance. Proponents of a skills approach adopt this position. They concentrate on describing what people are doing when performing two tasks simultaneously and what they are learning when practicing dual tasks. They avoid positing reified entities such as resources. For them, resources are a last resort rather than the major theoretical construct.
>
> (Hirst, 1986, pp. 132–133)

In his model, Hirst (1986) differentiates four aspects in order to account for the facilitation in simultaneous execution of tasks:

(a) Integration. This implies coordination and combination of two or several tasks in a task of higher level. This task reorganization can be done at stimulus or response level. One finds an illustration of reorganization at stimulus level in Seibel's study (1963). Subjects had to emit a sequence of responses by triggering different buttons arranged according to the sequence of presentation of luminous flashes. In subjects little familiarized with this task, RT depended on the number of flashes to which they had to react; on the other hand, after a long practice (more than 75,000 trials over 200 sessions), the response became independent of the number of flashes. As noted by Hirst (1986): 'Instead of responding to each light, subjects now saw the pattern of lights as a unit and responded with a unitary, integrated action' (p. 134). The author gives an illustration of an organized task at the level of response with the example of the beginner pianist who first has difficulties in executing semiquavers with the right hand while doing triplets with the left hand, a difficulty that will be overcome by organizing in six beats per bar this specific pattern of action.

(b) Automation. In describing Shiffrin and Schneider's model, we have stressed the much greater impact of practice on consistent mapping than on varied mapping. According to Hirst, other factors which remain to be defined and to be studied might explain why some tasks require less practice to pass from controlled to automatic processing. Does this automation specifically concern one of the two tasks – as in the example of car driving cited above – or both? What degree of automation must a task acquire to have no more impact on the concurrent task performance, etc? As stressed by the author, this type of study focusing on these different aspects of automation is highly unsatisfactory.

(c) The segregation between tasks includes all the factors that contribute to maintain them separated on the cognitive and/or neuronal level (cf. above: Navon's model). As stressed in the multiple resources model, interferences between tasks will be reduced and possibly absent if each task requires different entries or response modalities. In this case, the segregation of the tasks will be facilitated proportionally. Other factors would need a deeper study, such as those linked to strategies developed by the subject himself in order to maintain tasks separated from each other.

(d) Finally, time-sharing, which concerns the subject's capacity to conduct several tasks simultaneously by continuously and in rapid succession shifting his/her attention from one task to another. Indeed, in this case and as the author stresses, it no longer concerns divided attention strictly speaking. Hirst suggests training the subject with tasks the automation of which requires little practice and, in a second stage, adding a concurrent task in order to analyse the way in which the subject proceeds to shift alternately from one task to another, and finally succeeds in carrying both out to a successful conclusion.

Hirst concludes this model in the form of suggestions for further research by writing: 'The exact nature of these skills is poorly understood, but even the articulation of a taxonomy of attentional skills is a worthwhile endeavor' (p. 141).

3 Phasic alertness

This attentional component described by Posner and Boies (1971) and later specified as 'phasic alertness' (Posner and Rafal, 1987) corresponds to the 'Instantaneous generalized facilitation of performance induced by warning signal' (p. 183). Therefore, this attentional component reflects the optimization of the state of preparation, i.e. the subject's receptivity and reactivity when the information that he/she is going to have to process is preceded by a signal warning him/her of the imminence of the appearance of this information. This optimization constitutes a voluntary, sudden and transitory change: it occurs from 100 milliseconds after the signal beginning, the effect being maximal between 500 and 1,000 milliseconds in the paradigm used by Posner and Boies (1971). Their first paradigm can be summarized as follows.

A warning signal, for example a cross, appears for half a second on the screen. It is immediately followed by the appearance of a first letter which will remain displayed until the subject has given a response. At the end of an interval of a variable duration, from 0 to 1,000 msec (6 intervals: 0, 200, 400, 600, 800 and 1,000 msec), according to blocks of items, a second letter will appear and the distance between the two letters will form a visual angle of 3° at the foveal level. The subject has to trigger a specific response button according to whether, in the first condition, the letters are identical or different and, in the second condition, according to whether they are both consonants or vowels. In condition 1, only capital letters are used; in condition 2, it may be capital or small letters. Variables such as interval duration, letter type and expected response are counterbalanced within the different trial blocks to which the subjects are submitted. The main results are as follows:

- in condition 1, RT is shorter for responses 'same' than for responses 'different';
- in condition 2, the lowest RTs concern the comparison of physically identical letters, RTs slowing significantly when this correspondence is absent;
- finally, and especially as evidence of the alertness reaction, the form of RT curves is similar regardless of the matching condition or type of response expected: RTs decrease gradually for the shorter intervals and reach their lowest level with the interval of 500 msec, increasing again for longer intervals.

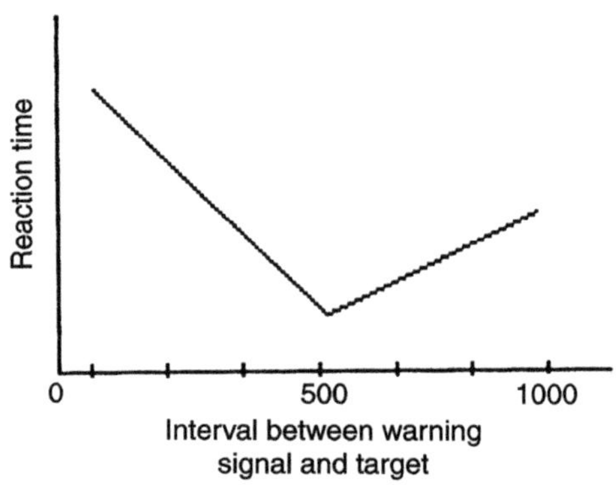

Figure 1.11 Alertness curve (adapted from Posner and Boies, 1971)

The specific form of this curve (Figure 1.11) confirms the state of the subject's preparation with an optimization of the performance for intermediate intervals: in the present case, 500 milliseconds. This state is transient since for longer intervals one records a lengthening of the RT. The difference between the RT levels for conditions 1 (low RT) and 2 (higher RT) in Posner and Boies's experiment demonstrates that the alertness does not act directly on information processing, which the authors have confirmed from others experimental paradigms. This optimization would be a function of a central mechanism allowing the programming of a response to the information (Siéroff, 1994).

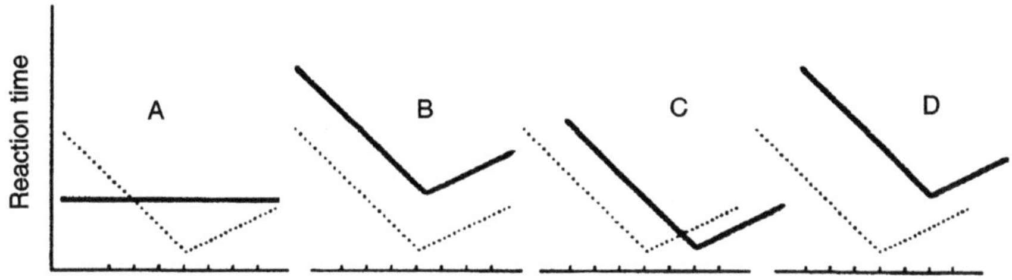

Figure 1.12 Different alertness protocols (adapted from Coyette, 1987). Dotted lines: curve of control subjects; solid lines: specific patients' curves

In pathology, different possibilities can appear (Figure 1.12). First, a simple and pure absence of alertness reaction (schema A): the subject's RT remains constant whatever the period separating the warning signal and the target presentation. The effect can be present despite the fact that the subject's RTs are systematically slower (schema B). Or, the effect is present but for intervals different from those obtained from control subjects (schema C); in this case, it will concern mainly longer intervals. Finally, a combination of the last two patterns: the effect is present in spite of globally slower RT and, comparatively to control subjects, only for longer intervals (schema D).

It is necessary to stress that the classic alert curve form comes from studies on groups of subjects and therefore is elaborated from RT averages; so, the absence of the expected curve in single-case studies requires caution before asserting the actual absence of alertness. Indeed, our current practice with this type of paradigm has frequently confronted us with the fact that some subjects cannot present the expected pattern of RT, and this in the absence of any complaint about this attentional component, even after a detailed interview. Most often in this case, the subject presents an effective decrease of his/her RT for items preceded by a warning signal, despite the fact that one seldom finds the expected correlation between the RT improvement and the progressive increasing of the delay separating the warning signal from the target presentation.

Note finally that alertness can produce cross-sensorial facilitation. Indeed, it appears that in tasks of visual detection, warning signals of auditory or kinaesthetic type have a greater facilitator effect than visual signals (Siéroff, 1994).

4 Vigilance and sustained attention

One must distinguish two aspects as regards this last attentional component: on the one hand, what Posner and Rafal (1987), in the model they propose, call 'tonic' alertness, which corresponds to the level of the subject's cortical activation (cf. notion of 'arousal') – it covers 'Diurnal fluctuation in wakefulness and performance' (p. 183); on the other hand, vigilance strictly speaking, which focuses on the subject's capacity to maintain a sufficient attentional efficacy level in monotonous tasks and tasks of long duration in which the number of stimuli to which he/she has to react is low. It concerns tasks of monitoring requiring the detection of events with rare occurrence. These two aspects are obviously interdependent.

Before developing these aspects, note that in the model elaborated by Posner and colleagues (Posner and Petersen, 1990; Posner and Rothbart, 1992), phasic alertness as well as tonic alertness would depend on a 'vigilance network' that would be underlain by the lateral portion of the right frontal lobe.

> When subjects have to maintain their state of alertness in the period that precedes a task using RT, or when they have to attend to a source of signals at the same time as they are waiting for the appearance of an infrequent target (vigilance), there is an important activity of this system. In Pet scan studies, this activity is brought to the fore in the lateral part of the right frontal lobe. Besides, a lesion of this area generates a deficit in the capacity to develop and to maintain a state of alertness.
>
> (Posner and Rothbart, 1992, p. 92, our translation)

4.1 Tonic arousal

This concerns a set of gradual, generalized, slow and involuntary changes of attention. It is mainly their involuntary aspect that identifies them in comparison with vigilance, this latter requiring a voluntary and conscious effort to maintain a sufficient level of efficiency in tasks of long duration. Arousal fluctuations during the day have a mostly physiological basis and their regulation is modulated by a large cerebral structure located in the cerebral trunk: the reticular formation (or reticular substance).

According to Lindsey (1950, 1962, cited in Cohen, 1993), patients with a lesion of the reticular formation are disorientated, confused and show severe problems in maintaining vigilance or cooperation in tasks of short duration. 'Often, they are abulic, as they tend to drift between states of sleep, drowsiness, and extreme lethargy ' (Cohen, 1993, p. 252).

Two nervous pathways come from the various peripheral sensorial receptors: one connecting these receptors to primary cortical areas (A), and the other (B) converging towards the reticular formation (Figure 1.13). Selective lesions of the reticular formation although saving somesthesic pathways have the effect of abolishing the cortical awakening reaction consecutive to peripheral stimulation. This observation indicates that it is not the inflow of sensorial impulses on the cortical level which elicits the awakening reaction. Furthermore, after selective destruction of the somesthesic pathway (A) so as to interrupt the impulses' inflow towards the cortical level, animals still present a normal electro-encephalographic pattern (Moruzzi and Magoun, 1949). Therefore, awakening is produced by pathways (B) connecting receptors with the reticular formation. Moreover, one can obtain the same effect of cortical awakening by direct stimulation of the reticular formation in the drowsy animal (Bonvallet, 1966).

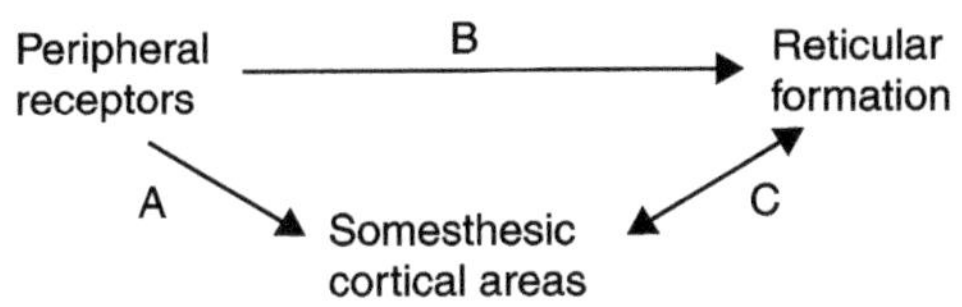

Figure 1.13 Schematic representation of the two pathways connecting receptors to reticular formation

As Richard stresses (1980):

> We are led to conclude that the reticular formation is stimulated by sensorial impulses and it is this structure which, in turn, elicits a cortical activation. These researches allow us to understand by which mechanism the effects of the sensorial dynamogenia demonstrated previously by Bremer act. These researches had shown that external stimulations play a preponderant role in maintaining the awake state: an isolated encephalon, deprived of most of its stimulations from the external world, falls into a state of somnolence. Cortical awakening depends on the level of activity of the reticular formation, also called reticular tonus, which depends in turn on external stimulations [B and C in our schema].
>
> (p. 20, our translation)

4.2 Vigilance strictly speaking

This notion is defined by Mackworth (1957) as: 'A state of readiness to detect and respond to certain small changes occurring at random time intervals in the environment' (pp. 389–390). This component is studied mainly through a series of detection tasks of rare events. These tasks are of long duration, most often of several ten-minute periods, requiring continuous monitoring by the subject. Performance in a vigilance task will depend mainly on the rate of correct detections, number of omissions and eventual false alarms, i.e. the erroneous reactions to non-relevant stimuli. Besides their respective rates for the whole task, these different parameters will also be analysed according to performance over the course of time. A performance decreasing with time is expected with healthy subjects but it is important to appreciate the change in performance with time and the extent of its degradation, so as to objectify some possibly pathological aspects.

The first specific studies concerning vigilance were conducted for the purpose of practical applications in the military, for example radar or sonar control. Mackworth (1950) is considered as a pioneer in this field. He submitted his subjects to a detection task, in front of a display simulating a radar screen. Subjects had to monitor the displacement of a needle which jumped forward one hundredth of a revolution, i.e. 7.5 mm approximately. At a distance of 2 metres from the display, they were instructed to press a response key each time the needle moved at an angle double that of the normal jump. These displacements happened twelve times per half-hour and were distributed in a pseudo-random manner for each half-hour period. The complete test was of two hours' duration. Subjects received no feedback as to the quality of their performance. Results schematized in Figure 1.14 show a significant omission rate at the end of the first half-hour, this rate remaining globally stable during the continuation of the test.

These results were confirmed in subsequent studies using the same type of task and, at first sight, these data seem univocal. Nevertheless, different

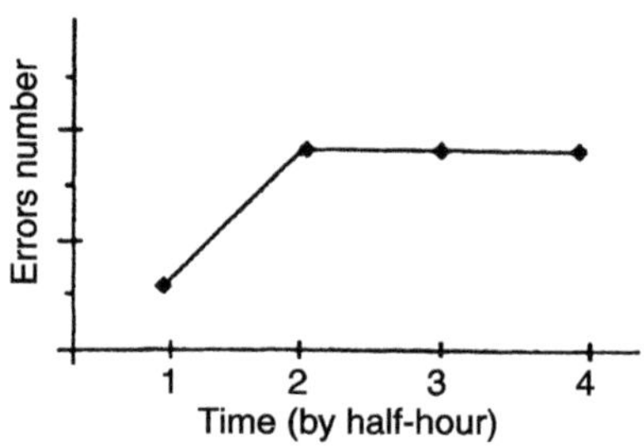

Figure 1.14 Schematic representation of error rate according to the time elapsed (adapted from Mackworth, 1950)

researches demonstrated that the subject's efficiency at this type of task depends on a series of factors specific to the subject, on the type of task to which he/she is submitted, and on the context in which the task takes place.

4.2.1 Readjustment of the subject's attitude according to the number of targets

Colquhoun and Baddeley (1964) studied the impact on the performance of the number of signals to be detected. They submitted their subjects to two successive tasks: a pre-test and the test itself. These tasks were differentiated by the frequency of the targets to be detected: high (18%) or low (2%). Their population was subdivided into four subgroups depending on whether the subjects were submitted during pre-testing and during testing time to a task including a high number (H) or a low number (L) of targets. Thus there were four conditions: H-H, H-L, L-L and L-H. The evolution of the performance during the test was analysed by calculating correct detection rates for six consecutive periods. Figure 1.15 summarizes data specific to period 1 (beginning) and period 6 (end) of the test. Two main findings emerge from these results:

- The rate of correct detection at the beginning of the test is related to the low or high frequency of the targets included in the pre-test: this rate is better for subjects who had been submitted in pre-test to a task including a high number of targets, and lower in the opposite case.
- The comparison between the performance at the beginning and at the end of the test demonstrates for each subgroup a decrease in the rate of detection; nevertheless, this decrease is significantly more marked for the subgroup submitted to a pre-test including a high number of targets and tested in a task including few targets.

These modulations of the subject's performance according to the

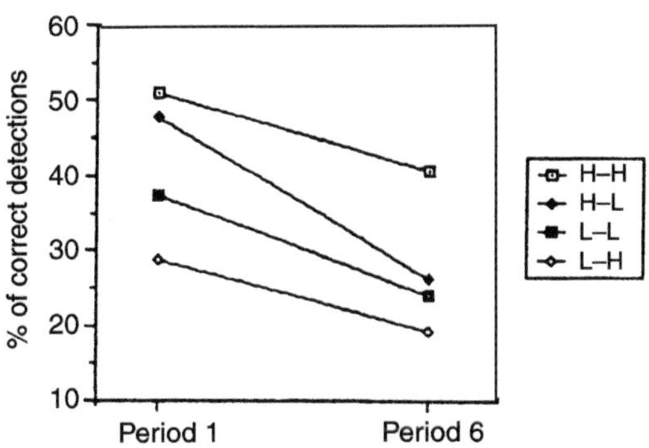

Figure 1.15 Schematic representation of results in Colquhoun and Baddeley's study (1964)

constraints specific to the training phase and to the test itself demonstrate the importance of the subject's expectations or his/her anticipatory attitude which change according to the constraints to which he/she is submitted. This attitude of anticipation, in the sense of a more or less rigorous respect for the constraints and a more or less important cautiousness according to the number of signals to which he/she is submitted, will affect his/her level of efficiency.

4.2.2 Effect of the number of distractors

Jerison and Pickett (1964) submitted their subjects to a task of 80 minutes' duration including twenty targets to detect. For half of the subjects, these twenty targets were presented among 400 distractors (5/min); for the other subgroup, the task included 2,400 distractors (30/min). The authors observe, on the one hand, that the performance of subjects who had been submitted to few distractors was significantly better and, on the other hand, that, in contrast to the subgroup who had been submitted to many distractors, their performance deteriorated less with time. So, a high number of distractors generated a poorer performance level and a more marked degradation with time. Richard (1980) interprets the observed decrease of the vigilance level when the number of non-critical signals is high as follows:

> Any new signal induces a reaction of observation, the repetition of the same signal induces an habituation, i.e. a weakening of this reaction, which is interpreted as a reaction of awakening. The more numerous the non-critical signals, and therefore the more they repeat themselves, the more important the habituation leading to a diminution of the activation, hence the decreasing of the activation which corresponds to the impression of monotony when one is confronted with a repetitive situation.
>
> (p. 27, our translation)

4.2.3 Effect of knowing the results:

Hardesty, Trumbo and Bevan (1963, cited in Mackworth, 1970) replicated Mackworth's princeps experiment (1950) using three groups of subjects. The first, control group, just as in the first experiment, received no information about the quality of its performance. The second group was verbally informed of the number of detected signals, omissions and false alarms. The third group received the same type of information but this time presented visually (lights). Results were as follows:

- The subjects composing the two informed subgroups obtained a performance significantly better than the control group;
- Comparatively to the control group, the performance degradation with time was less marked in the two informed subgroups;
- Comparatively to the subgroup who obtained visual information about the quality of its performance, the subgroup who had received verbal information showed a less marked degradation of detection rate with time.

In order to differentiate the informational versus motivational aspects of the feedback, Mackworth (1964) compared the performance of a group of subjects to whom objective information was given with that of another group receiving pseudo-information about the quality of their performance. The author observed that pseudo-information generated a lower performance than true information. However, comparatively to the performance obtained by subjects receiving no feedback, degradation of detection rate was less in the case of pseudo-information. This observation shows the activating effect of the information (true or false), to which is added a motivational effect and attitude readjustment from the subject according to the feedback that he/she receives when this latter corresponds to the reality of his/her performance.

4.2.4 Other factors

McGrath (1963) studied the impact of surrounding noises on the subject's performance in vigilance tasks. He demonstrated that noises (traffic and machines) improved the performance in a visual task when they were delivered with a frequency of twenty per minute. On the other hand, an exacerbation of efficiency degradation with time was observed when the frequency of these noises was sixty per minute.

Wilkinson (1963) studied the combined effect of noise and sleep deprivation.The author showed that the most important performance degradation with time concerned subjects deprived of sleep and carrying out the task within a quiet context; with the same subjects, this degradation was attenuated if the task was carried out in a noisy context. Inversely, for subjects having slept normally, performance was better in a quiet context than in a noisy one.

Mackworth (1969) showed that the detection rate remained more stable and without supplementary false alarms in subjects under amphetamine. So, this substance has an activator effect on vigilance. The effect of alcohol is more complex. Whereas it degrades the performance in subjects having slept normally, a low alcohol level in the blood improves the performance of subjects deprived of sleep; on the other hand, with these same subjects, a high level significantly degrades their performance (Wilkinson and Colquhoun, 1968). So, in the subject deprived of sleep, the effect of alcohol is double: first as an activator and later as a depressor, according to the level in the blood.

Finally, the introduction of short breaks leads to a decrease in the number of errors during vigilance tasks. This observation is proved correct when introducing breaks devoted to rest or to other tasks. Therefore the important factor is the changing of occupation. Furthermore, when one submits the subject to the same task but for successive sessions, taking place on different days, one observes: (a) the classic decreasing of the performance level in the course of the first session; (b) a higher performance level at the beginning of the second session comparatively to that corresponding to the end of the first session; and (c) a performance decreasing in the course of the second session. So, in this case, there is an attentional efficiency degradation with time to which are added some modifications in the subject's anticipative attitude according to the knowledge that he/she possesses about the task to which he/she has already been submitted during a first session (Mackworth, 1970).

4.2.5 Towards a multi-factorial approach

In a literature review and later publications, Parasuraman (1979, 1984, 1985) proposed a multi-factorial approach to vigilance and suggested operating different distinctions. First, he differentiated two aspects of vigilance: on the one hand, its *level*, assessed by the global performance in the task to which one submits the subject; and, on the other hand, its *decrement or degradation* characterized by the progressive increase of the number of errors in the course of the task. The level of cortical activation would affect mainly the level of vigilance rather than the vigilance decrement, strictly speaking. The only exception would concern vigilance tasks performed with a low level of activation from the very beginning of the task, as after sleep deprivation or in subjects suffering from intense tiredness. This dissociation finds confirmation in the fact that the vigilance level is sensitive to diurnal variations of cortical activation, which is not true for vigilance decrement. Indeed, Parasuraman (1985) demonstrated that the time of day at which the subject was tested had no influence on the performance stability, contrary to the global level of efficiency which proves to be higher in the morning than at the end of the day.

At the beginning of the task, the global vigilance level is a function of the cortical activation level (arousal). This level of activation itself depends on factors such as the environmental temperature, or the alcohol level in the blood, as well as some intrinsic variations according to the time of day at which the assessment is made. The author showed that if this level of cortical activation is low, the performance will be globally poor during the whole of the test. As a low level of activation reduces the subject's sensitivity, i.e. discrimination with respect to the background noise (in terms of the theory of signal detection: factor d'), a change in the response criteria will not improve the performance. Nevertheless, a low level of activation is not systematically associated with a decrease of performance. Other factors can intervene. Factors that decrease the sensitivity include the lengthening of the interval of time after which the signal is presented and the type of discrimination required by the task. Indeed, Parasuraman proposes to differentiate the tasks of discrimination into two categories: those in which stimuli are presented simultaneously; and those in which they are presented in succession. In tasks of simultaneous discrimination, all the information required to make the discrimination is presented simultaneously: for example, the subject has to discriminate a rectangular form among a set of other forms also appearing on the screen. On the other hand, successive discrimination tasks require that the subject detects a target presented separately and specified by the modification of one or another of the features: returning to the preceding example, the subject this time has to detect a rectangular form among different forms which appear in succession on the screen. Some observations show that successive discrimination is associated with a decreasing of sensitivity with time, which would not be the case in a paradigm of simultaneous discrimination. The author interprets these data in terms of resources demand or of more important effort required from the subject in successive discrimination compared to simultaneous discrimination. Cortical activation has an impact on the general performance level and the subject's sensitivity, whereas changes in the decision criterion and the task's requirements by affecting the sensitivity would be responsible for the progressive performance decrement in the course of the test. The author defends the idea according to which:

> only tasks requiring controlled or effortful processing show sensitivity decrement (and so a performance degradation, evidence of vigilance decrement). Nevertheless, it is not clear that all cases of sensitivity decrement can be attributed to control processing and all cases of stable vigilance performance to automatic processing.
>
> (Parasuraman, 1985, p. 507)

Table 1.2 List of the main factors having an impact on the subject's performance in vigilance tasks

Factors	*Activating effect*	*Deleterious effect*
A. Subject		
Cortical activation	If high	If low
Sleep deprivation, fatigue		++
B. External agents		
Noises	If of low frequency	If of high frequency
Alcohol	Slight dose	Strong dose
Stimulants (amphetamine)	Yes	
Pause times	Yes	
C. Task		
Type of task	Simultaneous discrimination	Successive discrimination
Targets number	High	Low
Distractors number	Few	Many
Inter-stimuli time interval	Short	Long
Knowledge of results	Chiefly verbal, pseudo-information included	No feedback

Table 1.2 summarizes the main factors we have reviewed, which sometimes have an activating, sometimes a negative impact on the stability of performance level in vigilance tasks. These factors can be subdivided into three main categories: factors (a) linked to the subject, (b) linked to external agents, and (c) intrinsic to the task.

Of course, this non-exhaustive list will have to be completed and perhaps remodelled according to further research. In addition, the incidence of these factors is not univocal and their impact on the performance will also depend on the synergies they can have with one another. For instance, as we have seen, surrounding noises which at high frequency have a deleterious effect on vigilance stability can have a favourable effect on a subject deprived of sleep or very tired, for whom the cortical level is low. Besides external agents which can have an impact on vigilance level, all the observations we have reviewed show that the subject's expectations, i.e. his/her anticipative attitude, have a crucial impact on the performance level in tasks requiring vigilance. This attitude can change during the task and lead to successive revisions of the decision criterion adopted by the subject. This decision criterion (β in terms of signal detection theory) consists of a state of observation below which the subject considers that the stimulus which is presented probably belongs to the background noise, and beyond which he/she identifies the signal as being the target to which he/she has to react (Bonnet, 1986). The change in decision criterion is considered as the successive readjustments of the subject's expectations towards the stimuli with which he/she is confronted (see among others Colquhoun and Baddeley's experiment, 1964, described above).

4.3 Sustained attention

We are permanently confronted with a continuous flow of information to process, the rhythm of this flow varying from one situation to another. In some studies the concepts of sustained attention and vigilance are used synonymously, probably because situations requiring vigilance are the most typical of sustained attention. In fact, vigilance strictly speaking constitutes one extreme of a continuum: as we have seen, little pertinent information has to be processed by the subject. Sustained attention concerns the other extreme of this continuum: it works in situations where the information flow is fast and, contrary to vigilance, requires from the subject a continuous active processing. If the rhythm is too high, there will be an excessive load on the system, exceeding the processing capacity and, finally, breakdown of the activity in question. The interpreter who carries out a simultaneous translation of a lecture constitutes a typical example of a situation of sustained attention during which the amount of information to process is important and in which the flow is rapid and continuous. The speaker speaking too fast risks overloading the system at any moment, and the interpreter has to warn the speaker to control his/her speech speed. The speaker who fails to do so runs the risk of being stopped during the lecture, or finding that the translation is riddled with silences corresponding to the 'system' interruptions.

Two other phenomena are linked with sustained attention: 'lapses of attention' and fatigability. Lapses of attention consist of transient attentional releases of short duration: some seconds at the most. They can express themselves either by the lack of response in any continuous task or by a sudden and marked lengthening of the RT, that is to say more than two standard deviations from the mean (van Zomeren and Brouwer, 1992).

Fatigability expresses itself by a progressive decreasing of attentional efficiency during continuous tasks, even of short duration, which include numerous events to process; this particularity differentiates this aspect from the notion of vigilance. A significant increase of the RT mean and of the standard deviation for the items corresponding to the end of the task, associated with a deterioration of the qualitative aspects of the responses during the task, reveals the subject's fatigability.

As pointed out by van Zomeren and Brouwer (1987): 'Sustained attention can never be regarded as an independent type of attention, as it involves sustained focused attention and sustained divided attention, as well as sustained supervisory control' (p. 399).

We conclude this presentation by stressing two problems inherent to the data we have reviewed: on the one hand, the attentional components' interdependency, and, on the other hand, the methodological constraints we are confronted with when we elaborate specific tasks for evaluating attention.

Attention cannot be studied in an isolated manner. Indeed, we always pay attention 'to something' and, then, the analysis of a given subject's attentional functions will be systematically dependent on other personal cognitive aspects: his/her perceptual capacities, mental representations, mnesic possibilities, etc. Moreover, each of the attentional components cannot be isolated as such, irrespective of the others. In others words, a 'pure' task of selective, sustained, divided attention, etc., does not exist. Whatever the task used, it will always recruit, although in different proportions, several different attentional competences. Therefore it will only be by cross-checking the subject's performance in different tasks, which have in common that they test some specific attentional aspect, that we will be able to give an opinion about the quality of the course of more specific processing.

Furthermore, direct observation leads us to envisage, beyond their interdependency, the existence of some hierarchical organization among attentional mechanisms. So, for example, it is obvious that the efficacy of the selective aspects of attention will depend on a sufficient arousal level, and that performances in a dual-task situation will depend on the alertness or overt and covert attentional orientation capacities of the subject. The understanding of the dynamic that these mechanisms have one over the other may be crucial in the choice of the type of intervention during the re-education phase (see Sturm *et al.*, Chapter 13 in this volume).

Finally we face the problem concerning the control of the different – and as we have seen numerous – variables leading to the designing and the adjustment of specific tasks. This problem exists for all the attentional components. In view of the number and diversity of factors which can have an impact on the subject's performance, the use of simple tasks (detection, analysis and/or selection of physically or semantically non-complex stimuli), the standardization of the conditions of administration and the normalization of these tasks with a sufficient number of control subjects constitute an essential preliminary to all reliable interpretation attempts. As underlined by Gronwall (1987): 'Because results from complex tasks have done little to add to our understanding of the effect of head injury on attention, it seems time to change direction, to examine simpler processes and simpler responses' (p. 386). The generalization to any neurological affection of this opinion formulated in the framework of a specific pathology, i.e. brain injury, could be beneficial to the understanding of these complex mechanisms.

References

Allport, D.A., Antonis, B. and Reynolds, P. (1972). On the division of attention: a disproof of the single channel hypothesis. *Quarterly Journal of Experimental Psychology*, *24*, 225–235.

Bonnet, C. (1986). La théorie de la détection du signal. *Manuel Pratique de Psychophysique*. Paris: Armand Colin, pp. 59–86.

Bonvallet, M. (1966). *Système nerveux et vigilance*. Paris: Presses Universitaires de France.

Broadbent, D.E. (1958). *Perception and Communication*. London: Pergamon Press.

Camus, J.F. (1988). La distinction entre les processus contrôlés et les processus automatiques chez Schneider et Shiffrin. In P. Perruchet (ed.) *Les Automatismes Cognitifs*. Liège: Mardaga, pp. 55–77.

Cherry, E.C. (1953). Some experiments on the recognition of speech with one or two ears. *Journal of the Acoustical Society of America*, *25*, 975–979.

Cohen, R.A. (1993). *The Neuropsychology of Attention*. New York: Plenum Press.

Colquhoun, W.P. and Baddeley, A.D. (1964). Role of pretest expectancy in vigilance decrement. *Journal of Experimental Psychology*, *68*, 156–160.

Corteen, R.S. and Dunn, D. (1974). Shock-associated words in a nonattended message: a test for momentary awareness. *Journal of Experimental Psychology*, *102*, 1143–1144.

Corteen, R.S. and Wood, B. (1972). Autonomic responses for shock-associated words in an unattended channel. *Journal of Experimental Psychology*, *94*, 308–313.

Coyette, F. (1987). Evaluation et rééducation des troubles de l'attention. Seminar. Service de neuropsychologie, Centre Hospitalier Universitaire, Liège.

Delis, D.C., Kiefner, M.G. and Fridlund, A.J. (1988). Visuospatial dysfunction following unilateral brain damage: dissociations in hierarchical and hemispatial analysis. *Journal of Clinical and Experimental Neuropsychology*, *10*, 421–431.

Delis, D.C., Robertson, L.C. and Efron, R. (1986). Hemispheric specialization of memory for visual hierarchical stimuli. *Neuropsychologia*, *24*, 205–214.

Deutsch, J.A. and Deutsch, D. (1963). Attention: some theoretical considerations. *Psychological Review*, *70*, 80–90.

Downing, C. and Pinker, S. (1985). The spatial structure of visual attention. In M.I. Posner and O.S.M. Marin (eds) *Attention and Performance*, vol. XI. Hillsdale, NJ: Lawrence Erlbaum, pp. 171–187.

Egly, R. and Homa, D. (1984). Sensitization of the visual field. *Journal of Experimental Psychology: Human Perception and Performance*, *10*, 778–793.

Eysenck, M.W. and Keane, M.T. (1991). *Cognitive Psychology: A Student's Handbook*. Hillsdale, NJ: Lawrence Erlbaum.

Grafman, J. (1989). Plans, actions, and mental sets: Managerial Knowledge Units in the frontal lobes. In E. Perecman (ed.) *Integrating Theory and Practice in Clinical Neuropsychology*. Hillsdale, NJ: Lawrence Erlbaum.

Gray, J.A. and Wedderburn, A.A. (1960). Grouping strategies with simultaneous stimuli. *Quarterly Journal of Experimental Psychology*, *12*, 180–184.

Gronwall, D. (1987). Advances in the assessment of attention and information processing after head injury. In S. Levin, J. Grafman and H.M. Eisenberg (eds) *Neurobehavioral Recovery from Head Injury*. Oxford: Oxford University Press.

Halligan, P.W. and Marshall, J.C. (1994). Toward a principled explanation of unilateral neglect. *Cognitive Neuropsychology*, *2*, 167–206.

Hampson, P.J. (1989). Aspects of attention and cognitive science. *Irish Journal of Psychology*, *10*, 261–275.

Hellige, J.B., Cox, B.J. and Litvac, L. (1979). Information processing in the cerebral hemispheres: selective activation and capacity limitations. *Journal of Experimental Psychology: General*, *108*, 251–279.

Hirst, W. (1986). The psychology of attention. In J.E. Ledoux and W. Hirst (eds) *Mind and Brain: Dialogues in Cognitive Neuroscience*. Cambridge: Cambridge University Press, pp. 105–141.

Hirst, W., Spelke, E.S., Reaves, C.C., Caharack, G. and Neisser, U. (1980). Dividing attention without alternation or automaticity. *Journal of Experimental Psychology: General*, *109*, 98–117.

Hughes, H.C. and Zimba, L.D. (1985). Spatial maps of directed visual attention. *Journal of Experimental Psychology: Human Perception and Performance*, *11*, 409–430.

Hughes, H.C. and Zimba, L.D. (1987). Natural boundaries for the spread of directed visual attention. *Neuropsychologia*, *25*, 5–18.

Humphreys, G.W. (1981). On varying the span of visual attention: evidence for two nodes of spatial attention. *Quarterly Journal of Experimental Psychology*, *33A*, 1–15.

Humphreys, G.W. and Bruce, V. (1989). *Visual Cognition: Computational, Experimental and Neuropsychological Perspectives*. Hillsdale, NJ: Lawrence Erlbaum.

Humphreys, G.W., Riddoch, M.J. and Quinlan, P.T. (1985). Interactive processes in perceptual organization: evidence from visual agnosia. In M.I. Posner and O.S. Marin (eds) *Attention and Performance*, vol. XI. Hillsdale, NJ: Lawrence Erlbaum.

James, W. (1890). *The Principles of Psychology*, vol. 1. New York: Holt & Co.

Jaspers, K. (1973). *Allgemeine Psychopathologie*. Berlin: Springer.

Jerison, H.J. and Pickett, R.M. (1964). Vigilance: the importance of the elicited observing rate. *Science*, *113*, 970–971.

Johnston, W.A. and Dark, V.J. (1985). Dissociable domains of selective processing. In M.I. Posner and O.S. Marin (eds) *Mechanisms of Attention: Attention and Performance*, vol. XI. Hillsdale, NJ: Lawrence Erlbaum.

Kahneman, D. (1973). *Attention and Effort*. Englewood Cliffs, NJ: Prentice Hall.

Kinchla, R.A. (1980). The measurement of attention. In R.S. Nickerson (ed.) *Attention and Performance*, vol. VIII. Hillsdale, NJ: Lawrence Erlbaum.

Kinchla, R.A., Solis-Macias, V. and Hoffman, J. (1983). Attending to different levels of structure in a visual image. *Perception and Psychophysics*, *33*, 1–10.

Kinsbourne, M. (1982). Hemispheric specialization and the growth of human understanding. *American Psychologist*, *37*, 411–420.

Kinsbourne, M. and Hicks, R. (1978). Functional cerebral space. In J. Requin (ed.) *Attention and Performance*, vol. VII. Hillsdale, NJ: Lawrence Erlbaum.

LaBerge, D. (1983). Spatial extent of attention to letters and words. *Journal of Experimental Psychology: Human Perception and Performance*, *9*, 371–379.

Lackner, J.R. and Garrett, M.F. (1972). Resolving ambiguity: effect of biasing context in the unattended ear. *Cognition*, *1*, 359–372.

Lane, D.L. (1982). Limited capacity, attention allocation, and productivity. In W.C.

Howell and E.A. Fleishman (eds) *Information Processing and Decision Making*. Hillsdale, NJ: Lawrence Erlbaum.

Lecas, J.-C. (1992). *L'Attention visuelle: de la conscience aux neurosciences*. Liège: Mardaga.

Lewis, J.L. (1970). Semantic processing of unattended messages using dichotic listening. *Journal of Experimental Psychology*, *85*, 225–228.

McCalley, L.T. (1995). Visual selective attention and aging. Eindhoven University: Doctoral thesis.

McGrath, J.J. (1963). Irrelevant stimulation and vigilance performance. In D.N. Buckner and J.J. McGrath (eds) *Vigilance: A Symposium*. New York: McGraw-Hill.

MacKay, D.G. (1973). Aspects of the theory of comprehension, memory and attention. *Quarterly Journal of Experimental Psychology*, *25*, 22–40.

Mackworth, J.F. (1964). The effect of true and false knowledge of results on the detectability of signals in vigilance tasks. *Journal of Psychology*, *18*, 106–117.

Mackworth, J.F. (1969). *Vigilance and Habituation: A Neuropsychological Approach*. Baltimore: Penguin Books.

Mackworth, J.F. (1970). *Vigilance and Attention*. Baltimore: Penguin Books.

Mackworth, N.H. (1950). Researches in the measurement of human performance. MRC Special Report Series, no. 268. London: HMSO. In Sinaiko (1961), Selected papers on human factors in the design and use of control systems. Dover Publications.

Mackworth, N.H. (1957). Some factors affecting vigilance. *Advancements in Science*, *53*, 389–393.

McLeod, P. (1977). A dual-task response modality effect: support for multiprocessor models of attention. *Quarterly Journal of Experimental Psychology*, *29*, 651–667.

Moray, N. (1959). Attention in dichotic listening: affective cues and the influence of instructions. *Quarterly Journal of Experimental Psychology*, *11*, 56–60.

Moruzzi, G. and Magoun, H.W. (1949). Brain stem reticular formation and activation of the EEG. *Electroencephalography and Clinical Neurophysiology*, *1*, 455–473.

Navon, D. (1977). Forest before the trees: the precedence of global features in visual processing. *Cognitive Psychology*, *9*, 353–383.

Navon, D. (1985). Attention division or attention sharing? In M.I. Posner and O.S.M. Marin (eds) *Attention and Performance*, vol. XI. Hillsdale, NJ: Lawrence Erlbaum.

Navon, D. and Gopher, D. (1979). On the economy of the human-processing system. *Psychological Review*, *86*, 214–255.

Neill, W.T. (1977). Inhibitory and facilitatory processes in selective attention. *Journal of Experimental Psychology: Human Perception and Performance*, *3*, 444–445.

Neisser, U. (1976). *Cognition and Reality: Principles and Implications of Cognitive Psychology*. San Francisco: Freeman.

Norman, D.A. (1968). Toward a theory of memory and attention. *Psychological Review*, *75*, 6, 522–536.

Norman, D.A. and Bobrow, D.G. (1975). On data-limited and resource-limited processes. *Cognitive Psychology*, *7*, 44–64.

Norman, D.A. and Shallice, T. (1980). Attention to action: willed and automatic control of behaviour. Center for Human Information Processing (Technical Report no. 99). Re-edited in a revised form in R.J. Davidson, G.E. Schwartz and D. Shapiro (eds) (1986). *Consciousness and Self-regulation*, vol. 4. New York: Plenum Press.

Parasuraman, R. (1979). Memory load and event rate control sensitivity decrements in sustained attention. *Science*, *205*, 924–927.
Parasuraman, R. (1984). Sustained attention in detection and discrimination. In R. Parasuraman and D.R. Davies (eds) *Varieties of Attention*. New York: Academic Press.
Parasuraman, R. (1985). Sustained attention: a multifactorial approach. In M.I. Posner and O.S.M. Marin (eds) *Attention and Performance*, vol. XI. Hillsdale, NJ: Lawrence Erlbaum.
Petersen, S.E., Robinson, D.L. and Morris, J.D. (1987). Contributions of the pulvinar to visual spatial attention. *Neuropsychology*, *25*, 97–105.
Poltrock, S.E., Lansman, M. and Hunt, E. (1982). Automatic and controlled attention processes in auditory target detection. *Journal of Experimental Psychology: Human Perception and Performance*, *8*, 37–45.
Posner, M.I. (1988). Structures and functions of selective attention. In T. Boll and B. Bryant (eds) *Master Lectures in Clinical Neuropsychology*. Washington, DC: American Psychological Association, pp. 173–202.
Posner, M.I. and Boies, S.J. (1971). Components of attention. *Psychological Review*, *78*, 391–408.
Posner, M.I. and Cohen, Y. (1984). Components of visual orienting. In H. Bouma and D.G. Bouwhuis (eds) *Attention and Performance*, vol. X. Hillsdale, NJ: Lawrence Erlbaum, pp. 531–556.
Posner, M.I., Nissen, M.J. and Ogden, W.C. (1978). Attended and unattended processing modes: the role of set for spatial location. In H.L. Pick and E. Saltzman (eds) *Modes of Perceiving and Processing of Information*. Hillsdale, NJ: Lawrence Erlbaum, pp. 137–157.
Posner, M.I. and Petersen, S.E. (1990). The attention system of the human brain. *Annual Review of Neuroscience*, *13*, 25–42.
Posner, M.I. and Rafal, R.D. (1987). Cognitive theories of attention and the rehabilitation of attentional deficits. In M.J. Meier, A.L. Benton and L. Diller (eds) *Neuropsychological Rehabilitation*. Edinburgh: Churchill Livingstone.
Posner, M.I. and Rothbart, M.K. (1992). Les mécanismes de l'attention et l'expérience consciente. *Revue de Neuropsychologie*, *2*, 85–115.
Posner, M.I., Walker, J.A., Friedrich, F.J. and Rafal, R.D. (1984). Effects of parietal injury on covert orienting of attention. *Journal of Neuroscience*, *4*, 7, 1863–1874.
Rafal, R., Posner, M.I., Friedman, J.H., Inhoff, A.W. and Bernstein, E. (1988). Orienting of visual attention in progressive supranuclear palsy. *Brain*, *111*, 267–280.
Richard, J.F. (1980). *L'Attention*. Paris: Presses Universitaires de France.
Rizzolatti, G., Riggio, L., Dascola, I. and Umilta, C. (1987). Reorienting attention across the horizontal and vertical meridians: evidence in favor of a premotor theory of attention. *Neuropsychologia*, *25*, 31–40.
Robertson, L.C. and Lamb, M.R. (1991). Neuropsychological contributions to part/whole organisation. *Cognitive Psychology*, *23*, 299–330.
Schank, R.C. (1982). *Dynamic Memory*. Cambridge: Cambridge University Press.
Schank, R.C. and Abelson, R. (1977). *Scripts, Plans, Goals, and Understanding*. Hillsdale, NJ: Lawrence Erlbaum.
Schneider, W., Dumais, S.T. and Shiffrin, R.M. (1984). Automatic and control processing and attention. In R. Parasuraman and D.R. Davies (eds) *Varieties of Attention*. New York: Academic Press.

Schneider, W. and Fisk, A.D. (1982). Concurrent automatic and controlled visual search: can processing occur without resource cost? *Journal of Experimental Psychology: Learning, Memory, and Cognition*, *8*, 4, 261–278.

Schneider, W. and Shiffrin, R.M. (1977). Controlled and automatic human information processing: 1. Detection, search and attention. *Psychological Review*, *84*, 1–66.

Seibel, R. (1963). Discrimination reaction time for a 1023-alternative task. *Journal of Experimental Psychology*, *66*, 215–226.

Sergent, J. (1982). The cerebral balance of power: confrontation or co-operation? *Journal of Experimental Psychology: Human Perception and Performance*, *8*, 253–272.

Shallice, T. (1982). Specific impairments of planning. *Philosophical Transactions of the Royal Society of London*, *B298*, 199–209.

Shallice, T. (1988). *From Neuropsychology to Mental Structure*. Cambridge: Cambridge University Press.

Shiffrin, R.M., Dumais, S.T. and Schneider, W. (1981). Characteristics of automatism. In J. Long and A. Baddeley (eds) *Attention and Performance*, vol. IX. Hillsdale, NJ: Lawrence Erlbaum.

Shiffrin, R.M. and Schneider, W. (1977). Controlled and automatic human information processing: 2. Perceptual learning, automatic attending and a general theory. *Psychological Review*, *84*, 127–190.

Shulman, G.L., Remington, R.W. and McLean, J.P. (1979). Moving attention through visual space. *Journal of Experimental Psychology: Human Perception and Performance*, *5*, 522–526.

Siéroff, E. (1990). Focusing on/in visual–verbal stimuli in patients with parietal lesions. *Cognitive Neuropsychology*, 7, 519–594.

Siéroff, E. (1994). Les mécanismes attentionnels. In X. Seron and M. Jeannerod (eds) *Neuropsychologie humaine*. Liège: Mardaga.

Spelke, E.S., Hirst, W. and Neisser, U. (1976). Skills of divided attention. *Cognition*, *4*, 215–230.

Sprengelmeyer, R., Zimmermann, P., Lange, H. and Homberg, V. (1993). Attention disorders in extrapyramidal disease: a preliminary report. In J. Stachowiack, R. De Bleser *et al.* (eds) *Developments in the Assessment and Rehabilitation of Brain-damaged Patients*. Tübingen: Gunter Narr Verlag, pp. 31–40.

Stroop, J.R. (1935). Studies of interference in serial verbal reactions. *Journal of Experimental Psychology*, *18*, 643–662.

Tipper, S.P. (1985). The negative priming effect: inhibitory priming by ignored objects. *Quarterly Journal of Experimental Psychology*, *37A*, 571–590.

Tipper, S.P. (1991). Less attentional selectivity as a result of declining inhibition in older adults. *Bulletin of Psychonomic Society*, 29, 45–47.

Tipper, S.P., Weaver, B., Cameron, S., Brehaut, J.C. and Bastedo, J. (1991). Inhibitory mechanisms of attention in identification and localization tasks: time course and disruption. *Journal of Experimental Psychology: Learning, Memory, and Cognition*, *17*, 681–692.

Treisman, A.M. (1960). Contextual cues in selective listening. *Quarterly Journal of Experimental Psychology*, *12*, 242–248.

Treisman, A.M. (1964). Verbal cues, language and meaning in selective attention. *American Journal of Psychology*, *77*, 206–219.

Treisman, A.M. (1992). L'attention, les traits et la perception des objets. In D. Andler (ed.) *Introduction aux Sciences Cognitives*. Paris: Gallimard (Folio-Essais collection) pp. 153–191. (This text formed the subject of a lecture in the International Arts Centre of Cerisy-la-Salle, France.)

Treisman, A.M. (1995). The perception of features and objects. In A. Baddeley and L. Weiskrantz (eds) *Attention: Selection, Awareness and Control. A Tribute to Donald Broadbent*. Oxford: Clarendon Press.

Treisman, A.M. and Gelade, G. (1980). A feature integration theory of attention. *Cognitive Psychology*, *12*, 97–136.

Treisman, A.M. and Schmidt, H. (1982). Illusory conjunctions in the perception of objects. *Cognitive Psychology*, *14*, 107–141.

Treisman, A.M., Sykes, M. and Gelade, G. (1977). Selective attention and stimulus integration. In S. Dornic (ed.) *Attention and Performance*, vol. VI. Hillsdale, NJ: Lawrence Erlbaum, pp. 333–361.

Underwood, G. (1974). Moray vs. the rest: the effects of extended shadowing practice. *Quarterly Journal of Experimental Psychology*, *26*, 368–372.

van Zomeren, A.H. and Brouwer, W.H. (1987). Head injury and concept of attention. In H.S. Levin, J. Grafman and H.M. Eisenberg (eds) *Neurobehavioral Recovery from Head Injury*. Oxford: Oxford University Press, pp. 398–415.

van Zomeren, A.H. and Brouwer, W.H. (1992). Assessment of attention. In J.R. Crawford, D.M. Parker and W.W. McKinlay (eds) A *Handbook of Neuropsychological Assessment*. Hillsdale, NJ: Lawrence Erlbaum, pp. 241–266.

van Zomeren, A.H. and Brouwer, W.H. (1994). *Clinical Neuropsychology of Attention*. Oxford: Oxford University Press.

Von Wright, J.M., Anderson, K. and Stenman, U. (1975). Generalization of conditioned GSRs in dichotic listening. In P.M.A. Rabbit and S. Dornic (eds) *Attention and Performance*, vol. V. New York: Academic Press.

Wagensonner, M. and Zimmermann, P. (1991). Die fähigkeit zur länger anhaltenden aufmerksamkeitszuwendung nach cerebraler schädigung. *Zeitschrift für Neuropsychologie*, *2*, 41–50.

Wickens, C.D. (1984a). Processing resources in attention. In R. Parasuraman and D.R. Davis (eds) *Varieties of Attention*. New York: Academic Press.

Wickens, C.D. (1984b). Attention, time-sharing, and workload. In C.D. Wickens (ed.) *Engineering Psychology and Human Performance*. New York: Bell & Howel.

Wilkinson, R.T. (1963). Interaction of noise with knowledge of results and sleep deprivation. *Journal of Experimental Psychology*, *66*, 332–337.

Wilkinson, R.T. and Colquhoun, W.P. (1968). Interaction of alcohol with incentive and sleep deprivation. *Journal of Experimental Psychology*, *76*, 623–629.

Zimmermann, P. and Fimm, B. (1994). *Tests d'Évaluation de l'Attention (TEA): Manuel D'Utilisation*. Würselen: Psychologische Testsysteme.

Zimmermann, P., North, P. and Fimm, B. (1993). Diagnosis of attentional deficits: theoretical considerations and presentation of a test battery. In J. Stachowiack, R. De Bleser *et al.* (eds) *Developments in the Assessment and Rehabilitation of Brain-damaged Patients*. Tübingen: Gunter Narr Verlag, pp. 3–15.

Chapter 2

Neuropsychological aspects of attentional functions and disturbances

Peter Zimmermann and Michel Leclercq

Introduction

Intact attentional functions are an important prerequisite for meeting daily demands. Whenever we are not able to rely on overlearned routines, we must concentrate on and continuously monitor our actions. This is not restricted to practical actions but holds equally well for every kind of social interaction and every kind of intellectual activity. In this sense, attentional functions can be considered as fundamental processes. When we are inattentive, 'unconcentrated', a number of things that go on around us escape our notice. We get distracted and digress, we do not remember details afterwards. Practical actions get difficult, and we make mistakes. Thus, impairments in attentional functions have far-reaching consequences for an individual's participation in almost every area of life, everyday activities, education, work, traffic, and nearly every other conceivable activity.

Seen from a neuropsychological standpoint, these attentional functions are especially important, because almost every kind of brain damage, brain pathology or brain illness is accompanied by different attentional impairments. This indicates a strong necessity to diagnose the different attentional disorders carefully and differentially after such damage or illnesses. However, the requirements for such a differentiated diagnosis prove to be a great challenge for the field of neuropsychology both from a theoretical and a clinical perspective.

Seen from the *theoretical perspective*, the first question that is raised concerns the definition or the identification of specific attentional functions. The absence of a standardized definition of attention is often criticized (e.g. by Johnston and Dark, 1986); however, such a demand can hardly be met, because the term, 'attention,' as it is generally used today, does not represent a unified construct (e.g. Mirsky, 1989; Posner and Petersen, 1990; Parasuraman, 1998). Rather, 'attention' refers to an entire bundle of specific functions that interact with every other cognitive function. In this sense, attentional functions are not autonomous but play a role in all cognitive processes, such as perception, memory, behavioural planning and actions, speech production and reception and orientation in space, to name some examples. For this reason, attentional functions are very difficult to separate both conceptually and functionally from other cognitive functions.

There are two modes of access for the development of the concept of attention and its functions. The first mode of access is through experimental research, where specific concepts are often based on circumscribed paradigms. Another mode of access is made possible by neuropsychological research: here the development of a differentiated concept of attention is usually based on the analysis of deficit patterns in individual cases of pathology. The results of experimental research and the neuropsychological analyses do not automatically lead to an identical perspective. Experimental concepts, which are usually based on specific paradigms, are in general operationally and thus unequivocally defined. However, the neuropsychological analyses of deficit patterns are limited because the deficits are intertwined with other intact or impaired cognitive processes, and because of the functional complexity of the diagnostic tools that are used. But we have to admit that the concepts derived from experimental paradigms with normal subjects do not automatically have a functional neuropsychological parallel. In other words, they are not always sufficient to explain specific deficit patterns observed in brain-injured patients.

From a *clinical perspective*, attentional processes are of central importance especially because of their significance for all other cognitive functions. Even more so, because according to findings to date, in addition to impairments in memory, impairments in attention are among the most common consequences of brain damage of very different kinds of etiologies (e.g. Oddy, Humphrey and Uttley, 1978; van Zomeren, 1981; van Zomeren and van den Burg, 1985; McLean *et al.*, 1983; Bohnen *et al.*, 1995; Levin, 1995; van Zomeren and Brouwer, 1994; see also Leclercq, Deloche and Rousseaux, Chapter 3 in this book), and they have far-reaching consequences. With this in mind, Lezak (1995) stated:

> When this sort of impairment (impaired attention and concentration) occurs, all the cognitive functions may be intact and the person may even be capable of better than average performance, yet overall cognitive productivity suffers from inattentiveness, faulty concentration and consequent fatigue.
>
> (Lezak, 1995, p. 40)

> In fact, when attentional problems are severe, the patient may be unable to benefit from rehabilitation even when motivation, reasoning, judgment, and memory functions are relatively intact. . . . Thus a careful analysis of the rehabilitation candidate's attentional deficits is often of primary importance both in evaluating the patient's rehabilitation potential and in determining the order in which training procedures can

> be effectively undertaken. When attentional problems are pronounced, they need to be dealt with before any other cognitive retraining efforts can be successful.
>
> (Lezak, 1987, p. 44)

Not only the disturbed attentional functions should be taken into consideration but also the *intact* attentional functions, because these constitute an important potential for the compensation of reduced performance in nearly all domains. Thus, a patient or an older person could try to compensate for his or her limited performance by concentrating on his deficits, e.g. a motor impairment or a language disorder. Conversely, it is also true that a patient with reduced attentional capacities is not able to constantly control his or her reduced function – for example, patients or older persons with gait disorders for whom walking or keeping balance demands full concentration risk falling if someone speaks to them or they have to respond to another task demanding attention (Wright and Kemp, 1992; Teasdale *et al.*, 1993).

Attentional performance from a clinical perspective

The importance that impaired attentional functions have for patients with closed head injuries was demonstrated by various studies (e.g. van Zomeren, 1981; van Zomeren and van den Burg, 1985; McLean *et al.*, 1983). The results of these reports are summarized in Table 2.1.

The investigation of patients with severe closed head injury by van Zomeren and his colleagues (van Zomeren, 1981; van Zomeren and van den

Table 2.1 Subjective symptoms reported by patients after severe CHI, shortly after insult (1) (van Zomeren, 1981, p. 9: 62 patients) and two years later (2) (van Zomeren and van den Burg, 1985: 57 patients), as well as following mild CHI (3) (McLean *et al.*, 1983: 20 patients with mild CHI)

	(1)	(2)	(3)
Memory problems	49%	54%	40%
Fatigue	41%	30%	65%
Increased need of sleep	39%	25%	—
Irritability	36%	39%	35%
Slowness	34%	33%	—
Attention problems	31%	33%	45%
Anxiety	31%	18%	35%
Intolerance of bustle	30%	19%	—
Dizziness	27%	26%	35%
Intolerance of noise	26%	23%	30%
Headache	25%	23%	35%
Loss of initiative	25%	23%	

Burg, 1985) revealed that more than half of these patients reported diminished memory performance, and a significant percentage reported impairments that could be attributed to a disorder in attentional performance (poor concentration, dizziness, fatigue, intolerance of noise, and not being able to do several things at once). These symptoms were reported in almost the same severity two years after the injury (van Zomeren and van den Burg, 1985). Only 9 out of 57 patients (16%) were symptom-free at this point in time.

The study by McLean *et al.* (1983) demonstrates that patients with mild head injury manifest the same complaints with almost the same frequency as the severely injured patients. But there is an important difference: while symptoms in severe head-injured patients are long-lasting, the deficits in mild head-injured patients, one month post insult, are no longer evident in objective assessment, even though the complaints, labelled as 'postconcussive syndrome', expressed by the patients persist (Binder, 1986; Dikmen, McLean and Temkin, 1986; Bernstein, 1999).

Of course, the findings of the studies cited above concern subjective reports and give no objective picture of the patients' deficiencies. However, several investigations in which attentional performance was tested confirm the occurrence and the frequency of such deficits. Worth mentioning here is an older study by Dencker and Löfving (1958) on pairs of twins: the comparison of the twins, where one of the twins had suffered brain damage (on average ten years ago, with a minimum of three years) and the other had not, demonstrated that even years after the accident, reduced performance is observed in the brain-injured twin. But also another important aspect was reported by these authors: the fact that the severity of the observed impairment was not directly related to the indicators of the severity of the insult. Also, a more recent study by Zoccolotti *et al.* (2000) confirms the existence of specific attentional deficits in a large sample of closed head-injury patients tested with an appropriate test battery.

Dencker and Löfving's observation (1958) that the severity of brain damage is not a reliable predictor of the extent of the resulting deficits (confirmed by others: Gennarelli *et al.*, 1982; Barth *et al.*, 1983) implies the risk that attentional deficits might go undetected, especially when no other neurological symptoms are apparent. Furthermore, because attentional problems are often not obvious, it is very hard for others to recognize the difficulties encountered by the patient in meeting everyday demands, and this can have serious consequences for the patient. This holds in particular for patients who do not appear to have noticeable impairments after brain damage such as a CHI and who are therefore often not taken seriously, when they report that they have trouble concentrating or tire easily, for example. In contrast, such patients are often suspected of refusing to make an effort or of letting themselves go. At worst, the complaints of difficulty meeting daily demands due to attentional deficits can be dismissed as a neurotic disorder, as was done by

Miller (1961) when he introduced the expression 'accident neurosis'. Van Zomeren, Brouwer and Deelman (1984), however, assume that the pressure exerted by others as well as the effort to compensate for the experienced deficiencies by the patients themselves can finally lead to the development of psychological or psychosomatic disturbances. Patients continuously taxed in this manner run the risk of developing vegetative disorders.

However, a patient's efforts to compensate are of great importance for psychological testing. This refers to the fact that the patient may be overachieving. In such cases, the patient's test score measures performance at the high end of his or her capacity and does not reflect the patient's effective performance level. This is illustrated by the report of a colleague who examined a patient for rehabilitation purposes. The young woman's performance was above average or even well above average in nearly all tests. However, one day the woman's occupational therapist asked the examiner what he was doing to the patient who was completely exhausted after each session with him. And indeed, it was not until the very last test session that the patient burst into tears and admitted that she was not able to continue!

Another important point is the fact that not every patient is aware of the cause or the extent of his/her difficulties, as shown by the inconsistency between the subjectively experienced deficits and those measured objectively (Lannoo *et al.*, 1998; Bernstein, 1999; see also Leclercq, Deloche and Rousseaux, Chapter 3 in this volume). Inaccurately judging one's actual abilities may either lead the patient to experience greater difficulties than can be assumed on the basis of objective assessment of his or her performance or, conversely, might make the patient tend to underestimate his or her difficulties. This discrepancy between the subjective experience of the impairment and its manifestation in test scores can be caused by many factors in addition to the increased compensatory effort mentioned above. For example, psychodynamic coping processes, insult-induced denial tendencies of an anosognosic nature or insult-related depression might play a role (for a detailed analysis see McGlynn and Schacter, 1989). It is important to bear in mind that a false impression of the patient's abilities might be created when inappropriate diagnostic tools are used.

Neuropsychological concepts of attention

We can assume that 'attention' is not to be considered a single function but rather an entire system of specific subprocesses (e.g. Mirsky, 1989; Posner and Petersen, 1990; Parasuraman, 1998), through which information processing and orientation, decisional processes and behaviour are controlled. It is important to remember that in our study of behaviour we are confronted with a much more complex phenomenon than appears at first glance. For example, take a simple reaction time task, probably the most basal behaviour and at the same time the simplest reaction we can study. The instruction is: 'When the stimulus appears, then push this button as quickly as possible.' To respond to this instruction, the subject must orient and keep his or her attention directed towards an area where the stimulus will appear, detect the stimulus, and identify it as a critical stimulus. The subject then has to decide that he or she should react and select the appropriate action programme. Finally, the subject must initiate the action and execute it by triggering the specific motor programme. It would be bold to assume that all these stages and processes are controlled by a uniform attentional function. Indeed, in the meantime there is a great deal of evidence that the flux of information processing is controlled by a large number of very specific processes, as will be illustrated in the following. Yet we are still far from having a complete overview of how the different subfunctions work, and have not identified all the underlying brain structures and processes involved. However, the analysis of attentional performance plays a key role in psychological research in general and in neuropsychology in particular. The problem has been approached from different directions: purely experimental research in normal functioning, neurophysiological and neuroanatomical studies in animals and humans, neuropsychological studies of brain-injured subjects and, recently, through investigations of attentional processes using neuroimaging techniques. The various research approaches have led to an increasingly fine-meshed view of attentional performance, and in the process the number of different aspects of attentional performance has became quite large. For example, the following aspects have been discussed: focused attention, selective attention, control, vigilance, sustained attention, concentration, arousal, alertness, divided attention, capacity, effort, alternating attention, attentional shift, flexibility, lapses of attention, fatigability, inhibition, supervisory control, and speed of information processing. None the less, as of yet, there is no generally accepted consensus about the classification of specific attentional functions.

Of course, the consistent use of these concepts in neuropsychology would be desired; however we are still far from such a standardized usage. This is surely less an expression of a lack of agreement and more likely the consequence of the fact that, despite all the intensive efforts deployed, until now we have not yet fully understood the phenomena underlying what we call attention. This is not only a theoretical problem but also a clinical one, because it raises questions as to which impairments in subprocesses we can expect in patients with brain damage or brain disease, what diagnostic tools we should use, and which treatment of specific deficits in attentional performance we should take into account.

One of the first attempts to systematize the different aspects of attention is reflected in the multi-component model of Posner and Boies (1971), which was made more precise in a paper by Posner and Rafal (1987). In addition to selectivity, Posner and Rafal's proposal included the concepts of 'alertness,' subdivided into 'tonic' and 'phasic arousal', as well as 'sustained concentration' or 'vigilance'.

Concerning the central aspect of selective attention, Posner and Rafal (1987) first distinguished between 'preconscious' and 'conscious' processes. Based on the James concept (1890), they emphasize the significance of selective attentional processes for more effective processing of relevant information. Here, selection can refer to a segment in space or to certain semantic attributes of the signal, and thus can be triggered by exogenic and endogenic conditions. A specific aspect of selective attention Posner and Rafal discuss is 'overt' and 'covert orienting of attention', whereby especially in reference to the latter they distinguish between facilitatory (favoured by valid cueing) and inhibitory (inhibition of return) components.

A second aspect within the framework of Posner and Rafal's model (1987) is the concept of 'alertness' including, on the one hand, a state of general arousal (tonic arousal) which varies characteristically in the course of the day, and, on the other hand, the capability of increasing the general level of attention with regard to an expected event (phasic arousal). The components of alertness modulate the responsiveness of the system and thus provide the necessary resources for selective attention. In particular, tonic arousal is closely associated with the aspect of 'sustained attention' or 'vigilance.'

Expanding Posner *et al.*'s component theory (Posner and Boies, 1971; Posner and Rafal, 1987), van Zomeren and Brouwer (1994) have attempted to create a heuristic framework for the central aspects of attention (see Table 2.2). This framework includes the distinction between the various

Table 2.2 Aspects of attention, after van Zomeren and Brouwer (1994, p. 38)

Intensity	alertness	CNV
		capacity
	sustained attention	time on task
		lapses of attention
		intra-individual variability
Selectivity	focused attention	distraction
		response interference
	divided attention	capacity
		resources

Supervisory attentional control
strategy; flexibility

components of attention made by Posner and Rafal (1987) as well as the distinction between the aspects of selectivity and intensity made by Kahneman (1973). The different subcomponents are placed in the two categories 'selectivity' and 'intensity'. Selectivity includes the components 'focused attention' and 'divided attention'. Intensity encompasses 'alertness' and 'vigilance'. Based on Shallice's (1982) cognitive model, they also propose 'supervisory attentional control' as a supra-modal function, which includes the subaspects of 'strategy' and 'flexibility'.

Selective attentional processes

The concept of focused attention appears to be quite vague at first and van Zomeren and Brouwer's model does not specify which processes control input and information flow. This is by no means a unitary process, as shown by an investigation conducted by Wagensonner (1986). In this study, patients with brain damage of different etiologies were examined for sustained attention using three procedures: the first two procedures were an acoustic and a visual variation of the Continuous Performance Test (CPT; Rosvold *et al.*, 1956); the third procedure involved cross-modality matching of an acoustic with a visual stimulus. The performance of patients with closed head injury is shown in Table 2.3. These results demonstrate that some patients have no problems in the kinds of tasks involving sustained attention, while other patients fail at all kinds of tasks, and still others show specific patterns of deficits. Of special interest are those patients who are unable to do one kind of unimodal task yet have no difficulty doing another type of unimodal task. In contrast, all patients with difficulties in either one or the other unimodal task were unable to successfully complete the cross-modality matching task. Patients were also observed who had no problem with unimodal tasks, but failed at

Table 2.3 Results of 7 (out of 21) CHI patients on three tests of sustained attention (15 minutes: visual, auditory, cross-model task) compared with the performance of 19 controls (Wagensonner, 1986)

Patient	*Visual test form*	*Auditory test form*	*Cross-modal test form*
01	reduced[1]	reduced	stopped[2]
02	+[3]	+	+
03	stopped	+	stopped
04	+	reduced	stopped
05	+	+	stopped
06	+	stopped	stopped
07	stopped	stopped	stopped

Notes:
[1] Large number of failures compared to controls
[2] Testing stopped after few minutes or testing not feasible
[3] Inconspicuous performance

cross-modality matching. The specific deficits in only one or the other single modality represent a double dissociation (Teuber, 1955; Shallice, 1988, 1991) in controlling the input from different sensory channels. This result supports the notion that there must exist specific mechanisms to control acoustic and visual input. Thus, there are some patients who cannot concentrate on listening, others who cannot concentrate on looking. But individual differences in the ability to control the input of the visual and auditory modality were also found in normal subjects (Lansman, Poltrock and Hunt, 1983). This idea of specific control mechanisms for the sensory input of different modalities was supported by a recent fMRI study done by Woodruff *et al.* (1996). In this study, a number from 1 to 9 was presented at the same time both visually and auditorily while the subjects had to attend to numbers presented either visually or auditorily in alternating blocks to detect a target number, the 8. The images showed differentially activated areas for attended stimuli in the visual and auditory modality, supporting the assumption of specific control mechanisms for different modalities.

Further investigations have shown that there are also more specific control mechanisms within a single modality. For example, within the visual modality, there are specific mechanisms and pathways for the analysis of form, colour, and movement, respectively (Livingstone and Hubel, 1987; Zeki, 1992). Each of these channels is under the control of specialized functions, which facilitates the analysis of the specific stimulus attributes, as shown by a PET study by Corbetta *et al.* (1991a, 1991b). Correspondingly, the brain structures which process the specific stimulus attributes were enhanced under PET (Corbetta *et al.*, 1991a, 1991b).

But there are also other functions of selective visual attention facilitating the processing of stimuli in a specific location in space: the 'localization-based' orienting of attention or 'covert shift of attention' (Posner, 1980) or, with respect to predefined attributes that characterize a specific object, the 'object-based' orienting of attention.

The localization-based orientation of attention was largely studied using Posner's covert-shift paradigm (e.g. Posner, 1980; Posner *et al.*, 1984). This paradigm revealed a facilitation of processing for stimuli in the precued location without eye movement. When this experimental paradigm was applied to patients with parietal lesions, it revealed that the patients' ability to orient attention to the contralesional side of the visual field was clearly impaired (Haufe, 1991; Egly, Driver and Rafal, 1994). This deficit is of practical clinical relevance because it is associated with disturbances of saccadic eye movement to the contralesional visual field, faulty detection of critical stimuli in the contralesional visual field, and impaired visual scanning (Haufe, 1991; Nobre *et al.*, 2000). However, not even the localization space-based orienting of attention constitutes a unitary function: the idea that this covert shift of attention underlies different specific functions, namely 'disengage', 'move', and 'engage' (Posner *et al.*, 1984; Posner and Rafal,

1987), is supported by numerous lesion studies (see Posner and Petersen, 1990).

Evidence of an object-based orientation of visual attention independent of the location-based orientation was provided by the results of experiments done by Kramer and Jacobson (1991) and by Vecera and Farah (1994), among others. Object-based orientation of visual attention means that on the basis of preattentive processing that position of the visual field is selected where the visual information can be grouped to a predefined object. It was Egly, Driver and Rafal (1994) who combined location- and object-based orienting of attention in a single experimental setting, thus demonstrating that both processes produce independent costs in RT and must therefore be considered independent processes. Applying the same experimental paradigm to patients with parietal lesions, they demonstrated a clear dissociation in performance between patients with left- and right-hemispheric lesions: while both groups of patients showed the expected difficulty in reorienting their attention to the contralesional side of the visual field, only patients with left hemispheric lesions had extremely elevated RT for tasks requiring object-based reorientation of attention in the contralesional field. As explained by Egly, Driver and Rafal (1994), an object-based deficit of attentional allocation seems characteristic for patients with Balint's syndrome. These patients are not able to see two overlapping forms at once and are also unable to shift from the presentation of one object to that of the other object.

The distinction of an 'object-based' or 'location-based' orientation of attention was also supported on a structural level by PET studies by Fink *et al.* (1997), Nobre *et al.* (1997) and Coull and Nobre (1998), and with fMRI by Kim *et al.* (1999).

At least for the visual modality, we see on a very basic level that the selection of visual input is warranted by a complex system of very specific processes, supporting the idea that 'selective attention', especially visual selective attention, is more than 'conscious' or 'preconscious' processing. Furthermore, with increasing evidence of differential processes for the input control not only in different modalities but also within a modality, it appears obvious that there must be supraordinate processes that ensure cross-modal matching or the integration of input arising from different channels to form a global impression. This was referred to by Luck (1998) as the 'binding problem', or by Treisman and colleagues within the visual modality as 'feature integration' (Treisman and Gelade, 1980; Treisman and Schmidt, 1982; Treisman, 1991, 1993). The study by Wagensonner (1986), mentioned above, demonstrated that specific deficits exist in cross-modal matching. For example, there is one patient presented in Table 2.3 (patient no 5) who had this kind of unequivocal cross-modal matching deficit due to the fact that he was unable to detect critical combinations of visual and auditory stimuli despite his intact unimodal control mechanisms. As demonstrated by Sprengelmeyer, Lange and Hömberg (1995), these kinds of integration processes are often disrupted in patients with Huntington's chorea. Recently, the involvement of specific brain areas in visual-tactile integration tasks that go beyond unimodal sensory processing was demonstrated by a PET study by Banati *et al.* (2000).

However, integrative processes are not only to be assumed close to the input level, but they are more likely to be organized in a hierarchically structured system with integrative processes at several stages of automatic or controlled processing (Mesulam, 1998). Integrative processes are also fundamental in visual-motor tasks, for example, which demand a continuous integration of visual input with the motor output system. According to Mirsky *et al.* (1991, p. 112) the 'attention for action' serves 'to link input with relevant output systems'.

However, there are also indications of another disorder in integration processes on a very high processing level. Thus, the disorders observed in patients with frontal lesions who are unable to correct their behaviour on the basis of feedback information, first reported by Luria and Homskaya (1963, 1964) and subsequently confirmed by Konow and Pribram (1970), must be seen as a disruption of integrative processes. Recently, the involvement of the frontal lobe structures in this sort of behavioural control was confirmed by fMRI studies by Carter *et al.* (1998) and MacDonald *et al.* (2000) and by an electrophysiological study by Luu, Flaisch and Tucker (2000).

Divided attention

Van Zomeren and Brouwer's model (1994) mentions 'divided attention' as the second component of selective attentional processes. Divided attention is of great importance in everyday life, as emphasized by Lane (1982, p. 121) who stated that 'situations that require divided attention are the rule, not the exception'.

The ability to meet simultaneous demands is especially crucial for brain-injured patients, because they frequently report these kinds of difficulties in daily activities or when they return to work. The situation is additionally aggravated for many patients by the fact that functions that were carried out automatically before the insult must be consciously controlled thereafter. For example, speaking requires a great deal of concentration in speech-impaired patients, and walking places high attentional demands on patients with motor difficulties so that it is hardly possible for them to carry out any competing activity.

None the less, the theoretical framework surrounding the concept of divided attention and the discussion about the underlying functions is very controversial. A number of authors support a capacity model of attention (e.g. Broadbent, 1958; Kahneman, 1973; Norman and Bobrow, 1975; Posner and Rafal, 1987), whereas other authors such as Neisser (1967, 1976; Allport, 1993; Sanders, 1997) emphatically reject the idea of a limited capacity.

Supporters of capacity models assume that simultaneous performance on two tasks demands that the available resources are divided among both tasks, whereby capacity and thus performance can be increased with increased effort. In contrast, opponents of a capacity model propose that simultaneous performance on several tasks is only possible when switching between the competing tasks is successful. In this case, performance is limited by the refractory period, that is, the minimum amount of time obligatorily devoted to a given task before switching back to the other task. On the basis of empirical evidence, it does not appear to be possible to choose between these conceptually different models at this time, although Pashler and Johnston (1998) feel that the data obtained thus far tend to speak against a capacity model.

The theoretical discussion above regarding whether dual-task performance is based on a capacity or a switching model is also important in clinical settings, because we need to know what functions cause the difficulties encountered by patients in dual-task situations. The impaired function should be accurately diagnosed before the treatment is planned so that the appropriate rehabilitation measures can be taken. In this sense, it is not unimportant whether a patient's performance deficit can be attributed to reduced capacity (i.e. reduced attentional resources), to general slowness, to impaired switching (i.e. reduced flexibility) or to impaired processing strategies, as van Zomeren and Brouwer (1994) assume with regard to patients with closed head injuries.

Control of the attentional focus and flexibility

Selective attention does not refer exclusively to the ability to focus attention or the ability to simultaneously perform competing tasks. When one speaks of focusing or directed and divided attention, one should also consider what controls the attentional focus. Controlling attentional focus represents a key aspect of selective attention which deserves to be addressed in its own right. In accordance with Parasuraman (1998, p. 6), attentional processes have the task of directing and monitoring behaviour when we are confronted with multiple, competing distractors. Adapting the guidance of attentional processes to the needs of the individual in a given situation is a central aspect of selective attentional performance. This is only possible when the individual has continuous control over the goals he or she has set and the internal and external conditions under which the goals are to be met. As early as 1890, James discussed the aspects of stimulus-driven attention and internally controlled attentional processes that were under the voluntary control of the subject.

Behaviour adapted to the needs of the individual and the situational conditions is only possible when external (stimulus-driven) and internal (intentionally driven) functions of attentional control are balanced. From a clinical standpoint, an imbalance between external and internal attentional control leads to specific syndromes: on the one hand, to increased distractibility, as is frequently observed in patients with frontal lobe lesions (e.g. Lhermitte, Pillon and Serdaru, 1986; Lhermitte, 1986); and on the other hand, to inflexible, perseverative behaviour which is a frequent, but not exclusive consequence of frontal lesions (Luria, 1966; Sandson and Albert, 1984; Goldberg and Bilder, 1987; Vilkki, 1989; Freedman *et al.*, 1998).

In general, the aspect of attentional control by means of external and internal factors can be subsumed under the concept of 'flexibility', described a quarter of a century ago by Zubin (1975) as an independent component of selective attention. Flexibility manifests itself in a large spectrum of activities: for example in perception, where the subject has to change his or her point of view continually, adapting his or her behaviour to the given and probably continuously changing conditions, and reorienting his or her goals of action when the adopted direction leads to no end. So, flexibility does not represent a single function, but is quite a comprehensive capacity that covers specific attentional functions as well as higher cognitive functions. Correspondingly, intelligence, creativity, problem solving and so on require flexible thinking. As a component of attention, however, flexibility is fundamental for nearly all kinds of practical as well as intellectual performance. In this vein, Eslinger and Grattan (1993) contend that: 'Cognitive flexibility commonly refers to the ability to shift avenues of thought and action in order to perceive, process and respond to situations in different ways. It is an essential feature of adaptive human behaviour that is frequently altered by brain damage' (Eslinger and Grattan, 1993, p. 17).

In addition, Lezak (1995) points out the importance of flexible behaviour in clinical settings:

> The capacity for flexibility in behavior extends through perceptual, cognitive, and response dimensions. Defects in mental flexibility show up perceptually in defective scanning and inability to change perceptual set easily. Conceptual flexibility appears in concrete or rigid approaches to understanding and problem solving, and also as stimulus-bound behavior in which these patients cannot dissociate their responses or pull their attention away from whatever is in their perceptual field or current thoughts. . . . Inflexibility of responses results in perseverative, stereotyped, nonadaptive behavior and difficulties in regulating and modulating motor acts.
>
> (Lezak, 1995, p. 666)

As is true of other attentional systems, flexibility is not a unitary function but a capacity that is involved in multiple stages of processing. Thus, specific forms of flexible behavioural control have been commonly referred to as 'shift' or 'orienting' (Posner and Petersen, 1990) in empirical investigations. The 'cross-modality shift' (Sutton *et al.*, 1961; Benton *et al.*, 1962) or the 'covert shift of attention' (Posner, 1980) are shift phenomena occurring near the sensory level, while set shifting (e.g. Brown and Marsden, 1988; Rogers *et al.*, 1998) or the performance required in the Wisconsin Card Sorting Test (WCST, e.g. Milner, 1963; Nelson, 1976; Lezak, 1995) or in fluency tasks (e.g. Luria, 1973; Jones-Gotman and Milner, 1977; Jason, 1985; Vilkki and Holst, 1994) is situated at a higher processing level. In summary, flexibility is not a single process but a hierarchically structured system of individual functions that are effective at very different levels of processing, from the control of the perceptual focus to the strategic control of actions and goals.

Flexibility is not only a cognitive process because emotional and motivational processes also play a significant role in both the external and the internal control of behaviour and thus also in attention. As Parasuraman (1998) put it, 'Of course, an organism's goals are themselves determined not only by the environment but by the organism's internal dispositions, both temporary and enduring; that is presumably what links attention to motivation and emotion' (Parasuraman, 1998, p. 6). One should not neglect the fact that attentional performances in their various forms are always motivated behaviour. Basically, the orientation of attention is directed by emotionally guided decision processes, whereas attentional focusing is maintained by motivational processes. The model developed by Deutsch and Deutsch (1963) is one of the few in which the significance of emotional processes for the guidance of attentional focus is explicitly discussed. Other authors tend to mention emotion only in passing, for example Kahneman (1973), or Posner and Rafal (1987), when they refer to control of conscious volition.

In advertising, it is self-evident that emotionally stimulating pictures or messages with a high emotional impact attract attention. This makes it even more surprising that this relationship was largely neglected in psychological research. Only in the past few years has the displacement of the attentional focus by emotionally relevant stimuli been the object of experimental research. First, emotional stimuli were shown to interfere with colour naming in Stroop tasks (see Mogg and Bradley, 1999). Then, different studies done by the group of Bradley and Mogg (Mogg and Bradley, 1999) indicated that diverse emotional stimuli induce a shift in attentional focus. This shift caused by emotional stimuli was first noted for threatening or anxiety-inducing stimuli (see Mogg and Bradley, 1999), and in general these effects were stronger in people with high trait anxiety (e.g. Bradley *et al.*, 1999) or in people suffering from pathological manifest anxiety disorders (e.g. Gilboa-Schechtman, Foa and Amir, 1999).

But also other emotionally relevant material attracts attention, as shown by Bradley *et al.* (1992). These authors presented subjects with pictures varying greatly in their affective valence (from pleasant to unpleasant) and found that those with higher valence were rated as more interesting and more arousing and provoked longer viewing time. As might be expected, recognition was highest for the highly arousing pictures. This finding remained stable in a follow-up study one year later independent of whether the pictures had been rated pleasant or unpleasant.

Recently, Lane *et al.* (1999) hypothesized that the anterior cingulate gyrus might be the anatomical structure that links emotional processes and selective attention. In the PET study by Lane *et al.* (1999) on the effects of emotional stimulation, it was this structure that showed a large activation. This was also the case in a great number of studies on selective attentional processes using a great variety of tasks (e.g. Pardo *et al.*, 1990; Corbetta *et al.*, 1991a, 1991b; Bench *et al.*, 1993; Paus *et al.*, 1997; Kawashima *et al.*, 1996; Tzourio *et al.*, 1997; Kim *et al.*, 1999).

However, a further PET study by Lane, Chua and Dolan (1999) with pictures varying in valence (pleasant, neutral, unpleasant) and in arousal under different levels of distraction did not observe cingulate gyrus activation. Yet this study demonstrated that valence of the stimuli as well as the different arousal levels influence both the very early (in accordance with other studies – see Lane, Chua and Dolan, 1999) and late stages of visual processing.

Intensity aspects of attention

The intensity aspects of attentional performance were proposed by van Zomeren and Brouwer (1994) as a further component of attention with the subprocesses of alertness and vigilance or sustained attention.

Alertness

Alertness is a basal function of arousal. Posner (1978; Posner and Boies, 1971) distinguishes between alertness functions that modulate the responsiveness of the attentional system over brief and long periods of time and calls them 'tonic' and 'phasic arousal' accordingly. In the long-term regulation of wakefulness, tonic arousal is maintained by the arousal system and is manifested in the variability in performance levels between sleep, drowsiness, and different levels of alertness throughout the course of the day. It is maintained by the reticular system of the brain stem which is modulated by time and activity factors or internal and external factors. In clinical terms, the various degrees of consciousness ranging from coma, unresponsiveness, disorientation, and a state of drowsiness to complete clarity and responsiveness represent different levels of tonic arousal.

Whether or not tonic arousal should be regarded as a specific aspect of attention or should be considered as a function on its own seems to be first a matter of definition, but one should not overlook that the aspects of vigilance and sustained attention are obviously closely linked to the processes of tonic arousal. Thus, Parasuraman, Warm and See (1998) raised the question of whether vigilance, in the sense of a state of general potential to act, might be distinguished from stages of tonic arousal. They eventually concluded that the basic processes that underlie arousal and vigilance overlap extensively, but despite this fact they consider that arousal cannot fully explain the vigilance decrement over time.

Phasic arousal refers to the temporary modulation of the attention system in expectation of or in response to a relevant stimulus (Posner, 1978; Posner and Petersen, 1990). The effect of a phasic alertness reaction can be illustrated by the situation in which an athlete in a race is waiting for a starting signal in order to reach maximal performance at that moment. According to Posner and Petersen (1990), the phasic alertness response has less of an influence on stimulus processing than on the conditions for a rapid reaction.

A phasic alertness reaction can be triggered by both external and internal factors (Posner, 1978), corresponding to a stimulus or an intentionally driven direction of the attentional focus. An intentionally triggered increase in the phasic arousal level takes place through the expectation of a relevant event on the basis of the knowledge of a situation (e.g. in sports, as mentioned above, in daily living or in the laboratory) or by the observation of a cue that is recognized as being meaningful. A stimulus-driven increase in phasic arousal occurs through the confrontation with an unexpected or an intense stimulus or with an attractive, aversive, or frightening stimulus. This is a further example of how emotional processes are linked to the orientation of attention.

A pronounced type of stimulus-driven modulation of the phasic arousal level is the orientation reflex (Pavlov, 1927) or orientation response (Sokolov, 1963). According to Pavlov (1927), the orientation reflex in humans and animals is triggered as a direct reaction to the smallest change in the environment. In this manner, the senses are directed to the cause of the change in order to investigate it more closely. This free direction of the attentional focus is accompanied by physiologically describable changes on all levels: changes in heart rate, skin conductance, pupil size and EEG (Rohrbaugh, 1984). The orientation response is thus a very comprehensive reaction which is involved in processes of focal attention as well as phasic arousal and probably also tonic arousal. The orientation response demonstrates how close aspects of focal attention and phasic arousal are. One might even ask to what extent processes of phasic alertness can be differentiated from focal attention. In another context, the reduction of reaction time to an imperative stimulus announced by a cue was explained by processes of focused attention: the 'covert shift of attention' (Posner, 1978; Posner *et al.*, 1984; Posner and Rafal, 1987). From the very beginning, the 'covert shift of attention' was discussed as a specific aspect of focused attention, and this may also be true of phasic arousal.

Furthermore, this raises the question of to what extent the temporal and spatial enhancement of responsiveness underlies similar processes. An investigation by Fernandez-Duque and Posner (1997) tried to answer this question by studying the overlap and interaction between orienting and alerting in different experimental settings. They concluded that orienting and alerting are separable and have different effects. They hypothesized that different transmitter systems underlie these two processes. But recent PET and fMRI studies by Coull and Nobre (1998) showed that, on a structural level, there is a large overlap of activation for spatial and temporal cueing. This result was confirmed and made more precise in a study done by Coull *et al.* (2000), demonstrating, in conjunction with the previous study (Coull and Nobre, 1998), the existence of a frontoparietal network both for temporal and for spatial orienting. Therefore, there is some evidence that phasic alertness as described by Posner (1978) should be considered as a covert orientation of attention in time and thus as a specific process of focused attention. By both temporal and spatial orientation, processes that may be competing are interrupted and the responsiveness to an expected stimulus is increased.

Vigilance and sustained attention

The ability to maintain attention using mental effort over a longer period of time, *sustained attention* or *vigilance*, is an additional component subsumed under the intensity aspect of attention. Many perceptual, practical and cognitive activities require sustained attention, if they are to be executed successfully and efficiently. In general, healthy persons do not have difficulty sustaining attention when doing interesting, moderately difficult tasks as opposed to monotonous or very demanding tasks. In contrast, patients, especially after a closed head injury, frequently report difficulties in working on a task for an extended period of time. When doing any task that takes time, they tire easily and must take frequent breaks.

In this context, the question is raised of to what extent the aspects of long-term maintenance of attention or vigilance can be distinguished from the processes of selective attention. With regard to this question, Parasuraman (1998) argues that selective attention and vigilance cannot be differentiated, but he suggests that they might stand for opponent processes, since in experimental research, stimulus frequency and cues have opposing effects on selectivity and vigilance.

An even more central aspect is the question of to what extent sustained attention and vigilance are procedurally and terminologically distinct. In fact, 'vigilance' and 'sustained attention' are frequently used as synonyms (e.g. Parasuraman, 1984, Coull *et al.*, 1996) and research has been dominated to a large extent by the study of the vigilance performance as established by Mackworth (1948); that is, the investigation of detection performance of rare, critical signals that were difficult to discriminate under extremely long and monotonous stimulus conditions. Characteristic for this experimental paradigm in healthy subjects is the increased number of 'misses' in response to critical stimuli, also known as the 'vigilance decrement', which begins after only a few minutes of observation (Parasuraman, Warm and See, 1998).

The standard use of extremely monotonous stimulus conditions in vigilance experiments makes these experiments clearly different from those with a higher stimulus rate or those having tasks demanding a higher cognitive processing load. We can assume that this difference is not merely of a conceptual nature, but that the drop in vigilance, on the one hand, and the consequences of fatigue during cognitively demanding tasks, on the other hand, are the result of different underlying processes. In accordance with such a perspective, a signal detection analysis of standard vigilance tasks in comparison to more cognitively demanding tasks exhibited that the decrement in the vigilance task is due to a criterion shift, that is, the subject is no longer responsive, while the reduced performance in tasks with more frequent critical signals and higher cognitive load is due to a decline in perceptual efficiency, that is, a loss of sensitivity due to fatigue (See, Howe, Warm and Dember, 1995). In agreement, Mathews and Holley (1993) reported that only tasks with rapid stimulus presentations requiring difficult discriminations can predict the performance decrements over longer periods in attentionally demanding tasks.

There is quite a bit of evidence in favour of the assumption that the monotonous stimulus conditions in the vigilance investigation evoke habituation processes as they have been described in the context of studies on the orientation response. Habituation is characterized by the reduction in the orientation response after repeated presentation of the stimulus that had originally triggered it. However, the occurrence of habituation processes does not only mean that the orientation response vanishes, but that these processes also evoke an inhibition of the arousal system. Thus, in an early study, Gastaud and Bert (1961, after Lynn, 1966) reported an experiment in which 156 normal adults were given repetitive stimulation for a period of eight minutes. Of the 102 subjects who had alpha rhythms, 45 developed EEG sleep rhythms during the repetitive stimulation and many subjects were definitely asleep (Lynn, 1966, p. 26). These processes are not the same as fatigue, as indicated by the fact that any change in stimulation, even a reduction in stimulus intensity, leads to an immediate restoration of the orientation reaction (Rohrbaugh, 1984). EEG registrations made during vigilance tasks seem to support the assumption of habituation processes, because, in the course of testing, the frequency spectrum goes from the alpha range to theta and delta activity, which is characteristic for a state of drowsiness and light sleep (e.g. Makeig and Inlow, 1993). Nevertheless, Parasuraman, Warm and See (1998) advocate that the vigilance decrement cannot be sufficiently explained by habituation processes.

Another point supporting the assumption that vigilance and sustained attention are distinct components of attentional functioning comes from studies with closed head-injured patients. Indeed, the majority of studies investigating vigilance in its strict sense in these patients confirm a preservation of this attentional function (Brouwer and van Wolffelaar, 1985; van Zomeren *et al.*, 1988; Stuss *et al.*, 1989; Parasuraman *et al.*, 1991; van Zomeren and Brouwer, 1994; Spikman *et al.*, 1996). Ponsford and Kinsella (1992) have even observed that patients with a severe head injury performed as well as controls on a continuous multiple-choice reaction time task that took 45 minutes. On the other hand, it has long been known that head-injured patients perform particularly poorly on tasks that are of short duration (a few minutes) but have a high stimulus rate and/or demand a high cognitive load – in other words, tasks requiring sustained attention. For example, the Paced Auditory Serial Addition Task (PASAT, Gronwall and Sampson, 1974; Gronwall, 1977) is a sensitive tool for assessing brain dysfunction even in patients with mild head injury. More recently, Robertson *et al.* (1997) examined patients with mild to extremely severe brain injury and demonstrated the existence of high correlations between the severity of brain damage and the attentional and performance failures observed and reported by relatives. In this investigation the Sustained Attention to Response Task (SART) was used in which the subject has to respond as quickly as possible to targets presented with a high frequency but has to withhold the response to some rare uncritical stimuli. These authors also showed the ecological validity of this paradigm in normal controls (Robertson *et al.*, 1997; Manly *et al.*, 1999). Therefore, it can be concluded that head-injured patients have frequently been observed to do well when the flow of information is slow and the targets are rare (vigilance) and poorly when there is a lot of information to process in a continuous stream (sustained attention). The contrast in performance points to the need for further research to differentiate these two subtypes of attentional mechanisms more precisely (for a detailed discussion, see also Manly and Robertson, 1997).

The question of to what extent vigilance decrement and sustained attentional performance – that is, mental concentration – represent different processes is of great clinical relevance, since in everyday life and at work demands on vigilance performance tend to be the exception, whereas long-term direction of attention with a high processing load is more likely to be the rule. In patients with brain damage, the investigation of vigilance performance seems to have low ecological validity. Thus, using a task making high demands on working memory load, Berberich (1996) could demonstrate that such tests have much higher predictive power than vigilance tasks in the proper sense. In this test, visual stimuli varying in form, colour, and size were displayed on a computer screen; the subjects had to detect when a stimulus had the same form or colour as the stimulus displayed just before (complex task), or the same form as the stimulus displayed just before (simple task). The results showed that this test requiring a high cognitive load allowed a good prediction of the patients' performance when they returned to work. None of those patients who were able to respond to the complex task reported having difficulty when returning to work, whereas all patients who were unable to manage the more difficult form of the test complained of attentional problems at work.

Consistent with these observations, Davies and Parasuraman (1982) proposed refraining from vigilance examinations in a narrow sense. They called for a:

> broadening of the scope of laboratory research, so that tasks with a complex response requirement, in which observation is not necessarily continuous and uninterrupted, and in which different types of multidimensional signals are presented which varying probabilities of occurrence during the work period, may be more extensively investigated in situations approximating more closely to the operational environment.
>
> (Davies and Parasuraman, 1982, p. 227)

Miscellaneous intensity aspects of attention

The classification of intensity aspects of attention is unclear and leaves questions open. The first of these questions involves *processing speed*. The second question involves the role that *fatigue* plays, a phenomenon many patients with brain damage complain about when working on tasks over a longer period of time.

Slowness in all cognitive and practical activities is frequently observed in patients after closed head injury or in those with lesions in the brain stem. Such general slowness can be considered an expression of reduced tonic arousal. In addition to this kind of general slowness, slowness in specific tasks should be seen as the expression of an impairment in an individual function. Thus, in patients with frontal lesions a marked contrast in reaction time in simple and complex tasks is sometimes observed. Some of these patients show an accelerated simple reaction time, whereas their reactions slow down markedly when a decision is required, as, for example, in simple Go–nogo tasks. Correspondingly, in patients with brain damage or brain illness, slowness in circumscribed tasks can reflect impaired performance areas, for, since Donders (1868; Sternberg, 1969), reaction time has been used to measure specific cognitive processes and serves as a measure of the efficiency of cognitive processing (Shum *et al.*, 1990; Shum, McFarland and Bain, 1994). Thus, slowness in a specific area is not necessarily an indicator of an attentional deficit but can be a result of any kind of cognitive impairment.

As mentioned above, *fatigue* is another open question. Fatigue occurs particularly in patients after closed head injury when they work on tasks demanding attention over extended periods of time (van Zomeren, Brouwer and Deelman, 1984). As discussed above, fatigue is more a consequence of sustained attention than of demands on vigilance. Whereas the factors leading to the experience of fatigue are seemingly obvious, there is no sufficient theoretical basis to explain this phenomenon. To date, there is also no way to objectively measure this state. Thus an important aspect of attentional performance eludes the scope of neuropsychological diagnostics.

Summary

The understanding of the attentional system is of central importance for neuropsychology and neuropsychological rehabilitation for several reasons. For one, attentional processes are fundamental to all cognitive skills. Second, disorders in these processes are relatively frequent compared to other neuropsychological disorders; and third, disorders in attentional processes can lead to a number of impairments in very different areas of performance, because attentional processes form the basis for the entire cognitive apparatus.

At this point in time, we cannot assume that we have a complete understanding of the attentional system and its individual components and specific functions. But one thing is clear: it is a complex system of highly interactive subprocesses, which overlaps with all other cognitive processes and systems in many ways and is therefore not easy to separate from them. However, it would certainly be wrong to consider attentional processes as merely a part of the cognitive system, because a key aspect of these selective processes is the fact that their control involves not only cognitive and strategic functions but, to a significant extent, also emotional and motivational processes.

Following the proposal of van Zomeren and Brouwer (1994), attentional processes can be divided heuristically into different components, or better still into different perspectives which play different roles within the attentional system. These components are based on very different theoretical foundations. The central aspect is *selective attention*, in particular focal attention, which is based on entire systems of specific functions for focusing on individual stimulus segments, for controlling the input or processing in different channels, and for integrating the input from different sensory channels or sources of processing. A further important aspect of selective attention is the ability to shift the attentional focus between stimuli or cognitive processes. Each of these systems seems to be hierarchically structured and extends from sensory-level control processes to the control of cognitive processing. Selective attention seems to link the emotional system with cognitive processes: in particular the control of the attentional focus in order to analyse relevant information more carefully seems to be under the control of emotional and motivational processes.

The aspect of *divided attention* is more of practical importance than it is a theoretically clear and distinct concept. Corresponding to its rather vague theoretical foundation, the specific subskills which are employed when carrying out dual tasks are ill-defined. Accordingly, within the framework of rehabilitation, the therapy for impairments in divided attention is far less specific than that for other functions (Sturm *et al.*, 1997).

Even less precise are the attentional components which van Zomeren and Brouwer (1994) group under the *intensity aspect*, namely, tonic and phasic arousal, vigilance and sustained attention. The *tonic arousal* function is a prerequisite for any efficient behaviour, and it is a question of definition whether it should be subsumed under the concept of attention. In the neuropsychology of brain-injured patients, tonic arousal (or vigilance in the sense of Parsuraman, Warm and See, 1998) is of great importance, because it is fundamental to a state of clear consciousness and general orientation.

In contrast, *phasic alertness* seems rather a specific aspect of focused attention, which directs the attentional focus toward an expected stimulus or an expected event in time, paralleling the orientation in space. Perhaps it is not a good conceptual solution to name these processes 'phasic alertness' or 'phasic arousal' because then they are immediately associated with the concept of tonic arousal, although they are clearly different.

The most intricate component of attentional processes is the concept of vigilance and/or sustained attention. Clinically, these aspects are of great importance but conceptually and functionally their distinction is not at all clear. Vigilance overlaps in many aspects with concepts or processes of phasic arousal and focused attention and, like sustained attention, is controlled to a large extent by motivation and effort. Serious doubts must be raised, however, as to whether vigilance, or more correctly the 'vigilance decrement', and sustained attention are functionally equivalent. Thus, the two concepts do not have the same ecological validity and the same predictive power in the context of neuropsychological rehabilitation.

In conclusion, we can say that the concept of attention refers to the function by which experience and thoughts are given a systematic and chronological structure. The processes underlying attention allow the individual to form a real-time percept of reality. This percept is based on relevant information from the different sense modalities, which are temporally integrated, selected, and associated with a hierarchy of conceptual categories. In this manner, a person comprehends his or her actual integration in time and space. At the same time, the attentional processes provide the basis requirements for nearly all cognitive performances. Every type of practical or intellectual activity can be greatly limited by impaired consciousness, fatigue or a reduced ability to concentrate. This is especially true for all forms of brain injury or disease. But every clinical therapist should be aware of the fact that attention cannot be conceptualized as a unitary function. Rather, it has to be assumed that control of the information flow in the cognitive system is controlled by a number of hierarchically organized, and in part, highly specific processes. However, it should also be taken into account that attention, emotion, and motivation are closely linked. Without considering emotional and motivational processes, the control of the attentional focus cannot be understood.

References

Allport, A.D. (1993). Attention and control: have we been asking the wrong questions? A critical review of twenty-five years. In D.E. Meyer, S. Kornblum *et al.* (eds) *Attention and Performance, 14*, 183–218.

Banati, R.B., Goerres, G.W., Tjoa, C., Aggleton, J.P. and Grasby, P. (2000). The functional anatomy of visual-tactile integration in man: a study using positron emission tomography. *Neuropsychologia, 38*, 115–124.

Barth, J.T., Macciocchi, S.N., Gioidani, B., Rimel, R., Jane, J.A. and Boll, T.J. (1983). Neuropsychological sequelae of minor head injury. *Neurosurgery, 13*, 529–532.

Bench, C.J., Frith, C.D., Grasby, P.M., Friston, K.J., Paulesu, E., Frackowiak, R.S.J. and Dolan, R.J. (1993). Investigations of the functional anatomy of attention using the Stroop Test. *Neurosurgery, 31*, 907–922.

Benton, A.L., Sutton, S., Kennedy, J.A. and Brokaw, M.A. (1962). The crossmodal retardation in reaction time of patients with cerebral disease. *Journal of Nervous and Mental Diseases, 135*, 413–418.

Berberich, S. (1996). Erprobung eines computergestützten Testverfahrens zur Erfassung von Daueraufmerksamkeit und Arbeitsgedächtnis bei Patienten mit Hirnschädigung. Psycholog. Institut der Universität Freiburg: Unpublished thesis.

Bernstein, D.M. (1999). Recovery from mild head injury. *Brain Injury, 13*, 151–172.

Binder, L.M. (1986). Persistent symptoms after mild head injury: a review of the postconcussive syndrome. *Journal of Clinical and Experimental Neuropsychology, 8*, 323–346.

Bohnen, N.I., Jolles, J., Twijnstra, A., Mellink, R. and Wijnen, G. (1995). Late neurobehavioral symptoms after mild head injury. *Brain Injury, 9*, 27–33.

Bradley, M.M., Greenwald, M.K., Petry, M. and Lang, P. (1992). Remembering pictures: pleasure and arousal in memory. *Journal of Experimental Psychology: Learning, Memory and Cognition, 18*, 379–390.

Bradley, B.P., Mogg, K., White, J., Groom, C. and de Bono, J. (1999). Attentional bias for emotional faces in generalized anxiety disorder. *British Journal of Clinical Psychology, 38*, 267–278.

Broadbent, D.E. (1958). *Perception and Communication.* New York: Pergamon Press.

Brouwer, W.H. and van Wolffelaar, P.C. (1985). Sustained attention and sustained effort after closed head injury: detection and 0.10 Hz heart rate variability in a low event rate vigilance task. *Cortex, 21*, 111–119.

Brown, R.G. and Marsden, C.D. (1988). An investigation of the phenomenon of 'set' in Parkinson's disease. *Movement Disorders, 3*, 152–161.

Carter, C.S., Braver, T.S., Barch, D.M., Botvinick, M.M., Noll, D. and Cohen, J.D. (1998). Anterior cingulate cortex, error detection, and the online monitoring of performance. *Science, 280*, 747–749.

Corbetta, M., Miezin, F.M., Dobmeyer, S., Shulman, G.L. and Petersen, S.E. (1991a). Attentional modulation of neural processing of shape, color, and velocity in humans. *Science*, *248*, 1556–1559.

Corbetta, M., Miezin, F.M., Dobmeyer, S., Shulman, G.L. and Petersen, S.E. (1991b). Selective and divided attention during visual discrimination of shape, color, and speed: functional anatomy by Positron Emission Tomography. *Journal of Neuroscience*, *11*, 2383–2402.

Coull, J.T., Frith, C.D., Büchel, C. and Nobre, A.C. (2000). Orienting attention in time: behavioural and neuroanatomical distinction between exogenous and endogenous shifts. *Neuropsychologia*, *38*, 808–819.

Coull, J.T., Frith, C.D., Frackowiak, R.S.J. and Grasby, P.M. (1996). A fronto-parietal network for rapid visual information processing: a PET study of sustained attention and working memory. *Neuropsychologia*, *34*, 1085–1095.

Coull, J.T. and Nobre, A.C. (1998). Where and when to pay attention: the neural systems for directing attention to spatial locations and to time intervals as revealed by both PET and fMRI. *Journal of Neuroscience*, *18*, 7426–7435.

Davies, D.R. and Parasuraman, R. (1982). *The Psychology of Vigilance*. London: Academic Press.

Dencker, S.J. and Löfving, B. (1958). A psychometric study of identical twins discordant for closed head injury. *Acta Psychiatrica et Neurologica Scandinavica*, *33*, Suppl. 122.

Deutsch, J.A. and Deutsch, D. (1963). Attention: some theoretical considerations. *Psychological Review*, *70*, 80–90.

Dikmen, S.S., McLean, A. and Temkin, N.R. (1986). Neuropsychological and psychosocial consequences of minor head injury. *Journal of Neurology, Neurosurgery, and Psychiatry*, *49*, 1227–1232.

Donders, F.C. (1868). Die Schnelligkeit psychischer Prozesse. *Archiv der Anatomie, Physiologie und wissenschaftlichen Medicin*, *1868*, 657–681.

Egly, R., Driver, J. and Rafal, R.D. (1994). Shifting visual attention between objects and locations: evidence from normal and parietal lesion subjects. *Journal of Experimental Psychology: General*, *123*, 146–160.

Eslinger, P.J. and Grattan, L.M. (1993). Frontal lobe and frontal-striatal substrates for different forms of human cognitive flexibility. *Neuropsychologia, 31*, 17–28.

Fernandez-Duque, D. and Posner, M.I. (1997). Relating the mechanisms of orienting and alerting. *Neuropsychologia*, *35*, 477–486.

Fink, G.R., Dolan, R.J., Halligan, P.W., Marshall, J.C. and Frith, C.D. (1997). Space-based and object-based visual attention: shared and specific neural domains. *Brain*, *120*, 2013–2028.

Freedman, M., Black, S., Ebert, P. and Binns, M. (1998). Orbitofrontal function, object alternation and perseveration. *Cerebral Cortex*, *8*, 18–27.

Gastaud, H. and Bert, J. (1961). Electroencephalographic detection of sleep induced by repetitive sensory stimuli. In G.E.W. Wolstenholme and M. O'Connor (eds) *The Nature of Sleep*. London: Churchill.

Gennarelli, T.A., Spielman, G.M., Langfitt, T.W., Gildenberg, P.L. Harrington, T., Jan, J.A., Marshall, L.F., Miller, J.D. and Pitts, L.H. (1982). Influence of the type of intracranial lesion on outcome from severe head injury. *Journal of Neurosurgery*, 56, 26–32.

Gilboa-Schechtman, E., Foa, E.B. and Amir, N. (1999). Attentional biases for facial expressions in social phobia: the face-in-the-crowd paradigm. *Cognition and Emotion, 13*, 305–318.

Goldberg, E. and Bilder, D.F. (1987). The frontal lobes and the hierarchical organization of cognitive control. In E. Perecman (ed.) *The Frontal Lobes Revisited*. New York: IRBN Press.

Gronwall, D. (1977). Paced Auditory Serial Addition Task: a measure of recovery from concussion. *Perceptual and Motor Skills*, *44*, 367–373.

Gronwall, D. and Sampson, H. (1974). *The Psychological Effects of Concussion*. Auckland: Auckland University Press.

Haufe, S. (1991). Visuelle Aufmerksamkeitsstörungen bei Patienten mit Läsionen des parietalen Kortex. Psycholog. Institut der Universität Freiburg: Unpublished thesis.

Howe, J.E., Warm, S.R. and Dember, W.N. (1995). Meta-analysis of the sensitivity decrement in vigilance. *Psychological Bulletin*, *117*, 230–249.

James, W. (1890). *Principles of Psychology*. New York: Holt.

Jason, G.W. (1985). Gesture fluency after focal cortical lesions. *Neuropsychologia*, *23*, 463–481.

Johnston, W.A. and Dark, V.J. (1986). Selective attention. *Annual Review of Psychology*, *37*, 43–75.

Jones-Gotman, M. and Milner, B. (1977). Design-fluency: the invention of nonsense drawing after focal cortical lesions. *Neuropsychologia*, *15*, 653–674.

Kahneman, D. (1973). *Attention and Effort*. Englewood Cliffs, NJ: Prentice Hall.

Kawashima, R., Satoh, K., Itoh, H., Ono, S. *et al.* (1996). Functional anatomy of GO/NO-GO discrimination and response selection – a PET study in man. *Brain Research*, *728*, 79–89.

Kim, Y.H., Gitelman, D.R., Nobre, A.C., Parrish, T.B., LaBar, K.S. and Mesulam, M.M. (1999). The large-scale neural network for spatial attention displays multifunctional overlap but differential asymmetry. *Neuroimage*, *9*, 269–277.

Konow, A. and Pribram, K.H. (1970). Error recognition and utilization produced by injury to the frontal cortex in man. *Neuropsychologia*, *8*, 489–491.

Kramer, A.F. and Jacobson, A. (1991). Perceptual organization and focused attention: the role of objects and proximity in visual processing. *Perception and Psychophysics*, *50*, 267–284.

Lane, D.L. (1982). Limited capacity, attention allocation, and productivity. In W.C. Howell and E.A. Fleishman (eds) *Information Processing and Decision Making*. Hillsdale, NJ: Erlbaum.

Lane, R.D., Chua, P.M.-L. and Dolan, R.J. (1999). Common effects of emotional valence, arousal and attention on neural activation during visual processing of pictures. *Neuropsychologia*, *37*, 989–997.

Lannoo, E., Colardy, F., Vandekerckhove, T., De Deyne, C., De Soete, G. and Jannes, C. (1998). Subjective complaints versus neuropsychological test performance after moderate to severe head injury. *Acta Neurochirurgica*, *140*, 245–253.

Lansman, M., Poltrock, S.E., Hunt, E. (1983). Individual differences in the ability to focus and divide attention. *Intelligence*, *7*, 299–312.

Levin, H.S. (1995). Neurobehavioral outcome of closed head injury: implications for clinical trials. *Journal of Neurotrauma*, *12*, 601–610.

Lezak, M. (1987). Assessment of rehabilitation planning. In R.J. Meier, A.C. Benton

and L. Diller (eds) *Neuropsychological Rehabilitation*. Edinburgh: Churchill Livingstone.
Lezak, M. (1995). *Neuropsychological Assessment* (3rd edn). New York: Oxford University Press.
Lhermitte, F. (1986). Human autonomy and the frontal lobes. Part II: Patients' behavior in complex social situations: 'The environmental dependency syndrome'. *Annals of Neurology*, *19*, 335–343.
Lhermitte, F., Pillon, B. and Serdaru, M. (1986). Human autonomy and the frontal lobes. Part I: Imitation and utilization behavior: a neuropsychological study of 75 patients. *Annals of Neurology*, *19*, 326–343.
Livingstone, M.S. and Hubel, D.H. (1987). Psychophysical evidence for separate channels for the perception of form, color, movement, and depth. *Journal of Neuroscience*, *7*, 3416–3468.
Luck, S.J. (1998). Neurophysiology of selective attention. In H. Pashler (ed.) *Attention*. Hove: Psychology Press.
Luria, A.R. (1966). *Higher Cortical Functions in Man*. New York: Basic Books.
Luria, A.R. (1973). *The Working Brain*. New York: Basic Books.
Luria, A.R. and Homskaya, E.D. (1963). Le trouble du rôle régulateur du langage au cours des lésions du lobe frontal. *Neuropsychologia*, *5*, 105–117.
Luria, A.R. and Homskaya, E.D. (1964). Disturbance in the regulative role of speech with frontal lobe lesions. In J.M. Waaren and K. Akert (eds) *The Frontal Granular Cortex and Behavior*. New York: McGraw-Hill.
Luu, P., Flaisch, T. and Tucker, D.M. (2000). Medial frontal cortex in action monitoring. *Journal of Neuroscience*, *20*, 464–469.
Lynn, R. (1966). *Attention, Arousal and the Orientation Reaction*. Oxford: Pergamon.
MacDonald, A.W., Cohen, J.D., Stenger, V.A. and Carter, C.S. (2000). Dissociating the role of the dorsolateral prefrontal and anterior cingulate cortex in cognitive control. *Science*, *288*, 1835–1838.
McGlynn, S.M. and Schacter, D.L. (1989). Unawareness of deficits in neuropsychological syndromes. *Journal of Clinical and Experimental Neuropsychology*, *11*, 143–205.
Mackworth, N.H. (1948). The breakdown of vigilance during prolonged visual search. *Quarterly Journal of Experimental Psychology*, *1*, 6–21.
McLean, A., Temkin, N.R., Dikmen, S. and Wyler, A.R. (1983). The behavioral sequelae of head injury. *Journal of Clinical Neuropsychology*, *5*, 361–376.
Makeig, S. and Inlow, M. (1993). Lapses in alertness: coherence and fluctuation in performance and EEG spectrum. *Electroencephalography and Clinical Neurophysiology*, *86*, 23–35.
Manly, T. and Robertson, I.H. (1997). Sustained attention and the frontal lobes. In P. Rabbitt (ed.) *Methodology of Frontal and Executive Function*. Hove: Psychology Press.
Manly, T., Robertson, I.H., Galloway, M. and Hawkins, K. (1999). The absent mind: further investigations of sustained attention to response. *Neuropsychologia*, *37*, 661–670.
Mathews, G. and Holley, P.J. (1993). Cognitive predictors of vigilance. *Human Factors*, *35*, 3–24.
Mesulam, M.M. (1998). From sensation to cognition. *Brain*, *121*, 1013–1052.
Miller, H. (1961). Accident neurosis. *British Medical Journal*, *1*, 919–925/992–998.
Milner, B. (1963). Effects of different brain lesions on card sorting. *Archives of Neurology*, *9*, 90–100.

Mirsky, A.F. (1989). The neuropsychology of attention: elements of a complex behavior. In E. Perecman (ed.) *Integrating Theory and Practice in Clinical Neuropsychology*. Hillsdale, NJ: Erlbaum.

Mirsky, A.F., Anthony, B.J., Duncan, C.C., Ahearn, M.B. and Kellam, S.G. (1991). Analysis of the elements of attention: a neuropsychological approach. *Neuropsychology Review*, *2*, 109–145.

Mogg, K. and Bradley, B.P. (1999). Selective attention and anxiety: a cognitive-motivational perspective. In T. Dalgleish and Mick J. Power (eds) *Handbook of Cognition and Emotion*. Chichester: Wiley.

Neisser, U. (1967). *Cognitive Psychology*. New York: Meredith.

Neisser, U. (1976). *Cognition and Reality. Principles and Implications of Cognitive Psychology*. San Francisco: Freeman.

Nelson, H.E. (1976). A modified card sorting test sensitive to frontal lobe defects. *Cortex*, *12*, 313–324.

Nobre, A.C., Gitelman, D.R., Dias, E.C. and Mesulam, M.M. (2000). Covert visual spatial orienting and saccades: overlapping neural systems. *Neuroimage*, *11*, 210–216.

Nobre, A.C., Sebestyen, G.N., Gitelman, D.R., Mesulam, M.M., Frackowiak, R.S. and Frith, C.D. (1997). Functional localization of the system for visuospatial attention using positron emission tomography. *Brain*, *120*, 515–533.

Norman, D.A. and Bobrow, D.G. (1975). On data-limited and resource-limited processes. *Cognitive Psychology*, 7, 44–64.

Oddy, M., Humphrey, M. and Uttley, D. (1978). Stress upon the relatives of brain-injured patients. *British Journal of Psychiatry*, *133*, 507–513.

Parasuraman, R. (1984). Sustained attention in detection and discrimination. In R. Parasuraman and D.R. Davies (eds) *Varieties of Attention*. Orlando: Academic Press.

Parasuraman, R. (1998). The attentive brain: issues and prospects. In R. Parsuraman (ed.) *The Attentive Brain*. Cambridge, MA: MIT Press.

Parasuraman, R., Mutter, S.A. and Molloy, R. (1991). Sustained attention following mild closed-head injury. *Journal of Clinical and Experimental Neuropsychology*, *13*, 789–811.

Parasuraman, R., Warm, J.S. and See, J.E. (1998). Brain systems of vigilance. In R. Parsuraman (ed.) *The Attentive Brain*. Cambridge, MA: MIT Press.

Pardo, J.V., Pardo, P.J., Janer, K.W. and Raichle, M.E. (1990). The anterior cingulated cortex mediates processing selection in the Stroop attentional conflict paradigm. *Neurobiology*, *87*, 256–259.

Pashler, H. and Johnston, J.C. (1998). Attention limitations in dual-task performance. In H. Pashler (ed.) *Attention*. Hove: Psychology Press.

Paus, T., Petrides, M., Evans, A.C. and Meyer, E. (1993). Role of the human anterior cingulate cortex in the control of oculomotor, manual, and speech responses: a positron emission tomography study. *Journal of Neurophysiology*, *70*, 453–469.

Paus, T., Zartorre, R.J., Hofle, N., Caramanos, Z., Gotman, J., Pertrides, M. and Evans, A.C. (1997). Time-change in neural systems underlying attention and arousal during the performance of an auditory vigilance task. *Journal of Cognitive Neuroscience*, *9*, 392–408.

Pavlov, I.P. (1927). *Conditioned Reflexes*. Oxford: Clarendon.

Ponsford, J. and Kinsella, G. (1992). Attentional deficits following severe closed head injury. *Journal of Clinical and Experimental Neuropsychology*, *14*, 822–838.
Posner, M.I. (1978). *Chronometric Explorations of Mind.* Hillsdale, NJ: Erlbaum.
Posner, M.I. (1980). Orienting of attention. *Quarterly Journal of Experimental Psychology*, *32*, 3–25.
Posner, M.I. and Boies. S.J. (1971). Components of attention. *Psychological Review*, *78*, 391–408.
Posner, M.I. and DiGirolamo, G.J. (1998). Executive attention. In R. Parasuraman (ed.) *The Attentive Brain*. Cambridge, MA: MIT Press.
Posner, M.I. and Petersen, S.E. (1990). The attention system of the human brain. *Annual Review of Neuroscience*, *13*, 25–42.
Posner, M.I. and Rafal, R.D. (1987). Cognitive theories of attention and the rehabilitation of attentional deficits. In R.J. Meier, A.C. Benton and L. Diller (eds) *Neuropsychological Rehabilitation*. Edinburgh: Churchill Livingstone.
Posner, M.I., Walker, J.A., Friedrich, F.A. and Rafal, R.D. (1984). Effects of parietal injury on covert orienting of attention. *Journal of Neuroscience*, *4*, 1863–1874.
Robertson, I.H., Manly, T., Andrade, J., Baddeley, B.T. and Yiend, J. (1997). 'Oops!': Performance correlates of everyday attentional failures in traumatic brain-injured and normal subjects. *Neuropsychologia*, *35*, 747–758.
Rogers, R.D., Sahakian, B.J., Hodges, J.R., Polkey, C.E. Kennard, C. and Robbins, T.W. (1998). Dissociating executive mechanisms of task control following frontal lobe damage and Parkinson's disease. *Brain*, *121*, 815–842.
Rohrbaugh, J.W. (1984). The orienting reflex: performance and central nervous system manifestations. In R. Parasuraman and D.R. Davies (eds) *Varieties of Attention*. Orlando: Academic Press.
Rosvold, H.E., Mirsky, A.F., Sarason, I., Bransome, D.E. and Beck, L.H. (1956). A continuous performance test for brain damage. *Journal of Consulting Psychology*, *20*, 343–350.
Sanders, A.F. (1997). A summary of resource theories from a behavioral perspective. *Biological Psychology*, *45*, 5–18.
Sandson, J. and Albert, M.L. (1984). Varieties of perseveration. *Neuropsychologia*, *22*, 715–732.
See, J.E., Howe, S.R., Warm, J.S. and Dember, W.N. (1995). Meta-analysis of the sensitivity decrement in vigilance. *Psychological Bulletin*, *117*, 230–249.
Shallice, T. (1982). Specific impairments of planning. In D.E. Broadbent and L. Weiskrantz (eds) *The Neuropsychology of Cognitive Functions*. London: The Royal Society.
Shallice, T. (1988). *From Neuropsychology to Mental Structure*. Cambridge: Cambridge University Press.
Shallice, T. (1991). Précis of 'From neuropsychology to mental structure'. *Behavioral and Brain Sciences*, *14*, 429–469.
Shum, D.H., McFarland, K. and Bain, J.D. (1994). Effects of closed-head injury on attentional processes: generality of Sternberg's additive factor method. *Journal of Clinical and Experimental Neuropsychology*, *16*, 547–555.
Shum, D.H., McFarland, K., Bain, J.D. and Humphreys, M.S. (1990). The effects of closed-head injury upon attentional processes: an information processing stage analysis. *Journal of Clinical and Experimental Neuropsychology*, *12*, 247–264.

Sokolov, Y.N. (1963). *Perception and the Conditioned Reflex*. New York: Macmillan.

Spikman, J., van Zomeren, A.H. and Deelman, B.G. (1996). Deficit of attention after closed-head injury: slowness only? *Journal of Clinical and Experimental Neuropsychology*, *18*, 755–767.

Sprengelmeyer, R., Lange, H. and Hömberg, V. (1995). The pattern of attentional deficits in Huntington's disease. *Brain*, *118*, 145–152.

Sternberg, S. (1969). The discovery of processing stages: extension of Donder's method. *Acta Psychologica*, *30*, 276–315.

Sturm, W., Willmes, K., Orgass, B. and Hartje, W. (1997). Do specific attention deficits need specific training? *Neuropsychological Rehabilitation*, *7*, 81–103.

Stuss, D.T., Stethem, L.L., Hugenholtz, H., Picto, T., Pivik, J. and Richard, M.T. (1989). Reaction time after head injury: fatigue, divided and focused attention, and consistency of performance. *Journal of Neurology, Neurosurgery and Psychiatry*, *52*, 742–748.

Sutton, S., Hakerem, G., Zubin, J. and Portnoy, M. (1961). The effect of shift of sensory modality on serial reaction time: a comparison of schizophrenics and normals. *American Journal of Psychology*, *74*, 224–232.

Teasdale, N., Bard, C., LaRue, J. and Fleury, M. (1993). On the cognitive penetrability of posture control. *Experimental Aging Research*, *19*, 1–13.

Teuber, H.L. (1955). Physiological Psychology. *Annual Review of Psychology*, *6*, 267–296.

Treisman, A. (1991). Search, similarity, and integration of features between and within dimensions. *Journal of Experimental Psychology: Human Perception and Performance*, *17*, 652–676.

Treisman, A. (1993). The perception of features and objects. In A. Baddeley and L. Weiskranz (eds) *Attention, Awareness, and Control*. Oxford: Clarendon.

Treisman, A.M. and Gelade, G. (1980). A feature-integration theory of attention. *Cognitive Psychology*, *12*, 97–136.

Treisman, A. and Schmidt, H. (1982). Illusory conjunctions in the perception of objects. *Cognitive Psychology*, *14*, 107–141.

Tzourio, N., El Massioui, F., Crivello, F., Joliot, M., Renault, B. and Mazoyer, B. (1997). Functional anatomy of human auditory attention studied with PET. *Neuroimage*, *5*, 63–77.

van Zomeren, A.H. (1981). Reaction time and attention after closed head injury. Riksuniversiteit Groningen: Dissertation.

van Zomeren, A.H. and Brouwer, W.H. (1994). *Clinical Neuropsychology of Attention*. New York: Oxford University Press.

van Zomeren, A.H., Brouwer, W.H. and Deelman, B.G. (1984). Attentional deficits: the riddles of selectivity, speed and alertness. In N. Brooks (ed.) *Closed Head Injury*. Oxford: Oxford University Press.

van Zomeren, A.H., Brouwer, W.H., Rothengatter, J.A. and Snoek, J.W. (1988). Fitness to drive a car after recovery from severe head injury. *Archives of Physical Medicine and Rehabilitation*, *69*, 90–96.

van Zomeren, A.H. and van den Burg, W. (1985). Residual complaints of patients two years after severe head injury. *Journal of Neurology, Neurosurgery and Psychiatry*, *48*, 21–28.

Vecera, S.P. and Farah, M.J. (1994). Does visual attention select objects or locations? *Journal of Experimental Psychology: General*, *123*, 146–160.

Vilkki, J. (1989). Perseveration in memory for figures after frontal lobe lesion. *Neuropsychologia*, *27*, 1101–1114.

Vilkki, J. and Holst, P. (1994). Speed and flexibility in word fluency-tasks after focal brain lesions. *Neuropsychologia*, *32*, 1257–1262.

Wagensonner, M. (1986). Vigilanzstörungen als eine spezifische Form von Aufmerksamkeitsstörungen nach zerebralen Läsionen. Psycholog. Institut der Universität Freiburg: Unpublished thesis.

Woodruff, P.W.R., Benson, R.R., Bandettini, P.A., Kwong, K.K., Howard, R.J., Talavage, T., Belliveau, J. and Rosen, B.R. (1996). Modulation of auditory and visual cortex by selective attention is modality-dependent. *Neuro Report*, *7*, 1909–1913.

Wright, D.L. and Kemp, T.L. (1992). The dual-task methodology and assessing the attentional demands of ambulation with walking devices. *Physical Therapy*, *72*, 306–312.

Zeki, S. (1992). The visual image in mind and brain. *Scientific American*, *257*, 43–50.

Zoccolotti, P., Matano, A., Deloche, G., Cantagallo, A., Passadori, A., Leclercq, M. *et al.* (2000). Pattern of attentional impairment following closed head injury: a collaborative European study. *Cortex*, *36*, 93–107.

Zubin, J. (1975). Problem of attention in schizophrenia. In M.L. Kietzman, S. Sutton and J. Zubin (eds) *Experimental Approaches to Psychopathology*. New York: Academic Press.

Part II

Assessment and diagnosis

Chapter 3

Attentional complaints evoked by traumatic brain-injured and stroke patients: frequency and importance

Michel Leclercq, Gérard Deloche and Marc Rousseaux

Unlike other cognitive disorders such as those affecting memory or language, attentional deficits resulting from neurological diseases have been the subject of objective, precise and detailed assessment only for the last twenty years or so (Richard, 1980; van Zomeren, 1981). Indeed the assessment of attentional efficiency was, until recently, mainly based on clinical observation (Benson and Geschwind, 1975; Hécaen and Albert, 1978). During the interview or psychometric investigations, the examiner based his/her observations on questions such as: in the course of conversation is the subject able to stay focused on the theme, to fix his/her gaze on the interlocutor without being distracted by some external or ideational interference unrelated to the content of the exchange? During the investigation is the patient able to maintain his/her attention on the task? Have surrounding noises a negative impact on his/her efficiency? Is the efficiency constant or, on the contrary, has it a tendency to decrease with time? And so on.

The assessment based on clinical observation leads to different situations. First, there is the situation in which one records a discrepancy between the complaints expressed by the patient or his/her close relatives and the behaviour during examination. Indeed, from the examiner's point of view, the attentional behaviour in many cases seems normal and adapted in spite of explicit complaints. This discrepancy between explicit complaints and the absence of clinical manifestation is due to the fact that the limitations described by the patient emerge exclusively in particular situations or can be revealed only by means of specific tools because they are sub-clinical. In spite of the lack of overt signs, these limitations act as a disabling brake on the subject's adaptation to domestic or social life. Moreover the sub-clinical attentional limitations are often underestimated or ignored by therapists or experts, with different prejudicial consequences for rehabilitation or for the evaluation of disability: failure to take into account the consequences of attentional disorders for other cognitive functions, inadequate adjustment of the treatment strategy, interpretation errors of the pathological aspect of some clinical pictures (for example, the notion of subjective post-concussional syndrome), underestimation of the degree of compensation during the evaluation by experts, etc. The risk of underestimation increases even more when there is no explicit complaint from the subject. Indeed, this will erroneously reinforce the idea in the examiner that the subject does not present any attentional deficit. In this case, only the observations coming from other health workers will be able to warn the examiner of attentional limitations.

Besides the absence of overt clinical signs, two other elements can also contribute to underestimating the presence and/or the importance of deficits. The first concerns the underestimation by the subject him/herself. Such underestimation can be in the form of reporting deficits as a banal feature of life, or it can be linked to a denial aiming to protect the subject's image of self, or it can reflect a more or less complete anosognosia of the deficits. The comparison of questionnaires of self- and hetero-evaluation allows us to measure these discrepancies of judgement according to the sources of information. The second concerns the examination situation itself which in several aspects is fundamentally different from everyday life situations. Indeed the examination situation is in itself unlikely to elicit the emergence of attentional difficulties: a quiet place without distractive elements, structured and sequentially presented solicitations, examiner's adaptation to the patient's rhythm, tasks of limited duration and breaks between tests, etc. Moreover, during the examination, the patient can use a set of strategies or compensatory mechanisms allowing him/her to cope correctly with the requirements he/she is confronted with. Resorting to less controlled and more automatic processes in everyday life situations can explain the frequent and sometimes marked discrepancy between the two types of situations.

One should also note that when evaluation of attentional disorders is restricted to clinical assessment, deficits are most often described in a global and undifferentiated manner. Indeed, one sometimes finds in examination reports observations limited to the presence of 'distractibility', 'concentration difficulties' and possibly 'fatigability' without other detail. Based on a holistic approach to attention, these vague descriptions do not consider the nature of the selectively disturbed attentional processes. This kind of information has a limited interest for the therapist, who is in the situation of a speech therapist who is asked to start a treatment with a patient who is presented only as suffering from 'some language difficulties'.

In usual clinical practice, complaints concerning the domain of attention are frequent in patients with a supposed or confirmed neurological dysfunction. The aim of this chapter is to attempt to clarify their frequency and, on the basis of available data, to evaluate their importance and their consequences for the adaptation to everyday life situations. It will take into account three main sources: complaints directly expressed by the patient, observations coming from close relatives and, finally, those collected by professionals involved in the treatment.

The patients' attentional complaints

The literature constitutes a first source of data. To our knowledge, most studies examining the frequency of complaints have concerned populations of traumatic brain-injury patients (TBI); this presentation will therefore be limited to this group. Table 3.1 shows for each source the number of patients in the relevant sample, the time elapsed between the injury and examination, and the duration of the post-traumatic amnesia (PTA). As one can see, the frequency of complaints varies considerably according to the series and the kind of disorders assessed. The analysis of Table 3.1 shows that this variability is related to the degree of severity (see PTA duration) and the time elapsed since the accident (see post-onset duration).

We have computed – somewhat arbitrarily considering the important variability of the data – the global mean of the frequency for each of the aspects studied; results were ordered with respect to decreasing frequency. For the cognitive and behavioural aspects, the most frequently formulated complaints concern memory processes (46.1%); followed by specific difficulties relevant to the attentional domain: mental fatigability, slowness, attention, somnolence, multiple tasks (global mean: 35.3%); and difficulties frequently described as a consequence of frontal dysfunction: lack of initiative,

Table 3.1 (Top) Data taken from the literature about the frequency (% of patients in each studied population) of subjective complaints expressed by victims of TBI. (Bottom) For each study the following are mentioned: the number of patients in the sample studied, the interval duration between the injury and the examination, and the duration of post-traumatic amnesia (PTA).

Sources:	[1]	[2]	[3]	[4]	[5]	[6]	[7]	[8]	[9]	[10]	%
Memory	49	54	38	69	40	6	41	35	76	53	46.1
Fatigability	41	30	33	69	65	23	—	26	62	—	43.6
Irritability	36	39	29	71	35	21	35	35	52	31	38.4
Slowness	34	33	—	67	—	—	67	17	6	—	37.3
Attention	31	33	29	—	45	14	21	22	69	46	34.4
Somnolence	39	25	—	—	—	—	—	—	—	—	32
Multiple tasks	—	21	—	—	—	—	—	9	59	28	29.3
Headaches	25	23	—	—	35	23	—	—	—	—	26.5
Dizziness	27	26	—	—	35	14	—	—	—	—	25.5
Noise intolerance	26	25	—	—	30	15	—	—	—	—	24
Lack of initiative	25	23	21	—	—	—	—	—	—	—	23
Indifference	—	16	—	—	—	—	—	—	—	28	22
Number of patients:	62	57	50	55	20	20	55	?	?	23	
Post-onset duration:	?	2 y	6 m	>3 m	>3 d	>3 d	?	<1 y	<1 y	7 y	
PTA duration:	>2 h	>2 h	>24 h	>2 d	>1 h	<10 mn	>2 d	<7 d	>7 d	>7 d	

Sources: [1] = van Zomeren, 1981; [2] = van Zomeren and van den Burg, 1985; [3] = Oddy *et al.*, 1978; [4] = McKinlay *et al.*, 1981; [5 + 6] = McLean *et al.*, 1983; [7] = McKinlay and Brooks, 1984; [8 + 9] = van Zomeren, 1994; [10] = Oddy *et al.*, 1985.

irritability and indifference (mean: 27.8%). Somatic complaints (headaches, dizziness and intolerance of noises) are last on the list with a mean of 26.8%.

Besides the high frequency of attentional complaints, it has to be emphasized that deficits often persist several years after the injury. For example, in the studies by van Zomeren and van den Burg (1985) and Oddy *et al.* (1985) respectively 29% and 46% of patients interviewed two and seven years after the injury still expressed some attentional complaints.

However, there is a relative doubt about some of these studies, since in most of them the subjective complaints expressed by the patient followed either explicit questions by the examiner during an interview, or the presentation of a questionnaire or checklist investigating possible limitations in different domains, including attention. Consequently, most of these studies do not concern complaints expressed *spontaneously*. The fact that these complaints are formulated in response to an explicit question probably increases their frequency.

In other respects, these data require some comment about their objectivity, i.e. their degree of concordance with the deficits measured by specific psychometric tests. Indeed, a patient can minimize his/her deficits especially if there is an anosognosia, a frequent and marked phenomenon during the period that immediately follows the injury, at least if the latter presents some degree of severity. Nevertheless, in the McLean *et al.* study (1983), 45% of the 20 patients showed a PTA of approximately one hour and when interviewed during the acute phase (between three days and one month) complained of attentional difficulties. This percentage dropped to 14% when the PTA was less than 10 minutes, this duration corresponding to a 'mild' injury (Jennett, 1976).

In some patients, the effect of underestimating difficulties can be partly compensated for by an accentuation of complaints, intentional or not, and on whatever grounds. Indeed, this possibility cannot a priori be discarded during the secondary phase, even if it will be more probable during assessments carried out later, in the context of medico-legal evaluation by experts, a situation which is not explicitly mentioned in any of the studies included in Table 3.1.

In order to verify this hypothesis we have studied the data recorded in 26 TBI patients assessed in the context of appraisals performed with the aim of estimating a percentage of residual handicap, and determining the amount of financial compensation (phase of consolidation). Table 3.2 displays the main data of this sample. There were 18 men and 8 women, with a mean age of 33 years (standard deviation = 12.5). These subjects were distributed in two subgroups according to the degree of severity of the injury: 10 had a mild or moderate TBI (PTA < 24 h) and 16 a severe TBI (PTA > 24 h), following Jennett's criteria (1976). In this population only two patients from the second group had a high level of education (university).

The assessment of the complaints was performed during an interview,

Table 3.2 Characteristics of 26 TBI patients assessed in the context of a medico-legal appraisal: number or mean [standard deviation]

	Mild or moderate TBI	*Severe TBI*
n	10	16
Gender	4 M + 6 W	14 M + 2 W
Age	32 [11]	34 [13]
Number years of schooling	8.4 [2.2]	10.2 [3.5]
Post-onset duration (months)	33 [21]	49 [50]
PTA duration	4.3 hours [4.9]	30 days [47]
IQ verbal	107 [10]	113 [14]
IQ performance	107 [12]	98 [18]
IQ total	107 [10]	107 [16]

before psychometric investigations. No specific type of difficulty was evoked by the examiner, who simply recorded spontaneous complaints following neutral questions such as: 'What difficulties do you experience now?' or during the interview: 'Do you still have other difficulties or problems?' The complaints were classified into three categories: somatic (headache, dizziness, pain, balance deficit, sensorial or motor disorders), affective (depression, suicidal thoughts, anxiety, nervousness, tension, irritability and anger) and cognitive (memory, attention, fatigue, language, orientation in place or time, and slowness). We will limit our analysis to this last category. Figure 3.1 shows for the two subgroups the frequency (% of patients) and the importance (score from 0 to 3) of complaints concerning these different cognitive aspects.

The severe TBI group (2) differed from the mild or moderate TBI group (1)

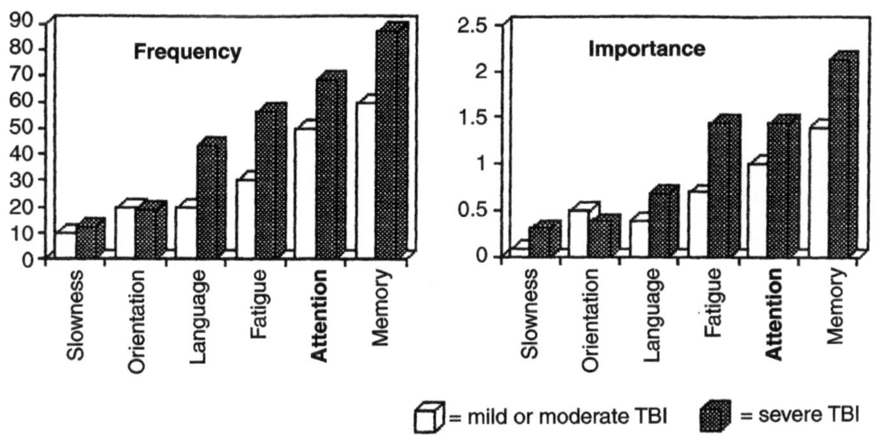

Figure 3.1 Types, frequency and importance of cognitive complaints spontaneously expressed by a group of 26 TBI patients assessed in the context of a medico-legal appraisal

in a higher frequency and severity of complaints. The difference reached a statistically significant level (Student's t-test: $p<.05$) in each case.

Complaints most frequently mentioned in both groups concerned memory, then attention. Indeed, the mean frequencies for memory disorders in groups 1 and 2 were 60% (6 out of 10 subjects) and 87.5% (14 out of 16 subjects) respectively, and for attentional impairments 50% (5 out of 10 subjects) and 68.7% (11 out of 16 subjects). The importance of these percentages tends to confirm the hypothesis that the mean frequency (59.4%) of complaints spontaneously expressed in the context of a medico-legal appraisal is significantly higher than in a standard examination (35.3%).

In other respects, 3 out of 10 subjects in the first group versus 10 out of 16 subjects in the second group expressed both memory and attentional difficulties; only two subjects from the first group and only one from second group did not spontaneously express difficulties in any of these domains. This observation emphasizes the interdependence of these two types of disorders (Craik and Lockhart, 1972; Russell, 1981; Baddeley, 1990) which increases corresponding to the severity of the TBI.

The importance of difficulties was assessed on a scale from 0 to 3: no repercussion (= 0), slight (= 1), moderate (= 2) or severe repercussions (= 3) on the subject's adaptation to daily life situations. Similarly to the frequency, the importance of complaints was more marked in the field of memory ($m = 2.13$), then attention ($m = 1.44$).

Finally, we found in both groups a highly significant correlation between the frequency and the importance of complaints (group 1: $r = 0.98$; group 2: $r = 0.96$). Indeed, as shown in Figure 3.1, the frequency of complaints increased simultaneously with the importance of their negative repercussions on the adaptation to daily life. In other words, and although these are fundamentally different aspects, a high complaint frequency was linked with the subjective feeling that the attentional difficulties were accompanied by various consequences limiting the quality of adaptation to everyday life situations.

Observations of close relatives

From the data collected in a survey initiated by the Integration group from the Biomed 1 network (Teasdale *et al.*, 1997; Deloche *et al.*, 1999), we have selected from the EBIQ (European Brain Injury Questionnaire) a set of seventeen items concerning different cognitive and behavioural disorders. They were classified into nine categories, discretely different from those of the princeps study (Teasdale *et al.*, 1997): mood lability, somatic complaints, frontal dysfunction, orientation in place and time, memory, anger, depression, attention and slowness (see Annex 1).

The main characteristics of the population (Teasdale *et al.*, 1997) were the following: 571 subjects presenting with a cerebrovascular accident (CVA),

258 TBI patients and 76 patients suffering from neurological diseases of different etiologies; 62% were male and 38% female, with a mean age of 47.6 years (standard deviation = 17.8). The mean level of education assessed on a scale of 7 points (1 = illiteracy, to 7 = university) was 4.6 (standard deviation = 1.7), and the mean time elapsed between onset of the disease and the filling in of the questionnaire was 31.8 months (standard deviation = 40.1). We excluded from the analysis the 76 subjects suffering from miscellaneous disorders ('different etiologies') other than CVA or TBI. The response alternatives to the items are 'not at all', 'a little' or 'a lot' and these are subsequently coded numerically as 1, 2, and 3 respectively.

Figure 3.2 shows for each category the importance of the expressed complaints according to the pathological group and to both sources (patient and close relatives) of information.

Figure 3.2 shows a marked trend for the close relatives to give a more severe estimation for most deficits than the patient. Such an observation has already been mentioned in TBI and CVA populations (Fahy *et al.*, 1967; Thomsen, 1974; Deloche *et al.*, 1996; Deloche and Dellatolas, 1997; Sherer *et al.*, 1998), even if the discrepancy in the estimation can be linked to the type of problem (somatic, cognitive, emotional) which is assessed (Hendryx, 1989). This difference in estimations is statistically significant (Student's t-test = 4.97, $p<.001$) for the two populations considered as a single group of patients. In the CVA group, the concordance in the estimation between the patients and their close relative was effective only for two of the categories, somatic complaints and anger. Furthermore, the global difference in estimations was statistically significant (Student's t-test = 4.318, $p<.002$). The lack of concordance between sources in the TBI group was the same for

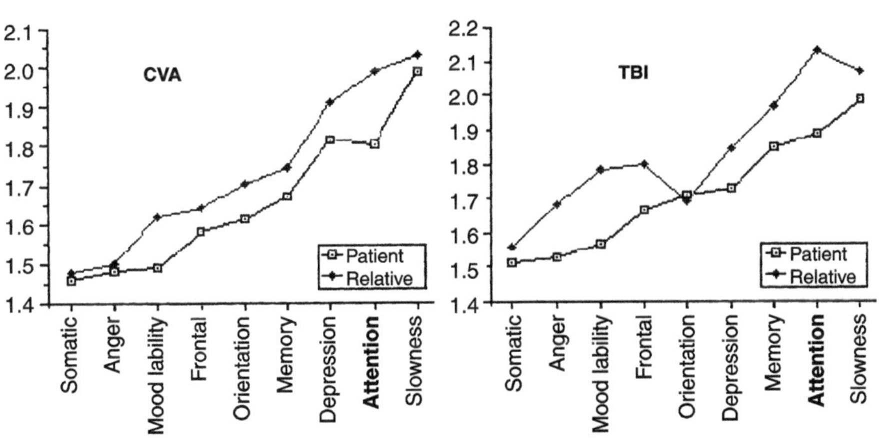

Figure 3.2 Comparative curves of the importance of complaints expressed by both populations of patients (CVA and TBI) on one hand, and by a close relative on the other hand

the number of domains (somatic complaints and orientation) but significantly more marked for the importance of the difference in estimation (Student's t-test = 4.97, p<.002).

Two hypotheses may explain these discrepancies in evaluations. The first is an underestimation by the patient of the importance of his/her own difficulties; this can be due to purely psychological (denial, narcissism, etc.) or to psycho-organic factors such as anosognosia (for a detailed analysis see McGlynn and Schacter, 1989). The second one is an overvaluation by the close relatives of the pathological aspect of the behaviour, because of the load (in time spent, anxiety) or even the 'burden' (London, 1967) that caring for a given patient represents. This feeling of burden tends to increase with time (Brooks *et al.*, 1986) and was probably important in this study as the mean interval between the onset of the disease and the filling in of the questionnaire was 31.8 months, i.e. more than two and a half years.

One other point, central for our subject, concerns the classification in increasing order of the importance of complaints. For both populations the difficulties of attention were at the second rank (in terms of severity) after slowness, which was the most marked complaint. It must be emphasized that some authors (among others Ponsford and Kinsella, 1991; van Zomeren and Brouwer, 1994) have considered that slowness is directly correlated with attentional complaints (van Zomeren *et al.*, 1984; van Zomeren and van den Burg, 1985; van Zomeren and Brouwer, 1994), and that slowness is even the core element explaining attentional difficulties, more especially in TBI patients (cf. van Zomeren and Brouwer's hypothesis of 'coping with', 1994). This interpretation leads on to include the slowness factor in the category of 'disorders of attention' (possibly representing a deficit of attention intensity). By doing so, the more marked complaint for both populations of this series was clearly in the field of attention, i.e. for the CVA population a mean score of 1.93 (mean standard deviation: 0.79) for patients, and 2.02 (mean standard deviation: 0.77) for close relatives, and for the TBI group a mean score of 1.95 (mean standard deviation: 0.79) for patients, and 2.09 (mean standard deviation: 0.76) for close relatives.

The professional's observations

In a multicentric[1] study, we have submitted 91 neurological patients and 91 normal control subjects, paired for age and education level, to a modified

1 We wish to thank the different colleagues who have contributed to the collection of the data: Lucia Braga (Hospital Sarah Kubistchek, Brasilia, Brazil), Josette Couillet (Hôpital Raymond Poincaré, Garches, France), Nadjette Cremel (Hospices Civils de Strasbourg, France), Nathalie Depoorter (Centre Hospitalier Vésale, Montigny-le-Tilleul, Belgium), Claudine Martin (Centre Hospitalier de Meaux, France), Yves Martin (Centre l'Espoir, Hellemes, France) and Emmanuel Strypstein (Le Cara, Bruxelles, Belgium).

version of Ponsford and Kinsella's rating scale of attentional behaviour (1991). The adaptation of this scale concerned the following aspects: the translation of the fourteen items into questions (self- and hetero-evaluations), while remaining as close as possible to the aspects targeted by the authors; the addition of three items (see Annex 2: nos. 15, 16 and 17) and of a final question (item 18) asking the subject (or the close relative) to compare his/her current attentional efficiency with that preceding the neurological disease; finally, the frequency gradient was reduced from 5 to 4 possibilities in order to prevent the subject from favouring the median grade. Three versions were constructed: one as a self-evaluation questionnaire addressing the patient (or the normal control subject); and both of the others as hetero-evaluation questionnaires for, on the one hand, the closest relative, and, on the other hand, a close health professional (psychologist or occupational therapist) involved in the treatment. A full version of the self-evaluation questionnaire to which patients and controls were submitted is presented in Annex 2; item 18 was not included in the questionnaire intended for the controls.

Table 3.3 shows the main characteristics of the study populations. Information concerning the coma duration was available for 39 of the 49 subjects (80%) in the TBI population: the mean duration was 24.1 days (standard deviation = 17.6). The information concerning the PTA duration was available in 30 cases (61%): the mean duration was 62.5 days (standard deviation = 18.6). These data show the general severity of the injury.

Besides the self- and the hetero-evaluations (close relative and professional), 20 CVA (48%) and 26 TBI patients (53%) were submitted to four tests extracted from Zimmermann and Fimm's computerized battery of attention (TEA, 1994): phasic alertness, divided attention, Go–nogo (condition 2) and visual vigilance (bar, low frequency of the targets). This assessment was done with the aim of searching for possible correlations with complaints in the self- and hetero-evaluations. Most often these tests were presented during one session, more rarely during separate sessions conducted over a short period of time (less than five days). From the objective data obtained by the subject in the four computerized tests (reaction times,

Table 3.3 Characteristics of the samples submitted to the self-evaluation questionnaire adapted from the scale elaborated by Ponsford and Kinsella (1991)

	CVA	*TBI*	*Controls*
Number of subjects	42	49	91
Mean age (standard deviation)	58.1 (14.1)	31.8 (12.1)	43.6 (18.3)
Proportions (%) of men and women	57 & 43	59 & 41	58 & 42
Number of successful years of schooling (standard deviation)	12.6 (4.3)	12.4 (3.5)	12.6 (4)
Duration of the disease in months (standard deviation)	21.9 (36.6)	22.8 (27.9)	—

number of errors, omissions, aberrant responses), each subject's performance was evaluated on a four-level scale (0 = absence of deficit, 1 = mild deficit, 2 = moderate deficit and 3 = marked deficit). In order to refine the correlations between questionnaire and psychometric tests, the different items of the questionnaire were distributed according to the representation of one of the following five attentional aspects: slowness (items 3, 4 and 5), selectivity and focusing (items 7, 8, 9, 11 and 12), sustained attention (items 2, 6, 13 and 14), divided attention (items 10 and 15) and shifting (item 16). The examiner supervising the psychometric assessment was different from the one filling in the hetero-evaluation questionnaire for the same patient; then both professionals carried out their respective assessments independently.

Finally, from the clinical observations and a classical neuropsychological examination, for 37 CVA (88%) and 46 TBI subjects (94%) the examiner carried out an assessment (also on a gradient with four levels: see above) of the dysexecutive syndrome, dissociating the cognitive (solving strategies, planification) from the behavioural aspects (character change, apathy, disinhibition). Indeed one knows the frequency and the diversity of attentional disorders associated with a frontal dysfunction (see among others: Wilkins *et al.*, 1987; Alivisatos and Milner, 1989; Godefroy and Rousseaux, 1996; Leclercq, 1999). In other respects, Baddeley *et al.* (1997) have demonstrated that attentional performances of patients with behavioural dysexecutive syndrome were deficient whereas they showed no impairment for several tasks that were sensitive to frontal dysfunction (Wisconsin Card Sorting Test, categorial evocation).

Considering the preceding elements, we have formulated the following hypotheses:

(I) Considered as a whole, patients (CVA and TBI) should obtain in the self-evaluation questionnaire scores significantly higher than paired controls.

(II) The self-evaluation of their difficulties should be lower than the close relative's hetero-evaluation, the latter being lower than that of the health professional.

(III)

- (a) Compared with CVA subjects, the discordance between sources (patient, close relative, professional) would be significantly more marked in TBI subjects;
- (b) in the same perspective, the underestimation of attentional difficulties compared with the pre-morbid functioning (cf. item 18: patient–close relative comparison) would be more marked in TBI subjects;
- (c) furthermore, in this TBI population, one would find more marked discrepancies between the self-evaluation of attention disorders and their more objective assessment using the TEA subtests.

(IV) More generally and independently of the etiology of the cerebral lesions, the existence of significant correlations between the scores on the questionnaires of self- and hetero-evaluation on the one hand, and the level of performance in the psychometric tests on the other hand, should reinforce the reliability of the tool and its ecological qualities.

(V)

(a) Low or even negative correlations should exist between the scores in the estimation of the dysexecutive syndrome and in the subtests of the TEA battery: the higher the estimations of dysexecutive disorders (cognitive and behavioural), the lower the performance in psychometric testing;
(b) moreover, following Baddeley *et al.*'s observations (1997) these correlations would exist mainly for behavioural, but not for cognitive aspects of the dysexecutive syndrome.

The statistical analyses were conducted with the SPSS software (SPSS Inc., Chicago, Illinois). Because of the lack of normal distribution of the data, analysis of variance (ANOVA) was done by means of the rank data (increasing classification of the raw data).

A first ANOVA compared the global scores obtained in both groups of patients and control subjects. In controls, women estimated their disorders as more severe than men, but there was no significant correlation between the subjective estimation and the age or the education level. Gender was then introduced as a covariance factor (men = 1; women = 0). Results of this analysis confirmed the first hypothesis: there was a group effect on the global score in self-evaluation ($p<.0001$), the severity of attention disorders being most important for CVA patients (mean = 18.4; mean rank = 117.3), followed by the TBI patients (mean = 14.6; mean rank = 99.2), and then the controls (mean = 10.7; mean rank = 47.1). Moreover, *post hoc* comparisons (Scheffé procedure) showed significant differences between CVA patients and controls ($p<.0001$), TBI and controls ($p = .005$), but not between CVA and TBI patients ($p = .14$). One can conclude that despite a possible underestimation of attentional difficulties (cf. above: feature of life, denial, anosognosia) both populations of patients complained of significantly more frequent attentional difficulties than paired healthy subjects.

Hypothesis II was partially confirmed. Indeed the ANOVA on the global score in the questionnaire showed a significant influence of the factor source (patient, close relative, health professional) ($p = .009$); *post hoc* analysis showed a significant difference ($p = .038$) between the patients's score (self-evaluation; mean = 16.3; mean rank = 115.5) and the close relative's (hetero-evaluation; mean = 19.9; mean rank = 145.0), and between ($p = .01$) patients and health professionals (hetero-evaluation; mean = 20.6; mean rank = 150.5), the latter being those who estimated the deficits the most severely. On the other hand, the two hetero-evaluations (close relatives vs. professionals) did not differ ($p = .89$). Indeed, where there was a progressive increase of the raw scores according to the sources (patients < close relatives < professionals), only the differences between the self- and hetero-evaluations were statistically significant. This general pattern according to the source factor has also been observed in the study by Fordyce and Rouesche (1986).

As already seen, the mean global score in the self-evaluation (hypothesis IIIa) was higher in CVA (mean = 18.4; mean rank = 50.8) than TBI subjects (mean = 14.6; mean rank = 41.9) but without significant difference ($p = .14$). For the close relative's hetero-evaluation, the global score of CVA subjects (mean = 19.1; mean rank = 43.6) was on the contrary lower than that of TBI patients (mean = 20.7; mean rank = 48.1), because the professional's assessment was less severe for CVA (mean = 19.4 ; mean rank = 43.0) than TBI subjects (mean = 21.7; mean rank = 48.6), but here also without significant difference ($p > .05$). In the same perspective (hypothesis IIIb) when they had to estimate their current attentional efficiency compared to their pre-morbid functioning (item 18 from the questionnaire), TBI patients obtained a mean score of deterioration significantly ($p = .017$) lower (mean = 0.88; mean rank = 40.3) than CVA subjects (mean = 1.21; mean rank = 52.6). In the same way the close relatives of the CVA subjects gave to this question a less severe estimate (mean = 1.0; mean rank = 39.2) than the close relatives of the TBI subjects (mean = 1.4; mean rank = 51.9).

One could therefore summarize the above results as follows: although the importance of complaints (global score in self-evaluation) and the comparison of the current attentional functioning with the premorbid efficiency showed the lowest scores in TBI subjects, it is nevertheless in this group that both the close relatives and professionals agreed to record the most important disorders. Moreover, although there also was a difference in the assessment according to the source in the population of CVA subjects, the discordance was much more marked for TBI patients. This underestimation of attentional difficulties by TBI subjects, an observation which can possibly be applied to other cognitive disorders, was reinforced by the existence (in both populations) of a significant correlation (Spearman's rho rank order correlation coefficient of 0.65, $p < .0001$) between the global score in the self-evaluation on the one hand, and the estimation of a possible deterioration of the attentional efficiency compared to the premorbid functioning on the other hand. Moreover a very significant correlation ($r = 0.51$, $p < .0001$) existed also between item 17 ('I have difficulties of attention') and item 18 (comparison of current/premorbid functioning) for both populations. These two correlations confirmed the coherence of the self-evaluations in the two populations of patients and, consequently, the underestimation of difficulties by TBI subjects.

We have also analysed the degree of concordance between the scores in the self-evaluation and the performance in the psychometric tests (TEA) for both populations of patients, using correlation analyses between the global score of the objective assessment of attention (performance score from 0 to 3, in the four psychometric tests of the TEA) and the five categories of attentional problems in daily life (from the questionnaire: slowness, selectivity, divided attention, sustained attention and shifting). The results confirmed hypothesis IIIc. Indeed, in the TBI population none of the 24 correlations was significant. On the other hand, for CVA patients almost half (11/24) of these correlations were significant. The data show that it is in the group of TBI patients that one finds the more marked discordance between the subjective estimation in self-evaluation (low frequency of complaints) and the (deficient) performance in the objective tests from the TEA battery.

In order to evaluate the degree of concordance between the score in the self- and hetero-evaluations on the one hand and the performance of the patients – as a whole – in the specific psychometric tests (hypothesis IV) on the other hand, we computed a set of correlations (see Table 3.4) differentiating the three sources of data: patient, close relative and professional. The analysis investigated correlations between the global score, item 17 of the questionnaire ('I have difficulties of attention'), and the five categories of attentional problems in daily life (see above) on the one hand, and the estimations of the performances in the four objective tests (TEA) on the other hand.

Table 3.4 shows a clearly higher number (24 out of 28) of significant correlations for the data from professionals, compared to the data from close relatives (12/28) or patients (9/28). This suggests that the hetero-evaluation questionnaire filled in by professionals has evident ecological qualities in the sense that these observations – strictly clinical and gathered outside any psychometrical investigations – correspond to a large extent with the data from objective testing. On the other hand, the degree of concordance between the observations realized by the close relative or the patient and the performance in the psychometric tests was much poorer. Of course, the degree of reliability of the collected data according to the different sources is itself to be relativized according to the degree of reliability that one can grant the so-called 'objective' tasks (TEA). This point is particularly crucial as, in the present study, patients were submitted to only one presentation of these tests. When we consider the importance of fluctuations in the cognitive efficiency of neurologic patients, especially in the domain of attention, it seems appropriate to carry out at least one test–retest for some tasks before stating with confidence the existence of a specific deficit. Despite this limitation, the number and the level of significance of correlations obtained with the professional's hetero-evaluation unequivocally suggest that this latter constitutes the more reliable of the three sources of observation. Our hypothesis IV was thus partially confirmed: the hetero-evaluation questionnaire is a sensitive tool and possesses evident ecological qualities when it is handled by professionals; but the concordance of the close relative's observations with the psychometric data is much poorer, even if it is better than that obtained using the self-evaluation by the patient.

Table 3.4 Rank order correlation coefficients between the scores in the self- and hetero-evaluations on the one hand and the performances in the psychometric tests (TEA) on the other hand

TEA tests →	*Go–nogo*	*Alertness*	*Divided attention*	*Vigilance*
1 Patient's questionnaire:				
Global score	0.141	0.293*	0.248	0.115
Item 17	0.309*	0.453***	0.243	0.151
Slowness	0.101	0.282	0.108	0.145
Selectivity	0.097	0.291*	0.268	0.019
Divided attention	−0.07	0.004	0.124	0.116
Sustained attention	0.203	0.305*	0.344*	0.17
Shifting	0.312*	0.453***	0.313*	0.182
2 Close relative's questionnaire:				
Global score	0.310*	0.342*	0.318*	0.242
Item 17	0.275	0.336*	0.279	0.325*
Slowness	0.283	0.301*	0.268	0.179
Selectivity	0.303*	0.277	0.294*	0.27
Divided attention	0.195	0.231	0.297*	0.163
Sustained attention	0.334*	0.384**	0.384**	0.151
Shifting	0.136	0.172	0.14	0.178
3 Professional's questionnaire:				
Global score	0.634***	0.528***	0.739***	0.396**
Item 17	0.549***	0.268	0.493***	0.362*
Slowness	0.48***	0.363*	0.579***	0.391**
Selectivity	0.649***	0.565***	0.742***	0.341*
Divided attention	0.56***	0.453***	0.647***	0.347*
Sustained attention	0.491***	0.537***	0.628***	0.276
Shifting	0.347*	0.219	0.458***	0.112

Notes:
* = p < .05 ** = p < .01 *** = p < .001

From our results, it was relatively difficult to interpret the pattern of correlations (significant or not) between the patient's and the close relative's questionnaires on the one hand, and the objective tests on the other hand. For the patient's questionnaire, for example (Table 3.4: upper part), it is difficult to understand why one of the most significant correlations links shifting to the alertness test, knowing that the latter does not require any alternation from one type of stimulus to another. Similar examples can be found in the analysis of the data from the close relative; however the pattern is more coherent for this source and one should underline the fact that the criteria 'global score' and 'vigilance' are the two parameters for which one records most of the significant correlations (3 of 4). These two parameters seem to constitute the most reliable indicators in the assessment done by the close relatives.

We carried out a correlation analysis of the assessment of the dysexecutive syndrome and the performances in the tests extracted from the TEA battery (hypothesis V). Table 3.5 shows the correlations between the two estimations of a possible frontal dysfunction (cognitive and behavioural level) on the one hand, and the global score, item 17 from the three sources, and performances in the four psychometric tests on the other hand.

The results confirmed the observations already mentioned above: the absence of significant correlation between the two parameters proper to the patient's self-evaluation (global score in the questionnaire and item 17) and the estimations of dysexecutive disorders. On the other hand, for the same criteria, 3 out of 4 correlations were significant for close relatives while they were all significant for professionals. This observation goes also in the sense of a graduation in the concordance between the data from the questionnaire (see above: patient < close relative < professional) and the psychometric data, and at the same time, the degree of reliability that one can attribute to each of these sources of assessment.

Furthermore, as shown in Table 3.5 (bottom part), three psychometric tests were significantly correlated to the cognitive aspects of the dysexecutive syndrome, whereas none of the correlations between psychometric tests and behavioural disorders reached the significance level. Our hypotheses were thus only partially confirmed. Indeed, as one could expect (hypothesis Va), patients with frontal cognitive deficits obtained lower performances in the different tests of attention, except for alertness. This association between cognitive disorders proper to the dysexecutive syndrome and attentional deficits has frequently been observed in the literature (see among others Stuss and Benson, 1986; Wilkins *et al.*, 1987; Messimy, 1988; Alivisatos and Milner, 1989; Fuster, 1989; Godefroy and Rousseaux, 1996; Leclercq, 1999). Similarly, the existence of an intact alertness reaction in patients with frontal

Table 3.5 Rank order correlation coefficients between the two estimations of a frontal dysfunction and different parameters of assessment

	Frontal cognitive	*Frontal behavioural*
Patient's total score	0.034	0.053
Item 17 Patient	0.147	0.069
Close relative's total score	0.289**	0.187
Item 17 Close relative	0.347***	0.313**
Professional's total score	0.5***	0.382***
Item 17 Professional	0.456***	0.322**
Alertness	0.177	–0.078
Selectivity	0.543***	0.155
Divided attention	0.46***	0.183
Vigilance	0.344*	0.001

Notes:
* = p < .05 ** = p < .01 *** = p < .001

lesions was also demonstrated in several studies assessing more specifically severe TBI patients (Ponsford and Kinsella, 1992; Whyte *et al.*, 1997; Azouvi *et al.*, 1998). On the other hand, the observation by Baddeley *et al.* (1997) (see above) was not confirmed (hypothesis Vb), as no significant correlation could be demonstrated between the estimation of behavioural disorders linked to a frontal dysfunction and psychometric testing; the only significant correlations were specifically related to the cognitive aspects of the dysexecutive syndrome.

It also seemed interesting for us to study among the population of CVA subjects the possible impact of the hemispheric lateralization of the lesion on the different variables. Only the subjects with a unilateral lesion (n = 37) were selected for these analyses. Table 3.6 shows the results of a first analysis of variance including age, gender and education level as covariance factors.

There was a significant difference between the global scores on the self-evaluation, according to the lesional lateralization, as the importance of the attentional complaints evoked by patients with right-hemispheric lesions (RHL) was higher than that of the left-hemispheric lesion (LHL) subjects. This observation was confirmed by the analysis of responses from the same subjects to item 17 ('I have difficulties of attention'): RHL subjects obtained a higher score than LHL subjects. Similar results were obtained using grouping of items from the questionnaire according to their degree of saturation for each main attentional component (see above). Indeed, the importance of complaints concerning the aspects of slowness, selectivity, sustained attention and shifting was significantly higher in RHL than LHL subjects. On the other hand a reversed profile was observed for divided attention, as the importance of complaints was significantly higher in LHL subjects.

Concerning the dysexecutive aspects, the RHL's scores of cognitive deficits were significantly higher than those of the LHL subjects; on the other hand, there was no significant difference for the estimation of behavioural dysexecutive disorders according to the lesional lateralization.

Table 3.6 Results of a first ANCOVA on different parameters according to the hemispheric lateralization of the lesion: mean [mean rank]

	RHL	*LHL*	*p*
Self-evaluation score	21.3 [51.7]	16.4 [44.8]	<.0001
Item 17	1.5 [49.7]	0.95 [37.5]	<.015
Slowness	1.35 [52.1]	0.92 [45.5]	<.0001
Selectivity	1.28 [52]	1.05 [42.9]	<.0001
Sustained attention	1.08 [50.6]	0.8 [41.7]	<.001
Shifting	1.0 [48.8]	0.62 [36.7]	<.019
Divided attention	1.22 [41.2]	1.5 [46.6]	<.017
Frontal cognitive	0.92 [20]	0.26 [14.1]	<.036
Frontal behavioural	0.3	0.21	ns

Finally, a last ANOVA including the same covariants (age, gender and education level) showed a significant difference between the performances in some psychometric tests according to the lesional lateralization. For the divided attention test, RHL subjects obtained a mean score (mean = 2.9; mean rank = 12.25) significantly ($p<.001$) higher than for LHL subjects (mean = 1.63; mean rank = 6.06). The pattern was similar for the vigilance test (RHL subjects: mean = 2.1; mean rank = 12.45. LHL subjects: mean = 0.5; mean rank = 5.81; significant difference: $p<.008$). There was no significant difference according to the lesional lateralization for the alertness ($p = .092$) and selectivity ($p = .106$) tests.

Although the significant differences observed for divided attention and vigilance agree with data from the literature (see among others: Heilman *et al.*, 1983; Posner and Petersen, 1990; Posner and Rothbart, 1992; Sturm, 1999), these results must be interpreted with caution. One is well aware of the current trend to consider attention and its more specific mechanisms as underlined by a complex network of structures distributed all through the brain. Furthermore, the macroscopic aspect of the analyses we have conducted in terms of a simple left–right dichotomy hides the existence of possible privileged links between one or another of the specific attentional components and some more delimited cerebral structures.

In conclusion, victims of a CVA or a TBI express more frequently than healthy subjects complaints about their attentional functioning. These patients complain about difficulties which are more important in terms of repercussions on everyday life adaptation than the ordinary attentional difficulties with which normal subjects are confronted. The frequency and the importance of these complaints are related to different factors, especially the situation of examination (standard vs. medico-legal appraisal), the severity of the lesions, their possible hemispheric lateralization, the etiology of the disease (CVA or TBI) and its duration. The lack of awareness of the disorders (anosognosia) or their degree of acceptance (feature of life, denial) also probably contribute to modulate the complaints' frequency and importance. Compared to victims of a CVA, severe TBI patients have a more marked underestimation of their attentional disorders and of their repercussions. It is also in this specific population that one records the most marked discrepancies between the data from self-evaluation (patient) and hetero-evaluations (close relative and professional) on the one hand, and the complaints expressed in the self-evaluation and the quality of the performance in different psychometric tests on the other hand. Furthermore, the presented data suggest that in CVA patients with a unilateral hemispheric lesion, the most severe attentional complaints (in frequency and repercussions) are evoked by patients with a right-hemispheric injury.

Finally, the adaptation of Ponsford and Kinsella's scale (1991) in the form of a hetero-evaluation questionnaire seems to have a fair ecological validity (observation reliability), but only when used by health professionals.

References

Alivisatos, B. and Milner, B. (1989). Effects of frontal or temporal lobectomy on the use of advance information in a choice reaction time task. *Neuropsychologia*, *27*, 4, 495–503.

Azouvi, P., Couillet, J. and Agar, N. (1998). Troubles de l'attention après traumatisme crânien sévère: aspects théoriques et rééducation. *Revue de Neuropsychologie*, *8*, 1, 125–154.

Baddeley, A. (1990). *Human Memory: Theory and Practice*. Boston: Allyn & Bacon.

Baddeley, A., Della Sala, S., Papagno, C., and Spinnler, H. (1997). Dual-task performance in dysexecutive and nondysexecutive patients with a frontal lesion. *Neuropsychology*, *11*, 2, 187–194.

Benson, D.F. and Geschwind, N. (1975). Psychiatric conditions associated with focal lesions of the central nervous system. In S. Ariety and M. Reiser (eds) *American Handbook of Psychiatry: Organic Disorders and Psychosomatic Medicine*, vol. 4. New York: Basic Books, pp. 208–243.

Brooks, D.N., Hosie, J., Bond, M.R., Jennett, B. and Aughton, M. (1986). Cognitive sequelae of severe head injury in relation to the Glasgow Outcome Scale. *Journal of Neurology, Neurosurgery and Psychiatry*, *49*, 549–553.

Craik, F.I. and Lockhart, R.S. (1972). Levels of processing: a framework for memory research. *Journal of Verbal Learning and Verbal Behavior*, *11*, 671–684.

Deloche, G. and Dellatolas, G. (1997). Appréciations subjectives des difficultés des patients cérébrolésés (TC et AVC). *Handicaps et Inadaptations, Cahiers du CTNERHI*, *75–76*, 101–114.

Deloche, G., Dellatolas, G. and Christensen, A.L. (1999). The European Brain Injury Questionnaire: patients' and families' subjective evaluation of brain-injured patients current and prior to injury difficulties. In A.L. Christensen and B.P. Uzzell (eds) *International Handbook of Neuropsychological Rehabilitation*. New York: Kluwer Academic Plenum Publishers, pp. 81–92.

Deloche, G., North, P., Dellatolas, G., Christensen, A.L., Cremel, N., Passadori, A., Dordain, M. and Hannequin, D. (1996). Le handicap des adultes cérébrolésés: le point de vue des patients et de leur entourage. *Annales de Réadaptation et de Médecine Physique*, *39*, 1–9.

Fahy, T.J., Irving, M.H. and Millac, P. (1967). Severe head injuries: a six year follow-up. *Lancet*, *2*, 475–479.

Fordyce, D.J. and Rouesche, J.R. (1986). Change in perspectives of disability among patients, staff, and relatives during rehabilitation of brain injury. *Rehabilitation Psychology*, *31*, 4, 217–229.

Fuster, J.M. (1989). *The Prefrontal Cortex: Anatomy, Physiology and Neuropsychology of the Frontal Lobe*. New York: Raven Press.

Godefroy, O. and Rousseaux, M. (1996). Divided and focused attention in patients with lesion of the prefrontal cortex. *Brain and Cognition*, *30*, 155–174.

Hécaen, H. and Albert, M. (1978). *Human Neuropsychology*. New York: Wiley.

Heilman K.M., Watson R.T., Bower D. and Valenstein E. (1983). Dominance hémisphérique droite pour l'attention. *Revue Neurologique*, *139*, 15–17.

Hendryx, P.M. (1989). Psychosocial changes perceived by closed head injury adults and their families. *Archives of Physical Medicine and Rehabilitation*, *70*, 526–530.

Jennett, B. (1976). Assessment of the severity of head injury. *Journal of Neurology, Neurosurgery and Psychiatry*, *39*, 647–655.

Leclercq, M. (1999). Lobes frontaux et attention. In M. Van der Linden, X. Seron, D. Le Gall and P. Andrès (eds) *Neuropsychologie des lobes frontaux*. Marseille: Solal, pp. 137–166.

London, P.S. (1967). Some observations on the course of events after severe injury of the head. *Annals of the Royal College of Surgeons of England*, *41*, 460–479.

McGlynn, S.M. and Schacter, D.L. (1989). Unawareness of deficits in neuropsychological syndromes. *Journal of Clinical and Experimental Neuropsychology*, *11*, 143–205.

McKinlay, W.W. and Brooks, D.N. (1984). Methodological problems in assessing psychosocial recovery following severe head injury. *Journal of Clinical Neuropsychology*, *6*, 87–99.

McKinlay, W.W., Brooks, D.N., Bond, M.R., Martinage, D.P. and Marshall, M.M. (1981). The short-term outcome of severe blunt head injury as reported by relatives of the injured persons. *Journal of Neurology, Neurosurgery and Psychiatry*, *44*, 527–533.

McLean, A., Temkin, N.R., Dikmen, S. and Wyler, A.R. (1983). The behavioral sequelae of head injury. *Journal of Clinical Neuropsychology*, *5*, 361–376.

Messimy, R. (1988). *Le cortex préfrontal. Ses relations avec les systèmes sous-corticaux. Données expérimentales, cliniques et physiopathologiques*. Paris: Expansion Scientifique Française.

Oddy, M., Coughlan, T., Tyerman, A. and Jenkins, D. (1985). Social adjustment after closed head injury: a further follow-up seven years after injury. *Journal of Neurology, Neurosurgery and Psychiatry*, *48*, 564–568.

Oddy, M., Humphrey, M. and Uttley, D. (1978). Subjective impairment and social recovery after closed head injury. *Journal of Neurology, Neurosurgery and Psychiatry*, *41*, 611–616.

Ponsford, J. and Kinsella, G. (1991). The use of a rating scale of attentional behaviour. *Neuropsychological Rehabilitation*, *1*, 241–257.

Ponsford, J. and Kinsella, G. (1992). Attentional deficits following severe closed head injury. *Journal of Clinical and Experimental Neuropsychology*, *14*, 822–838.

Posner, M.I. and Petersen, S.E. (1990). The attention system of the human brain. *Annual Review of Neuroscience*, *13*, 25–42.

Posner, M.I. and Rothbart, M.K. (1992). Les mécanismes de l'attention et l'expérience consciente. *Revue de Neuropsychologie*, *2*, 85–115.

Richard, J.-F. (1980). *L'attention*. Paris: Presses Universitaires de France.

Russell, E.W. (1981). The pathology and clinical examination of memory. In S.B. Filskov and T.J. Boll (eds) *Handbook of Clinical Neuropsychology*. New York: Wiley.

Sherer, M., Boake, C., Levin, E., Silver, B.V., Ringholz, G. and High, W.M. (1998). Characteristics of impaired awareness after traumatic brain injury. *Journal of the International Neuropsychological Society*, *4*, 380–387.

Sturm, W. (1999). Rééducation des troubles de l'attention. In P. Azouvi, D. Perrier and M. Van der Linden (eds) *La Rééducation en Neuropsychologie*. Marseille: Solal, pp. 125–145.

Stuss, D.T. and Benson, D.F. (1986). *The Frontal Lobes*. New York: Raven Press.

Teasdale, T.W., Christensen, A.L., Willmes, K., Deloche, G., Braga, L., Stachowiak, F., Vendrell, J.M., Castro-Caldas, A., Laaksonen, R.K. and Leclercq, M. (1997). Subjective experience in brain-injured patients and their close relatives: a European Brain Injury Questionnaire study. *Brain Injury*, *11*, 543–563.

Thomsen, I.V. (1974). The patient with severe head injury and his family: a follow-up study of 50 patients. *Scandinavian Journal of Rehabilitation Medicine*, 6, 180–183.
van Zomeren, A.H. (1981). *Reaction Time and Attention after Closed Head Injury*. Lisse: Swets and Zeitlinger.
van Zomeren, A.H. (1994). Attentional disorders after severe closed head injury. In C. Bergego and P. Azouvi (eds) *Neuropsychologie des traumatismes crâniens graves de l'adulte*. Paris: Édition de la Société de Neuropsychologie de Langue Française.
van Zomeren, A.H. and Brouwer, W.H. (1994). *Clinical Neuropsychology of Attention*. Oxford: Oxford University Press.
van Zomeren, A.H., Brouwer, W.H. and Deelman, B.G. (1984). Attentional deficits: the riddles of selectivity, speed, and alertness. In N. Brooks (ed.) *Closed Head Injury: Psychological, Social, and Family Consequences*. Oxford: Oxford University Press.
van Zomeren, A.H. and van den Burg, W. (1985). Residual complaints of patients two years after severe head injury. *Journal of Neurology, Neurosurgery and Psychiatry*, *48*, 21–28.
Whyte, J., Fleming, M., Polansky, M., Cavalucci, C. and Coslett, H.B. (1997). Phasic arousal in response to auditory warnings after traumatic brain injury. *Neuropsychologia*, *35*, 313–324.
Wilkins, A.J., Shallice, T. and McCarthy, R. (1987). Frontal lesions and sustained attention. *Neuropsychologia*, *25*, 359–365.
Zimmermann, P. and Fimm, B. (1994). *Tests d'Évaluation de l'Attention (TEA)*. Würselen: Psytest.

Annex I

List of the seventeen items extracted from the EBIQ questionnaire (Teasdale *et al.*, 1997) and classified into nine categories:

1 Mood lability:
   Mood swings without reason (item 13)
2 Somatic complaints:
   Headaches (item 1)
   Faintness or dizziness (item 16)
   Sleep problems (item 32)
3 Frontal dysfunction:
   Being unable to plan activities (item 8)
   Behaving tactlessly (item 62)
4 Orientation in time and place:
   Difficulty finding way in new surroundings (item 42)
   Forgetting the day of the week (item 46)
5 Memory:
   Trouble remembering things (item 4)
   Forgetting appointments (item 54)
6 Anger:
   Having temper outbursts (item 10)
   Throwing things in anger (item 57)

7 Depression:
    Feeling hopeless about the future (item 9)
    Feeling sad (item 18)
8 Attention:
    Trouble concentrating (item 22)
9 Slowness:
    Failing to get things done on time (item 2)
    Having to do things slowly in order to be correct (item 15)

Annex 2

Adapted version of the Ponsford and Kinsella rating scale (1991): protocol intended for the patients or the control subjects (for the latter, item 18 is not included in the protocol).

Please tick off for each sentence the box corresponding to your *current* behaviour.

	Never	*Sometimes*	*Often*	*Always*
1. I lack energy	0	1	2	3
2. I am easily tired	0	1	2	3
3. I am slow in my movements	0	1	2	3
4. I am slow to respond verbally	0	1	2	3
5. My mind has slowed down	0	1	2	3
6. I need prompting to get on with things	0	1	2	3
7. I stare into space for long periods	0	1	2	3
8. I have difficulties in staying concentrated	0	1	2	3
9. I am easily distracted	0	1	2	3
10. I am unable to pay attention to more than one thing at a time	0	1	2	3
11. I make mistakes due to inattention	0	1	2	3
12. In some activities I miss important details	0	1	2	3
13. I have difficulties in sticking to what I am doing	0	1	2	3
14. I am unable to focus on an activity for a long period of time	0	1	2	3
15. I am unable to do two things at the same time	0	1	2	3
16. I have difficulties in shifting easily from one activity to another	0	1	2	3
17. I have difficulties of attention	0	1	2	3
18. Compared to the time before my disease I feel that my attention is:	0	1	2	3

as before (0) slightly degraded (1) clearly degraded (2) very deficient (3)
(please underline the statement which seems the most appropriate)

Chapter 4

A test battery for attentional performance

Peter Zimmermann and Bruno Fimm

Introduction

All of the actions we carry out that are not based on overlearned routines must be controlled by functions that can be summarized under the concept of 'attention'. Every moment that we experience consciously is determined by the information that the attentional system has filtered and conveyed. As discussed earlier (see Chapter 2), there is no conceivable cognitive or non-automatic practical action that is not under the control of the attentional system. When we explore our environment, even if only to take a closer look, when we move through space in order to reach a goal or to avoid an obstacle, when we make a coordinated movement or adjust the accuracy of a manipulation, when we follow a conversation or contemplate what we want to say, when we plan a sequence in a series of actions or look for the solution to a problem, the efficiency of our behaviour is determined by the capacity of the attentional system. As said before, attention functions can be considered fundamental processes. When we are inattentive, 'unconcentrated', a number of things that go on around us escape our notice. We get distracted and digress, we do not remember details afterwards. Practical actions get difficult, and we make mistakes. Thus, impairments in attentional functions have far-reaching consequences for an individual's participation in almost every area of life: everyday activities, education, work, traffic, and nearly every other conceivable activity (see Chapter 2).

Even the diverse demands that are made when controlling different perceptual actions, movements and activities as well as cognitive performance clearly show that attention must be based on a complex system of specific functions. The fact that specific attentional performances are linked to every kind of cognitive, perceptual, or motor action, which each have different cerebral representations, indicates that 'attention' cannot have a circumscribed localization. Rather, the attention system is represented in a cerebral network which is closely linked to almost every function under our conscious control.

In this sense, Margulis (1985) concludes:

> 'Paying attention' requires the coordinate activity of many brain systems. The complexity of the precursor processes by which the brain shifts through inputs to interpret, prioritize, learn and coordinate efferent activities tends to discourage thought that there may be any relatively simple mechanism or substratum to mediate as intricate an activity as attention.
>
> (p. 222)

The complexity of this system, which involves nearly every brain structure, has been well documented by recordings of cerebral activation patterns using neuroimaging techniques (e.g. Posner and Raichle, 1994; Corbetta *et al.*, 1998; Coull and Nobre, 1998; Johannsen *et al.*, 1997; Kim *et al.*, 1999; Sturm *et al.*, 1999). However, a network of structures involving almost every larger brain area could be demonstrated even for specific individual performances. For example, this was found to be the case for saccadic eye movements, certainly one of the most efficient mechanisms of selective visual attention. According to the studies by Robinson and McClurkin (1989) and Fischer and Boch (1991), the following, though not exhaustive, list of structures has been associated with attentional processes: striate cortex, prestriate cortex, medial temporal cortex, inferior parietal cortex, frontal eye fields, prefrontal cortex, cingulate gyrus, nucleus pulvinaris, lateral geniculate nucleus, substantia nigra, superior colliculus, as well as the network of neuronal connections and feedback loops between these structures.

The fact that the cerebral representation of attentional performance takes the form of a widespread network makes the attentional system extremely vulnerable. There is hardly a brain lesion or brain disease imaginable which does not affect substructures relevant to attention. This explains why impairments in attentional performance are one of the most frequently observed deficits following brain lesions or brain disease of various etiologies. However, in accordance with the complexity of the system, very specific impairments can occur which each have very different effects on everyday performance.

Quoting Lezak (1995):

> When this sort of impairment (impaired attention and concentration) occurs, all the cognitive functions may be intact and the person may even be capable of better than the average performance, yet overall cognitive productivity suffers from inattentiveness, faulty concentration and consequent fatigue.
>
> (Lezak, 1995, p. 40)

As mentioned before (see Chapter 2), intact attentional performance can also have important potential for compensation for impairments and restrictions in various cases of brain damage and brain disease. This implies the necessity of carefully examining the attentional performance in each individual patient. This is the only way to guarantee efficient therapeutic treatment and counselling of the patient with regard to the rehabilitation at home and at work and appropriate suggestions to cope with problems of everyday life. The 'Test battery for Attentional Performance' (TAP) was developed with these goals in mind.

1 Development of the test battery

The 'Test for Attentional Performance' was initially developed for the assessment of attentional deficits in patients with cerebral lesions (Zimmermann and Fimm, 1993, 1995). The core of the procedures is reaction time tasks of low complexity allowing the evaluation of very specific deficiencies. The tasks consist of simple and easily distinguishable stimuli that the patients react to by a simple motor response. Thus, the influence of a number of factors that would have an inhibiting effect on testing is kept to a limit. As much as possible, it was attempted to account for factors that may disrupt testing, such as hemiparesis, ataxia, visual disorders, and aphasic symptoms. With few exceptions, the stimuli make no demand on verbal capacities. The standardization and validation of the test battery were supported by institutions in Belgium, Germany, France and Italy.[1]

The test battery is a computerized procedure running on PC under MS-DOS or pure DOS mode within Windows 95 or 98. It makes no special demands on the hardware configuration. Results can be presented as lists or graphics on the screen or printed out.

The subtests permit us to assess a variety of attentional aspects such as alertness, divided attention, overt and covert shift of attention, vigilance, neglect, visual search, working memory, inhibitory processes, intermodal comparison and the flexibility of focused attention.

2 Description of the testing procedures

The test battery comprises thirteen subtests which allow us to examine a large spectrum of specific attentional performances. In the following, a short description of the different subtests will be given.

Alertness

This test is designed to measure processes of tonic and phasic alertness (Posner and Rafal, 1987). It includes a simple and a cued reaction time task

1 The tests are available in German, French, English, Italian, Spanish, Catalan and Dutch. These language adaptations were made possible partly due to support of the E.S.C.A.P.E project of the European Community (Stachowiak, 1993).

with a visual test stimulus and an acoustic cue. The range of reaction times is of special interest in that there is great variability, which may be the expression of 'lapses of attention' (van Zomeren and Brouwer, 1987).

Covert shift of attention

The examination consists of a simple visual reaction time task with preceding cue, an arrow in the centre of the screen pointing with high probability to the side where the target stimulus will appear (valid cues: 80% of the presentations) or in rare cases to the opposed side (invalid cues: 20% of the presentations). The ability to shift the attentional focus is evaluated by the RT with valid cues and the difference in RT between the trials with valid and invalid cues (Posner, 1980).

Divided attention

This dual-task procedure is supposed to assess the capacity of attention, according to Kahneman (1973), by minimizing the extent of structural interference between the two tasks. In the present examination, this is realized by use of visual and acoustic stimuli. The visual task consists of crosses that appear in a random configuration in a 4 × 4 matrix. The subject has to detect whether the crosses form the corners of a square. The acoustic task includes a regular sequence of high and low beeps. The subject has to detect an irregularity in the sequence. In practice tasks, it can be established that the subject can perform the single task without difficulty.

Eye movement

Disengagement of attention and subsequent eye movements to the left and right hemispace are measured in this test by a reaction time paradigm: on the left or the right side of the fixation point, a stimulus is presented to which the subject has selectively to react. The stimulus consists of a square of dim contrast which is open on the upper side in 50% of the presentations. The square with one side open is the target stimulus. In a GAP condition the fixation point disappears 200 msec prior to the presentation of the target stimulus, whereas in the OVERLAP condition the fixation point remains on the screen, thus making disengagement of attention more difficult.

Flexibility

In this examination the flexibility of focused attention is tested by a mental alternation between two sets of targets. There are two alternatives for testing, a verbal and a non-verbal version. In the verbal version the sets of targets consist of letters and numbers; in the non-verbal version of angular and round forms. For testing, two stimuli, one from each set, are presented simultaneously and randomly on the left or the right side of the fixation point. From one presentation to the other, the target changes either from letter to number or from angular to round forms and vice versa. The subject has to press as quickly as possible the key on the side of the target (left or right).

Go–nogo

This task examines the ability to suppress a response in the presence of irrelevant stimuli as well as the response latency during stimulus selection. For testing, two different Go–nogo tasks were realized: an easy form with only two stimuli (an upright and an inclined cross), and a version with a higher memory load with five stimuli, squares with different textures, where two are targets.

Incompatibility

The aim of this test is the assessment of the capacity of focused attention, that is the capacity to reject irrelevant information ('focused attention deficit' = FAD according to Schneider and Shiffrin, 1977). Such FAD was described for patients with frontal lesions in the form of interference tendencies (Luria, 1966; Drewe, 1975; Mesulam, 1985). This interference tendency is tested by a stimulus–response incompatibility (e.g. Fitts and Seeger, 1953; Nicoletti *et al.*, 1982). Arrows pointing to the left or the right are presented on the left or the right of the fixation point on the screen. The subject has to press a key on the side indicated by the direction of the arrow – independent of the position of the arrow. If the side of presentation of the arrow and the side of response are in accordance, the condition is classified as compatible, otherwise as incompatible.

Crossmodal integration

In the present examination, the capacity to integrate information out of different modality channels (supramodal control), which is a basic process of selective attention (Mesulam, 1981; Lansman, Poltrock and Hunt, 1983; Wagensonner and Zimmermann, 1991), is tested by the presentation of sounds (high or low) and arrows (directed up or down). A concordance of pitch and direction of the arrow has to be detected by pressing the response key.

Vigilance

There are four tasks with different stimuli (3 unimodal tasks: 1 acoustic, 2 visual; and 1 bimodal task: visuo-acoustic) which assess sustained attention or vigilance. Each task can be run with a high or low event rate of critical stimuli. The different forms of testing in different modalities were chosen because the sensorial channels or the integration of information out of different channels can be impaired selectively (Mesulam, 1981; Beaumont, 1983: Fimm, 1988; Mirsky, 1989; Wagensonner and Zimmermann, 1991).

Visual field examination/neglect

The primary purpose of this test is to provide a rough assessment of the visual field. An intact central visual field is a prerequisite for most of the tests in this battery. This test is also designed to differentiate between hemianopia and half-field neglect. In the present test, numerical stimuli appear in random locations within the central visual field. The stimulus appears with a random time delay and the subject should respond as quickly as possible whenever a number is presented. During its presentation, the three-digit integer is randomly changing its value, thus appearing to slightly flicker. The maximal stimulus presentation is limited to three seconds, after which the stimulus is judged as not seen. In the test for visual neglect, the presence of a critical stimulus is simultaneously masked by several other numerical stimuli. It is assumed that, in cases of visual neglect, the patient attends predominantly to the ipsilesional visual field, and thus, by means of extinction, misses the critical stimuli presented in the contralesional visual field (Heilman, 1979; Mesulam, 1985; Karnath, 1988; Weintraub and Mesulam, 1989).

Visual search

This examination investigates the ability to actively scan the visual field in search of a specific stimulus. A target pattern, a square opened on the upper side, has to be detected in a 5 × 5 arrangement of squares with openings on other sides. Besides latency and quality of visual search, the ability to establish and retain an efficient search strategy is measured.

Working memory

The present task requires a continuous control of the information flow through short-term memory. Numbers are presented on the screen which must be compared with previously exposed numbers. The repetition of a number within a short interval has to be indicated by pressing a key. The test can be administered with three levels of difficulty.

The majority of tasks have been normalized on healthy subjects, with age (children: 6–12 years; adults: 20–85 years), education (less than, equal to or more than 12 years of education) and sex being taken into consideration.

On the bases of these normative data, the split-half reliability of the different parameters for the Alertness, Divided attention, Go–nogo, Incompatibility, Visual search, Working memory and Flexibility tests was estimated for the samples of children, adults and patients with varying etiologies and lesions. For all procedures, the reliabilities for the reaction time measures were throughout higher than .98. The reliabilities of false alarms and omissions were somewhat lower but satisfactory. Only in healthy subjects, where the number of omissions or false alarms was extremely low, did the reliabilities drop markedly.

Data on the retest reliability of the TAP and the stability of test performance of closed head-injury patients (Zoccolotti *et al.*, 2000) and 7–10-year-old children (Földényi *et al.*, 2000b) have recently been provided.

Concerning the validity of the TAP, it could be shown that its subtests are measuring different and statistically independent attentional aspects (see Zimmermann and Fimm, 1995). Furthermore, they provide detailed information on attentional deficits in the single case (see e.g. Fimm, 1996; Weniger *et al.*, 1995).

3 Applications of the test battery

Besides classic neuropsychology additional fields of application emerged, such as ADHD in children, neurotoxicology and pharmacology, sleep disorders and psychiatry. Below we present sample applications of the TAP in different domains including case reports of patients with selective attentional impairments.

3.1 Normal attentional function

A number of studies have used the TAP to describe attentional functioning in normal subjects. Fahrenberg *et al.* (1999) investigated diurnal changes of performance; Kunert *et al.* (1996) and Földényi *et al.* (1999) published normative data for the TAP based on samples of 6–12-year-old children; Becker *et al.* (1996) did a normalization study in adults. Weeß *et al.* (2000) stress the importance of the TAP in somnology; Niemann and Döhner (1999) demonstrate the use of the TAP within traffic psychology.

3.1.1 Lifespan data on several attentional functions

3.1.1.1 THE DEVELOPMENT OF ATTENTIONAL FUNCTIONS IN CHILDREN

Attentional capacities are particularly important for children, especially in conjunction with academic performance, because school instruction demands continuous, distraction-resistant orienting of attention. With this in mind, it is worthwhile to look into how attentional functions develop in children, in particular those of school age. Studies of neuronal developmental processes indicate that the development of the brain, in particular the myelenization of neural tissue, can be observed up until puberty, and beyond in certain cases (Gibson, 1991). The complexity of the cortical networks on which the various attentional functions are based implies that the different attentional aspects might show a comparable course of development.

Investigations thus far, however, have produced contradictory results. A few studies reported an improvement with age in attentional performance in school-aged children, for example, with regard to reaction time in attention tests (Mitchell *et al.*, 1990; Halpering *et al.*, 1994), in selective attention (Maccoby, 1969), or in divided attention (Manis, Keating and Morison, 1980). Yet other studies could not confirm these results entirely (Halpering *et al.*, 1994 for selective attention; Birch, 1978 for divided attention).

The data gathered during the process of standardizing the TAP[2] enable a cross-section analysis of performance in different tests according to different parameters in different age groups. In the following, the development of attentional performance in children aged 6 to 12 years on selected tests will be described. The simple reaction time was measured using the Alertness test; here, the age covers a range from 6 to 18 years. Selective attention was tested with the Go–nogo task and attentional capacity with the Divided attention and Flexibility (non-verbal form) test.

The distribution of reaction times (medians of simple reaction time: Alertness without warning; see Figure 4.1) shows a marked reduction with increasing age and does not appear to stabilize before the age of 13 or 14 years. Also worth noting in this context are the individual standard deviations of reaction times during the course of testing, which represent the stability of individual performance. The ranges of the individual reaction times are still very broad at the age of 6 to 7 years, illustrating the enormous variability in performance in this age group. This variability decreases significantly as the children get older, and begins to stabilize when the children reach the age of 14 or 15.

Another interesting aspect is the fact that the variability in the median as well as in the individual standard deviation of RT tends to decrease with age. This might result from the fact that children in lower age groups are in different stages of development. It is not until development begins to slow down that the differences in performance caused by these different developmental stages decrease. This explanation is supported by the fact that the heterogeneity in performance is highly correlated with age in almost all parameters (with the exception of the medians of the reaction times in the Flexibility test).

In a similar way, the medians and the individual standard deviations of

2 We are indebted to Kunert, Derichs and Irle (1996) and to Földényi, Giovanoli, Tagwerker-Neuenschwander, Schallberger and Steinhausen (2000a) who gathered a great part of these data.

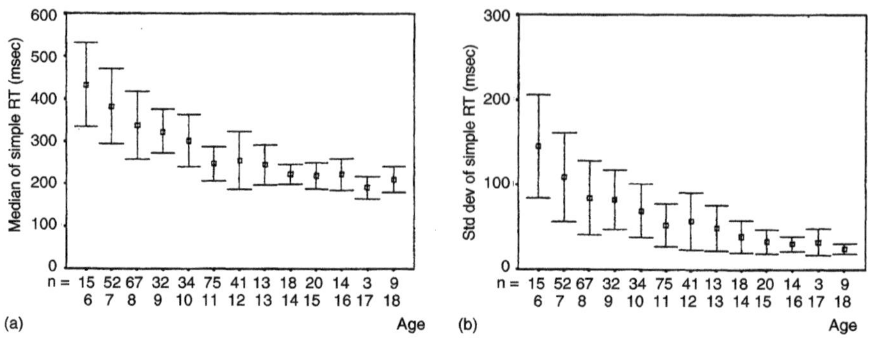

Figure 4.1 Means and standard deviations of the medians (a) and the standard deviations within subjects (b) in simple reaction times (test: Alertness without warning) in different age groups (6 to 18 years)

reaction time in the other tests, with the exception of Divided attention, correlate with age (see Tables 4.1 and 4.2). Also the correlations of medians of reaction time between the tests are highly significant, with the exception of Flexibility and Divided attention. The highest correlations are those between the simple reaction time (Alertness without warning) and the medians of the reaction times in the Go–nogo and Divided attention tests.

These correlations persist after the partialling out of age, with the exception of the Flexibility test. For the Flexibility test, all correlations vanish after the control of age. This shows two things: first, the parameters of reaction time of the Flexibility test grasp aspects of attentional performance other than those of the other tasks and, second, the parameters of the Flexibility test represent a specific aspect of development in children since the correlations of these parameters with age are the highest. This becomes even more tangible after a further step: when the simple reaction time (median of the reaction time in the Alertness without warning test) is removed from the correlation of age with the median of the reaction time in Flexibility, the correlation remains practically unchanged ($r = -.674$ as compared to the original value of $r = -.658$).

Comparable developmental trends can also be observed in the individual standard deviation of the reaction times (see Table 4.2): those correlate strongly with age, but for Divided attention this correlation is somewhat lower. In the same way, the correlation between tests is consistently very high. The high correlations with age indicate that the individual performances, as far as they are measured by reaction time, are a function of age and stabilize as the child matures. After removing age, the correlations drop significantly and vanish nearly completely with Flexibility. Here, too, removing the individual variability in the simple reaction times leads to an almost unchanged correlation of the individual standard deviation in the Flexibility test with

Table 4.1 The correlations of the medians of the reaction times for the age group of 6–12-year-old children in different tests, with age and with each other. The correlations written in italics represent partial correlations excluding age

		Age	*Alertness*	*Go–nogo*	*Divided attention*
Alertness	N	316			
		–.613**			
Go–nogo	N	387	.300		
		–.525**	.595**		
			*407***		
Divided attention	N	202	116	185	
		–.106	.435**	.258**	
			*.343***	*.253***	
Flexibility	N	235	150	235	85
		–.658**	.312**	.386**	.070
			–.154	*.063*	*–.048*

Note: ** The correlation is significant at the 0.01 level (2-sided)

age (r = –.532 as compared to the original r = –.596). This fact underlines, once again, the specific relevance of reaction times in the Flexibility test.

A somewhat different picture emerges when looking at the incorrect responses in the different tests: the false alarms in the Go–nogo and Flexibility tests as well as the omissions in the Divided attention test. Neither in the Go–nogo test (r = –.049, not significant; see Figure 4.2a) nor in the Flexibility test (r = –.075, not significant; see Figure 4.2c) is there a significant relationship between the number of incorrect responses and age. However, the omissions in the Divided attention test show a clear dependence on age (r = –.539; see Figure 4.2b). The differences with regard to age and the types of errors made are possibly due to the fact that younger children are somewhat more cautious when confronted with a speed–accuracy trade-off, whereas in the Divided attention test there is no such time dependence in the missing of critical signals.

In summary, it can be said that developmental tendencies in children in the age range from 6 to 12 years clearly leave their mark in both the median and in the individual variability of reaction times. Several paths of development can be observed: in the age range from 6 to 12 years, the simple reaction time continues to decrease and stabilize. Independently, the flexibility in the

Table 4.2 The correlations of the standard deviations of the individual reaction times in the various tests with age and with each other. The correlations written in italics represent partial correlations excluding age

		Age	*Alertness*	*Go–nogo*	*Divided attention*
Alertness		–.491**			
	N	316			
Go–nogo		–.538**	.418**		
			*.209***		
	N	387	300		
Divided attention		–.319	.351**	.283**	
			*.236***	*.139***	
	N	350	264	333	
Flexibility		–.596**	.319**	.415**	.264**
			.038	*.139**	*.097*
	N	235	150	235	233

Notes:
* The correlation is significant at the 0.01 level (2-sided)
** The correlation is significant at the 0.05 level (2-sided)

control of the attentional focus increases as the child matures. Finally, the attentional capacity grows as the child does, but independently from the changes in reaction time and flexibility.

3.1.1.2 AGEING AND CHANGES IN ATTENTIONAL PERFORMANCE

The fact that cognitive skills tend to decline with age seems be generally accepted. In addition to memory functions, the various attentional functions are particularly affected by this kind of degeneration. A large number of investigations seem to support this relationship (see Van der Linden and Collette, Chapter 7 in this volume). However, almost all investigations are based on a generality hypothesis which assumes that these kinds of developmental tendencies can be studied in ageing persons as a group by comparing the means or by using regression models. This approach leaves several questions unanswered: for example, when does performance begin to decline, what course does it follow, and are older persons in the same age group affected by such declines in performance in the same way? It is obvious that the ageing process varies greatly between individuals and that an exclusively statistical comparison between the different age groups does not accurately reflect the

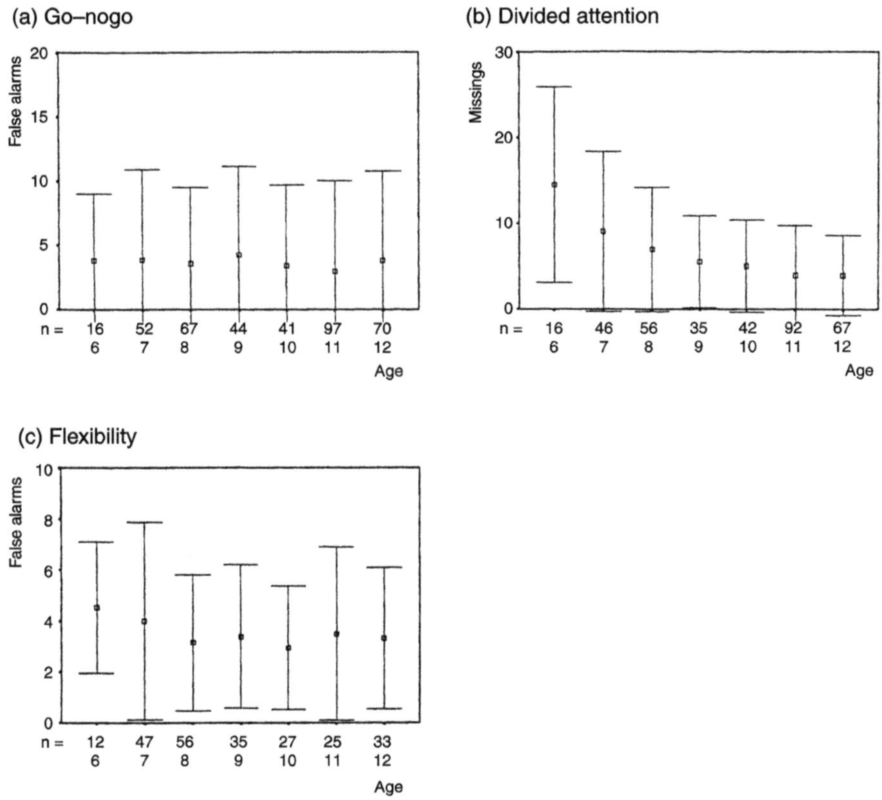

Figure 4.2 Means and standard deviations of (a) false alarms in the Go–nogo test, (b) omissions in the Divided attention test and (c) false reactions in the Flexibility test in different age groups (6 to 12 years)

variation in changes occurring during the ageing process. To be sure, the above-mentioned differential perspective is of great practical relevance: the capability of living independently depends in part on the extent to which intact attentional functions enable an individual to cope with the diverse demands of everyday activities. This concerns last but not least the ability to safely operate a motor vehicle (see Brouwer, Chapter 8 in this volume). Mobility, ensured for many older persons by the possibility of driving a car, is an important prerequisite for their independence. Furthermore, sufficient attentional capacities are essential for general efficiency in daily living and the intellectual alertness necessary for social interactions. Therefore, intact attentional functions are, among other things, an important basis for the quality of life and the maintenance of a satisfying lifestyle while ageing.

The findings that individual attentional functions are based on different cerebral circuits which are connected to very different cerebral structures and systems imply that just as these structures differ in their vulnerability, the attentional functions do not degenerate in a unified manner. However, several questions remain open: first, there is the question of whether the various attentional functions are affected to the same extent. The second question concerns the age at which significant deficits in attentional performance can be expected. The last question is whether all individuals are affected equally by a decline in performance.

The data obtained while establishing the norms for the various subtests of the TAP provide a good starting point to answer these questions. We will address them using the results from tests that are considered central. The following data will be discussed: the general reaction time, findings from parts of the test on selective attention using the Go–nogo tests, the ability to redirect the focus of attention using the Covert shift of attention and the Flexibility test, and attentional capacity using the Divided attention test.

Table 4.3 provides a first impression of the relationship between test performance and age. In order to illustrate the differential effects, the changes in the course of age will be given by examples of scatterplots for some tests. This form of presentation elucidates not only the general trend, but also the variability of performance as well as minimum and maximum performance in the different age groups. It is important to note that the results presented for different tests were obtained from different samples, since the length of the

Table 4.3 Correlations and trends in different parameters with age for the Alertness, Go–nogo, Divided attention, Covert shift of attention, and Flexibility tests

				Trends		
	N	*r*	*p*	*linear*	*quadratic*	*cubic*
Alertness without warning: median of RT	243	.21	.001			×
Alertness without warning: std dev of RT	243	.25	.000	×	×	
Go–nogo: median of RT	352	.35	.000			×
Go–nogo: std dev of RT	352	.28	.000		×	
Go–nogo: false alarms	352	.28	.000	×	×	
Go–nogo: speed–accuracy trade-off	352	.22	.000		×	
Divided attention: median of RT	590	.32	.000			×
Divided attention: std dev of RT	590	.32	.000	×	×	×
Divided attention: omissions	590	.29	.000		×	×
Covert shift: median of RT/compatible	136	.63	.000	×		
Covert shift: median of RT/incompatible	136	.57	.000		×	
Covert shift: F-value incomp./comp.	136	.15	.014		×	
Flexibility: median of RT	641	.58	.000	×	×	×
Flexibility: std dev of RT	641	.51	.000	×	×	×
Flexibility: false reactions	641	.01	.116			
Flexibility: speed–accuracy trade-off	641	.41	.000	×	×	×

test battery does not allow norms for all of the tests to be obtained on the same sample.

The analyses of all of the tests displayed in Table 4.3 and almost all of the parameters showed a change with age, seldom linear, mostly non-linear. The median and the individual standard deviation of the reaction times were used as test parameters, as well as omissions or false alarms, depending on the tests. Where possible, the relationship of omissions or false alarms to the median of the reaction times was used as an indicator of the speed–accuracy trade-off of the individual participants.

The different tests produced very different linear or non-linear correlations between test performance and age: these range from .21 (median of RT for Alertness without warning) to .58 (median of RT for Flexibility). As the results show, there tend to be very low correlations with the parameters of the simpler tests (Alertness, Go–nogo), whereas for Flexibility, the most complex task, as well as for the Covert shift, the results show a much stronger age dependency.

The course of the decline in performance with age also differs for the different attentional functions, which is reflected in the different trends in the individual tests and parameters. Linear, quadratic and cubic trends can be observed. A linear trend usually means a continuous decrease in performance from youth to old age. A quadratic trend occurs when performance is mainly stable through middle age and then begins to decline rapidly as age progresses. A cubic trend indicates that very good performance begins to drop slightly in early adulthood, remains stable for the most part in middle age, and then drops continuously with increasing age.

A number of parameters show a linear trend overlapping a cubic trend. This often indicates a decrease in performance developing over the entire adult years and picking up speed at high ages. This is the case for the parameters of Flexibility, the most complex test. In contrast, the medians of the reaction times in the simpler tasks (Alertness, Figure 4.3; Go–nogo, Figure 4.4; Divided attention) consistently showed an exclusive cubic trend, which indicates a relatively stable performance level in middle-aged adulthood. Performance generally drops noticeably for an increasing number of older persons beginning at the age of 60 years.

The trends in the individual standard deviation in reaction times in all of the tests indicate that performance becomes increasingly unstable with age. With the exception of the very simple tests (Alertness, Go–nogo), cubic trends emerge here as well. Based on these data, performance in many persons appears to become increasingly unstable between the ages of 50 and 60 years. The Flexibility test having a multiple correlation of $R = .51$ demonstrates quite the strongest effect of ageing.

The errors made in the various tests (false alarms in Go–nogo, Figure 4.4c; incorrect reactions in the Flexibility test, Figure 4.5c; omissions in the Divided attention test) reveal different trends according to whether the tests

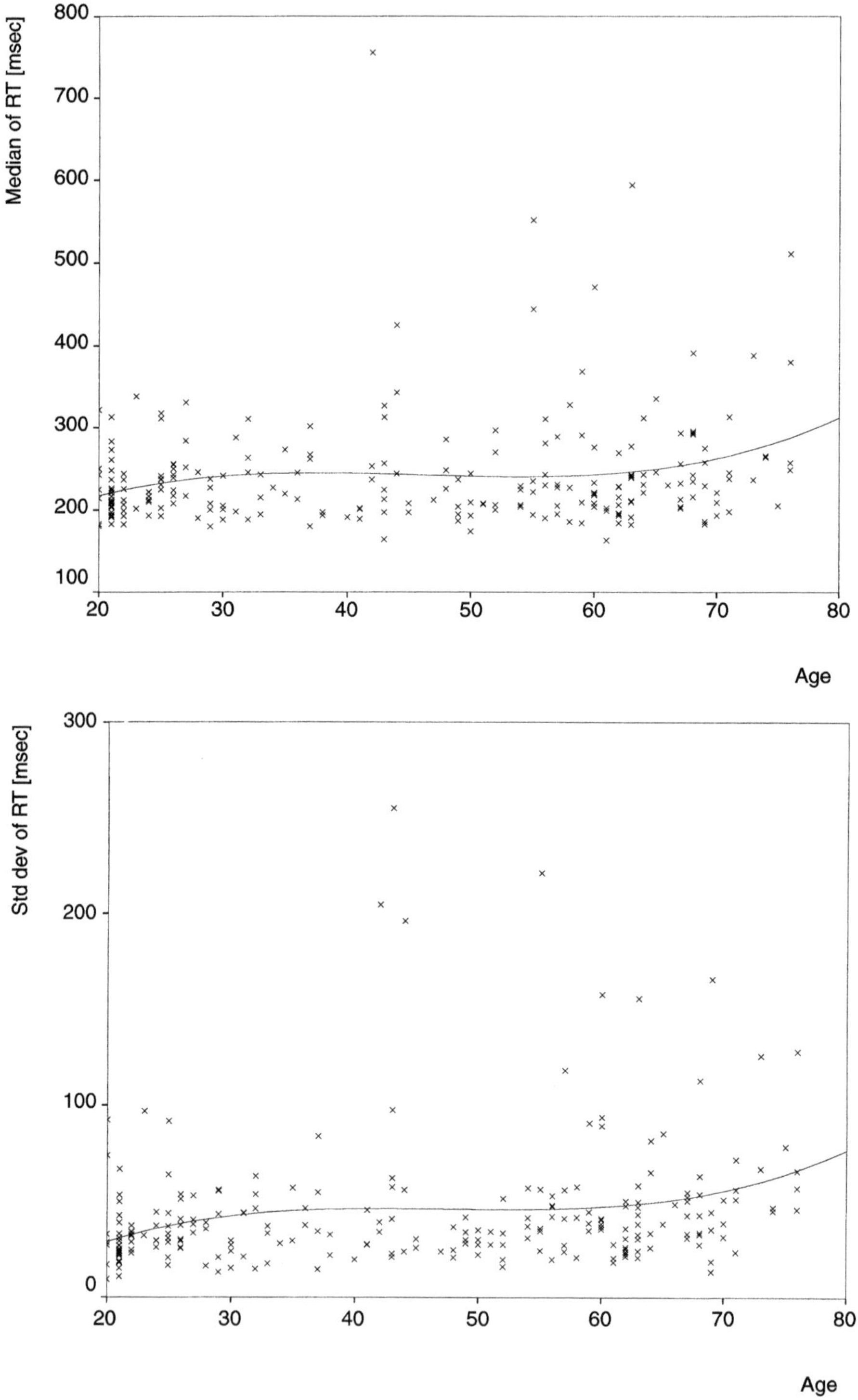

Figure 4.3 Trends in the medians and the standard deviations of simple reaction time with age in the Alertness (without warning) test; (N = 243)

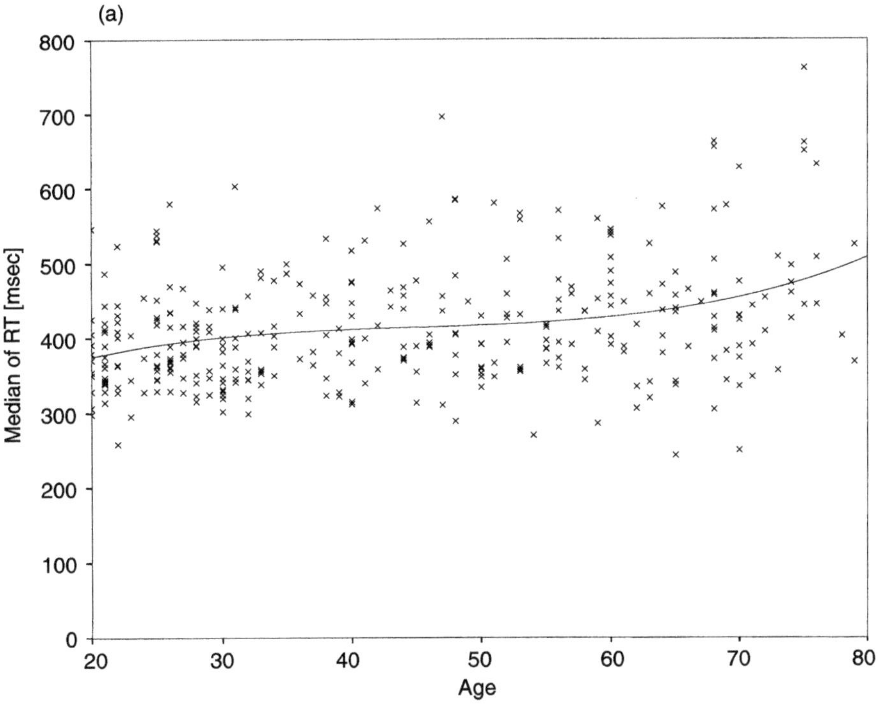

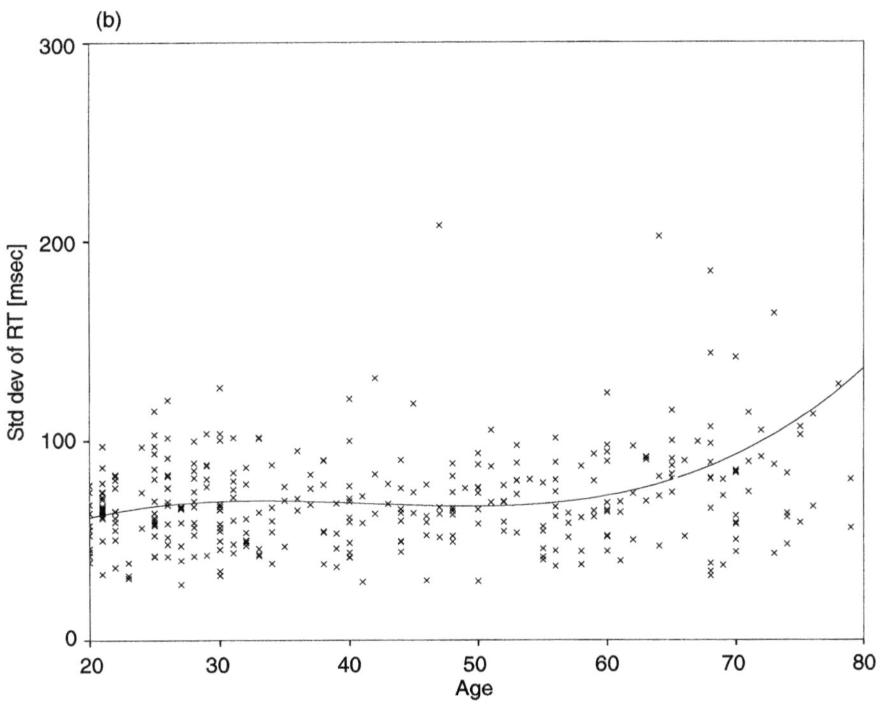

Figure 4.4 Trends in (a) the medians (b) the standard deviations of reaction time (c) false alarms and (d) speed–accuracy trade-off with age in the Go–nogo test (version 1: one critical stimulus out of two; N = 352)

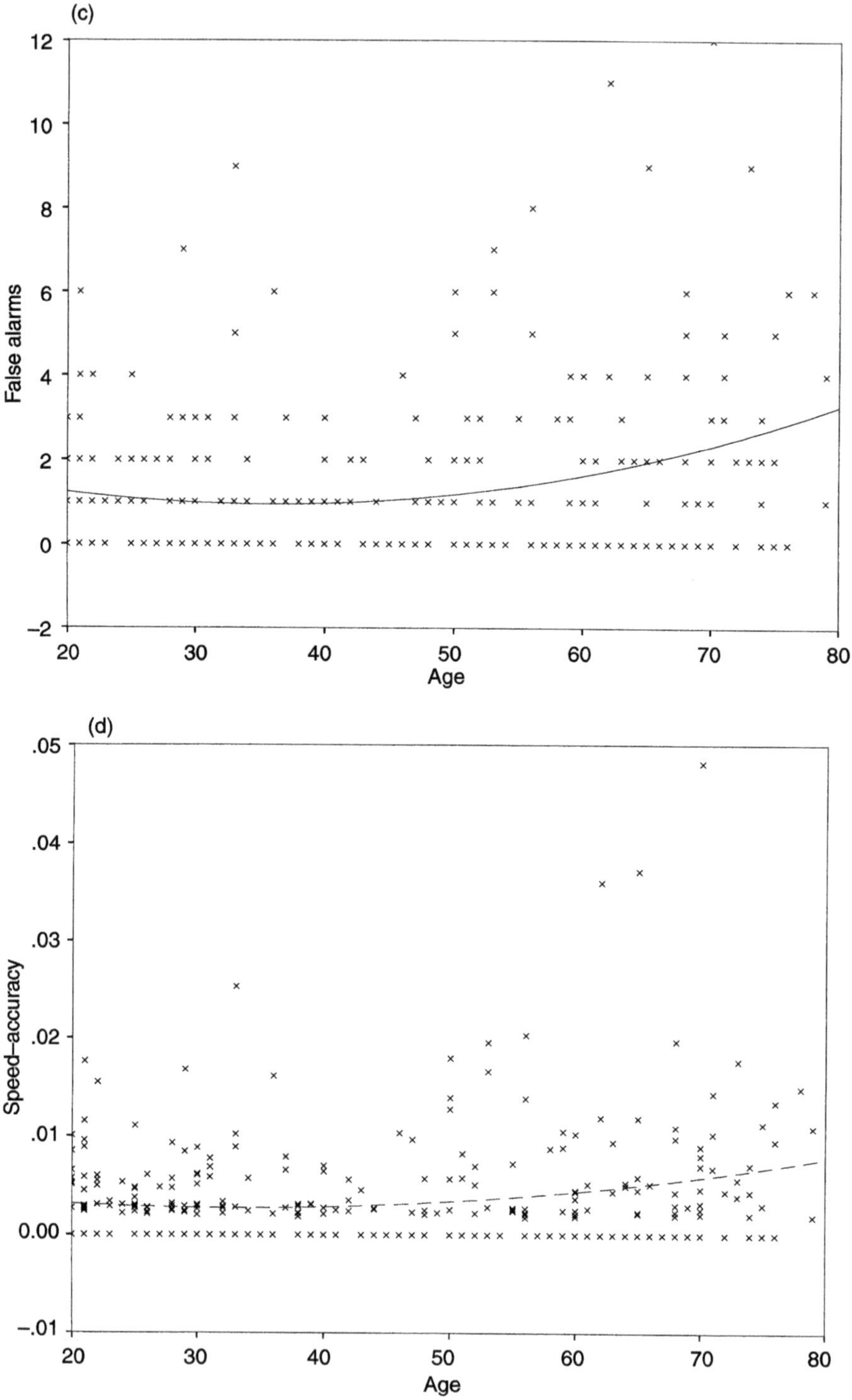

Figure 4.4 (continued)

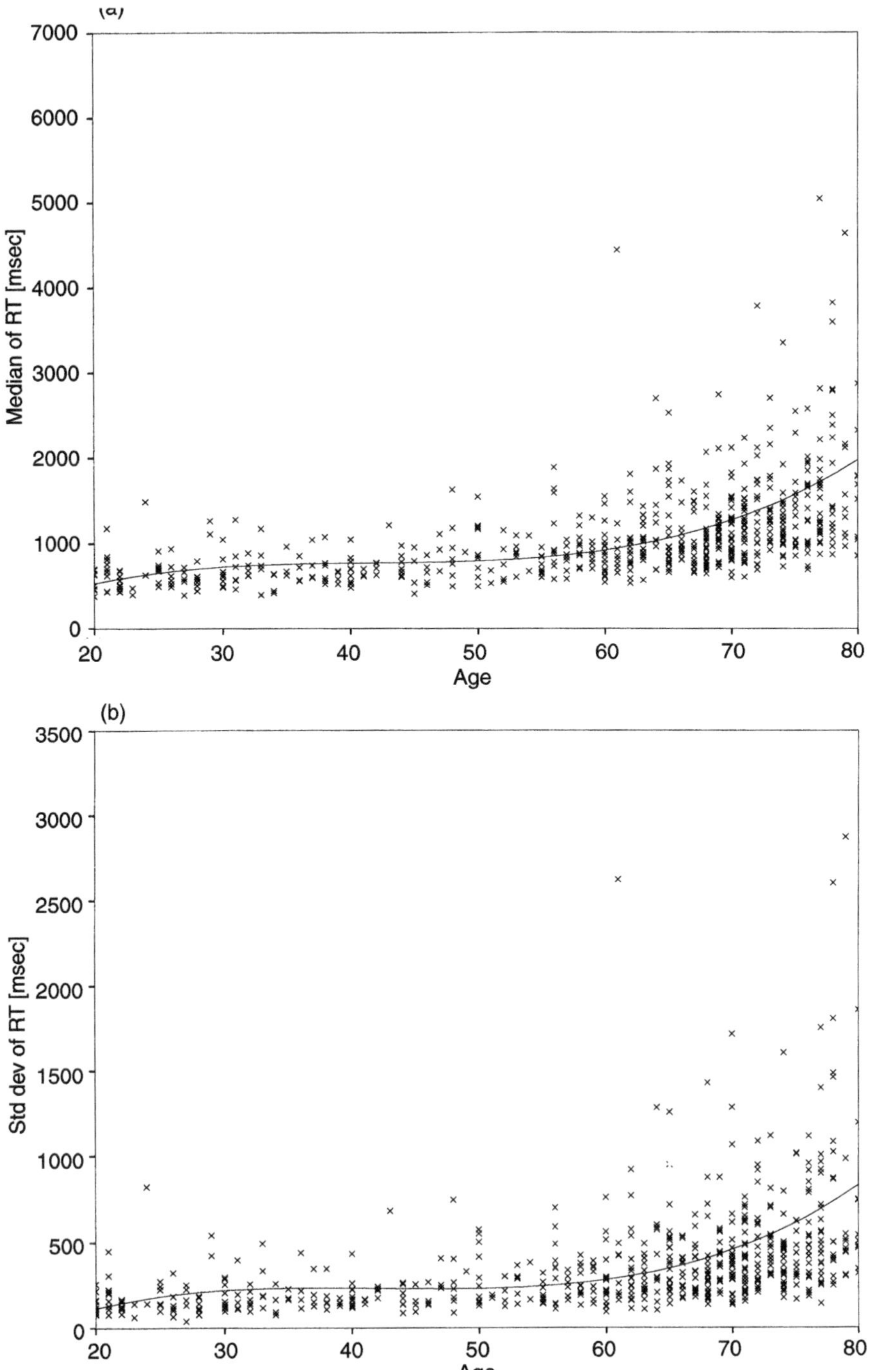

Figure 4.5 Trends in (a) the medians (b) the standard deviations of reaction time (c) false reactions and (d) speed–accuracy trade off with age in the Flexibility test (N = 641)

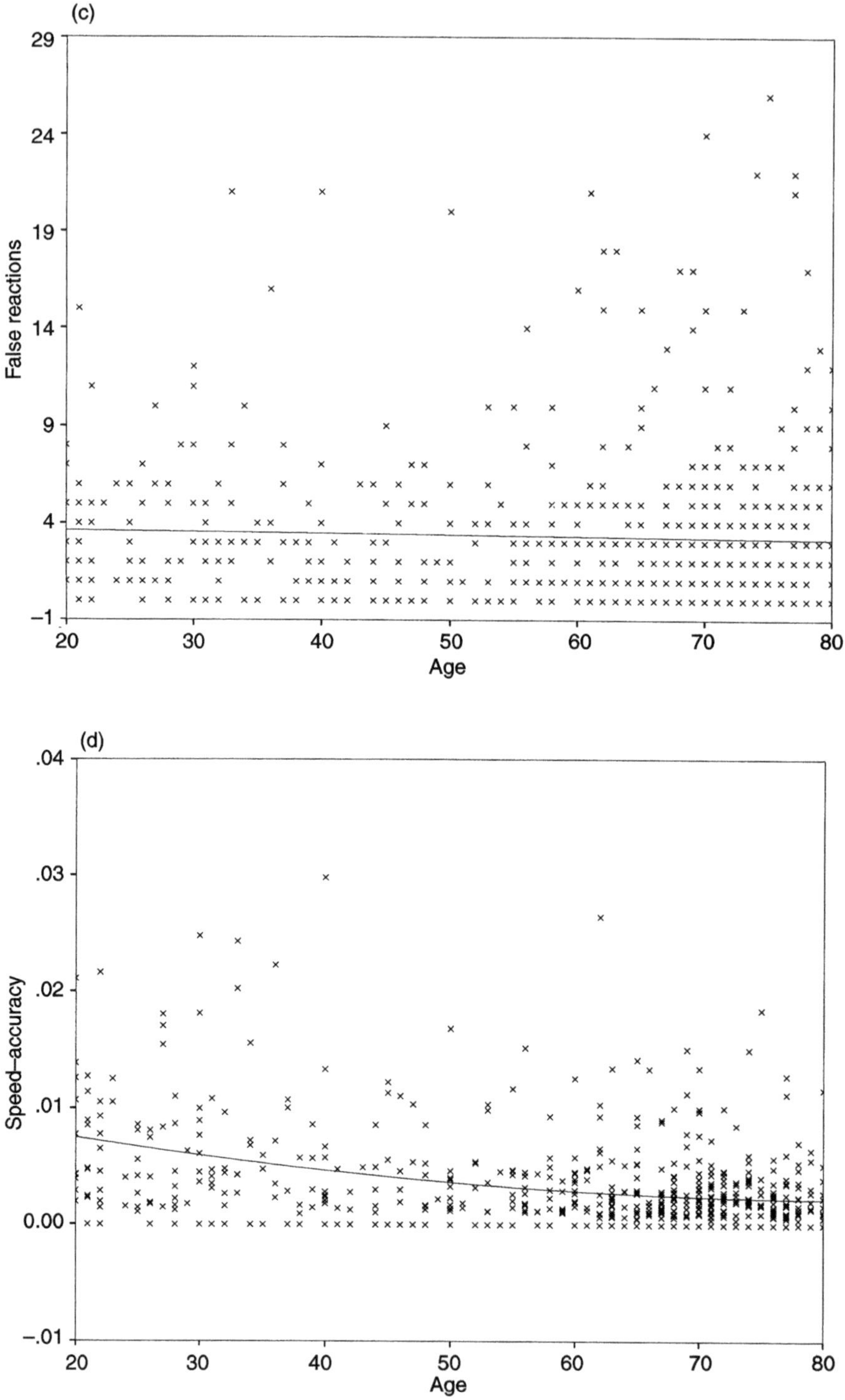

Figure 4.5 (continued)

are simple or complex. In the Go–nogo and Divided attention tests, trends emerge that confirm a decrement in performance with age.

The errors made on the Flexibility test show a clear departure from the otherwise consistent trend in the error rate. However, here one can observe a 'speed–accuracy trade-off,' which, in contrast to the other tasks, shows a falling tendency (R for trend = .41). The scatterplot of the parameter for the 'speed–accuracy trade-off' related to age shows that the behaviour of younger adults tends to be more risk oriented, then becomes increasingly more controlled in middle adulthood, and remains stable for the rest of the lifespan. This implies that older persons tend to make an effort to compensate for their losses in performance. The Flexibility test is particularly well-suited to recording this tendency, because it entails a direct relationship between reaction speed and error risk, and feedback on the errors is made immediately. This kind of immediate error control is not provided to the participants for omissions in the Divided attention test.

Nevertheless, the discussion of the general trends in the different performances during ageing must not lose sight of the differential perspective. Not all people age in the same way. In addition to those who begin to show signs of ageing comparatively early, there are others who retain high performance up until old age. This is, however, dependent on the area of performance. A general trend can be observed in which in almost all tests starting between the ages of 55 and 60 years the heterogeneity in the various age groups increases. In other words, there is a gap between those older persons who perform poorly and those who perform well above average. As a rule, this holds for reaction time, the stability of the performance measured as the standard deviation from the reaction time, and the error rate. Despite this, there are differences: in all tests, with the exception of Alertness, there are individuals over 80 years of age or even as old as 90, whose performance lies within the average range of the 20-year-olds or is even comparable with the best performance in this age group. The fact that such trends are not observed in the Alertness test is most likely explained by the fact that the data base for the age group over 70 years is very small for this test (N = 18). However, other investigations using the TAP have reported that a few participants close to the age of 90 showed reaction times below 200 msec for Alertness. Conversely, one must not overlook the fact that there are also persons of younger ages who perform very poorly.

In summary, with advanced age, there is a trend towards a decrease in accuracy combined with slower reaction times and increasing instability in performance in practically all tests and parameters. This development usually begins between 50 and 60 years of age. The performance decrement is much greater in the complex test (Flexibility) than in simple tests (Alertness, Go–nogo, Divided attention). However, the individual ageing processes show very different patterns: whereas some older persons retain a high performance level up to a very advanced age, others show a significant drop in performance.

3.2 Pathologic attentional function

In this section, the application of the TAP in cerebrovascular disease, degenerative disease (Huntington's disease) and neurotoxicology is briefly exemplified. Furthermore a variety of applications exist in psychiatry (Beblo *et al.*, 2000; Irle *et al.*, 1998; Rentrop *et al.*, 1999). In addition, the test battery has been used in patients with whiplash syndrome (Radanov *et al.*, 1999), with hypoxia (Cremel *et al.*, 1993), with tumours (Tucha *et al.*, 1999), microangiopathy (Sabri *et al.*, 1999), cerebellar disease (Drepper *et al.*, 1999), degenerative prefrontal damage (Kessler *et al.*, 1999) and Parkinson's disease (North *et al.*, 1993). The clinical validity of the TAP with respect to the diagnosis of ADHD has been shown by Földényi *et al.* (2000a). Apart from diagnostic issues the TAP has also proved to be a valuable instrument for the evaluation of rehabilitation effects (Sturm *et al.*, 1994, 1997; Hildebrandt *et al.*, 1998; Plohmann *et al.*, 1998; Höschel *et al.*, 1996).

3.2.1 Cerebrovascular disease

The TAP was used in a variety of single-case and group studies of patients with cerebrovascular disease. Weniger *et al.* (1995) described a 51-year-old male patient with intracerebral haemorrhage in the left neostratum and basal forebrain, who showed profound anterograde and retrograde mnemonic deficits and additional marked impairments in visual search and working memory. Markowitsch *et al.* (1999) were able to show intact tonic alertness in a patient with impaired retrograde knowledge system. In patients after rupture and repair of the anterior communicating artery Böttger *et al.* (1998) found an impairment of divided attention. Fimm (1996) described a patient with a right-sided haemorrhage in the basal ganglia who showed clear attentional asymmetry in the visual search task. Such an asymmetry was also described by Hildebrandt *et al.* (1999) in the visual search task after infarction of the right middle cerebral artery. Furthermore, Schuppert *et al.* (2000) did not find any correlation between basic attentional aspects (tonic alertness) and amusia in a sample of patients with unilateral right- or left-sided cerebrovascular lesion.

3.2.1.2 ATTENTIONAL DEFICITS IN APHASIC PATIENTS

In aphasic patients, attentional deficits have a clear impact on language comprehension and production, as emphasized by Murray (1999) in her review. But furthermore, attentional capacities are essential for the way a patient will profit from speech therapy. Therefore, assessment and treatment of attention deficits have to be taken into consideration in the rehabilitation of aphasic patients.

The subtests Alertness, Go–nogo 2 and Divided attention of the TAP were administered to an unselected sample of 107 chronic subjects with left-hemisphere vascular lesions to evaluate the necessity of attention therapy in the single case. Figure 4.6 shows the percentage of patients with impaired performance (i.e. T<43 or percentile rank <25) compared to normal subjects of their age.

It is evident that a poor performance in Alertness (tonic and phasic) is not much more frequent than in normal subjects (25%). The frequency of patients with increased rate of false alarms in the Go–nogo task is also comparable to normal subjects. However, the percentage of patients with impairment (or below average range) in the Divided attention test and with respect to the median reaction time in the Go–nogo 2 test is clearly higher than in the normal population. It is not surprising that the aphasic patients do not have frequent problems of alertness, since this has been shown to be predominantly associated with right-hemisphere structures (Sturm *et al.*, 1999) which are not affected in these patients.

A subsample of patients was additionally examined by the single-task (unimodal) versions of the Divided attention test, i.e. with only visual (squares) or acoustic (tonal sequence) stimuli. A detailed analysis of the omissions in the simple and complex versions of this task suggests that the dual-task situation leads predominantly to an impairment in the processing of acoustic but not visual stimuli, as can be deduced from Figure 4.7. Treatments of this divided attention deficit as well as language therapy should consider this.

These results might suggest that the assessment of attention in aphasic patients could be confined to selective and divided attention. This conclusion

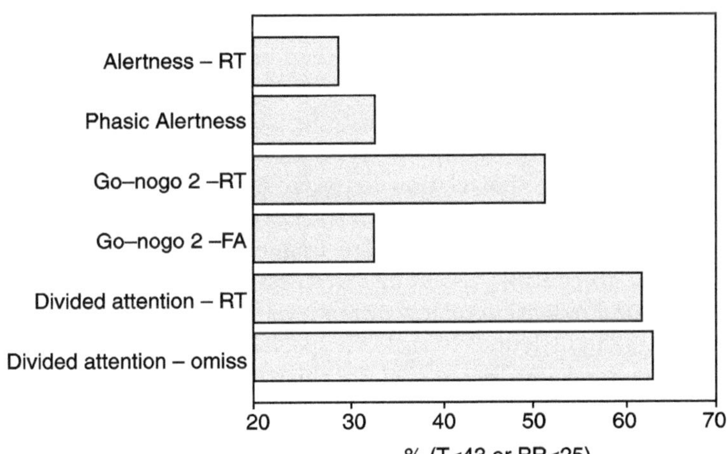

Figure 4.6 Percentage of aphasic patients with T-values less than 43 in different-TAP tests

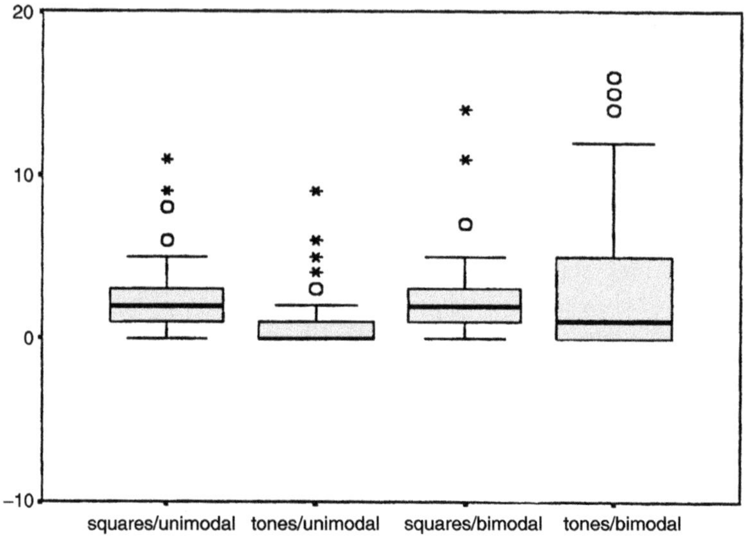

Figure 4.7 Boxplots of the omissions in the unimodal (squares or tones) and bimodal (squares and tones) Divided attention test

is misleading, as Figure 4.8 shows. Comparing the activation level (tonic alertness) of the patients with the control group, not just by using the T-values but by looking at the raw median reaction times, reveals a profound impairment of several patients, whose performance lies completely outside the normal range, i.e. comparable to outliers and extreme values in the control group. Patients with median reaction times (condition without warning tone) above 400 msec have a seriously reduced activation level which certainly affects the performance in other attentional domains. This is exemplified in a non-significant Spearman rank-order correlation of 0.13 for the control group and a highly significant correlation of 0.41 ($p<.001$) for the patient group concerning the relation between Alertness (median reaction time) and the total number of omissions in the Divided attention test. Therefore, even if Alertness is not much more frequently impaired in aphasic patients compared to controls, assessing Alertness is recommended since in single cases profound reductions of activation level influencing more complex attentional aspects can be found. In this case specific therapy for this deficit is necessary (see Chapter 13 by Sturm *et al.*, in this volume).

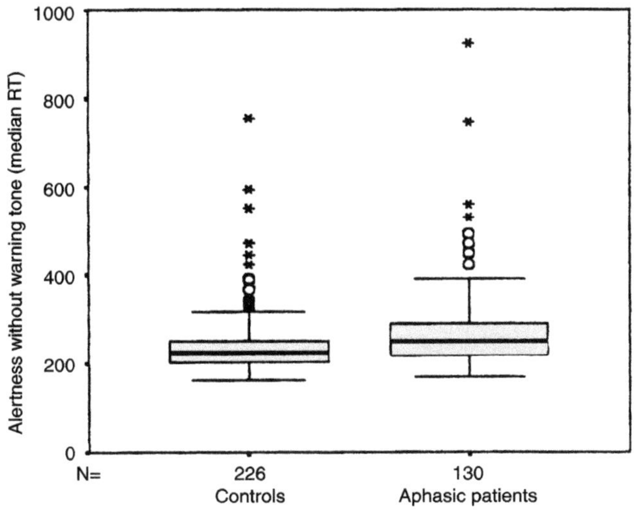

Figure 4.8 Boxplots of the median reaction times in the Alertness test condition without warning tone in aphasic patients and controls. Both samples have the same distribution of age

3.2.2 Degenerative disease

3.2.2.1 HUNTINGTON'S DISEASE AND IMPAIRMENTS OF ATTENTION

Depending on the kind of degenerative disease and its main focus of cerebral damage, different attentional impairment profiles can be found (see Chapter 7 by Van der Linden and Collette, in this volume, for a review of degenerative syndromes). In this section data on patients with Alzheimer's disease and Huntington's disease being assessed with the TAP and other tests are presented.

In a comprehensive study of attentional deficiencies in Huntington's disease, Sprengelmeyer *et al.* (1995) described profound impairments in a group of patients in an advanced stage of disease. He administered the subtests Alertness, Vigilance, Intermodal comparison, Flexibility and Divided attention. The simultaneous monitoring of visual and acoustic stimuli in the Divided attention task as well as the ability to perform intermodal integration were severely impaired in the patients. Furthermore, flexibility and selective visual attention in the Go–nogo task were impaired in the patients. Although this suggests a rather homogeneous and typical performance profile, a closer look at data of single patients reveals that even in patients with the same etiology and comparable duration of disease attentional impairments only partially overlap. Figure 4.9 shows the results of two Huntington patients in several subtests of the TAP. The performance is displayed in

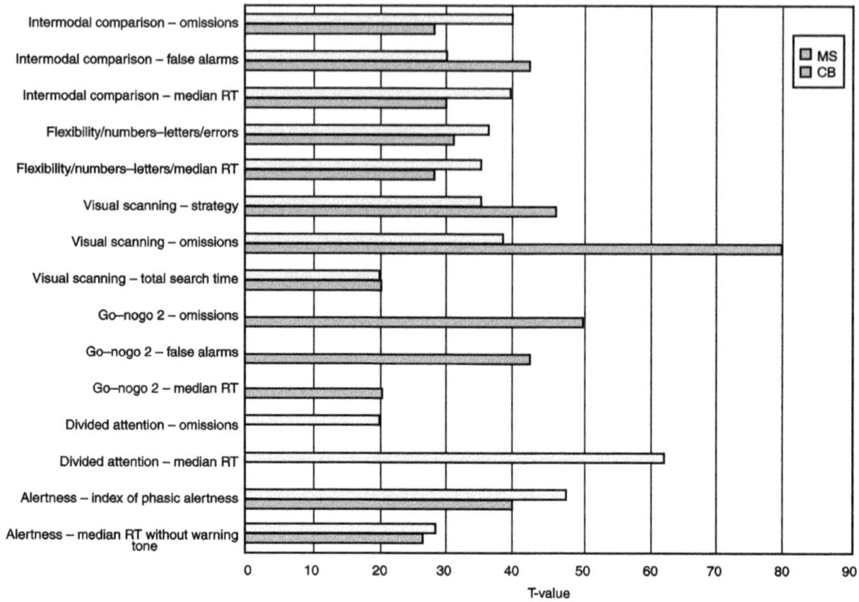

Figure 4.9 TAP results of two Huntington patients (T-values are displayed)

T-values that denote the performance relative to a group of control subjects of the same age. A T-value of 43 is equivalent to a percentile rank of 25, a T-value of 57 means a PR of 75. Per test up to three relevant parameters are displayed.

Patient CB is female, 45 years old and has been symptomatic for approximately one year. She is still working as an employee in administration but is imputed by her employer to be incapable of doing her work. Verbal and non-verbal memory span is impaired, as well as verbal working memory and verbal memory (Hopkins Verbal Learning Test, Rivermead Behavioural Memory Test). However, recognition and delayed recall are not reduced. Her performance in the Conditional Associative Learning Test is profoundly impaired (even after 68 trials the criterion is not reached), as well as her result in the Wisconsin Card Sorting Test (a lot of perseverative and non-perseverative errors). No language difficulties (Token Test, Boston Naming Test) and no visuo-spatial deficits (test battery for visual Object- and Space-perception) exist. Phonologic and semantic word fluency is still within the average range. Her vocabulary is still normal, whereas the performance in the WAIS Block Design subtest is below average as a result of reduced planning and unsystematic work on the task. Trail Making Test A and B are clearly impaired.

Patient MS is male, 48 years old and is working in a power station at the time of examination. In his job he has to monitor machines and displays. For four years he has complained of increasing hyperkinesia and irritability. He judges his memory and concentration to be normal. Verbal and non-verbal memory span are reduced, as well as verbal working memory. Phonologic and semantic word fluency are in the lower average range. In learning tasks, free recall (Buschke Selective Reminding Test) is moderately impaired, but recognition (Verbal and Nonverbal Learning Test) and delayed recall (one hour delay) are normal, as are visuo-constructive abilities (WAIS-Block Design). Profound deficits can be found in the Wisconsin Card Sorting Test (a lot of perseverations) and the Conditional Associative Learning Test (criterion not reached).

Both patients show profound deficits in their speed of visual search and in their alertness (the latter can be explained in terms of a deficit in the initiation of simple manual movements, which can also be observed in other extrapyramidal diseases) and they also show comparable impairments of cognitive flexibility and intermodal comparison. However phasic alertness does not seem to be an attentional aspect that is impaired in Huntington's disease. The reduced performance of patient MS in the Divided attention test is predominantly caused by his deficient visual scanning abilities since he missed six critical visual stimuli in this dual-task paradigm. Even in the unimodal visual control condition of the procedure he missed seven targets. These results suggest that, in addition to the well-known deficits of Huntington patients, namely reduced free recall, impaired cognitive flexibility with perseverations or reduced planning ability, a disorder of visual scanning or search exists, which might influence the patient's performance in a variety of tasks relying on this function. The main disorder hereby is a reduced visual scanning speed without any attentional asymmetry, which might be accompanied by an increasing error rate or reduced strategy.

3.2.2.2 ALZHEIMER'S DISEASE AND IMPAIRMENTS OF ATTENTION

Deficits in attentional performance in persons with early stage Alzheimer's disease have been the subject of numerous studies (see Collette and Van der Linden, Chapter 11 in this volume); however, they mainly consist of statistical comparisons of groups with different pathologies or comparisons between patients at the early stages of Alzheimer's disease and normal persons in the same age groups. But this strategy gives no answer to the question of whether there is a general decline in performance or only in specific functions, nor to the question of whether all patients or only individual ones are affected by such a decline. For this reason, the individual performances of patients diagnosed as having Alzheimer's in an early stage will be compared with healthy older persons in three tests of the TAP.

The differences in simple reaction time shown below (see Figure 4.10) are based on the performance in the Alertness (without warning) test. The data

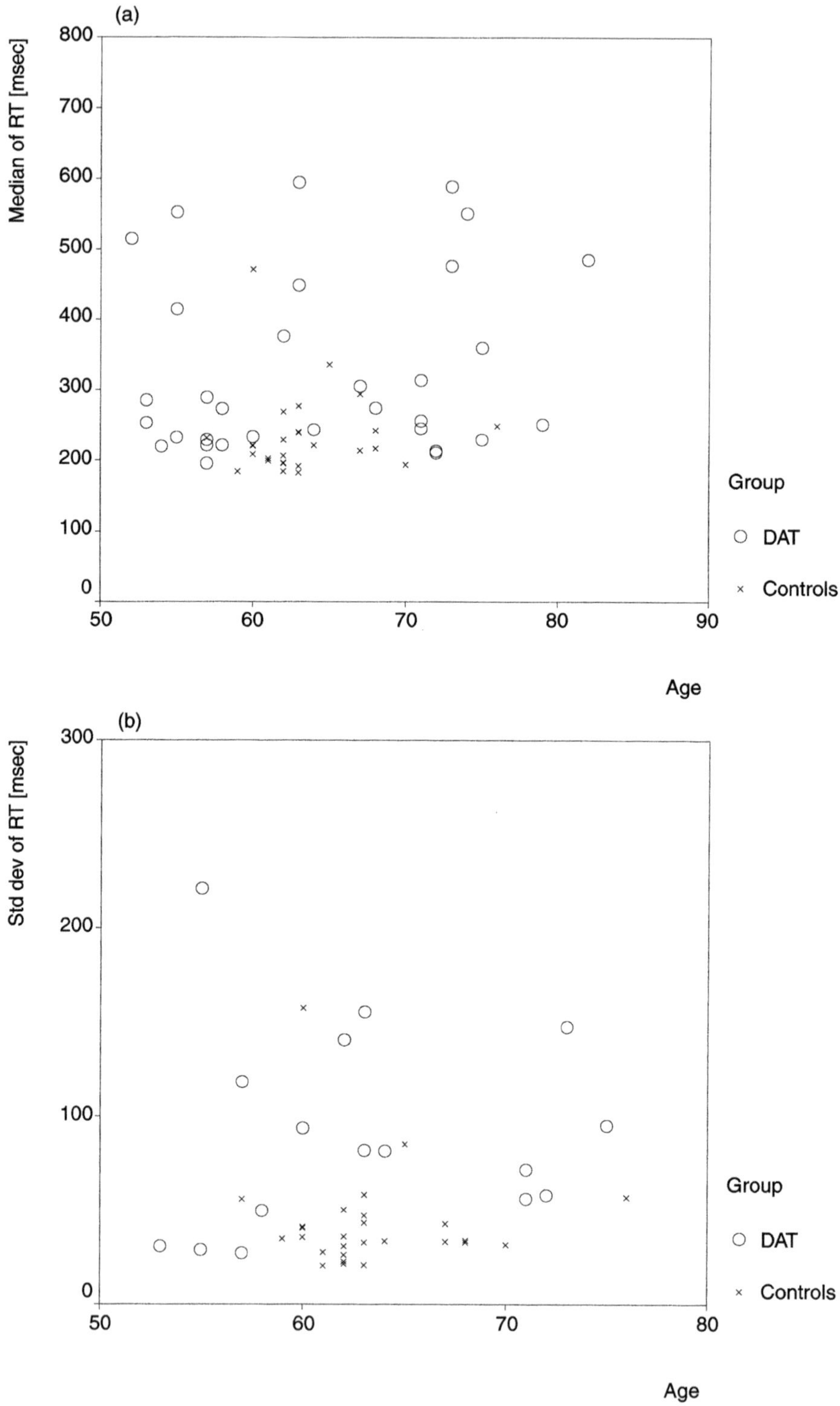

Figure 4.10 Medians (a) and standard deviations (b) of simple reaction times (Alertness without warning) for patients with early stage Alzheimer's disease (DAT: N = 31) and healthy controls (N = 27) of different age

presented stem from 27 healthy older persons[3] as controls and from 33 persons who had been diagnosed as having early stage Alzheimer's disease.[4] Only two of the 27 participants show noticeable slowing with a median reaction time over 300 msec. On the other side, 22 patients with early stage Alzheimer's disease show slow reaction times, but 11 Alzheimer patients are within the average range of the normal controls, and some are significantly faster than 300 msec. Thus, on the basis of these data, one cannot speak of a general slowness of the patients in an early stage of the illness.

The standard deviation of the patients' reaction times is somewhat more striking, because only three to four patients show stable performance within the normal range (Figure 4.10b).

The performance of 29 patients with early stage dementia of the Alzheimer type and 265 healthy normal controls was examined using the Divided attention and Flexibility tests as part of the project 'Preclinical Markers of Alzheimer's Disease'[5] (Monsch *et al.*, in preparation).

The results of the test on Divided attention (Figure 4.11) show that there is no clear distinction between patients with Alzheimer's disease and the controls in any of the parameters. A great number of the patients with Alzheimer's disease perform as well as healthy controls up to a very advanced age regarding both average reaction time and the distribution of reaction times. With regard to omissions, there is a somewhat greater number of patients who show, with numerous omissions, a reduced attentional capacity, but there are also nine patients with three omissions only, thus performing within the normal range. On the basis of these results, one cannot conclude that there is a general decline in divided attention in patients with early stage Alzheimer's disease.

The results of the Flexibility test show tendencies similar to those in the above described tests (see Figure 4.12); however, the number of patients with normal performance is clearly lower. Only seven respectively eight patients scored within the average range (performance above the 10th percentile rank of the healthy controls) with regard to the median and individual standard deviation of the reaction times, and the number of false reactions. When the speed–accuracy trade-off (the ratio of false reactions to the median of reaction times; Figure 4.12d) is used as a criterion, the deficiency of the majority of the patients becomes still more obvious; however, the performance of nine patients still falls above the 10th percentile rank of the healthy subjects.

3 We are very grateful to Ann Truche, psychologist in a centre for retirees near Lyon, France, for these data.

4 These data stem by evaluations from Barbara Romero, at the Psychiatrische Klinik in Munich, Manfred Herrmann, at the Neurologische Klinik in Magdeburg and Bruno Fimm, at the Neurologische Klinik in Aachen.

5 Project 'Preclinical Markers of Alzheimer's Disease', Monsch, Stähelin, Pflüger, Zimmermann; with support of the Schweizerischen Nationalfont (Swiss National Fund), Project NF 3200–49107.96.

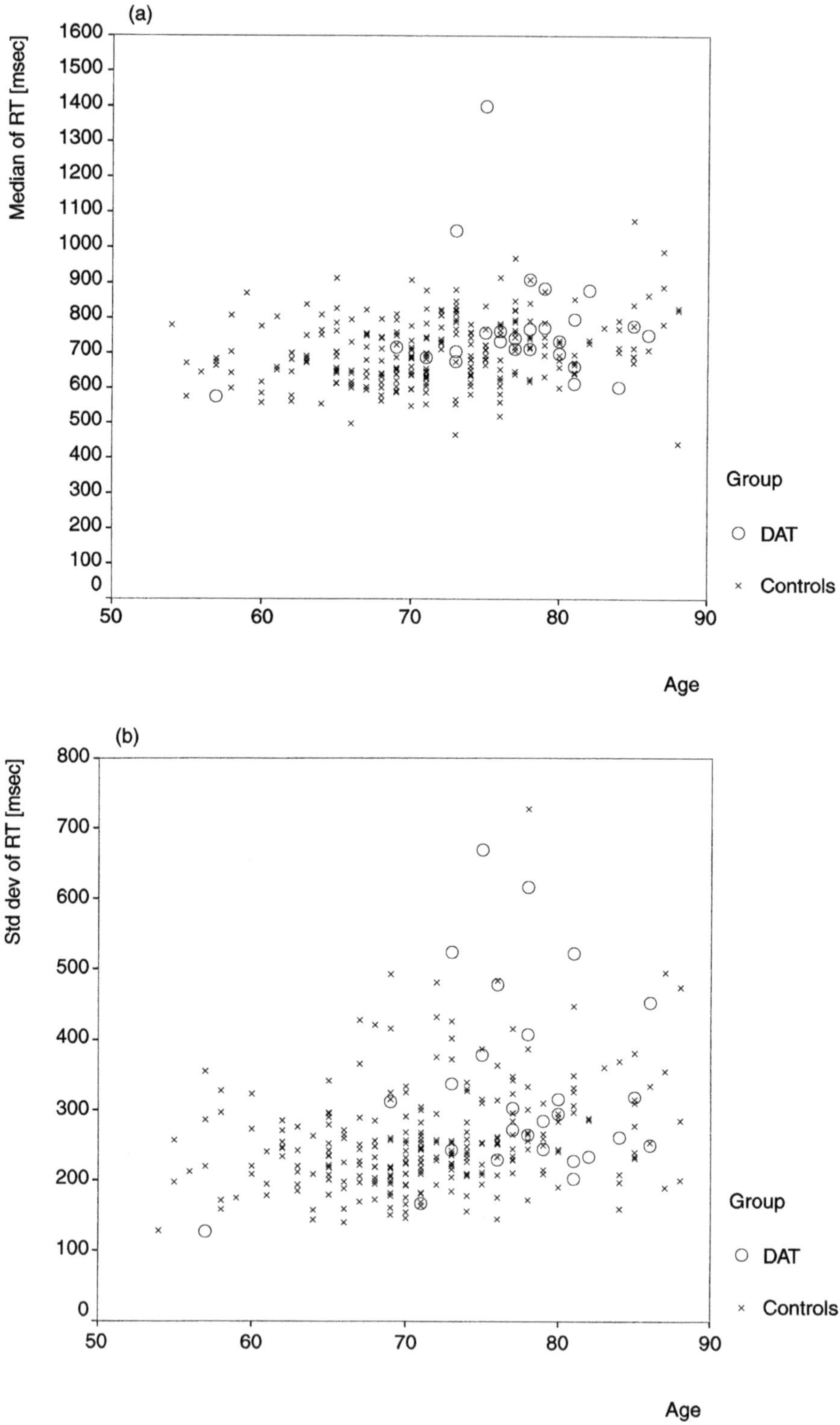

Figure 4.11 Medians (a), individual standard deviations of reaction times (b) and omissions (c) in the Divided attention tests for patients with early stage dementia of the Alzheimer type (DAT: N = 29) and healthy controls (N = 265)

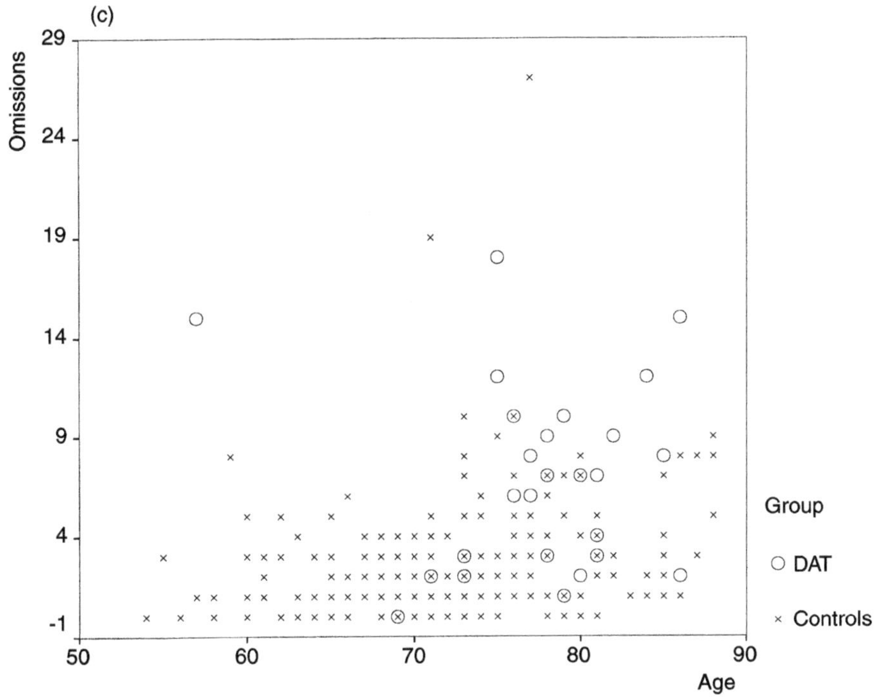

Figure 4.11 (continued)

In summary, there is no hint of a general decline in attentional capacities in patients with early stage Alzheimer's disease. It is obvious that a majority of these patients demonstrate reduced performance but there are always some patients who perform at a normal level.

3.2.3 Attention in children with attention-deficit/hyperactivity disorder (ADHD)

Because of its frequency, attention-deficit/hyperactivity disorder (ADHD) is one of the most important developmental disorders, specifically with regard to attentional functions. In a meticulously conducted secondary analysis of the literature available from 1975 to 1997, Goldman *et al.* (1998) found that according to studies based on standardized diagnostic criteria, the prevalence rate of ADHD among school children can be estimated at 3% to 6%. Today, the diagnosis of ADHD is based on the DSM-IV guidelines, which categorize the criteria in two different 'symptom domains', the first being *impulsivity and hyperactivity*, the second comprising *attentional disorders*. The predominant

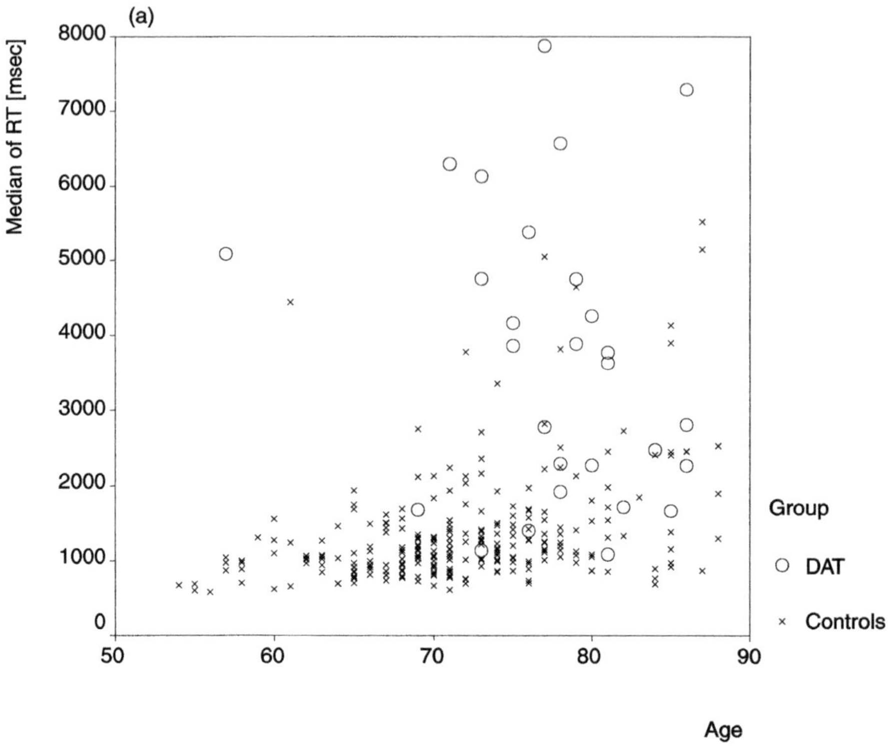

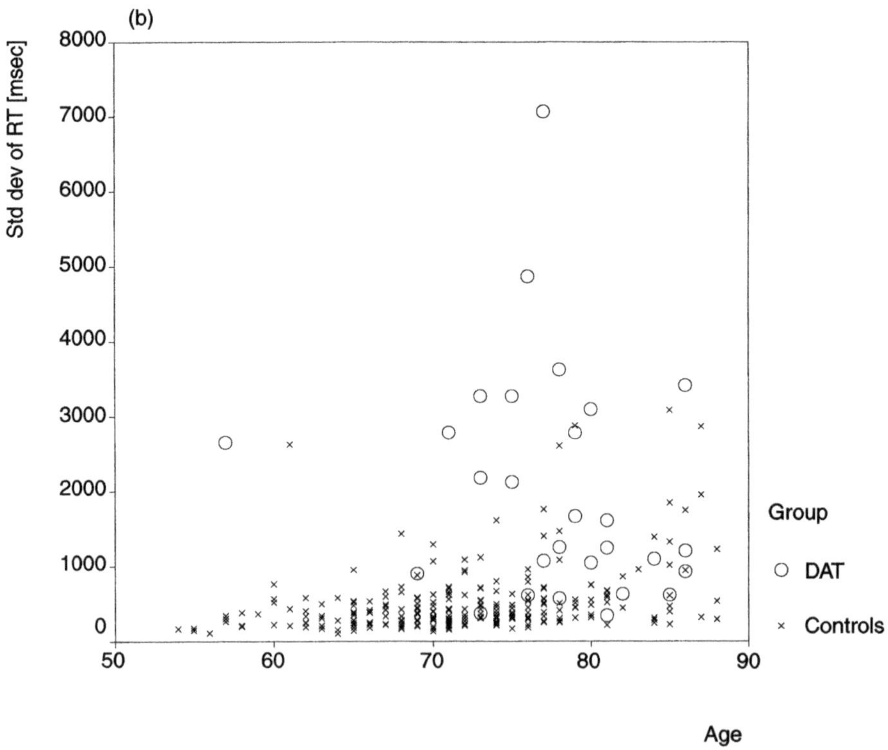

Figure 4.12 Medians (a) and individual standard deviations of reaction times (b), false reactions with reference to age (c) and false reactions with reference to the medians of reaction time (d) in the Flexibility test for patients with early stage dementia of the Alzheimer type (DAT: N = 29) and healthy controls (N = 265)

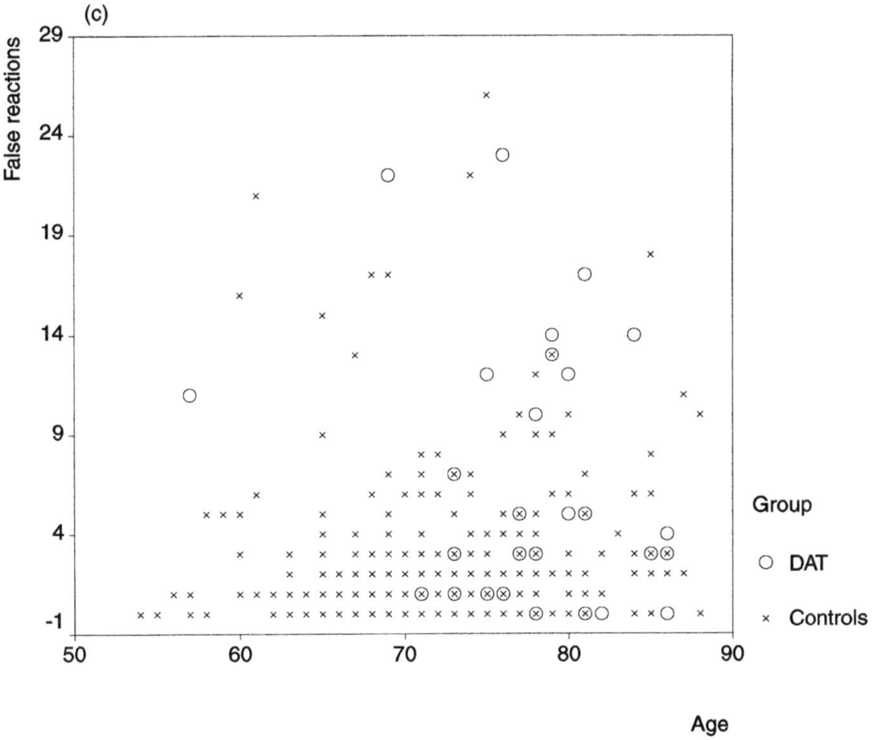

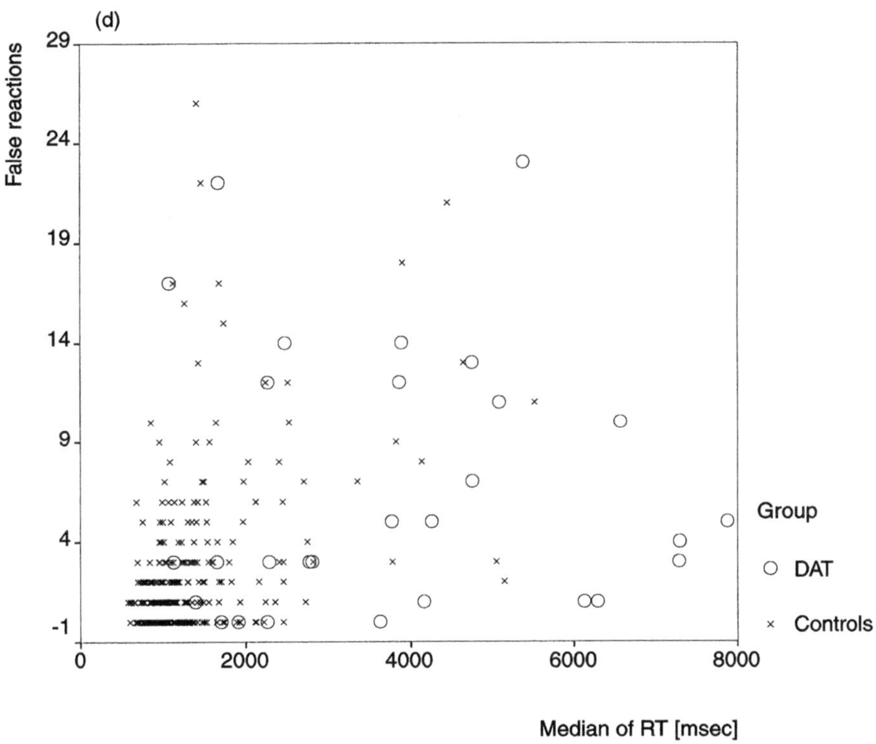

Figure 4.12 (continued)

symptom is reflected in three groups of disorders: predominant hyperactive/impulsive, predominant attentional disorder, and a combination of the two.

This raises the question as to which specific aspects of attentional performance are impaired in children diagnosed as having ADHD. In their review article, Swanson *et al.* (1998) summarized the results of the disorders observed in ADHD as being in the areas of alerting (vigilance), orienting, and executive control based on the model of attention proposed by Posner and Raichle (1994). Based on Sergeant's investigations using tasks of the Continuous Performance Test (CPT) type with a high presentation rate (Sergeant, 1989), the authors came to the conclusion that children with ADHD were observed to have a lower base rate with regard to the aspect of 'alerting' but a comparable performance decrement as compared to children without ADHD symptoms. In contrast, investigations of orienting based on Posner's covert shift paradigm (Posner, 1980) showed inconsistent results. Significant differences in performance could only be observed in very specific stimulus conditions or very specific subgroups. The clearest finding appears in the tasks concerning executive control. For example, according to Pennington and Ozonoff (1996), the deficits in these children's performance can be demonstrated most clearly using the Stroop tasks. Studies using stop tasks, requiring the suppression of an initiated action, produced similar results.

Klein (in preparation) studied, with subtests of the TAP, 43 children (7 to 15 years of age) diagnosed with ADHD according to ICD-10 and DSM-IV criteria, by experienced clinical psychologists and psychiatrists on the basis of parent rating scales (Steinhausen, 1993), video-based behavioural observations of social interactions with the accompanying parent (in most cases, the mother) within the clinical setting, and anamnestic interviews with the parent including the relevant sections of the Diagnostic Interview for Psychiatric Disorders for Children (DIPS-K, Unnewehr, Schneider and Margraf, 1995), and 50 children without ADHD symptoms (8 to 15 years of age). At the time of examination, the children with ADHD had been Ritalin-free for 12–18 hours. The subtests of the TAP used for this research were the 'Alertness' test and the 'Incompatibility' test. The first task falls under the category 'alerting' (excluding the vigilance component) and the second can be placed within the category of executive control. The differences in performance between children with and without the diagnosis ADHD were examined with regard to age.

In the 'Alertness' test, the medians and the individual variability in reaction times in the course of development are presented in Figure 4.13. The curvilinear trends indicate that performance becomes stable as age increases. In children with ADHD as well as in healthy controls, performance stabilizes in both parameters as age increases ($p<.01$). In order to examine how the children with ADHD differ from controls, covariate analyses were conducted in which age served as a covariate. When age is controlled in this manner, a difference in the median of reaction time between the two groups cannot be established statistically ($F = 1.8$; $df_1 = 1$;

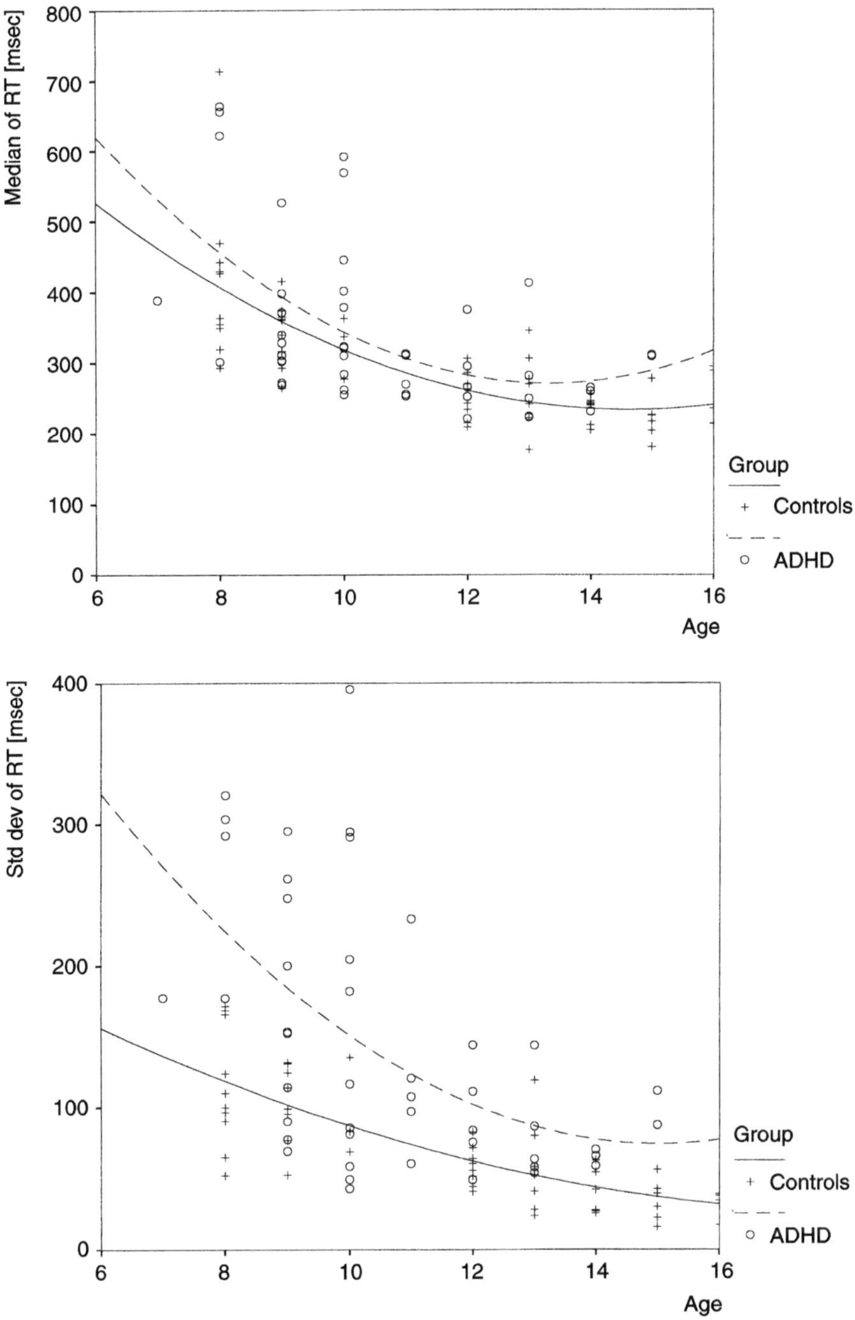

Figure 4.13 Medians (a) and the individual standard deviations of the simple reaction times (b) (Alertness without warning) in the course of development in children diagnosed with ADHD (N = 43) and controls (N = 50)

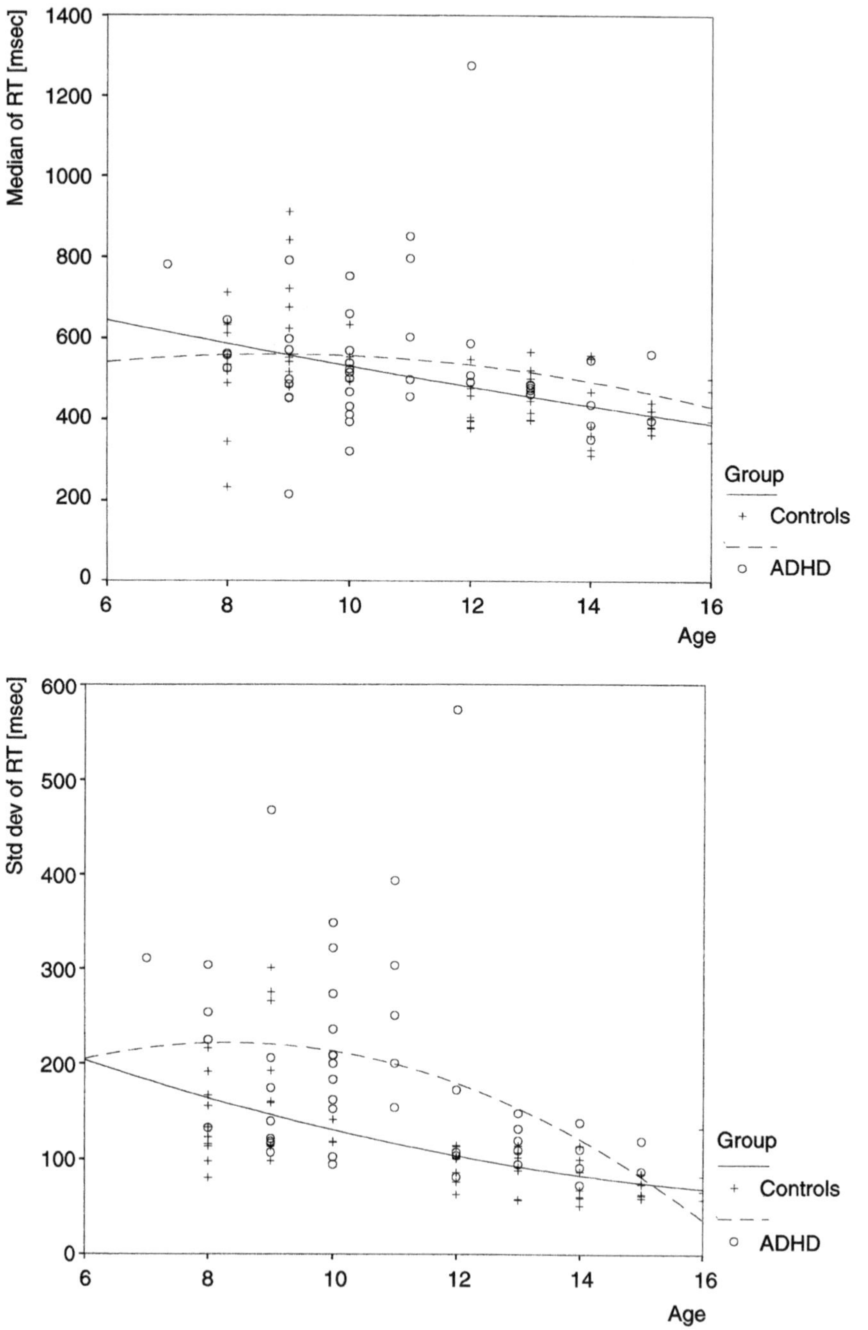

Figure 4.14 Medians (a), the individual standard deviations of the reaction times (b) and false reactions (c) in the Incompatibility test in the course of development in children diagnosed with ADHD (N = 43) and controls (N = 50)

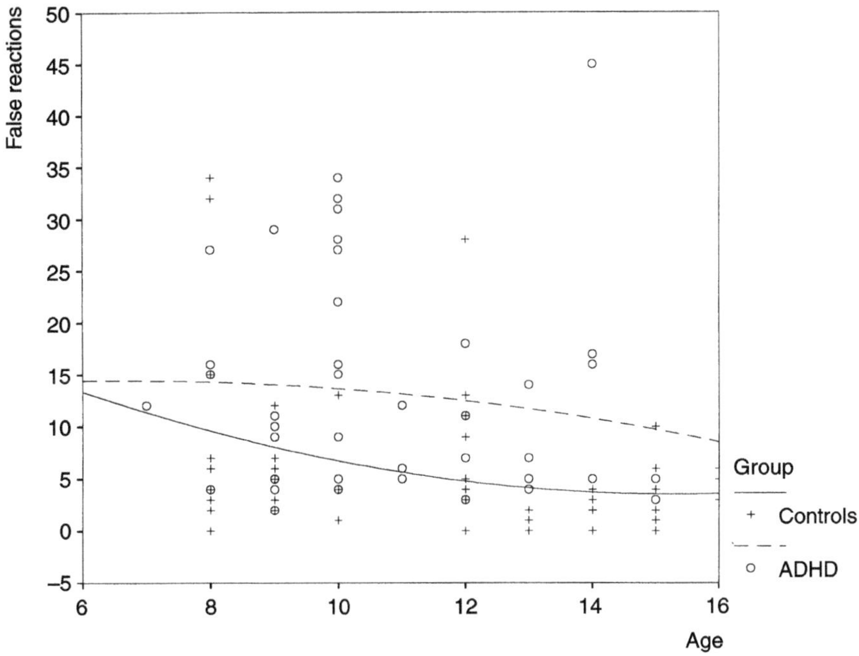

Figure 4.14 (continued)

$df_2 = 93$; $p = .177$). However, the variability in individual performance between the two groups is highly significant (standard deviation of RT: $F = 22.8$; $df_1 = 1$; $df_2 = 93$; $p = .000$). These results indicate that children with and without ADHD differ less in overall reaction speed and more in the stability of their performance. Children diagnosed as having ADHD show significantly more variability in their performance than do healthy controls.

The performance in the 'Incompatibility' test was analysed on the basis of the medians and individual standard deviations of the reaction times and errors (false reactions). The course of development for these parameters is presented in Figure 4.14.

For both groups, the performance in the Incompatibility test improves with age ($p<.05$ for all parameters). There is no difference between groups in the reaction time (median of RT with control of age: $F = 1.6$; $df_1 = 1$; $df_2 = 90$; $p = .208$), whereas the individual standard deviations of reaction times ($F = 18.4$; $df_1 = 1$; $df_2 = 90$; $p = .000$) and errors ($F = 11.8$; $df_1 = 1$; $df_2 = 90$; $p = .001$) show a clear difference in performance between children with ADHD and healthy controls.

In summary, the results demonstrate that the difference in attentional performance in simple as well as complex tasks is not in reaction time but in the stability of the reactions (demonstrated by the difference in the individual standard deviations of RT) as well as in the control of reactions (errors in the Incompatibility test). Thus, based on these results hyperactivity is reflected in a reduction in the control of action.

4 Summary

The Test battery for Attentional Performance has gained wide acceptance within neuropsychology and related fields of application. It enables us to assess a variety of attentional functions in a reliable way and can be easily administered with few apparatus prerequisites – only a PC is required. The test procedures are rather simple in structure and can even be applied in children from the age of 6 and aged people of 80 years and more.

References

Beaumont, J.G. (1983). *Introduction to Neuropsychology*. Oxford: Blackwell.

Beblo, Th., Baumann, B., Bogerts, B., Wallesch, C.-W. and Herrmann, M. (2000). Neuropsychological correlates of major depression: a short-term follow-up. *Cognitive Neuropsychiatry*, *4*, 333–341.

Becker, M., Sturm, W., Willmes, K. and Zimmermann, P. (1996). Normierungsstudie zur Aufmerksamkeits-testbatterie (TAP) von Zimmermann und Fimm. *Zeitschrift für Neuropsychologie*, 7, 3–15.

Birch, L.L. (1978). Baseline differences, attention, and age differences in time-sharing performance. *Journal of Experimental Child Psychology*, *25*, 79–85.

Böttger, S., Prosiegel, M., Steiger, H.-J. and Yassouridis, A. (1998). Neurobehavioural disturbances, rehabilitation outcome, and lesion site in patients after rupture and repair of anterior communicating artery aneurysm. *Journal of Neurology, Neurosurgery and Psychiatry*, *65*, 93–102.

Corbetta, M., Akbudak, E., Conturo, T.E. *et al.* (1998). A common network of functional areas for attention and eye movement. *Neuron*, *21*, 761–773.

Coull, J.T. and Nobre, A.C. (1998). Where and when to pay attention: the neural system for directing attention to spatial locations and the time intervals as revealed by both PET and fMRI. *Journal of Neuroscience*, *18*, 7426–7435.

Cremel, N., North, P., Rizzo, L., Sellal, F. and Zimmermann, P. (1993). Attention performances in a case of post anoxic amnesia. In F.J. Stachowiak *et al.* (eds) *Developments in the Assessment and Rehabilitation of Brain-damaged Patients*. Tübingen: Gunter Narr.

Drepper, J., Timmann, D., Kolb, F.P. and Diener, H.C. (1999). Non-motor associative learning in patients with isolated degenerative cerebellar disease. *Brain*, 122, 87–97.

Drewe, E.A. (1975). Go–nogo learning after frontal lobe lesions in humans. *Cortex*, *11*, 8–16.

Fahrenberg, J., Brügner, G., Foerster, F. and Käppler, C. (1999). Ambulatory assessment of diurnal changes with a hand-held computer: mood, attention and morningness-eveningness. *Personality and Individual Differences*, *26*, 641–656.

Fimm, B. (1996). Mikroanalyse von Aufmerksamkeitsprozessen. In S. Gauggel and G. Kerkhoff (eds) *Fallbuch Neuropsychologie*. Göttingen: Hogrefe.

Fimm, B., Zahn, R., Schütz, J., Block, F., Mull, M. and Schwarz, M. (1996). Neuropsychological disorders in patients with circumscribed subcortical lesions. *Neurology*, *243*, Suppl. 2, 28.

Fischer, B. and Boch, R. (1991). Cerebral cortex. In R.H.S. Carpenter (ed.) *Vision and Visual Dysfunction. Vol. 9: Eye Movement*. London: Macmillan.

Fitts, P.M. and Seeger, C.M. (1953). S-R compatibility: spatial characteristics of stimulus and response codes. *Journal of Experimental Psychology*, *46*, 199–210.

Földényi, M., Giovanoli, A., Tagwerker-Neuenschwander, F., Schallberger, U. and Steinhausen, H.-C. (2000b). Reliabilität und Retest-Stabilität der Testleistungen bon 7–10-jährigen Kindern in der computergestützten TAP. *Zeitschrift für Neuropsychologie*, *11*, 1–11.

Földényi, M., Imhof, K. and Steinhausen, H.-C. (2000a). Zur klinischen Validität der computerunterstützten Testbatterie zur Aufmerksamkeitprüfung (TAP) bei Kindern mit Aufmerksamkeits-/Hyperaktivitätsstörungen. *Zeitschrift für Neuropsychologie*, *11*, 154–167.

Földényi, M., Tagwerker-Neuenschwander, F., Giovanoli, A., Schallberger, U. and Steinhausen, H.-C. (1999). Die Aufmerksamkeitsleistungen von 6–10-jährigen Kindern in der computerunterstützten Testbatterie zur Aufmerksamkeitsprüfung (TAP). *Zeitschrift für Neuropsychologie*, *10*, 87–101.

Gibson, K.R. (1991). Myelination and behavioral development: a comparative perspective on questions of neoteny, altriciality and intelligence. In K.R. Gibson and A.C. Petersen (eds) *Brain Maturation and Cognitive Development: Comparative and Cross-cultural Perspectives*. New York: Aldine De Gruyter.

Goldman, L.S., Genel, M., Bezman, R.J. and Slanetz, P.J. (1998). Diagnosis and treatment of attention-deficit/hyperactivity disorder in children and adolescents. *Journal of the American Medical Association*, *279*, 1100–1107.

Halpering, J.M., McKay, K.E., Mattier, K. and Sharma, V. (1994). Attention, response inhibition and activity level in children: developmental neuropsychological perspectives. In M.G. Tramontana and S.R. Hooper (eds) *Advances in Child Neuropsychology*, vol. 2. New York: Springer.

Heilman, K.M. (1979). Neglect and related disorders. In K.M. Heilman and E. Valenstein (eds) *Clinical Neuropsychology*. New York: Oxford University Press.

Hildebrandt, H., Benetz, J., Schröder, A. and Sachsenheimer, W. (1998). Behandlungserfolge bei Gesichtsfeldausfall und Neglect durch kompensatorisches Training und sensible Anbahnung. *Neurologische Rehabilitation*, *4*, 132–136.

Hildebrandt, H., Gieβelmann, H. and Sachsenheimer, W. (1999). Visual search and visual target detection in patients with infarctions of the left or right posterior or the right middle brain artery. *Journal of Clinical and Experimental Neuropsychology*, *21*, 94–107.

Höschel, K., Uhlendorff, V., Biegel, K., Kunert, H.J., Weniger, G. and Irle, E. (1996). Effektivität eines ambulanten neuropsychologischen Aufmerksamkeits – und Gedächtnistrainings in der Spätphase nach Schädel-Hirn-Trauma. *Zeitschrift für Neuropsychologie*, *7*, 69–82.

Irle, E., Exner, C., Thielen, K., Weniger, G. and Rüther, E. (1998). Obsessive-compulsive disorder and ventromedial frontal lesions: clinical and neuropsychological findings. *American Journal of Psychiatry*, *155*, 255–263.

Johannsen, P., Jakobsen, J., Bruhn, P., Hansen, S.B., Gee, A., Støgkilde-Jørgensen, H. and Gjedde, A. (1997). Cortical sites of sustained and divided attention in normal elderly humans. *Neuroimage*, *6*, 145–155.

Kahneman, D. (1973). *Attention and Effort*. Englewood Cliffs, NJ: Prentice Hall.

Karnath, H.O. (1988). Deficits of attention in acute and recovered visual hemi-neglect. *Neuropsychologia*, *26*, 27–43.

Kessler, J., Markowitsch, H.J., Ghaemi, M., Rudolf, J., Weniger, G.H. and Heiss, W.D. (1999). Degenerative prefrontal damage in a young adult: static and dynamic imaging and neuropsychological correlates. *Neurocase*, *5*, 173–179.

Kim, Y.H., Gitelmann, D.R., Nobre, A.C., Parrish, T.B., LaBar, K.S. and Mesulam, M.M. (1999). The large-scale network for spatial attention displays multifunctional overlap but differential asymmetry. *Neuroimage*, *9*, 269–277.

Kunert, H.J., Derichs, G. and Irle, E. (1996). Entwicklung von Aufmerksamkeitsfunktionen im Kindesalter: Ergebnisse einer vorläufigen Normierung der computergestützten Testbatterie zur Aufmerksamkeitsprüfung (TAP) and 9–12 jährigen Kindern. *Zeitschrift für Neuropsychologie*, *7*, 92–113.

Lansman, M., Poltrock, S.E. and Hunt, E. (1983). Individual differences in the ability to focus and divide attention. *Intelligence*, *7*, 299–312.

Lezak, M. (1995). *Neuropsychological Assessment* (3rd edn). New York: Oxford University Press.

Luria, A.R. (1966). *Higher Cortical Functions in Man*. New York: Basic Books.

Maccoby, E.E. (1969). The development of stimulus selection. In J.P. Hill (ed.) *Minnesota Symposium on Child Psychology, 3*. Minneapolis: University of Minnesota Press.

Manis, F.R., Keating, D.P. and Morison, F.J. (1980). Developmental differences in the allocation of processing capacity. *Journal of Experimental Child Psychology*, *29*, 156–169.

Margulis, D.M. (1985). Selective attention and the brain: a hypothesis concerning the hippocampal-ventral striatal axis, the mediation of selective attention, and the pathogenesis of attentional disorders. *Medial Hypothesis*, *18*, 221–264.

Markowitsch, H.J., Calabrese, P., Neufeld, H., Gehlen, W. and Durwen, H.F. (1999). Retrograde amnesia for world knowledge and preserved memory for autobiographic events. A case report. *Cortex*, *35*, 243–252.

Mesulam, M.M. (1981). A cortical network for directed attention and unilateral neglect. *Annals of Neurology*, *10*, 309–325.

Mesulam, M.M. (1985). Attention, confusional states, and neglect. In M.M. Mesulam (ed.) *Principles of Behavioral Neurology*. Philadelphia: Davis.

Mirsky, A.F. (1989). The neuropsychology of attention: elements of a complex behavior. In E. Perecman (ed.) *Integrating Theory and Practice in Clinical Neuropsychology*. Hillsdale, NJ: Erlbaum.

Mitchell, W.G., Chavez, J.M., Baker, S.A., Guzman, B.L. and Azen, S.P. (1990). Reaction time, impulsivity, and attention in hyperactive children and controls: a video game technique. *Journal of Child Neuropsychology*, *5*, 195–204.

Murray, L.L. (1999). Attention and aphasia: theory, research and clinical implications. *Aphasiology*, *13*, 91–111.

Nicoletti, R., Anzola, G.P., Luppino, G., Rizzolatti, G. and Umilta, C. (1982).

Spatial compatibility effects on the same side of the body midline. *Journal of Experimental Psychology: Human Perception and Performance*, *8*, 664–673.

Niemann, H. and Döhner, A. (1999). Fahreignung von Patienten mit Schädigung des ZNS. In B. Schlag (ed.) *Empirische Verkehrspsychologie*. Lengerich: Pabst Science Publishers.

North, P., Rizzo, L., Fimm, B. and Zimmermann, P. (1993). Early attention impairment in Parkinson's disease. In F.J. Stachowiak *et al.* (eds) *Developments in the Assessment and Rehabilitation of Brain-damaged Patients*. Tübingen: Gunter Narr.

Pennington, B.F. and Ozonoff, S. (1996). Executive functions and developmental psychopathology. *Journal of Child Psychology and Psychiatry and Allied Disciplines*, *37*, 51–87.

Plohmann, A.M., Kappos, L., Ammann, W., Thordai, A., Wittwer, A., Huber, S., Bellaiche, Y. and Lechner-Scott, J. (1998). Computer assisted retraining of attentional impairments in patients with multiple sclerosis. *Journal of Neurology, Neurosurgery and Psychiatry*, *64*, 455–462.

Posner, M.I. (1980). Orienting of attention. *Quarterly Journal of Experimental Psychology*, *32*, 3–25.

Posner, M.I. and Rafal, R.D. (1987). Cognitive theories of attention and the rehabilitation of attentional deficits. In R.J. Meier, A.C. Benton and L. Diller (eds) *Neuropsychological Rehabilitation*. Edinburgh: Churchill Livingstone.

Posner, M.I. and Raichle, M.E. (1994). *Images of Mind*. New York: Scientific American Library.

Radanov, B.P., Bicik, I., Dvorak, J., Antinnes, J., von Schulthess, G.K. and Buck, A. (1999). Relation between neuropsychological and neuroimaging findings in patients with late whiplash syndrome. *Journal of Neurology, Neurosurgery and Psychiatry*, *66*, 485–489.

Rentrop, M., Hakk, K., Freisleder, F.J., Kissling, W. and Kockott, G. (1999). Kindstötung und hebephrenes Syndrom bei metachromatischer Leukodystrophie. *Nervenarzt*, *70*, 276–280.

Robinson, D.L. and McClurkin, J.W. (1989). The visual superior colliculus and pulvinar. In R.H. Wurtz and M.E. Goldberg (eds) *The Neurobiology of Saccadic Eye Movements*. Amsterdam: Elsevier.

Sabri, O., Ringelstein, E.-B., Hellwig, D., Schneider, R., Schreckenberger, M., Kaiser, H.-J., Mull, M. and Buell, U. (1999). Neuropsychological impairment correlates with hypoperfusion and hypometabolism but not with severity of white matter lesions on MRI in patients with cerebral microangiopathy. *Stroke*, *30*, 556–566.

Schneider, W. and Shiffrin, R.M. (1977). Controlled and automatic human information processing I: Detection, search and attention. *Psychological Review*, *84*, 1–66.

Schuppert, M., Münte, Th.F., Wieringa, B.M. and Altenmüller, E. (2000). Receptive amusia: evidence for cross-hemispheric neural networks underlying music processing strategies. *Brain*, *123*, 546–559.

Sergeant, J. (1989). In search of processing deficits of attention in Add-H children. In L. Bloomingdale and J. Swanson (eds) *Attention Deficits Disorder: Current Concepts and Emerging Trends*. Oxford: Pergamon Press.

Sprengelmeyer, R., Lange, H. and Hömberg, V. (1995). The pattern of attentional deficits in Huntington's disease. *Brain*, *118*, 145–152.

Stachowiak, F.J. (ed.) (1993). *Developments in the Assessment and Rehabilitation of Brain-damaged Patients*. Tübingen: Gunter Narr.

Steinhausen, H.C. (1993). *Psychische Sörungen bei Kindern und Jugendlichen*. München: Urban and Schwarzenberg.

Sturm, W., Hartje, W., Orgaβ, B. and Willmes, K. (1994). Effektivität eines computergestützten Trainings von vier Aufmerksamkeitsfunktionen. *Zeitschrift für Neuropsychologie*, *5*, 15–28.

Sturm, W., de Simone, A., Krause, B.J., Specht, K., Hesselmann, V., Radermacher, I., Herzog, H., Tellmann, L., Müller-Gärtner, H.-W. and Willmes, K. (1999). Functional anatomy of intrinsic alertness: evidence for a fronto-parietal-thalamic-brainstem network in the right hemisphere. *Neuropsychologia*, *37*, 797–805.

Sturm, W., Willmes, K., Orgaβ, B. and Hartje, W. (1997). Do specific attention deficits need specific training? *Neuropsychological Rehabilitation*, *7*, 81–103.

Swanson, J., Posner, M.I., Cantwell, D., Wigal, S., Crinell, F., Filipek, P., Emerson, J., Tucker, D. and Nalcioglu, O. (1998). Attention-deficit/hyperactivity disorder: symptom domains, cognitive processes and neural networks. In R. Parasuraman (ed.) *The Attentive Brain*. Cambridge, MA: MIT Press.

Tucha, O., Smely, C. and Lange, K.W. (1999). Verbal and figural fluency in patients with mass lesions of the left or right frontal lobes. *Journal of Clinical and Experimental Neuropsychology*, *21*, 229–236.

Unnewehr, S., Schneider, S. and Margraf, J. (1995). *DIPS-K – Diagnostisches Interview bei psychischen Störungen im Kindes- und Jugendalter*. Berlin: Springer.

van Zomeren, A.H. and Brouwer, W.H. (1987). Head injury and concepts of attention. In H.S. Levin, J. Grafman and H.M. Eisenberg (eds) *Neurobehavioral Recovery from Head Injury*. New York: Oxford University Press.

Wagensonner, M. and Zimmermann, P. (1991). Die Fähigkeit zur länger anhaltenden Aufmerksamkeitszuwendung nach cerebraler Schädigung. *Zeitschrift für Neuropsychologie*, *2*, 41–50.

Weeβ, H.-G., Sauter, C., Geisler, P., Böhning, W., Wilhelm, B., Rotte, M., Gresele, C., Schneider, C., Schulz, H., Lund, R. and Steinberg, R. (2000). Vigilanz, Einschlafneigung, Daueraufmerksamkeit, Müdigkeit, Schläfrigkeit – Diagnostische Instrumentarien zur Messung müdigkeits- und schläfrigkeitsbezogener Prozesse und deren Gütekriterien. *Somnologie*, *4*, 1–19.

Weintraub, S. and Mesulam, M.M. (1989). Neglect: hemispheric specialisation, behavioral components and anatomical correlates. In F. Boller and J. Grafman (eds) *Handbook of Neuropsychology*, vol. 2. Amsterdam: Elsevier.

Weniger, G., Markowitsch, H.J. and Irle, E. (1995). Anterograde and retrograde mnemonic deficits after unilateral damage of neostriatal, ventral striatal and basal forebrain structures. *Neurocase*, *1*, 231–238.

Zimmermann, P. and Fimm, B. (1993). *Testbatterie zur Aufmerksamkeitsprüfung. Version 1.02*. Freiburg: Psytest.

Zimmermann, P. and Fimm, B. (1995). *Test for Attentional Performance (TAP)*. English version 1.02. Herzogenrath: Psytest.

Zimmermann, P., North, P. and Fimm, B. (1993). Diagnosis of attentional deficits: theoretical considerations and presentation of a test battery. In F.J. Stachowiak *et al.* (eds) *Developments in the Assessment and Rehabilitation of Brain-damaged Patients*. Tübingen: Gunter Narr.

Zoccolotti, P., Matano, A., Deloche, G., Cantagallo, A., Passadori, A., Leclercq, M., Braga, L., Cremel, N., Pittau, P., Renom, M., Rousseaux, M., Truche, A., Fimm, B. and Zimmermann, P. (2000). Patterns of attentional impairment following closed head injury: a collaborative European study. *Cortex*, 36, 93–107.

Chapter 5

Psychometric characteristics of attention tests in neuropsychological practice

Pierluigi Zoccolotti and Barbara Caracciolo

In order to be used profitably in clinical neuropsychological practice, tests must fulfil a number of requirements in terms of validity, reliability, ease of administration and sensitivity with pathological populations. With respect to these problems, attention is peculiar in at least two ways as compared to other cognitive functions, such as memory and language. One question concerns the nature of the measurement itself; a second question regards the historical development of tests of attention. A brief outline of these two issues follows.

Attention refers to a class of processes by which we modulate our intake of ongoing environmental (or inner) stimulation. Thus, attention qualifies the active capacity of the perceiver to allocate his/her limited cognitive resources. In these terms, attention is not an independent entity as much as a process modulating the action of other cognitive processes such as perception or memory. This view has a number of measurement implications. On the one hand, there is no 'pure' test of attention. Even though an effort is commonly made to use stimulus materials and tasks that are as simple as possible, attentional tests always rely on a number of motor and cognitive processes (see van Zomeren and Brouwer, 1994, for an extensive discussion of this aspect). Thus, for example, even when measuring reaction times (RT) to simple unstructured visual stimuli, one must be aware that the task requires integrity of visual detection and motor responding; consequently, individual performance cannot be considered as a 'direct' measure of attention. On the other hand, following the idea of attention as a modulator of cognitive processes, measurement of attention is best seen as a *change in performance between different conditions*. In our previous example, the measuring of RTs does not necessarily identify a single attentional process. For example, in measuring the ability to hold attention over time, RTs at the beginning and at the end of the testing period will have to be compared. Only a *reduction* in performance with time (often called time-on-task effect) will point to a specific deficit in vigilance. In the case of phasic alertness, a measure of the changes in RTs between trials with or without a warning signal will be required. Similar considerations may apply to other attentional processes such as selective or divided attention. In all these cases, the attentional component of the task lies in the change in performance between two conditions. In the literature, this has been dealt with in a variety of ways. In some cases, only the most critical condition has been used (e.g. only a dual-task condition for evaluating divided attention); alternatively, various indices of performance have been developed including difference scores and various coefficients or regression formulas. The choice among these alternatives poses relevant measurement questions and may have important implications in the evaluation of individual performances. A discussion of this point will be presented in the 'Issues of measurement' section.

In a historical perspective, it may be noted that experimental investigation and theoretical analysis of attentional processes have undergone considerable development in the last decades. As an effect of this, also, research in the neuropsychological correlates of attention has received a new impetus, as demonstrated by much of the content of the present volume. However, one may wonder how much of this knowledge has actually transferred to clinical practice. In general, if one examines the instruments used to evaluate attentional processes, they fall into two broad categories. On the one hand, there are some 'classical' instruments which anticipate the development of current theories of attention. Well-known examples are the Trail Making Test developed by Reitan (1955, 1958) and the PASAT (Paced Auditory Serial Addition Test) developed by Gronwall (1977). These tests received a wide clinical use. Further, there is now a body of evidence concerning their characteristics in terms of reliability, validity, sensitivity in pathological populations and so on. At the same time, one must be aware that these instruments were generally developed with the idea of detecting the presence of attentional disorder, not with that of specifying the nature of the disturbance. In contrast, most of the subsequent research and theory has focused on the observation that attention should be qualified as a set of independent, although related, processes (see Zimmermann and Leclercq, Chapter 2 in this volume). In terms of clinical practice, the logical consequence of these theoretical advancements would be to develop measures of attention which are both unidimensional and psychometrically valid. This is clearly not an easy achievement for a variety of theoretical and empirical reasons. To name just a few, it must be noted that, in spite of important developments, there is clearly no general agreement about the relevant dimensions. Also, experimental studies characteristically use a number of manipulations that cannot be directly transferred into the clinical setting; further, the frequent use of complex apparatus and measures is a further delay in the transfer to a clinical use. In spite of these difficulties, some new instruments for the measure of attention have been developed. Examples in this second category of tests are the Test for Attentional Performance by Zimmermann and Fimm (1992) or the Test of Everyday Attention by Robertson *et al.* (1994a). Based on the experimental literature on attention, these batteries provide a wide spectrum of tests that intend to capture different and independent attentional processes. However, due to their relatively recent development, the use of these instruments has not been widespread and clinical validation requires further work.

Based on this framework, the first aim of this chapter is to review the psychometric information regarding tests of attention relevant to clinical neuropsychological use. A special focus of our presentation will be on an analysis of the measurement characteristics of the tests and of the validity studies. Further, information concerning reliability of attentional tests and the effect of repetitive presentation on performance will be presented. Following the above distinction, we will refer to both classical and newly constructed tests and attempt to describe their relative strengths and weaknesses. Note that the presentation aims to highlight the psychometric problems that have a more direct impact on the clinical neuropsychological evaluation of attention; consequently, the presentation will focus on a limited number of informative cases. In contrast, a comprehensive evaluation of the psychometric characteristics of all available tests of attention is beyond the scope of this chapter and the reader is referred to test handbooks such as Lezak (1995) and Spreen and Strauss (1998).

A second aim of the chapter is to describe a study on the psychometric characteristics of the Test for Attentional Performance by Zimmermann and Fimm (1992) in its use with traumatic brain injury (TBI) patients. This study is used to illustrate the problems in establishing a clinically oriented approach for the evaluation of an individual patient's performance.

Issues of measurement

Measuring performance in attentional tasks raises problems that are in part common to other neuropsychological dimensions. In particular, it is well known that many neuropsychological measures do not possess the characteristics of an interval scale.[1] This is the case for most tests with a fixed number of items where performance is measured in terms of the number of correct responses (or errors). In these cases, we can assume that higher scores indicate higher performances (ordinal property) but we cannot consider that the numeric differences in the variable we are measuring are consistent along the scale (interval property). More generally, there is no certainty that differences in the measured dimensions directly relate to differences in the source dimension that they are intended to capture.

Lack of the interval property raises several problems. One debated question refers to the possibility of using parametric statistics (such as analysis of variance) on these data. While strictly not allowed, statisticians generally

1 A systematic presentation of these problems is beyond the scope of this presentation. The reader should refer to general reviews of this topic (e.g. Capitani and Laiacona, 1999).

consider that parametric analyses may be appropriate with ordinal measures provided that other conditions are met (e.g. Capitani and Laiacona, 1999). A second problem refers to the possibility of comparing different data based on ordinal scales. This may prove an important step in the clinical evaluation of a patient, particularly in the field of attention. As an example, let us assume that we are interested in establishing how far a patient is able to deal with multiple sources of information (divided attention). One way to proceed is to measure the performance of a patient in two tasks separately and then to examine it when the tasks are performed simultaneously. The difference between the basic and the dual-task conditions should provide information on the divided attention ability of the patient. However, an important characteristic of an ordinal scale is that *the ordinal property is lost when a difference score is used*. In our example, a relatively small or large difference between the basic and dual-task conditions cannot be taken to reliably reflect corresponding differences in divided attention.

Apart from this general measurement consideration, raw difference scores present the additional problem of being particularly sensitive to differences in variability between the two relevant measures. This problem was referred to as the 'cow–canary' effect (Capitani *et al.*, 1999). When measuring the difference in weight between these two animals, the obtained value will clearly be influenced more by variations in the weight of the cow than in that of the canary. In general terms, the difference score will be more correlated with the measure with the larger variability. In the case of attentional tests, complex tasks usually yield greater variability than basic tasks. For example, Giovagnoli *et al.* (1996) observed that the difference in performance between parts A and B in the Trail Making Test was more correlated with the complex part B task ($r = .97$) than with the basic part A task ($r = .57$). In this particular case, the difference score in fact generated results that were nearly identical to those of the complex task alone (part B).

Another question regarding difference scores concerns their reliability. In general terms, reliability refers to the proportion of true versus error variance in obtained test scores. It has been noted that the reliability of a difference score stems from two fallible scores and sums their error variances (Guilford, 1954). Operationally, the reliability of a difference score depends on the respective reliabilities of the two scores and on their intercorrelation.[2] In

2 The reliability of a difference score is expressed as:

$$r_{dd} = \frac{r_{jj} + r_{kk} - 2r_{jk}}{2(1 - r_{jk})}$$

where r_{dd} is the reliability of the difference $Xj - Xk$; r_{jj} and r_{kk} are the reliabilities of Xj and of Xk, respectively; and r_{jk} is the intercorrelation between Xj and Xk (Guilford, 1954).

general, the higher the correlation between the two original measures the lower the reliability of the difference score; in the particular case in which the two original measures are perfectly correlated, reliability is zero. In other words, if two measures are highly correlated, the difference between them will capture a small proportion of true variance. However, a fair degree of correlation is probably the rule rather than the exception; in the previous example by Giovagnoli *et al.* (1996), parts A and B of the Trail Making Test correlated .75.

It is thus clear that the way of considering differences in performance represents a key issue in the evaluation of attentional processes. How can this problem be dealt with? One possible way of proceeding is to use non-parametric analyses which bypass the problem of considering differences between ordinal measures. Alternatively, one should refer to measures that do possess the interval property. These two approaches will be briefly described.

Capitani and colleagues (1999) presented an in-depth analysis of the use of bi-variate non-parametric tolerance limits with attentional tests. Performances in a basic task and in a complex task were examined with the aim of evaluating the best way to measure 'interference', i.e. the additional cognitive load present in the complex as compared to the basic task. Several indices of interference were calculated[3] and compared on two attentional tests (Visual reaction tests and Colour-word Stroop test). Results indicated that the various indices were generally correlated in terms of group analyses. However, results were quite variable at the individual level; the identification of extreme subjects varied depending on the index of performance used. This finding highlights the difference between an experimentally focused approach based on group comparisons and a clinically focused approach where the interest is in reliably establishing the position of an individual patient with respect to normal standards. It also makes clear that the choice of a measure of performance does not represent an abstract statistical problem but is an unavoidable step in developing valid and reliable tests of attention.

Tolerance limits define a region of space including a part of the population (e.g. 'normal' subjects). If the position of a subject is to be placed against two joint measures, multivariate tolerance limits may be used. In this case, the region of space defining the acceptance of normality can be defined in various ways. However, in the most frequent and relevant case in which the performances in the two tasks are correlated, the shape of the non-parametric tolerance region may be usefully defined with reference to the regression of the simple over the complex task (see Capitani *et al.*, 1999 for details of the procedure). This procedure has a number of advantages over traditional

3 These included the raw difference between the basic and complex tasks, the difference divided by the performance in the basic test, the performance in the complex task adjusted for the performance on the basic task on the basis of a regression analysis, and the difference in the two tasks after they have been standardized.

methods and may prove useful in providing a base for individual analysis of attentional performance.

An alternative approach is that of using measures of performance for which one can safely assume the interval property. On logical grounds one such case is the use of time measurements. A large body of cognitive literature has been devoted to the chronometric analysis of mental processes (Posner, 1978). Reaction times represent a particularly sensitive measure of performance and have proved quite effective in separating different stages of processing. By the end of the nineteenth century, F.C. Donders proposed the idea that the time taken in a specific mental operation can be evaluated by subtraction between two separate time estimates (subtractive method). This idea was developed by Sternberg (1969) who proposed the additive factor method; accordingly, variables affecting different stages have additive effects on the overall RT while variables affecting the same stage would have interactive effects. Sternberg's method was applied by Shum and colleagues in a series of studies on TBI patients (Shum *et al.*, 1990, 1994a). In their studies, attention was operationalized in terms of four processing stages (feature extraction, stimulus identification, response selection and motor adjustment). Each of these stages was evaluated by means of a specific manipulation; e.g. feature extraction was examined by contrasting undegraded and degraded imperative signals; stimulus identification was manipulated by varying the similarity of the imperative signal and so on. Shum and colleagues were successful in making manipulations that produced main effects (but no interactions) on all four expected processing stages. Using this paradigm, it proved possible to detect specific attentional deficits in TBI patients: severe short-term TBI patients were impaired in the identification and response selection stages; severe long-term TBI patients were impaired in the response-selection stage only. Results appear robust in that they were replicated for a physical directional matching task (Shum *et al.*, 1990) and for a name-matching task (Shum *et al.*, 1994a).

However, the question remains as to whether this procedure can be useful in clinical practice. A step in this direction comes from a study by Shum, McFarland and Bain (1994b) in which various indices of information processing derived from the described RT paradigm were compared with standard tests of attention. A fuller description of this study is beyond the scope of this presentation; however, it seems interesting that several meaningful relationships between these two quite different sets of measures were obtained (Shum *et al.*, 1994b). This finding indicates the possibility of a bridge between the traditional psychological testing and the information processing approach (Shum *et al.*, 1994b).

At the same time, it should be considered that these results still apply to groups of subjects and no proof that the approach developed by Shum and colleagues may provide a reliable basis for analysis of attentional performance at the individual level is yet available. A further note of caution should be added. For time measures, an interval quality of the measure can be assumed. However, many of the additional problems, which we have noted to intervene when examining differences in performance, hold also in the case of the RT measures.[4] Thus, as stated above, when comparing RTs in two conditions we can expect variability to be higher for the more complex task, as expected in the 'cow–canary' effect. In view of these empirical considerations, Capitani *et al.* (1999) proposed the use of the bi-variate non-parametric tolerance limits also when comparing RTs in a simple and a Go–nogo paradigm.

Overall, the use of time measures appears to provide a potentially important method of evaluating attentional deficits for a variety of reasons. First, this approach has proved effective in identifying the stage at which the attentional deficit produced by a cerebral damage can be located. Second, unlike most standard psychological tests, it has the advantage of yielding measures with an interval quality. In spite of these advantages, up to recent years the actual use of these procedures in clinical practice has been limited, in part because of the need for relatively complex apparatus. However, with the increased use of PCs, it has been possible to develop standardized test batteries, such as that of Zimmermann and Fimm (1992), which have inverted this tendency, by making the chronometric approach feasible at the clinical level.

Validity studies

Validity refers to the capacity of a test to effectively measure the psychological dimension that it is supposed to map. Much information converges in evaluating the validity of a test. In general, both theoretical and empirical considerations are important. As to the former, we expect a test to be based on an explicitly stated theoretical formulation of the psychological dimension to be measured. The inner structure of the test should be logically compatible with this formulation; this refers to the *construct validity* of the test. It may be noted that, in all psychological domains, tests have often been developed on the basis of limited theoretical statements. Consequently, it has not been uncommon for most research on the validity of a given test to be performed after the instrument has gained considerable clinical popularity.[5] This is also the case for measures of attention; in fact, as mentioned in the introductory remarks, several attentional tests that have gained considerable clinical usage were devised before the development of formal models of attention. Empirically,

4 In this presentation, we will not refer to a number of classical questions with reaction time measures, such as anticipations or outliers, relationship with accuracy and selection of the appropriate dependent measure (for a discussion of these issues see Viggiano, 1999).

5 An example of this may be provided by the well-known WISC scale. This was originally thought of in terms of a verbal and a performance subscale. Factor-analytic studies have shown that the scale is best understood in terms of three factors, with one of them (called the 'attention-concentration' factor) cutting across the two hypothesized subscales. Interestingly, the verbal and performance distinction is still widely used in clinical practice.

validity can be examined by correlating the performance in a given test with other established instruments. When a measure correlates well with other tests purported to measure the same construct this indicates good *convergent validity*. Also important is the concept of *divergent validity:* this indicates that a test measures something specific that is not measured by other tests tapping other psychological dimensions. Empirically, this is demonstrated when theoretically unrelated tests are found to be unrelated to the test object of study.

In exemplifying validity studies we will refer to two widely used classical tests: the Trail Making Test and PASAT. We will also briefly refer to evidence concerning two batteries of tests of attention: the Test for Attentional Performance by Zimmermann and Fimm (1992) and the Test of Everyday Attention by Robertson *et al.* (1994a).

The Trail Making Test

The Trail Making Test (TMT) was created in a military environment as part of the Army Individual Test Battery (1944) and was then chosen by Halstead (1947) to form the nucleus of what then became the popular Halstead–Reitan Neuropsychological Test Battery (Reitan and Wolfson, 1985). Soon the test became known for its effectiveness in discriminating subjects with brain damage from the rest of the population (Armitage, 1946; Reitan, 1958; Spreen and Benton, 1965). However, it seems that the test is not able to discriminate brain-damaged from psychiatric patients (Spreen and Benton, 1965; Orgel and McDonald, 1967; Heaton, Baade and Johnson, 1978).

The test consists of two parts. In part A, the subject has to connect the numbers from 1 to 25 randomly scattered on a sheet of paper. Part B is more complex: the trail consists of connecting alternating numbers (from 1 to 13) and letters (from 'a' to 'l'). Classically it was held that part A measures motor and visual-spatial abilities and part B, besides these, more complex cognitive abilities such as mental flexibility and divided attention (Reitan, 1971; Stuss, Stethem and Poirier, 1987; van Zomeren and Brouwer, 1994; Lezak, 1995). In this view, the TMT is potentially useful since it is one of the few evaluation instruments able to offer a comparison between the performances of a single subject on two tasks that differ only in terms of the complexity of the cognitive abilities required.

Correlational studies generally support the TMT as a general measure of attention (e.g. McCaffrey *et al.*, 1992). In a factor-analytic study, it was found that TMT contributes highly to the total variance of the same factor as other tests of attention such as the Digit Symbol, a Stroop measure and a letter cancellation task (Mirsky *et al.*, 1991). Since these tests have in common a requirement for focused mental processing speed, the factor was defined as 'focus execute'. A related study also found a similar factor with high loadings of PASAT and part B of the TMT (O'Donnell, *et al.*, 1994). Similar findings were also reported in another factor study where TMT, and especially part B, had high loading on an attention factor (Schmidt, Trueblood and Merwin, 1994). Note that this factor was interpreted as 'visuo-motor scanning' but resulted from the association of the same measures of attention (such as the Digit Symbol and Stroop test) previously included in Mirsky's 'focus execute' factor.

In general, these studies indicate that TMT loads on an attentional factor and, at least in factor-analytic studies, it seems that this pattern is clearer for part B than for part A. A more direct test of the different processes involved in the two tasks was performed by Crowe (1998). Examining a non-pathological population, it was found that motor ability and visual search predicted performance in part A while visual search and ability to alternate attention predicted performance in part B. Interestingly, the pattern of predictors was considerably less clear when the difference score between parts B and A was used; this is understandable if one considers that difference scores between correlated measures have low reliability, i.e. capture a small proportion of true variance.

With regard to the divergent validity of the TMT, some studies have found moderate correlations with measures of non-attentional constructs, such as intelligence (Waldmann *et al.*, 1992) and educational level (Kennedy, 1981; Stanton *et al.*, 1984).

Another aspect linked to the validity of the TMT concerns the difference between the two parts of the test. In principle, differences between parts A and B should only depend upon the different cognitive processes involved. However, structural differences between the two trails may contribute to such differences. Fossum, Homberg and Reinvang (1992) compared the basic version of the TMT with a modified version in which the trails remained unchanged but the stimuli were inverted; in part A, the numbers were replaced by alternated numbers and letters, and in part B only numbers were used. Alphanumeric stimuli were in general more difficult, as expected; however, the effect of path structure and an interaction between task complexity and path structure were also present: the path of part B was more difficult than that of part A over and above the cognitive requirements of the task. Several factors may contribute to such an effect. First, the total length of the part B route was found to be about 32% longer than that of part A (Rossini and Karl, 1994). Further, the path of part B requires a more complex visual search since there are more stimuli between one target and the next (Gaudino, Geisler and Squires, 1995). Vickers, Vincent and Medvedev (1996) noted that the paths are not truly random in the sense that they were chosen on the basis of some (unspecified) constraints. Of interest is that the paths are self-avoiding; i.e. the continuous line that links the circles never intersects itself. This constraint considerably limits the number of possible paths.

These observations do not necessarily contradict the idea that performance in parts A and B depends upon partially different processes. However, they make clear that the raw difference between the two parts is not a quantitatively appropriate measure by which to judge the contribution of the attentional processes additionally present in part B. As we have seen, difference scores also have measurement and reliability problems (Capitani *et al.*, 1999).

The Trail Making Test has been widely used because of its simplicity of administration and potentially useful clinical meaning. The use of a basic and a complex condition provides a format open to an attentional interpretation of the results. However, multiple processes are involved in both parts. Consequently, low performance in part B cannot be uniquely ascribed to an attentional deficit. Further, scoring is made complex by the structural differences between the paths.

PASAT

In the Paced Auditory Serial Addition Test (PASAT) the subject is presented with a series of numbers and is requested to add every successive number. In the original report, four different versions corresponding to different presentation rates of the numbers (1.2, 1.6, 2.0, 2.4 seconds) were described (Gronwall and Sampson, 1974). The task proves relatively difficult. An example makes this point clear. Let us assume that the subject is given a list of numbers (3, 6, 2, 8 and so on). After adding the first and second number (i.e. 9), the subject has to inhibit the resulting sum in order to pass to the next sum (between the second and third number; i.e. 8).

Gronwall and Sampson (1974) posited that PASAT was a test of attention with a strong component linked to speed of processing. Classically, it is thought that this test is linked to the individual capacity of dividing attention, considered as the amount of information that can be handled at one time (Spreen and Strauss, 1998). Gronwall and Sampson (1974) reported that PASAT is very sensitive in detecting attentional deficits following TBI.

Several correlational studies provide information on the convergent validity of PASAT. It presents moderate to high correlations with a variety of tests such as the Brown–Peterson Consonant Trigrams Test (Sherman, Strauss and Spellacy, 1997), the d2 Cancellation Test (de Vries *et al.*, 1992; Sherman *et al.*, 1997), the Stroop Test (Sherman *et al.*, 1997), the Trail Making Test (O'Donnell *et al.*, 1994; Sherman *et al.*, 1997), the Vigilance and the Distractibility tasks from the Gordon Diagnostic System (Burg, Burright and Donovick, 1995) and the Visual Search and Attention Test (O'Donnell *et al.*, 1994).[6]

6 It should be noted that different PASAT measures were used in different studies. For example, Sherman *et al.* (1997) reported separate correlations for the 2.0 and 1.6 sec versions; other studies referred to the general score based on the four versions (e.g. Burg *et al.*, 1995).

More direct evidence on the convergent validity of PASAT stems from factor-analytic studies. A number of them indicated that performance on PASAT loads highly on factors variously defined as 'freedom from distractibility', 'attention/concentration' or 'attention/information processing' (Gronwall and Wrightson, 1981; Deary *et al.*, 1991; Schmidt *et al.*, 1994; Larrabee and Curtiss, 1995; Crawford *et al.*, 1998; Sherman *et al.*, 1995). In a recent study, O'Donnell and co-workers (1994) obtained a factor characterized by loadings of PASAT, the Trail Making Test, part B, and the Visual Search and Attention Test (VSAT). Based on the Mirsky (1989) classification, they interpreted this factor as 'focal execute'. These tests did not contribute to a second 'conceptual' factor linked to the performance on the Category test and the Wisconsin Card Sorting Test. Thus, the O'Donnell *et al.* (1994) study provides information on both the convergent and the divergent validity of PASAT.

Converging evidence on validity may also stem from neurophysiological investigations. Using single positron emission tomography, Deary and colleagues (1994) found that during PASAT performance there was a significant increase in tracer uptake in right anterior cingulate and left posterior cingulate areas, regions previously associated with mechanisms of attention in humans and other animals.

As to the divergent validity, Gronwall and Sampson (1974) claimed that PASAT has minimal relations with other cognitive components such as intelligence and individual arithmetic abilities. Several studies have focused on checking this assumption.

PASAT and arithmetic ability

In Sherman *et al.*'s (1997) study, the highest correlation between PASAT and several other tests referred to the Arithmetic subtest of the WAIS-R. They concluded that, although PASAT measures a component related to attention, it is also strongly influenced by the arithmetic ability of the subjects. Similar findings were observed in a study examining a larger sample of subjects (Crawford, Obonsawin and Allan, 1998). PASAT had a higher correlation with Arithmetic than with any other subtest of the WAIS-R. However, it must be pointed out that this subtest measures arithmetic performance within a time limit and has been classically considered as part of the 'attention-concentration' factor of the WAIS-R, along with the Digit Symbol and the Digit Span subtests.

Other studies approached this problem from a different perspective. Ward (1997) found that young adults performed on the PASAT more poorly than older subjects; this finding was interpreted as an effect of lower arithmetic competence of the new generation, due to the widespread use of pocket calculators. Accordingly, these data would indicate poor divergent validity of the PASAT due to the preponderance of arithmetic skills in the PASAT performance. However, in a study on a larger sample of subjects, Crawford *et al.* (1998) failed to confirm the non-linear relationship between age and performance on the PASAT, disproving Ward's hypothesis.

Chronicle and MacGregor's (1998) study used a more articulated experimental paradigm. These authors constructed a computer version of an arithmetic task, including all four basic operations. Performance on the PASAT was highly correlated with the mean reaction time on this arithmetic task. Chronicle and MacGregor (1998) posited that performance on the PASAT is strongly dependent on arithmetic competence and, therefore, in the absence of information on this ability, it should not be used as a test of attention. Although well-structured, this study may also be subject to criticism. It is of note that the arithmetic test involved a timed task: the stimuli were presented for 1,200 msec and the subject was instructed to respond as quickly as possible. Under these conditions, one may suppose that the arithmetic task itself has become loaded with an attentional component.

Overall, several studies cast doubt on the Gronwall and Sampson (1974) assumption that performance on PASAT is independent of arithmetic ability. At the same time, the observation that PASAT correlates with other arithmetic tasks is open to different interpretations. In particular, characteristics of several arithmetic tasks may themselves call into play attentional factors.

PASAT and intelligence

This topic has also been the target of many studies aimed at verifying whether, contrary to what was originally stated (Gronwall and Sampson, 1974; Gronwall and Wrightson, 1981), the test was correlated with a general intelligence factor.

High correlations between performance in PASAT and different measures of intellectual functioning have been reported in studies based on both healthy and pathological samples. Kanter (1984) found a strong correlation between PASAT scores and speeded non-verbal intellectual tasks in a sample of head-injured patients. Brittain *et al.* (1991) reported similar findings using the Shipley score as a measure of general intellectual functioning along with Levin's version of PASAT. A number of other studies have used partial or total scores from the WAIS-R to relate PASAT and intelligence. For example, Deary and colleagues (1991) found a positive relationship between the two measures in a sample of diabetic patients, and Egan (1988) reported high correlations between PASAT scores and IQ in a non-clinical population. Roman *et al.* (1991) documented only moderate correlations between PASAT and an abbreviated version of WAIS-R, dismissing this correlation as not clinically relevant. In contrast, Wiens, Fuller and Crosser (1997) suggested caution in using PASAT as an attention test in the case of patients with low IQ due to the presence of a large variability of performance in this type of subject.

Crawford and colleagues (1998) carried out a particularly thorough study on this problem. The authors administered the entire WAIS-R battery, the PASAT and the NART (Nelson, 1982) to a large group of healthy subjects. A factor analysis carried out using the subtests of the WAIS-R and the PASAT showed a first component related to a general intelligence factor 'g'. PASAT had a high loading on this component. When the varimax rotation was carried out, a second factor emerged which the authors defined as 'attention/concentration'. PASAT had a high loading on this factor (.75). The subsequent analysis of the relationship between the WAIS-R and the PASAT led to four possible explicative models: (a) PASAT is explained by both the 'g' factor and the attention/concentration factor; (b) PASAT is not explained by any of the factors of the WAIS-R; (c) PASAT is explained only by the attention/concentration factor; (d) PASAT is explained only by the 'g' factor. Based on an estimation of fitness using chi-square, the model that is best adapted to the data is the first: i.e. general intelligence 'g' plus attention/concentration. Thus, Crawford *et al.*'s (1998) study confirms the convergent validity of PASAT but also poses some limits to its divergent validity.

The overall picture seems to reveal a mild to moderate link between general intellectual abilities and performance on the PASAT. Clinicians using PASAT should consider this finding. Further research might allow for a possible adjustment of normative data based on the general intelligence 'g' factor.

Batteries of tests of attention

In recent years, various test batteries based on explicit models of attention have been devised. These instruments have several potential advantages over the classical tests of attention. Based on the idea that attention is predicated on a set of interrelated processes (Zimmermann and Leclercq, Chapter 2 in this volume), they cover with independent measures the various attentional processes that have been revealed by the experimental studies in these fields. This may allow us to build a profile of the attentional abilities of an individual (Crawford, Sommerville and Robertson, 1997). At the same, the choice to use highly specific attentional constructs may enhance the construct validity of each task. In fact, the emphasis is on discriminating specific, well-defined constructs.

This concept becomes clear with reference to the Test for Attentional Performance (TAP) by Zimmermann and Fimm (1992). Here, the subject is examined with a wide spectrum of tasks closely derived from the large body of experimental research in this area. To name just a few, these include the capacity to respond promptly to an unstructured stimulus (alertness) or only to specific targets (selective attention), to maintain an adequate level of responsiveness to monotonous repetitive signals (vigilance), or to perform adequately in the presence of multiple sources of signals (divided attention). A comprehensive description of this battery as well as of the evidence on its validity is presented in the chapter by Zimmermann and Fimm (Chapter 4 in this volume).

A different approach characterizes the Test of Everyday Attention devised by Robertson *et al.* (1994a, 1994b). While this battery retains a close connection with the literature on multiple attentional systems, an attempt is also made to use a test format that has some ecological validity. Thus, the subject is told to imagine himself on a vacation trip to Philadelphia (USA); the various subtests of the scale refer to different tasks that could have occurred during this trip (e.g. searching a map to find restaurants or counting the number of floors on an elevator). The use of tasks and materials relatively similar to those of everyday life is aimed to foster motivation in the subjects and to reduce uneasiness with experimental conditions. Another feature of this battery is that it requires minimal instrumentation; visual tasks use paper and pencil, and acoustic tasks are presented by means of a simple cassette tape recorder.

The battery features eight subtests that intend to capture the various aspects of attention. To establish their convergent validity, Robertson and colleagues (1994a, 1994b) gave all subtests of the battery along with other standard tests of attention to a group of normal subjects stratified for age and education. A factor analysis indicated four factors. The first factor identified subtests such as Map Search and Telephone Search with a strong requirement for 'visual selective attention/speed'; the Brickenkamp (1981) d2 visual search task, the Stroop test and the TMT part B also showed high loadings on this factor. The second factor was characterized as 'attentional switching'. The Visual Elevator subtest loading on this factor requires the subject to change a mental operation (from counting upwards to counting backwards and vice versa); the Wisconsin Card Sorting Test also had a high loading on this factor. A third factor, defined as sustained attention, included three subtests: Lottery, Elevator Counting and Telephone Search while Counting. The first two tests require attention to repetitive stimuli while the third is a dual attention task; Robertson and colleagues (1994a) posited that this latter test shares with the other two a strong requirement for sustained attention. A fourth factor identified four tests, two from the battery (Elevator Counting with Reversal, Elevator Counting with Distraction) and two standard tests (Backward Digit Span and PASAT). These tests appear to share a load on working memory and auditory selective attention ('auditory-verbal working memory' factor).

Robertson and colleagues (1994a) reported that scores in the Test of Everyday Attention were uncorrelated with a measure of verbal intelligence (NART), once the effect of age was partialled out. Furthermore, they evaluated the possible effect of sensory constraints on the task performance. In particular, since several subtests feature an acoustic presentation, Robertson and colleagues (1994a) evaluated the effect of moderate hearing loss on performance. Once the effect of age was partialled out, no correlation was present between performance in any of the acoustic subtests of the Test of Everyday Attention and a measure of hearing impairment (Four Alternative Auditory Features Test).

To date, the Test of Everyday Attention has received relatively limited validation in pathological samples (Chan, 2000). However, Robertson and colleagues (1994a) quoted data referring to both CVA and TBI patients. Recently, Crawford and colleagues (1997) applied to this test a procedure to evaluate the reliability of subtest differences, originally developed by Silverstein (1982) and Knight and Godfrey (1984). This method is based on the idea of checking each subtest with the mean from all subtests rather than analysing differences between individual subtests, and has the advantage of compromising type I and type II errors. Further, they presented a procedure to compare the observed subtest differences with those of a normative sample, so as to establish their expected frequency. These methods may prove particularly useful in the evaluation of the profile of a patient's individual performance.

Reliability studies

As stated above, test reliability indicates the proportion of true variance or alternatively the relative independence from random errors, which can be due to many causes. Reliability is commonly expressed as a correlation between two administrations of the same test (or of parallel forms of the same test) or of two parts of the same test (e.g. first–second part). The former refers to how stable the test measures are over a period of time; the latter provides information on the internal consistency of a test. Based on the between-subjects variability of a test and on its reliability, it is possible to establish the confidence limits of individual performance (standard error of measurement); this indicates the true score of a subject with a controlled risk. In examining the evidence on reliability we will use as examples the same studies described in the validity tests section.

In the TMT, high test–retest correlations have been reported in various studies (Giovagnoli *et al.*, 1996; McCaffrey *et al.*, 1992); however, in one study low values were reported for both parts A and B (Matarazzo *et al.*, 1974). Stuss *et al.* (1989) reported a good level of test reliability in the case of severe head trauma patients.

In the case of PASAT, good levels of reliability have generally been reported. In the case of test–retest, reliability has been found to be high both in healthy and pathological samples (McCaffrey *et al.*, 1995). Similar results have been reported in children using the CHIPASAT (Dyche and Johnson, 1991), and in the case of severe head trauma (Stuss *et al.*, 1989). Also the internal consistency has been found to be high both in terms of Cronbach alpha (Crawford *et al.*, 1998) and with the split-half method (Egan, 1988; Johnson *et al.*, 1988). Different versions of the test using different rates of presentation of the stimuli were found to be highly correlated (Sherman *et al.*, 1997; MacLeod and Prior, 1996).

Zimmermann and Fimm (1992) report both test–retest and Cronbach alphas for the subtests of the Test for Attentional Performance (1992). These values will be examined in the research section of this chapter along with the data on a sample of TBI patients (see also Chapter 4 by Zimmermann and Fimm, in this volume).

In the case of the Test of Everyday Attention, Robertson and colleagues (1994a) report Pearson correlations between three parallel forms of the battery on a large sample of healthy subjects. For five subtests, medium to high correlations were present (range .66–.87). An exception is provided by the Telephone Search while Counting, a subtest measuring divided attention. Robertson and colleagues (1994a) posited that low reliability in this subtest may be due to the presence of strategic learning in dual-task conditions. However, in this case performance is assessed by means of a coefficient which includes a difference between the search time in this subtest and in the Telephone Search subtest; as we have seen, difference scores may yield low reliability coefficients in cases where the two original measures are highly correlated (as is likely to happen in this case). For two subtests (Elevator Counting and Lottery), performance of control subjects showed a ceiling effect and values for a sample of stroke patients were used instead; in both cases, adequate levels of reliability were present.

Effect of practice on attention tests

The effect of practice is particularly important when examining patients longitudinally, as when evaluating spontaneous recovery or assessing the effectiveness of rehabilitative training. However, only a few systematic investigations have studied the effect of repetitive presentation upon a subject's performance, perhaps because it has been assumed that the simplicity of stimulus material characteristic of attentional tests would yield small learning effects (Feinstein, Brown and Ron, 1994). However, the available evidence indicates that practice effects are in fact present in several attentional tests.

In the case of PASAT, it was originally proposed that performance improved between the first and second administration (Gronwall, 1977; Stuss *et al.*, 1987; Macciocchi, 1990; see Dyche and Johnson, 1991, for data concerning the children's version, CHIPASAT) but would level out afterwards (Gronwall, 1977; Sampson, 1961). Contrasting findings have been reported by Feinstein *et al.* (1994). Giving the PASAT eight times with a 2–4-week interval, they observed learning effects beyond the second administration of the test. These effects were more marked in young (25- to 35-year-old) as opposed to older (41- to 57-year-old) subjects who reached a plateau by the sixth presentation. Similar results were reported for several other tests including the PVSAT (a visual version of PASAT), a multiple choice reaction time test and the Stroop test. This latter test had been reported as stable in a previous study (Sacks *et al.*, 1991). No improvement was observed in the case of simple reaction times; in fact, performance deteriorated somewhat across sessions. This finding was taken to indicate that no actual improvement is possible in such simple tasks and a fall-off in vigilance may also occur.

Significant improvements in multiple testing have been reported for the Trail Making Test (McCaffrey, Ortega and Haase, 1993) and for multiple choice reaction time tests (Johnson, Hock and Johnson, 1991). These improvements were observed also when testing was given along with 'slowing' substances such as marijuana and alcohol (Peeke, Jones and Stone, 1976; Maylor *et al.*, 1992).

Systematic observations in pathological populations have been more limited. In the case of PASAT and the Trail Making Test, Stuss *et al.* (1989) gave the two tests five times at growing intervals (from four days to around two months). Both mild TBI patients and matched controls showed a slight but continuous tendency to improve. Godefroy, Lhullier and Rousseaux (1994, exp. II) reported significant improvements with choice RTs over a four-session span in a group combining frontal and parietal lesions; improvements were less marked in the control subjects. Unimodal (visual and auditory) simple stimuli yielded less clear-cut practice effects over a three-session span (Godefroy *et al.*, 1994, exp. I). Dodrill and Troupin (1975) examined performance on the TMT in a group of epileptic patients and found no learning effects; however, this finding may depend upon the intervention of a pharmacological treatment.

Most other studies only examined performances across two sessions. Significant improvements at the retest were reported for the Trail Making Test (Matarazzo *et al.*, 1974; Dye, 1979; Stuss *et al.*, 1987; Wiederholt *et al.*, 1996; Dikmen *et al.*, 1999), for a choice reaction times test (Schweinberger, Buse and Sommer, 1993) and for the Stroop test (Dulaney and Rogers, 1994). For the d2 Cancellation test, a learning effect was reported for normal controls (Spreen and Strauss, 1998) but not for patients with cerebral damage (Sturm *et al.*, 1983).

Zimmermann and Fimm (1992) reported improvements on only some of the tests of their battery. On the second testing, at least some improvement was observed in the case of the Flexibility test, Working memory (only for error scores) and Incompatibility test (only for false alarms). In contrast, no change was present for several other tests (Alertness, Go–nogo, Divided attention).

Since practice effects are present in some subtests of the Test of Everyday

Attention (Robertson *et al.*, 1994a), three parallel forms of the battery were devised. In order to evaluate the influence of practice these parallel forms must be administered in a fixed sequence. Robertson and co-workers (1994a) provide norms to distinguish between spontaneous fluctuations of performance and actual changes in performance (Appendix 9 of the Manual, Robertson *et al.*, 1994a).

The evidence indicates that performance in several attentional tests improves over sessions. These changes in performance occur in both normal controls and pathological populations. In general, changes appear more marked with relatively 'complex' tasks such as PASAT or the Trail Making Test; in contrast, no improvement is present in the case of RT to unstructured visual stimuli. However, it should be pointed out that we are far from having a thorough comprehension of the factors underlying these practice effects. The complexity of interpretation is evident when considering the commonly used conditions that require speeded responses to choice stimuli. In these cases, performance depends upon a number of factors which may produce contrasting influences (Fisk and Schneider, 1981). For example, one may obtain a rise in performance as the learning of the task consolidates, as well as a fall-off due to fatigue as the task proceeds. Thus, general performance may depend upon the degree of practice prior to the actual test and the overall duration of the test. Differences in these parameters may be at the base of different outcomes, such as in the case of choice reaction tests (Schweinberger *et al.*, 1993; Zimmermann and Fimm, 1992). Further, it has been proposed that learning is slower but quantitatively greater in difficult-to-automatize tasks while smaller but faster in easy-to-automatize tasks (Fisk and Schneider, 1981). It is of note that this proposal moves the interpretation away from the difficulty of the tasks *per se*, while it emphasizes the control–automatic dimension and the role of conditions favouring or inhibiting learning.

In conclusion, at least under some specific conditions, improvements in performance may not be restricted to the first retest but continue in several successive presentations. While an interpretation of these effects awaits further analysis, the reviewed evidence suggests caution in the use of multiple administration of attention tests. A typical example is that in which the influence of rehabilitative training is evaluated by repeated presentation of the same test.

An investigation of the psychometric characteristics of the Test for Attentional Performance (Zimmermann and Fimm, 1992) in patients with traumatic brain injury

The above comments underscore the importance of basing the clinical evaluation of attention on diagnostic instruments for which psychometric characteristics have been carefully verified. As a part of the BIOMED-I-ESCAPE project (European Standardised Computerised Assessment Procedure for the Evaluation and Rehabilitation of Brain Damaged Patients), sponsored by the European Community, a joint study was carried out to evaluate the psychometric characteristics of the Zimmermann and Fimm (1992) battery in the case of patients with traumatic brain injury. The study was carried out at various centres in Europe (Belgium: Centre Neurologique William Lennox, Ottignies-Louvain-la-Neuve. France: CIRLEP, Université de Reims, Centre de Réadaptation de Mulhouse, Mulhouse, Service de Rééducation et Convalescence Neurologiques, Lille, and Centre de Rééducation et d'Etude des Activités Mnésiques, Tassin La Demi-Lune. Germany: Neurologische Klinik, Aachen, and Psychologisches Institut der Universität, Freiburg. Italy: IRCCS S. Lucia, Rome, Rehabilitative Medicine Unit, Ferrara, and Neurological Division of Grosseto Hospital, Grosseto. Spain: EPL Hospital de la Santa Creu i Sant Pau, Barcelona) and in Brazil (Sarah Kubistchek Hospital, Brasilia). An analytical description of the research is presented in Zoccolotti *et al.* (2000).

Special interest in assessing attentional processes in TBI patients is understandable in view of the high frequency of such pathology; further, TBI characteristically occurs in young adults with a long life expectancy. It is well known that TBI patients often complain of severe difficulties in concentration and report being slow and inefficient under time pressure. At least in part, difficulties in returning to work have been traced back to attentional disorders (e.g. van Zomeren and van den Burg, 1985). Experimental evidence indicates that these patients are particularly deficient in situations of divided and selective attention (e.g. Stablum *et al.*, 1994; Azouvi *et al.*, 1996); in contrast, deficits in the intensive dimension of attention are relatively infrequent. Thus, TBI patients as a group show normal alertness reactions (White *et al.*, 1992); furthermore, most evidence indicates spared sustained attention processes in these patients (e.g. Brouwer and van Wolffelaar, 1985). Here, we would just like to point out that, to date, most studies have focused on an experimental analysis of the attentional disorders in these patients. Thus, group comparisons were typically used, cancelling out individual variability; further, experimental tasks are usually specifically constructed to test the specific hypotheses of a given study and their clinical usage is consequently limited. As stated above, the Zimmermann and Fimm (1992) battery of attentional tests offers a wide spectrum of computerized tasks that allow us to assess the major facets of attention. While each subtest has been based on the relevant theoretical literature, an effort has been made to make the tasks feasible in a clinical setting in terms of ease of administration, standardization of instructions and normal control reference norms. The only requirement is the use of a PC. A through description of the battery is presented in Chapter 4 by Zimmermann and Fimm, in this volume.

Following van Zomeren and Brouwer's (1994) classification of attentional processes, we chose those subtests that most closely map the major basic attentional processes: alertness and vigilance (intensive dimension) and selective and divided attention (selective dimension).

The Zimmermann and Fimm (1992) battery includes an *Alertness* test. The subject sees a cross at the centre of the screen presented at irregular intervals and presses a button as quickly as possible. In one block, the stimulus onset is anticipated by an acoustic signal (warning condition). Reaction times (RT) with or without warning are the measure of performance; further, a coefficient of phasic attention is calculated based on the difference between RT to warned and unwarned trials divided by the general median RT. In the *Optical vigilance* subtest, the subject is presented with a bar moving regularly up and down in the middle of the screen. The subject has to press the button when the bar shows a larger oscillation. The task is given continuously for 15 minutes. RTs and number of errors (omissions and false alarms) are the critical measures of performance. Reference norms refer to both the total period of testing and to blocks of 5-minute periods. The *Go–nogo* subtest measures selective attention. Two patterned squares serve as target stimuli and three as non-target stimuli. The subject has to press the button on presentation of a target and must not press it on presentation of a non-target. Main parameters are reaction times for correct responses, number of false reactions and number of omissions. In the *Divided attention* subtest, two simultaneous tasks (one visual and one acoustic) are given. In the visual task, matrices, consisting of a regular array of sixteen dots with seven little 'x's superimposed randomly upon them, are displayed on the screen. The subject has to press a key whenever four 'x's form a square. In the acoustic task, the patient listens to a sequence of alternating high and low sounds and has to detect a change in this sequence and press a button. Reaction times, number of omissions and false reactions are taken as measures of the subject's performance.

In many tests, raw scores are subjected to correction formulas to take into account the effect of age and education. When required, corrected scores were used in the following analyses; this permitted comparing patients' data with standardized norms (Zimmermann and Fimm, 1992).

The aim of the study was to investigate the psychometric characteristics of the scale in its use with TBI patients. More specifically we evaluated: (a) reliability of attentional measures (to this aim, a subsample of patients was tested twice, with a one-month interval); (b) consistency of different dependent measures (e.g. errors vs. reaction times); (c) error of measurement of individual performance; (d) stability of performance, i.e. range of individual fluctuations on each test in the absence of rehabilitative treatment; (e) frequency with which patients fall into the pathological range on each of these attentional processes; and (f) relationship of performance to the severity of trauma.

A total sample of 106 patients (75 males and 31 females) was tested.

Patients were relatively young (mean age = 28.2; SD = 9.7); average schooling was 10.6 years (SD = 3.0). Patients were assessed with a stabilized symptomatology (at least five months after injury); on average testing occurred 22.6 months (SD = 22.0) after injury. Note that TBI was relatively severe as assessed by coma duration (mean = 27.4 days; SD = 28.6); 62 patients had a coma lasting between one week and one month, and 23 more than one month. A subset of 62 patients was examined a second time at least one month after the first evaluation.

Reliability

Reliability was assessed by computing Pearson correlations between the first and second examination (Table 5.1). In addition, test–retest correlations based on a sample of 35 normal controls, collected by Dr Heinze and reported by Zimmermann and Fimm (1992), are given. It is of note that the composition of this sample is very similar to that of the TBI group of patients for

Table 5.1 Test–retest correlations for TBI patients and for a group of control subjects (data from Zimmermann and Fimm, 1992). Realiability coefficients based on Cronbach alpha values are also shown for comparison

	TBI patients			*Controls*			*Controls*		
Test/parameter	*N*	*r*		*N*	*r*		*N*	*Cronbach alpha*	
Alertness									
RT (no warning)	62	0.87	**	35	0.81°		200	0.975	***
RT (warning)	62	0.86	**	35	0.81°		200	0.972	***
phasic index	62	0.15	ns	35	−0.07	ns	200	—	
Optical vigilance									
RT	31	0.18	ns						
false reactions	31	0.40	*						
omissions	31	0.67	**						
Go–nogo									
RT	62	0.53	**				199	0.922	***
false reactions	62	0.59	**						
omissions	62	0.16	ns						
Divided attention									
RT	57	0.33	**	35	0.48	***	200	0.588	***
false reactions	57	0.65	**	35	0.64	***			
omissions	57	0.73	**	35	0.44	**			

Notes:
* $p < .05$ ** $p < .01$ *** $p < .001$
° Warned and unwarned reaction times were analysed together

age, sex and education; further, the interval of testing was also very similar (about 25 days). Data refer to only two out of four subtests because of differences in the actual versions of the tests used. Also reported are Cronbach alphas based on a larger sample of control subjects from Zimmermann and Fimm (1992); these values are available for three out of the four tests and only in terms of RT.

An inspection of Table 5.1 indicates that for TBI patients correlations were generally significant, although highly variable (ranging from .15 to .87). Note that different parameters in the same test showed considerably different levels of reliability. Thus, in both the Optical vigilance and the Divided attention test reliability was highest for number of omissions and lowest for RTs. In the Go–nogo test, moderate values of reliability were present for RTs and number of false reactions. Omissions were very rare in this test (not shown in the table) making this measure unreliable. The picture for the Alertness test is somewhat different. RTs (both with and without warning) were quite stable; in contrast, the reliability coefficient for the phasic index alertness was very low and non-significant, indicating need for caution in interpreting this parameter.

Test–retest correlations for the control subjects showed a similar although not identical pattern. Thus, RTs in the Alertness test were quite stable but for this group also reliability was very low for the phasic index. In the Divided attention test, correlations were generally lower although significant. However, the pattern was somewhat different in TBI patients and controls. Among patients, RTs showed the lowest value and omissions the highest; in control subjects, smaller differences among parameters were present. Cronbach alphas yielded reliability values generally higher than test–retest coefficients for both TBI and control subjects.

Overall, these data indicate the importance of taking into account the different parameters of attentional performance. In general, RTs are expected to provide more 'fine grained' measures of individual performance. However, in order to be reliable, this measure requires a relatively high number of trials and low error rates. Low number of target trials may be responsible for the low reliability in the Optical vigilance test. In the normative data, Zimmermann and Fimm (1992) refer to a 30-minute presentation. This period of testing seemed too taxing for TBI patients. Therefore, the present results indicate that, at least for a 15-minute presentation, omissions may be a more useful index of performance than RTs. The Divided attention test proved particularly difficult for the TBI patients who made a high number of omissions; this restricted the number of valid RTs to target trials, thus yielding a low reliability for this measure.

The index of phasic alertness showed low levels of reliability in both TBI and control subjects. As we have seen, measures capturing the difference between conditions have a potentially important theoretical value but they often fail at the psychometric level. As stated above, reliability of a difference score is lower when the two original measures are highly correlated. In the case of the Alertness task, Zimmermann and Fimm (1992) report a .84 correlation between warned and unwarned conditions. An in-depth study of the task parameters, such as ISI duration and variability, and of the distributions of scores in the unwarned and warned conditions may be needed to establish a more reliable index of phasic alertness performance. Also, the application of bi-variate non-parametric tolerance limits may prove useful in detecting the region defining an expected difference between warned and unwarned trials (Capitani *et al.*, 1999).

Error of measurement of individual performance

The standard error of measurement (SEM) allows us to estimate the extent to which a score is expected to vary on repeated measurement (Domholdt, 1993). Standard error of measurement is expressed as

$$\mathrm{SEM} = s\sqrt{1 - r}$$

where s is the standard deviation and r the reliability coefficient.

Since measurement errors are expected to be normally distributed, the SEM allows for evaluating the probability with which a second measure will fall within a given range. Since we know that, in a normal distribution, around 68% of cases fall within one standard deviation, approximately 68% of the time the repeated measurement will be within one SEM. This information is clinically important when trying to understand fluctuations of performance. For example, one may want to judge whether a change in performance after a period of training should be considered as meaningful or whether it may be considered as a random fluctuation.

Standard deviations and standard errors of measurement associated with each parameter are reported in Table 5.2. For comparison, data from Zimmermann and Fimm (1992) on control subjects are reported. An inspection of the table indicates that TBI patients are considerably more variable than normal controls, i.e. show larger standard deviations on all measures. This finding may be expected since injury may selectively affect performance in some but not all patients. Of particular interest is the observation that SEMs are also considerably larger in TBI patients, ranging from a factor of about three to one of about six. This indicates that individual performance can show considerably larger spontaneous fluctuations in TBI patients as compared to normal controls. However, it must be observed that, in TBI patients, the reliability coefficient used in calculating the SEM was the test–retest correlation, while it was the Cronbach alphas in the case of normal controls. As shown in Table 5.1, Cronbach alphas yielded generally higher values of reliability in both TBI patients and controls. Even with a note of caution, these

Table 5.2 Standard deviations and standard errors of measurement for TBI patients and for control subjects (data from Zimmermann and Fimm, 1992)

	TBI patients			*Controls*		
Test/parameter	*N*	*SD*	*SEM*	*N*	*SD*	*SEM*
Alertness						
RT (no warning)	62	129	46.51	200	43.97	6.95
RT (warning)	62	132	49.39	200	42.27	7.70
phasic index	62	.13	0.12			
Optical vigilance						
RT	31	98	88.74			
false reactions	31	15.1	11.70			
omissions	31	2.7	1.55			
Go–nogo						
RT	62	99	67.87	199	61.45	17.16
false reactions	62	4.2	2.69			
omissions	62	2.7	2.47			
Divided attention						
RT	57	173	141.61	200	91.56	58.77
false	57	6.2	3.67			
omissions	57	4.7	2.44			

findings underscore the importance of analysis of individual fluctuations being based on errors of measurement appropriate for a pathological population.

It is of note that factors other than random fluctuations due to error of measurement may contribute in generating actual differences in performances. In particular, as we have seen, several attentional tests show systematic changes with repetitive administrations (this problem is assessed in the next section).

Stability of perfomance: test–retest comparisons

Table 5.3 presents the means (and standard deviations) of the difference between the first and second session of the various tests and the relative Student t-statistics. For comparison, data on control subjects from Zimmermann and Fimm (1992) are shown.

As for the TBI patients, RTs in the Alertness test were faster in the second session in the warning condition, yielding a larger index of phasic alertness. For the Optical vigilance subtest, RTs were significantly faster in the second test; in contrast, errors (both omissions and false alarms) showed no systematic change. In the Go–nogo subtest, false alarms reduced in the second test while no changes were present for RTs and omissions (very rare in this task).

Table 5.3 Difference in performance between first and second administration for the TBI patients and for control subjects (data from Zimmermann and Fimm, 1992)

	TBI patients					*Controls*	
Test/parameter	*N*	*Mean difference*	*Standard deviation*	*t*	*p*	*N*	*p*
Alertness							
RT (no warning)	62	−11.25	86.97	1.02	ns	36	ns°
RT (warning)	62	−27.47	79.78	2.71	0.009	36	ns°
phasic index	62	0.5	0.16	−2.34	0.02	36	ns
Optical vigilance							
RT	31	−60.21	133.82	2.51	0.018		
false	31	−2.29	17.71	0.72	ns		
omissions	31	0.23	3.34	−0.38	ns		
Go–nogo							
RT	62	−9.03	109.32	0.65	ns		
false	62	−1.74	4.12	3.33	0.002		
omissions	62	−0.71	4.01	1.4	ns		
Divided attention							
RT	57	−29.12	178.46	1.23	ns	36	ns
false	57	−0.81	5.99	1.02	ns	36	ns
omissions	57	−.79	3.34	1.79	ns	36	ns

Note: ° Warned and unwarned reaction times were analysed together

In the Divided attention subtest, no changes in performance were observed between the two testing sessions either in terms of RTs or errors.

In the case of control subjects, no effect of practice was present for any of the tests in which this comparison was available.

In evaluating stability of performance on repetitive testing, it seems important to focus on the most critical and reliable parameters of performance. In this vein, omissions on the Optical vigilance and the Divided attention subtests indicate that performance in these tasks was relatively stable. As we have seen, RTs in the Optical vigilance test were quite unreliable; consequently, their change with time may not be clinically critical.

Note that patients were tested in the chronic phase; consequently, the obtained changes are likely to be due to the effect of practice on the actual tasks not to actual changes in the patient's symptomatology.

Overall, performance changes upon repetitive testing were limited, particularly if one considers the most critical and reliable parameters of performance. However, some specific changes did occur and should be taken into consideration when interpreting individual changes of performance over time. It is of note that these changes did not vary in a clear way with the complexity of the task. Thus, no change was observed in the Divided attention subtest, which was certainly the most complex task.

Individual analysis of pathological performance

Performance of the group of TBI patients was generally lower than expected for their age group in all measures. However, what appears more interesting is to examine the effect of head trauma on individual performances. Therefore, we calculated the proportion of patients who performed equal to or below a cut-off point (5th percentile) based on the reference norms (Zimmermann and Fimm, 1992). These results are presented in Figure 5.1. An inspection of the figure indicates striking differences between tests. Only a relatively small proportion of patients fall below the cut-off point in the intensive tests. Only 9% of patients were pathological in the Optical vigilance test (number of omissions). Also in this test no clear effect of time-on-task was present. Thus, when examining separately the performance in the first, second and third 5-minute periods, pathological cases were 9%, 11% and 8%, respectively. These findings confirm previous observations indicating spared vigilance in

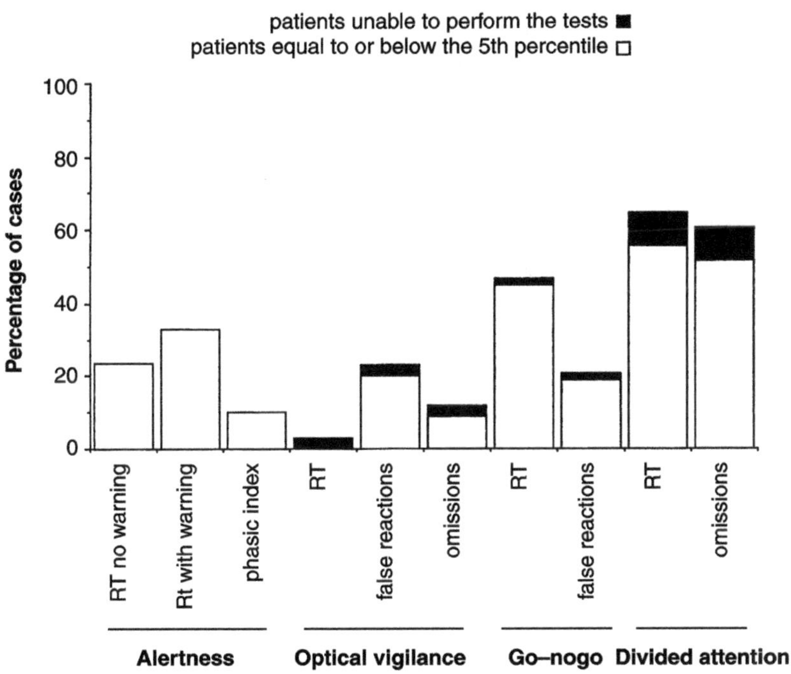

Figure 5.1 Proportion of patients who performed equal to or below the 5th percentile in four attentional tests; percentiles are based on the reference norms of Zimmermann and Fimm (1992)

traumatic patients (e.g. Brouwer and van Wolffelaar, 1985). Proportions of pathological performances were also relatively low in the Alertness test.

Considerably higher proportions of patients were pathological in the selective attention tests. Thus, more than half of patients were pathological in the Divided attention test, both in terms of number of omissions and RTs. Further, note that a sizeable proportion of patients were unable to perform this test. A similar proportion were impaired in the Go–nogo test in terms of RTs, although not in terms of false reactions.

A difference between intensive and selective tests of attention was present also in terms of severity of trauma, as assessed by coma duration. To evaluate this factor we considered four separate subgroups of patients: those with a coma of less than one day (N = 13), those with a coma of between one day and one week (N = 8), between one week and one month (N = 62) and over a month (N = 23). A set of ANOVAs indicated no effect of coma duration on any of the intensive measures of attention. In contrast, RTs in the Go–nogo test were slower for patients with longer coma duration. As for the Divided attention test, there was a trend for increased numbers of omissions for patients in the longer coma duration categories. Further, it must be noted that a few patients were unable to complete this test and they were all in the two subgroups with longer coma duration.

The effect of age, schooling and time since trauma on the attentional measures was evaluated by means of Pearson correlations. Neither age nor schooling exerted any significant effect on any of the measures, indicating no effect of these parameters once the correction formulas are applied. Also, in the case of time since trauma, all correlations were near zero and non-significant, indicating that attentional performance was relatively stable five months from the time of injury.

In general, a difference between intensive and selective tests of attention was present. Patients were more likely to be impaired in tests of selective attention and their performance in these tests varied as a function of trauma severity. In contrast, their performances in tests mapping the intensity dimension of attention were less affected. These observations appear generally consistent with previous findings based on group comparisons. Performance in vigilance tests has been reported as spared in patients with stabilized symptomatology (Brouwer and van Wolffelaar, 1985; Parasuraman, Mutter and Molloy, 1991). RTs to simple visual stimuli were generally lower in the TBI as a group. However, most patients performed within normal limits and no effect of trauma severity was present for this variable in spite of the large variability present in the sample.

Concluding remarks

Knowledge of attentional processes has undergone a dramatic improvement in recent decades. However, the process by which these theoretical advancements are converted into usable instruments suitable for clinical practice is complex and certainly requires further work. In the present chapter, we have tried to highlight a number of psychometric questions concerning the use of attentional tests. In particular, our presentation has focused on some measurement problems. As we have seen, analysis of individual attentional performance calls for a comparative evaluation across different conditions; however, while theoretically relevant, difference scores raise a number of measurement and reliability problems. A number of interesting proposals have been recently advanced to deal with this question. These include the use of bi-variate non-parametric tolerance limits proposed by Capitani and colleagues (1999) and the subtest profile analysis proposed by Crawford and colleagues (1997). Further research is clearly needed to substantiate these methodological contributions and prove their clinical usefulness.

Another important aspect for clinical usage of tests is that they should be validated on pathological samples. The European collaborative study on TBI patients presented in the last part of the chapter represents a contribution in this direction. When applying the Test for Attentional Performance by Zimmermann and Fimm (1992) to TBI patients, several interesting observations emerged. For example, it was observed that different dependent measures may prove more effective in capturing individual performances in different tests and that this pattern may be different in healthy versus pathological subjects. Further, clear differences between these two groups were also present in terms of errors of measurement. These considerations are important when analysing individual patients particularly if one is interested in the longitudinal analysis of performance.

Acknowledgements: This research was supported by a BIOMED1 grant from the European Community. We would like to thank Donatella Spinelli, Anna Cantagallo and Bruno Fimm for their comments on this chapter.

References

Armitage, S.G. (1946). An analysis of certain psychological tests used for the evaluation of brain injury. *Psychological Monographs*, *60* (Whole Number 277).

Army Individual Test Battery (1944). *Manual of Directions and Scoring*. Washington, DC: War Department, Adjutant General's Office.

Azouvi, P., Jokic, C., Van der Linden, M., Marlier, N. and Bussel, B. (1996). Working memory and supervisory control after severe closed-head injury. A study of dual task performance and random generation. *Journal of Clinical and Experimental Neuropsychology*, *18*, 317–337.

Brickenkamp, R. (1981). *Testd2: Aufmerksamkeists-Belastungs-Test* (Handanweisung, 7th edn) [Test d2: Concentration-Endurance-Test: Manual, 7th edn]. Gottingen, Toronto, Zurich: Verlag für Psychologie, C. J. Hogrefe.

Brittain, J.L., La Marche, J.A., Reeder, K.P., Roth, D.L. and Boll, T.J. (1991). Effects of age and IQ on paced auditory serial addition task (PASAT) performance. *Clinical Neuropsychologist*, *5*, 163–175.

Brouwer, W.H. and van Wolffelaar, P.C. (1985). Sustained attention and sustained effort after closed head injury: detection and 0.10 Hz heart rate variability in a low event rate vigilance task. *Cortex*, *21*, 11–119.

Burg, J.S., Burright, R.G. and Donovick, P.J. (1995). Performance data for traumatic brain-injured subjects on the Gordon Diagnostic System (GDS) tests of attention. *Brain Injury*, 9, 395–403.

Capitani, E. and Laiacona, M. (1999). The evaluation of experimental data in neuropsychology. In G. Denes and L. Pizzamiglio (eds) *Handbook of Clinical and Experimental Neuropsychology*. Hove: Psychology Press.

Capitani, E., Laiacona, M., Barbarotto, R. and Cossa, F.M. (1999). How can we evaluate interference in attentional tests? A study based on bi-variate non-parametric tolerance limits. *Journal of Clinical and Experimental Neuropsychology*, *21*, 216–228.

Chan, R.C.K. (2000) Attentional deficits in patients with closed head injury: a further study of the discriminative validity of the test of everyday attention. *Brain Injury*, *14*, 227–236.

Chronicle, E.P. and MacGregor, N.A. (1998). Are PASAT scores related to mathematical ability? *Neuropsychological Rehabilitation*, *8*, 3, 273–282.

Crawford, J.R., Obonsawin, M.C. and Allan, K.M. (1998). PASAT and components of WAIS-R performance: convergent and discriminant validity. *Neuropsychological Rehabilitation*, *8*, 255–272.

Crawford, J.R., Sommerville, J. and Robertson, I.H. (1997). Assessing the reliability and abnormality of subtest differences on the Test of Everyday Attention. *British Journal of Clinical Psychology*, *36*, 609–617.

Crowe, S.F. (1998) The differential contribution of mental tracking, cognitive flexibility, visual search, and motor speed to performance on parts A and B of the Trail Making Test. *Journal of Clinical Psychology*, *54*, 585–591.

Deary, I.J., Ebmeier, K.P., MacLeod, K.M., Dougall, N., Hepburn, D.A., Frier, B.M., and Goldwin, G.M. (1994). PASAT performance and the pattern of uptake of 99mTc-exametazime in brain estimated with single photon emission tomography. *Biol. Psychol.*, *38*, 1, 1–18.

Deary, I.J., Langan, S.J., Hepburn, D.A. and Frier, B.M. (1991). Which abilities does the PASAT test? *Personality and Individual Differences*, *12*, 983–987.

de Vries, H., van Houte, L.R., Lindeboom, J., van Eijk, J.T. and de Haan, M. (1992). [Paced addition. A neuropsychological test for assessment of divided attention] (Article in Dutch). *Tijdschr. Gerontol. Geriatr.*, *23*, 4, 147–156.

Dikmen, S.S., Heaton, R.K., Grant, I. and Temkin, N.R. (1999). Test–retest reliability and practice effects of expanded Halstead–Reitan Neuropsychological Test Battery. *Journal of the International Neuropsychological Society*, *5*, 346–356.

Dodrill, C.B. and Troupin, A.S. (1975). Effects of repeated administrations of comprehensive neuropsychological battery among chronic epileptics. *Journal of Nervous and Mental Disease*, *161*, 3, 185–190.

Domholdt, E. (1993). *Physical Therapy Research: Principles and Application*. Philadelphia: W.B. Saunders Company.

Dulaney, C.L. and Rogers, W.A. (1994). Mechanisms underlying reduction in Stroop interference with practice for young and old adults. *Journal of Experimental Psychology: Learning, Memory and Cognition*, *20*, 2, 470–484.

Dyche, G.E., and Johnson, D.A. (1991). Development and evaluation of CHIPASAT, an attention test for children: II. Test–retest reliability and practice effect for a normal sample. *Perceptual and Motor Skills*, *72*, 563–572.

Dye, O.A. (1979). Effects of practice on trail making test performance. *Perceptual and Motor Skills*, *48*, 296.

Egan, V. (1988). PASAT: observed correlations with IQ. *Personality and Individual Differences*, *9*, 179–180.

Feinstein, A., Brown, R. and Ron, M. (1994). Effects of practice of serial tests of attention in healthy subjects. *Journal of Clinical and Experimental Neuropsychology*, *16*, 436–447.

Fisk, A.D. and Schneider, W. (1981). Control and automatic processing during tasks requiring sustained attention: a new approach to vigilance. *Human Factors*, *23*, 737–750.

Fossum, B., Homberg, H. and Reinvang, I. (1992). Spatial and symbolic factors in performance on the Trail Making Test. *Neuropsychology*, *2*, 71–75.

Gaudino, E.A., Geisler, M.W. and Squires, N.K. (1995). Construct validity in the Trail Making Test: what makes Part B harder? *Journal of Clinical and Experimental Neuropsychology*, *17*, 529–535.

Giovagnoli, A.R., Del Pesce, M., Mascheroni, S., Simoncelli, M., Laiacona, M. and Capitani, E. (1996). Trail Making Test: normative values from 287 normal adult controls. *Italian Journal of Neurological Sciences*, *17*, 305–309.

Godefroy, O., Lhullier, C. and Rousseaux, M. (1994). Reliability of reaction times measurements in brain damaged patients. *Journal of Neurological Sciences*, *126*, 168–171.

Gronwall, D.M. (1977). Paced Auditory Serial Addition Task: a measure of recovery from concussion. *Perceptual and Motor Skills*, *44*, 367–373.

Gronwall, D.M. and Sampson, H. (1974). *The Psychological Effects of Concussion*. Auckland: Oxford University Press.

Gronwall, D.M. and Wrightson, P. (1981). Memory and information processing capacity after closed head injury. *Journal of Neurology, Neurosurgery and Psychiatry*, *44*, 889–895.

Guilford, J.P. (1954). *Psychometric Methods* (2nd edn). New York: McGraw-Hill.

Halstead, W.C. (1947). *Brain and Intelligence*. Chicago: University of Illinois Press.

Heaton, R.K., Baade, L.E. and Johnson, K.L. (1978). Neuropsychological test results associated with psychiatric disorders in adults. *Psychological Bulletin*, *85*, 141–162.

Johnson, B.F., Hock, K. and Johnson, J. (1991). Variability in psychometric test scores: the importance of the practice effect in patient study design. *Prog. Neuropsychopharmacol. Biol. Psychiatry*, *15*, 5, 625–635.

Johnson, D.A., Roething-Johnson, K. and Middleton, J. (1988). Development and evaluation of an attentional test for head-injured children: 1. Information processing capacity in a normal sample. *Journal of Child Psychology and Psychiatry*, *2*, 199–208.

Kanter, G. (1984). PASAT performance and intelligence: A relationship? *International Journal of Clinical Neuropsychology*, *6*, 84.

Kennedy, K.J. (1981). Age effects on Trail Making Test performance. *Perceptual and Motor Skills*, *52*, 671–675.

Knight, R.G. and Godfrey, H.P.D. (1984) Assessing the significance of differences between subtests on the Wechsler Adult Intelligence Scale – Revised. *Journal of Clinical Psychology*, *40*, 808–810.

Larrabee, G.J. and Curtiss, G. (1995). Construct validity of various verbal and visual memory tests. *Journal of Clinical and Experimental Neuropsychology*, *17*, 4, 536–547.

Lezak, M.D. (1995). *Neuropsychological Assessment* (3rd edn). New York: Oxford University Press.

McCaffrey, R.J., Cousins, J.P., Westervelt, H.J., Martynowicz, M., Remick, S.C., Szebenyi, S., Wagle, W.A., Bottomley, P.A., Hardy, C.J. and Haase, R.F. (1995). Practice effects with the NIMH AIDS Abbreviated Neuropsychological Battery. *Archives of Clinical Neuropsychology*, *10*, 3, 241–250.

McCaffrey, R.J., Ortega, A. and Haase, R.F. (1993). Effects of repeated neuropsychological assessments. *Archives of Clinical Neuropsychology*, *8*, 519–524.

McCaffrey, R.J., Ortega, A., Orsillo, M., Nelles, W. and Haase, R.F. (1992). Practice effects in repeated neuropsychological assessments. *Clinical Neuropsychologist*, *6*, 32–42.

Macciocchi, S.N. (1990). 'Practice makes perfect': retest effects in college athletes. *Journal of Clinical Psychology*, *46*, 628–631.

McLeod, D. and Prior, M. (1996). Attention deficits in adolescents with ADHD and other clinical groups. *Child Neuropsychology*, *2*, 1–10.

Matarazzo, J.D., Wiens, A.N., Matarazzo, R.G. and Goldstein, S.G. (1974). Psychometric and clinical test–retest reliability of the Halstead–Reitan Impairment Index in a sample of healthy, young, normal men. *Journal of Nervous and Mental Disease*, *158*, 37–49.

Maylor, E.A., Rabbitt, P.M., James, G.H. and Kerr, S.A. (1992). Effects of alcohol, practice, and task complexity on reaction time distributions. *Quarterly Journal of Experimental Psychology*, *44*, 119–139.

Mirsky, A.F. (1989). The neuropsychology of attention: elements of a complex behaviour. In E. Perecman (ed.) *Integrating Theory and Practice in Clinical Neuropsychology*. Hillsdale, NJ: Erlbaum, pp. 75–91.

Mirsky, A.F., Anthony, B.J., Duncan, C.C., Ahearn, M.B. and Kellam, S.G. (1991). Analysis of the elements of attention: a neuropsychological approach. *Neuropsychology Review*, *2*, 109–145.

Nelson, H.E. (1982). *National Adult Reading Test (NART): Test Manual*. Windsor: NFER Nelson.

O'Donnell, J.P., MacGregor, L.A., Dabrowski, J.J., Oestreicher, J.M. and Romero, J.J. (1994). Construct validity of neuropsychological tests of conceptual and attentional abilities. *Journal of Clinical Psychology*, *50*, 4, 596–600.

Orgel, S. and McDonald, R. (1967). An evaluation of the Trail Making Test. *Journal of Consulting Psychology*, *31*, 77–78.

Parasuraman, R., Mutter, S.A. and Molloy, R. (1991). Sustained attention folowing mild closed head injury. *Journal of Clinical and Experimental Neuropsychology*, *13*, 789–811.

Peeke, S.C., Jones, R.T. and Stone, G.C. (1976). Effects of practice on marijuana-induced changes in reaction time. *Psychopharmacology*, *48*, 159–163.

Posner, M.I. (1978). *Chronometric Explorations of Mind*. Hillsdale, NJ: Erlbaum.

Reitan, R.M. (1955). The relation of the Trail Making Test to organic brain damage. *Journal of Consulting Psychology*, *19*, 393–394.

Reitan, R.M. (1958). The validity of the Trail Making Test as an indicator of organic brain damage. *Perceptual and Motor Skills*, *8*, 271–276.

Reitan, R.M. (1971). Trail Making Test results for normal and brain-damaged children. *Perceptual and Motor Skills*, *33*, 575–581.

Reitan, R.M. and Wolfson, D. (1985). The Halstead–Reitan Neuropsychological Test Battery. Tucson, AZ: Neuropsychology Press.

Robertson, I.H., Ward, T., Ridgeway, V. and Nimmo-Smith, I. (1994a). *The Test of Everyday Attention*. Bury St Edmunds: Thames Valley Test Company.

Robertson, I.H., Ward, T., Ridgeway, V. and Nimmo-Smith, I. (1994b). The structure of normal human attention: the test of Everyday Attention. *Journal of the International Neuropsychological Society*, *2*, 525–534.

Roman, D.D., Edwall, G.E., Buchanan, R.J. and Patton, J.H. (1991). Extended norms for the Paced Auditory Serial Addition Test. *Clinical Neuropsychologist*, 5, 33–40.

Rossini, E.D. and Karl, M.A. (1994). The Trail Making Test A and B: a technical note on their structural non-equivalence. *Perceptual and Motor Skills*, *78*, 625–626.

Sacks, T.L., Clark, C.R., Pols, R. and Geffen, L.B. (1991). Comparability and stability of performance on six alternative forms of the Dodrill–Stroop Color–Word Test. *Clinical Neuropsychologist*, *5*, 220–225.

Sampson, H. (1961) Effects of practice on paced performance. *Australian Journal of Psychology*, 13, 185–194.

Schmidt, M., Trueblood, W. and Merwin, M. (1994). How much do 'attention' tests tell us? *Archives of Clinical Neuropsychology*, *9*, 383–394.

Schweinberger, S.R., Buse, C. and Sommer, W. (1993). Reaction time improvements with practice in brain-damaged patients. *Cortex*, *29*, 333–340.

Sherman, E.M.S., Strauss, E., Spellacy, F. and Hunter, M. (1995). Construct validity of WAIS-R factors: neuropsychological correlates in adults referred for possible head injury. *Psychological Assessment*, 7, 440–444.

Sherman, E.M.S., Strauss, E. and Spellacy, F. (1997). Validity of the Paced Auditory Serial Addition Test (PASAT) in adults referred for neuropsychological assessment after head injury. *Clinical Neuropsychologist*, *11*, 1, 34–45.

Shum, D.H.K., McFarland, K.A., Bain, J.D. and Humphreys, M.S. (1990). The effects of closed-head injury upon attentional processes: an information processing stage analysis. *Journal of Clinical and Experimental Neuropsychology*, *12*, 247–264.

Shum, D.H.K., McFarland, K.A. and Bain, J.D. (1994a). Effects of closed-head injury on attentional processes: generality of Stenberg's additive factor method. *Journal of Clinical and Experimental Neuropsychology*, *16*, 547–555.

Shum, D.H.K., McFarland, K.A. and Bain, J.D. (1994b). Assessment of attention: relationship between psychological testing and information processing approaches. *Journal of Clinical and Experimental Neuropsychology*, *16*, 531–538.

Silverstein, A.B. (1982). Pattern analysis as simultaneous statistical inference. *Journal of Consulting and Clinical Psychology*, *50*, 234–240.

Spreen, O. and Benton, A. (1965). Comparative studies of some psychological tests for cerebral damage. *Journal of Nervous and Mental Disease*, *140*, 323–333.

Spreen, O. and Strauss, E. (1998). *A Compendium of Neuropsychological Tests* (2nd edn). New York: Oxford University Press.

Stablum, F., Leonardi, G., Mazzoldi, M., Umiltà, C. and Morra, S. (1994). Attention and control deficits following closed head injury. *Cortex*, *30*, 603–618.

Stanton, B.A., Savageau, J.A., Aucion, R., Jenkins, C.D. and Zyzanki, S.J. (1984). Age and educational differences on the Trail Making Test. *Perceptual and Motor Skills*, *58*, 311–318.

Sternberg, S. (1969). On the discovery of processing stage. *Acta Psychologica*, *30*, 276–315.

Sturm, W., Dahmen, W., Hartje, W. and Wilmes, K. (1983). Ergebnisse eines Trainingsprogrammems zur Verbesserung der visuellen Auffassungsschnelligkeit und Konzentrationsfähigkeit bei Hirngeschädigten [Results of a programme for the training of perceptual speed and concentration in brain-damaged patients]. *Archiv für Psychiatrie und Nervenkrankheiten*, *233*, 9–22.

Stuss, D.T., Stethem, L.L., Hugenholtz, H. and Richard, M.T. (1989). Traumatic brain injury: a comparison of three clinical tests, and analysis of recovery. *Clinical Neuropsychologist*, *3*, 145–156.

Stuss, D.T., Stethem, L. and Poirier, C.A. (1987). Comparison of three tests of attention and rapid information processing across six age groups. *Clinical Neuropsychologist*, *1*, 139–152.

van Zomeren, A.H. and Brouwer, P. (1994). *Clinical Neuropsychology of Attention*. Oxford: Oxford University Press.

van Zomeren, A. and van den Burg, W. (1985). Residual complaints of patients two years after severe head injury. *Journal of Neurology, Neurosurgery and Psychiatry*, *48*, 21–28.

Vickers, D., Vincent, N. and Medvedev, A. (1996). The geometric structure, construction, and interpretation of path following (Trail-Making) tests. *Journal of Clinical Psychology*, *52*, 651–661.

Viggiano, M.P. (1999). Behavioural methods in neuropsychology. In G. Denes and L. Pizzamiglio (eds) *Handbook of Clinical and Experimental Neuropsychology*. Hove: Psychology Press.

Waldmann, B.W., Dickson, A.L., Monahan, M.C. and Kazelskis, R. (1992). The relationship between intellectual ability and adult performance on the Trail Making Test and the Symbol Digit Modalities Test. *Journal of Clinical Psychology*, *48*, 360–363.

Ward, T. (1997). A note of caution for clinicians using the Paced Auditory Serial Addition Task. *British Journal of Clinical Psychology*, *36*, 303–307.

White, J., Fleming, M., Polansky, M., Cavallucci, C. and Coslett, H.B. (1992). Phasic arousal in response to auditory warnings after traumatic brain injury. *Neuropsychologia*, *35*, 313–324.

Wiederholt, W.C., Kritz-Silverstein, D.K., Salmon, D.P. and Barrett-Connor, E. (1996). Effects of sequential neuropsychological testing of an elderly community-based sample. *Neuroepidemiology*, *15*, 257–268.

Wiens, A.N., Fuller, K.H. and Crosser, J.R. (1997). Paced Auditory Serial Addition Test: adult norms and moderator variables. *Journal of Clinical and Experimental Neuropsychology*, *19*, 473–483.

Zimmermann, P. and Fimm, B. (1992). *Test for Attentional Performance (TAP)*. Würselen: Psytest.

Zoccolotti, P., Matano, A., Deloche, G., Cantagallo, A., Passadori, A., Leclercq, M., Braga, L., Cremel, N., Pittau, P., Renom, M., Rousseaux, M., Truche, A., Fimm, B. and Zimmermann, P. (2000). Patterns of attentional impairments following a closed head injury: a collaborative European study. *Cortex*, *36*, 93–107.

Chapter 6

Neuropsychological assessment of attention disorders using non-computerized tasks: impairment and disability

Anna Cantagallo

Introduction

Attention refers to a class of intensive and selective processes (van Zomeren and Brouwer, 1994; see the models proposed by Posner and Petersen in 1990, Norman and Shallice in 1986, Baddeley in 1986, Shiffrin and Schneider in 1977, and described in the previous chapters) and we usually base our assessment proposal upon a classification of three subtypes of attention (selective attention, divided attention, sustained attention) all derived from clinical and experimental assessment, functional imaging, and cognitive event-related potentials. Consequently the clinical assessment of attention would embrace the examination of each attentional process: only in this way is it possible to delimit the specific pattern of attentional disorders in each patient and suggest an individualized programme of neuropsychological rehabilitation. Many non-computerized tests have been designed to assess selective attention, divided attention and sustained attention.

Selective attention permits us to focus only on some *stimuli* (target stimuli) while ignoring others (non-target stimuli or distractors), in the same or in different sensory modalities (inter- or intra-modal). In daily life we are often engaged in two or more tasks simultaneously, utilizing another very important attentional process, divided attention. Even if selective attention and divided attention, always working together, cannot be conceived as entirely separate processes, it seems very useful to distinguish the processes in order to assess them separately. Finally, in the same way, we separate sustained attention over long periods of time from other attentional processes, even if ecologically both selective attention and divided attention could be sustained in time. For this reason, the term 'vigilance' is more correct when referring to sustained attention in a low-event-rate situation or in a low level of stimulation. Performance in a sustained attention task could decrease slowly and gradually in time ('time-on-task effect') or suddenly, only for a few seconds ('lapses of attention') (van Zomeren and Brouwer, 1994).

In this chapter we will present the most common non-computerized tests for bedside examination of attention and for the specific assessment of selective attention, divided attention and sustained attention. We have chosen only the tasks supported with coded rules for administration and scoring, and above all with normative data; generally these tasks have been used in many clinical researches applied to different etiologies of brain damage, and for this reason most of them are familiar to clinicians.

The advantages of paper-and-pencil tests are easy administration and the presence of standardization. Some advantages are intrinsic to the test, such as the Digit Span: it is so easy that it could be used in bedside assessment and it follows the patient's recovery from the beginning. Some advantages are historical: there is a great deal of information about the paper-and-pencil tests because they have been used for a long time in clinical and experimental settings; moreover these tests show relatively high sensitivity.

As far as their disadvantages are concerned, first, they often have low specificity because they involve not only attention processes, but also working memory, visuo-spatial abilities, and calculation. Secondly, most of them (with the exception of a few, such as the Test of Everyday Attention by Robertson and co-workers, 1994) predate current theoretical models of attention, and for this reason their best use is for screening and global quantification rather than qualification of the disorder: they are frequently difficult to place in a cognitive model of attention processes (Perry and Hodges, 1999).

While experimental research with instrumental devices is closer to the cognitive model of attention, but often does not take into account the clinical aspects of the patient, the paper-and-pencil tasks are more clinical and simple, and follow the patient's recovery.

Moreover, in a clinical approach (as compared to experimental), a complete assessment of attention disorders is influenced by general disorders of each patient (for instance, visual or auditory perception deficits in input direction, and speech or motor diseases in output direction), which could impair the patient's performance regardless of real attention disorders. Hypovision, or dysarthria, if a verbal answer is required, or mild hemiparesis, may impede the utilization of some paper-and-pencil tests: it is, therefore, necessary to control the task conditions for each patient with regard to sensory and motor requirements.

After the first or acute phase following cerebral vascular accident (CVA) or traumatic brain injury (TBI), a bedside examination is advisable due to general and severe attention disorders, whereas in the post-acute and chronic phase, when the patient is more collaborative, it is possible to begin the assessment of attention with direct or indirect observation (through relatives, friends and colleagues) and description of the patient's behaviour during daily activities at home, in a social situation, and at work. This preliminary behaviour assessment is helpful for the specific assessment of attention processes.

Furthermore, the time interval between examination and onset should modify the choice of tests in a clinical approach: in this chapter we will indicate the best timing for using each test. Different etiologies (CVA and TBI patients, for example) involve variations in time of neuropsychological recovery.

Finally, spatial exploration and executive functions overlap with attention functions and should be assessed in the general neuropsychological assessment of the patient, since hemi-neglect and impairments in supervisory attentional control may affect performance in attention tasks (Perry and Hodges, 1999); the devices used to assess spatial attention and executive functions are not discussed in this chapter; we therefore refer the reader to other specialized books (Lezak, 1995; Spreen and Strauss, 1998).

The aforementioned books are also suggested for more details of administration, scoring, normative data, and psychometric properties of the following non-instrumental tests for attention process assessment.

Bedside examination

The initial assessment of attention in the departments of neurology or rehabilitation should be short (since the patient may be confused, easily distracted, and exhausted), as well as simple (the assessment in this phase is rarely made by neuropsychologists, but more frequently by medical doctors). Furthermore, it should focus mainly on short-term memory for auditory stimuli (Digit Span Forward), or on elaboration of stimuli requiring activation of working memory (Digit Span Backward, Serial Seven Test), or the counting of all the target stimuli engaging selective and sustained attention (Brief Test of Attention, Attentional Capacity Test). Using tasks with auditory stimuli can be useful for a quick examination of the patients while they are lying in a bed or on a gymnasium carpet. Good responsiveness and patient compliance are essential for the tests presented in this chapter: assessment of visual attention in minimally responsive brain-injured patients is not dealt with here (Whyte and Di Pasquale, 1995).

The Digit Span test used in the Wechsler batteries (Wechsler Adult Intelligence Scale – Revised or WAIS-R: Wechsler, 1981; Wechsler Memory Scale – Revised or WMS-R: Wechsler, 1987) comprises two different tests, Digit Forward and Digit Backward, which involve different attention processes. The examiner reads aloud random number sequences at the rate of one number per second, and the subject is required to repeat each sequence exactly as it is given in Digit Forward, and in reverse order in Digit Backward. The examiner then reads longer and longer number sequences, continuing until the subject fails two sequences of the same length. Both tasks involve short-term memory; Digit Backward also involves working memory, mental tracking as well as both verbal and visual scanning processes, as hypothesized by Weinberg and co-workers (1972). Concerning normal performance of Digit Forward, 'it is easy to remember that spans of 6 or better are well *within normal limits*, a span of 5 may be marginal to *normal limits*, a span of 4 is definitely *borderline*, and 3 is *defective*' (Lezak, 1995). The span tends to decline only minimally beyond the ages of 65 or 70 (Craik, 1990). The normal raw score difference between Digit Forward and Digit Backward tends to range a little above 1.0 (Kaplan *et al.*, 1991). Therefore Lezak (1995) considers a raw score of 4 or 5 in Digit Backward as *within normal limits*, 3 as *borderline or defective*, depending on the patient's level of education, and 2 totally *defective* for everyone. The Digit Backward decreases by about one point during the seventh decade. It is sensitive to many kinds of focal or diffuse brain damage and is very frequently used in the clinical approach to the patient.

Other 'tests of mental control' (Stuss and Benson, 1986), used more frequently than Digit Span Forward and Backward, are the Serial Subtraction Tests: the simplest of these tests requires counting backwards from 10, whereas in the Serial Seven Test (Smith, 1967) the patient has to subtract 7 from 100 at least five times (100–93–86–79–72–65). The test is very useful in discriminating between normal and severe brain-injured populations, not simply on the presence or absence of errors (Smith found that 25% of normal subjects made three or more errors, even if only 2% of normal subjects were either unable to complete the task or made five errors; Smith, 1967), but also on behavioural observations. For example, it is possible to note the reduction in performance after the first or second number, or the bad working memory for test instructions, provided that addition ability is good.

The Brief Test of Attention (BTA) (Schretlen, 1996; Schretlen *et al.*, 1996a and 1996b) is an auditory perception task for non-aphasic hearing adults, including those with visual and motor impairments that preclude tests requiring visual scanning or manual dexterity. The BTA consists of two parallel forms presented via audio cassette. On form N (Numbers), a voice reads ten lists of letters and numbers that increase in length from 4 to 18 items; the respondent must count how many numbers were read aloud, disregarding the letters presented. Form L (Letters) consists of the same ten lists, but the respondent must now count the letters. The total score is the sum of correctly monitored lists across both forms, with raw scores ranging from 0 to 20. About ten minutes are required for administering and scoring the entire test. A manual is available with information about administration, scoring, interpretation, normative procedures, reliability, and validity of the BTA (Schretlen, 1996). The test is standardized for use with adults aged from 17 to 82 years, with a decline in performance after 60 years, males producing significantly lower scores than females; the two forms have acceptable reliability and test–retest stability, and research supports the construct validity of BTA in relation to other accepted measures of working memory. BTA (Schretlen *et al.*, 1996a and 1996b) correlates more strongly with the 'complex' tests of selective attention (Digit Span Backward, Trail Making Test – part B) than with the 'simple' ones (Digit Span Forward, Trail Making – part A), and more strongly with measures of attention than with other cognitive tasks (memory or language). Amnesic patients can therefore be assessed with this test because BTA does not require intact memory for successful performance.

While auditory selective attention is assessed in the BTA, the Attentional Capacity Test (ACT; Weber, 1988) involves the sequential presentation of stimuli over a progressively longer period of time: this taped sustained attention test consists of eight progressively complex levels with three trials within each level. The subject must count how many target letters or numbers are read aloud, and the total score ranges from 0 to 24. Normative study has shown that controls never perform below 12, although no subject has achieved the maximum score of 24; neither sex nor age seems to affect this normative group. High correlation has been demonstrated with the Paced Auditory Serial Addition Test (PASAT), but with the additional advantage that number addition ability is not required.

In conclusion, the advantage of the bedside tests is that they may be used in the early phase as an initial evaluation, following the patient from the beginning, and may lead to further, more specific, tests at the right moment. In this initial phase some tests (Serial Seven test and Digit Span) do not allow easy distinction between attentive and mnesic processes of short-term memory and working memory, whereas other tests (BTA and ACT) have been designed to eliminate the verbal memory component from the evaluation so that assessment is more focused on attention.

Behavioural and social consequences of attentional deficits: work and driving

Observation of everyday life behaviour is important not only for assessing disability secondary to attention impairment, but also for describing performance during attention assessment which may constitute a useful predictive factor for complex daily life activities, such as return to work, or driving.

Ainsley and Gliner (1989) found a high correlation between therapist observation of attentional disorders (such as distraction and bad concentration) and employability.

In research on the prediction of return to work for 98 TBI patients seven years post-onset, Brooks and colleagues (1987) found that age, cognitive, behavioural and personality changes are related to bad work status, and that, in the domain of cognitive disorders, memory and attention deficits seem to be the best predictors, the latter having been measured by fast presentation of PASAT (explained in detail later on). Gronwall and Wrightson (1974) also reported that speed and efficiency of information processing in PASAT are related to readiness to return to work in mild TBI.

More recently, Ruff and co-workers (1993) demonstrated that once again age and slowness of information processing could critically affect return to work at one year post-trauma. Also fast attentional switching measured by the Trail Making Test – part B (Teasdale *et al.*, 1997) and preserved dual-task capacity (Girard *et al.*, 1996; Witol *et al.*, 1996) are good predictors for return to work. The slowness in information processing and response elaboration revealed also by a choice reaction time paradigm significantly correlates with return to work (van Zomeren and van den Burg, 1985).

Finally, no research has studied sustained attention and demonstrated it as a useful factor to predict employability, even if Gronwall (1987) pointed out the high frequency of TBI patients' subjective complaints about lapses of attention and reduced performance in time in the workplace.

Besides return to work, complex instrumental ability, such as car driving, can be compromised by the presence of attentional disorders.

When dividing driving competence into driving skills and motor/cognitive fitness to drive, van Zomeren and Brouwer (1994) underlined that some driving skills, such as safety, time or space constraints, could permit the patient to bypass attention disorders. For this reason the authors considered speed of information processing, as indicated by reaction time measures, as an unreliable factor to predict driving ability. In this way assessment of attention (with the Symbol Digit Test: see below; Gouvier *et al.*, 1989) may help to delineate the good and bad drivers, but this indicator is not sufficient. More information seems to be necessary, and should be collected not only in the laboratory (regarding other neuropsychological functions, or in driving simulation; Gouvier *et al.*, 1989), but also 'on the road' in a natural setting (Gregory, 1989).

Behavioural assessment and disability

1 Questionnaires

In a clinical approach to attention assessment, concomitant with bedside assessment, the hospital staff and professionals should report on any behaviour (or *disability assessment*) that could reflect the patient's attentional *impairment* for visual or auditory stimuli. Moreover relatives and caregivers should be interviewed about the patient's concentration and mental rapidity in daily life activities (another approach to the disability assessment) (Kinsella, 1998). Many rating scales aimed at quantifying patient disability resulting from neuropsychological disorders include some items for the description of attention disorders. An example of these may be seen in the Neurobehavioural Rating Scale (Levin *et al.*, 1987) where at least three out of 27 items are related to attention problems reported by clinicians after TBI. 'Fatigability: rapidly fatigues on challenging cognitive tasks or complex activities, lethargic' or 'Inattention/Reduced alertness: fails to sustain attention, easily distracted, fails to notice aspects of environment, has difficulty directing attention, decreased alertness' are some examples of these items. The scale has reported satisfactory inter-judge reliability.

Another questionnaire is the Trauma Complaints List (van Zomeren and van den Burg, 1985) which contains ten items for the relatives' point of view with regard to the patient's attentional difficulties: 'does your relative have more trouble doing two things simultaneously, since the accident?' or 'is the subject slower now?' This second scale has reported good content validity.

However, the first rating scale specifically constructed for attentional disorders is the Attentional Rating Scale (Ponsford and Kinsella, 1991): fourteen items describe distraction, slowness, reduction in sustained attention, difficulty in dual tasks ('had difficulty in concentration' or 'performed slowly on mental tasks' or 'was easily distracted' or 'was unable to pay attention to more than one thing at once'). A 5-point scale scores the frequency of the problem (from 'never' to 'always'). The inter-observer reliability of the scale is high.

2 The Test of Everyday Attention (TEA)

At times patients may be anosognosic about their attentional disorders, and their relatives are not always objective observers of their behaviour in daily life. For this reason Robertson and co-workers developed a battery of eight tests of attention based on ecologically plausible activities: for example, in an imaginary scenario of a vacation trip to Philadelphia, looking at maps, counting the floor level in a visual or auditory lift, looking through telephone directories and listening to lottery numbers; and through these role-playing situations the clinician can judge the difficulties secondary to the attentional impairments (Test of Everyday Attention or TEA: Robertson *et al.*, 1994, 1996).

An important advantage is that TEA structure is based on Posner and Peterson's (1990) model of attention which has identified at least three attention processes: selective attention (for selecting relevant stimuli and inhibiting irrelevant stimuli), sustained attention (and vigilance), and orientation (for engaging, moving and disengaging attention in space). Besides appearing to correlate to the functional status of the patient, the TEA has good test–retest reliability in all the three parallel forms available, and for each subtest, except for the dual-task decrement where a large practice effect may occur. The TEA performance correlates with existing measures of attention (e.g. d2 test, PASAT, Trail Making Test – part B: see below) and shows low relation to verbal intelligence. Normative data are available on 154 age- sex- and IQ-stratified subjects, and comparative results have been collected on 15 TBI patients (Robertson *et al.*, 1994). By means of factor analysis, Robertson and colleagues (1996) identified four independent factors in normal subjects: sustained attention, selective attention, attentional switching and auditory-verbal working memory. Selective attention and sustained attention performance significantly discriminated between TBI and controls.

Moving on to the presentation of the tests assessing the attentional impairment, the assessment is described here separately for each attention process of the previous classification: selective attention, divided attention, and sustained attention.

Assessment of selective attention

Selective attention permits us to pick out some inputs in perceiving and responding, and is usually assessed visually with paper and pencil, or, at times, by auditory means.

The tasks most commonly used are the Cancellation Tests (d2 test, the 2 and 7 Test, Digit Cancellation, Visual Search and Attention Test or VSAT): these classical paper-and-pencil tests require visual search, activation and inhibition of responses, visual-motor coordination, and, moreover, rapidity both in input analysis and in output execution (Lezak, 1995). The basic format is an A4 sheet of paper (sometimes A3 paper) where all stimuli (with low or high density, with low or high ratio between targets and non-targets) are randomly designed or tape-written, scattered, or, more frequently, ordered in rows: all these variables can be modified in order to decrease or increase the task difficulty (Diller *et al.*, 1974). The performance is scored either for errors (omissions and false alarms) within a limited amount of time, or for time used to complete the search for all stimuli. A characteristic of cancellation tasks is that they are self-paced, even if the subject is always instructed to complete the test as quickly as possible, so the patient can adjust his own rate of working and speed/accuracy index. Apart from the score, therefore, they are useful for observing patient behaviour (e.g. slow but accurate, or fast but not accurate). In order for the tests to be valid and reliable, some conditions are to be respected: for example, the patient must not present visual perception reduction, neglect, motor disorders in cancelling symbols, or low visual coordination capacity.

The Digit Cancellation Test (Della Sala *et al.*, 1992) and the Letter Cancellation Test (also used to assess hemineglect; Diller *et al.*, 1974) are simple cancellation tasks. The first one is a standardized task with age-, education- and sex-adjusted normative data, designed to assess selective attention in Alzheimer patients, but now also used for clinical assessment of other cerebral lesions. Two digits are to be crossed out in the first matrix, three in the second one, within a time limit of 45 seconds for each matrix; the total score is calculated by assigning one point for each 'hit response' and a negative coefficient for each 'false alarm'.

The Concentration Endurance d2 Test (Brickenkamp, 1981) was designed to assess visual scanning in selective and sustained attention: the target is the letter d with two quotation marks placed above, or below, or separated, one above and one below (d" d„ 'd,); distractors are visually very similar to targets (p with one, two, three or four marks, or d with one, three or four marks); targets and distractors are scattered in 14 lines; the time limit is 20 seconds per line and the total time is about 5 minutes. Even if mild practice effect is present, test–retest reliability is high, ranging from .89 to .92 after 5 hours, and from .92 after 12 months; performance declines from 40 years on, and is better in females. Moreover it is fairly independent of intelligence test results (Spreen and Strauss, 1998).

The 2 and 7 Test (Ruff *et al.*, 1986, 1992) should differentiate between *automatic information processing* (selection of target stimuli from very different stimuli of another category) and *voluntary or controlled information processing* (selection of target stimuli from very similar stimuli of the same category): in the first part the subject must recognize and cancel the 2s and 7s randomly interspersed among other digits (part N from Numbers), in the second part the distractors are alphabetical letters (part L from Letters). The test comprises 20 blocks of three lines with a time limit of 15 seconds for each block; the total time is about 5 minutes. Test–retest reliability is very high (from .84 to .97), even if a mild practice effect is present. Neither gender nor education-level effects appeared on normative studies; the performance decreases linearly with age as far as both conditions are concerned. Using the 2 and 7 Test the authors have found that after right-hemispheric damage, with the obvious exception of cases with left neglect, performance is overall very slow, whereas the maximum difference between automatic and controlled information processing has been demonstrated in frontal lesions (Ruff *et al.*, 1992).

Another cancellation test is the Visual Search and Attention Test (VSAT; Trenerry *et al.*, 1990), consisting of four parts, of which the first two are practice for the patient in crossing out a letter or symbol; parts 3 and 4 require the patient to cancel a letter or symbol printed in blue, among distractors printed in blue, red or green. Each part is a matrix of 10 rows × 40 stimuli, of which 10 are targets; the time limit is 60 seconds for each part. The authors have reported good test–retest reliability (.95), although their study group was restricted to only 28 normal subjects. Moreover the test offered satisfactory discrimination between a larger group of normal and brain-injured individuals (Trenerry *et al.*, 1990). A low correlation was found between VSAT and other neuropsychological tests for attention processes and executive functions, whereas a factor analysis separated VSAT, Trail Making B, PASAT (explained further on) by collecting them in an 'attention' factor, and Verbal Fluency and Wisconsin Card Sorting Test by collecting them in an 'intelligence' factor (O'Donnell *et al.*, 1994). Normative data are available, stratified for age groups, while sex and education have no effect on VSAT performance (Trenerry *et al.*, 1990).

Derived and modified from the original task of the Wechsler Adult Intelligence Scale, the Symbol Digit Modalities Test (SDMT) (Smith, 1982) aims at measuring visual selective attention, but all the skills used in the cancellation tasks and orthographic ability contribute to performance. In SDMT the symbols are printed above and the patient must write the number below in the blank squares, following the association between symbols and numbers reported at the bottom of the page. The time limit is 90 seconds, and for subjects who are unable to write quickly, an oral version is available. In a study involving the effect of practice on a group of attention tasks presented to 10 volunteers, tested at 2- and 4-weekly intervals, SDMT did not significantly improve (Feinstein *et al.*, 1994). Motor speed is related to performance of the written version of SDMT (Polubinsky and Melamed, 1986), and this datum reduces its specificity. Normative data are collected for both versions, written and oral; educational level and age are both correlated with SDMT performance. Good discriminative power between TBI patients and normal controls has been demonstrated for the written version (Ponsford and Kinsella, 1992).

The Trail Making Test (TMT), originally part of the US Army Test Battery for the selection of military forces, and later added to the Halstead–Reitan Battery (Reitan and Wolfson, 1985), was developed to assess visual search, selective attention, switching of attention and motor speed. It requires the patient to connect, by pencil, 25 numbers, randomly arranged on a sheet of paper, in increasing order (part A), and 25 numbers and letters in alternating order (1-A-2-B-3-C-4-D; part B). The time required is about 5–10 minutes, and scoring is expressed in terms of the time required to complete part A and part B separately; a difference score (B – A) removes the component of movement speed from the test evaluation (Giovagnoli *et al.*, 1996), and the authors collected normal data for the B minus A score. Normative data for part A and part B separately have been collected in adults by Stuss and co-workers (1987); the difference score B – A is strongly affected by educational level (Bornstein, 1985; Ernst, 1987), IQ (Warner *et al.*, 1987) and age (Stanton *et al.*, 1984; Stuss *et al.*, 1987, 1988). Alekoumbides *et al.* (1987) published correction factors for age and education. The reliability coefficients considerably varied in different studies, from .60 to .90 (as reported by Spreen and Strauss, 1993), but part B remains the more sensitive task of the Trail Making Test, and can be used for predicting outcome in mild, moderate and severe TBI (Acker and Davis, 1989; Leininger *et al.*, 1990).

Even if the Paced Auditory Serial Addition Test (PASAT) (Gronwall and Sampson, 1974; Gronwall, 1977) has been presented in articles and books as a test designed to assess divided attention, it actually measures the rapidity of information processing, the switching of attention from one stimulus to another, and response inhibition; for this reason we present it in the section on selective attention. A random taped series of digits from 1 to 9 is presented to the subject, who must add progressively the last number heard to the one immediately preceding it: the second is added to the first, the third to the second, the fourth to the third, and so on. The test comprises four different trials with different rates of digit presentation (2.4, 2.0, 1.6, 1.2 seconds): the faster the rate, the more difficult the task. The total time for administration is about 15 minutes; the score is the total number of correct responses for each trial (range 0–60) and the mean time per correct response. If the proportion of correct responses is less than 80 per cent, and if more than one trial differs by more than 0.6 seconds from all other trials in time per correct response, data from all the trials are difficult to interpret. Not surprisingly, performance in this test, as in other tests with high speed, declines with age (Brittain *et al.*, 1991; Wiens *et al.*, 1997), but does not present gender differences (Roman *et al.*, 1991). A mild practice effect has been noticed but it disappears with the second administration (Gronwall, 1977). PASAT performance is influenced by sensorial modality, and is enhanced when stimuli are presented visually (Hiscock *et al.*, 1998). According to the authors of this test, PASAT is not a primary test for working memory (Gronwall and Wrightson, 1981), and it only weakly correlates with arithmetic ability and general intelligence (.28 for both) (Gronwall and Sampson, 1974; Gronwall and Wrightson, 1981): the PASAT performance is an indicator of information-processing capacity without the influence of verbal activities and complex motor skills. However, some other authors have suggested that the test could be as much a test of general intelligence (Crawford *et al.*, 1998) and mathematical ability (Sherman *et al.*, 1997; Chronicle and MacGregor, 1998) as of attention. Sherman and co-workers (1997) have found that in head-injured patients, WAIS-R Arithmetic is the strongest predictor of PASAT performance. Thus, low PASAT performance should be interpreted as an indicator of impaired selective attention only in the absence of poor performance on mathematics, verbal ability and general intelligence tests. The implication is that the PASAT has high sensitivity in high-functioning patients or in mild head-injured patients (Kessels *et al.*, 1998), but shows low specificity.

Fast rate of digit presentation is useful in discriminating between mild TBI and normal subjects (Gronwall and Sampson, 1974; Gronwall and Wrightson, 1974). Roman and colleagues (1991) underline that PASAT's ability to detect consequences of head injury is best in lesions secondary to acceleration/deceleration forces and for this reason associated with diffuse brain damage mainly in white matter and subcortical structures.

Because of all the processes involved in the PASAT, we suggest using it only in non-dysarthric, high-functioning patients; moreover, special care should be used with anxious subjects because the test is frustrating (Lezak, 1995).

Some subtests of TEA, 'Map Search' and 'Telephone Search', which are visual scanning and cancellation tasks, involve a considerable degree of visual selective attention: the ability to select target stimuli, while ignoring competing distractors, seems to be a common factor between subtests (Robertson *et al.*, 1994). They are timed tests and so speed of processing may play a part.

Moreover, the subtest of TEA loading the attention-switching factor is 'Visual Elevator': subjects have to count each elevator door up and down following the direction of an upward or downward arrow, and have to reverse direction whenever an arrow appears which is opposite in direction to that in which they are counting.

In conclusion, among selective attention tests, cancellation tasks are popular and simple; they require fair performance in visual perception, spatial scanning, and visual-motor coordination; they are able to distinguish between severe brain-damage cases and normal subjects; but they are relatively insensitive for mild brain-injured patients.

The SDMT also requires orthographic ability. The Trail Making Test measures the detection of target stimuli mixed with distractors, and, moreover, the switching of attention capacity. Unlike the other tests, PASAT is an auditory test with a more restricted application and focuses on discrimination of mild attention disorders. More prerequisites are necessary for its utilization, namely, absence of deficits in auditory perception, calculation and speech production, and absence of anxiety status. Finally, subtests of TEA loading the selective attention factor are the most recent paper-and-pencil tools designed following the cognitive model of attention processes.

Assessment of divided attention

In contrast to the many tools assessing selective attention, including shifting of attention, few standardized tests are available for the assessment of divided attention, although many experimental studies on this function are reported in the literature. Moreover, in this domain the boundary line between attention and executive functions is not always clear.

Some tests, such as the PASAT and Trail Making Test, have been considered as assessing divided attention because they explore the ability to attend to two or more stimuli simultaneously. However, there is only one task to be performed at one time (and not two or more tasks), so it could be argued that these tests assess selective attention.

Observation of behaviour in daily life could reveal not only evident disorders of divided attention, but also mild disturbances of this process: in fact, much daily activity involves division of attention between two or more tasks. For example, for normal subjects walking is an automatic activity, whereas walking, with or without devices, in hemiparetic patients usually requires high voluntary attentional control; thus, walking and talking together, or walking and performing a reaction times test in a dual-task paradigm, obviously requires even more attention (as measured by Wright and Kemp, 1992).

A typical non-instrumental dual task is the combination of visual tracking and verbal digit span repetition used by Baddeley and co-workers (1997a, 1997b; Della Sala *et al.*, 1995). In one task, tracking, the subject must follow, with a pen, a chain of boxes linked to form a path laid out on a piece of paper, in a time limit of 2 minutes; the other task is the baseline digit span for a period of 2 minutes. In the dual-task condition patients perform the two tests simultaneously for 2 minutes and the dual-task decrement is calculated with a formula provided by the authors.

Normative data from 108 control subjects were collected, and no correlations were found between the dual-task decrement and age, sex, educational level, and digit span (Della Sala *et al.*, 1995). The test–retest reliability of the dual-task performance is low (.44), most likely due, in part, to interference of a memory component. The authors suggest improving the reliability by testing a larger sample of subjects and over 4 minutes, rather than 2 minutes.

Using this dual task in two groups of patients with frontal lobe lesions, patients with dysexecutive behaviour differ significantly from the non-dysexecutive patients: therefore the task seems to be more sensitive to dysexecutive behaviour than other classical tests for frontal lobe lesion, such as the Verbal Fluency Test and Wisconsin Card Sorting Test (Baddeley and Della Sala, 1996; Baddeley *et al.*, 1997b).

The subtest of the TEA 'Telephone Searching While Counting' is a dual task and has the advantage of being a clinical paper-and-pencil test, even if its application in brain-damaged subjects has been limited to stroke patients and a small group of TBI patients (Robertson *et al.*, 1994). The reliability of the TEA is good for almost all subtests, with only one exception: the dual-task decrement.

In conclusion, most divided attention tests are either experimental tasks, and are not used in clinical assessment, or instrumental, and for this reason they are not presented in this chapter. We must hope that new paper-and-pencil tests of divided attention will be devised in the future.

Assessment of sustained attention

By observing the behaviour in daily life activities and during neuropsychological assessment, it is possible to gain a lot of information about sustained attention (the time limit of maintenance of selective attention at a good level, and lapses of attention) and about vigilance in very monotonous work such as a task with a very low-frequency stimulation. Some cancellation tests can be used with doubled time (at least 15 minutes) for the assessment of sustained attention (Lezak, 1995) but normative data are not available.

The most widely used test for assessing sustained attention is the Continuous Performance Test (CPT) (Rosvold *et al.*, 1958, in Lezak, 1995): in the original version a random series of letters appears on the screen and the subject must press a button when the letter X appears (for the assessment of sustained attention), and in the second condition (assessing sustained attention and also working memory and response inhibition) only if the X is preceded by an A (the distractors are X preceded by a B, Y preceded by an A or a B); in an auditory version the subject is required to respond each time he/she hears the letter A (Strub and Black, 1985; Grafman *et al.*, 1990). Several CPT versions are available commercially and the best-known is the Conners version (1995), with six blocks of increasing interstimulus intervals (1, 2 or 4 seconds) for a total time of about 15 minutes. Low practice effect has been demonstrated, and both age and sex can affect CPT performance (Conners *et al.*, 1995).

The Sustained Attention to Response Test (SART) (Robertson *et al.*, 1997) requires the subject to pay attention to low-frequency stimuli (one target in nine inputs) presented visually on the screen and gives equal importance to accuracy and speed. In 75 normal subjects SART performance correlated with self-reports of attentional failures, and it discriminated 34 TBI patients from age-, sex-, IQ-matched controls.

The SART results are determined by the duration of the test and by the frequency of targets: 'the high frequency acts as external (exogenous) support to performance and hence reduces the need of internal (endogenous) attention allocation to response selection' (Manly *et al.*, 1999, p. 668).

Moreover, coma duration is the principal predictor of SART performance, whereas PASAT is associated with both coma duration and post-traumatic amnesia duration. In considering these relationships, it is known that coma severity, as assessed by the Glasgow Coma Scale, is associated with sustained attention deficits measured by SART, whereas PASAT is a more complex task demanding greater cortical involvement (Robertson *et al.*, 1997).

Since most sustained attention tests are instrumental or computerized, we have made an exception from the scope of the present chapter and presented two such tests, selecting them from those most commonly used. However, it is clear that the need for technical devices limits their use in clinical practice.

Once again, some TEA subtests (Robertson *et al.*, 1994), 'Lottery' and 'Elevator counting', have been designed with the goal of a clinical assessment; they involve the ability to sustain attention to repetitive stimuli; the first one with a very low frequency of stimuli (about one a minute) is a vigilance task; the second one is a sustained attention test. In 'Lottery', the subject listens to a series of letters and numbers and must write the letters following two identical numbers. In 'Elevator counting', subjects must count tones in some strings of tones.

In conclusion, few paper-and-pencil tests are available for assessing sustained attention: some utilize the 'time-on-task' effect (they are longer), and others utilize the decrement in performance in a monotonous task (such as some TEA subtests that are shorter).

Conclusions

The choice of the test in assessment of attention greatly depends on the goals, which vary according to the context in which they are carried out (clinical or experimental, and within a clinical context, in a neurology or rehabilitation department, or in a forensic environment). In neurology, for example, since the aim is diagnostic, assessment is focused on the impairment rather than the disability. In rehabilitation, on the other hand, the assessment contributes to the prognosis and the treatment, and therefore concentrates more on overcoming the disability. In the forensic setting emphasis is placed on measuring the percentage loss of abilities in order to quantify the compensation.

The assessment of attention impairment provides information on the subject's difficulties, in a relatively objective, standardized, reliable way, but it does not explore the subject's functioning in daily life. In contrast, the assessment of disability secondary to attention impairment allows us to investigate the subject's ability to cope with the difficulties in ecological situations: the disability assessment focuses more on individual functions, so it is more realistic, but often less objective and reliable.

Moreover, in a clinical context, a screening examination should be brief and sensitive to disorders secondary to a cerebral lesion, whereas, in a rehabilitation setting, the assessment should be large and exhaustive, with verbal or auditory and visual stimuli, in order to determine all relevant areas of weakness and strength. For general screening, when the goal is to identify persons with general neuropsychological disorders, a sensitive test such as SDMT should be selected. However, this test is not very specific, and so is of little value to the examiner hoping to delineate a specific attention disorder.

In experimental neuropsychology the tasks are designed for the specific domain of research. Since the paper-and-pencil tests are so universally used, they could also provide further application as a baseline assessment in order to define inclusion/exclusion criteria.

Acknowledgements: I would like to thank Leonard Diller, Pierluigi Zoccolotti and the editors of this book for their observations and very helpful suggestions.

References

Acker, M.B. and Davis, J.R. (1989). Psychology test scores associated with late outcome in head injury. *Neuropsychology*, *3*, 123–133.

Ainsley, M.B. and Gliner, J. (1989). Factors in the employability of the brain injured adult. *Cognitive Rehabilitation*, *7*, 28–33.

Alekoumbides, A., Charter, R.A., Adkins, T.G. and Seacat, G.F. (1987). The diagnosis of brain damage by the WAIS, WMS, and Reitan Battery utilising standardised scores corrected for age and education. *International Journal of Clinical Neuropsychology*, *9*, 11–28.

Baddeley, A. (1986). *Working Memory*. Oxford: Oxford University Press.

Baddeley, A. and Della Sala, S. (1996). Working memory and executive control. *Philosophical Transactions of the Royal Society of London*, *351*, 1397–1404.

Baddeley, A., Della Sala, S., Gray, C. and Papagno, S. (1997a). Testing central executive functioning with a pencil-and-paper test. In P. Rabbit (ed.) *Methodology of Frontal and Executive Functions*. Hove: Psychology Press.

Baddeley, A., Della Sala, S. and Papagno, S. (1997b). Dual-task performance in dysexecutive and nondysexecutive patients with a frontal lesion. *Neuropsychology, 11*, 187–194.

Bornstein, R.A. (1985). Normative data on selected neuropsychological measures from a nonclinical sample. *Journal of Clinical Psychology, 41*, 651–659.

Brickenkamp, R. (1981). *Test d2: Aufmerksamkeits-Belastungs-test: Handanweisung* (7th edn) (Test d2: Concentration-Endurance-Test: Manual, 7th edn). Gottingen: Verlag fur Psychologie.

Brittain, J.L., La Marche, J.A., Reeder, K.P., Roth, D.L. and Boll, T.J. (1991). Effects of age and IQ on Paced Auditory Serial Addition Test (PASAT) performance. *Clinical Neuropsychologist, 5*, 163–175.

Brooks, N., McKinlay, W., Symington, B., Beattie, A. and Campsie, L. (1987). Return to work within the first seven years of severe head injury. *Brain Injury, 1*, 15–19.

Chronicle, E.P. and MacGregor, N.A. (1998). Are PASAT scores related to mathematical ability? *Neuropsychological Rehabilitation, 8*, 273–282.

Conners, C.K. and Multi-Health Systems Staff (1995). *Conners' Continuous Performance Test (CPT)*. Toronto: MHS.

Craik, F.I.M. (1990). Changes in memory with normal aging: a functional view. In R.J. Wurtman *et al.* (eds) *Advances in Neurology, vol. 51: Alzheimer's Disease*. New York: Raven Press.

Crawford, J.R., Obonsawin, M.C. and Allan, K.M. (1998). PASAT and components of WAIS-R performance: convergent and discriminant validity. *Neuropsychological Rehabilitation, 8*, 255–272.

Della Sala, S., Baddeley, A., Papagno, S. and Spinnler, H. (1995). Dual-task paradigm: a means to examine the central executive. In J. Grafman, K.J. Holyoak and F. Boller (eds) Structure and functions of the human prefrontal cortex. *Annals of the New York Academy of Sciences, 769*, 161–172.

Della Sala, S., Laiacona, M., Spinnler, H. and Ubezio, C. (1992). A cancellation test: its reliability in assessing attentional deficits in Alzheimer's disease. *Psychological Medicine, 22*, 885–901.

Diller, L., Ben-Yishay, Y. and Gerstman, L.J. (1974) *Studies in Cognition and Rehabilitation in Hemiplegia* (Rehabilitation Monograph, N.50). New York: New York University Medical Center, Institute of Rehabilitation Medicine.

Ernst, J. (1987). Neuropsychological problem-solving skills in the elderly. *Psychology and Aging, 2*, 363–365.

Feinstein, A., Brown, R. and Ron, M. (1994). Effects of practice of serial tests of attention in healthy subjects. *Journal of Clinical and Experimental Neuropsychology, 16*, 436–447.

Giovagnoli, A.R., Del Pesce, M., Mascheroni, S., Simoncelli, M., Laiacona, M. and Capitani, E. (1996). Trail making test: normative values from 287 normal adult controls. *Italian Journal of Neurological Sciences, 17*, 305–309.

Girard, D., Brown, J., Burnett-Stolnack, M., Hashimoto, N., Hier-Wellmer, S., Perlman, O.Z. and Seigerman, C. (1996). The relationship of neuropsychological status and productive outcomes following traumatic brain injury. *Brain Injury, 10*, 663–676.

Gouvier, W.D., Maxfield, M.W., Schweitzer, J.R., Horton, C., Shipp, M., Neilson, K. and Hale, P. (1989). Psychometric prediction of driving performance among the disabled. *Archives of Physical Medicine and Rehabilitation, 70*, 745–750.

Grafman, J., Litvan, I., Gomez, C. and Chase, T.N. (1990). Frontal lobe function in progressive supranuclear palsy. *Archives of Neurology*, *47*, 553–558.

Gregory, S. (1989). Functional evaluation of the driver with acquired brain damage. In V. Anderson and M. Bailey (eds) *Theory and Function: Bridging the Gap*. Melbourne: ASSBI.

Gronwall, D. (1977). Paced auditory serial addition task: a measure of recovery from concussion. *Perceptual and Motor Skills*, *44*, 367–373.

Gronwall, D. (1987). Advances in the assessment of attention and information processing after head injury. In H.S. Levin, J. Grafman and H.M. Eisenberg (eds) *Neurobehavioural Recovery from Head Injury*. New York: Oxford University Press.

Gronwall, D. and Sampson, H. (1974) *The Psychological Effects of Concussion*. New Zealand: Auckland University Press.

Gronwall, D. and Wrightson, P. (1974). Delayed recovery of intellectual function after minor head injury. *Lancet*, *2*, 995–997.

Gronwall, D. and Wrightson, P. (1981). Memory and information processing capacity after closed head injury. *Journal of Neurology, Neurosurgery and Psychiatry*, *44*, 889–895.

Hiscock, M., Caroselli, J.S. and Kimball, L.E. (1998). Paced Serial Addition: modality-specific and arithmetic-specific factors. *Journal of Clinical and Experimental Neuropsychology*, *20*, 463–472.

Kaplan, E., Fein, D., Morris, R. and Delis, D. (1991). *WAIS-R as a Neuropsychological Instrument*. San Antonio, TX: The Psychological Corporation.

Kessels, R.P., Keyser, A., Verhagen, W.I. and van-Luijtelaar, E.L. (1998). The whiplash syndrome: a psychophysiological and neuropsychological study towards attention. *Acta Neurologica Scandinavica*, *97*, 188–193.

Kinsella, G.J. (1998). Assessment of attention following traumatic brain injury: a review. *Neuropsychological Rehabilitation*, *8*, 351–375.

Leininger, B.E., Grambling, S.E., Farrell, A.D., Kreutzer, J.S. and Peck, E.A. (1990). Neuropsychological deficits in symptomatic minor head injury patients after concussion and mild concussion. *Journal of Neurology, Neurosurgery and Psychiatry*, *53*, 293–296.

Levin, H.S., High, W.M. and Goethe, K.E. (1987). The Neurobehavioural Rating Scale: assessment of the behavioural sequelae of head injury by the clinician. *Journal of Neurology, Neurosurgery and Psychiatry*, *50*, 183–193.

Lezak, M.D. (1995). *Neuropsychological Assessment* (3rd edn). New York: Oxford University Press.

Manly, T., Robertson, I.H., Galloway, M. and Hawkins, K. (1999). The absent mind: further investigations of sustained attention to response. *Neuropsychologia*, *37*, 661–670.

Norman, D.A. and Shallice, T. (1986). Attention to action. Willed and automatic control of behavior. In R.J. Davidson, G.E. Schwartz and D. Shapiro (eds) *Consciousness and Self-regulation. Advances in Research and Theory*, vol. 4. New York: Plenum Press.

O'Donnell, J.P., MacGregor, L.A., Dabrowjki, J.J., Oestreicher, J.M. and Romero, J.J. (1994). Construct validity of neuropsychological test of conceptual and attentional abilities. *Journal of Clinical Psychology*, *50*, 596–600.

Perry, R.J. and Hodges, J.R. (1999). Attention and executive deficits in Alzheimer's disease. A critical review. *Brain*, *122*, 383–404.

Polubinsky, J.P. and Melamed, L.E. (1986). Examination of the sex differences on a symbol digit substitution task. *Perceptual and Motor Skills*, *62*, 975–982.

Ponsford, J.L. and Kinsella, G.J. (1991). The use of a rating scale of attentional behaviour. *Neuropsychological Rehabilitation*, *1*, 241–257.

Ponsford, J.L. and Kinsella, G.J. (1992). Attentional deficits following closed-head injury. *Journal of Clinical and Experimental Neuropsychology*, *14*, 822–838.

Posner, M.I. and Peterson, S.E. (1990). The attention system of the human brain (Review). *Annual Review of Neurosciences*, *13*, 25–42.

Reitan, R.M. and Wolfson, D. (1985). *The Halstead–Reitan Neuropsychological Test Battery*. Tucson: Neuropsychology Press.

Robertson, I.H., Manly, T., Andrade, J., Baddeley, B.T. and Yiend, J. (1997). 'Oops!': performance correlates of everyday attentional failures in traumatic brain injured and normal subjects. *Neuropsychologia*, *35*, 747–758.

Robertson, I.H., Ward, T., Ridgeway, V. and Nimmo-Smith, I. (1994). *The Test of Everyday Attention*. Bury St Edmunds: Thames Valley Test Company.

Robertson, I.H., Ward, T., Ridgeway, V. and Nimmo-Smith, I. (1996). The structure of normal human attention: the Test of Everyday Attention. *Journal of International Neuropsychological Society*, *2*, 525–534.

Roman, D.D., Edwall, G.E., Buchanan, R.J. and Patton, J.H. (1991). Extended norms for the Paced Auditory Serial Addition Test. *Clinical Neuropsychologist*, *5*, 33–40.

Ruff, R.M., Evans, R.W. and Light, R.H. (1986). Automatic detection vs controlled search: a paper-and-pencil approach. *Perceptual and Motor Skills*, *62*, 407–416.

Ruff, R.M., Marshall, L.F., Crouch, J., Klauber, J., Levin, H.S., Barth, J., Kreutzer, J., Blunt, B.A., Foulkes, M.A., Eisenberg, H.M., Jane, J.A. and Marmarou, A. (1993). Predictors of outcome following severe head trauma: follow-up data from the Traumatic Coma Data Bank. *Brain Injury*, 7, 101–111.

Ruff, R.M., Niemann, H., Allen, C.C., Farrow, C.E. and Wylie, T. (1992). The Ruff 2 and 7 selective attention test: a neuropsychological application. *Perceptual and Motor Skills*, *75*, 1311–1319.

Schretlen, D. (1996). *BTA. Brief Test of Attention. Professional Manual*. Odessa: PAR, Psychological Assessment Resources, Inc.

Schretlen, D., Bobholz, J.H. and Brandt, J. (1996a). Development and psychometric properties of the Brief Test of Attention. *Clinical Neuropsychologist*, *10*, 80–89.

Schretlen, D., Brandt, J. and Bobholz, J.H. (1996b). The validation of the Brief Test of Attention in patients with Huntington's disease and amnesia. *Clinical Neuropsychologist*, *10*, 90–95.

Sherman, E.M.S., Strauss, E. and Spellacy, F. (1997). Testing the validity of the Paced Auditory Serial Addition Test (PASAT) in adults with head injury. *Clinical Neuropsychologist*, *11*, 34–45.

Shiffrin, R.M. and Schneider, W. (1977). Controlled and automatic human information processing: II. Perceptual, learning, automatic attending, and a general theory. *Psychological Review*, *84*, 127–190.

Smith, A. (1967). The Serial Sevens Subtraction Test. *Archives of Neurology*, *17*, 78–80.

Smith, A. (1982). *Symbol Digit Modalities Test (SDMT). Manual*. Los Angeles: Western Psychological Services.

Spreen, O. and Strauss, E. (1993). *A Compendium of Neuropsychological Tests. Administration, Norms, and Commentary*. New York: Oxford University Press.

Spreen, O. and Strauss, E. (1998). *A Compendium of Neuropsychological Tests. Administration, Norms, and Commentary* (2nd edn). New York: Oxford University Press.

Stanton, B.A., Jenkins, C.D., Savageau, J.A., Zyzanski, S.J. and Aucoin, R. (1984). Age and education differences on the Trail Making Test and Wechsler Memory Scales. *Perceptual and Motor Skills*, *58*, 311–318.

Strub, R.L. and Black, F.W. (1985). *The Mental Status Examination in Neurology*. Philadelphia: FA Davis.

Stuss, D.T. and Benson, D.F. (1986). *The Frontal Lobes*. New York: Raven Press.

Stuss, D.T., Steheem, L.L. and Poirier, C.A. (1987). Comparison of three tests of attention and rapid information processing across six age groups. *Clinical Neuropsychologist*, *1*, 139–152.

Stuss, D.T., Steheem, L.L. and Pelchat, G. (1988). Three tests of attention and rapid information processing: an extension. *Clinical Neuropsychologist*, *2*, 246–250.

Teasdale, T.W., Skovdahl, H.H., Gade, A. and Christensen, A.L. (1997). Neuropsychological test scores before and after brain-injury rehabilitation in relation to return to employment. *Neuropsychological Rehabilitation*, *7*, 23–42.

Trenerry, M.R., Crosson, B., DeBoe, J. and Leber, W.R. (1990). *Visual Search and Attention Test*. Odessa: Psychological Assessment Sources.

van Zomeren, A.H. and Brouwer, W.B. (1994). *Clinical Neuropsychology of Attention*. Oxford: Oxford University Press.

van Zomeren, A.H. and van den Burg, W. (1985). Residual complaints of patients two years after severe head injury. *Journal of Neurology, Neurosurgery and Psychiatry*, *48*, 21–28.

Warner, M.H., Ernst, J., Townes, B.D., Peel, J. and Preston, M. (1987). Relationship between IQ and neuropsychological measures in neuropsychiatric populations: within-laboratory and cross-cultural replications using WAIS and WAIS-R. *Journal of Clinical and Experimental Neuropsychology*, *9*, 545–562.

Weber, A.M. (1988). A new clinical measure of attention: the Attentional Capacity Test. *Neuropsychology*, *2*, 59–71.

Wechsler, D. (1981). *WAIS-R Manual*. New York: The Psychological Corporation.

Wechsler, D. (1987). *Wechsler Memory Scale Manual*. San Antonio, TX: The Psychological Corporation.

Weinberg, J., Diller, L., Gerstman, L. and Schulman, P. (1972). Digit span in right and left hemiplegic. *Journal of Clinical Psychology*, *28*, 361.

Whyte, J. and Di Pasquale, M.C. (1995). Assessment of vision and visual attention in minimally responsive brain injured patients. *Archives of Physical Medicine and Rehabilitation*, *76*, 804–810.

Wiens, A.N., Fuller, K.H. and Crossen, J.R. (1997). Paced Auditory Serial Addition Test: adult norms and moderator variables. *Journal of Clinical and Experimental Neuropsychology*, *19*, 473–483.

Witol, A.D., Sander, A.M., Seel, R.T. and Kreutzer, J.S. (1996). Long-term neurobehavioral characteristics after brain injury: implications for vocational rehabilitation. *Journal of Vocational Rehabilitation*, *7*, 159–167.

Wright, D.L. and Kemp, T.L. (1992). The dual-task methodology and assessing the attentional demands of ambulation with walking devices. *Physical Therapy*, *72*, 306–314.

Chapter 7

Attention and normal ageing

Martial Van der Linden and Fabienne Collette

Over the past twenty-five years, a great deal of evidence has been accumulated indicating that advancing age is accompanied by a systematic decline in performance on a wide variety of cognitive tasks, both in the laboratory and in everyday life. However, age-related decline is not observed in all situations, and older adults may even show a relative advantage in some tasks. In this perspective, a life-span theory of intellectual development has been proposed which distinguishes between two components of cognitive functioning: the mechanics and the pragmatics of cognition (Baltes, Staudinger, and Lindenberger, 1999). The mechanics of cognition are considered as an expression of basic and biological information processing, while the pragmatics of cognition are associated with acquired knowledge mediated through culture. Abilities that critically involve mechanics, such as reasoning, spatial orientation, or perceptual speed, generally show roughly linear decline during adulthood. In contrast, more pragmatic abilities, such as verbal (semantic memory) knowledge, have weak, and even sometimes positive, age relations.

Other labels have been used to characterize this distinction between declining and stable cognitive abilities in ageing, such as fluid versus crystallized intelligence (Cattell, 1971) or intelligence A/intellectual power and intelligence B/intellectual products (Hebb, 1949). More recently, Salthouse (2000) suggested that the terms *process* and *product* constitute a more adequate description of the intended distinction. The term *process* refers to the efficiency of processing at the time of testing, and reflects the ability to solve novel problems or to manipulate and transform familiar material. The term *cognitive product* covers the accumulated products of processing carried out in the past and, consequently, refers to various types of acquired knowledge. It should be noted that these two components of cognition are not necessarily independent. Indeed, the cognitive products need to be acquired through the operation of processes, and the current level of products may influence the efficiency of some processes.

There exists some consensus concerning the existence of an age-related decline of process cognition (or cognitive mechanics). In addition, several interpretations have been proposed for these negative age–process relations.

According to the analytical approaches, these changes are to be explained in terms of the efficiency of task-specific structural or processing components. In contrast, global approaches suggest that they may be attributed to age-related differences in a few general factors intervening between the age variable and the performance in a large variety of cognitive tasks. In other words, contrary to the analytical ('task-specific') interpretations which postulate the existence of multiple specific deficits (inefficient strategies or defective components), the global approach considers that a large proportion of age-related differences on various cognitive variables are shared and are not independent and, consequently, that the number of explanations is much lower than the number of variables exhibiting age-related declines (see Salthouse, 2000). Currently, the global approach seems to dominate the cognitive ageing literature.

I The global interpretations

A large part of the recent research aims at identifying age differences in some general factors and specifying the contribution of these differences in various aspects of cognition. In recent years, several such general factors or mechanisms have been identified: a decline in the speed of processing, a decline in working memory capability, a decline in inhibitory efficiency, and a decline in sensory functioning (see Park, 2000). Some of these general factors (especially inhibition and working memory) clearly belong to the attentional domain.

Processing speed

The processing speed hypothesis considers that a reduction in the speed with which elementary processing operations can be executed strongly contributes to the age-related differences observed with many measures of cognition (Birren and Fisher, 1995; Salthouse, 1996). The speed hypothesis has been a pervasive one in the cognitive ageing literature, and is perhaps the most general of the three hypotheses. Salthouse (1996) presented a large amount of evidence suggesting that nearly all age-related variance on various cognitive tasks (even tasks that may not appear to have an obvious speed component) can be explained by knowledge of the rate at which subjects make rapid comparisons on perceptual speed tasks (for example, same–different judgements about pairs of digits or letter strings). With regard to the attentional tasks, this position argues that what appear to be age differences in attention are simply expressions of a general slowing down of cognitive operations in old age. According to Salthouse (1996), reduction in speed leads to declines in cognitive functioning because relevant operations cannot be successfully executed (the limited time mechanism) and because the products of early processing may no longer be available when later processing is complete (the simultaneity mechanism). In other words, age-related differences are observed because the elderly subjects are slower in performing early operations in a complex cognitive task, and, due to this cognitive slowing, they may not have the products of earlier mental operations, which are necessary to perform later steps, available to them.

Working memory

The working memory hypothesis postulates that age-related cognitive deficits are due to a reduction in the amount of cognitive resources that are needed for temporarily storing new information while simultaneously performing mental operations on incoming or recently accessed information (Baddeley, 1986). Working memory is classically measured by asking subjects to both store and process information simultaneously (for example, in the computation span task, subjects are asked to solve a series of addition problems, but also to remember the second number in each equation). Many studies have found that older adults do show significantly poorer working memory (e.g. Van der Linden, Brédart, and Beerten, 1994; Van der Linden, Beerten, and Pesenti, 1998), and there is much evidence that the age-related variance in many cognitive tasks may be largely mediated by working memory differences (e.g. Kirasic *et al.*, 1996; see also Van der Linden *et al.*, 1999).

Inhibition

The inhibition hypothesis proposes that age-related differences in cognitive function may occur because older adults have a deficit in those inhibitory attentional mechanisms that ordinarily prevent irrelevant information from gaining access to working memory (Hasher and Zacks, 1988; Zacks and Hasher, 1994). More specifically, the inhibition deficit is supposed to limit both the ability of older participants to prevent irrelevant information from entering working memory during the processing of target information, and their ability to de-activate contextually related but less relevant information, or information that is no longer relevant. For example, in the domain of language comprehension, both types of failure are thought to impair comprehension processes if activation of off-goal information is sustained during the construction of a coherent text-based representation. Findings from various studies by Hasher, Zacks, and co-workers support this explanation (for a review, see Zacks and Hasher, 1994). However, in a recent critical assessment of the inhibition deficit theory as applied to language processing, Burke (1997) pointed out that many other inconsistent data have been reported and she argued that alternative explanations can also be proposed in any cases where data seem to support the inhibition view (for a reply, see Zacks and Hasher, 1997).

Sensory function

Some recent work clearly identifies a strong age-based relationship between sensorimotor functioning (vision, hearing and balance/gait) and cognitive performance (Baltes and Lindenberger, 1997; Lindenberger and Baltes, 1994). For example, Baltes and Lindenberger (1997) explored a life-span sample including subjects ranging in age from 25 to 103 years. They demonstrated systematic decline across the life span in all aspects of cognition and they observed strong evidence for mediation of cognitive decline by sensory function. In addition, Lindenberger and Baltes (1997) showed that the decline gradient did not vary as a function of education, occupation, social class, and income. This suggests that the connection between the sensory and cognitive domains might be the outcome of a fourth common (biological) factor, namely the integrity of brain structure and functions (the 'common cause' hypothesis).

In conclusion, there exists some evidence suggesting that different general factors, namely processing speed, working memory, inhibition capability, and sensory function, play a role in the effects of ageing on cognitive functioning. However, there also exists much debate as to which hypothesis best accounts for age declines in different cognitive domains.

Relationships between the general factors

Most researchers do agree that these general indices of processing efficiency might be interdependent, and therefore the debate has more recently addressed the question of how much each factor contributes to ageing effects. For example, Kwong See and Ryan (1995), using hierarchical regression analyses to compare young and old participants' performances, suggested that age-related variations in language and memory are partially and independently mediated by speed and inhibition but, when these factors are controlled, the contribution of age remains significant. In addition, after variability associated with speed and inhibition had been controlled, working memory measures did not predict language and memory performance.

More recently, we also conducted a study aimed at determining how much processing speed, working memory capacity, and inhibition capability contribute to the effects of ageing on language performance (Van der Linden *et al.*, 1999). An individual differences approach was used to examine the mediators that predict performance in language comprehension and verbal long-term memory tasks. A total of 151 participants (ages 31–80) completed language and verbal memory tasks and a battery of tasks designed to assess processing speed, working memory, and resistance to interference. Latent-construct structural equation modelling (see Bollen and Long, 1993) was used to examine the relationships of these factors and age to different types of language tasks. The results of this study may be summarized as follows. The best-fit model postulates that all significant relationships between age and measures of language comprehension/verbal memory are indirect and mediated through age-related reductions in speed, resistance to interference and working memory; no direct links were found. These findings indicate that the three general factors of cognitive functioning are to be considered as useful constructs in explaining age-related differences in language comprehension and verbal long-term memory. More generally, they confirm the validity of the general-factor approach to age-related differences in cognitive performance across a range of verbal tasks. In addition, the best-fit model also showed that the contribution of speed and resistance to interference is indirect and mediated by working memory which appears to play a crucial role in explaining age-related differences in language performance.

Our results, obtained by means of a cross-sectional analysis, clearly need to be confirmed by studies using other methods, namely longitudinal studies, in order to examine both individual trends and cohort effects (e.g. Hultsch *et al.*, 1992). Whatever the discrepancies might be between the two types of approach, it is worth noting that in their longitudinal study, Hultsch *et al.* (1992) also found a relationship between age and working memory which was not completely explained by processing speed differences. Similarly, in a more recent monograph, Hultsch *et al.* (1999) reported further longitudinal results much in line with our findings, showing that change in working memory drives changes in comprehension and memory and also showing that the influence of speed is mediated through changes in working memory. Our findings are in contradiction with Kwong See and Ryan's (1995) final conclusion that working memory cannot be retained as a central explanatory principle to account for older adults' poorer performance in language tasks. A plausible interpretation of the discrepancy between their findings and ours seems to be that the language and verbal memory tasks used in our study are more demanding than those used by Kwong See and Ryan.

Other studies also suggest that the relative contribution of processing speed, working memory and inhibition actually depends on the type of cognitive task or the type of information to be remembered. For example, Mayr and Kliegl (1993) and Kliegl, Mayr, and Krampe (1994) propose a two-factor model of age differences which includes speed (which is associated with sequential processing complexity) and working memory (which is associated with coordinative processing complexity). More recently, Park *et al.* (1996) confirmed that speed is a central construct in explaining age-related variance in different types of memory performance. In addition, they found that working memory also contributed to explain variance in some memory tests (especially verbal free and cued recall) but not in others (such as spatial memory). More generally, Park *et al.*'s findings suggest that the contribution of working memory increases as memory becomes more effortful (see also Whiting and Smith, 1997, for similar conclusions). Finally, Kirasic *et al.* (1996) found that working memory was a more important mediating factor than processing speed in declarative learning when assessed by means of tasks that resemble those in daily learning situations (such as learning a menu, a round-trip bus schedule or a spatial arrangement). More specifically, with this set of memory tasks, they showed that the contribution of processing speed was small and mediated by working memory capacity. In conclusion, it appears that these various studies lead to divergent or even contradictory conclusions, especially regarding the contribution of working memory. As suggested by Park *et al.* (1996), this is probably because the extent to which different general factors contribute to cognitive performance is likely to be determined by the specific demands of the task under investigation.

Analytical exploration of general factors

The global factor approach is confronted with the problem that there is no agreement within the scientific community on the proper measurement of speed, inhibition and working memory. It appears that such a measurement can only be validated by a thorough analysis of the underlying mechanisms. For example, there is convincing evidence that working memory is composed of distinct subsystems: a phonological loop, a visuo-spatial sketchpad, and a central executive which itself is a cluster of several control processes (Baddeley, 1996a, 1996b). Measures of working memory usually involve many of these components and this is probably why they predict performance in complex tasks. Further research is needed to understand how performance on different complex cognitive tasks depends on elementary operations performed on the input to the working memory system, on the speed of their execution, and on the ability of the system to select the relevant information. It should also be noted that an important function of working memory, especially the central executive component, consists in the goal-directed (executive) control of action and thought. In addition, some neuropsychological data have indicated that the central executive may not be a unitary system (Shallice and Burgess, 1993; see also Seron, Van der Linden, and Andrès, 1999). Rather, there seem to be several control functions, which are commonly labelled 'executive' and which may operate quite independently. Recently, Baddeley (1996b) suggested distinguishing different central executive abilities, especially the ability to select and manipulate information in long-term memory, the ability to act as an attentional controller, selecting certain information and rejecting (inhibiting) others, and the ability to coordinate two or more concurrent activities. According to Morris and Jones (1990, see also Van der Linden *et al.*, 1994), another important function of the central executive is the updating of working memory. As suggested by Baltes *et al.* (1999), this raises doubts about the status of working memory as a basic, 'primitive' mediator of age-related differences in cognitive functioning.

In the same vein, a more precise specification of the inhibitory construct and its relationships with interference, working memory, and processing speed, along with the development of multiple reliable measures of inhibition, is clearly needed. Actually, the relationships between inhibition and interference still remain unclear. Some authors suggest that interference (such as measured by the Stroop test) and negative priming might result from independent inhibitory mechanisms (Stoltzfus *et al.*, 1993). The negative priming effect occurs when subjects are asked to provide some response to a given stimulus (the target), while at the same time ignoring an irrelevant stimulus. If the distractor on one trial (the prime trial) becomes the target in the next trial (the test trial), performance is usually hampered (as suggested by an increased response time or, sometimes, more errors). The dominant interpretation of this effect is that it indicates inhibitory attentional processes: in the prime trial, the representation of the distractor is inhibited, and subsequently, when it is presented as a target in the test trial, additional processing time is required to overcome the inhibition generated in the previous trial.

In the interference situation, inhibitory processes should intervene to reduce interference during concurrent response selection; in the negative priming situation, inhibitory processes should act to prevent recently rejected information from influencing the current task. However, evidence for this interpretation is controversial (see Kieley and Hartley, 1997). This clearly shows that any further progress in our understanding of how inhibition capability contributes to age-related differences in cognition will require a better identification of the mechanisms that underlie the inhibitory function.

2 The analytical interpretations

The analytical approaches to normal ageing consider that it is possible to fractionate the cognitive performance in a specific task into its different constitutive elements (systems and processes), and that age-related differences in cognitive functioning can be interpreted in terms of the relative efficiency of task-specific components or strategies. From a neuropsychological point of view, these analytical approaches suggest that the cognitive declines observed in elderly subjects may result from localized dysfunction of specific neural structures. In that perspective, it appears that the frontal lobes and the medial temporal regions are particularly vulnerable to ageing (see Reuter-Lorenz, 2000; Raz *et al.*, 1998).

With regard to the age-related differences in attentional function, the analytical position postulates that separate components of attention can be distinguished, both at a functional and, to some extent, at an anatomical level, and that separate attentional systems are differentially affected by the ageing process. In other words, this view predicts that there exist specific age-related effects on attention, which are not simply artefacts of more fundamental age differences, such as a general slowing down.

The attentional systems and cerebral networks

According to Berger and Posner (2000), attention may be examined in terms of three major functions: orienting to sensory stimuli, executive functions, and maintaining the alert state. The executive function has been related to the control of goal-directed behaviour, target detection, error detection, conflict resolution and inhibition of automatic responses. The alertness function is involved in establishing a vigilant state and maintaining readiness to react. The orienting function concerns all the processes that are responsible for the selection of one stimulus among many, for shifting from one stimulus to the next, and for focusing only on those stimulus characteristics that are relevant to the task.

The precise neural mechanisms that are responsible for these operations are still not known but many of the brain areas and networks that are involved have been identified (see Posner and Dehaene, 1994; Posner and Raichle, 1996; LaBerge, 1992; Posner and Petersen, 1990). Evidence from cognitive neuroscientific research suggests that there are at least two distinct attentional networks in the brain, which are thought to be primarily responsible for different attentional processes. The posterior attentional network (superior parietal cortex, pulvinar and superior colliculus) is largely responsible for focusing attention on specific visual stimuli when relevant information in the visual field can be filtered on the basis of peripheral attributes such as location, shape, etc. The anterior attentional network (midline frontal areas including the anterior cingulate gyrus, SMA, and portions of the basal ganglia) has been related to the executive control function. It is also involved in selecting visual stimuli when the instructions emphasize properties of the object. More specifically, it serves, when central processing is required, to focus only on those stimulus characteristics that are relevant to the task, while inhibiting further processing of competing sets of information. This anterior attentional system is a general one and does not appear to be associated with any particular sensory modality or cognitive content. Lateral areas of the frontal cortex have also often been identified with executive functions. Besides these two anterior/posterior systems, a network of brain areas devoted to alertness function has also been identified and includes the right frontal lobe (especially the superior region of Brodmann area 6), the right parietal lobe and the locus coeruleus.

There exists some evidence suggesting that all attentional systems are not similarly affected by ageing. This point will be illustrated in the domain of selective attention.

Ageing and selective attention

A number of studies show age-related differences in the ability to select or focus on a single input in the presence of competing inputs (for a review, see

Hartley, 1992; McDowd and Birren, 1990). Evidence for this was obtained from different paradigms, including visual search tasks (e.g. Plude and Doussard-Roosevelt, 1989), the Stroop task (e.g. Cohn, Dustman, and Bradford, 1984; Bruyer *et al.*, 1995; Spieler, Balota, and Faust, 1996) and response competition tasks (see Hahn and Kramer, 1995).

However, these age differences diminish or disappear under certain task parameters, in particular when a relevant stimulus is precued by a physical attribute such as location, diminishing the need to process irrelevant stimuli that do not contain those physical characteristics (see Madden and Plude, 1993). Nevertheless, it remains to identify the details of cueing effects on ageing, especially the time course, the degree of validity of the cue, and so forth (Rogers, 2000).

In contrast, the magnitude of age differences increases when central processing is required to focus attention on one among several types of information that are not dissociable on the basis of peripheral cues, such as when the location of target information is uncertain, or when the target information is physically integrated with distracting information. For example, Hartley (1993) compared the performance of young and elderly subjects on two versions of the Stroop test: the Color–Block Task which consists in identifying the colour of a box that appears in a fixed location while ignoring the adjacent colour name printed in black and the Color–Word Task which consists in identifying the ink of the colour name presented while ignoring the semantic meaning of the colour name. Young and older adults showed equivalent performances on the Color–Block Task while substantial age differences emerged on the Color–Word Task. According to Hartley (1993), this dissociation is attributable to differential ageing of the distinct anterior/posterior attentional processes required by each task. In a recent study, Brink and McDowd (1999) replicated Hartley's results. In addition, they also showed that task complexity, as manipulated quantitatively by degree of choice (a two- and four-colour choice condition), affected young and older subjects in a similar manner and was explained by a generalized slowing down. However, task type affected the age groups differently, suggesting that the effect of generalized slowing down due to quantitative manipulation of complexity cannot account for the age differences in performance on the two tasks.

Age differences in selective attentional tasks were originally interpreted as evidence of a specific age-related deficit in the ability to ignore irrelevant information. More recently, failures to ignore irrelevant information have been attributed to an age-related decline in the efficiency of inhibitory processes (see Zacks and Hasher, 1994). Support for this hypothesis comes especially from a number of studies demonstrating reduced negative priming effects in elderly subjects.

In a recent meta-analysis, Verhaeghen and De Meersman (1998) found that younger and older adults are susceptible to the negative priming effect, and this is true for both identity and location negative priming: identity priming refers to negative priming in tasks in which the response is related to the identity of a stimulus (e.g. naming a pictured object or reading a letter), while location priming refers to negative priming in tasks in which the response is related to the location of a stimulus (e.g. pressing a key corresponding to the location of a particular stimulus). They also observed that the identity negative priming effect was smaller in older than in younger adults, while no evidence for a differential age deficit was found in location negative priming (this last conclusion has to be taken cautiously because the number of studies on location tasks is rather limited). In addition, there was no evidence for the influence of moderator variables (such as pacing of the task, exposure duration, etc.) on the location or identity negative priming effect, as indicated by the homogeneity of effect sizes.

These results suggest that older adults have more difficulty inhibiting irrelevant aspects of a stimulus than younger adults. However, recent studies suggest that, besides inhibition mechanisms, a memorial process may also be active in the negative priming effect (e.g. Kane *et al.*, 1997): this view considers that in the prime trial, the distractor provides information that has to be ignored; this information ('ignore it') will be retrieved when the distractor becomes the target in the test trial, which may slow down processing. Consequently, it is quite possible that the reduction of negative priming in elderly subjects is due to age-related problems with the memory component of the task, rather than to an age-related deficit in inhibitory processes.

In a recent study, Intons-Peterson *et al.* (1998) showed that both older and younger adults displayed negative priming when tested at preferred times (in the morning for older adults, later in the day for the young subjects), but not when tested at non-preferred times. As suggested by Verhaeghen and De Meersman (1998), these results indicate that inasmuch as primary researchers did not test their subjects at their optimal time of day, this may have confounded the results (it should be noted that another source of confusion in the literature is the potential lack of power in individual studies, due to the fact that the size of the average negative priming effect is quite small and sample sizes are typically modest). According to Intons-Peterson *et al.* (1998), peak times in negative priming performance may reflect the involvement of the attentional system of the frontal lobes (Posner and Petersen, 1990), which presumably show individual and circadian differences in peak alertness times. More generally, some evidence suggests that inhibitory functioning is impaired at the individual's non-optimal relative to optimal times, while excitatory functioning (assessed for example by means of access to well-learned, familiar, or highly practised responses) does not vary through the day (see Yoon, May, and Hasher, 2000). The consequences of synchrony can be greater for older than for younger adults given the age-related deficits in inhibition.

Besides the optimal testing time, it seems important to control other factors which can contribute to age differences in selective attention, especially sensory loss. For example, Murphy, McDowd and Wilcox (1999) showed that, when the listening situation was adjusted to correct for individual differences in hearing, younger and older adults were similarly influenced by unattended auditory information. These results suggest that age-related auditory attentional deficits may be due more to sensory or perceptual difficulties experienced by older subjects in understanding speech in a noisy environment than to any inhibitory decline. In addition, it is also possible that there exist different inhibitory mechanisms underlying auditory and visual selective attention, with visual inhibition being more affected by age than auditory inhibition.

Another interpretation of age differences in selective attention, based on a limited-capacity approach to selective attentional situations (Lavie, 1995), has been proposed by Maylor and Lavie (1998). They considered that ageing of selective attention seems to involve (at least) two mechanisms: a reduction of an active inhibition mechanism and a reduced processing capacity. In their study, young and older subjects were asked to make rapid choice responses indicating which of two target letters was present in a relevant set of letters in the centre of the display while they attempted to ignore an irrelevant distractor in the periphery. The perceptual load of relevant processing was manipulated by varying the central set size. The results show that when the relevant set size was small, the adverse effect of an incompatible distractor was much greater for the older than for the younger subjects. However, with larger relevant set sizes, this was no longer the case, with the periphery distractor effect becoming irrelevant at lower levels of perceptual load for older than for younger subjects. The interpretation suggests that a low perceptual load condition leaves spare capacity which is then automatically allocated to the processing of irrelevant information (in both young and older subjects). Due to a reduction in the active inhibition mechanism, this is more disruptive in old age, leading to a greater distracting effect. In a high perceptual load condition, capacity is exhausted by the relevant processing, which leads to simply not processing the distractor (passive selectivity), and this intervenes with smaller increases of load in older than in younger subjects. Moreover, the age difference in the distractor effect under conditions of low perceptual load was significantly greater than expected solely on the basis of generalized slowing down. Indeed, when baseline response time differences were taken into account, the distractor effect remained three times greater for the older than for the younger adults. Finally, the age differences cannot be due to age-related changes in peripheral acuity: indeed, the influence of perceptual load on the age-related differences in the distractor effect has been observed with the distractor item presented at a constant distance from fixation in all conditions. In conclusion, Maylor and Lavie's results suggest that, besides an inhibition deficit, age-related differences in selective attention are also due to a reduced cognitive capacity. Furthermore, they demonstrated that these age differences are not simply the consequence of a generalized slowing down.

Typically, the cognitive capacity reduction in old age has been inferred from the observation of age differences in divided attention (dual tasks). In the next section, we will examine the studies which have explored the effect of age on divided attention.

Ageing and divided attention

A common assumption in the ageing literature is that there is some fundamental resource (cognitive capacity) upon which all cognitive operations draw and that this resource is reduced in old age. Dual-task studies appear to constitute the ideal test for this assumption: they are thought of as requiring the division of attention between the two simultaneous tasks. If the cognitive capacity of elderly subjects is reduced, then a primary task should require a greater proportion of the available resource, leaving less for a secondary task and thus leading to a poorer secondary-task performance in older than in younger subjects.

At first sight, empirical evidence appears to be consistent with the claim of a reduced resource in older adults. Indeed, Hartley (1992) reported a meta-analysis conducted by Kieley (1990) which showed that age-related differences in dual tasks are reliable. Greater dual-task costs have also been found in the rare studies which have equated younger and older groups on single-task performance (e.g. Crossley and Hiscock, 1992; Korteling, 1991). However, some studies (e.g. Somberg and Salthouse, 1982) showed that the older adults were able to divide their attention between the two tasks as well as the younger adults. These dissociations may be due to differences in task complexity. In addition, the amount of practice provided may also contribute to the studies' heterogeneity (see Rogers, 2000).

Hartley and Little (1999) consider that it is premature to attribute age differences in dual tasks to a reduction in resource. Indeed, in most studies, dual tasks are complex: for example, McDowd and Craik (1988) required their subjects to monitor an orally presented list of words, to detect words which denoted living things, while simultaneously determining whether a visually presented character was a vowel, consonant, odd digit, or even digit. Performance in such a dual task requires many operations to be carried out. In addition, the duration and the ordering of operations may change from trial to trial, and, consequently, aggregate measures could mask specific sources of interference. In other words, there is no way of knowing which operations in the primary task interfere with particular operations in the secondary task.

In this perspective, Hartley and Little (1999) compared the performance of younger and older adults in dual tasks in which two simple, well-learned tasks were carried out on each trial. The relative onsets of the stimuli for the two tasks were controlled. Each trial began with the presentation of a white X. After 500 msec, the colour was changed to red or green. In Task 1, subjects had to give a response identifying the colour. Some time later, the colour changed (a stimulus onset asynchrony (SOA) of 50, 150, 500 or 1,000 msec), and the X was also replaced by an A or B (but the colour remained the same). In Task 2, subjects had to identify the letter. They were instructed to carry out both tasks as quickly as possible. This procedure has a number of advantages: the tasks are simple; they involve relatively few operations; they are repeated in the same order from trial to trial; and finally, controlling the SOA permits us to manipulate the interference between the tasks (at very short SOAs, there should be considerable interference between tasks). Seven experiments were conducted which manipulated different dimensions (especially, eliminating the requirement for a rapid response to Task 2, vocal rather than key press response, and task difficulty).

The general reduced-resource model predicted that older adults would be slower (or less correct) than young adults in responding to Task 2 and that the age difference would increase as the overlap between the two tasks increased (that is, when the SOA decreased). It also predicted that any factor that increased the difficulty of either task would result in increased dual-task interference for both tasks, and that this complexity manipulation should have its greatest effect with minimal SOA. Finally, it predicted that the interaction between SOA and complexity manipulation would be larger in older than in younger adults. Several aspects of the results provided by the seven experiments were inconsistent with this model. In contrast, the results were globally more consistent with a task-switching model in which a single response-selection mechanism can process only one task at a time, in which the architecture of task management is the same in younger and older adults, and in which age was assumed to produce generalized slowing down. Moreover, there was no evidence for a specific impairment in the ability of older adults to manage simultaneous tasks. However, there exists some evidence indicating that input and output interference are greater in older adults. Hartley and Little (1999) suggest that the other studies which obtained results suggesting a reduction of processing resource used more complex tasks, in which the variability of operations may have led to changes appearing widespread and non-specific. Another possibility is that more complex tasks activate executive processes and that these processes are particularly affected by ageing.

In the last part of this chapter, we will consider more specifically the effect of ageing on executive functions (or the central executive component of working memory).

Ageing and executive system

Executive processes are clearly an amalgam of control processes and a wide range of cognitive functions has been ascribed to this system. For an explanation of the function of the central executive, Baddeley (1986) adopted Norman and Shallice's model (see Shallice, 1988) which describes the control of information processing. This model consists of two control systems: contention scheduling activates semi-automatic schemata necessary to accomplish routine tasks, whereas the supervisory attentional system (SAS) is needed in novel or problematic situations, such as planning of future actions, decision-making, and trouble-shooting. Baddeley (1986) suggested that the SAS and the central executive are essentially the same structure. In addition, according to Shallice (1988), dysfunction of the SAS could plausibly account for the cognitive deficits following frontal-lobe lesions.

Several studies have suggested that ageing is characterized by a decline in the capacity of the central executive component of working memory (e.g. Van der Linden, Brédart, and Beerten, 1994; Van der Linden, Beerten, and Pesenti, 1998). It has also been proposed that this reduced central executive ability could be, at least partially, associated with the decline in frontal function which is considered to be a feature of normal ageing (see Braun and Lalonde, 1990; Moscovitch and Winocur, 1992; Daigneault and Braun, 1993; West, 1996).

For example, in a recent study (Van der Linden *et al.*, 1998), we investigated the effects of age on a random generation task. According to Baddeley (1986, 1996b), attempting to generate random sequences of items is an activity that places significant demands on the central executive component of working memory. Indeed, when subjects are required to produce random sequences of letter names or digits, they have to select new strategies, to keep the sequence as random as possible, prevent the occurrence of schematic responses (e.g. alphabetic stereotypes, such as 'LMN'), check that the responses are suitably random and, if not, change the strategy. All these selection and control functions correspond exactly to the role that is assigned by Baddeley (1986) to the central executive system. In Experiment 1, young and elderly subjects were asked to generate random strings of letters at 1-, 2- and 4-second rates. The elderly subjects produced more alphabetical stereotype responses than young subjects, even in the slowest rate condition. Furthermore, as faster rates were imposed, elderly subjects could no longer keep in step and missed responses. In Experiment 2, subjects were required to generate letters at the same time as they were sorting cards into 1, 2, 4 or 8 categories. Age-related differences were observed on most of the measures of randomness (stereotypes, zero-order and first-order measures). In addition, the number of errors increased with the number of sorting alternatives, especially for elderly subjects. These results suggested the existence of a reduction of central executive resources, along with reduced inhibition ability, in the elderly subjects.

In another study (Van der Linden *et al.*, 1994), we explored the effect of ageing on the central executive in two experiments using a working memory updating task (Pollack, Johnson, and Knaft, 1959; Morris and Jones, 1990). The task requires subjects to watch strings of consonants whose length is unknown to them, and then to recall serially a specific number of recent items. The updating task requires considerable flexibility of information processing and a progressive shift of attention, i.e. discarding some items while new ones are registered. Morris and Jones (1990) showed that the updating task requires two independent working memory mechanisms: the phonological loop which is involved in the serial recall component of the task, and the central executive which is involved in the updating process. In a first experiment, we administered to young and elderly subjects a task in which they were asked to watch strings of 4 to 10 consonants and then to recall serially the four most recent items. Results revealed no effect of age. A second experiment was then carried out using a memory load that was close to memory span: lists of 6 to 12 consonants were presented and subjects had to recall the last six items. The results showed that the effect of ageing on the updating component and on the serial recall component of the updating task may be dissociated: age interacted with the number of required updating operations but not with serial position. These data support the idea that older subjects have decreased central executive resources: holding a memory load close to, or beyond, the memory span while carrying out online updating exceeded the processing capacities of the elderly subjects' central executive. In addition, the absence of interaction between age and serial position suggests that the phonological loop (storage) component is not affected by age.

However, the existence of a central executive dysfunction (presumably due to a 'frontal' decline) has been questioned by Fisk and Warr (1996). These authors compared older and younger subjects on a random generation task. They asked subjects to generate letters in a random sequence, at each of three production rates (4, 2 and 1 second). Two measures of randomness were taken at each of the elicitation rates: the number of times any letter pair was repeated and the number of letter pairs that were alphabetically ordered (this yielded a total of six scores). Significant positive age correlations for five of the six scores were observed, which seems to indicate a decline of central executive function with age. In addition, the age effect in random generation (measured by one score which combined the above measures) remained significant after statistical control for the phonological loop function (measured by word span and digit span). However, these age differences in random generation were largely eliminated after controlling for age deficits in perceptual speed (measured by means of a letter comparison and a pattern comparison speed task). These findings are consistent with the numerous studies conducted by Salthouse (see Salthouse, 1996) who showed that although increased age is associated with lower performance on working memory tasks, many of these age-related differences appear to be mediated by a slower speed of processing. Therefore, it appears that the main part of the age-related variations observed in random generation could be due to a general reduction of perceptual speed rather than to a specific problem affecting the central executive. More specifically, slowing (through either limited time or simultaneity mechanisms) would disrupt the different operations of the central executive needed for random generation – that is, to switch strategies, to access new strategies, and to monitor response output (Baddeley, 1996a).

In the same vein, Fisk and Warr (1996) argued that, as no control was present in our updating study, it is possible that the observed age differences were in fact due to speed differences. However, in a recent study (Van der Linden and Adam, 2000), we confirmed the existence of a significant age-related decline in the performance of the updating task (the task was administered to 151 subjects spanning five age categories, from 30 to 80 years; see Van der Linden *et al.*, 1999, for a more detailed description of the sample and the updating task). In addition, a regression analysis showed that the age differences in working memory updating remained very significant after statistical control of processing speed (measured by means of a letter comparison task and a colour naming task) and also after control of interference (measured by means of two methods taken from the Stroop task; see Van der Linden *et al.*, 1999). These results suggest that age-related declines in central executive functioning cannot be attributed only to a generalized slowing down (or to a reduced resistance to interference).

However, other studies are indicative of an intact functioning of the central executive in normal ageing. Belleville, Rouleau, and Caza (1998) explored the central executive functioning of young and elderly subjects using the alpha span task. The alpha span task requires simultaneous storage and manipulation of information. This task consists in presenting word lists whose length corresponds to the span minus one of each individual. In the first condition, subjects have to recall the words in serial order. In the second condition, the words have to be recalled in alphabetical order. The storage requirement being equated between the two conditions, the only difference concerns the intervention of the central executive during alphabetical recall. Results indicate a decrease in performance from the serial recall condition to the alphabetical recall condition. However, this decrease in performance is similar in young and elderly subjects, indicating the presence of intact manipulation in working memory abilities. The presence of discrepant results between studies exploring central executive function can be related to the fractionation of that system (Baddeley, 1996b): random generation, updating and alpha span tasks would evaluate different aspects of the central executive function, and normal ageing would lead to deficits in only some of these aspects.

Other studies have suggested that cognitive decline in ageing is linked to a deficit of executive functions (e.g. Daigneault, Braun, and Whitaker, 1992;

Brennan, Welsh, and Fisher, 1997; Parkin and Java, 1999). However, Parkin and Java (1999) showed that a large proportion of age-related variance on measures of frontal-lobe function may be attributed to a more general factor characterized jointly by the Digit Symbol Substitution Test (from the WAIS-R; it is a task typically used in order to measure perceptual speed; see Salthouse, 1996) and the AH4 test of fluid intelligence. On the other hand, when performance on a Digit Cancellation Task was used as a covariate (a task which has no memory load, minimal attentional demands, and only a small motor component, and, consequently, which seems to meet admirably the criteria proposed by Salthouse, 1996, to assess perceptual speed), it does not, contrary to the Digit Symbol Substitution Test, reduce age differences on frontal tasks to non-significant levels. In conclusion, the Digit Cancellation Task and the Digit Symbol Substitution Test are not functionally equivalent in the extent and nature of their interactions with age-sensitive changes in cognition. More generally, as suggested by Parkin and Java (1999), if the perceptual speed interpretation of cognitive ageing is to progress, the concept of perceptual speed should have an unambiguous operational definition.

In a recent study (Andrès and Van der Linden, 2000), we also explored the hypothesis of a link between cognitive ageing and executive functions by using tasks designed to assess specific executive operations and which have been proved to be sensitive to frontal dysfunction. The theoretical framework on which this study was based is the attentional control of action model developed by Norman and Shallice (1980). Three tasks were used (the Tower of London task, Shallice, 1982; the Hayling test, Burgess and Shallice, 1996a; the Brixton test, Burgess and Shallice, 1996b) in order to examine three executive processes (planning, inhibition, and rule detection). The performance of the elderly participants was significantly poorer than that of the young participants in all three tasks. In addition, processing speed, measured by means of a colour naming task, explained some but not all of the age-related differences. Globally, these age-related differences in executive functions are consistent with the studies showing a frontal decline in the elderly (Raz *et al.*, 1997; Raz *et al.*, 1998).

Sustained attention and vigilance in normal ageing

An important attentional function is the ability to prepare and sustain alertness to process high-priority signals (Posner and Petersen, 1990, p. 35). This function was explored in normal ageing with attentional tasks defined as phasic alertness and vigilance. Phasic alertness represents the capability to enhance response readiness following a warning stimulus. Vigilance requires the subject to stay alert for a prolonged period of time in order to detect relevant but very infrequent stimuli, which appear at irregular intervals during the task. In contrast, sustained attention concerns the ability to detect a large number of items over a brief period of time (Sturm *et al.*, 1997).

Some studies have more specifically explored the changes in alertness in normal elderly subjects. Nebes and Brady (1993) explored phasic alertness in young and elderly subjects by a choice reaction time (RT) task in which subjects had to press one of two switches depending on the position of a square. In this task, the stimulus was usually preceded by an auditory warning signal. The time subjects needed to attain maximal phasic alertness was determined by varying the stimulus onset asynchrony (SOA) between the warning and the stimulus. Results indicate that elderly subjects have longer reaction times (RTs) than young subjects, but the distribution of the RTs in relation to the interval between the warning signal and the presentation of the stimulus is similar in both groups. Thus, the elderly subjects did not appear to need more time than the young to attain a maximal level of preparedness and they benefited in the same way from the presence of a warning signal. These results seem to indicate that phasic alertness is relatively unchanged by normal ageing.

In another study, Pate *et al.* (1994) administered to young and elderly subjects a simple reaction time task (SRT; to press a single response key every time one numeral appeared) and a choice reaction time task (CRT; to press one of two key responses following the presentation of one of two numerals). In both tasks, each trial begins with the presentation of a warning signal. Both groups responded more quickly on the SRT than on the CRT task. Moreover, although elderly subjects were slower than young subjects, the increase in the RT was not disproportionately larger in older subjects from the SRT to the CRT task. In a second experiment, the authors explored the effects of various warning conditions on normal ageing. They administered the CRT task with a warning signal occurring 2,500, 4,500 or 6,500 msec before the target stimuli. Unwarned trials were also administered. The results indicated that both groups benefited from a warning signal, responding more rapidly on warned than on unwarned trials. These data are also in agreement with the existence of intact phasic alterness in normal ageing, although these subjects have slower RTs.

With regard to the vigilance function, the few studies that do exist show little evidence for age-related declines (see Giambra, 1993, for a review). Nebes and Brady (1993) explored more specifically whether there exists a vigilance decrement over time (resulting in increased RTs from the beginning to the end of the task) in elderly subjects. Older subjects again exhibited longer RTs than the young ones. However, both groups showed a similar monotonic rise in their RT with increasing time-on-task, indicating also intact vigilance functions in normal ageing. In a more recent study, Mouloua and Parasuraman (1995) found that performance in a vigilance task requiring target identification across 30-minute sessions deteriorated across time at a faster rate for old adults than for young adults when event rate was high and target location certainty was low (that is, when demands on visual attention are great).

Conclusions

In 1992, Hartley presented a detailed and critical review of the empirical findings on age-related changes in attention. He concluded that ageing and attention was not a mature field, that there was little data and that the field contained loosely specified theories. A decade later, much additional data has accumulated and some progress has been made in the identification of brain structures involved in different aspects of attention, as well as in the comprehension of the effect of ageing on the brain. However, from a theoretical and methodological point of view, it is not evident that the situation has substantially improved.

In some attentional domains, a great number of factors (some cognitive, others non-cognitive; some specific, others more general) have been identified that contribute to age-related differences. For example, in the selective attention domain, age differences have been related to generalized slowing, reduced inhibition, reduced processing capacity, optimal testing time, sensory loss, etc. Some data also suggest the existence of a differential effect of ageing on the posterior/anterior attentional systems. However an integrative and predictive theory is still lacking.

In other domains, such as the executive one, the exploration of the effect of ageing has been confronted with important conceptual and methodological problems, related to the definition of executive functions and the elaboration of tasks specifically designed to assess these functions (see Van der Linden *et al.*, 2000). In many studies, tasks are complex and multi-determined and, consequently, it is not easy to determine the nature of the age-related declines. Some recent studies have attempted to elaborate more controlled procedures (for example, see the dual-task procedure used by Hartley and Little, 1999). There also exist domains such as sustained attention in which the data are still rare and mixed: some researches reported age differences, whereas others did not. In addition, it appears that age differences can often be attributed to other aspects of the tasks, such as discriminability of the task, duration of stimulus presentation, or working memory load.

It could be argued that the global approach to ageing contributes to demonstrating confidently that task-specific interpretations such as inefficient strategies or defective components are unlikely to play a major role in accounting for age-related differences in cognition (see Salthouse, 2000). Indeed, more and more data suggest that some age-related differences cannot be explained by general factors such as generalized slowing. Furthermore, it has recently become clear that the global approach needs a more precise specification of the general constructs (such as speed, inhibition, working memory) and their mutual relationships, along with the development of multiple reliable measures of these mediators. In a sense, the future of global approaches to cognitive ageing is likely to consist in more analytic investigations of the variables that hide within the general factors.

Another point concerns the fact that little is known about the nature of the relations between pragmatic and mechanic abilities (or process and product), and between age and the joint effect of these cognitive abilities. As suggested by Salthouse (2000), this is unfortunate inasmuch as most everyday activities involve a combination of the two types of cognition.

More generally, it appears that more applied work is essential for understanding the meaning of age-related attention difficulties for everyday life. A particularly important issue is to determine how declines in cognitive function may be offset by the experience and knowledge the elderly adults possess (Park and Hall Gutchess, 2000; Van der Linden and Hupet, 1994). There is a wealth of evidence suggesting that the decrements in cognitive performance that occur with age do not impact on everyday activities as negatively as one might expect. For example, meta-analyses have consistently failed to find a relationship between age and job performance (Rhodes, 1983; Waldman and Avolio, 1986). Similarly, several studies showed that adults aged 60 to 75 made almost no errors in their medication-taking behaviours, despite the fact that medication adherence is a task that appears to be highly cognitive and resource driven (Morrel *et al.*, 1997; Park *et al.*, 1999). These findings suggest that environmental supports, elaborated knowledge structures, tacit (procedural) knowledge, experience of older adults, and automaticity may serve as compensatory mechanisms in familiar environments. In contrast, the impact of cognitive decline on everyday activities is most pronounced in unfamilar environments and novel tasks.

Additional progress in understanding the effects of age-associated cognitive decline (and more specifically, attention decline) on everyday behaviour will require clear models of the cognitive processes involved in various tasks (a 'daily life cognitive psychology'). For example, in the attention domain, an important issue concerns the relationship of attention processes (ability to divide attention, ability to ignore distractors, processing speed) to driving and ageing (see Park and Hall Gutchess, 2000).

References

Andrès, P. and Van der Linden, M. (2000). Age-related differences in Supervisory Attentional System functions. *Journal of Gerontology: Psychological Sciences*, *55B*, 373–380.

Baddeley, A.D. (1986). *Working Memory*. New York: Oxford University Press.

Baddeley, A.D. (1996a). The concept of working memory. In S.E. Gathercole (ed.) *Models of Short-term Memory*. Hove: Psychology Press.

Baddeley, A. (1996b). Exploring the central executive. *Quarterly Journal of Experimental Psychology*, *49A*, 5–28.

Baltes, P.B. and Lindenberger, U. (1997). Emergence of a powerful connection between sensory and cognitive functions across the adult life span: a new window to the study of cognitive aging. *Psychology and Aging*, *12*, 12–21.

Baltes, P.B., Staudinger, U.M., and Lindenberger, U. (1999). Lifespan psychology: theory and application to intellectual functioning. *Annual Review of Psychology*, *50*, 471–507.

Belleville, S., Rouleau, N., and Caza, N. (1998). Effects of normal aging on the manipulation of information in working memory. *Memory and Cognition*, *26*, 572–583.

Berger, A. and Posner, M.I. (2000). Pathologies of brain attentional networks. *Neuroscience and Biobehavioral Reviews*, *24*, 3–5.

Birren, J.E. and Fisher, L.M. (1995). Aging and speed of behavior: possible consequences for psychological functioning. *Annual Review of Psychology*, *46*, 329–353.

Bollen, K.A. and Long, J.S. (1993). *Testing Structural Equation Models*. Newbury Park, CA: Sage.

Braun, C.M.J. and Lalonde, R. (1990). Les déclins des fonctions cognitives chez la personne âgée: une perspective neuropsychologique. *Canadian Journal of Aging*, *9*, 135–158.

Brennan, M., Welsh, M.C., and Fisher, C.B. (1997). Aging and executive function skills: an examination of a community-dwelling older adult population. *Perceptual and Motor Skills*, *84*, 1187–1197.

Brink, J.M. and McDowd, J.M. (1999). Aging and selective attention: an issue of complexity or multiple mechanisms? *Journal of Gerontology: Psychological Sciences*, *54B*, 30–33.

Bruyer, R., Van der Linden, M., Rectem, D., and Galvez, C. (1995). Effects of age and education on the Stroop interference. *Archives de Psychologie*, *63*, 257–267.

Burgess, P.W. and Shallice, T. (1996a). Response suppression, initiation and strategy use following frontal lobe lesions. *Neuropsychologia*, *34*, 263–273.

Burgess, P.W. and Shallice, T. (1996b). Bizarre responses, rule detection and frontal lobe lesions. *Cortex*, *32*, 241–259.

Burke, D.M. (1997). Language, aging, and inhibitory deficits: evaluation of a theory. *Journal of Gerontology: Psychological Sciences*, *52B*, 254–264.

Cattell, R.B. (1971). *Abilities: Their Structure, Growth, and Action*. Boston, MA: Houghton Mifflin.

Cohn, N.B., Dustman, R.E., and Bradford, D.C. (1984). Age-related decrements in Stroop color test performance. *Journal of Clinical Psychology*, *40*, 1244–1250.

Crossley, M. and Hiscock, M. (1992). Age-related differences in concurrent task performance of normal adults: evidence for a decline in processing resources. *Psychology and Aging*, 7, 499–506.

Daigneault, S. and Braun, C.M.J. (1993). Working memory and the self-ordered pointing task: further evidence of early prefrontal decline in normal aging. *Journal of Clinical and Experimental Neuropsychology*, *15*, 881–895.

Daigneault, S., Braun, C.M.J., and Whitaker, M.A. (1992). Early effects of normal aging on perseverative and non-perseverative prefrontal measures. *Developmental Neuropsychology*, *8*, 99–104.

Fisk, J.E. and Warr, P. (1996). Age and working memory: the role of perceptual speed, the central executive, and the phonological loop. *Psychology and Aging*, *11*, 316–323.

Giambra, L.M. (1993). Sustained attention in older adults: performance and process. In J. Cerella, J. Rybash, W. Hoyer, and M.L. Common (eds) *Adult Information Processing: Limits on Loss*. San Diego, CA: Academic Press.

Hahn, S. and Kramer, A.F. (1995). Attentional flexibility and aging: you don't need to be 20 years of age to split the beam. *Psychology and Aging*, *10*, 597–609.

Hartley, A.A. (1992). Attention. In F.I.M. Craik and T.A. Salthouse (eds) *The Handbook of Aging and Cognition*. Hillsdale, NJ: Erlbaum.

Hartley, A.A. (1993). Evidence for the selective preservation of spatial selective attention in old age. *Psychology and Aging*, *8*, 371–379.

Hartley, A.A. and Little, D.M. (1999). Age-related differences and similarities in dual-task interference. *Journal of Experimental Psychology: General*, *128*, 416–449.

Hasher, L. and Zacks, R.T. (1988). Working memory, comprehension and aging: a review and a new view. In G.H. Bower (ed.) *The Psychology of Learning and Motivation*, vol. 2. San Diego, CA: Academic Press.

Hebb, D.O. (1949). *The Organization of Behavior*. New York: Wiley.

Hultsch, D.F., Herzog, C., Small, B.J., McDonald-Miszczak, and Dixon, R.A. (1992). Short-term longitudinal change in cognitive performance in later life. *Psychology and Aging*, *7*, 571–584.

Hultsch, D.F., Dixon, R.A., Small, B.J., and Hertzog, C. (1999). *Memory Change in the Aged*. Cambridge: Cambridge University Press.

Intons-Peterson, M.J., Rocchi, P., West, T., McLellan, K., and Hackney, A. (1998). Aging, optimal testing times, and negative priming. *Journal of Experimental Psychology: Learning, Memory, and Cognition*, *24*, 362–376.

Kane, M.J., May, C.P., Hasher, L., Rahhal, T., and Stoltzfus, E.R. (1997). Dual mechanisms of negative priming. *Journal of Experimental Psychology: Human Perception and Performance*, *23*, 632–650.

Kieley, J. (1990). A meta- analysis and review of aging and divided attention. Claremont Graduate School, Department of Psychology, Claremont, CA: Unpublished manuscript.

Kieley, J.M. and Hartley, A.A. (1997). Age-related equivalence of identity suppression in the Stroop color–word task. *Psychology and Aging*, *12*, 22–29.

Kirasic, K., Allen, G.L., Dobson, S.H., and Binder, K.S. (1996). Aging, cognitive resources, and declarative learning. *Psychology and Aging*, *11*, 658–670.

Kliegl, R., Mayr, U., and Krampe, R. (1994). Time–accuracy functions for determining process and person differences: an application to cognitive aging. *Cognitive Psychology*, *26*, 134–164.

Korteling, J.E. (1991). Effects of skill integration and perceptual competition on age-related differences in dual-task performance. *Human Factors*, *33*, 35–44.

Kwong See, S.T. and Ryan, E. (1995). Cognitive mediation of adult age differences in language performance. *Psychology and Aging*, *10*, 458–468.

LaBerge, D. (1992). Thalamic and cortical mechanisms of attention suggested by recent positron emission tomographic experiments. *Journal of Cognitive Neuroscience*, *2*, 358–372.

Lavie, N. (1995). Perceptual load as a necessary condition for selective attention. *Journal of Experimental Psychology: Human Perception and Performance*, *21*, 451–468.

Lindenberger, U. and Baltes, P.B. (1994). Sensory functioning and intelligence in old age: a strong connection. *Psychology and Aging*, *9*, 339–355.

Lindenberger, U. and Baltes, P.B. (1997). Intellectual functioning in old and very old age: cross-sectional results from the Berlin Aging Study. *Psychology and Aging*, *12*, 410–432.

McDowd, J.M. and Birren, J.E. (1990). Aging and attentional processes. In J.E. Birren and K.W. Schaie (eds) *Handbook of the Psychology of Aging*. San Diego, CA: Academic Press.

McDowd, J.M. and Craik, F.I.M. (1988). Effects of aging and task difficulty on divided attention performance. *Journal of Experimental Psychology: Human Perception and Performance*, *14*, 267–280.

Madden, D.J. and Plude, D.J. (1993). Selective preservation of selective attention. In J. Cerella, J. Rybash, W. Hoyer, and M.L. Common (eds) *Adult Information Processing: Limits on Loss*. San Diego, CA: Academic Press.

Maylor, E.M. and Lavie, N. (1998). The influence of perceptual load on age differences in selective attention. *Psychology and Aging*, *13*, 563–573.

Mayr, U. and Kliegl, R. (1993). Sequential and coordinative complexity: age-based processing limitations in figural transformations. *Journal of Experimental Psychology: Learning, Memory, and Cognition*, *19*, 1297–1320.

Morrel, R.W., Park, D.C., Kidder, D.P., and Martin, M. (1997). Adherence to anti-hypertensive medications over the lifespan. *The Gerontologist*, *37*, 609–619.

Morris, R.N. and Jones, D.M. (1990). Memory updating in working memory: the role of the central executive. *British Journal of Psychology*, *81*, 111–121.

Moscovitch, M. and Winocur, G. (1992). The neuropsychology of aging. In F.I.M. Craik and T.A. Salthouse (eds) *The Handbook of Aging and Cognition*. Hillsdale, NJ: Erlbaum.

Mouloua, M. and Parasuraman, R. (1995). Aging and cognitive vigilance: effects of spatial uncertainty and event rate. *Experimental Aging Research*, *21*, 17–32.

Murphy, D.R., McDowd, J.M., and Wilcox, K.A. (1999). Inhibition and aging: similarities between younger and older adults as revealed by the processing of unattended auditory information. *Psychology and Aging*, *14*, 44–59.

Nebes, R.D. and Brady, C.B. (1993). Phasic and tonic alertness in Alzheimer's disease. *Cortex*, *29*, 77–90.

Norman, D.A. and Shallice, T. (1980). Attention to action: willed and automatic control of behavior. Center for human information processing (Technical report No. 99). Reprinted in revised form in R.J. Davidson, G.E. Schartz and D. Shapiro (eds) (1986) *Consciousness and Self-regulation. Advances in Research*, 4. New York and London: Plenum Press.

Park, D.C. (2000). The basic mechanisms accounting for age-related decline in cognitive function. In D. Park and N. Schwartz (eds) *Cognitive Aging: A Primer*. Hove: Psychology Press.

Park, D.C. and Hall Gutchess, A. (2000). Cognitive aging and everyday life. In D. Park and N. Schwartz (eds) *Cognitive Aging: A Primer*. Hove: Psychology Press.

Park, D.C., Smith, A.D., Lautenschlager, G., Earles, J.L., Frieske, D., Zwahr, M., and Gaines, C.L. (1996). Mediators of long-term memory performance across the life span. *Psychology and Aging, 11*, 621–637.

Park, D.C., Herzog, C., Leventhal, H., Morrel, R.W., Leventhal, E., Birchmore, D.,

Martin, M., and Bennett, J. (1999). Medication adherence in rheumatoid arthritis patients: older is wiser. *Journal of the American Geriatrics Society*, *47*, 172–183.

Parkin, A.J. and Java, R.I. (1999). Deterioration of frontal lobe function in normal aging: influences of fluid intelligence versus perceptual speed. *Neuropsychology*, *13*, 539–545.

Pate, D.S., Margolin, D.I., Friedrich, F.J., and Bentley, E.E. (1994). Decision-making and attentional processes in ageing and in dementia of the Alzheimer's type. *Cognitive Neuropsychology*, *11*, 321–329.

Plude, D. and Doussard-Roosevelt, J. (1989). Aging, selective attention, and feature integration. *Psychology and Aging*, *4*, 98–105.

Pollack, I., Johnson, L.B., and Knaft, P.R. (1959). Running memory span. *Journal of Experimental Psychology*, *57*, 137–146.

Posner, M.I. and Dehaene, S. (1994). Attentional networks. *Trends in Neurosciences*, *17*, 75–79.

Posner, M.I. and Petersen, S.E. (1990). The attention system of the human brain. *Annual Review of Neuroscience*, *13*, 25–42.

Posner, M.I. and Raichle, M. (1996). *Images of Mind*. Washington, DC: Scientific American Books.

Raz, N., Gunning, F.M., Head, D., Dupuis, J.H., McQuain, J., Briggs, S.D., Loken, W.J., Thorton, E., and Acker, J.D. (1997). Selective aging of the human cerebral cortex observed in vivo: differential vulnerability of the prefrontal gray matter. *Cerebral Cortex*, 7, 268–282.

Raz, N., Gunning-Dixon, F.M., Head, D., Dupuis, J.H., and Acker, J.D. (1998). Neuroanatomical correlates of cognitive aging: evidence from structural magnetic resonance imaging. *Neuropsychology*, *12*, 95–114.

Reuter-Lorenz, P. (2000). Cognitive neuropsychology of the aging brain. In D. Park and N. Schwartz (eds) *Cognitive Aging: A Primer*. Hove: Psychology Press.

Rhodes, S.R. (1983). Age-related differences in work attitudes and behavior: a review and conceptual analysis. *Psychological Bulletin*, *93*, 328–367.

Rogers, W.A. (2000). Attention and aging. In D. Park and N. Schwartz (eds) *Cognitive Aging: A Primer*. Hove: Psychology Press.

Salthouse, T.A. (1996). The processing-speed theory of adult age differences in cognition. *Psychological Review*, *103*, 403–428.

Salthouse, T.A. (2000). Pressing issues in cognitive aging. In D. Park and N. Schwartz (eds) *Cognitive Aging: A Primer*. Hove: Psychology Press.

Seron, X., Van der Linden, M. and Andrès, P. (1999). Le lobe frontal: a la recherche de ses connectivités fonctionnelles. In M. Van der Linden, X. Seron, D. Le Gall and P. Andrès (eds) *Neuropsychologie des lobes frontaux*. Marseilles: Solal.

Shallice, T. (1982). Specific impairments of planning. *Philosophical Transactions of the Royal Society of London, B*, *298*, 199–209.

Shallice, T. (1988). *From Neuropsychology to Mental Structure*. Cambridge: Cambridge University Press.

Shallice, T. and Burgess, P. (1993). Supervisory control of action and thought selection. In A.D. Baddeley and L. Weiskrantz (eds) *Attention: Selection, Awareness and Control. A Tribute to Donald Broadbent*. Oxford: Oxford University Press.

Somberg, B.L. and Salthouse, T.A. (1982). Divided attention abilities in young and old adults. *Journal of Experimental Psychology: Human Perception and Performance*, *8*, 651–663.

Spieler, D.H., Balota, D.A., and Faust, M.E. (1996). Stroop performance in healthy younger and older adults and in individuals with dementia of the Alzheimer's type. *Journal of Experimental Psychology: Human Perception and Performance*, *22*, 461–479.

Stoltzfus, E.R., Hasher, L., Zacks, R.T., Ulivi, M.S., and Goldstein, D. (1993). Investigations of inhibition and interference in younger and older adults. *Journal of Gerontology: Psychological Sciences*, *48*, 179–188.

Sturm, W., Willmes, K., Orgass, B., and Hartje, W. (1997). Do specific attention deficits need specific training? *Neuropsychological Rehabilitation*, *7*, 81–103.

Van der Linden, M. and Adam, S. (2000). Age-related differences in central executive functioning: the contribution of processing speed, resistance to interference, and phonological ability. In preparation.

Van der Linden, M. and Hupet, M. (1994). L'optimalisation du fonctionnement cognitif de la personne âgée: les interventions cognitives. In M. Van der Linden and M. Hupet (eds) *Le Vieillissement cognitif*. Paris: Presses Universitaires de France.

Van der Linden, M., Brédart, S., and Beerten, A. (1994). Age-related differences in updating working memory. *British Journal of Psychology*, *85*, 145–152.

Van der Linden, M., Beerten, A., and Pesenti, M. (1998). Age-related differences in random generation. *Brain and Cognition*, *38*, 1–16.

Van der Linden, M., Hupet, M., Feyereisen, P., Schelstraete, M.A., Bestgen, Y., Bruyer, R., Lories, G., El Ahmadi, A., and Seron, X. (1999). Cognitive mediators of age-related differences in language comprehension and verbal memory performance. *Aging, Neuropsychology, and Cognition*, *6*, 32–55.

Van der Linden, M., Meulemans, Th., Seron, X., Coyette, F., Andrès, P., and Prairial, C. (2000). L'évaluation des fonctions exécutives. In X. Seron and M. Van der Linden (eds) *Traité de Neuropsychologie Clinique*. Marseilles: Solal.

Verhaeghen, P. and De Meersman, L. (1998). Aging and the negative priming effect: a meta-analysis. *Psychology and Aging*, *13*, 435–444.

Waldman, D.A. and Avolio, B.J. (1986). A meta-analysis of age differences in job performance. *Journal of Applied Psychology*, *71*, 33–38.

West, R.L. (1996). An application of prefrontal cortex function theory to cognitive aging. *Psychological Bulletin*, *120*, 272–292.

Whiting, L.W. and Smith, A.D. (1997). Differential age-related processing limitations in recall and recognition tasks. *Psychology and Aging*, *12*, 216–224.

Yoon, C., May, C.P., and Hasher, L. (2000). Aging, circadian arousal patterns, and cognition. In D. Park and N. Schwartz (eds) *Cognitive Aging: A Primer*. Hove: Psychology Press.

Zacks, R.T. and Hasher, L. (1994). Directed ignoring. Inhibitory regulation of working memory. In D. Dagenbach and T.H. Carr (eds) *Inhibitory Processes in Attention, Memory and Language*. San Diego, CA: Academic Press.

Zacks, R.T. and Hasher, L. (1997). Cognitive gerontology and attentional inhibition: a reply to Burke and McDowd. *Journal of Gerontology: Psychological Sciences*, *52B*, 274–283.

Chapter 8

Attention and driving: a cognitive neuropsychological approach

Wiebo H. Brouwer

1 Introduction

If I ask how much attention must be given to drive a car safely through the rush hour, you might consider this a rhetorical question because it obviously takes a lot of attention. But occasionally I hear that only very little attention is needed, for example if I ask colleagues working in the area of dementia and driving.

They interpret the word attention as a label for a cognitive function or a set of cognitive functions which can be tested with tests of selective attention, both focused and divided attention, e.g. the Stroop test, and a complex reaction-time test. When such tests are presented according to normal clinical practice, persons with mild dementia usually score far outside the normal range. Occasionally there are perfectly safe drivers among them even in complex driving situations, as officially confirmed by driving experts of the licensing authority (Withaar, Brouwer and van Zomeren, 2000). Of course, demented drivers need co-drivers (usually their spouses) to plan and remember the route for all non-routine trips, but with regard to the control of speed and lane-position and the interaction with other traffic, some are fluent and safe.

The answer that quite a lot of attention must be given is based on the subjective feeling of high alertness which accompanies driving in the busy rush hour. Also many people have experienced a near miss while driving when their attention was focused on another task, e.g. changing a radio station. Although the experienced awareness of intense selective attention cannot be denied, the question is how much of this attention was actually deliberately *given* by the driver in the sense of an active conscious allocation of attention? Could it be that the attention was more or less reflexively *taken* (captured) by the driving task once the driver started off? And exactly how necessary is conscious awareness for driving? To illustrate the importance of automatic unconscious processes in driving I refer to two cases of persons with somnambulism, reported by Schenck and Mahowald (1995), who managed to get into their cars and drive distances of 8 and 23 km respectively without an accident while presumably being asleep. In one subject polysomnograms produced in the sleep lab demonstrated that almost every night he had a combination of behavioural activation and persisting sleep on the EEG throughout most of the recording. It is likely that this combination also occurred during the nightly ride. Of course, these nightly rides were made in quiet traffic conditions, but, still, quite a lot of selective information processing must have gone on.

Two different conceptualizations of attention are behind the apparent confusion about how much attention is needed for driving (van Zomeren and Brouwer, 1994). In one view, attention is considered to be a collection of selective brain mechanisms which can be localized as separate entities both in functional and neuroanatomical terms and which can be investigated with neuropsychological tests. In this view, the fact that persons can be found who drive safely but who repeatedly and consistently fail on tests of a key aspect of attention, implies that this aspect of attention is not necessary for safe driving.

The alternative view on attention is not primarily concerned with specific brain mechanisms but with anticipatory mental representations or schemata (Neisser, 1976). Attention refers to a continuously changing cognitive state characterized by a selective bias for processing certain internal or external stimuli. Important aspects of attention in this sense are selectivity, intensity and its dynamic character. Attention anticipates the processing of task-relevant information by way of its selective bias. This continuously changing state is multiply determined by both stimulus- and context-triggered automatic information processes, by momentary conscious intentions and thoughts, and by enduring motivational and emotional dispositions (van Zomeren and Brouwer, 1994). In this framework, attention is seen as the proximal or immediate cause of task performance. Brain injury is not viewed as something that directly impairs attention but as a condition which, dependent on its nature and severity, impairs perceptual and cognitive functions which in their turn constrain the (maximally obtainable) quality and intensity of the attentional state. Whether perceptual and cognitive impairments actually lead to serious attention problems in real life also strongly depends on the nature of the external task requirements and the previous experience with the corresponding tasks (skill level).

This cognitive conceptualization of attention gives a better fit with the driving literature and the medico-legal concept of fitness to drive than the 'basic mechanisms approach' because it leaves ample room for accommodating task- and domain-specificity and because it naturally allows for multiple determination of attentional problems. Therefore I adopt it for this chapter. The alternative approach where specific attentional mechanisms are conceptualized can be easily accommodated in the cognitive approach if these specific attentional mechanisms are viewed as perceptual or cognitive functions that constrain the attentional state.

Regulations with regard to fitness to drive are often formulated in terms of a wide variety of seemingly unrelated disease categories all of which are thought to impair the state of attention. A closer look reveals that the implicit assumption is that the diseases specified can lead to one or more of the following three types of attentional problems.

- There are problems with *sustaining attention*. For example, there is a more than negligible probability of sudden and unpredictable lapses of control over behaviour, as in certain types of epileptic insults and in diseases leading to excessive daytime sleepiness, such as narcolepsy and the sleep apnoea syndrome. In our attention framework such impairments interfere with the state of attention by their abnormal brain activation.
- There are problems with *selective attention* and basic information processing functions. In the realm of neuropsychology, one primarily thinks here of severe impairments of visual perception and spatial function, e.g. a visual hemi-inattention syndrome where one side of visual space is poorly represented. Also, one should think here of more general limitations of information processing such as mental slowness which easily results in divided attention deficits in time-pressured situations.
- There are problems with *executive functions*. This may have to do with judgement when a situation absolutely requires a deviation from routine or a change of goals for safety or courtesy reasons, the emotional evaluation of such situations, and the ability to inhibit and regulate automatisms. One might think of certain forms of dementia and hemi-neglect with strong denial of illness, and of course prefrontal brain injuries. Also Attentional Deficit Hyperactivity Disorder (ADHD) and related conditions as they extend into adulthood may be included here.

In the third part of the chapter, frequent neuropsychological disorders which may have serious consequences for attention in driving will be discussed, ordered according to the problem categories distinguished above. Before that, we will look in more detail at the cognitive architecture of driving in order to understand better how much and what type of attention is actually needed. We begin with a look at driving from the outside: how can the subtasks that comprise driving be globally ordered and what is the consequence of this ordering and its inherent hierarchy for attention requirements? Subsequently we look at driving from the inside: how is driving knowledge represented in memory, how is this knowledge accessed, and how does this relate to attention?

2 The driving task

2.1 Hierarchical task analysis

A first, very global distinction of subtasks in driving is in terms of the hierarchical task analysis proposed by Michon (1971) and adapted for application in neuropsychology and rehabilitation by van Zomeren, Brouwer and Minderhoud (1987). It describes traffic behaviour as a hierarchy of subtasks on the strategic, tactical and operational level. On the *strategic* level, choices and decisions are made concerning mode of transportation, route, time of day, and so on. These decisions are usually made without time pressure and often before engaging in actual driving. On the *tactical* level, preparatory actions are taken while driving (e.g. deciding to reduce speed when a traffic sign indicates the vicinity of a school or hospital). A slight time pressure is usually present on this level. Finally, the *operational* level comprises the numerous perceptions and actions performed from second to second to hold the car on course, to avoid parked vehicles, etc. On this level the task exerts a constant time pressure, as the driver has only limited time for avoiding or dealing with dangerous situations.

An analysis in terms of this hierarchy reveals that time pressure exists in particular on the operational level (escaping from acute danger). An almost universal consequence of impairments of perception and cognition resulting either from brain injuries or from sensory losses is that the afflicted person needs more time to identify and respond to an object or situation. Because of the inherent time pressure this has its most extensive effects on the operational level. However, decisions on higher levels can strongly influence the probability of running into time pressure on lower levels. For example, when driving more slowly near a school, there will be less time pressure if a child crosses unexpectedly. The existence of such opportunities for compensation in the driving task must be taken into account when formulating the ability requirements.

2.2 Driving as an expert domain

Driving is one of the instrumental activities of daily living (IADL), those everyday activities in and around the house which are necessary for independent functioning. Most adults have obtained a high level of skill in driving, based not only on experience when driving a car or motorcycle but also on experience in dynamic locomotion tasks such as running and cycling from an early age. Because it concerns such natural and highly practised skills, the correspondence between functions as assessed by psychological and ophthalmologic tests, and fitness to drive may be different from that expected on the basis of face-validity of tests. Because visual information is essential in driving, it seems logical to expect that persons with poor visual acuity have more crashes and drive less safely than those with good eyesight do. However, the studies done in this area quite convincingly demonstrate that the correlation between visual acuity and crash involvement is very low (Shinar and Schieber, 1991). For specific subtasks of driving like reading meters and road signs, of course poor visual acuity is annoying. However, unless it is extremely poor, it does not corrupt the visual information processing involved in the basic driving tasks of steering and speed regulation in interaction with the road environment and other traffic. Maybe this is because the visual information required for these basic tasks is in the low spatial frequencies. Visual functions relevant here have to do with perception of and adaptation to dynamically changing time-to-collision information (Gibson, 1979; Bruce, Green and Georgeson, 1996). Even then, the minimal requirements are low because the driving task leaves plenty of space for compensation on the tactical and operational level. Van Winsum and Brouwer (1997; Van Winsum, 1996) found a strong relationship between an individual's skill in adapting to abrupt speed changes of a lead vehicle, and that same individual's preferred car-following distance, in healthy adult drivers. This fits with the idea that drivers take their maximal performance level in operational subtasks of driving into account when choosing safety margins on the tactical level (see also Summala, 1997).

To be able to talk about the minimal function requirements with regard to attention for driving one must know about a person's level of skill. To paraphrase Welford (1983, pp. 153–154), the more skilled one is, the less function is required when that skill is applied. But it also appears that the nature of functions most predictive of skilled performance changes with the stage of expertise (Ackerman, 1988). In the literature on skill acquisition three phases of development are often distinguished, following a terminology proposed by Fitts (1964): the cognitive, the associative, and the autonomous phase of skill. This distinction is related to the memory representation, as declarative or procedural knowledge or as a combination. When a skill is in the early cognitive phase, as when you start to learn to drive, driving knowledge is declarative and primarily verbal. Knowledge can only influence action through deliberate conscious attention to each separate element of skill. To drive away from a parking lane, you first check the car controls, then start the engine, kick down the clutch, put the gear lever in first, look behind, aside and ahead, wait if necessary and then repeat the looking, indicate direction, release the hand-brake while slowly releasing the clutch and slightly pushing the accelerator down, and steer the vehicle into the lane. With growing experience all these elements presumably combine into one rule in procedural memory, triggered when you step into the car with the intention to go somewhere. The autonomous phase is that stage in skill development in which no deliberate conscious attention is required for applying the skill once the context is right. The example in the introduction of the unconscious driver who drove 23 km illustrates this stage. In the intermediate associative phase, given the proper environmental conditions, elements get associated in short chains, with a requirement for conscious attention only at the start of each short chain. In the example, you might have chunks for 'starting the engine', 'looking', and 'driving away'.

In real life, well-practised actions always require some checks on their progress to establish whether they are running according to plan and whether the plan itself is adequate to achieve the desired outcome. Automatic actions are susceptible to errors (slips of action), because an inappropriate schema is triggered by an ambiguous situation, but presumably also because of spontaneous fluctuations of alertness. Also conscious control is necessary to check for unlikely events which the schemata, which are for routine events, do not foresee. Errors that occur because a required shift to the conscious control mode was not made are sometimes called slips of attention. A train driver who always has a green signal when leaving a certain station will ultimately forget to check it unless he is very disciplined, because it is not informative. One day, however, it may be red; if he hasn't looked, drives off and has an accident, such an accident is assigned to a slip of attention. So the practice of everyday driving is probably more like the associative phase, where shorter or longer chains of chunked elements are alternated with conscious checks and occasional transitions to a consciously controlled mode of information processing. It is believed that even in perfectly healthy persons most accidents are 'caused' by slips of action or slips of attention as described above. These slips do not generally occur because people *cannot* pay attention, but rather because they *do* not. In this respect it is important to refer to a distinction made by Näätänen and Summala (1974, quoted by Summala, 1997) between behaviour ('do') and performance ('can do'): 'Crucial to traffic safety is what the driver actually does in any given traffic situation, rather than his maximal level of performance.'

Ackerman's modified radex model (Ackerman, 1988) describes the relation of 'function classes' to phases of skill acquisition and can be used to predict the association between individual differences in functions and individual differences in performance across levels of skill. In the cognitive phase of skill acquisition, general intellectual functions such as figural, verbal and numerical aptitudes are most predictive of performance. Performance in the associative phase wherein learners develop streamlined procedures depends more on task-specific associations and less on general declarative knowledge. As speed and efficiency of performance develop, the learner becomes less dependent on conscious mediation, and the dependence of performance on general intellectual functions is reduced. Ackerman has shown that performance in this phase is predicted best by perceptual speed, a function that can be measured, e.g. by the proficiency in detection of stimuli that are presented at very short duration. Finally, in the autonomous phase, procedures have been automated and performance is free of demands on conscious processes. In this phase, psychomotor functions such as simple reaction time, movement time, and precision of aiming and movement control become most predictive.

3 Attention and driving in frequent neuropsychological disorders

Frequent neuropsychological disorders will be discussed with regard to their effects on perceptual and cognitive functions that constrain attention in driving. First, conditions affecting sustained attention will be discussed. In view of the hierarchical model of driving and the distinction in levels of skill, it can be expected that particular conditions where the temporary loss of attention is unpredictable and relatively frequent and where it also impairs automatic action are incompatible with driving. Subsequently conditions primarily affecting focused and divided attention will be discussed. On the basis of the previous section we can expect that in experienced drivers there will be little relationship between impairments of general cognitive functions and driving. On the other hand, it can be expected that impaired perceptual and psychomotor speed, important factors in many clinical tests of attention, will be predictive of the quality of driving performance. Because of its hierarchical structure driving allows much compensation for speed limitations, at least as far as safety of driving is concerned. It can be expected therefore that, to be relevant for driving safety, the impairments must be severe and/or accompanied by lacking tactical and strategic compensation. The latter problem will be discussed in relation to impairments of executive functions.

3.1 Problems of sustained attention

3.1.1 Epilepsy

Epilepsy is a condition characterized by *recurrent* electrographic seizures. Epileptic seizures are very common; 1 person in 20 will experience at least one seizure during their lifetime. The prevalence of multiple seizures is much lower, about 1 in 200 (Kolb and Whishaw, 1990).

The principal problem for sustained attention is a complete loss of consciousness after an epileptic insult, resulting in a loss of control of the vehicle and a possible crash. But epilepsy might also have negative effects on driving safety by its influence on electrographic activation and psychological processes in the interrictal period (between seizures) and by the effects of anti-epileptic medication. In practice, in the regulations and guidelines for the assessment of fitness to drive, only the probability of crashing because of a seizure is addressed, and this is based mainly on epidemiological and statistical arguments.

Sonnen (1997) argued that in society there is an over-awareness of this crash risk because of the presumed (a) sudden start, (b) unpredictable nature, (c) high frequency, (d) complete loss of consciousness, and (e) loss of driving ability. In response to these presuppositions he points out that (a) up to 50% of patients have an aura that warns them; (b) provoking circumstances such as sleep, awakening, rest after exercise, photic stimulation, premonition hours ahead, make many seizures not totally unpredictable; (c) many people have only one or two seizures a year; (d) in many seizures consciousness is retained; and (e) some seizures, such as some types of simple partial or myoclonic seizures, do not impair driving ability. From this he concludes that general statements about epilepsy and driving are misleading and rules should be detailed and take individual differences into account. This opinion is shared by many experts in the area of epilepsy and driving, as becomes clear from the consensus statement of the European working group on epilepsy and driving organized by the International Bureau for Epilepsy, formulated in meetings in 1995 and 1996 in Brussels (*Epilepsy and Driving*, 1997).

In this meeting a clear distinction was made between regulations for 'group 1 licences' for private drivers (non-commercial drivers) and 'group 2 licences' for professional drivers, such as bus drivers and lorry drivers (commercial drivers). An important reason for this distinction is that professional drivers usually drive more, have less choice with regard to the time and circumstances of driving, and may have to drive with many passengers. For non-commercial drivers it is argued that a 1% risk of a seizure-related traffic accident in the next year is acceptable based on a comparison with other known risk factors. This leads to only a slight increase in a person's annual risk of being involved in a crash (from 10 to 11%), comparable in size to the effects of gender or region of living, but much smaller than the effect of young age, so this can be considered a conservative approach, erring on the safe side. Calculating this through for the different subcategories of epilepsy and seizures, based on the frequency and nature of recurring seizures, the working group have come to the consensus with regard to the recommended principles for the assessment of fitness to drive for non-commercial drivers (group 1 licences) that is shown in Table 8.1.

According to the working group these principles are completely within the limits of the European Directives for the assessment of fitness to drive issued by the European Commission. The working group states that their directives are as liberal as possible to stimulate compliance with domestic laws, but commensurate with public safety. In countries with very restrictive directives with regard to epilepsy and driving, patients often do not report epilepsy. As a result they might not seek proper medical attention and medication, so the net result of strict regulations may be a decrease in public safety.

With regard to other possible negative effects of epilepsy on driving safety there are a few studies which look at driving behaviour in relation to subclinical epileptiform activity in the EEG. Kasteleijn-Nolst Trenité *et al.* (1987) observed that in dense traffic the frequency of sub-clinical epileptiform EEG discharges was lower than in quiet conditions. This might be a

Table 8.1 Recommended principles for the assessment of fitness to drive (from *Epilepsy and Driving*, 1997)

First seizure	
– No neurological disorder	3–6 months' driving ban
– Neurological disorder	individual assessment, at least 6 months' ban
Epilepsy (>1 seizure, more than 24 hours apart)	1 year driving ban
Exceptions	
– In last year, seizures only during sleep	no ban, but licence only of limited duration (for example, 1 year)
– Sporadic seizures (interval >2 years)	assessment as in case of first seizure
– Progressive neurological disorder	individual assessment, at least 1 year ban
Change of medication	
– Change of medication	driving ban during 0–3 months
– Recurrence in the course of withdrawal or change of medication	assessment as in case of first seizure
– Withdrawal:	
after < 3 years' seizure freedom	driving ban during withdrawal + 3 months
after > = 3 years' seizure freedom	no driving ban during withdrawal or thereafter

contributing factor to the fact that epilepsy-related accidents are often one-sided (Hansotia and Broste, 1991).

The effects of different types of anti-epileptic medication on driving behaviour have not to my knowledge been systematically studied. It is generally assumed, however, that anti-convulsant medication, with the exception of phenobarbital, has only limited perceptual and cognitive side effects, as assessed with neuropsychological measures (e.g. Meador *et al*., 1990).

3.1.2 Excessive daytime sleepiness

Sleep apnoea and narcolepsy cause excessive daytime sleepiness (EDS) and difficulty remaining alert and attentive. In sleep apnoea the alertness problem is a symptom of chronic fatigue caused by an incomplete nocturnal sleep pattern. Because of oxygen shortage that results from respiratory arrests, deep sleep stages are not sustained. Narcolepsy is a chronic clinical syndrome characterized by intermittent episodes of uncontrollable sleep in daytime. The nocturnal sleep of narcoleptics is usually unremarkable. Sleep attacks may occur several times daily under appropriate or inappropriate circumstances, with or without warning. These attacks last from minutes to hours. There may be hypnagogic hallucinations at the onset of sleep and an inability to move in the interval between sleep and arousal (sleep paralysis). Sudden transient loss of muscle tone and pathological muscle weakness during emotional reactions, e.g. laughing and crying, may also occur (cataplexy). Narcolepsy usually persists throughout life. The attacks of somnolence and sleep may be relieved by medical treatment but the emotional muscle weakness is usually not affected by drug therapy (de Groot and Chusid, 1988).

In a number of studies with relatively few subjects these disorders were found to be associated with an increased risk of automobile crashes (e.g. Aldrich, 1989). Detailed analysis of the accident scenarios is lacking but, as with epilepsy, the first risk factor to be considered is that of becoming unconscious (in this case falling asleep) while driving. There is also some published evidence for poor performance on laboratory tests of sustained attention in EDS patients when they are awake. At present, there are no studies in which their actual performance on the road is investigated, however.

When considering the risk of falling asleep while driving, methods for assessing the ease of falling asleep and the ability to stay awake seem to be relevant diagnostic tools (Sangal, Thomas and Mitler, 1992a and b). Surprisingly these two types of tools may measure quite different abilities. The standard test for assessing the ease of falling asleep is the 'Multiple Sleep Latency Test (MSLT)'. After a night's sleep, subjects are asked to get into bed four times throughout the day and try to sleep. Measuring the EEG to mark the onset of sleep and hence the time it takes to fall asleep (sleep latency) is the standard tool for determining pathologic EDS. Often untreated patients have sleep latencies of less than 5 minutes while in healthy controls they are usually above 20 minutes. A test for the ability to stay awake is the 'Maintenance of Wakefulness Test (MWT)' in which subjects are seated upright in bed and are asked to stay awake for 40 minutes; this is also repeated four times over the day after a night's sleep. The sleep latency is the test score, with untreated patients having a median score of 23 minutes while healthy controls seldom fall asleep within the 40 minutes. In their first study Sangal and co-workers found that some patients with abnormal MSLT scores were able to stay awake when asked to do so on the MWT and, conversely, some patients who failed to stay awake on the MWT were unable to fall asleep quickly on the MSLT. In their second study, assessing the effect of treatment, Sangal *et al.* showed a further and more interesting dissociation. In the study, 47 patients with sleep disorders leading to EDS were treated by various therapeutic means ranging from surgery to medication. Before and after treatment the MSLT and MWT were assessed. It appeared that the effect of treatment was strong and significant in the MWT measure but only small and insignificant in the MSLT measure. Sangal *et al.* suggested that 'since the ability to stay awake (and not ability to fall asleep) is a prerequisite for all job-related duties, an objective, physiologically based test such as the MWT should be used to assess the impact of sleep disorders in cases where there is a clinical concern about fitness to drive or work' (1992b, p. 699). Poceta *et al.* (1990) suggested earlier that a patient with an MWT of less than 15 minutes should be advised not to drive, and this opinion appears to be supported by Sangal and co-workers (1992b). Earlier doubts with regard to the validity of the MSLT as a measure for assessing fitness to drive were raised by Aldrich (1989) who found no difference in MSLT between patients with EDS who had been involved in accidents and those who had not.

With regard to the second risk factor, reduced alertness while awake, two recent studies revealed very strong performance decrements (in respectively a visual vigilance task and a visual divided attention task) within a 30 minute period in untreated patients with sleep apnoea and narcolepsy (Findley *et al.*, 1995; George, Boudreau and Smiley, 1996). Interestingly enough, in both studies, the MSLT score was only weakly related to the functional measurements which are more similar to actual driving behaviour. This raises still further doubts about the validity of the MSLT as an index for fitness to drive. Nevertheless, the MSLT is mentioned in some American directives or guidelines as the relevant index (Pakola, Dinges and Pack, 1995).

3.2 Problems with selective attention and basic information processing functions

Many neurological conditions impair basic information processing functions which could have consequences for attention and driving. The discussion will be restricted to three of these, namely stroke, traumatic brain injury and ageing-related cognitive impairments. Most questions regarding fitness to drive asked of a clinical neuropsychologist concern these three frequent conditions. Also, most research concerns these conditions, including some recent studies with large sample sizes. These recent studies will be given most emphasis because older studies have been extensively reviewed previously (e.g. van Zomeren *et al.*, 1987; Brouwer and Withaar, 1997; Withaar, Brouwer and van Zomeren, 2000).

3.2.1 Stroke

Stroke has a high incidence. Yearly in Europe and North America at least 150 in 100,000 persons suffer from a first stroke. Between 30 and 50% of stroke survivors who drove before the stroke resume driving, particularly those who are less disabled in terms of everyday skills (Fisk, Owsley and Vonne Pulley, 1997).

From the perspective of attention and driving, the visual and visuo-spatial impairments after stroke are most important because of their effects on the mental representation of space and on the speed and efficiency of visual scanning. Right-hemisphere stroke is most suspect because of its connection with visuo-spatial impairments, especially the hemi-neglect or hemi-inattention syndrome. The syndrome is characterized by a relative or absolute failure to perceive or to orient to objects in the hemi-space contralateral to the lesion and is more frequent and more persistent after right-hemisphere strokes. In its clinical form hemi-neglect is easy to detect with cancellation tests (many targets missed, most on the left side of the paper) and by observation of IADL performance, e.g. the patient ignoring persons and objects in the room at his left-hand side. The consensus is that hemi-neglect in its clinical form is incompatible with safe driving. In early articles about driving after stroke (reviewed by van Zomeren, Brouwer and Minderhoud, 1987) one finds frequent references to hemi-neglect observed during the test-ride as a reason for test failure. Patients with persistent hemi-neglect may be difficult to convince of their unfitness as the spatial impairments are often accompanied by a lack of awareness of the disability.

Because driving is a spatial task, it can be expected that on average right-hemisphere stroke patients do worse on driving tests than left-hemisphere cases. Indeed most studies in the field indicate somewhat higher percentages of unfitness in right-hemisphere cases (Sundet, Goffeng and Hofft, 1995). The latter authors warn that, due to differences in sample selection, the precise numbers should be treated with caution and not be taken as true estimates of hemisphere differences. Rather they indicate that impairments after lesions in either hemisphere may render the patient unfit for driving.

An important recent study, which has a predominance of subjects with left-hemisphere stroke, was published by Hannen, Hartje and Skreczek (1998) who assessed 116 persons with acquired brain injuries (94 CVA, 19 TBI and 3 from other etiologies) with a test battery aimed at driving-relevant basic information processing functions and an on-road driving test. Neurological and ophthalmologic assessments also took place. Fifty-seven per cent of the subjects had a diagnosis of aphasia, and, related to that, there were more cases with left than with right-hemisphere damage (LH 62%, RH 14%, bilateral 24%). The average age of the sample was 46 and they were tested on average 22 months after disease/injury. Twenty-four per cent had resumed driving.

The psychological test battery consisted of tests of information processing speed in simple tasks (tachistoscopic perception, visual reaction time, and visual search) and in more complex tasks (divided attention). An intelligence test was also administered. The on-road driving assessment was made on the basis of a 50 km drive with city, rural and highway driving. Patients drove an automatic car that could be adapted for hemiplegia. During the ride some 300 items were judged as correct or incorrect. The outcome was summarized in thirteen driver behaviour categories, e.g. lateral position control in ongoing conditions (Spurhalten), and when merging or after turning

(Spurverhalten) and actively creating a safety margin when changing lanes, at intersections and narrowing of the lane (Sichern). Also the inspector sometimes made an intervention to prevent a crash or serious traffic conflict; these were separately noted in the protocol. Immediately after the ride, the inspector judged the global quality of performance on a score from 1 to 6, where 1 is very good and 6 is insufficient. For the purpose of this study, scores of 5 and 6 were considered as failing.

Results: 42% failed the test-ride. No significant effects were found of the laterality of brain damage and of the presence of aphasia or hemiplegia, but the effect of a visual field defect appeared to be very strong: 11 out of 13 patients with this impairment failed the on-road test; in 10 it came to an intervention. The pass/fail scores of the persons who had resumed driving were not significantly better than those of the others. In a step-wise discriminant analysis procedure, the score on a divided attention condition of the Wiener Determinations Gerät (WDG-R) was a significant predictor of passing the on-road driving test (67% correct predictions). Taking this variable already into account, other psychological test scores did not contribute significantly. With the combined medical and psychological scores the percentage of correctly predicted pass–fail scores is 73 at maximum (predictors: WDG-R score and presence of visual field defects; 20% false negatives, 7% false positives).

In the study discussed above, visual field defect was a strong predictor of unfitness to drive. Unfortunately the procedures for assessing the field defects are not explained in the article so it is impossible to assess how far hemi-inattention or more subtle spatial impairments could have been involved besides pure visual field defects such as homonymous hemianopia. Many persons with hemi-neglect also suffer from homonymous hemianopia. In hemianopia there is blindness for one side of the visual field because of post-chiasmatic damage of the optic tract.

According to Zihl (1995) pure hemianopia may be compensated for effectively. He presented a visual scanning test to 60 subjects with pure hemianopia. Cases with associated neuropsychological syndromes such as hemi-neglect and aphasia were excluded. Zihl found that scanning behaviour in 40% of this group was completely normal, as were search times. In the subgroup which did not compensate effectively, CT and NMR examination often revealed additional damage to the ipsilateral posterior thalamus or the parieto-occipital cortex. This suggests that the scanning problems that hemianopes may have are related more to spatial impairments than to the visual field loss.

A similar suggestion, namely that it is not so much the hemianopia, but rather co-occurring cognitive and spatial impairments, which determine poor scanning behaviour, was made by the medical department of the Dutch licensing authority (Centraal Bureau Rijvaardigheidsbewijzen, Rijswijk). In an ongoing research project they have officially assessed the driving performance of more than 100 hemianopes (Warmink, personal communication). In most countries it is illegal to drive with hemianopia. In the Netherlands, however, following an early convincing demonstration by Vos and Riemersma (1976) that a hemianope can be a safe driver, the policy has been to decide on their fitness on the basis of a test-ride for the assessment of 'practical fitness to drive'. In this ride the effectiveness of scanning behaviour is critically assessed. In a majority of cases this policy led to a positive decision with regard to fitness to drive in hemianopes who opted for the test-ride (Warmink, personal communication). Although this may not be a representative sample of hemianopes, the high proportion of positive decisions strongly raises the question of whether the absolute ban on driving for hemianopes that many countries apply is justified. In my department this is currently being tested in a study of how far neuropsychological test performance in the areas of visual perception and selective attention can predict fitness to drive in hemianopes both before and after visual scanning training.

3.2.2 Traumatic brain injury

Traumatic brain injury (TBI) has a high incidence. In the Netherlands almost 1 per 1,000 inhabitants is yearly admitted into hospital because of TBI, usually a closed head injury (CHI). These figures include cases of widely varying severity, with durations of disturbed consciousness (coma and post traumatic amnesia, PTA) varying between around six hours and permanent. In only a small minority is the question of fitness to drive ever officially considered – usually in very severe patients with long coma durations who have been treated in a rehabilitation hospital after the acute stage.

Leaving aside the incidental cases of post-traumatic epilepsy, problems with sustaining attention are *not* more frequent in CHI patients than in healthy control subjects (reviewed in van Zomeren and Brouwer, 1994). When reaction time tasks or visual search tasks are used as tests of sustained attention, CHI patients perform more slowly on average than healthy controls, but the difference is present already from the beginning and does not increase with time-on-task. Therefore it is better understood as another manifestation of the very general finding that perceptual, cognitive and psychomotor processes take significantly more time after CHI. The extent of slowing appears to be determined by the severity of the CHI, the time since injury and the complexity of the task.

As driving has many elements of time pressure, slow information processing can be a problem, particularly when it is very extreme. On the operational level there is little opportunity for compensation and therefore it is not surprising that there is much evidence for negative effects of severe TBI in studies where operational aspects of driving are studied in detail. In the Netherlands, four studies with small samples of severe TBI patients – mostly young male adults tested years after injury – have been performed in which important operational aspects of driving were studied in quantitative terms, alongside a comprehensive neuropsychological test battery of visual search and visuo-motor functions (see Brouwer and Withaar, 1997, for a review). The operational driving tasks comprised lateral position control (steering skill), braking speed and gap judgement latency at an intersection. Patients were significantly impaired with regard to the speed or precision of these operational tasks. In the patients, the quantitative measures of operational level driving skills had moderate to high correlations with scores on corresponding neuropsychological tests of visual search, visual reaction time and visual–motor coordination.

In two of these studies tactical aspects of driving were also assessed in the form of expert judgements of traffic insight and traffic perception made during a comprehensive test-ride in various traffic conditions. The tactical aspects had only very low correlations with test scores of information processing speed and visual–motor coordination and also with scores on tests of verbal memory and planning. What did appear to be important here was driving experience. Significant positive relationships were found between the total distance driven and the judged quality of tactical driving skill.

Brooke *et al.* (1992) studied 13 moderately to severely concussed patients 3 to 6 months post-injury. A neuropsychological evaluation was carried out as well as an on-road test, resulting in a global pass/fail rating and a driving performance score. They found a moderately high correlation between a composite score of the Tactual Performance Test and the Trail Making Test and the global pass/fail rating but no appreciable correlations of the latter rating with general measures of intelligence and verbal skills. Brooke *et al.* clinically characterized those patients who failed the on-road test (5 out of 13) as suffering from visuo-spatial deficits or attentional impairments resulting in extreme slowness or distractibility.

Korteling and Kaptein (1996) studied 38 very severe TBI subjects (mean coma duration of 33 days), at least one year after injury, who wanted to resume driving. Four neuropsychological tests were selected: a perceptual speed test, the Symbol Digit Substitution test, a time estimation task and a tracking/reaction dual task. Severity of injury and previous driving experience were included as predictive measures as well. These measures were compared with the criterion standard, the outcome of an on-road test carried out by the Division of Adaptations of the Dutch Licensing Authority (CBR). Driving competence was judged on an 8-point scale covering temporal and attentional aspects, flexibility, technical driving and traffic rules. The study found that the perceptual speed and time estimation tasks correlated most highly with the criterion measures. These two measures, together with coma duration and previous driving experience, resulted in the best regression equation and together could explain 35% of the variance.

Lundqvist *et al.* (1997) tested 29 patients with brain injury (16 with TBI and 13 with subarachnoidal haemorrhage) on average 3.7 years after injury/illness. Also, 29 healthy control subjects were tested, individually matched to the patients on age, gender and education. Mean age was 45 and more than 80% in each group had held a licence for over ten years. All subjects underwent a structured interview, a neuropsychological examination, a test-ride in an advanced driving simulator, and an on-road driving test. In the interview, driving history and driving habits were assessed, e.g. avoidance of specific driving situations. In the neuropsychological examination, chronometric tests were used of both simple (e.g. finger tapping speed) and complex information processing (e.g. the PASAT and a computerized divided attention test) while problem-solving and memory functions were also tested. In the advanced driving simulator, high and low predictability scenarios were used; a distracting task was presented three times during driving. Measures of tactical aspects of driving reflecting safety margins collected in the predictable situation were (minimal) time and distance to collision. A measure of operational driving skill was the brake reaction time to unexpected complex visual stimuli (e.g. sudden emergency stop of the lead vehicle) in the unpredictable situation. On-road testing took place in the subject's own car on a 25 km standardized route with a variety of traffic situations, including city, country road and highway. A certified driving inspector scored five aspects of driving (speed, manoeuvring, lateral position, traffic behaviour, attention) on scales from 1 to 5 with ratings of 1 or 2 failing. Speed was evaluated in relation to current traffic demands. Manoeuvring was the handling and control of the vehicle, e.g. steering and braking. Lateral position was the placing of the vehicle in lanes, at roundabouts and at intersections. Attention referred to noticing relevant traffic signs, directions and other road users. Traffic behaviour included planning the ride and adjusting to traffic rules and other road users. Based on these scores, an overall rating of driving quality was made. The same inspector rated both the patient and the matched control subject. The inspector did not know beforehand which pair member was the patient.

In the interview, patients reported significantly more avoidance of long-distance driving. Also generally they had reduced the frequency of driving. The neuropsychological tests indicated very significant differences between the groups in memory and problem-solving, and in timed and time-pressured complex information processing tests. On average, the patient group appeared to be aware of deficits because they rated their own performance as slower and less efficient than the control group. The simulated driving revealed a slightly slower reaction to the unpredictable visual stimuli and a tendency towards larger safety margins (giving themselves more time) in the patient group. The effects of distraction were equal in both groups.

In the on-road driving test, the traffic inspectors classified 41% of the patients and 10% of the controls as failing on the overall quality score. The difference between the groups was present on all subscales but only significantly so on the scales of attention and traffic behaviour. When looking at correlations between neuropsychological measures and the on-road driving scores it appeared that the timed and time-pressured information processing tests were most strongly related to the on-road test scores, with correlations in the order of +.50. Interestingly enough there was no appreciable correlation between the simulator scores and either the neuropsychological or on-road test scores. Also gender, age, diagnosis and residual neurological symptoms were not significantly correlated with the on-road test scores.

Group studies on TBI injury run the danger of losing sight of the individual differences caused by the location of lesions. Most TBI patients are concussions, and therefore diffuse axonal injury, which is most easily linked to mental slowness and divided attention, may be a central problem. Nevertheless, with increasing severity, the probability of additional focal contusions increases. If manifestly abnormal driving behaviour is observed in a subject who also has severe focal brain damage, it is tempting to causally relate these. In one of our studies on the effect of very severe concussion on driving competence we assessed the quality of everyday driving with the so-called Test for Advanced Drivers (van Zomeren *et al.*, 1988). During the test, one patient featured particularly dangerous driving, rigidly sticking to his rights and failing to take into account traffic-rule-breaking behaviours of other traffic participants. For example, when approaching an intersection where he must turn left he 'pre-sorted' towards the outer left side of his lane although he saw a bus approaching from the opposite direction which drove in the middle of the road and could not do otherwise because of parked vehicles. This behaviour would either lead to a collision or a blocked traffic situation. Confronted with a critical comment of the driving examiner, he answered that he always stuck to his rights whatever the behaviour of others. At the time he participated in our research he had given up driving. In a very short period he had been involved in three crashes and he could not understand why these crashes had occurred. In addition to diffuse brain injury, he had sustained severe left prefrontal penetrating damage. When casually discussing our findings with a good friend of the subject, the friend said that our subject had always been like that, even before the accident. It is very difficult to weigh the evidence in such a case. Given the nature of the accidents that cause TBI, it is not unlikely that persons with a premorbid accident-prone behavioural style are overrepresented in the population of TBI victims.

3.2.3 Studies on ageing-related cognitive impairment

In many countries old age is a significant factor in the driving legislation in the sense that, starting from a certain age, usually 70, a medical and/or ophthalmologic assessment of fitness to drive is obligatory. Traditionally, the emphasis has been on detecting poor visual acuity. In recent years this has been criticized and it has been suggested that assessment of higher-order aspects of visual perception (e.g. as assessed in tests of visual selective attention) or dementia screening is more relevant (Shinar and Schieber, 1991;

Brouwer and Ponds, 1994). This is based on the evidence that persons with dementia and/or higher-order impairments of visual perception are overrepresented in accidents (Lundberg *et al.*, 1997; Owsley *et al.*, 1998). Also, it has been known for many years that situations that older drivers find particularly difficult and where they are overrepresented in crash statistics are characterized by divided attention and time pressure (Brouwer and Ponds, 1994).

Because of the large numbers of older drivers, it is comparatively easier to do research on crash involvement in relation to impairments than in the neurological conditions discussed above. As crashes are very infrequent and most often have multiple causes, crash involvement must be viewed as a relatively unreliable indicator of individual unsafe traffic behaviour and therefore many subjects are required in such studies.

In a series of articles, Ball, Owsley and co-workers (see Owsley *et al.*, 1998) described a procedure for validating their measure of the 'Useful Field of View' (UFOV). The UFOV is meant to measure spatial visual attention and is composed of several subtests tapping speed of processing of centrally and (near) peripherally presented visual stimuli, both in focused (central or peripheral task only) and divided attention conditions (central and peripheral detection), with and without distraction stimuli in the periphery.

In the state of Alabama, they selected a large sample of 294 drivers aged between 55 and 90 years on the basis of the number of at-fault accidents during the five preceding years. They obtained equally sized and equally aged subgroups of drivers, without any crashes, with 1–3, and with four or more crashes. All took part in an extensive research protocol involving a visual examination and a cognitive evaluation, including the Mattis Organic Mental Status Syndrome Examination and the UFOV. The UFOV did best in explaining crash frequency.

Apart from *post hoc* explanations of crash involvement, the UFOV score was also shown to predict crashes in a prospective study in the same sample (Owsley *et al.*, 1998). Of the 294 drivers aged between 55 and 87 followed over a three-year period 56 were involved in at least one and 11 of them experienced two or more crashes. They found that older drivers with a UFOV reduction of 40% or more were 2.2 times more likely to crash than those with less reduction. This association was primarily mediated by performance in the divided attention condition under brief target durations. In their computations the authors adjusted for age, sex, race, chronic medical conditions, mental status and days driven per week. Unfortunately, they put all the emphasis on UFOV results, without analysing or discussing the predictive value of other cognitive and perceptual tests, except for mental status. Therefore it is not known at this moment how unique the strong association with crash involvement is for the UFOV. The finding that the divided attention condition of the UFOV is more sensitive than the visually demanding distraction condition suggests that cognitive impairment is an important element in the association with crashes.

A further study on subjects selected on the basis of crash involvement was carried out in Sweden by Johansson *et al.* (1996) who studied 37 drivers over 65 years old convicted for various traffic violations, and a matched control group. In 62% of the convicted drivers the reason for conviction was a crash. The other 38% were convicted for other violations such as speeding, not stopping at a stop sign or red light, and driving outside the right lane. Subjects received a thorough medical evaluation. Cognitive status was assessed by the Clinical Dementia Rating Scale (CDR), the MMSE, a five-item recall test, and a test for visual-spatial abilities (copying a cube). The medical clinical evaluation did not reveal differences between the convicted drivers and the controls. However, significant differences were found in the cognitive evaluation, with the drivers convicted for crashes obtaining lower scores on all tests, including the CDR and the MMSE. Questionable dementia (CDR = 0.5) and mild dementia (CDR = 1) were found significantly more frequently in this group with crashes, but not in the subgroup convicted for violations.

There are at least six recent studies where on-road driving performance and neuropsychological functions of cognitively impaired older subjects and age-matched healthy control subjects are assessed. These studies are discussed by Withaar, Brouwer and Van Zomeren (2000). Findings in these studies may be summarized as follows: (1) cognitively impaired subjects as a group perform significantly worse than controls on both neuropsychological and driving measures. (2) Moderately high correlations between specific neuropsychological test scores and driving performance measures could be established. Performance on a number of tests in the domain of attention is a better predictor of driving behaviour than MMSE scores or other global indicators of severity of illness. (3) However, a large range in test scores has been found, both in subgroups of poor and good performing drivers, making it difficult to discriminate between cognitively impaired subjects who are fit or unfit to drive. The review goes on to discuss the methodological difficulties in the field of dementia and driving (subject selection, the choice of tests, and the operationalization of driving performance) and concludes with suggestions for future research.

3.3 Impairments of executive functions: attentional deficit hyperactivity disorder

Several recent papers suggest unsafe driver behaviour in adolescents and young adults with ADHD symptoms. As discussed below, this may be partly determined by attentional impairments, but behavioural disorders, more related to comorbidity than to ADHD as such, may also be implicated. The cardinal symptoms of Attentional Deficit Hyperactivity Disorder (ADHD) are hyperactivity, impulsivity and distractibility. As such symptoms have also been observed after frontal lesions, the hypothesis of frontal lobe dysfunction in ADHD has been popular. This hypothesis is supported by several recent studies of brain physiology, which demonstrate relative hypofrontality in unmedicated ADHD. In cognitive terms the cardinal symptoms are explained by a deficit in the executive function of inhibition. Pennington and Ozonoff (1996) did a meta-analysis on tests of executive function in ADHD and found the most consistent group effects in specific measures of response inhibition, e.g. Go–nogo tasks. In the reviewed studies other cognitive functions had also been assessed and in most cases ADHD was not found to impair verbal and visuo-spatial measures and general intelligence.

Murphy and Barkley (1996) estimated that the disorder persists into adolescence in 50–70% and into adulthood in 30–50% of cases. In ADHD comorbidity is often observed. In the realm of traffic safety particularly, comorbidity with conduct disorder (CD) appears important. CD has as its cardinal symptom multiple antisocial behaviours that are repetitive and persistent. Pennington and Ozonoff (1996) reported on many studies on CD where relationships were found with verbal deficits and a lower IQ, but they did not find any reports on executive or attentional dysfunction in CD when the effects of ADHD had been controlled. So, the effects of CD on driving safety must not be viewed as attentional effects in the conventional sense.

Barkley *et al.* (1993) compared two groups of teenagers and young adults 3–5 years after original diagnosis, an ADHD group (n = 35) and a control group without ADHD, with regard to parent ratings of negative driving outcomes and a rating scale of driving behaviour. In comparison with the control group, subjects with ADHD had more, and more serious, car crashes for which they were legally at fault more often, and got more traffic citations, particularly for speeding. These effects were more pronounced in a subgroup with comorbid oppositional defiant and CD symptoms.

Realizing the limitations of working with parent ratings only, Barkley, Murphy and Kwasnik (1996) did a further study with an extensive collection of dependent variables:

- Self-ratings of driving history, traffic violations, and crashes.
- Self- and other-ratings of driving habits (e.g. driving within the speed limits).
- A video test of driving knowledge.
- A computer simulated driving test combining steering with visual reaction time.
- Official state driving records from the Department of Motor Vehicles in their region.

Twenty-five young adults with ADHD were compared with an age-, gender- and education-matched control group. It appeared that the groups particularly differed in terms of unsafe aspects of driving behaviour as indicated by the behavioural ratings and corroborated by the official driving records.

ADHD young adults were cited more often for speeding, were more likely to have their licences suspended, were involved in more, and more serious, crashes, and were rated by themselves and others as using poorer driving habits. No differences were found between the groups in the video test of driving knowledge. The ADHD young adults performed slightly worse on the computer-simulated driving test, in a measure of steering control.

In their conclusion the authors proposed that 'ADHD does not interfere with driving knowledge so much as with actual performance (motor control) during vehicle operation' (p. 1089). This formulation suggests a possible contribution to unsafe driver behaviour in ADHD of impaired motor control processes, which could easily be related to the attentional impairment with regard to response inhibition discussed above.

However, it cannot be assessed from this study what the role of comorbid disorders may have been. In a study by Nada-Raja *et al.* (1997), a relatively pure group of adolescents with CD was compared with an adolescent ADHD group with regard to driving offences in a two-year period following assessment of their mental health status at age 15. The groups were selected from a birth cohort of 916 New Zealand adolescents. The authors concluded that most of the driving offences were associated with CD rather than ADHD symptoms. So, in conclusion, there is no convincing evidence for implicating the attentional impairment as such in ADHD as a causal factor in ADHD young adults' high involvement in car accidents and driving offences.

4 Summary and discussion

A cognitive framework was chosen where attention is viewed as a multiply determined dynamic cognitive state which is triggered by and anticipates the task context. In this framework, problems of attention in driving can emerge in many ways but only some are related to brain injury. The most common causes of unsafe traffic behaviour are *slips of attention*, when conscious attention is allocated to non-driving activities, e.g. telephoning or worrying about daily hassles. Such incidents typically are not related to neuropsychological impairments but rather to motivational factors or inadequate risk estimation (Summala, 1997). Bluntly speaking, there is enough attention but it is inappropriately spent on non-driving tasks.

The situation is quite different in the cases described under the heading of *sustained attention*. Instead of wrongly allocated attention, occasionally there is *no attention at all*. Epilepsy, narcolepsy or sleep apnoea can cause such a temporary loss of attention while driving. Directives for assessing the risk of individual cases with these disorders were given; for epilepsy following the suggestions of the International Bureau for Epilepsy (*Epilepsy and Driving*, 1997). For narcolepsy and sleep apnoea which both lead to excessive daytime sleepiness (EDS) it was argued that methods assessing maintenance of wakefulness and sustained task performance are more relevant than the frequently used sleep latency tests. As a research issue I suggest comparing and validating the various clinical measurements for assessing and treating EDS. Driving simulator scenarios representing difficult situations for EDS patients could be used as external criteria. The same measurements and scenarios might also be used to research effects of subclinical epileptiform EEG discharges and partial seizures. The epilepsy directives are possibly too strict for partial seizures.

In disorders characterized by impairments of selective attention and basic information processing functions, unsafe traffic behaviour may occur in spite of the fact that no distracting activities are undertaken and the person is fully alert. In hemi-neglect and related spatial disorders, *spatial deficits of attention* occur because the spatial coordinates for shaping the attentional schema are impaired. Hemi-neglect, as clinically observed and objectified with cancellation tests, is incompatible with driving. In cases of pure homonymous hemianopia, fitness to drive may be preserved, particularly if visual search test scores are normal. It should be urgently investigated whether the absolute ban on driving for hemianopes that many countries apply is justified. The hypothesis is that in those hemianopes who are actually unfit, there are additional cognitive impairments.

Apart from these specific visuo-spatial impairments, more global impairments after brain injury were also discussed. In the areas of stroke, traumatic brain injury and ageing-related cognitive impairments the literature quite convincingly supports the expectations formulated on the basis of Ackerman's model (1988). General intelligence, language and memory functions do not correlate with driving quality at all. In studies where brain-damaged subjects with only a little driving experience were included, these subjects performed relatively poorly. This suggests that a higher level of skill reduces the negative effects of brain injury on performing that skill. As expected, perceptual and psychomotor speed, important factors in many clinical tests of attention, were correlated moderately highly with driving quality, particularly on the operational level.

The speed-related deficits of attention we are talking about here could be called *divided attention deficits* because too much information must be processed through the attentional schemata in too little time. In a number of studies it proved that particularly time-pressed divided attention tasks had moderately strong relationships with measures of driving quality. Also, in on-road tests the largest difference between brain-injured and healthy groups tends to occur in divided attention situations. The practical consequence is that divided attention conditions should be part of the neuropsychological assessment with regard to fitness to drive. A more theoretical question, to be approached separately for different disorders, is what determines the greater sensitivity of divided attention conditions.

Although correlations between neuropsychological test scores and on-road driving competence are moderately high, they are too low to permit the use of neuropsychological tests as an exclusive basis for deciding unfitness. Rather, neuropsychological testing should be part of a multidisciplinary assessment, also including the expertise of a specialized driving examiner. This combination of expertise is particularly important when the question arises as to whether and how poor driving competence in a particular client could be improved with training and instruction.

In the last section on *executive functions and driving*, ADHD and related disorders as they extend into young adulthood were discussed. The literature revealed that most of the driving offences are associated with conduct disorder, a frequent comorbidity, rather than ADHD symptoms. It was concluded that there is no convincing evidence for implicating cognitive impairments in ADHD as a causal factor in the high involvement of ADHD young adults in car accidents and driving offences. Nevertheless, for practical purposes, it quite relevant to look at combinations of individual risk factors. As early as 1932 Bingham stressed the importance of a combination of risk factors in his classic article about the accident-prone driver.

References

Ackerman, P.L. (1988). Determinants of individual differences during skill acquisition: cognitive abilities and information processing. *Journal of Experimental Psychology: General*, *117*, 288–318.

Aldrich, M.S. (1989). Automobile accidents in patients with sleep disorders. *Sleep*, *12*, 487–494.

Barkley, R.A., Guevremont, D.C., Anastopoulos, A.D., Du Paul, G.J. and Shelton, T.L. (1993). Driving-related risks and outcomes of attention deficit hyperactivity disorder in adolescents and young adults: a 3- to 5-year follow-up survey. *Pediatrics*, *92*, 212–218.

Barkley, R.A., Murphy, K.R. and Kwasnik, D. (1996). Motor vehicle driving competencies and risks in teens and young adults with attention deficit hyperactivity disorder. *Pediatrics*, *98*, 1089–1095.

Bingham, W.V. (1932). The accident-prone driver. *The Human Factor*, *6*, 158–169.

Brooke, M.M., Questad, K.A., Patterson, D.R. and Valois, T.A. (1992). Driving evaluation after traumatic brain injury. *American Journal of Physical Medicine and Rehabilitation*, *71*, 177–182.

Brouwer, W.H. and Ponds, R.W.H.M. (1994). Driving competence in older persons. *Disability and Rehabilitation*, *16*, 149–161.

Brouwer, W.H. and Withaar, F.K. (1997). Fitness to drive after traumatic brain injury. *Neurospsychological Rehabilitation*, *7*, 177–193.

Bruce, V., Green, P.R. and Georgeson, M.A. (1996). *Visual Perception, Physiology, Psychology, and Ecology*. Hove: Psychology Press.

de Groot, J. and Chusid, J.G. (1988). *Correlative Neuroanatomy*. East Norwalk, CT: Appleton and Lange.

Epilepsy and Driving, A European View (1997). Ed. A.E.H. Sonnen. Heemstede, the Netherlands: International Bureau for Epilepsy.

Findley, L., Unverzagt, M., Guchu, R. *et al.* (1995). Vigilance and automobile accidents in patients with sleep apnea or narcolepsy. *Chest*, *108*, 619–624.

Fisk, G.D., Owsley, C. and Vonne Pulley, L. (1997). Driving after stroke: driving exposure, advice, and evaluations. *Archives of Physical Medicine and Rehabilitation*, *78*, 1338–1345.

Fitts, P.M. (1964). Human motor learning. In A.W. Melton (ed.) *Categories of Human Learning*. New York: Academic Press, pp. 253–265.

George, C.F.P., Boudreau, A.C. and Smiley, A. (1996). Comparison of simulated driving performance in narcolepsy and sleep apnea patients. *Sleep*, *19*, 9, 711–717.

Gibson, J.J. (1979). *The Ecological Approach to Visual Perception*. Boston, MA: Houghton Mifflin.

Hannen, P., Hartje, W. and Skreczek, W. (1998). Beurteilung der Fahreignung nach Hirnschädigung: Neuropsychologische Diagnostik und Fahrprobe. *Nervenarzt*, *69*, 864–872.

Hansotia, P. and Broste, S.K. (1991). The effect of epilepsy or diabetes mellitus on the risk of automobile accidents. *New England Journal of Medicine*, *343*, 22–26.

Johansson, K., Bronge, L., Lundberg, C., Persson, A., Seideman, M. and Viitanen, M. (1996). Can a physician recognize an older driver with increased crash risk potential? *Journal of the American Geriatrics Society*, *44*, 1198–1204.

Kasteleijn-Nolst Trenité, D.G.A., Riemersma, J.B.J., Binnie, C.D., Smit, A.M. and Meinardi, H. (1987). The influence of subclinical epileptiform EEG discharges on driving behaviour. *Electroencephalography and Clinical Neurophysiology*, *67*, 167–170.

Kolb, B. and Whishaw, I.Q. (1990). *Fundamentals of Human Neuropsychology*. New York: Freeman and comp.

Korteling, J.E. and Kaptein, N.A. (1996). Neuropsychological driving fitness tests for brain-damaged subjects. *Archives of Physical Medicine and Rehabilitation*, *77*, 138–145.

Lundberg, C., Johansson, K., Ball, K. *et al.* (1997). Dementia and driving: an attempt at consensus. *Alzheimer's Disease and Associated Disorders*, *11*, 28–37.

Lundqvist, A., Alinder, J., Alm, H., Gerdle, B., Levander, S. and Rönnberg, J. (1997). Neuropsychological aspects of driving after brain lesion: simulator study and on-road driving. *Applied Neuropsychology*, *4*, 220–230.

Meador, K.J., Loring, D.E., Huh, K., Calagher, B.B. and King, D.W. (1990). Comparative cognitive effects of anticonvulsants. *Neurology*, *40*, 391–394.

Michon, J.A. (1971). *Psychonomie Onderweg (inaugural lecture)*. Groningen: Wolters Noordhoff.

Murphy, K. and Barkley, R.A. (1996). Attentional Deficit Hyperactivity Disorder adults: comorbidities and adaptive impairments. *Comprehensive Psychiatry*, *37*, 6, 393–401.

Nada-Raja, S., Langley, J.D., McGee, R., Williams, S.M., Begg, D.J. and Reeder, A.I. (1997). Inattentive and hyperactive behaviors and driving offenses in adolescence. *Journal of the American Academy of Child and Adolescent Psychiatry*, *36*, 4, 515–522.

Neisser, U. (1976). *Cognition and Reality*. San Francisco, CA: Freeman.

Owsley, C., Ball, K., McGwin, G., Sloane, M.E., Roenker, D.L., White, M.F. and Overley, T. (1998). Visual processing impairment and risk of motor vehicle crash among older adults. *JAMA*, *279*, 1083–1088.

Pakola, S.J., Dinges, D.F. and Pack, A.I. (1995). Driving and sleepiness: review of regulations and guidelines for commercial and noncommercial drivers with sleep apnea and narcolepsy. *Sleep*, *18*, 9, 787–796.

Pennington, B.F. and Ozonoff, S. (1996). Executive functions and developmental psychopathology. *Journal of Child Psychology and Psychiatry*, *37*, 51–87.
Poceta, J.S., Ho, S., Jeong, D. and Mitler, M.M. (1990). The maintenance of wakefulness test in obstructive sleep apnea syndrome. *Sleep Research*, *19*, 268.
Sangal, R.B., Thomas, L. and Mitler, M.M. (1992a). The maintenance of wakefulness test (MWT) and the multiple sleep latency test (MSLT) measure different abilities in patients with sleep disorders. *Chest*, *101*, 898–902.
Sangal, R.B., Thomas, L. and Mitler, M.M. (1992b). Disorders of excessive sleepiness: treatment improves ability to stay awake but does not reduce sleepiness. *Chest*, *102*, 699–703.
Schenck, C.H. and Mahowald, M.W. (1995) A polysomnographically documented case of adult somnambulism with long-distance automobile driving and frequent nocturnal violence: parasomnia with continuing danger as a noninsane automatism? *Sleep*, *18*, 9, 765–772.
Shinar, D. and Schieber, F. (1991). Visual requirements for safety and mobility of older drivers. *Human Factors*, *33*, 507–519.
Sonnen, A.E.H. (1997). General principles of assessment and the concept of acceptable risk. In A.E.H. Sonnen (ed.) *Epilepsy and Driving, A European View*. Heemstede, the Netherlands: The International Bureau for Epilepsy, pp. 13–32.
Summala, H. (1997). Hierarchical models of behavioural adaptation and traffic accidents. In T. Rothengatter and E. Carbonell Vaya (eds) *Traffic and Transport Psychology, Theory and Application*. Oxford: Elsevier, pp. 41–52.
Sundet, K., Goffeng, L. and Hofft, E. (1995). To drive or not to drive: neuropsychological assessment for driver's licence among stroke patients. *Scandinavian Journal of Psychology*, *36*, 47–58.
Van Winsum, W. (1996) From adaptive control to adaptive driver behaviour. University of Groningen: Doctoral dissertation.
Van Winsum, W. and Brouwer, W.H. (1997). Time-headway in car-following and operational performance during unexpected braking. *Perceptual and Motor Skills*, *84*, 1247–1257.
van Zomeren, A.H. and Brouwer, W.H. (1994). *The Clinical Neuropsychology of Attention*. New York: Oxford University Press.
van Zomeren, A.H., Brouwer, W.H. and Minderhoud, J.M. (1987). Acquired brain damage and car driving: a review. *Archives of Physical Medicine and Rehabilitation*, *68*, 697–705.
van Zomeren, A.H., Brouwer, W.H., Rothengatter, J.A. and Snoek, J.W. (1988). Fitness to drive a car after recovery from severe head injury. *Archives of Physical and Medical Rehabilitation*, *69*, 90–96.
Vos, J.J. and Riemersma, J.B.J. (1976). On the behavior in traffic of a homonymous hemianope. *Ophthalmologia*, *173*, 427–428.
Welford, A.T. (1983). Motor skills and aging. In J.A. Mortimer, F.J. Pirozzolo and G.J. Maletta (eds) *The Aging Motor System*. New York: Praeger.
Withaar, F.K., Brouwer, W.H. and van Zomeren, A.H. (2000). Fitness to drive in older drivers with cognitive impairment. *Journal of the International Neuropsychological Society*, *6*, 480–490.
Zihl, J. (1995). Visual scanning behavior in patients with homonymous hemianopia. *Neuropsychologia*, *33*, 287–303.

Part III

Pathologies of attention

Chapter 9

Attention after traumatic brain injury

Michel Leclercq and Philippe Azouvi

Traumatic brain injury (TBI) is probably the neurological condition that has been the most extensively studied in the neuropsychological literature on attentional impairments. Indeed, attentional disorders are, along with memory problems and personality and behavioural modifications, among the most prominent problems exhibited by TBI patients. Moreover, these problems may be long-lasting, particularly in severely injured individuals, and may compromise social and vocational reintegration. Attentional difficulties may be reported by TBI patients themselves, or, more frequently, by their relatives or by rehabilitation professionals (for a comparison of complaints frequency between different sources see Leclercq, Deloche and Rousseaux, Chapter 3 in this book). Attentional deficits may interfere with the rehabilitation programme of the TBI person. As pointed out by Lezak (1987):

> A careful analysis of the rehabilitation candidate's attentional deficits is often of primary importance both in evaluating the patient's rehabilitation potential and in determining the order in which training procedures can effectively be undertaken. When attentional problems are pronounced, they need to be dealt with before any other cognitive retraining efforts can be successful.
>
> (p. 44)

However, although there is a consensus among rehabilitation professionals on the high prevalence of attentional deficits after TBI, there is much less consensus on the nature and mechanisms of underlying cognitive impairments.

The first part of this chapter presents clinical and behavioural data on attentional impairments after TBI. The second part is a review of experimental studies on each main attentional component, as described in detail in the two theoretical chapters of this book (Chapters 1 and 2), with particular emphasis on the van Zomeren and Brouwer (1994) framework. A tentative synthesis of the currently available data will be presented. Most of the data cited in this chapter come from studies on severe or very severe TBI. However, mild or moderate TBI individuals may also complain of attentional problems (Binder, 1986; Bernstein, 1999) and show objective deficits on neuropsychological tests, particularly in the early post-injury phase (McLean *et al.*, 1983). These deficits, although they may not be clinically obvious, should not be underestimated as they may interfere with outcome (for details, see Zimmermann and Leclercq, Chapter 2 in this book).

Clinical and behavioural data

Attentional disorders are among the most frequent complaints of survivors of TBI. In a group of 57 severe TBI patients interviewed two years after the injury, 33% complained of mental slowness, 33% of poor concentration, and 21% of inability to do two things simultaneously (van Zomeren and van den Burg, 1985). In addition, mental fatigue, which may exacerbate attentional difficulties, was reported by 30% of the patients. Some of these complaints were significantly correlated with severity of injury. For example, while poor concentration was reported by 18% of patients with a post-traumatic amnesia (PTA) of seven days or less, it increased to 40% for patients with a PTA lasting more than seven days. Attentional complaints were also significantly correlated to vocational outcome, particularly the inability to do two things simultaneously ($r = .56$) and mental slowness ($r = .36$). Relatives' reports may be assumed to be more realistic than patients' complaints, due to a frequent lack of awareness. Oddy *et al.* (1985) found that 50% of the relatives of severe TBI patients reported difficulty in concentrating seven years post-injury. In the Brooks *et al.* (1986) study, 67% of relatives reported mental slowness five years post-injury.

Attentional problems are also frequently reported by rehabilitation professionals. Ponsford and Kinsella (1991) devised a Rating Scale of Attentional Behaviour, designed to provide an ecological assessment of attention in a rehabilitation setting. Of the fourteen items of the scale, the two most severe problems reported by therapists of severe TBI patients were 'performed slowly on mental tasks' and 'unable to pay attention to more than one thing at once' (Ponsford and Kinsella, 1991) (see also Leclercq, Deloche and Rousseaux, Chapter 3 in this book). Other problems that also obtained a high rating (more impaired) were 'made mistakes because he/she wasn't paying attention properly', and 'missed important details in what he/she is doing'. More recently, Whyte *et al.* (1996, 2000) devised a quantitative assessment of behavioural inattentiveness, based on videotaped recordings of patients performing independent work in quiet or distracting environments. Subacute moderate to severe TBI patients exhibited more off-task behaviour (such as looking away from the task material) than matched controls, both in the presence of distractors and in their absence. The duration of episodes of off-task behaviour was also longer in the patient group. However, contrary to expectations, patients did not seem to be more influenced by the presence of distractors than controls.

These different behavioural data suggest that TBI may be associated with a wide range of attention-related problems such as slowness, difficulty in concentrating, difficulty in doing two things simultaneously, increased distractibility. However, experimental studies have given quite contrasting results, and the nature of attentional impairments after TBI is not yet fully understood.

Slowness of information processing

Although speed of processing is not an attentional function *per se*, mental slowness is usually considered as closely related to impairments of attention. Indeed, tasks tapping attention almost always involve time pressure, and include a timed measure of performance. Mental slowness is an extremely frequent consequence of acquired brain damage (Blackburn and Benton, 1955; Hicks and Birren, 1970; Benton, 1986). Slowed information processing has been one of the most robust findings across all neuropsychological studies after TBI, including very early reports (Conkey, 1938; Ruesch, 1944; Norrman and Svahn, 1961; Miller, 1970; van Zomeren and Deelman, 1976; van Zomeren, 1981; Ponsford and Kinsella, 1992). Studies using reaction times (RTs) found that speed of processing was significantly inversely correlated with severity of injury (van Zomeren and Deelman, 1976). Slowness may have important consequences for daily life skills. It has been found to be one of the best neuropsychological predictors of the ability to return to work seven years after the injury (Brooks *et al.*, 1987).

As underlined by van Zomeren and Brouwer (1994), slowed processing can be demonstrated across numerous different tasks, simple or complex, automatic or controlled, perceptual, cognitive or motor. In clinical practice, any timed task, such as the Trail Making Test, the Digit Symbol, the Paced Auditory Serial Addition Task (PASAT; Gronwall and Sampson, 1974), or RT tasks (van Zomeren, 1981), may be used to demonstrate mental slowness. However, although TBI patients perform more slowly, they do not make more errors than controls, at least in self-paced tasks where they are able to sacrifice speed to achieve greater accuracy (Ponsford and Kinsella, 1992). This has been called the speed–accuracy trade-off. Generally speaking, multiple-choice RTs are more sensitive to TBI than simple RTs (Norrman and Svahn, 1961; Miller, 1970; van Zomeren and Deelman, 1976; Ponsford and Kinsella, 1992). The RT difference between controls and patients has been found to depend on the number of response alternatives, and thus on task complexity (Miller, 1970; van Zomeren and Deelman, 1978). Van Zomeren and Deelman (1976) also found a significant interaction between severity of injury and task complexity, related to an increasing difference between simple and choice reaction time with increasing severity. Two studies (van

Zomeren, 1981; Ponsford and Kinsella, 1992) used an experimental device that permitted the authors to split the total RT into two components: decision time and movement time. Both studies found that, although there was a mild trend for prolonged movement times, the complexity effect, i.e. the greater sensitivity to increased number of alternatives, was indeed due to prolonged decision times. Van Zomeren and Brouwer (1994) carried out a meta-analysis of seven RT studies in subacute (<1 year) TBI subjects. They found a remarkably constant relationship between the RTs of TBI patients and controls, with a ratio that was about 1.4. However, this ratio appeared slightly larger in more complex tasks, producing RTs of 700 msec or more in control subjects.

There has been little research on recovery of speed of information processing after TBI. Van Zomeren and Deelman (1978) carried out a longitudinal study of simple and four-choice visual RT up to two years after the injury. They found a significant three-way interaction between severity of injury, task complexity and time. Two years post-injury, the most severe group (coma >1 week) performed significantly more slowly than less severely injured groups on the four-choice RT task, while all groups performed within the normal range on simple RT. More recent longitudinal studies have addressed the question of recovery using a more complex multilevel analysis, which permits us to take into account confounding factors, such as retest effects or individual differences in performance level or recovery (Zwaagstra *et al.*, 1996; Spikman *et al.*, 1999). Zwaagstra *et al.* (1996) found that recovery was significantly predicted by age (younger patients recovering more than older patients), and severity of injury (recovery being faster for the more severely injured patients, which does not mean that these patients end up on a higher performance level than the less severely injured). Spikman *et al.* (1999) assessed recovery in the first year post-trauma in a group including patients with mild, moderate and severe TBI. To control for practice effects, control subjects were tested at the same intervals as patients. An improvement, greater than the retest effect shown by the controls, occurred on most attentional tests, but the patient group still demonstrated mental slowness one year post-trauma. More severe patients started at a lower level but showed more recovery than less severe ones, thus suggesting a possible ceiling effect in the amount of improvement of patients starting with a better score. Most improvement seemed to occur within the first six months. In this study, recovery rate was not related to age or vocational status.

The origin of the mental slowness is still debated. Early studies, within the Shiffrin and Schneider (1977) framework, assumed that slowness mainly concerned controlled processing (as opposed to automatic processing) (van Zomeren *et al.*, 1984). Indeed, several studies found that TBI patients' RTs were greatly dependent on the number of stimulus alternatives and on stimulus–response compatibility, both variables that are thought to influence the more controlled stages of information processing, such as decision-making and response selection (Gronwall and Sampson, 1974; Miller, 1970; van Zomeren and Deelman, 1976). Other studies used Sternberg's additive model (Smith, 1968; Sternberg, 1969) to disentangle the effect of TBI on successive stages of the information processing chain, such as stimulus encoding, memory comparison, decision-making, reponse selection and execution (Schmitter-Edgecombe *et al.*, 1992; Shum *et al.*, 1990, 1994). These studies reported contradictory results. For example, Schmitter-Edgecombe *et al.* (1992) found in a group of severe and chronic (>18 months) TBI patients a selective slowness in the stimulus encoding and the response selection/decision-making stages, while the memory comparison stage was preserved. Shum *et al.* (1990, 1994) reported that subacute TBI patients were specifically slowed in the stimulus identification and response selection stages, while chronic patients were slowed only in the response selection stage. Stokx and Gaillard (1986) obtained different results in a group of chronic severe TBI patients. They analysed separately four stages of the information processing chain (stimulus encoding, memory comparison, response selection and motor preparation) and found a similar deficit on all of these stages. They concluded that there was a general and non-specific slowness of information processing.

Examined as a whole, these studies tend to suggest that slowed processing after TBI is not limited to a particular stage of information processing (van Zomeren and Brouwer, 1994). It seems that slowness may be more reliably related to a global reduction of available processing resources. Data presented above reporting that some stages were differentially impaired could be related to the different attentional demands of the experimental tasks. Some stages may have been found preserved only because they were less resource-demanding (Schmitter-Edgecombe *et al.*, 1992). To explain this non-specific slowing, van Zomeren and Brouwer (1994) proposed a physiopathological hypothesis based on a reduction of the signal-to-noise ratio in information processing, possibly as a result of diffuse functional (in the acute and subacute stage) and structural axonal damage.

In summary, there is no doubt that mental slowness is a pervasive problem after severe TBI. However, whether slowness by itself is sufficient to explain all attention-related difficulties experienced by brain-injured individuals is still a matter of controversy. This question will be addressed in the following parts of this chapter.

Focused attention

Distractibility and difficulty in concentrating are frequent complaints after TBI, suggesting a decrease of response selectivity. However, as mentioned earlier, contrary to expectations, a behavioural study showed that the number and duration of off-task behaviours of TBI patients were not particularly influenced by the presence of distractors (Whyte *et al.*, 1996, 2000).

Experimental studies have also given contrasting results, some of them failing to demonstrate disproportionate distraction and sensitivity to interference.

Several studies used the Stroop paradigm. In the interference Stroop condition, subjects are asked to name the ink colour of colour names: e.g. the word 'green' written with a red ink. Colour naming requires the inhibition of the strong automatic reading tendency. Several studies reported that TBI patients performed the task more slowly than controls, but without being more distracted by the interference condition (Chadwick *et al.*, 1981; Stuss *et al.*, 1985; Ponsford and Kinsella, 1992). However, discrepant results were obtained by McLean *et al.* (1983), who found that the most severely injured patients showed a disproportionate interference effect, but limited to the subacute phase (before six months). Vakil *et al.* (1995) used a modified Stroop task including two additional conditions: habituation and negative priming. This study was based on theoretical accounts suggesting that selective attention may be subdivided into two complementary processes (Neill, 1977; Tipper, 1985): an excitatory mechanism (selecting the relevant stimulus), and an inhibitory one (ignoring irrelevant stimuli). An additional mechanism, habituation, occurs when stimuli are presented repeatedly (Tipper, 1985; Lorch and Horn, 1986). The experimental task required subjects to name the colour of stimuli under four conditions (Tipper *et al.*, 1989): neutral (coloured X), Stroop (colour names printed in conflicting colours), habituation (only one word, 'GREEN', with different colours), and negative priming (stimuli printed in the same colour of ink as the name of the word in the previous trial). Negative priming is demonstrated by a slowing down of response to a target stimulus that had been a distractor on the previous trial. Vakil *et al.* (1995) found that, contrary to most previous studies, moderate and severe subacute (<1 year) TBI patients were more sensitive to interference than controls (Stroop effect). However, they were not different from controls for the habituation effect. Furthermore, there was no negative priming effect in TBI patients. Indeed, the controls were significantly slower under the negative priming condition, compared to the Stroop condition, while there was no significant difference between these two conditions for the TBI group. These results suggest a deficit of the inhibitory mechanisms of selective attention. However, these results have not been confirmed in a more recent study using a different experimental paradigm of negative priming with chronic patients (Simpson and Schmitter-Edgecombe, 2000). In this latter study, subjects were presented with two successive displays with two words each, one target (in bold type) and one distractor. The first display was called the prime and the second the probe. The task was to read aloud the target word and to ignore distractor words. In the negative priming condition, the distractor prime was the same as the subsequent target probe. Chronic (>1 year) severe TBI patients showed the same amount of inhibition as controls. The differences between the two studies on negative priming may be related to the different nature of the tasks (Stroop vs. reading), or to different recovery stages (subacute vs. chronic). Nevertheless, these results suggest that an inability to inhibit distracting information may not underlie the difficulties in distractibility and selective attention of chronic severe TBI patients.

Other studies used experimental paradigms based on response interference, in which distractors strongly elicit response tendencies competing with those of the target stimuli. Here again, contrasting results have been reported. Stablum *et al.* (1994) asked subjects to read large capital letters composed of small capital letters that were either congruent or incongruent with the large letter. They found that TBI patients were not disproportionately affected by the conflict condition. Van Zomeren and Brouwer (1987) studied the effect of response interference using a four-choice visual RT. The stimuli were buttons that had to be pressed as quickly as possible when they were lit up. In the distraction condition, a distractor button – similar and in close proximity to the targets – lit up simultaneously with each target button. Patients had to push down only the set of buttons first specified as targets. Subacute (3 to 6 months post-injury) TBI patients showed a significant interference effect. However, van Zomeren and Brouwer (1994) assumed that this effect was not necessarily related to a deficit of focused attention but rather to the fact that TBI patients needed more time to deal with the response interference. The same experiment was recently replicated in two studies on subacute severe TBI persons by the same team (Veltman *et al.*, 1996; Spikman *et al.*, 1996). Veltman *et al.* (1996) failed to find a significant group × condition interaction. Although the increase in raw decision time produced by the distraction was larger in the patient group, the proportional increase was almost the same in both groups. Spikman *et al.* (1996) tested a larger group of patients (n = 60) and used a covariance analysis to control for a possible confounding effect of basic slowness. When the RT in the non-distraction condition was taken as a covariate, there was no difference between patients and controls on distraction RT. Moreover, the non-distraction RT appeared to be a very good predictor of the distraction RT (r = 0.80). These data are indeed in agreement with van Zomeren and Brouwer's (1994) slowed processing assumption.

In a choice RT task without any inherent response conflict, Stuss *et al.* (1989) found that some TBI patients showed difficulties in ignoring redundant information. The stimuli had three attributes: shape, colour and line orientation within the shapes. In a multiple-choice redundant condition, no attribute specific to the target could ever appear in a distractor, so that patients could detect the target by attending to only one dimension, excluding systematically from their analysis the non-informative attributes. Patients, in comparison with controls, were disproportionately slowed in this condition, suggesting that they were processing irrelevant information. However, this finding was limited to one patient subgroup and to one testing session. It was considered by the authors themselves as 'somewhat elusive' (p. 747).

Whyte *et al.* (1998) studied distractibility in a way that was supposed to be more analogous to the inappropriate orienting to irrelevant stimuli that occurs in naturalistic settings. They tested subacute moderate to severe TBI patients with a visual Go–nogo reaction time task in which the target was preceded or followed by a brightly coloured moving stimulus, appearing above the target location. They found that distractors occurring before the target actually improved subjects' performance, probably because they served as warning stimuli. In contrast, distractors occurring simultaneously or shortly after the target produced slowing of RT which was significantly greater for patients than controls. Response accuracy was not significantly modified by the distractor, which only influenced speed of response. These data were interpreted as reflecting a greater distractibility of TBI patients, due to a greater impact of the visual distractor on response preparation and execution rather than target detection. Another finding of this study was that the differential distraction impact between TBI and control groups waned with practice, and disappeared at the third experimental session.

Visual selective attention was studied in severe chronic (>1 year) TBI by Schmitter-Edgecombe and Kibby (1998) with a visual search task. Participants were asked to detect the presence of a target among visual displays containing 1, 4 or 8 items under two conditions: a search condition and a non-search condition, in which the location of the target was cued with an arrow. Only the non-search condition was assumed to assess focused attention, as subjects had to focus on one source of information and ignore irrelevant stimuli. Patients performed as well as controls in the non-search task. However, the authors replicated this experiment under a more difficult condition, with high target–distractor similarity, and found that TBI participants had more difficulty than controls in ignoring irrelevant information. These results have important implications, since they suggest that the presence of a deficit of focused attention may depend on the specific requirements of the task. As emphasized by the authors:

> severe CHI participants' selective attention difficulties may reflect not only the presence of irrelevant information, but the manner in which relevant information is made distinct from irrelevant information by virtue of stimulus differences. In conditions where discriminability between targets and distractors is difficult . . . CHI participants may experience more difficulties than controls.
>
> (Schmitter-Edgecombe and Kibby, 1998, p. 157).

In conclusion, empirical studies currently present an inconsistent picture of focused attention after TBI. Although patients, relatives and rehabilitation professionals frequently complain of distractibility and difficulty in concentrating, experimental and behavioural data do not clearly support the assumption of a specific deficit of the ability to suppress irrelevant information. Discrepancies between the different studies may be related to a number of confounding factors, such as the selection of different patient populations, but also to different operational definitions on how focused attention should be measured. Moreover, the ability to focus on a relevant stimulus and the susceptibility to disruption by extraneous distractors may represent independent phenomena (Whyte *et al.*, 1998). In their detailed review of the topic, van Zomeren and Brouwer (1994) suggested that focused attention may be preserved in chronic TBI patients (more than one year post-injury), while subacute patients may show increased sensitivity to interference. However, recent data from the same group suggested that this effect may have been, at least in part, contaminated by the confounding effect of slowed processing (Veltman *et al.*, 1996; Spikman *et al.*, 1996). Nevertheless, other factors, such as practice with task (Whyte *et al.*, 1998), task difficulty, or target–distractor discriminability (Schmitter-Edgecombe and Kibby, 1998) may also have an influence.

Divided attention

Clinicians frequently report difficulties in doing two things simultaneously after TBI. Such difficulties may interfere with daily-life demands. Cazalis *et al.* (in press) studied the ability to generate and reconstitute scripts corresponding to sequences of actions necessary to achieve a given goal. TBI patients did not have specific impairments of action knowledge, but they had more difficulties than controls when they had to deal with multiple different scripts at the same time. These difficulties have also been found to interfere with return to work (van Zomeren and van den Burg, 1985; Vilkki *et al.*, 1994; Crépeau and Scherzer, 1993). Indeed, work situations frequently require us to deal with multiple simultaneous sources of information under time pressure. However, once again, experimental data are controversial. The mechanisms underlying these difficulties remain unclear.

Divided attention is determined by at least two factors (Shallice, 1988; van Zomeren and Brouwer, 1994). The first one is speed of processing, the second corresponds to control mechanisms involved in sharing resources and switching between tasks. If one of these components is impaired, a divided attention deficit should be anticipated for (van Zomeren and Brouwer, 1994).

Brouwer, van Zomeren and their colleagues have conducted a series of influential studies which led them to the conclusion that, when speed of processing is controlled for, there is little additional specific deficit of divided attention after TBI. Brouwer *et al.* (1989) used a dual task combining a visual choice RT and a driving simulator task, in which the difficulty of each single task was adjusted to the individual's performance level. Such adjustment permitted them to control for differences in speed. The dual task was performed under three different emphasis conditions (i.e. subjects were asked to give most emphasis to visual RT, or to driving, or equal emphasis to both tasks). TBI patients did not show any disproportionate dual-task decrement as compared with controls. However, this study only included chronic patients with a good recovery. Veltman *et al.* (1996) replicated this experiment with subacute (<6 months) severe TBI patients. As in the Brouwer *et al.* (1989) study, patients were as able as controls to share their attention between the tasks and to allocate preferentially their attentional resources to one task or another according to instructions. Similar results were obtained with a different dual-task paradigm, combining a four-choice visual and a simple auditory RT (Veltman *et al.*, 1996). The proportional increase in RT under the dual-task condition did not differ in patients and controls. The same dual RT task was also used in a larger (n = 60) group of patients with moderately severe and severe TBI at the subacute phase, again with similar results (Spikman *et al.*, 1996). When simple RT was used as a covariate, there was no significant group difference under the dual-task condition. The simple RT appeared to be a good predictor (r = 0.61) of the dual-task RT.

These data suggest that the ability to divide and shift attention may be preserved after TBI, at least as far as slowed processing and impairment in single-task performance are controlled for. However, two studies mentioned above (Brouwer *et al.*, 1989; Veltman *et al.*, 1996) reported a significant correlation within the patient group between injury severity and divided attention cost in the driving simulator divided attention task. Indeed, the performance of patients with a PTA of more than two weeks was poorer, and also showed a different pattern compared with less severely injured participants. Very severely injured patients tended to overemphasize visual RT at the expense of the driving task. Veltman *et al.* (1996) proposed a tentative analysis of their findings suggesting that the less severely injured patients would use a compensatory strategy characterized by cautiousness and increased mental effort, which allows them to obtain a performance close to (or even better) than that of controls. But such strategies would not be available to more severely injured patients. On average, this would lead to the absence of any significant difference between TBI and control participants. Finally, a more recent study by the same team (Withaar, 2000) brought further insights into the relative contribution of speed and control processes to divided attention after TBI. A group of severe TBI participants at a very early phase (<3 months) performed three tasks of increasing complexity, which were assumed to put increasing demands on control processes. The simplest task, assumed to be essentially 'stimulus-driven' (i.e. responses are simply determined by the stimulus configuration), was a dual RT task (visual and auditory), as previously described. The second task was the Trail Making Test, assumed to be 'memory-driven' (performance depends on mental sets that have to be actively kept in working memory by the subjects). The more complex task ('strategy-driven'), combining a driving simulator and an arrow identification task, was assumed to rely on the subject's ability to decide when and how to shift between tasks under high time pressure. The more complex task was performed under two conditions: easy (after individual adjustment of task difficulty) and difficult (patients performed under the same conditions as controls). The main result was that a specific impairment of control processes, apart from slowness, could only be demonstrated in the third, 'strategy-driven' dual task. Moreover, in this latter task, this impairment became even more pronounced in the more difficult condition. Finally, dual-task measures under the most difficult condition showed the highest correlations with performance in activities of daily living, thus suggesting the ecological validity of divided attention performance under high time pressure. The authors conclude that deficits in divided attention after TBI are task-dependent. Although slowed information processing seems sufficient to explain impairments in simple and relatively automatic dual tasks, additional impairments in control processes emerge in more complex tasks, performed under high time pressure.

Several other studies tended to confirm this hypothesis and suggested the existence of deficits of control and coordination mechanisms in dual-task processing after TBI in complex tasks performed under time pressure. Stablum *et al.* (1994) studied 14 severe TBI patients with apparent good recovery but persisting subjective complaints more than six months after the injury. Stimuli were pairs of letters presented vertically one above the other on a computer screen, left or right of a fixation point. In the single-task condition, subjects had to respond to the position (left or right) of the stimuli by pressing one of two keys on a response panel. In the dual-task condition, subjects had in addition to say aloud if the letters were identical or not. Compared to controls, patients had a disproportionate increase of RT under the dual-task condition. Vilkki *et al.* (1996) compared the dual-task performance of acute (<1 month) and subacute mild to severe TBI patients with that of patients with non-traumatic frontal or posterior lesions, and with that of healthy controls. The experiment included a cancellation task and backwards counting. Only acute TBI patients showed a significant performance decrement under the dual-task condition.

Azouvi *et al.* (1996) assessed severe subacute TBI patients with two different dual tasks. The first one was performed without time pressure and combined a modified Stroop paradigm and a random generation task. No disproportionate dual-task impairment was found in the TBI group. The second experiment included a greater time pressure. Patients were asked to perform a card sorting task of variable difficulty level combined with random generation of letters (Baddeley, 1966). These latter tasks were not self-paced but performed at a predetermined rate. A disproportionate decrease in performance occurred under the dual-task condition in the TBI group, even after statistical control for slowed information processing. These results again suggest (i) that the presence of divided attention deficits in TBI depends on the attentional demands of the task, and (ii) that in complex resource-demanding conditions, slowness is not sufficient to explain the subject's limitations in divided attention. Recently, Leclercq *et al.* (2000) assessed 16 very severe

TBI persons with a dual task combining self-paced random number generation with a simple visual RT. Compared to controls, TBI patients showed a disproportionate increase of reaction time under the dual-task condition. However, there was no disproportionate dual-task decrement in random generation. Couillet *et al.* (2000) replicated this study with a larger sample (n = 43) of very severe TBI patients. However, this time a more demanding Go–nogo visual RT task was used, in association with self-paced random number generation. Compared to controls, the TBI group showed here a disproportionate dual-task decrement on each of the two component tasks. However, in two other conditions, subjects were instructed to emphasize alternately each of the tasks in a balanced order. TBI patients were able to allocate their resources according to task instructions as efficiently as controls, while they had difficulties in managing the two tasks simultaneously.

Two recent studies yielded similar results (McDowell *et al.*, 1997; Park *et al.*, 1999). McDowell *et al.* (1997) used a simple visual RT performed concurrently with articulation or digit span tasks. Subacute TBI patients had greater decrements in performance during dual-task conditions. However, single-task performance was also significantly poorer in the TBI group, and this could be a source of confusion. To address this concern, a separate analysis was performed by pairing a subsample of TBI patients with control subjects matched to within 6 msec for single-task reaction time. The dual-task decrement assessed in this way was still significantly higher for TBI patients than controls. The authors also report the results of a factorial analysis which showed that a common factor does exist between dual-task performance and other measures of executive functions.

Park *et al.* (1999) looked at the interaction between divided attention and working memory load. They used the PASAT, in association with a delayed (lag) recall task. In this latter task, participants were asked to decide which one of two test letters was identical to a letter that had been presented just immediately before (lag 0) or one trial back (lag 1). They found that chronic severe TBI persons were significantly impaired, compared to controls, in the dual task combining PASAT and lag 1 recall, while they performed as well as controls on each task alone. However, the study sample was quite small (n = 6), and the patients were older than the usual TBI patients (mean age about 50). These interesting findings should be replicated in a larger TBI group. In addition, Park *et al.* (1999) reported a meta-analysis including seven studies on divided attention after TBI, plus their own research. They calculated an effect size estimate, which is a statistical measure used in meta-analyses to permit the comparison of results across studies. The effect size was defined as the difference between mean performance by the TBI group and the control group, divided by the standard deviation. A positive value indicates a greater divided attention cost in the TBI group, while a value close to zero would suggest that there is no significant difference between groups. They found that the effect size varied considerably from one study to another (range: 0.03 to 1.28). They concluded that the degree of impairment on divided attention after TBI is task-dependent. TBI patients would perform normally when the divided attention tasks could be performed relatively automatically, while they would be impaired relative to controls on tasks involving substantial working memory load (Park *et al.*, 1999).

Several conclusions can be drawn from these different studies on divided attention after TBI. First, it is clear that TBI patients have difficulty in dealing with two concurrent tasks at the same time. Second, slowed processing is without doubt a major factor contributing to divided attention deficit after TBI. Third, impairments in control processes apart from slowed processing, may be demonstrated in more complex situations, under time pressure or high working memory load, and/or in the more severely injured patients.

Phasic alertness

There has been much less research on phasic alertness than on selective attention after TBI. Most neuropsychological studies agree on the fact that phasic alertness, as assessed by the shortening of RT when the targets are preceded by a warning signal, is preserved after TBI (Ponsford and Kinsella, 1992; van Zomeren and Brouwer, 1994; Whyte *et al.*, 1997).

Ponsford and Kinsella (1992) studied the effect of an auditory warning signal on simple and choice visual RT in severe subacute TBI patients. The benefit led by the warning signal was the same for patients and controls. Similar results were obtained by Whyte *et al.* (1997), also with an auditory warning signal and a visual RT task. Whyte *et al.* (1997) found that, after adjustment for baseline performance, the effects of auditory warnings on performance accuracy, reaction time and response bias did not differ between patients and controls. More recently, Zoccolotti *et al.* (2000) also studied the effect of an auditory warning stimulus on visual RT. Patients' performance was not compared to a matched control group, but to normative data from a large sample of healthy subjects. They found that the number of patients who performed outside the normal range was nearly similar with or without a warning signal.

Surprisingly, however, these behavioural data are contradictory to electrophysiological studies using the 'contingent negative variation' (CNV). The CNV is an electroencephalographic signal occurring between the warning signal and the imperative stimulus requiring response execution. Indeed, several studies demonstrated a reduced amplitude of the CNV, and particularly of its early component, after TBI (Rizzo *et al.*, 1978; Curry, 1981; Rugg *et al.*, 1989; Segalowitz *et al.*, 1992). The early component is believed to be associated with orienting to the warning stimulus, while the later central negativity would be associated with response preparation (Segalowitz *et al.*, 1992). Segalowitz *et al.* (1992) found that the amplitude of the early frontal component of the CNV of TBI participants was significantly correlated to performance on neuropsychological tests sensitive to frontal damage. The clinical significance of these findings, however, is unknown.

In conclusion, phasic alertness, at least as operationally defined by the effect of an acoustic warning signal on visual RT, seems preserved in TBI patients but the discrepancies between behavioural and electrophysiological data remain to be clarified. As suggested by Whyte *et al.* (1997), further research should investigate other modalities of warning and of response preparation. For example, a recent study suggested that the length of the preparatory interval on the preceding trial had a disproportionate effect in the TBI group as compared to controls (Zahn and Mirsky, 1999). This finding was interpreted as suggesting that the process of preparation to unexpected stimuli may be retarded in TBI. This deserves further investigations of response preparation.

Vigilance and sustained attention

As underlined in a review by Foster *et al.* (1994), the definition of sustained attention strongly varies from one study to another. Briefly, this concept may be related to two different experimental situations. The first one addresses the stability of performance over long periods of time during which the subject is required to detect the occurrence of low-frequency stimuli. Low stimulus frequency and the monotonous aspect of the task make it difficult to maintain a sufficient level of arousal and monitoring. Such a condition will be referred to as a vigilance task. In the second situation, which will be referred to as a sustained attention task, the subject is asked to respond to a rapid and continuous flow of information. Such situations include a high time pressure which may overload the individual's processing resources. Deficits in sustained attention may also appear as increased intra-individual variability or brief and transitory lapses of attention producing either a lack of response or the sudden occurrence of irrelevant automatic responses.

Although clinicians frequently report that TBI patients have difficulty in maintaining attention, once again laboratory measures of sustained attention and vigilance have produced conflicting results. Most studies on vigilance after TBI found no disproportionate time-on-task effect (Stuss and Benson, 1986; van Zomeren *et al.*, 1988; van Zomeren and Brouwer, 1994; Spikman *et al.*, 1996). This means that, although TBI persons' overall level of performance is usually low, it does not decrease more than controls' with time. For example, van Zomeren and Brouwer (1994) used a dot cancellation task (a modified Bourdon task) and found that subacute patients worked more slowly, but maintained their initial level of performance (during 15 minutes) just as well as controls. Tasks of longer duration have also been used with quite similar results. Brouwer and van Wolffelaar (1985) found that eight subacute moderate and severe TBI patients did not show more performance decrement with time than matched controls on an auditory vigilance task lasting 40 minutes. They also found no evidence for a decrease of mental effort with time, as operationally measured by heart rate variability. Van Zomeren *et al.* (1988), in a research study on driving skills, found that chronic severe TBI patients did not present any specific time-on-task effect during an actual one-hour ride on a quiet, straight highway, although their overall performance was poorer than that of matched controls. Similarly, Ponsford and Kinsella (1992) found that the performance of severely head-injured subjects on a continuous choice RT task lasting 45 minutes did not deteriorate more over time than that of controls. Zoccolotti *et al.* (2000) used a visual RT task lasting 15 minutes with low-frequency stimuli in a large (n = 106) group of TBI patients. They found that only a few patients fell below the cut-off point (9% for omissions, 20% for false reactions), and they did not report any clear effect of time-on-task.

However, one recent study reported different results. Whyte *et al.* (1995) used a visual Go–nogo RT task lasting 15 minutes. Stimuli were pairs of vertical lines. Subjects were asked to press a response key if two lines were of equal length. Distractors were pairs of grossly unequal lines, and represented half of the stimuli. The interstimulus interval ranged from 4 to 8 seconds. They found that RT, RT variability and response bias (more conservative responses, i.e. the subject's threshold of certainty used for deciding when to respond) deteriorated more with time in a group of moderate and severe TBI participants in subacute phase (<1 year) compared to controls. Furthermore, analysis of individual data showed that only 15% of patients showed no abnormal vigilance decrement. The authors relate their findings to an increase of lapses of attention with time. The discrepancy with previous studies might be related to the fact that the task was more resource-demanding, and was performed under greater time pressure. Indeed, they used a limited-hold paradigm (the stimulus disappears whether or not the subject responds), associated to short individualized stimulus durations (adapted to each subject's baseline performance). These task characteristics may have produced a greater susceptibility to lapses of attention.

Several studies reported evidence suggesting that sustained attention – strictly speaking – may be impaired after TBI (Stuss and Benson, 1986; Gronwall, 1987; Ponsford and Kinsella, 1992; Robertson *et al.*, 1997). These deficits appear in continuous tasks requiring an active processing of a rapid flow of information (Gronwall, 1987) or the inhibition of highly automatized responses (Robertson *et al.*, 1997). Robertson *et al.* (1997) found that the performance of TBI patients on a test of sustained attention was significantly correlated to everyday slips of attention. In such tasks, greater intra-individual variability of performance and the presence of sudden and transitory lapses of attention suggest the presence of a sustained attention deficit (van Zomeren and Brouwer, 1994).

Stuss *et al.* (1989, 1994) assessed consistency of performance on RT tasks both within an experimental session, by comparing individual standard deviations of patients and controls, and over longer periods of time, by comparing performance between repeated testing sessions. They found that TBI patients had greater inconsistency of performance as compared to controls, both within a test and across assessments. However, the mechanism and clinical significance of inconsistency are debated. Stuss *et al.* (1994) found that inconsistency of performance was not significantly related to injury severity. According to van Zomeren and Brouwer (1994), 'there is no specific increase of intraindividual variability . . . as variability measures show increases that are proportional to the increases in mean or median RT' (p. 86). However, new insights on performance variability came from an electrophysiological study of a simple auditory RT task (Segalowitz *et al.*, 1997). Segalowitz *et al.* (1997) found that in chronic (>1 year) TBI subjects, the variability (but not the speed) of RT was related to the amplitude of the P300 wave, which reflects attentional allocation, and to the preresponse component of the CNV, which reflects sustained attention. In contrast, in normal subjects, it was the speed of RT that was significantly related to P300 amplitude. The authors conclude that after TBI it is the variability but not the speed of RT that is sensitive to the ability to allocate and sustain attention.

Fatigue is another problem that may be related to vigilance and sustained attention. Mental fatigue is a highly frequent complaint after TBI. It was found in 72% of patients two years post-injury (Ponsford *et al.*, 1995). In the Brooks *et al.* (1986) study, 62% of relatives reported tiredness five years post-injury. However, fatigue has received little attention in TBI research, probably because it is difficult to measure objectively. According to van Zomeren *et al.* (1984), mental fatigue could be due to the constant compensational effort required in meeting the demands of everyday life ('the coping hypothesis'). Riese *et al.* (1999) assessed the performance of eight very severe TBI patients in a continuous dual task lasting 50 minutes. They used both physiological (heart rate, blood pressure) and subjective measures of mental effort and distress. They found that, after experimental control for individual differences in single-task performance, sustained task performance and measures of mental effort were not significantly different between TBI and control subjects. However, TBI patients did show more distress than controls. They reported higher levels of task load and more visual complaints. Moreover, while in the controls systolic blood pressure decreased from pre- to post-test, it showed the reverse pattern in the TBI group. These results suggest that TBI may produce higher psychophysiological costs to sustain task performance, and that this may be related to subjective mental fatigue.

In conclusion, the contradictory results on vigilance and sustained attention suggest that, once again, the nature of the task might be of importance to the subject's performance. While less demanding tasks do not seem to be associated with any disproportionate time-on-task effect after TBI, this may not be true for more demanding tasks, such as the one used in the study by Whyte *et al.* (1995). Although TBI is commonly associated with greater inconsistency of performance, the clinical significance of this finding is yet unknown.

General conclusion

Attentional disorders are among the most frequent neuropsychological impairments following TBI. They are significantly correlated with severity of injury and with social and vocational outcome. The most consistent finding is mental slowness, related to a global, non-specific slowing of information processing. Whether attentional functions are additionally impaired remains largely debated. Van Zomeren and Brouwer (1994) claimed that, when slowed information processing is controlled for, there is little if any additional impairment of higher aspects of attention. More recent findings, however, suggest that the presence of specific impairments of attentional functions may depend on the nature and complexity of the task. Studies using complex resource-demanding tasks performed under time pressure suggested that TBI may actually be associated with some degree of impairment of focused attention, of vigilance and sustained attention, and of divided attention. Severity and chronicity of injury may also be of importance (Veltman *et al.*, 1996). It is also possible, as recently suggested by Zoccolotti *et al.* (2000), that there may be distinct patterns of impairment within the TBI population.

The brain dysfunctions underlying attentional impairments remain to be elucidated. The fact that attentional deficits are significantly correlated with severity of injury strongly suggests that they are related to diffuse axonal injury. This may explain why these deficits have not been found related to focal contusions of the brain as assessed with structural neuroimaging techniques (for a review, see Azouvi, 2000). For example, Spikman *et al.* (2000) found no difference between patients with or without detectable focal prefrontal damage with respect to several attention test measures. Recent studies using functional neuroimaging, such as PET (Fontaine *et al.*, 1999) or functional MRI (McAllister *et al.*, 1999), provided new insights into the understanding of the functional neuroanatomy of cognitive impairments after TBI. Fontaine *et al.* (1999) showed that the performance on neuropsychological tests of attention after severe TBI was significantly correlated with hypometabolism at rest in prefrontal and cingulate areas. McAllister *et al.* (1999) found that mild TBI patients at a very early phase had a modified pattern of activation in prefrontal and parietal regions in response to an increasing working memory load. These data suggest that attentional deficits may be related to a defective activation or modulation of attentional/executive networks including but not limited to the prefrontal cortex.

Finally, it is surprising that TBI patients have repeatedly performed better than expected in most experimental studies of attention. Ponsford and Kinsella (1992) emphasized the fact that the laboratory tasks used to assess attention are quite different in nature from real life situations. The latter may be much more complex and unstructured, and may last over much longer periods of time, than structured neuropsychological tasks. This may explain the discrepancy between neuropsychological measures and clinical observations in naturalistic settings. To get a complete picture of a patient's attentional difficulties, clinicians should try to collect all available information, including but not limited to the results of neuropsychological tests. Information about subjective complaints and the patient's behaviour in daily life situations (from health-care professionals, close relatives, work colleagues) should be carefully recorded and taken into consideration. Such information may be crucial for adequate decision-making in rehabilitation and community re-entry programmes.

References

Azouvi, P. (2000). Neuroimaging correlates of cognitive and functional outcome after traumatic brain injury. *Current Opinion in Neurology*, *13*, 665–669.

Azouvi, P., Jokic, C., Van der Linden, M., Marlier, N. and Bussel, B. (1996). Working memory and supervisory control after severe closed head injury. A study of dual task performance and random generation. *Journal of Clinical and Experimental Neuropsychology*, *18*, 317–337.

Baddeley, A.D. (1966). The capacity for generating information by randomization. *Quarterly Journal of Experimental Psychology*, *18*, 119–129.

Benton, A.L. (1986). Reaction time in brain disease: some reflections. *Cortex*, *22*, 129–140.

Bernstein, D.M. (1999). Recovery from mild head injury. *Brain Injury*, *13*, 151–172.

Binder, L.M. (1986). Persistent symptoms after mild head injury: a review of the postconcussive syndrome. *Journal of Clinical and Experimental Neuropsychology*, *8*, 323–346.

Blackburn, H.L. and Benton, A.L. (1955). Simple and choice reaction time in cerebral disease. *Confinia Neurologica*, *15*, 327–338.

Brooks, D.N., Campsie, L., Symington, C., Beattie, A. and MacKinlay, W. (1986). The five year outcome of severe blunt head injury: a relative's view. *Journal of Neurology, Neurosurgery and Psychiatry*, *49*, 764–770.

Brooks, N., McKinlay, W., Symington, C., Beattie, A. and Campsie, L. (1987). Return to work within the first seven years after severe head injury. *Brain Injury*, *1*, 5–19.

Brouwer, W.H., Ponds, R.W., Van Wolffelaar, P.C. and van Zomeren, A.H. (1989). Divided attention 5 to 10 years after severe closed head injury. *Cortex*, *25*, 219–230.

Brouwer, W.H. and van Wolffelaar, P.C. (1985). Sustained attention and sustained effort after closed head injury: detection and 0.10 Hz heart rate variability in a low event rate vigilance task. *Cortex*, *21*, 111–119.

Cazalis, F., Azouvi, P., Sirigu, A., Agar, N. and Burnod, Y. (in press). Script knowledge after severe traumatic brain injury. *Journal of the International Neuropsychological Society*.

Chadwick, O., Rutter, M., Brown, G., Shaffer, D. and Traub, M. (1981). A prospective study of chidren with head injuries: II. Cognitive sequelae. *Psychological Medicine*, *11*, 49–61.

Conkey, R.C. (1938). Psychological changes associated with head injuries. *Archives of Psychology*, *33*, 232.

Couillet, J., Leclercq, M., Martin, Y., Rousseaux, M. and Azouvi, P. (2000). Divided attention after severe diffuse traumatic brain injury. Paper presented at the European Brain Injury Association meeting, Paris, 20–23 September 2000.

Crépeau, F. and Scherzer, P. (1993). Predictors and indicators of work status after traumatic brain injury: a meta-analysis. *Brain Injury*, *3*, 5–35.

Curry, S.H. (1981). Event-related potentials as indicants of structural and functional damage in closed head injury. *Progress in Brain Research*, *54*, 507–515.

Fontaine, A., Azouvi, P., Remy, P., Bussel, B. and Samson, Y. (1999). Functional anatomy of neuropsychological deficits after severe traumatic brain injury. *Neurology*, *53*, 1963–1968.

Foster, J.K., Eskes, G.A. and Stuss, D.T. (1994). The cognitive neuropsychology of attention: a frontal lobe perspective. *Cognitive Neuropsychology*, *11*, 133–147.

Gronwall, D. (1987). Advances in the assessment of attention and information processing after head injury. In H.S. Levin, J. Grafman and H.M. Eisenberg (eds), *Neurobehavioral Recovery from Head Injury*. New York: Oxford University Press, pp. 355–371.

Gronwall, D. and Sampson, H. (1974). *The Psychological Effects of Concussion*. Auckland: Auckland University Press.

Hicks, L. and Birren, J.E. (1970). Aging, brain damage and psychomotor slowing. *Psychological Bulletin*, *74*, 377–396.

Leclercq, M., Couillet, J., Azouvi, P., Marlier, N., Martin, Y., Strypstein, E. and Rousseaux, M. (2000). Dual task performance after severe diffuse traumatic brain injury or vascular prefrontal damage. *Journal of Clinical and Experimental Neuropsychology*, *22*, 339–350.

Lezak, M.D. (1987). Assessment for rehabilitation planning. In M.J. Meier, A.L. Benton and L. Diller (eds) *Neuropsychological Rehabilitation*. Edinburgh: Churchill Livingstone, pp. 41–58.

Lorch, E.P. and Horn, D.G. (1986). Habituation of attention to irrelevant stimuli in elementary school children. *Journal of Experimental Child Psychology*, *41*, 84–197.

McAllister, T.W., Saykin, A.J., Flashman, L.A., Sparling, M.B., Johnson, S.C., Guerin, S.J., Mamourian, A.C., Weaver, J.B. and Yanofsky, N. (1999). Brain activation during working memory 1 month after mild traumatic brain injury. A functional MRI study. *Neurology*, *53*, 1300–1308.

McDowell, S., Whyte, J. and Desposito, M. (1997). Working memory impairments in traumatic brain injury: evidence from a dual-task paradigm. *Neuropsychologia*, *35*, 1341–1353.

McLean, A., Temkin, N.R., Dikmen, S. and Wyler, A.R. (1983). The behavioral sequelae of head injury. *Journal of Clinical Neuropsychology*, *5*, 361–376.

Miller, E. (1970). Simple and choice reaction time following severe head injury. *Cortex*, *6*, 121–127.

Neill, W.T. (1977). Inhibition and facilitation processes in selective attention. *Journal of Experimental Psychology: Human Perception and Performance*, *3*, 444–450.

Norrman, B. and Svahn, K. (1961). A follow-up study of severe brain injuries. *Acta Psychiatrica Scandinavia*, *37*, 236–264.

Oddy, M., Coughlan, T., Tyerman, A. and Jenkins, D. (1985). Social adjustment after closed head injury: a further follow-up seven years after injury. *Journal of Neurology, Neurosurgery and Psychiatry*, *48*, 564–568.

Park, N.W., Moscovitch, M. and Robertson, I.H. (1999). Divided attention impairments after traumatic brain injury. *Neuropsychologia*, *37*, 1119–1133.

Ponsford, J. and Kinsella, G. (1991). The use of a rating scale of attentional behaviour. *Neuropsychological Rehabilitation*, *1*, 241–257.

Ponsford, J. and Kinsella, G. (1992). Attentional deficits following severe closed head injury. *Journal of Clinical and Experimental Neuropsychology*, *14*, 822–838.

Ponsford, J.L., Olver, J.H. and Curran, C. (1995). A profile of outcome: 2 years after traumatic brain injury. *Brain Injury*, *9*, 1–10.

Riese, H., Hoedemaeker, M., Brouwer, W.H., Mulder, L.J.M., Cremer, R. and Veldman, J.B.P. (1999). Mental fatigue after very severe closed head injury: sustained performance, mental effort, and distress at two levels of workload in a driving simulator. *Neuropsychological Rehabilitation*, *9*, 189–205.

Rizzo, P., Amabile, C., Caporali, M., Spadaro, M., Zanasi, M. and Morocutti, C. (1978). A CNV study in a group of patients with traumatic head injuries. *Electroencephalography and Clinical Neurophysiology*, *45*, 281–285.

Robertson, I.H., Manly, T., Andrade, J., Baddeley, B.T. and Yiend, J. (1997). 'Oops!': Performance correlates of everyday attentional failures in traumatic brain injured and normal subjects. *Neuropsychologia*, *35*, 747–758.

Ruesch, J. (1944). Intellectual impairment in head injuries. *American Journal of Psychiatry*, *100*, 480–496.

Rugg, M.D., Cowan, C.P., Nagy, M.E., Milner, A.D., Jacobson, I. and Brooks, D.N. (1989). CNV abnormalities following closed head injury. *Brain*, *112*, 489–506.

Schmitter-Edgecombe, M. and Kibby, M.K. (1998). Visual selective attention after severe closed head injury. *Journal of the International Neuropsychological Society*, *4*, 144–159.

Schmitter-Edgecombe, M., Marks, W., Fahy, J.F. and Long, C.J. (1992). Effects of severe closed head injury on three stages of information processing. *Journal of Clinical and Experimental Neuropsychology*, *14*, 717–737.

Segalowitz, S.J., Dywan, J. and Unsal, A. (1997). Attentional factors in response time variability after traumatic brain injury: an ERP study. *Journal of the International Neuropsychological Society*, *3*, 95–107.

Segalowitz, S.J., Unsal, A. and Dywan, J. (1992). CNV evidence for the distinctiveness of frontal and posterior neural processes in a traumatic brain-injured population. *Journal of Clinical and Experimental Neuropsychology*, *14*, 545–565.

Shallice, T. (1988). *From Neuropsychology to Mental Structure*. Cambridge: Cambridge University Press.

Shiffrin, R.M. and Schneider, W. (1977). Controlled and automatic human information processing. II: Perceptual learning, automatic attending, and a general theory. *Psychological Review*, *84*, 127–190.

Shum, D.H.K., McFarland, K., Bain, J.D. and Humphreys, M.S. (1990). Effects of closed head injury on attentional processes: an information stage analysis. *Journal of Clinical and Experimental Neuropsychology*, *12*, 247–264.

Shum, D.H.K., McFarland, K. and Bain, J.D. (1994). Effects of closed head injury on attentional processes: generality of Sternberg's additive factor method. *Journal of Clinical and Experimental Neuropsychology*, *16*, 547–555.

Simpson, A. and Schmitter-Edgecombe, M. (2000). Intactness of inhibitory attentional mechanisms following severe closed-head injury. *Neuropsychology*, *14*, 310–319.

Smith, E.E. (1968). Choice reaction time: an analysis of the major theoretical positions. *Psychological Bulletin*, *69*, 77–110.

Spikman, J.M., Deelman, B.G. and van Zomeren, A.H. (2000). Executive functioning, attention and frontal lesions in patients with chronic CHI. *Journal of Clinical and Experimental Neuropsychology*, *22*, 325–338.

Spikman, J.M., Timmerman, M.E., van Zomeren, A.H. and Deelman, B.G. (1999). Recovery versus retest effects in attention after closed head injury. *Journal of Clinical and Experimental Neuropsychology*, *21*, 585–605.

Spikman, J.M., van Zomeren, A.H. and Deelman, B.G. (1996). Deficits of attention after closed-head injury: slowness only? *Journal of Clinical and Experimental Neuropsychology*, *18*, 755–767.

Stablum, F., Leonardi, G., Mazzoldi, M., Ulmita, C. and Morra, S. (1994). Attention and control deficits following brain injury. *Cortex*, *30*, 603–618.

Sternberg, S. (1969). The discovery of processing stages: extensions of Donder's method. *Acta Psychologia*, *30*, 276–315.

Stokx, L.C. and Gaillard, A.W.K. (1986). Task and driving performance of patients with a severe concussion of the brain. *Journal of Clinical and Experimental Neuropsychology*, *8*, 421–436.

Stuss, D.T. and Benson, D.F. (1986). *The Frontal Lobes*. New York: Raven Press.

Stuss, D.T., Ely, P., Hugenholtz, H., Richard, M.T., Larochelle, S., Poirier, C.A. and Bell, I. (1985). Subtle neuropsychological deficits in patients with good recovery after closed head injury. *Neurosurgery*, *17*, 41–47.

Stuss, D.T., Pogue, J., Buckle, L. and Bondar, J. (1994). Characterization of stability of performance in patients with traumatic brain injury: variability and consistency on reaction time tests. *Neuropsychology*, *8*, 316–324.

Stuss, D.T., Stethem, L.L., Hugenholtz, H., Picto, T., Pivik, J. and Richard, M.T. (1989). Reaction time after head injury: fatigue, divided and focused attention, and consistency of performance. *Journal of Neurology, Neurosurgery and Psychiatry*, *52*, 742–748.

Tipper, S.P. (1985). The negative priming effect: inhibitory priming by ignored objects. *The Quarterly Journal of Experimental Psychology*, *37A*, 571–590.

Tipper, S.P., Bourque, T.A., Anderson, S.H. and Brehaut, J.C. (1989). Mechanisms of attention: a developmental study. *Journal of Experimental Child Psychology*, *48*, 353–378.

Vakil, E., Weis, H., Jedwab, L., Groswasser, Z. and Aberbuch, S. (1995). Stroop color–word task as a measure of selective attention: efficiency in closed-head-injured patients. *Journal of Clinical and Experimental Neuropsychology*, *17*, 335–342.

van Zomeren, A.H. (1981). *Reaction Time and Attention after Closed Head Injury*. Lisse: Swets and Zeitlinger.

van Zomeren, A.H. and Brouwer, W.H. (1987). Head injury and concepts of attention. In H.S. Levin, J. Grafman and H.M. Eisenberg (eds) *Neurobehavioral Recovery from Head Injury*. New York: Oxford University Press, pp. 398–415.

van Zomeren, A.H. and Brouwer, W.H. (1994). *Clinical Neuropsychology of Attention*. New York: Oxford University Press.

van Zomeren, A.H., Brouwer, W.H. and Deelman, B.G. (1984). Attentional deficits:

the riddles of selectivity, speed and alertness. In D.N. Brooks (ed.) *Closed Head Injury: Psychological, Social and Family Consequences*. Oxford: Oxford University Press, pp. 74–107.

van Zomeren, A.H., Brouwer, W.H., Rothengatter, J.A. and Snoeck, J.W. (1988). Fitness to drive a car after recovery from severe head injury. *Archives of Physical Medicine and Rehabilitation*, *69*, 90–96.

van Zomeren, A.H. and Deelman, B.G. (1976). Differential effects of simple and choice reaction time after closed head injury. *Clinical Neurology and Neurosurgery*, *79*, 81–90.

van Zomeren, A.H. and Deelman, B.G. (1978). Long term recovery of visual reaction time after closed head injury. *Journal of Neurology, Neurosurgery and Psychiatry*, *41*, 452–457.

van Zomeren, A.H. and van den Burg, W. (1985). Residual complaints of patients two years after severe head injury. *Journal of Neurology, Neurosurgery, and Psychiatry*, *48*, 21–28.

Veltman, J.C., Brouwer, W.H., van Zomeren, A.H. and van Wolffelaer, P.C. (1996). Central executive aspects of attention in subacute severe and very severe closed head injury patients: planning, inhibition, flexibility and divided attention. *Neuropsychology*, *10*, 357–367.

Vilkki, J., Ahola, K., Holst, P., Öhman, J., Servo, A. and Heiskanen, O. (1994). Prediction of psychosocial recovery after head injury with cognitive tests and neurobehavioral ratings. *Journal of Clinical and Experimental Neuropsychology*, *16*, 325–338.

Vilkki, J., Virtanen, S., Surma-Aho, O. and Servo, A. (1996). Dual task performance after focal cerebral lesion and closed head injuries. *Neuropsychologia*, *34*, 1051–1056.

Whyte, J., Fleming, M., Polansky, M., Cavalluci, C. and Coslett, H.B. (1997). Phasic arousal in response to auditory warnings after traumatic brain injury. *Neuropsychologia*, *35*, 313–324.

Whyte, J., Fleming, M., Polansky, M., Cavalucci, C. and Coslett, H.B. (1998). The effect of visual distraction following traumatic brain injury. *Journal of the International Neuropsychological Society*, *4*, 127–136.

Whyte, J., Polansky, M., Cavalucci, C., Fleming, M., Lhulier, J. and Coslett, H.B. (1996). Inattentive behavior after traumatic brain injury. *Journal of the International Neuropsychological Society*, *2*, 274–281.

Whyte, J., Polansky, M., Fleming, M., Coslett, H.B. and Cavalucci, C. (1995). Sustained arousal and attention after traumatic brain injury. *Neuropsychologia*, *33*, 797–813.

Whyte, J., Schuster, K., Polansky, M., Adams, J. and Coslett, H.B. (2000). Frequency and duration of inattentive behavior after traumatic brain injury: effects of distraction, task, and practice. *Journal of the International Neuropsychological Society*, *6* 1–11.

Withaar, F. K. (2000). Divided attention and driving: the effects of aging and brain injury. Rijksuniversiteit, Groningen: Unpublished PhD dissertation.

Zahn, T.P. and Mirsky, A.F. (1999). Reaction time indicators of attention deficits in closed head injury. *Journal of Clinical and Experimental Neuropsychology*, *21*, 352–367.

Zoccolotti, P., Matano, A., Deloche, G., Cantagallo, A., Passadori, A., Leclercq, M.,

Braga, L., Cremel, N., Pittau, P., Renom, M., Rousseaux, M., Truche, A., Fimm, B. and Zimmermann, P. (2000). Patterns of attentional impairment following closed head injury: a collaborative European study. *Cortex*, *36*, 93–107.

Zwaagstra, R., Schmidt, I. and Vanier, M. (1996). Recovery of speed of information processing in closed-head injury patients. *Journal of Clinical and Experimental Neuropsychology*, *18*, 383–393.

Chapter 10

Attention disorders in cerebrovascular diseases

Marc Rousseaux, Bruno Fimm and Anna Cantagallo

Introduction

Cerebrovascular diseases are, with degenerative disorders, those that most frequently affect brain functioning in adult patients. They are also those that better allow, together with focal surgical resections, analysing consequences of circumscribed brain lesions, therefore contributing to identifying neural systems underlying cognitive functions. These considerations apply to non-spatial attention. However, this remains rather poorly evaluated, despite many studies being presented in the last decade. One main problem is that the concept of attention and its different components remains controversial. Detecting and investigating such problems have become far more important since specific rehabilitation techniques have demonstrated a clear efficiency (Sturm and Willmes, 1991).

In this chapter, we will therefore briefly present the concepts that are most widely accepted, then switch to specific methodological problems of patient assessment, before considering the main consequences of focal vascular injury. We will later consider to what extent cerebrovascular disorders can contribute to validate the main cognitive (Broadbent, 1958; Schneider and Shiffrin, 1977; Posner, 1980; Baddeley, 1986) or anatomo-functional (Mesulam, 1981; Watson *et al.*, 1981; Posner and Petersen, 1990; LaBerge, 1995) models of non-spatial attention. The last part of this chapter deals with more ecological and pragmatic considerations.

The main components of attention

Attention is the selective aspect of perception and action, consisting first in a preparation and orientation of the individual toward one or several specific perceptual channels, and one or several particular stimuli. To be able to control attention has three advantages for the individual: precision, speed of processing, and maintainence of mental treatment (LaBerge, 1995). Data collected in the context of behavioural analysis, experimental psychology, neuropsychology, and animal experimentation suggest that attention is not a unitary capacity, but is formed by a conjunction of complementary components, subtended by multimodular brain systems (Mesulam, 1981; Posner and Petersen, 1990; LaBerge, 1995). Most authors have differentiated concepts of preparation, intensity and selectivity (Richard, 1980; van Zomeren and Brouwer, 1987). In this chapter, we will discriminate alertness, perceptuo-motor slowing, vigilance and sustained attention, focused attention, and divided attention. Alertness is a state of arousal and preparation to respond, which has phasic and tonic dimensions. Vigilance is the capacity to maintain a level of performance for a prolonged time, for targets that appear less frequently and in an unpredictable way. Focalization is the capacity of self-fixation on a source of stimulations or on a cognitive activity. Divided attention corresponds to the capacity to respond simultaneously to several demands (Broadbent, 1958; Posner and Boies, 1971; Schneider and Shiffrin, 1977; Shiffrin and Schneider, 1977; Parasuraman, 1984; Posner and Rafal, 1987; van Zomeren and Brouwer, 1992, 1994; LaBerge, 1995; Zimmerman and Leclercq, Chapter 2 in this book).

In addition to these general considerations, three points must be emphasized, which are rarely taken into account in the general context of experimental or cognitive psychology, but which pathology and brain activation studies require us to consider.

The first one is the distinction between spatial and non-spatial attention capacities, which was emphasized by LaBerge (1995). Some attention processes (and networks) we have previously considered have been described in the context of spatial attention. Posner and Rafal (1987) have related some elementary attention processes to specific cortical or subcortical structures, especially frontal, parietal, and cingulate. The participation of these areas in non-spatial processing must be discussed. Some are probably involved, for example those that are implicated in decision processes; others are probably distinct, especially those that are associated with the spatial components of attention (posterior hemispheric areas). A second point is that a number of attention components are tightly associated with other cognitive capacities; for example, selectivity, in its intentional and controlled aspects is linked to the decision processes and to working memory. It may therefore be suggested that the pathological impairment of one of these late processes can severely disturb patients' efficiency in tasks assessing selectivity. Relations between attention disorders, decision processes and working memory need to be more precisely evaluated. Pathological condition can contribute to demonstrating dissociations (Godefroy *et al.*, 1999; Leclercq *et al.*, 2000). A third point is that previous distinctions do not (or poorly) take into account the fundamental notions of learning and motivation. The study of these processes in the specific frame of attention or attention dysfunction must also be valorized.

Methodological problems associated with the study of patients with cerebrovascular diseases

Problems arise in relation to the imaging techniques used in the localization of lesions and the definition of their volume and of the stage of disease (post-stroke interval), but also in relation to systematic control of pathologies which are often associated with focused vascular disorders, especially degenerative processes and hypometabolism in brain territories which are relatively remote from the lesion (diaschisis).

Authors have often used CT scans in order to define the topography of anatomic lesions, and their volume. Now, it is difficult to precisely evaluate the topography of a brain insult using CT performed in a routine way, even when a tridimensionnal reconstruction of lesions is performed. The superiority of MRI has clearly been demonstrated in a study of frontal syndrome associated with unilateral lenticulo-striate infarcts (Godefroy *et al.*, 1992): the frontal dysfunction, demonstrated by inverse tapping, motor sequences of Luria, the Trail Making Test, and behavioural study seemed to be related to subcortical lesions when CT was used, while it was evidently due to the extension of lesions in the temporal and fronto-temporal cortices when MRI images were taken into account. In a similar way, lesions resulting from rupture of aneurysms of the anterior communicating artery (AACA) are always more severe on MRI, especially on the T2 sequences, than on conventional CT scans. Importantly, these MRI lesions are tightly correlated to the drop of regional cerebral blood flow and metabolic dysfunction in the same areas (Rousseaux *et al.*, 1994). The problem of the role of the lesion volume has been emphasized by Boller *et al.* (1970) and Tartaglione *et al.* (1986), but has received little attention in most of the other studies. These authors have observed a strong correlation between the volume of the lesion estimated using isotopic brain scans and the slowing down of simple visual and auditory reaction time (RT), especially in patients with a right hemispheric lesion (vascular or tumoral), approximating Lashley's principle of mass action.

In cerebrovascular diseases, remote consequences, usually called 'diaschisis', must also be taken into account. They can be demonstrated using regional cerebral blood flow (SPECT or PET technique), or metabolic (consumption of oxygen or glucose with PET) studies. This appears to be especially important following subcortical (Baron *et al.*, 1986; Rousseaux *et al.*, 1986) and even frontal (Rousseaux *et al.*, 1994) lesions.

Problems of brain imaging can help to explain discrepancies in the literature. If we consider AACA, an extension of lesions in the anterior or antero-lateral temporal area is frequent, and explains the exclusion of such patients in some studies (Rousseaux *et al.*, 1996). Furthermore, the involvement of the anterior striatum (head of the caudate nucleus, Heubner artery territory) can explain some of the dysexecutive and behavioural disorders (Irle *et al.*, 1992).

In another domain, patients with posterior vascular infarcts, especially in the territory of the posterior cerebral artery (classical temporal-occipital lesion), can present with a subcortical injury of the posterolateral or even the medial thalamus. Now, this thalamic insult can by itself explain the occurrence of spatial or non-spatial attention disorders (Sandson *et al.*, 1991; Malamut *et al.*, 1992; Sturm *et al.*, 1999).

Another element to be controlled is the period of time since the lesion onset. In many studies, patients have been included after markedly different delays following the stroke event. However, the analysis of single cases or series of patients has suggested that, even in severe frontal or subcortical lesions, attention and executive disorders are quite rapidly reversible with time (Eslinger and Damasio, 1985; Rousseaux *et al.*, 1996; D'Esposito *et al.*, 1996). Following a stroke or other acute brain affection, it seems highly desirable to clearly discriminate three distinct phases in the evolution and recovery processes: the initial phase usually extends from the lesion onset to 3 or 4 weeks post-onset; the secondary phase from the first to the sixth to eighth month; the late phase usually begins after 10–12 months. Indeed, the severity and even the presence of non-spatial attention disorders can vary considerably over time.

A third problem concerns the evaluation of the premorbid cognitive status of CVA patients. Recent studies have shown that, after 60 years of age, a pre-existing cognitive deterioration is frequent. In patients presenting with dementia three months after a stroke, more than one-third probably had Alzheimer's disease (Tatemichi *et al.*, 1992). Pohjasvaara *et al.* (1998) observed a cognitive decline before the stroke in 9.1% of patients aged 55–70 years, and in 15.7% of patients aged 71–85 years. Using a standardized questionnaire for the detection of pre-existing dementia demonstrated a higher frequency (Henon *et al.* 1997). Discrete cognitive disorders are even more frequent than dementia (Colantonio *et al.*, 1993). In none of the series of patients with attention disorders following stroke, has the presence of a discrete or moderate pre-existing cognitive decline been formally addressed. A few studies mention the exclusion of patients with obvious dementia. In haemorrhagic vascular pathology, the potential risk of secondary hydrocephalus must also be taken into account, especially following aneurysm rupture. This hydrocephalus can by itself be the source of a discrete to severe cognitive decline, and especially of attention disorders.

Instrumental assessment of attention processes in patients with cerebrovascular disease

The approach of most authors has consisted in identifying the components of attention that could be principally or selectively affected by focused CVA lesions, with the aim of discriminating, often roughly, the subjacent systems. They have mainly evaluated the effect of the localization of lesions on a sagittal axis, by investigating selectively, or in a comparative way, the consequences of anterior and posterior brain injury. Other have more specifically addressed the discrimination of the effect of right and left lesions. Most recent studies have attempted to more precisely define the critical structures whose lesions are correlated with the severity of the attention disorders, mainly in the anterior prefrontal and cingular brain areas.

We will consider successively these different approaches. They are complementary to the investigations of the consequences of circumscribed surgical cortical resections (Wilkins *et al.*, 1987; Richer *et al.*, 1993) or focused tumoral lesions.

Effect of the anterior or posterior localization of lesions

In the context of non-spatial attention, this remains the principal subject of reflections and investigations. However, alteration of attention processes has been poorly evaluated in patients with posterior brain injury, although some authors have discussed whether they could suffer from impaired discrimination between stimuli (Cohen, 1993). Most often, they have been used as a reference group in the analysis of consequences of anterior brain lesions.

Perceptuo-motor slowing and alertness

Perceptuo-motor slowing has been distinguished from purely attentional dysfunction. However, it can be induced by altered alertness, notably by repeated 'lapses of attention', even when the task is associated with relatively frequent responses, and it can be considered as a disorder of the 'intensive' aspect of attention. It should be considered first, as it can explain more severe impairment of brain-injured patients in more complex tasks investigating focused or divided attention, in comparison with simple tasks (van Zomeren and Brouwer, 1994).

In patients with frontal lesions, perceptuo-motor slowing has been observed in most studies using simple visual or auditory RT (Benton and Joynt, 1958; Godefroy *et al.*, 1996). One of these (Godefroy *et al.*, 1996) has suggested that it is relatively well correlated with the presence of a lesion in the frontal dorsolateral cortex of the left hemisphere. This slowing is not specific to anterior pathology, and seems to be of similar amplitude in patients with posterior brain injury (Benton and Joynt, 1958; Godefroy *et al.*, 1996).

Vigilance and sustained attention

One single study has specifically investigated this problem in the context of CVA, in patients presenting with frontal, anterior cingulate and basal forebrain lesions (Godefroy *et al.*, 1994a). The authors have assessed 11 patients in the secondary stage of disease (see definition above) using a visual Go–nogo test lasting for 24 minutes (two consecutive sessions of 12 minutes each) and infrequent target stimuli. Patients were slower than controls, but without any increase in RT between the first and the second part. Mean RT and variance had a tendency to be reduced in the second session, in both groups. Equivalent results were observed for omission and false alarms (commission errors), which were more frequent in patients than controls. A further argument for the absence of vigilance disorder came from the study of fatigability in unimodal (visual or auditory), and bimodal (visual and auditory) RT tasks. Patients and controls showed a comparable increase in RT with time. This study showed an absence of vigilance disorders in patients with well-defined frontal insult. The severe slowing and higher frequency of errors rather suggested a disorder of focused attention. Such a dissociation justified the differentiation between vigilance and selective attention.

It must be emphasized that these results are in relative contradiction to those of two other studies evaluating the consequences of lesions of a different nature. Wilkins *et al.* (1987) investigated patients who had undergone localized cortical resection for relief of epilepsy, using a task of counting series of auditory or tactile stimuli presented at increasing frequencies (1 to 7 Hz). Subjects with removals involving the right frontal lobe made a greater number of errors than those with a left frontal injury or a right or left temporal lesion, and this was selectively observed at a low frequency of stimulation (1 Hz). These results were interpreted as reflecting a vigilance disorder. However, the concepts and the task were both different from those used by most other authors. Furthermore, the frontal patients' impairment could have been induced by slowness in learning the procedure (novelty effect), as low-frequency stimulations were always presented before high-frequency ones. Rueckert and Grafman (1996) investigated patients the majority of whom had received a penetrating brain injury. In a simple RT task which lasted for 30 minutes (3 × 10), patients had increased slowness and omissions, and this was more important in right than in left lesions. However, the decrement in performance with time was similar in patients and controls. In a conditional RT task (Go–nogo; two sets of trials, 2 × 5 minutes each), patients with a right frontal injury were the only ones to show a significant increase in RT. They also showed a more severe increase in omissions with time than the other groups. Furthermore, there was no effect of the lesion volume on RT and omissions.

In conclusion, the assertion that frontal lobe lesions are associated with vigilance disorders must be considered with caution. The differences in results between studies are most likely related to methodological (and perhaps conceptual) discrepancies. They might also have been caused by the diversity of lesions.

Focused attention

Focusing has been the most frequently investigated attention capacity. Most studies have used chronometric measures with Go–nogo tasks.

Salmaso and Denes (1982) examined 10 patients with anterior and 10 others with unilateral posterior damage of vascular origin. Two tachitoscopic tasks were presented, one with pairs of letters, the other with pairs of lines. Patients had to respond to selected stimuli (1 out of 5). Non-parametric estimates of sensitivity and criterion (false positive rate) were calculated. The main result was that patients with anterior lesions had reduced sensitivity and an increased false positive rate (more liberal criterion), in comparison with those with posterior lesions and normal controls, who did not show any inter-group difference. Furthermore, there was no effect of the lateralization of lesions on both variables.

Godefroy and Rousseaux (1996a) and Godefroy *et al.* (1996) analysed focused attention in patients with anterior (11 cases) or posterior lesions (11 cases), at the secondary phase after the onset of CVA, using bimodal RT tasks (visual and auditory). In the Go–nogo test, they had to respond to one type (visual or auditory) of stimulus presented at random. Reaction times were compared to those obtained in a simple bimodal task, with systematic response to both types of stimuli. In the bimodal test, two distinct situations were compared: the ipsimodal one, where the preceding stimulus was of similar modality (visual–visual or auditory–auditory), and the crossmodal one, where it was not (visual–auditory or auditory–visual). Reaction times were significantly longer in patients than in controls, in the Go–nogo as well as in the simple bimodal condition, and in the crossmodal as well as in the ipsimodal situation. The most important finding was a severe crossmodal prolongation of RT of the anterior frontal group in the Go–nogo test. This increase in RT in the Go–nogo test was similar in patients with posterior stroke and controls. Errors were more frequent in frontal patients, in the crossmodal situation, and were more often of the commission (false alarm) than of the omission type. Sensitivity (Grier, 1971) was reduced, and the response criterion was increased in frontal patients. This was similar in both conditions (ipsimodal and crossmodal). Furthermore, the crossmodal retardation was correlated with the severity of lesions in the head of the left caudate nucleus, but not with the lesion volume.

It must be emphasized that some of these results were quite similar to those obtained in a more limited study of patients with frontal or posterior lesions of other etiology (Drewe, 1975).

Other investigations of focused attention have been performed using the Stroop test, which specifically addresses the interference effect between reading (automatic processing), and colour naming (controlled processing).

Rousseaux *et al.* (1996) evaluated 21 patients presenting with frontal lesions after rupture of an AACA. At the secondary phase, they were significantly slower than controls, and this slowness was more severe in the interferential than in the simple naming task. The error rate was higher in patients, in the interferential condition. However, both deficits disappeared at the late phase (10 to 16 months post-stroke). These results therefore suggest a disorder of focused attention in frontal patients, which is largely reversible with time. Furthermore, the error rate correlated with the severity of lesions in the left anterior cingulate cortex. Results obtained at the secondary phase were close to those demonstrated by Vendrell *et al.* (1995) in a series of 32 patients with frontal lesions, most often post-traumatic or tumoral.

The sensitivity to distracting sensory information has been evaluated by Chao and Knight (1995) in three groups of patients presenting (>6 months post-onset of lesion) with a dorsolateral frontal (7 cases), temporoparietal (5 cases), or posteromedial temporal (hippocampic or parahippocampic, 5 cases) lesion. The task consisted of a similarity decision (yes–no) between two stimuli (environmental sounds) presented successively at various intervals of 4 to 12.6 seconds. Intervals were (distractor condition) or were not (no-distractor condition) occupied by the presentation of interfering stimuli (pure tones). In the no-distractor trials, patients exhibited a higher percentage of errors than normal control subjects, without any between-groups difference. In the distractor condition, prefrontal patients were impaired at all delays, and deficits increased at longer delays. Hippocampic patients were impaired at longer delays, related to long-term memory disorders, while temporoparietal patients were comparable to controls. These data then suggested that the dorsolateral prefrontal cortex is critical for gating irrelevant sensory inputs.

In conclusion, most studies of focused attention suggest specific impairment of patients with frontal lesions, as compared with patients with posterior injury or normal controls. Furthermore, relations with more specific frontal structures were relatively variable, but principally concerned the dorsolateral frontal cortex and the anterior cingulate gyrus.

Divided attention

Divided attention is considered as one of the key functions of the central executive system of working memory (Baddeley, 1986). Usually, it is operationally defined by the capacity to simultaneously perform different tasks (most often two). However, it can also be assessed, at a more basic level, by the control of inputs arising from different perceptual channels (simultaneous monitoring).

Division and switching of attention between perceptual channels (visual and auditory) has been investigated in the groups of patients previously described (Godefroy and Rousseaux, 1996a; Godefroy *et al.*, 1996), presenting with anterior or posterior vascular lesions. Three RT tasks were compared:

one unimodal visual task, one unimodal auditory task, and one bimodal task using similar visual or auditory stimuli, in a pseudo-random order of presentation. Unimodal and bimodal tests only differed in the number of perceptual channels to be monitored. Patients with frontal lesions were slower than controls, and their RT more markedly increased than in patients with posterior lesions and normal controls, while changing from the unimodal to the ipsimodal situation of the bimodal task. Furthermore, this result was especially marked at brief interstimuli intervals (1 second, in comparison with 4, 7 and 10 seconds). Patients with posterior lesions were slower in the crossmodal than in the ipsimodal situation, and in the ipsimodal than in the unimodal condition, but this was comparable to what was observed in normal subjects. Furthermore, the index of divided attention correlated with the clinical evaluation of distractibility, and was explained by the presence of lesions in the left dorsolateral prefrontal cortex, and the right lesion volume. Two separate phenomena could therefore be described in frontal patients: the ipsimodal and the crossmodal retardations of RT. The ipsimodal retardation showed that these patients are more sensitive to the uncertainty of the modality of the next stimulus to be presented, suggesting a deficit of divided attention between perceptual channels. The crossmodal retardation is a priori related to a slowing in shifting from one perceptual channel to the other.

Division of attention between tasks was more recently investigated (Leclercq *et al.*, 2000) in patients with vascular prefrontal lesions (9 cases with AACA) or traumatic brain injury (TBI; 16 cases). Tasks consisted of simple visual RT and random number generation (RNG) (Baddeley, 1966; Rosenberg *et al.*, 1990), in single- and dual-task conditions. RT was lengthened in stroke and TBI patients in comparison with normal controls, with no difference between them. In AACA and TBI patients, RT was more markedly increased in the dual- than in the single-task condition. Furthermore, the ratio of RT obtained in patients and controls (patients' RT/controls' RT) increased from 1.34 in the single-task condition to 1.55 in the dual task, suggesting that this result was not simply related to perceptuo-motor slowing (van Zomeren and Brouwer, 1994). In the RNG task, frontal stroke patients were less random than TBI patients and controls, who had a similar level of performance. Furthermore, forward and backward digit spans were well preserved, and significant correlations were observed between randomization ability and digit span backward or literal and categorical fluency. These results suggested that divided attention, altered in both patient groups (as shown by the severe increase of RT in the dual-task condition), is quite independent of working memory (preserved in both patient groups), and of the ability to randomize (deficit only in the group of patients with vascular prefrontal lesions).

In conclusion, studies of CVA patients have shown strong associations between divided attention and frontal structure, especially the dorsolateral frontal cortex. These results are congruent with evidence arising from PET scan and functional MRI studies of normal subjects (D'Esposito *et al.*, 1995).

Attention in subcortical lesions

No exhaustive study of attention components has been performed, even in patients presenting with thalamic lesions, but several authors have suggested that this nuclear structure could play a major role in attention processes (Watson *et al.*, 1981; Mesulam, 1981, 1990; LaBerge, 1995).

In the case of thalamic CVA, exhaustive case studies have been reported, in which attention performance was partially evaluated. Following anterior thalamic lesions, perceptuo-motor slowing has been described on the basis of increased simple RT (Rousseaux *et al.*, 1991). Increase in time or interference errors are frequently observed in the Stroop test (Bogousslavsky *et al.*, 1986; Sandson *et al.*, 1991; Pepin and Auray-Pepin, 1993). In internal and paramedial thalamic lesions, attention disorders have sometimes been described on clinical and behavioural grounds, but formal assessment has rarely and even then only partially been performed; Malamut *et al.* (1992) reported mild impairment in sustained and focused attention (Continuous Performance Test, Stroop test) in one patient. In another patient with a dorsolateral infarct, there was neither slowness nor increased errors in the Stroop test, cancellation test (omissions, false alarms), and Trail Making Test (Rousseaux *et al.*, 1995). In other cases with more extended unilateral injury, authors often observed non-specific cognitive slowing in simple RT tasks, or in some investigations of the dysexecutive syndrome, but the impairment of focused attention (Stroop test) was inconstant (Hashimoto *et al.*, 1995; Rousseaux *et al.*, 1998). Overall, these studies suggest a role of the anterior thalamus in focused attention. It must be emphasized that the anterior and medial thalamic nuclei are tightly associated with the mediobasal and dorsolateral prefrontal cortex (Powell, 1973).

In striatal vascular lesions, the presence of attention disorders has never been assessed using chronometric tasks. When the striatum is selectively altered, patients do not present perceptuo-motor slowing in simple visual or auditory RT tasks (Godefroy *et al.*, 1992). Slowing can be demonstrated in more complex tasks, such as the Trail Making Test, but without a concomitant increase in errors. Furthermore, it seems that frontal lobe dysfunction principally arises when the subcortical lesions are associated with a frontal or temporal cortex injury.

Effect of the right or left lateralization of lesions

Several studies have suggested that consequences of lesions of the right and left cerebral hemispheres are not equivalent – some of the attention components such as tonic arousal or vigilance being more specifically impaired by right-hemispheric (and most often anterior) lesions; others such as focused or divided attention (non-spatial) being more severely altered following left injuries. However, results of various studies are somewhat heterogeneous.

Perceptuo-motor slowing and alertness

A certain number of studies on simple RT have suggested that patients with right lesions are slower than those with left injury.

De Renzi and Faglioni (1965) have investigated an important series of patients presenting with left- (98) or right-hemispheric (68) lesions, which were most often of vascular origin. In a simple visual RT task, they were slower than normal controls, especially in the case of right-hemisphere insult. Slowing was confirmed by Benson and Barton (1970), in a heterogeneous population of patients, whose lesions were principally tumoral and sometimes vascular. Simple visual and auditory RTs were more severely increased in patients with right than left lesions, with no difference between the latter and controls. Furthermore, patients with anterior lesions were discretely slower than those with posterior lesions, but without significant difference. The results of the study of Howes and Boller (1975) went in the same direction. The patient sample was heterogeneous with respect to etiology, with a predominance of brain tumours. Simple auditory RT was much more increased in patients with non-dominant hemisphere lesions (most often the right one) than with dominant hemisphere lesions. Furthermore, RT was usually prolonged at shorter (4 seconds) rather than longer (15 seconds) interstimuli intervals, namely in patients with non-dominant hemisphere lesions. Slowing was not correlated with the size of the lesions, but with the site within the non-dominant hemisphere, with parietal and basal ganglia structures playing an important role. Nakamura and Taniguchi (1977) evaluated 22 patients presenting with a minor hemiparesis as a sequel of a unilateral stroke. They had to extend the middle finger, as quickly as possible, in response to a brief sound presentation. The premotor time (from the sound presentation to the onset of surface EMG activity) was differentiated from the motor time (from the onset of EMG activity to the beginning of the finger move). The overall RT was significantly increased in both hands in the case of left hemiparesis, and in the right hand in the case of right hemiparesis. The premotor time was increased on both hands in left, but not in right, hemiparesis. The motor time was increased in both groups in the hand affected by the hemiparesis. These results then suggested that right lesions are responsible for premotor slowing and for an increase in motor time on the contralateral arm, while left ones only induce an increase in the contralateral motor time.

However, the more severe slowness of patients with right lesions has been challenged by other authors. The first study on consequences of unilateral lesions was presented by Benton and Joynt (1958). Most patients suffered from a brain neoplasm or CVA. In a simple RT task, visual stimuli were preceded by an auditory warning signal. Increased RTs were observed in patients with right or left injury, with higher values in the latter group, but without between-groups difference. Results from Dee and Van Allen (1973) were quite similar: patients with right or left lesions exhibited comparable RTs in a simple visual detection task. Tartaglione *et al.* (1986) have re-evaluated the problem of simple RT slowing, in order to elucidate the potential influence of the lesion side and of an alerting stimulus on the right–left asymmetry. Indeed, it appeared from the previous studies that the increase in RT of patients with right-hemisphere lesions could have been triggered by the use of a warning signal. The sample consisted of 74 patients with unilateral vascular or neoplastic lesion (right: 34; left: 40) and 30 controls. The simple visual RT task with and without an auditory warning signal was used. Both groups of patients showed longer RTs than controls. Without a warning stimulus, patients with right lesions were slightly slower than those with left ones, but the difference was not significant. No difference was observed in the presence of a warning stimulus. Furthermore, slowing was correlated with the lesion volume in right-hemisphere patients, but not in the left ones, as previously suggested by Boller *et al.* (1970); and in the left-hemisphere group, aphasic patients were slower than non-aphasics, in spite of a relatively similar lesion volume. Audet *et al.* (2000) investigated a series of 46 right-brain-damaged and 37 left-brain-damaged patients, using Go–nogo tasks. The presence of a warning signal resulted in an improvement in RT which was discretely more important (just above significance) in the second patient group.

In conclusion, more severe increase in RT has often been suggested to be associated with right-hemisphere injuries. However, this assumption must be relativized by two considerations: the first one is that subjects presenting with relatively severe aphasia (and a left injury) may have been partially discarded from the series which demonstrated a clear-cut right–left asymmetry; the second one is that the spatial neglect of some of the patients with right-hemisphere lesions may have favoured the RT slowing down for stimuli presented in the central part of the visual field. Furthermore, the few investigations of alertness presented diverging results. Therefore, considering the relative heterogeneity of the literature and these methodological problems, further studies are indispensable, using a more precise analysis of the localization and importance of lesions, and of the influence of associated factors.

Vigilance and sustained attention

Several works have analysed the differential influence of the lesion side on prolonged tasks which potentially assess vigilance or sustained attention. In the study already cited above of De Renzi and Faglioni (1965), patients were presented with a continuous choice RT task, in which they had to respond exclusively to the simultaneous occurrence of a black circle and a white square, and to ignore other combinations of stimuli. Tests lasted for 12.5 minutes, but the frequency of configurations to respond to was relatively high (34%). Dependent variables were correct responses and the sum of omissions and false alarms, without evaluation of their progression with time. Patients showed weaker performance than controls, but without differential effect of the lesion side. Results were interpreted as reflecting a vigilance disorder, but this does not correspond to the criteria we have previously reported (Parasuraman, 1984), and especially that of a performance decrement. They more probably reflected a disorder of focused attention, as in the classical Go–nogo tasks. As previously reported, Rueckert and Grafman (1996) have analysed sustained attention in patients presenting with frontal lobe lesions (most often of traumatic origin). The decline in performance was more severe in patients with right frontal injury. Korda and Douglas (1997) have searched for vigilance disorders in a group of 21 aphasic stroke patients. Processing speed (verbal or visual material) was reduced, and this increased with the task complexity. Vigilance was assessed by the continuous identification of a target letter with rare occurrence for as long as 32 minutes. There was a decline of performance in aphasics and controls, as demonstrated by increased RT. However, this decline was comparable in both groups, suggesting that aphasic patients with a left-hemispheric lesion have preserved vigilance. Audet *et al.* (2000) investigated the time course of RT across four blocks of trials in a Go–nogo task, in the two groups of patients with right- or left-hemispheric stroke previously reported. The decrease in RT was modest and perfectly similar in both groups.

In conclusion, investigations of CVA patients have most often failed to demonstrate a clear effect of the lesion side, even if older studies have suggested that vigilance and sustained attention could be associated with the right hemisphere (Jerison, 1977; Dimond, 1979).

Focused attention

Very little information is available about the effect of the lateralization of lesions on focused attention. Benton and Joynt (1958) have assessed patients with right (20 cases) or left (20 cases) brain lesions in comparison with a similar control group (20 cases), using a visual two-choice task. Slowing was observed in both groups of patients and was discretely more severe in the case of left-hemisphere injury. Dee and Van Allen (1973) evaluated patients presenting with unilateral and mostly vascular lesions, in a variable (1, 2, 3, 4) choice RT task. The performance in the simple RT test (one choice) was comparable in the two groups of patients. Furthermore, RT increased in line with the number of choices. This increase was similar in patients with a right lesion and controls, but much more severe in those with a left lesion. Salmaso *et al.* (1976; Salmaso, 1980; Salmaso and Denes, 1982) obtained controversial results. In the first studies, there seemed to be a difference in the severity of alteration of the estimates of sensitivity and criterion, according to the hemispheric side of the brain injury. However, in a more recent investigation (Salmaso and Denes, 1982), no difference could be observed in both indices with respect to the lateralization of the vascular lesion. In a simple Go–nogo task, Audet *et al.* (2000) similarly observed no difference in RT between patients with right- or left-brain stroke.

In conclusion, there are weak arguments for a more severe impairment of focused attention in left than right lesions. This is in line with the studies that have shown significant relations between indices of focused attention (cross-modal retardation and commission rate in the Go–nogo task) and the left caudate nucleus (Godefroy *et al.*, 1996) or the left anterior cingulum (Rousseaux *et al.*, 1996). It must be emphasized that the left–right asymmetry has not been observed in studies of patients with lesions of other origin (Drewe, 1975)

Divided attention

As far as we know, no study of the consequences of vascular disorders has investigated the effect of the lateralization of the lesions on divided attention. In the Godefroy *et al.* (1996) study, the index of divided attention (ipsimodal RT – unimodal RT, in bimodal and unimodal visual and/or auditory RT tests) depended on the presence of a lesion in the left dorsolateral cortex and the lesion volume in the right frontal lobe. The implication of the left dorsolateral cortex has also been reported in the PET-scan assessment of divided attention by D'Esposito *et al.* (1995) (but see Corbetta *et al.*, 1991, for challenging results).

Conclusion

The observation that, in certain studies, sustained attention and vigilance were more severely impaired in patients with right lesions, and focused or selective attention was more clearly affected by left-hemispheric lesions, has led several authors to propose that the two cerebral hemispheres hold two different attention systems (Jerison, 1977; Dimond, 1979). However, these oppositions have not been clearly confirmed by more recent studies, and the proposition remains hypothetical.

Specific studies of processes associated with attention

During the past forty years, a few studies have addressed the impairment of some processes tightly associated with attention, and especially motivation and decision processes. These processes have a main role in most of the tasks used, and most importantly in vigilance and focused attention.

Motivation

The effect of motivation has been studied in simple and choice RT tests. Blackburn (1958) investigated the effect of motivating instructions in patients with vascular or tumoral lesions, without taking into account the lateralization and the anterior–posterior situation. In a visual choice RT task, stimuli were presented on the right or the left. Following standard non-motivating instructions, patients were slower than controls. Introducing 'urging and evaluating' instructions resulted in a marked improvement in RT in both pathological and control groups. The effect was discretely more important in patients. However, the observation that their RTs were basically longer than those of controls must be taken into account. The presentation of 'relaxing and reassuring' instructions resulted in a modest reduction of RT in both groups. The simple repetition of the first standard task showed an increase in RT in brain-damaged patients, related to fatigability, while RT of the control group was not really modified. Shankweiler (1959) tried to more precisely define the relative influence of success or failure experience, using a similar paradigm. The standard retest instruction did not change the RT of control subjects and brain-damaged patients. The failure instruction, delivered during the retest period, resulted in an important and significant gain in speed in both groups, and especially in brain-damaged patients. The success instruction resulted in a small but statistically significant gain in both groups, which was more important in brain-damaged patients. The effect of motivating instructions on the performance in choice RT tasks in brain-damaged patients and controls was also investigated by Sturm and Büssing (1982). They found a comparable increase in performance in patients and controls with increasing motivational content of the instruction. This increase in performance was statistically significant in the response-driven but not in the stimulus-driven choice RT task.

This problem of the role of motivation has been more recently re-evaluated in patients presenting with a prefrontal and cingulate lesion (Godefroy *et al.*, 1994a), using simple visual, auditory or bimodal (visual and auditory) RT tests. The tests were first presented in a standard condition, thereafter following strong motivating instructions. A moderate effect of instructions was observed, with a reduction in RT, but without difference between patients and controls.

These results demonstrate that patients presenting with relatively non-localized or frontal and cingulate injury are still able to improve their performance level in simple RT or binary choice RT tasks, in spite of the classical involvement of the anterior limbic system in internal motivation. This could argue for the usefulness of distinguishing internal from external motivations, as one of these components seems to be relatively preserved.

Novelty effect and decision process

The importance of taking into account the novelty effect in tasks classically used in the evaluation of attention has recently been emphasized. Most paradigms used in the assessment of attention, vigilance and principally focused and divided attention, indeed require the subject to build up relations between a stimulus and the appropriate response. In most cases, this link is described verbally to the subject, and included in the instructions which are presented orally, before the task onset. This link is established in an unstable way by the use of training trials of limited number. In a first study of decision processes, Godefroy and Rousseaux (1996b) have shown, using binary choice RT tests, that prefrontal patients were slightly slower than controls, but were not more impaired than patients with posterior lesions and controls in choice RT versus simple RT. Furthermore, their hit rate was comparable to that of controls, except in the first choice test with which they were confronted, suggesting a sensitivity to novel operations. In a second study (Godefroy and Rousseaux, 1997), these authors have re-evaluated the application of new decision rules by comparing overlearned stimulus–response associations to new ones, in choice RT tests similar to the previous ones. Patients were slower than controls, and this was more obvious in the frontal than in the posterior group. Reaction time was longer for new stimuli. Furthermore, the increase in RT for the trials requiring a response that differed from the previous one was more marked in frontal patients, especially when the trial involved novel stimuli. Hit scores were less frequent for novel stimuli and the novelty effect was more marked in the frontal group. Further analysis using the Relative Judgement Theory (Link, 1975) showed that the threshold of activation of the appropriate response was lower for novel decisions, and that the decision time was longer for novel stimuli. This phenomenon was more specifically observed in frontal patients. It must be emphasized that these results were observed in patients who did not present with any disorder of working memory, as assessed by the Sternberg's paradigm (Godefroy *et al.*, 1999). There was no correlation between the reduction in correct responses for new stimuli and the assessment of short-term (digit span) and long-term memories. The novelty effect is of major importance in the understanding of the impairment of frontal patients. It is a priori linked to their difficulties in establishing internal referents (Fuster, 1989; Shallice and Burgess, 1991). This impairment is likely to be one of the main consequences of the prefrontal injury, which largely helps to explain patients' disorders on more complex tasks. Furthermore, this disorder can be observed independently of the working memory capacity, which remains largely unaffected in such patients.

Relations between non-spatial and spatial attention

Even if it seems appropriate to separate non-spatial from spatial attention processes, especially in studying consequences of cerebral injury, tight links do exist between the two functions. These relations have been evaluated by Robertson *et al.* (1997) in 44 patients presenting with a right-hemisphere stroke. Significant correlations were observed between performance in a test of sustained attention (monotonous tone counting) and investigations of spatial attention (visuo-manual tasks). According to the authors, this finding can be explained on the basis of Posner's model (Posner and Petersen, 1990; Posner, 1995), which proposed that the system subserving sustained attention exerts a strong modulatory influence on the functioning of the spatial attention system located in the posterior part of the right hemisphere.

Electrophysiological studies of attention

Other ways of investigating attention disorders in circumscribed vascular lesions do exist. One of them, which has been extensively used by Knight (1991), consisted in studying either middle-latency evoked potentials (MAEPs; 0 to 50 msec), which evaluate the activity in the sensory paths and the primary sensory cortex, or late latency evoked potentials (LLEPs; 50 to 1,000 msec), which assess motor preparation, orientation and attention.

A first group of studies has evaluated the differential effect of restricted cortico-subcortical lesions on the amplitude of middle-latency evoked potentials. Knight *et al.* (1989) have recorded auditory evoked potentials in a group of patients presenting with dorsolateral prefrontal and premotor damage centred in Brodmann areas 9 and 46, most often of vascular origin, at least six months post lesion onset. A widespread increase in the amplitude of the Pa component (22–38 msec) was found, which was comparable for stimuli presented ipsilateral or contralateral to the lesion. This phenomenon was not due to peripheral factors, since the amplitudes of earlier waves were comparable between frontal patients and controls. The increase in the amplitude of Pa suggested a selective loss of inhibitory prefrontal control of input to the primary auditory regions. This phenomenon was later evaluated with a focus on the somatosensory input (Yamaguchi and Knight, 1990). The amplitude of the P26 somatosensory evoked potential was also enhanced in the frontal group, while the earlier components were preserved. In the Wisconsin Card Sorting Test, patients achieved significantly fewer categories and made more errors than controls, due to perseverative errors. These results were similarly interpreted as resulting from loss of inhibitory control of frontal origin on the early somatosensory selection capacity.

A second group of investigations assessed the consequences of prefrontal damage on the late components of evoked potentials (event-related potentials: ERPs), and especially on the P300 component, and the frontally distributed

N200-P300. Knight (1984) observed an alteration of the responses to novel and unexpected auditory stimuli in patients with prefrontal dorsolateral lesion. The normal N200 enhancement was absent, and the P300 response was altered in its latency and spatial distribution. It was significantly smaller at fronto-central sites, in relation to an alteration of the early fronto-centrally distributed component of the P300 (P3a), which is tightly associated with the occurrence of an unexpected stimulus. This result was later confirmed by the study of visual and somatosensory afferences (Yamaguchi and Knight, 1991; Knight, 1997). The P3a impairment occurs for both ipsilateral and contralateral presentations, but is maximal for contralateral stimulation.

Theoretical consequences of attention disorders observed in patients with cerebrovascular diseases

Several consequences of the study of patients with circumscribed CVA must be emphasized. The first one is that non-spatial attention must be partially differentiated from spatial attention. Patients with a posterior hemispheric stoke (left or right) did not present with clear divided non-spatial attention disorders, and are relatively able to shift between sources of stimuli (for example, visual to auditory), when this does not imply a spatial disengagement. This is clearly divergent from what has been described in visuo-spatial tasks, for which patients with posterior parietal lesions (right more often than left) are especially impaired. Furthermore, disorders of non-spatial shifting are tightly associated with frontal lesions, more specifically of the left prefrontal cortex. Then, some modulations can be suggested for Posner's model (Posner, 1980, 1995; Posner and Petersen, 1990) which proposes that three attentional networks can be described: one prefrontal system involved in the controlled processes of attention, one parietal system associated with the automatic orientation of attention, and one right-hemispheric system responsible for alertness and phasic cortical arousal; the second network (orientation of attention) is strongly associated with prefrontal structures and not posterior ones in non-spatial tasks.

A second consequence is that non-spatial attention is not a unitary process and that various attentional components must be separated. The main evidence for this comes from dissociations observed in group and single case studies. Group studies suggest that at least two attention components could be related to different lesion situations. The intensity aspect of attention, corresponding to alertness, sustained attention and vigilance, would be principally altered following right-hemisphere lesions, especially in an anterior and prefrontal situation (Rueckert and Grafman, 1996). In contrast, the selective component of attention could be mainly affected by the left-hemisphere injury, especially of the anterior type (Benton and Joynt, 1958; Dee and Van Allen, 1973). It must be emphasized that this simple dissociation has not been confirmed by other studies of patients with similar CVA or tumours (De Renzi and Faglioni, 1965; Salmaso and Denes, 1982; Drewe, 1975). Group studies also allow the analysis of correlations between the performance level and the severity of lesions in various anatomical sites. Such studies have suggested that the different attentional processes are associated with various frontal or subcortical lesion sites (Vendrell *et al.*, 1995; Godefroy *et al.*, 1996; Rousseaux *et al.*, 1996): simple perceptuo-motor speed with the left dorsolateral cortex, focused attention with the anterior striatum and the left anterior cingulum, divided attention with the left dorsolateral prefrontal cortex. Other evidence justifying the discrimination of different attentional processes comes from dissociations observed in multiple single case studies. In homogeneous samples of patients, a selective impairment of focused or divided attention could be demonstrated in some selected cases (Godefroy *et al.*, 1996).

A third consequence is that some of the attention processes must be separated from working memory. Godefroy *et al.* (1999) and Leclercq *et al.* (2000) have demonstrated dissociations between focused and divided attention and working memory components. This problem is of special importance, as attention and control processes have always been considered as being tightly associated with short-term or working memory, and more especially with its 'central executive' component (Baddeley, 1986).

The fourth consequence refers to anatomo-functional models of attention processes. The observation that different cognitive processes associated with attention are dissociable and associated with different prefrontal and anterior cingulate structures suggests a complex architecture of control processes and working memory in the anterior brain and subcortical structures (Mesulam, 1981, 1990; Fuster, 1989; Posner and Petersen, 1990). This multimodular organization is clearly supported by most of the recent activation studies of normal subjects which used PET scan or functional MRI (Corbetta *et al.*, 1991; D'Esposito *et al.*, 1995; Sturm *et al.*, 1999). In fact, the functional organization of attention and control processes cannot be represented by simple models, as was recently proposed (LaBerge, 1995, 1998).

Functional correlates of attention disorders and practical considerations

Relations between behavioural disorders of patients and results observed in laboratory testing have received limited attention. In frontal patients Godefroy *et al.* (1994a) observed that correlations between distractibility or aspontaneity and vigilance level (defined by RT) were absent or modest, while distractibility correlated with errors (false alarms plus omissions), in a vigilance test. Furthermore, distractibility but not aspontaneity was correlated with measures of divided and focused attention (Godefroy *et al.*, 1996). These correlations argue for the validity of studying attention processes using 'laboratory' RT tasks.

Leclercq *et al.* (see Chapter 3 in this book) have investigated the relations between attentional complaints of patients, close relatives and close health professionals and objective deficits in attention assessment (Zimmermann and Fimm's computerized battery of attention tests (TEA), 1994: phasic alertness, divided attention, Go–nogo test, and visual vigilance). Important findings were that: close relatives and professionals gave more severe estimations of disorders than patients did; patients with strokes had a more accurate estimation of their problem than those suffering from traumatic brain injury; self-estimation of attention disorders was relatively well correlated with the performance level in attention tests, especially those analysing alertness, focused attention (Go–nogo), and divided attention; and attentional complaints by patients with right-hemispheric injury were higher than those by the left-hemispheric lesion subjects. These results partially confirm the usefulness of objective estimation of the main attention components, as regards correlations with the subjective estimation by patients, and especially by close relatives and professionals.

More precise knowledge about the impairment of attention processes in brain-injured patients has important consequences for the organization of care. This is especially important as Sturm and Willmes (1991; see also Chapter 12 'Rehabilitation of attention disorders: a literature review', and Chapter 13 'Computerized training of specific attention deficits in stroke and brain-injured patients: a multicentric efficacy study' in this book) have shown that rehabilitation techniques have a clear efficiency when they are specifically dedicated to the care of a single attention component. Programmes for alleviating non-spatial attention disorders must be systematically introduced in neurorehabilitation centres, and these programmes must be adapted to the impairments which can be potentially observed in patients.

Conclusion

In conclusion, the study of patients presenting with CVA can bring clear insights into the organization of attentional processes in two separate and complementary ways. The first one is the differentiation of attention components by dissociating affected from non-affected processes. The second refers to the anatomo-functional models of attention (attention networks) and controlled processing, as lesions involving circumscribed and well-defined brain structure can selectively impair restricted and unitary processes associated with attention. Furthermore, in a given patient, a better specification of the non-spatial attentional disorders resulting from the cerebrovascular injury is indispensable before setting up rehabilitation programmes.

References

Audet, T., Mercier, L., Collard, S., Rochette, A. and Réjan, H. (2000). Attention deficits: is there a right hemisphere specialisation for simple reaction time, sustained attention, and phasic alertness? *Brain and Cognition*, *43*, 17–21.

Baddeley, A.D. (1966). The capacity for generating information by randomization. *Quarterly Journal of Experimental Psychology*, *18*, 119–129.

Baddeley, A. (1986). *Working Memory*. Oxford: Clarendon Press.

Baron, J.C., D'Antona, R., Pantano, P., Serdaru, M., Samson, Y. and Bousser, M.G. (1986). Effects of thalamic stroke on energy metabolism of the cerebral cortex. *Brain*, *109*, 1243–1256.

Benson, D.F. and Barton, M.I. (1970). Disturbance in constructional ability. *Cortex*, *6*, 19–46.

Benton, A.L. and Joynt, R.J. (1958). Reaction time in unilateral cerebral disease. *Confina Neurologica*, *19*, 247–256.

Blackburn H.L. (1958). Effect of motivating instructions on reaction times in cerebral diseases. *Journal of Abnormal and Social Psychology*, *56*, 359–366.

Bogousslavsky, J., Regli, F. and Assal, G. (1986). The syndrome of unilateral tuberothalamic artery territory infarction. *Stroke*, *17*, 434–441.

Boller, F., Howes, D. and Patten, D.H. (1970). A behavioral evaluation of brain-scan estimates of lesion size. *Neurology*, *20*, 852–859.

Broadbent, D.E. (1958). *Perception and Communication*. Oxford: Pergamon.

Chao, L.L. and Knight, R.T. (1995). Human prefrontal lesions increase distractibility to irrelevant sensory inputs. *Neuroreport*, *6*, 1605–1610.

Cohen, R.A. (1993). Neuroanatomical disorders of attention affecting sensory selection. In R.A. Cohen (ed.) *The Neuropsychology of Attention*. New York: Plenum Press, pp. 189–218.

Colantonio, A., Kasl, S.V., Ostfeld, A.M. and Berkman, L.F. (1993). Psychosocial predictors of stroke outcomes in an elderly population. *Journal of Gerontology*, *48*, 261–268.

Corbetta, M., Miezin, F.M., Dobmeyer, S., Shulman, G.L. and Petersen, S.E. (1991). Selective and divided attention during visual discriminations of shape, color, and speed: functional anatomy by positron emission tomography. *Journal of Neurosciences*, *11*, 2383–2402.

Dee, H.L. and Van Allen, M.W. (1973). Speed of decision-making processes in patients with unilateral cerebral disease. *Archives of Neurology*, *28*, 163–166.

De Renzi, E. and Faglioni, P. (1965). The comparative efficiency of intelligence and vigilance tests in detecting hemispheric cerebral damage. *Cortex*, *1*, 410–433.

D'Esposito, M., Alexander, M.P., Fischer, R., McGlinchey-Berroth, R. and O'Connor, M. (1996). Recovery of memory and executive function following anterior communicating artery aneurysm rupture. *Journal of the International Neuropsychological Society*, *2*, 565–570.

D'Esposito, M., Detre, J.A., Alsop, D.C., Shin, R.K., Atlas, S. and Grossman, M. (1995). The neural basis of the central executive system of working memory. *Nature*, *378*, 279–281.

Dimond, S.J. (1979). Disconnection and psychopathology. In J.H. Gruzelier and P.

Flor-Henry (eds) *Hemispheres' Asymmetries of Function in Psychopathology*. Amsterdam: Elsevier, pp. 35–47.

Drewe, E.A. (1975). Go No-Go learning after frontal lobe lesions in humans. *Cortex*, *11*, 8–16.

Eslinger, P.J. and Damasio, A.R. (1985). Severe disturbance of higher cognition after bilateral frontal lobe ablation. *Neurology*, *35*, 1731–1741.

Fuster, J.M. (1989). *The Prefrontal Cortex. Anatomy, Physiology, and Neuropsychology of the Frontal Lobe* (2nd edn). New York: Raven Press.

Godefroy, O., Cabaret, M., Petit-Chenal, V., Pruvo, J.P. and Rousseaux, M. (1999). Control functions of the frontal lobes. Modularity of the central-supervisory system? *Cortex*, *35*, 1–20.

Godefroy, O., Cabaret, M. and Rousseaux, M. (1994a). Vigilance and effects of fatigability, practice and motivation on simple reaction time tests in patients with lesion of the frontal lobe. *Neuropsychologia*, *32*, 983–990.

Godefroy, O., Lhullier, C. and Rousseaux, M. (1996). Non-spatial attention disorders in patients with frontal or posterior brain damage. *Brain*, *119*, 191–202.

Godefroy, O. and Rousseaux, M. (1996a). Divided and focused attention in patients with lesion of the prefrontal cortex. *Brain and Cognition*, *30*, 155–174.

Godefroy, O. and Rousseaux, M. (1996b). Binary choice in patients with prefrontal or posterior brain damage. A relative judgment theory analysis. *Neuropsychologia*, *34*, 1029–1038.

Godefroy, O. and Rousseaux, M. (1997). Novel decision making in patients with prefrontal or posterior brain damage. *Neurology*, *49*, 695–701.

Godefroy, O., Rousseaux, M., Leys, D., Destée, A., Scheltens, Ph. and Pruvo, J.P. (1992). Frontal lobe dysfunction in unilateral lenticulostriate infarcts. *Archives of Neurology*, *49*, 1285–1289.

Grier, J.B. (1971). Nonparametric indexes for sensitivity and bias: computing formulas. *Psychological Bulletin*, *75*, 424–429.

Hashimoto, R., Yoshida, M. and Tanaka, Y. (1995). Utilization behaviour after right thalamic infarction. *European Neurology*, *35*, 58–62.

Henon, H., Pasquier, F., Durieu, I., Godefroy, O., Lucas, C., Lebert, F. and Leys, D. (1997). Preexisting dementia in stroke patients. Baseline frequency, associated factors, and outcome. *Stroke*, *28*, 2429–2436.

Howes, D. and Boller, F. (1975). Simple reaction time; evidence for focal impairment from lesions of the right hemisphere. *Brain*, *98*, 317–332.

Irle, E., Wowra, B., Kunert, H.J., Hampl, J. and Kunze, S. (1992). Memory disturbances following anterior communicating artery rupture. *Annals of Neurology*, *31*, 473–480.

Jerison, H.J. (1977). Vigilance: biology, psychology, theory and practice. In R.R. Mackie (ed.) *Vigilance (NATO conference series)*. New York: Plenum Press, pp. 27–40.

Knight, R.T. (1984). Decreased response to novel stimuli after prefrontal lesions in man. *Electroencephalography and Clinical Neurophysiology*, *59*, 9–20.

Knight, R.T. (1991). Evoked potentials studies of attention capacity in human frontal lobe lesions. In H.S. Levin, H.M. Eisenberg and A.L. Benton (eds) *Frontal Lobe Function and Dysfunction*. Oxford: Oxford University Press, pp. 139–156.

Knight, R.T. (1997). Distributed cortical network for visual attention. *Journal of Cognitive Neuroscience*, *9*, 75–91.

Knight, R.T., Scabini, D. and Woods, D.L. (1989). Prefrontal cortex gating of auditory transmission in humans. *Brain Research*, *504*, 338–342.

Korda, R.J. and Douglas, J.M. (1997). Attention deficits in stroke patients with aphasia. *Journal of Clinical and Experimental Neuropsychology*, *19*, 525–542.

LaBerge, D. (1995). *Attentional Processing*. Cambridge, MA: Harvard University Press.

LaBerge, D. (1998). L'attention comme amplificateur de l'activité corticale. *Revue de Neuropsychologie*, *8*, 53–81.

Leclercq, M., Couillet, J., Marlier, N., Azouvi, P., Martin, Y., Strypstein, E. and Rousseaux, M. (2000). Dual task performance after severe diffuse traumatic brain injury or vascular prefrontal damage. *Journal of Clinical and Experimental Neuropsychology*, *22*, 339–350.

Link, S.W. (1975). The relative judgement theory of two choice response time. *Journal of Mathematical Psychology*, *12*, 114–135.

Malamut, B.L., Graff-Radford, N., Chawluk, J., Grossman, R.L. and Gur, R.C. (1992). Memory in a case of bilateral thalamic infarction. *Neurology*, *42*, 163–169.

Mesulam, M.-M. (1981). A cortical network for directed attention and unilateral neglect. *Annals of Neurology*, *10*, 309–325.

Mesulam, M.-M. (1990). Large-scale neurocognitive networks and distributed processing for attention, language, and memory. *Annals of Neurology*, *28*, 597–615.

Nakamura, R. and Taniguchi, R. (1977). Reaction times in patients with cerebral hemiparesis. *Neuropsychologia*, *15*, 845–848.

Parasuraman, R. (1984). Sustained attention in detection and discrimination. In R. Parasuraman and D.R. Davies (eds) *Varieties of Attention*. New York: Academic Press, pp. 243–267.

Pepin, E.P. and Auray-Pepin, L. (1993). Selective dorsolateral frontal lobe dysfunction associated with diencephalic amnesia. *Neurology*, *43*, 733–741.

Pohjasvaara, T., Erkinjuntti, T., Vataja, R. and Kaste, M. (1998). Correlates of dependent living 3 months after ischemic stroke. *Cerebrovascular Disorders*, *8*, 259–266.

Posner, M.I. (1980). Orienting of attention. *Quarterly Journal of Experimental Psychology*, *32*, 3–25.

Posner, M.I. (1995). Attention in cognitive neuroscience, an overview. In M.S. Gazzaniga (ed.) *The Cognitive Neurosciences*. Cambridge, MA: MIT Press.

Posner, M. and Boies, S.J. (1971). Components of attention. *Psychological Review*, *78*, 391–408.

Posner, M.I. and Petersen, S.E. (1990). The attention system of the human brain. *Annual Review of Neuroscience*, *13*, 25–42.

Posner, M.I. and Rafal, R.D. (1987). Cognitive theories of attention and the rehabilitation of attentional deficit. In R.J. Meier, L. Diller and A.C. Benton (eds) *Neuropsychological Rehabilitation*. London: Livingstone, pp. 343–350.

Powell, E.W. (1973). Limbic projections to the thalamus. *Experimental Brain Research*, *17*, 394–401.

Richard, J.F. (1980). *L'Attention*. Paris: Presses Universitaires de France.

Richer, F., Decary, A., Lapierre, M.-F., Rouleau, I., Bouvier, G. and Saint-Hilaire, J.M. (1993) Target detection deficits in frontal lobectomy. *Brain and Cognition*, *21*, 203–211.

Robertson, I.H., Manly, T., Beschin, N., Daini, R., Haeske-Dewick, H., Homberg,

V., Jehkonen, M., Pizzamiglio, G., Shiel, A. and Weber, E. (1997). Auditory sustained attention is a marker of unilateral spatial neglect. *Neuropsychologia*, *35*, 1527–1532.

Rosenberg, S., Weber, N., Crocq, M.C., Duval, F. and Macher, J.P. (1990). Random number generation by normal, alcoholic and schizophrenic subjects. *Psychological Medicine*, *26*, 953–960.

Rousseaux, M., Cabaret, M., Benaïm, C. and Steinling, M. (1995). Déficit du rappel verbal par infarctus thalamique dorso-latéral gauche. *Revue Neurologique*, *151*, 36–46.

Rousseaux, M., Cabaret, M., Bernati, T., Pruvo, J.P. and Steinling, M. (1998). Déficit résiduel du rappel verbal après un infarctus de la veine cérébrale interne gauche. *Revue Neurologique*, *154*, 401–407.

Rousseaux, M., Godefroy, O., Cabaret, M., Benaïm, C. and Pruvo, J.P. (1996). Analyse et évolution des déficits cognitifs après rupture des anévrysmes de l'artère communicante antérieure. *Revue Neurologique*, *152*, 678–687.

Rousseaux, M., Huglo, D. and Steinling, M. (1994). Cerebral blood flow after surgery and prefrontal lesions of anterior communicating artery aneurysms. *Stroke*, *25*, 135–140.

Rousseaux, M., Kassiotis, P., Signoret, J.L., Cabaret, M. and Petit, H. (1991). Syndrome amnésique par infarctus restreint du thalamus antérieur droit. *Revue Neurologique*, *147*, 809–818.

Rousseaux, M., Steinling, M., Petit, H., Lesoin, F., Dubois, F. and Vergnes, R. (1986). Perturbations débimétriques hémisphériques et hématomes profonds. *Revue Neurologique (Paris)*, *142*, 480–488.

Rueckert, L. and Grafman, J. (1996). Sustained attention deficits in patients with right frontal lesions. *Neuropsychologia*, *34*, 953–963.

Salmaso, D. (1980). Hemispheric differences in a novel task requiring attention. *Perceptual and Motor Skills*, *51*, 383–391.

Salmaso, D. and Denes, G. (1982). Role of the frontal lobes on an attention task: a signal detection analysis. *Perceptual Motor Skills*, *54*, 1147–1150.

Salmaso, D., Denes, G. and De Stavola, G. (1976). Interhemispheric differences in attention to novelty. *Italian Journal of Psychology*, *3*, 273–283.

Sandson, T.A., Duffner, K.R., Carvalho, P.A. and Mesulam, M.M. (1991). Frontal lobe dysfunction following infarction of the left-sided medial thalamus. *Archives of Neurology*, *48*, 1300–1303.

Schneider, W. and Shiffrin, R.M. (1977). Controlled and automatic human information processing. I. Detection, search, and attention. *Psychological Review*, 84, 1–66.

Shallice, T. and Burgess, P. (1991). Higher-order cognitive impairments and frontal lobe lesions in man. In H.S. Levin, H.M. Eisenberg and A.I. Benton (eds) *Frontal Lobe Function and Dysfunction*. Oxford: Oxford University Press, pp. 125–138.

Shankweiler, D.P. (1959). Effects of success and failure instructions on reaction time in patients with brain damage. *Journal of Comparative Physiology and Psychology*, *52*, 546–549.

Shiffrin, R.M. and Schneider, W. (1977). Controlled and automatic human information processing. II. Perceptual learning, automatic attending, and a general theory. *Psychological Review*, *84*, 127–190.

Sturm, W. and Büssing, A. (1982). Zum Einfluβ motivierender Testinstruktionen auf die Reaktionsleistung hirngeschädigter Patienten. *Nervenarzt*, *53*, 395–400.

Sturm, W., de Simone, A., Krause, B.J., Specht, K., Hesselmann, V., Radermacher, I., Herzog, H., Tellmann, L., Muller-Gartner, H.W. and Willmes, K. (1999). Functional anatomy of intrinsic alertness: evidence for a fronto-parietal-thalamic-brainstem network in the right hemisphere. *Neuropsychologia*, *37*, 797–805.

Sturm, W. and Willmes, K. (1991). Efficacy of a reaction training on various attentional and cognitive functions in stroke patients. *Neuropsychological Rehabilitation*, *1*, 259–280.

Tartaglione, A., Bino, G., Manzino, M., Spadavecchia, L. and Favale, E. (1986). Simple reaction time changes in patients with unilateral brain damage. *Neuropsychologia*, *24*, 649–658.

Tatemichi, T.K., Desmond, D.W., Mayeux, R., Paik, M., Stern, Y., Sano, M., Remien, R.H., Williams, J.B.W., Mohr, J.P., Hauser, W.A. and Figueroa, M. (1992). Dementia after stroke: baseline frequency, risks, and clinical features in a hospitalized cohort. *Neurology*, *42*, 1185–1193.

van Zomeren, A.H. and Brouwer, W.H. (1987). Head injury and concepts of attention. In H.S. Levin, J. Grafman and H.M. Eisenberg (eds) *Neurobehavioral Recovery from Head Injury*. New York: Oxford University Press, pp. 398–415.

van Zomeren, A.H. and Brouwer, W.H. (1992). Assessment of attention. In J.R. Crawford, D.M. Parker and W.W. McKinlay (eds) *A Handbook of Neuropsychological Assessment*. London: Lawrence Erlbaum, pp. 241–265.

van Zomeren, A.H. and Brouwer, W.H. (1994). *Clinical Neuropsychology of Attention*. Oxford: Oxford University Press.

Vendrell, P., Junqué, C., Pujol, J., Jurado, L., Molet, J. and Grafman, J. (1995). Role of prefrontal regions in the Stroop task. *Neuropsychologia*, *33*, 341–352.

Watson, R.T., Valenstein, E. and Heilman, K.M. (1981). Thalamic neglect: possible role of the medial thalamus and nucleus reticularis thalami in behaviour. *Archives of Neurology*, *38*, 501–506.

Wilkins, A.J., Shallice, T. and McCarthy, R. (1987). Frontal lesions and sustained attention. *Neuropsychologia*, *25*, 359–365.

Yamaguchi, S. and Knight, R.T. (1990). Gating of somatosensory inputs by human prefrontal cortex. *Brain Research*, *521*, 281–288.

Yamaguchi, S. and Knight, R.T. (1991). Anterior and posterior association cortex contributions to the somatosensory P300. *Journal of Neurosciences*, *11*, 2039–2054.

Zimmermann, P. and Fimm, B. (1994). *Tests d'Evaluation de l'Attention (TEA)*. Würselen: Psytest.

Chapter 11

Attention disorders in neurodegenerative diseases

Fabienne Collette and Martial Van der Linden

A number of neuropsychological studies in recent years have shown that demented patients do not necessarily present a global deterioration and that the disease can impair some cognitive processes or systems, while sparing others. Moreover, qualitatively different patterns of cognitive impairment have been identified in association with different types of neurodegenerative dementias, such as Alzheimer's disease, Huntington's disease, Parkinson's disease, or frontotemporal dementia.

Among these cognitive impairments, deficits of attention are typically observed in neurodegenerative disorders (see Parasuraman and Haxby, 1993; Perry and Hodges, 1999; Spinnler, 1991; Van der Linden, 1994; Zakzanis, 1998). Cognitive models of attention such as that proposed by Posner and Petersen (1990) suggest that attention is not a homogeneous system and that separate subcomponents of attention can be distinguished, both at a functional and, to some extent, at an anatomical level. In particular, attention has been classically divided into the global categories of phasic alertness, vigilance, selective attention, and divided attention (Sturm *et al.*, 1997).

In this context, the purpose of the present chapter is to characterize the attentional disorders specifically observed in Alzheimer's disease and to compare the pattern of preserved and impaired attentional abilities observed in this disease to those associated with other types of dementia, especially Parkinson's disease, Huntington's disease, progressive supranuclear palsy and frontotemporal dementia.

1 Attentional deficits in Alzheimer's disease

Alzheimer's disease (AD) is characterized by the progressive accumulation of deficits affecting several cognitive domains, almost without any specific neurological signs. Neuropsychological studies have long been guided by a concept of a generalized and homogeneous impairment in AD patients. Consequently, neuropsychologists have searched for a typical cognitive profile (the 'essence') in AD patients. The application of cognitive psychology concepts and methods in the neuropsychological approach to AD has largely modified this point of view (Van der Linden, 1994; Venneri, Turnbull and Della Sala, 1996).

It is now widely acknowledged that the disease does not affect all cognitive processes or systems in a similar way. In addition, a large number of studies have shown that both the nature of the defective processes and the impairment progression can vary considerably from one AD patient to another. Such heterogeneity can be seen both between cognitive functions (for example, between language and visuo-spatial abilities, see Martin, 1990) and within a particular cognitive domain (for example, in the memory domain, see Baddeley, Della Sala and Spinnler, 1991b; Belleville, Peretz, and Malenfant, 1996; Collette *et al.*, 1999).

Memory (especially episodic memory) and attention (especially divided attention and some aspects of selective attention) deficits are among the first clinical manifestations to develop in Alzheimer's disease (Almkvist, 1996; Fabrigoule *et al.*, 1998; Lafleche and Albert, 1995; Parasuraman and Haxby, 1993; Perry and Hodges, 1999; Small *et al.*, 1997; Tierney *et al.*, 1996). The memory deficits have been related primarily to lesions of the hippocampus and medial temporal structures (Fox *et al.*, 1996; Kaye *et al.*, 1997; Laakso *et al.*, 1998), while the attention deficits are considered to be associated with lesions of cortical areas in the parietal and frontal lobes (Johannsen *et al.*, 1999).

1.1 Alertness, vigilance and sustained attention

An important attentional function is the ability to prepare and sustain attention alertness to process high-priority signals (Posner and Petersen, 1990, p. 35). In a recent study, Sturm *et al.* (1997) proposed, in line with Posner's theoretical propositions, the following definition of phasic and tonic alertness, vigilance and sustained attention. *Phasic alertness* represents the capability to enhance response readiness following a warning stimulus. Typical tasks for the assessment of phasic alertness are simple reaction time paradigms with and without presentation of a warning signal preceding the target stimulus. The reduction in response times (RT) after warning serves as an indicator of phasic alertness. *Tonic alertness* on the other hand is a relatively stable level of activation which changes only slightly and involuntarily. Tonic changes of alertness are mostly attributed to physiological, diurnal changes in the organism. *Vigilance* requires the subject to stay alert for a prolonged period of time in order to detect relevant but very infrequent stimuli, which appear at irregular intervals during the task. In contrast, *sustained attention* is concerned with the ability to detect a large number of items over a brief period of time.

Some studies have more specifically explored the phasic changes in alertness in AD. Nebes and Brady (1993) examined phasic alertness in AD patients and control subjects by a choice RT task in which subjects had to press one of two switches depending on the position of a square. In this task, the stimulus was usually preceded by an auditory warning signal. The time subjects needed to attain maximal phasic alertness was determined by varying the interval between the warning and the stimulus (stimulus onset asynchrony, SOA). Results indicated that AD patients showed a degree of benefit due to the tone warning, globally similar to control subjects, supporting the claim that phasic alertness is relatively unaffected by Alzheimer's disease. However, the benefit due to a warning signal is short-lived in AD patients and it takes a slightly longer time to reach the RT minimum. In another study, Pate *et al.* (1994) administered to mild and very mild AD patients and control subjects a simple reaction time task (SRT; to press a single response key every time one numeral appeared) and a choice reaction time task (CRT; to press one of two response keys following the presentation of one of two numerals). In both tasks, each trial began with the presentation of a visual warning signal and the target remained on the screen until either the subjects responded or 5 seconds had elapsed. All groups responded more quickly on the SRT than on the CRT task. Moreover, the two AD groups were disproportionately slower on the CRT task but only the mild AD patients were slower on the SRT task. The normal performance of very mild AD patients on the SRT task suggests that these patients benefited from the warning signal. The impairment of both groups of AD patients in the CRT task indicated that AD patients are disproportionately impaired on more complex cognitive attentional tasks.

A classical task used to evaluate vigilance and sustained attention is the Continuous Performance Test (Rosvold *et al.*, 1956), in which the targets are specific letters appearing occasionally and randomly in a series of non-target letters. Taken as a whole, the earlier studies using this task showed unimpaired sustained attention in AD patients (e.g. Lines *et al.*, 1991). Nebes and Brady (1993) explored more specifically whether there exists a vigilance decrement over time (resulting in increased reaction times from the beginning to the end of the task) in mild to moderate AD patients. They administered to AD patients and control subjects a task consisting in the presentation of a square in one of four possible positions on a screen. The subjects had to press one of four switches depending on the position of the square. AD patients were found to be slower overall in their reactions, but the difference in RT from the beginning to the end of the task was the same as in the control subjects, suggesting no deficit in vigilance. Slightly different results were found by Brazzelli *et al.* (1994) in a group of mildly impaired AD patients. In that study, deficits in vigilance in the group of AD patients were demonstrated by the increased difficulty in accurately discriminating targets and non-targets over time, although the changes in RT during the task were globally similar in the groups of AD patients and control subjects.

In conclusion, these studies suggest a normal sustained attention (Lines *et al.*, 1991), but some vigilance deficits seem to be present in more impaired AD patients (Brazzelli *et al.*, 1994). Similarly, no deficits in phasic alertness were found (at least when simple cognitive tasks were used), although AD patients needed more time to reach an optimal level of alertness (Nebes and Brady, 1993; Pate *et al.*, 1994).

1.2 Selective attention

Selective attention refers to the ability to shift attention between different sensory inputs in order to screen out irrelevant stimuli. Selective attention processes are involved in the orienting and shifting of spatial attention ('spatial-based attentional tasks') as well as in the detection, filtering and selection of appropriate targets from distractors ('object- and feature-based attentional tasks'). Specifically, these selective attention tasks include engaging or focusing attention on a location or on an attribute of the stimulus, disengaging attention, and shifting (or moving) to another location or attribute of the stimulus. In addition, selective attention may also involve inhibition of irrelevant stimuli (Posner and Cohen, 1984; Tipper, 1985). There is substantial evidence that a posterior attentional network controls these processes of spatial selective attention (Posner and Petersen, 1990) while inhibition processes require supplementary anterior cerebral areas (e.g. Taylor *et al.*, 1997). We will consider studies which have explored spatial selective attention, feature- and object-based selection and inhibition of irrelevant stimuli.

Spatial-based attention

Parasuraman *et al.* (1992) examined cue-directed shifts of spatial attention for a letter discrimination task in mild to moderate AD patients and elderly normal subjects. Before the presentation of the item, a visual warning cue was used. This cue could be valid, invalid or neutral regarding the location of the target. Two types of cues were used: symbolic (endogenous) cues presented at the fixation point (an arrow) and highly salient (exogenous) cues presented in the periphery near the expected stimulus location cue (brightening the side of the screen). Exogenous shifts of attention driven by peripheral cues have been found to be most effective at short SOAs, perhaps because such cues elicit an automatic or involuntary process which is short-lived and replaced by a subsequent, long-lasting voluntary process which is elicited by central, symbolic cues (Parasuraman and Greenwood, 1998). The results obtained in this study indicate a pattern of intact and impaired functioning in component operations underlying shifts of visuo-spatial attention. More precisely, AD patients showed an advantage similar to that of control subjects when the target was preceded by a valid cue compared to a neutral or invalid cue. This advantage exists for exogenous and endogenous cues, suggesting no impairment in engaging or focusing attention in the early stages of AD. In contrast, response to invalid cues led to a relative increase in response time in AD patients compared to controls, suggesting a specific impairment in disengaging or reorienting spatial attention. With regard to the type of cues used, the AD group showed a deficit in exogenous attention-shifting only at short SOAs, whereas endogenous attention-shifting was impaired at long SOAs. These data indicate that both automatic and voluntary orientations of attention are impaired in Alzheimer's disease. Finally, Parasuraman *et al.* showed that increased reaction time to invalid cues was associated with right parietal hypometabolism and argued that early-impaired disengagement of visuo-spatial functioning in AD may be linked to a dysfunction of cortico-cortical attentional networks linking the posterior parietal and frontal lobes.

Using a rather similar cue-directed spatial attention task, Oken *et al.* (1994) again showed there was a disproportionately worse performance following the presentation of invalid cues in AD patients compared to control subjects. The existence of a specific impairment in spatial attention in Alzheimer's disease was also found in a study by Scinto *et al.* (1994) using a different methodology. In that study, moderately affected Alzheimer patients were instructed in a first condition to attend to and fixate a target appearing randomly at the right or left of a central marker, and, in a second condition, to direct attention to and fixate a target appearing randomly in one of four peripheral locations. Eye movements were measured during the execution of the two tasks and they demonstrated that AD patients are less accurate in orienting and present longer saccade latencies in both tasks. Moreover, the performance of AD patients (but not control subjects) was worse in the second task which placed increased demand on attention. Finally, AD patients produced a high number of perseverative (incorrect initial fixation without subsequent correction or fixation of previously cued locations) and impersistence or impulsivity (the subject being unable to maintain fixation) errors. The number of perseverative responses recorded by AD patients also suggests problems with disengagement.

The ability to direct covert visual spatial attention was also examined by Maruff, Malone and Currie (1995) using a modified version of the Covert Orienting of Visual-spatial Attention Task (COVAT; Posner, 1980; Petersen, Robinson and Currie, 1989). This task provides a valid and reliable measure of an individual's ability to direct visual spatial attention to areas of the visual field without accompanying eye movements. The procedure consists in presenting a central fixation point flanked by two peripheral circles. The target of the task was a red spot that appeared at the centre of the peripheral circles. Spatial (valid and invalid) cues for the appearance of a target consist of a brief doubling of the luminance of one of the peripheral circles, and non-spatial (diffuse) cues consist of a weak diffuse luminance increase over the entire attended area of the visual field; they provide the same temporal information as the spatial cues but lack directional information. The RTs of AD patients on this task were significantly longer than those of a matched control group. However, the facilitation of RT for validly cued trials compared with reaction times for both invalidly and diffusely cued trials was similar in the two groups, but both invalid and diffuse effect sizes were larger for the Alzheimer's disease subgroup compared to control subjects. These data confirm that AD patients were able to utilize the peripheral cue to direct attention to the target location, but had some difficulties in disengaging attention from a previously cued location.

However, other studies using target detection rather than discrimination tasks failed to show the existence of a disengagement deficit in AD patients. For example, in the study by Parasuraman *et al.* (1992), a letter detection task was administered to a group of mild to moderate AD patients. This task consisted in detecting the appearance of a letter on the screen. Again, cues presented were valid, invalid or neutral, and the type of cues presented was endogenous or exogenous. Results indicated that, unlike the letter discrimination task, the reaction time following the presentation of both valid and invalid spatial location cues did not differ significantly between AD patients and control subjects. The authors interpreted these results as indicating a greater need for focal attention in the letter discrimination task, which required a choice RT response to one of several letters, compared with the letter detection task, where a simple RT response was required for a single letter.

These studies have examined attention-shifting in relatively impoverished visual environments. Typically, participants were required to engage or disengage attention to targets presented in an otherwise empty visual field. However, any difficulty in redirecting or disengageing visuo-spatial attention should become more evident if repeated shifts of attention are required to search for a target surrounded by distractors. In that context, Parasuraman, Greenwood and Alexander (1995) administered to a group of mild AD patients and healthy elderly subjects a cued visual search task. Following a central fixation point, a rectangular location cue appeared before the presentation of an array of letters. The cue varied in size, and hence in the precision of the localization information. The display size was also varied (10 or 15 letters) and letters were one of three colours and one of three consonants. Two search conditions were presented: (1) single feature (colour) search, in which only one item in the display had the salient target propriety of colour; and (2) conjoined feature (colour + letter) search, in which both target colour and form appeared with equal frequency in the display but appeared together only in the target. The single feature search may be relatively automatic and occur in parallel (with no or minimal eye movements), inducing the 'pop-out' phenomenon, while the conjoined feature search is more demanding and takes place in 'series', with saccadic eye movements occurring from one stimulus to the next (Treisman and Gelade, 1980). The effects of display size and cue size on reaction time for single feature search were similar in AD subjects and controls, although the former had slower overall search RTs. These results are compatible with the hypothesis of preservation of single feature search in AD. However, the conjoined search process was impaired in AD patients, as indicated by more difficulties than control subjects in directing their search according to the location of a previously presented spatial cue in the conjoined search task. These data suggest an impairment in the spatial focusing of attention during more complex visual search.

Taken as a whole, these studies suggest deficits of spatially-based selective attention in AD. More precisely, although AD patients demonstrated no impairments in engaging or focusing attention, a specific impairment in disengaging or reorienting attention was found (Oken *et al.*, 1994; Parasuraman *et al.*, 1992; Scinto *et al.*, 1994). These patients also experienced difficulties when they had to change the focus of spatial attention during the search task (Parasuraman *et al.*, 1995). However, these deficits were found only for more complex attentional tasks: no difficulties of disengagement were found when subjects had to perform a detection task or a single feature search task, while such difficulties were found in discrimination or conjoined feature search tasks (Parasuraman *et al.*, 1992, 1995).

Object- and feature-based attention

The above tasks concern switching between spatial locations. Other studies have explored the selection of a target on the basis of one or several features from multiple distractors in the same field of vision. In a first study, Nebes and Brady (1989) showed that simple-feature selection was not markedly affected in AD patients. They presented an array of six letters to the subjects. On half of the trials, all the letters were black, and on the rest of the trials, two of the letters were black and the others red. The subjects had to decide whether a target letter was present or not but were told that the target would always be black. Results indicated that AD patients showed the same RT advantage as the controls when a colour cue was available to select a target among others. In order to confirm these results, in a second experiment, the RTs, when subjects had to detect a target between six black distractors, were compared to the RTs when only two black letters were presented. Indeed, if subjects were able to ignore totally the four irrelevant letters in the cued condition, then the RT difference between the non-cued and cued conditions in the first experiment should have been as large as between the six- and two-letter conditions in the second experiment. Results indicated that the subjects could not totally ignore the irrelevant letters in the cued condition, but that this effect was similar in normal controls and AD patients, confirming that the latter can focus their attention on relevant information as effectively as can normal subjects.

However, other studies are indicative of feature-based attentional impairment in AD. Parasuraman and Haxby (1993) reported a study (Haxby *et al.*, 1991) which used a matching-to-sample reaction time task in which one of the two choice stimuli shared a visual feature with a sample stimulus. The matching could be made on more than one feature: for example, colour, shape or number. Four tasks were employed: a baseline choice RT task and three forced-choice RT tasks. On the first visual matching task, the matching feature was the same for all items, and the irrelevant items were held constant. The second task also used the same matching feature for all items, but the other features varied, increasing selective attention demand. The third task used similar items but the matching feature changed in every item. Alzheimer patients demonstrated equivalent increase of RT relative to control subjects on the baseline choice RT task and the first visual matching task (matching feature and irrelevant items held constant). By contrast, AD patients were slower on the second and third visual matching tasks, which required more selective attention demand (variation of the irrelevant items or matching feature). From these results, the authors concluded that patients in the early stages of AD had a specific impairment in switching attention between multiple attributes of compound stimuli.

Another study, exploring switching between dimension stimuli, was conducted by Filoteo *et al.* (1992) who investigated the level of perceptual organization within the same stimulus. In their study, digits, made up of arrays of smaller digits (for example, a 2 constructed from smaller 1s), were presented visually. On each trial, subjects were asked to identify the target stimulus as either a '1' or a '2'. Across consecutive trials, the target stimulus could appear at either the same level (e.g. local – local), or could change level between trials (e.g. local – global). Results indicated that switching between local and global features led to a much longer response time in AD patients, whereas when the target remained at the same level across consecutive trials, RT was relatively unaffected in AD patients. These data also suggest a specific deficit in switching between the different attributes of an item in these patients. In another study, Massman *et al.* (1993) administered a similar paradigm to a group of AD patients and normal control subjects. They showed that RTs of individuals with AD were disproportionately affected for detection of targets at a particular level if the opposing level contained a conflicting target (e.g. discriminating a 1 from a 2 at the local level with a 2 at the global level). These findings also suggest a disengagement deficit in AD, but this time between different hierarchical levels of a composite object. Thus the attention-shifting in AD applies not only to locations *per se* but also to different levels of perceptual organization at different locations within a complex stimulus.

Finally, in a more recent study, Foster, Berhmann and Stuss (1999) investigated selective attention in AD using a visual search procedure similar to that of Parasuraman *et al.* (1995). They compared the performance of mild and moderate AD patients and control subjects in a simple and conjoined visual feature search task. Participants had to respond as quickly as possible whenever a target stimulus was present. Whereas in the simple feature condition, the target differed from the background distractors by a single feature, in the conjoined task, the target was differentiated from the background distractors by a conjunction of two features. In both conditions, the number of distractors presented was varied. Their results indicated that AD patients had significant deficits in visual attention, as revealed by their differentially lower target detection speed on the conjoined feature task, although simple feature search (involving less resource-demanding capabilities) remained relatively preserved. The impairment of AD patients on the conjoined feature task also increased with a larger array size. Moreover, the number of errors made by AD patients was lower (and globally similar to that of control subjects) on the simple feature condition than on the conjoined feature condition. These findings imply that AD patients have substantial and specific problems with visual attention when the target item shares common features with other stimuli in the background.

In conclusion, studies which explored feature-based selective attention in AD showed a preservation of single-feature search (Nebes and Brady, 1989; Foster *et al.*, 1999). However, other studies demonstrated that AD patients have specific selective attention impairments when the task requires them to switch attention not only between different attributes of items (e.g. Haxby *et al.*, 1991; Foster *et al.*, 1999) but also between different levels of perceptual organization within a single complex stimulus (Filoteo *et al.*, 1992; Massman *et al.*, 1993).

Inhibition

Cognitive inhibition is defined as a mechanism which actively suppresses distracting information. The existence of inhibition deficits in AD has been demonstrated in several studies using different procedures, such as the Stroop task (Stroop, 1935), the negative priming procedure (Neill, 1977; Tipper, 1985), and the Hayling task (Burgess and Shallice, 1996). The interference Stroop effect refers to the increased latency time taken to name the colour of the ink with which an item is printed when the item is the name of another colour (e.g. the word 'red' printed in green) in comparison to neutral stimuli (e.g. the item 'XXX' also printed in green). In the negative priming procedure, subjects are simultaneously shown two letters of the alphabet, one red (target) and the other green (the distractor). Subjects are instructed to name the red letter as quickly as possible and to ignore the green one. The observed effect (called 'negative priming') is that response time increases when the letter serving as the distractor in one trial (prime) is used as the target in the very next trial (probe). The explanation for this effect (called the 'suppression effect') is that the distractor is actively inhibited in the prime trial.

Spieler, Balota and Faust (1996) measured interference effects using the Stroop task in a group of AD patients and normal elderly subjects. They showed increased reaction times and naming errors (i.e. reading the printed word instead of naming the colour of the ink) in AD patients relative to control subjects. From these results, the authors concluded that there was a larger sensitivity to interference in AD. Simone and Baylis (1997) also demonstrated the presence of exaggerated interference effects. These authors administered to AD patients and control subjects a task in which a red key remained illuminated on a board until touched. In some trials, a green distractor could also appear at a different key. Reaction times for error trials and trials immediately following an error were excluded from the analyses. In this task, AD patients showed longer RTs than normal elderly adults when a distractor was simultaneously presented. Moreover, AD patients experienced more difficulties than control subjects in preventing themselves from responding to distractors, while positive priming rather than negative priming was seen when a target appeared at a location where a distractor had been previously located. These findings were interpreted in terms of AD patients' inability to use inhibitory processes efficiently. However, in a more recent study, Rouleau, Belleville and Van der Linden (2001) found normal interference effects with the Stroop task in a group of AD patients. One possible explanation for these discrepant results could be the measure used in the different studies: Rouleau *et al.* calculated the interference effect on the basis of RTs for both correct and incorrect naming trials, whereas Spieler *et al.* and Simone and Baylis used only RTs for correct trials. Since Spieler *et al.* showed that response times for incorrect responses are significantly faster for Alzheimer patients, the possibility that the measure of response times for incorrect responses may have obscured the abnormal interference effect in AD patients cannot be excluded.

Another series of studies investigated inhibition processes in AD using the negative priming procedure. Identity negative priming was first explored by Sullivan, Faust and Balota (1995) in two experiments using overlapping pictures and written words with controlled exposure times. The results of both experiments produced reliable identity negative priming in elderly adults but not in the individuals with AD, indicating impairment of the inhibitory component underlying selective attention. However, a more recent study also using overlapping letters demonstrated no evidence of an AD-related decline in inhibitory processes (Langley *et al.*, 1998). More specifically, neither reaction times nor error scores differed between AD patients and control (young and elderly) subjects. Contrary to Sullivan *et al.*, these authors recorded reading times for entire lists and allowed self-pacing of stimulus exposure time. The existence of normal inhibition processes in Alzheimer's disease was also demonstrated by Rouleau *et al.* (2001) in a study using non-overlapping letters. Again, no differences were found between groups in the identity negative priming condition for the RT and error score analysis. These authors, like Sullivan *et al.* (1995), used controlled exposure time and measured reading time for correct individual trials only.

Faust and Balota (1997) specifically explored inhibition of return in AD. They administered a selective attention task to normal elderly subjects and AD patients, in which the subjects fixed their gaze on a central location and had to detect the appearance of targets in one of two peripherally located boxes following the presentation of a brightening (valid or invalid) cue in the outline of one of the boxes. In half of the trials, the target appeared shortly after the peripheral cue (single-cue trials) and, in the other half, a second cue was presented (double-cue trials) to elicit reflexive reorientation of attention to central fixation. The authors predicted that the single-cue trials would yield to a traditional cue validity effect and the double-cue trials to a reversal of this effect (i.e. inhibition of return). Indeed, once attention was reflexively reoriented to the centre, the natural tendency for previously attended locations to be inhibited would have become apparent in subsequent detection performance (Posner *et al.*, 1985). The results clearly yielded equivalent inhibition of return in AD patients and control (young and elderly) subjects when a second exogenous cue was presented. This was interpreted as a relative preservation of lower-level inhibitory mechanisms in AD.

More recently, Danckert *et al.* (1998) used a task similar to the single-cue trials condition in the Faust and Balota experiment (1997) in order to explore inhibition of return in AD. Short and long intervals between the onset of the cue and the onset of the target (stimulus onset asynchrony, SOA) were presented. Indeed, previous studies showed a RT advantage for targets appearing at the cued location at early SOAs (expressing facilitation in target detection), whereas at longer SOAs an RT advantage for targets appearing at a location contralateral to the cue was found (expressing a reorientation of attention and a bias against responding to a previously attended location; Posner *et al.*, 1985). The results of this experiment also indicate normal inhibition of return in AD: patients show an initial RT advantage for targets appearing at the cued location at early SOAs and a subsequent RT advantage for targets appearing contralateral to the cued location at longer SOAs.

Finally, Rouleau *et al.* (2001) measured inhibition of return in a group of AD patients and elderly subjects with a different procedure. It consisted in the simultaneous presentation of two letters, one of them having to be named and the other to be inhibited. The inhibition of return was expressed by changes in the RTs between a condition in which the letter to process was presented in the same location as that of the letter to inhibit in the previous trial, and a control condition in which the letter to process was presented in a different location from that of the letter to inhibit in the previous trial. AD patients showed faster RTs and fewer errors in the inhibition of return condition than in the control condition while control subjects showed the reverse profile. In other words, AD patients failed to show the inhibitory effect, but they also exhibited a large facilitation effect. The authors suggest that this facilitation probably reflects a deficit in visual selective attention, since it indicates some form of attentional grasping or disengagement deficit.

Although negative priming is a very useful tool for the exploration of inhibitory processes, this paradigm assesses only some aspects of the phenomenon. Indeed, the inhibition processes investigated are automatic (as opposed to controlled or voluntary), and fast (measured in differences of milliseconds), and they reflect visual selective attention and use lexical material. Thus, it seems essential to explore inhibition processes by using tasks measuring other aspects of inhibition. In this context, recent studies (Collette, Van der Linden and Salmon, 2001a; Rouleau *et al.*, 2001) showed semantic inhibition deficits in Alzheimer's disease by using the Hayling task (Burgess and Shallice, 1996). In this task, subjects are asked to complete sentences in which the final word is omitted, either with an appropriate word (*'initiation'* condition) or with a word that makes no sense at all in the context of the sentence (*'suppression'* condition). In comparison to the first condition, the second condition requires inhibiting the automatically activated word in order to provide a word unrelated to the context of the sentence. The response latency in the suppression condition was found to be greater in the Alzheimer group, and the overall semantic relatedness of the responses to the sentences in the suppression condition was higher in the AD patients than in the control subjects. Moreover, the response times in the suppression condition were found to be correlated to the cerebral metabolism at rest of AD patients in the left and right superior frontal gyrus (Collette, Van der Linden and Salmon, 2000), these cerebral areas being relatively close to those found in cerebral activation studies when normal subjects performed the suppression condition (Collette *et al.*, 2001b).

In conclusion, studies which have explored inhibition processes in AD have shown some discrepant results. However, methodologies varied greatly between these studies and controlled replications will be needed to determine which factors led to conflicting results. Nevertheless, these studies indicated the presence of a large sensitivity to interference in AD patients (Spieler *et al.*, 1996; Simone and Baylis, 1997), as well as semantic inhibition deficits (Collette *et al.*, 2001a; Rouleau *et al.*, 2001). However, with regard to the negative priming paradigm, most of the studies showed no deficit affecting inhibition of identity and inhibition of return processes (e.g. Langley *et al.*, 1998; Danckert *et al.*, 1998; see, however, Rouleau *et al.*, 2001).

1.3 Divided attention

Divided attention has been frequently explored in AD patients by using a dual-task procedure which requires the subject to perform two tasks separately before performing both tasks simultaneously. According to Baddeley (1996), divided attention abilities can be clearly related to the concept of working memory and constitute one of the most important functions of the central executive system. The central executive is assumed to be an attentional control system responsible for strategy selection, control and coordination of the various processes involved in short-term storage and more general processing tasks. Baddeley (1986) has suggested that the supervisory attentional system component of attentional control in the action model proposed by Norman and Shallice (1986) might be an adequate approximation of the central executive system.

The cerebral areas involved in the coordination of dual tasks were explored in normal subjects by D'Esposito *et al.* (1995). Using fMRI, these authors compared the changes in cerebral metabolism when subjects had to perform two tasks successively or simultaneously. The two tasks (a semantic judgement task and a spatial rotation task) were chosen because they do not require central executive functioning and they activate only posterior cerebral areas. When the two tasks were performed simultaneously, increases of cerebral activity were found bilaterally in the dorsolateral prefrontal cortex and in the cingulate area. For the authors, these activation foci would be specifically related to the dual-task performance and not to task difficulty. Indeed, no supplementary frontal activity was found when the spatial rotation task was performed at different levels of difficulty.

Baddeley *et al.* (1986) have administered to AD patients and normal (young and elderly) control subjects a dual task composed of a pursuit tracking task, which requires the patient to hold a light pen over a moving stimulus on a computer screen, while executing a digit repetition task. The difficulty of both tasks was adjusted between patients and control subjects so as to equate performance across the groups when the tasks were performed alone. When both tasks were performed simultaneously, the deterioration in performance shown by AD patients was particularly marked, compared to control subjects. A follow-up study explored the same patients after a six-month delay (Baddeley *et al.*, 1991a). It revealed that the dual-task performance had deteriorated significantly, whereas the single-task performance remained stable. Similar results were obtained with a paper-and-pencil version of the task (Greene, Hodges and Baddeley, 1995). This version consisted in the successive and simultaneous execution of a digit repetition task and a motor task requiring the subject to put a cross in boxes following a predetermined trail. Again, the performance was equated between control subjects and AD patients in the single condition, but only for the digit repetition task. The majority of patients in the moderate stage of the disease showed marked impairment in the dual-task condition. However, patients in the very early stages of the disease showed no marked decrement relative to controls. Taken as a whole, these data suggest that AD patients exhibit impaired ability to perform two tasks simultaneously, which is compatible with impairments at the level of the central executive system.

Divided attentional deficits in AD patients were also found in dual tasks requiring no storage of the information to be processed. In Baddeley *et al.*'s (1986) study, another dual-task condition required subjects to perform the pursuit tracking task while detecting tones. AD patients also demonstrated impairments, compared to control subjects, during the simultaneous execution of these two tasks. These results were confirmed by Nestor *et al.* (1991) who used a probe reaction time method. In that study, the two primary tasks consisted of a simple auditory reaction time task and a visual matching paradigm (in which the subject has to indicate whether two items simultaneously presented are similar or different). Again, AD patients experienced more difficulties than control subjects in the dual-task condition. However, in these two experiments, the difficulty of the tasks performed in isolation was not equated between subjects, and the performance of AD patients was already lower during the realization of the single tasks. Moreover, the authors also explored the relationships between dual-task performance and cerebral metabolism, and showed that the simultaneous execution of an auditory reaction time and a visual matching task was associated in mild AD patients with reduced brain metabolism in right parietal and frontal premotor association regions. Finally, impairments in dual-task coordination also exist for relatively automatic processes such as talking and walking, leading to a higher probability of falls when AD patients have to talk while walking (Camicioli *et al.*, 1997). Taken as a whole, these studies indicate that reduced divided attentional capacities are a main feature of AD.

However, interpretations other than dual-task coordination deficits could be proposed to explain these results (Morris, 1992). For example, these deficits could be only the reflection of the difficulties experienced by AD patients in the single tasks. These deficits could also be due to an abnormal effect of structural interference. In other words, AD patients would exhibit difficulties in all tasks involving similar cognitive processes. Finally, these deficits could come from the global complexity of the task. However, these various interpretations can hardly explain the results obtained by Baddeley *et al.* (1986, 1991a) since in these studies the level of difficulty for each individual task was controlled and the tasks were chosen in order to minimize structural interference (e.g. a verbal and a visuo-spatial task).

In a more recent study, Collette *et al.* (1999) explored dual-task abilities in a group of early AD patients using two tasks: a classic dual-task paradigm and an alphabetical span task. The dual-task paradigm was a paper-and-pencil version of the task initially described by Baddeley and collaborators, in which subjects have (successively and then simultaneously) to repeat sets of digits at their span level and to put a cross in boxes following a predetermined trail (see Greene *et al.*, 1995). Results indicate a marginally greater decrease of performance in the dual-task condition in mild AD patients than in control subjects. The alphabetical span task (Belleville, Rouleau and Caza, 1998) requires simultaneous storage and manipulation of information. This task consists in presenting word lists whose length corresponds to the span minus one of each individual. In the first condition, subjects have to recall the words in serial order. In the second condition, the words have to be recalled in alphabetical order. The storage requirement being equated between the two conditions, the only difference concerns the intervention of the central executive during alphabetical recall. Although AD patients and control subjects display a similar performance when they have to perform serial recall of information, AD patients show a much poorer performance than control subjects when they have to recall information in alphabetical order (see also Belleville *et al.*, 2001, for similar results).

However, dual-task coordination abilities do not represent the only central executive dysfunction suffered by Alzheimer patients. Indeed, recent reports have demonstrated that individuals with Alzheimer's disease are impaired relatively early on a variety of tasks that have been commonly considered as measures of executive control, such as verbal fluency, planning abilities, inhibition processes and the random generation task (for a review, see Collette *et al.*, 1999b). These data are in agreement with other recent studies which showed that, despite an important heterogeneity of cognitive deficits observed in AD patients, there exists a prevalence of certain types of deficits early in the disease (for a review see Juillerat *et al.*, 2000). More specifically, two types of impairment seem to be particularly frequent and occur early in the course of AD: episodic memory deficits assessed by explicit memory tests such as recall or recognition tasks (Albert, 1996; Small *et al.*, 1997), and deficits affecting some executive (or controlled) processes (Fabrigoule *et al.*, 1998; Salthouse and Becker, 1998).

In that context, we recently explored the hypothesis of dissociation between automatic and controlled processes in early Alzheimer patients with reference to a theoretical model integrating the distinction between controlled and automatic processes. In a first study (Collette *et al.*, 1999), we used the framework of the Baddeley working memory model (Baddeley, 1986). The integrity of the phonological loop (considered as relatively automatic) and the central executive (involved in controlled processes) of working memory was evaluated in a group of AD patients and normal elderly subjects. Results indicate that AD patients in the first stages of the disease exhibit impairments in tasks assessing the central executive, with a preservation of the subcomponents of the phonological loop (phonological store and articulatory rehearsal system), while impairments of the phonological loop are found in more severely demented AD patients. In a second study (Adam, 2000), the process dissociation procedure proposed by Jacoby (1991) was used to explore the dissociation of automatic and controlled processes in early Alzheimer's disease. It enables us to separate contributions of automatic and consciously controlled memory processes in the same task and can be described in the following way. In the word-stem version of the procedure, subjects perform two tasks, one involving inclusion, and the other exclusion. In the inclusion task, subjects are asked to complete a stem with a previously studied word and, if they are unable do so, to use the first word that comes to mind. In the exclusion task, they are asked to complete a stem with a new word that was not encountered during the earlier study phase and to avoid old, studied words. Controlled processes can be estimated by subtracting the probability of responding with a studied word in the exclusion task from the probability of responding with an old word in the inclusion task. Once an estimate of controlled processes has been obtained, the contribution of automatic processes corresponds to the probability of completing a stem with the studied word in the exclusion condition divided by one minus the probability of completing a stem with the studied word in the inclusion condition. This process dissociation procedure was administered to a group of AD patients and control subjects. In this task, the length of the intervals between the encoding of an item and the presentation of the corresponding radical was varied in the inclusion and exclusion condition (0, 3 and 12 items inserted). Results indicated that the contribution of controlled processes in this memory task was significantly lower in AD patients than in control subjects. Moreover, this deficit of controlled processes increased in the AD group with the length of the interval. With regard to the automatic processes, no significant difference was found between the two groups for the three intervals.

These two studies showed that a preservation of automatic processes associated with an impairment of controlled processes characterizes the cognitive functioning of AD patients in the early stages of the disease. These data are in agreement with the hypotheses of Fabrigoule *et al.* (1998) and Salthouse and Becker (1998) in which the impairment of a general factor could be responsible for a large part of the cognitive deficits presented by AD patients from the beginning of the disease.

1.4 Conclusions

The studies reviewed earlier support the existence of attentional deficits in Alzheimer's disease (see Table 11.1 for a summary of these deficits). These deficits appear relatively early in the disease, and more precisely after memory impairment but before language and visuo-spatial impairments (Grady *et al.*, 1988; Reid *et al.*, 1996). Recently, Perry, Watson and Hodges (2000) explored attentional functioning as well as other cognitive domains in a group of minimal (MMSE 24–30) and mild (MMSE 18–23) AD patients. They confirmed that there is an initial amnestic stage with profound deficits in episodic memory before impairments of attention become manifest.

However, it is regrettable that few studies have systematically explored the longitudinal course of attentional dysfunctions in Alzheimer's disease in

Table 11.1 Attentional deficits in Alzheimer's disease

Phasic alertness	Relatively unaffected when simple tasks are used	Nebes and Brady, 1993; Pate *et al.*, 1994
Sustained attention	Unimpaired	Lines *et al.*, 1991
Vigilance	Contradictory results	Nebes and Brady, 1993; Brazzelli *et al.*, 1994
Sustained attention:		
Spatial-based	No impairment in engaging or disengaging attention during detection tasks	Parasuraman *et al.*, 1992
	Selective impairment in disengaging attention during discrimination tasks	Parasuraman *et al.* 1992; Oken *et al.*, 1994; Scinto *et al.*, 1994; Maruff *et al.*, 1995
	Impairment in the spatial focusing of attention during complex search tasks only	Parasuraman *et al.*, 1995
Object- and feature-based	Impairment in conjoined-feature search tasks	Nebes and Brady, 1989; Foster *et al.*, 1999
	Impairment in switching attention between multiple attributes of compound stimuli	Haxby *et al.*, 1991; Filoteo *et al.*, 1992; Massman *et al.*, 1993
Inhibition:		
Interference	Increased sensitivity	Spieler *et al.*, 1996; Simone and Baylis, 1997
Inhibition of identity	Contradictory results	Sullivan *et al.*, 1995; Langley *et al.*, 1998
Inhibition of return	Contradictory results	Faust and Balota, 1997; Danckert *et al.*, 1998; Rouleau *et al.*, 2001
Semantic inhibition	Impaired	Collette *et al.*, 1999b; Rouleau *et al.*, 2000
Divided attention	Impaired	Baddeley *et al.*, 1986, 1991a; Camicioli *et al.*, 1997; Collette *et al.*, 1999a; Greene *et al.*, 1995; Nestor *et al.*, 1991

order to determine whether there exists a simultaneous impairment of all attentional processes. Thus, Pate *et al.* (1994) observed that choice reaction time tasks are affected before simple reaction time tasks. Several studies compared AD patients at different stages of the disease and reported that visual attentional shifting may be preserved early in the course of the disease (Faust and Balota, 1997; Oken *et al.*, 1994; Parasuraman *et al.*, 1992; Sahakian *et al.*, 1990) but impaired in a more severe subgroup of AD patients

(Sahakian *et al.*, 1990). In a similar way, an increase of inhibitory dysfunction was also found along with the progression of the disease (Simone and Baylis, 1997). Then, Greene *et al.* (1995) showed a preservation of divided attention capacity in the very early stages of the disease. Finally, Perry *et al.* (2000) explored different aspects of attention in the same group of very mild and mild AD patients, and administered to patients and control subjects tasks of sustained, selective and divided attention. Results suggest that there is no deficit in sustained and divided attention in the minimally demented AD patients, and impairment of these domains only becomes manifest as the disease progresses. In contrast to the normal performance shown on tests of sustained and divided attention, the minimal AD group was significantly impaired on tasks of selective attention, more precisely on a feature-based task (to count strings of low tones whilst ignoring higher-pitched tones) (Robertson *et al.*, 1996) and on an inhibition task (the Stroop task).

The pattern of deficits presented by AD patients in attentional tasks reviewed here could be interpreted in terms of preserved automatic and impaired controlled attentional processes. Indeed, choice RT tasks, requiring target discrimination, are impaired before simple RT tasks, requiring only target detection (e.g. Pate *et al.*, 1994). Similarly, single-feature search was intact in AD patients while conjoined-feature search, which requires subjects to switch continuously between the different attributes of items, was impaired (e.g. Foster *et al.*, 1999). Finally, in the inhibitory domain, normal inhibition of return was found when detection tasks were used (Faust and Balota, 1997; Danckert *et al.*, 1998). However, inhibitory deficits were found when subjects had to suppress actively interfering information (e.g. Spieler *et al.*, 1996): to name a letter which was inhibited in the previous trial (Rouleau *et al.*, 2001), or to inhibit actively semantic information (Collette *et al.*, 2001a; Rouleau *et al.*, 2001). These latter tasks, but not the item detection task, require active processing of the information to inhibit. However, these different attentional tasks probably require the intervention of both controlled and automatic attentional processes. Consequently, it would be particularly interesting to use the process dissociation procedure described by Jacoby (1991) in order to explore systematically the integrity of the automatic and controlled processes in the different subcomponents of the attentional domain. Indeed, from a clinical viewpoint, the use of tasks contrasting the requirement of controlled and automatic processes in several cognitive domains could be useful in the early detection of the disease, while tasks requiring only the intervention of automatic processes could be used in follow-up studies of AD populations.

2 Attentional deficits in other types of dementias

Some studies have also investigated attentional functioning in dementia other than Alzheimer's disease, especially in Parkinson's disease (PD), Huntington's disease (HD), progressive supranuclear palsy (PSP) and frontotemporal dementia (FTD). However, these studies generally did not focus specifically on attentional processes but were interested in the more general cognitive functioning of the patients. Consequently, the integrity of the different subcomponents of attention was not investigated as thoroughly as in Alzheimer's disease. Otherwise, few studies have directly compared the abilities of different dementia groups and these studies were mainly interested in selective attentional abilities. In this section, we will briefly describe the studies that have explored attentional functioning in these different pathologies, and then the question of differential attentional impairments in these groups of patients will be illustrated in the domain of selective attention.

2.1 Attentional deficits in Parkinson's disease

Parkinson's disease is a progressive neurodegenerative disorder characterized by a severe loss of neurons in the substantia nigra, resulting in a depletion of the neurotransmitter dopamine. Neuropsychological impairments described in the disease concern the learning of new information in episodic memory, executive functioning and visuo-spatial processing (Lawrence and Sahakian, 1996).

With regard to attentional functioning, Parkinson's disease patients exhibit a slowing down of the response times for all modalities of presentation of the stimulus but the presentation of a warning signal improves in a similar way the RTs of these patients and control subjects (Bloxham, Dick and Moore, 1987; Jahanshahi, Brown and Marsden, 1992).

The studies that have explored attentional functioning in Parkinson's disease are focused mainly on spatial selective attention processes and on divided attentional abilities. In a first study, Wright *et al.* (1990) explored spatially-based covert orientation of attention in a group of patients with idiopathic Parkinson's disease and normal elderly subjects, using an RT task which measured disengagement, covert movement and engagement of attention. In this task, trials consisted of a central cue stimulus presented at a fixation point and followed by a peripheral target stimulus. The cue stimulus indicated valid location with an 80% probability. Results indicated that, despite an overall slowing down of response time, patients with PD showed a response time benefit similar to that of the control group, indicating relatively normal covert movement and engagement of attention. However, these patients showed a reduced cost of invalid cueing compared to controls. From these data, Wright *et al.* concluded that PD patients may exhibit abnormally rapid disengagement of attention relative to normal subjects, and that this may reflect a deficit in maintaining attention. Using a similar procedure, Sharpe (1990) also found that PD patients disengaged attention from the cued target more rapidly than control subjects. Similar results were obtained by Bennet *et al.* (1995) who also showed a preserved ability to modulate the focus of attention according to the size of the area that must be focused upon. Finally, Yamada *et al.* (1990) reported that PD patients who were older, with a longer duration of illness and more disabled did not exhibit a time benefit for the valid trials in comparison to neutral trials.

In a recent study, Lee *et al.* (1999) obtained slightly different results. They administered to PD patients and normal subjects a task in which a target stimulus (the letter S or H) was displayed in a cued location. Subjects had to type the presented letter as quickly as possible while distractors (similar or not to the target letters) were displayed at various distances. PD patients responded significantly more slowly and less accurately than control subjects across all interference conditions and spatial distances. However, they did not show significantly greater interference or facilitation effects, indicating normal maintenance and disengagement processes. It is important to note, nevertheless, that in this study response times greater than 1,000 msec were not included in the analysis. As many PD patients suffer from a slowing down of motor execution, this procedure may have resulted in excluding a large number of trials in which PD patients experienced difficulties of selective attention.

Finally, these patients also present inhibition deficits. Indeed, Bellaj (1999) showed that in the Hayling task (requiring subjects to complete a sentence with a word unrelated to the context of the sentence), PD patients had similar RTs to control subjects but experienced more difficulties in providing a word that did not have any semantic relationship with the sentence. Moreover, there also exists an increased sensitivity to interference, as demonstrated in the Stroop task (e.g. Brown and Marsden, 1988; Taylor, Saint-Cyr and Lang, 1990).

Divided attention abilities have been frequently explored in PD patients by using various dual-task procedures. Dual-task coordination deficits were also found with the dual-task paradigm initially described by Baddeley and collaborators (1986, 1991a; for a description of the tasks see p. 311): even when the performance in the single task was equated between PD patients and control subjects, the patients experienced more difficulties than control subjects in performing the two tasks simultaneously (Dalrymple-Alford *et al.*, 1994; Bellaj, 1999). Discrepant results were nevertheless obtained by Fournet *et al.* (1996) who showed no deficit in the dual-task coordination abilities of a group of PD patients. However, the interfering tasks used in that study were articulatory suppression and counting. These tasks do appear to be relatively automatic and may not have been sufficiently demanding on attentional resources to disrupt the central executive functioning.

The role of dopamine in the divided attention tasks was clearly demonstrated by Fournet *et al.* (2000). In that study, the performance in a task ('the double span task') assessing the coordination and integration functions of the central executive was compared in PD patients treated or not with L-Dopa. In this task, words are presented in grids that subjects have to memorize in order to recall (following the condition) the words (verbal span), their spatial location (visuo-spatial span) or both (double span). Although no effect of medication was found on simple verbal and visuo-spatial span tasks, the withdrawal of dopaminergic medication affects performance on the double span task.

In conclusion, these studies seem to indicate the presence in PD patients of a slowing down (Jahanshashi *et al.*, 1992), of spatially-based selective attention impairment (Wright *et al.*, 1990) as well as divided attention and executive dysfunction (e.g. Dalrymple-Alford *et al.*, 1994; Bellaj, 1999). However, these results must be discussed with caution because these studies do not systematically control the medication of the patients and the presence or absence of dopamine depletion could explain some discrepant results (e.g. normal or impaired performance, depending on the studies, when similar components of attention are assessed). Moreover, these studies evaluated PD patients at different stages of the disease, which could also influence the pattern of performance observed.

2.2 Attentional deficits in Huntington's disease, progressive supranuclear palsy and frontal lobe dementia

Huntington's disease (HD) is a progressive neurodegenerative disorder, characterized by involuntary choreiform movements, slowed-down voluntary movements, cognitive deterioration and affective disturbances. Surprisingly, although there is a large body of knowledge covering the motor abnormalities and neuropsychological deficits in Huntington's disease (see for example Brandt and Butters, 1996), there have been few studies investigating basic attentional capacities in this disorder. In that context, Sprengelmeyer, Lange and Hömberg (1995) have explored the integrity of a large range of attentional processes in Huntington's disease. They administered to a group of HD patients and control subjects subtests of the Test for Attentional Performance (TAP) of Zimmermann and Fimm (1994), namely an alertness task (to react to the appearance of a cross on the screen, the cross being preceded in one condition by a warning signal but not in another condition), a divided attention task (to respond successively and then simultaneously to the presentation of a visual and acoustic signal), response flexibility (consisting in the simultaneous presentation of one letter and one digit, the subjects having, in one trial, to press the button on the side where the letter appeared and, for the next trial, on the side where the digit appeared), response inhibition (a Go–nogo task requiring subjects to react when a specific stimulus appears but not when other stimuli are presented). The results obtained on these tasks are as follows. Despite an overall slowing down in their motor responses, HD patients were not disproportionately impaired in the phasic alertness task.

Like controls, they were able to speed up their RTs when an acoustic warning signal preceded the imperative stimulus. Otherwise, the divided attention task was severely affected by the disease: HD patients had an increase of RT similar to that of control subjects from the single to the dual conditions, but the number of errors was more important for the patients, which indicates a problem in allocation of attentional resources to different modalities. The performance of the HD patients in the response flexibility task shows that these patients were impaired in shifting the focus of attention selectively to different aspects of a task without external guidance. Finally, HD patients were also impaired in reacting selectively to Go–nogo stimuli in the response inhibition task. These results suggest a specific pattern of attentional deficits in HD patients. Further studies will obviously be necessary to determine the influence of these attentional deficits on other cognitive domains (such as memory functioning).

Progressive supranuclear palsy (PSP) is a progressive subcortical disease which predominantly affects the cholinergic and dopaminergic neurotransmitter systems. From a neuropsychological viewpoint, executive dysfunction and slowed information processing appear early in the course of PSP. However, memory, although impaired, is less severely affected (Grafman, Litvan and Stark, 1995). Concerning the attentional domain, several studies have indicated that PSP patients have difficulties on tasks requiring auditory or visual attention (such as detection of a target letter among a set of distractors). Moreover, these patients demonstrated significantly impaired vigilance by gradually identifying fewer targets over time compared to controls (Grafman *et al.*, 1995). Using the visuo-spatial attention task initially described by Posner (1980), several investigators found that PSP patients were impaired in orienting their attention (Rafal and Posner, 1988; Kertzman *et al.*, 1990; Rafal, 1992) and the severity of this impairment was related to the duration of the disease (Kertzman, Robinson and Litvan, 1990). Deficits were also found in the domain of selective attention and cognitive flexibility (assessed with the Trail Making Test part B or the Wisconsin Card Sorting Test; Grafman *et al.*, 1990; Pillon *et al.*, 1986). However, these patients did not exhibit a larger sensitivity to interference in the Stroop task (Grafman *et al.*, 1990).

The term frontotemporal dementia (FTD) represents a heterogeneous group of disorders with variable clinical and neuropathological manifestations. The term encompasses a number of conditions in which progressive dementia with degeneration of the frontal cortex occurs (in association or not with degeneration of the temporal cortex). These patients are mainly characterized by behavioural disorders and impairments in tasks assessing executive functioning as well as memory retrieval processes. Few studies were interested in attentional functioning in FTD. Miller *et al.* (1991) showed that selective attention was impaired in the disease using the Stroop task and the Trail Making Test part B. At present, only one study has explored the integrity of different attentional processes in a group of FTD patients (Pasquier, 1994; Pasquier and Lebert, 1995). FTD patients and control subjects were administered attentional tasks that explored: (a) vigilance (digit ordination over five minutes) and sustained attention with and without warning signal; (b) selective attention using an object-feature-based task (to detect a target item between distractors) and a spatial-based task (to detect a target item following the presentation of valid or invalid cues); (c) inhibition processes (using the Stroop task and Trail Making Test part B). Results indicated intact vigilance abilities but an impairment of sustained attention, with an increase of RTs in the FTD patients, which are not improved with the warning signal. Selective attention processes are affected for the object-feature-based task only (with slowing down increasing with the number of targets to detect). Finally, inhibition processes were also found to be impaired by the disease.

2.3 Comparison of attentional disorders in different degenerative diseases

The pattern of performance in attentional tasks of patients suffering from different degenerative diseases was explored in several studies. These studies mainly explored the abilities of these patients on tasks assessing selective attentional processes (and more precisely feature-based selective attention). Filoteo *et al.* (1995) administered a global/local divided attention task to three dementia groups (AD, PD and HD patients) using visual hierarchical stimuli consisting of large numbers composed of several smaller numbers (e.g. a large 1 composed of smaller 2s; Filoteo *et al.*, 1992). On each trial, subjects were asked to identify the target stimulus as either a '1' or a '2'. Across consecutive trials, the target stimulus could either appear at the same level (e.g. local – local), or it could change level between trials (e.g. local – global). As described previously, the AD group was differentially slower in comparison to control subjects when the target level changed from global to local or local to global across the trials. In contrast, individuals with PD were faster to respond than controls when the target level changed across trials, and slower when the target level remained the same, which is consistent with a deficit in maintaining attention on a specific attribute of the items. Finally, the HD group did not show a deficit in shifting attention across trials in this task, a result which suggests that they had neither a disengagement nor a maintenance deficit. Recently, Roman *et al.* (1998) also used the procedure of Filoteo *et al.* (1992) to explore the influence of distracting stimuli on selective attention in Parkinson's disease and Huntington's disease. They administered to patients and control subjects a task in which stimuli consisted of global–local forms that were either consistent (e.g. a large 1 made of smaller 1s) or inconsistent (e.g. a large 1 made of smaller 2s). In one group of trials, subjects were required to focus their attention on and identify the global-level form; in another group of trials, they had to focus on and identify the local-level form. Results indicate that, compared to control subjects, PD patients were not disproportionately slower in responding to inconsistent stimuli relative to consistent stimuli, whereas patients with HD had greater increases in their RTs to inconsistent compared to consistent stimuli. These results indicate that patients with HD manifested a deficit in focusing attention in the presence of distracting stimuli, whereas patients with PD exhibited no such impairments.

The dichotic listening task was another procedure also classically used to explore selective attentional processes. Claus and Mohr (1996) administered to AD, PD (with and without dementia) and HD patients and control subjects a verbal dichotic listening task in which subjects were simultaneously presented with conflicting auditory stimuli to the right and left ear. In a first stage, subjects had to recall the items presented without reference to order of recall. This was followed by a left or right ear first order of recall condition. Results indicate that demented subjects performed at a comparable level regardless of specific diagnosis; likewise those without dementia also achieved similar (and superior to demented subjects,) levels of performance. Moreover, AD and HD patients showed consistent right ear preference under all recall conditions, while PD (demented and non-demented) patients and controls could selectively allocate attention to each ear. From these data, the authors concluded that non-selective attentional processing is affected by dementia, but not by a specific disease, while selective attentional processing shows disease-specific impairments, regardless of the presence of dementia.

Taken as a whole, these studies indicate that patients with different cortical and subcortical degenerative disorders may exhibit qualitatively distinct impairments in the different components of attention. More precisely, selective attention tasks showed deficits in maintaining attention in Parkinson's disease, while AD patients showed selective impairment of disengagement and HD patients exhibited neither a maintaining nor a disengagement deficit (Filoteo *et al.*, 1995; Wright *et al.*, 1990).

3 Conclusion

At present, a classic view of attentional processes considers that attention is not a homogeneous system and that separate subcomponents of attention can be distinguished at a functional level. In agreement with this conception, recent functional imagery studies in young healthy subjects demonstrated that attention processes are not subserved by a single brain region but by distributed anterior and posterior neural systems (for a review, see Posner and Dehaene, 1994; Posner and Petersen, 1990).

The exploration of specific impaired and preserved functions in brain-damaged populations could contribute to define more precisely the role of the different structures involved in attentional processes, and also to dissociate better the various cognitive components intervening in tasks used to explore different attentional systems. Indeed, the studies described in this chapter have shown that diseases affecting subcortical structures (such as Parkinson's and Huntington's disease and progressive supranuclear palsy) lead to deficits different from those described in cortical degeneration (such as Alzheimer's disease or frontotemporal lobe dementia). Moreover, the patterns of impairment also differ within the different subcortical or cortical dementias. For example, with regard to selective attention, AD patients exhibit disengagement deficits, while PD patients exhibit difficulties in maintaining attention and PSP patients in the orientation of attention (Filoteo *et al.*, 1995; Kertzman *et al.*, 1990; Wright *et al.*, 1990). Otherwise, no deficits were found in phasic alertness and vigilance tasks for AD, PD and HD patients, while such deficits were found in PSP patients (Grafman *et al.*, 1995; Jahanshahi *et al.*, 1992; Nebes and Brady, 1993; Sprengelmeyer *et al.*, 1995). Finally, divided attention impairments seem to be a general characteristic of all dementia disorders (Baddeley, 1986; Dalrymple-Alford *et al.*, 1994; Sprengelmeyer *et al.*, 1995).

Taken as a whole, these data underline the necessity to compare systematically attentional functioning in different degenerative diseases (as well as to explore the relationships between cognitive performance and cerebral metabolism dysfunction of these patients). Such studies constitute a fruitful alternative to the exploration of the cognitive components intervening in attentional tasks in normal subjects, as well as to the exploration of the role of the different cerebral areas in the execution of these tasks. Moreover, the comparison of the relationships between patterns of performance and changes in cerebral metabolism in different degenerative diseases could permit us to isolate the cerebral areas (and neurotransmitter systems) that are essential to the realization of specific attentional tasks. However, it is important to note that an important heterogeneity characterizes the cognitive functioning of the different types of dementia, and a fruitful approach to the group studies described in the present chapter would be to perform multiple single-case analysis in a group of patients. Such studies would permit a better characterization of attentional functioning in pathological ageing, by identifying various patterns of association/dissociation between attentional processes.

An important question which was not systematically discussed in the studies exploring attentional deficits in degenerative disorders concerns the existence of a generalized slowing down which could influence the performance of the patients on the different attentional tasks. Such a cognitive slowing down was demonstrated in Alzheimer's disease. More precisely, a larger increase of RTs was found in AD patients compared to control subjects when the difficulty of the attentional task increased (Nebes and Madden, 1988). However, other studies have shown that the increased RT of AD patients, when the task becomes more difficult, is similar to that found in elderly subjects. Indeed, AD patients exhibit RTs approximately 2.3 times longer than those of control subjects (Nebes and Brady, 1992). In this context, further studies will be necessary in order to determine whether the slowing down observed in AD represents only a generalized low-level increase of the reaction time (increase of RT proportional to that of control subjects) or a qualitative change in cognitive functioning (larger increase of RT in relation to the complexity of the task).

From a clinical viewpoint, a better characterization of attentional disorders in pathological ageing will have repercussions on the efficiency of early diagnosis of Alzheimer's disease. Indeed, at this time, it appears that some measures of episodic memory and executive functioning are good predictors of the disease. If some attentional processes are also found frequently associated with the early stage of the disease, the inclusion of tasks involving these processes in neuropsychological examination will increase the sensitivity and specificity of diagnosis. Similarly, the exploration of attentional functioning in pathological ageing will lead to a better characterization of the deficits specific to the different diseases and to a better accuracy in differential diagnosis. Furthermore, an important goal for neuropsychologists is to identify the consequences of cognitive disorders, in particular attentional disorders, in everyday activities. More precisely, clinical observation of AD patients in everyday situations suggests that they have problems in maintaining attention, whilst performing tasks, fairly early in the course of the disease. In that context, a recent work by Perry *et al.* (2000) showed that the first attentional deficits to appear in the disease are selective attention deficits. Moreover, as indicated earlier, Fabrigoule *et al.* (1998) and Salthouse and Becker (1998) showed that the performance of AD patients in tasks assessing attentional functioning can be interpreted as a defect in controlled processes. These deficits of a general factor representing controlled processes can explain the performance of AD patients in various tasks depending (at least in part) on that factor.

From these data it appears that a better understanding of the attentional processes intervening in everyday life activities should enable us to draw up specific rehabilitation programmes in order to improve the efficiency of brain-damaged patients in their daily activities (at least in the first stages of the disease). In this perspective, Adam *et al.* (2000) elaborated an assessment and intervention programme which was conducted in a day-care centre in order to minimize the impact of cognitive deficits on knitting activity at home in a 70-year-old Alzheimer patient (AM). The first step of this intervention programme consisted in a detailed analysis of the cognitive processes involved in knitting. This analysis revealed that knitting requires particularly important working memory resources, selective attention and planning, as well as procedural abilities and semantic knowledge about the knitting stitches. Neuropsychological evaluation of these components showed that AM's semantic and procedural knowledge associated with knitting was intact. However, there were selective attention deficits (and more precisely impaired inhibition processes) as well as a reduction of working memory capacity and planning impairment. In order to minimize the impact of selective attention deficits, the knitting pattern was adapted by suppressing the irrelevant information and enlarging the original pattern. Furthermore, AM had problems maintaining the relevant information in working memory when she had to pass from the pattern to the knitting operation (i.e. to count and to maintain in working memory the number of stitches to do), and she also showed considerable difficulty in mentally planning the succession of patterns designed to guide her in her knitting task. Taking into account AM's planning deficits, the diagram was copied, cut and pasted according to the needs of each knitting section. Since AM could not mentally plan the succession of diagrams, all the necessary information was visually presented to her. In order to reduce the demands on the central executive resources, the patient was encouraged to cross out the stitches already knitted, and numbers were inserted in the diagram every time the number of stitches concerning one colour block was superior to two. Following these adaptations, the knitting performance of AM improved substantially. Moreover, the benefit of the intervention was not limited only to the knitting activity but became generalized to other everyday life activities: the patient took more initiatives and become more active especially in housework. At a behavioural level, the intervention significantly decreased AM's apathy and depressive mood as well as her husband's burden.

In conclusion, the studies reviewed in this chapter clearly demonstrate the importance of a better specification of impaired and preserved attentional deficits in degenerative diseases. Indeed, from a theoretical viewpoint, these studies have provided a better knowledge of the different attentional domains. From a clinical viewpoint, such a specification would permit the elaboration of attentional tasks useful to the differential diagnosis of degenerative diseases. Moreover, a better understanding of the attentional deficits in the various degenerative diseases will be necessary for the elaboration of attentional training programmes related to the specific impairments presented by these patients in daily life activities.

References

Adam, S. (2000). Exploration of controlled and automatic processes in early Alzheimer's disease with the process dissociation procedure of Jacoby. In preparation.

Adam, S., Van der Linden, M., Juillerat, AC., and Salmon, E. (2000). The cognitive management of daily life activities in patients with mild to moderate Alzheimer's disease in a day-care center: a case report. *Neuropsychological Rehabilitation*, *10*, 485–509.

Albert, M.S. (1996). Cognitive and neurobiological markers of early Alzheimer disease. *Proceedings of the National Academic of Sciences, USA*, *93*, 13457–13551.

Almkvist, O. (1996). Neuropsychological features of early Alzheimer's disease: preclinical and clinical stages. *Acta Neurologica Scandinavia*, *165*, 63–71.

Baddeley, A.D. (1986). *Working Memory*. Oxford: Clarendon Press.

Baddeley, A.D. (1996). Exploring the central executive. *Quarterly Journal of Experimental Psychology*, *49A*, 5–28.

Baddeley, A.D., Bressi, S., Della Sala, S., Logie, R., and Spinnler, H. (1991a). The decline of working memory in Alzheimer's disease. A longitudinal study. *Brain*, *114*, 2521–2542.

Baddeley, A.D., Della Sala, S., and Spinnler, H. (1991b). The two-component hypothesis of memory deficit in Alzheimer's disease. *Journal of Clinical and Experimental Neuropsychology*, *13*, 372–380.

Baddeley, A.D., Logie, R., Bressi, S., Della Sala, S., and Spinnler, H. (1986). Dementia and working memory. *Quarterly Journal of Experimental Psychology*, *38A*, 603–618.

Bellaj, T. (1999). Dysfonctionnement de la mémoire de travail dans la maladie de Parkinson. Université de Tunis: Unpublished doctoral thesis.

Belleville, S., Peretz, I., and Malenfant, D. (1996). Examination of the working memory components in normal aging and in dementia of the Alzheimer type. *Neuropsychologia*, *34*, 195–207.

Belleville, S., Rouleau, N., and Caza, N. (1998). Effects of normal aging on the manipulation of information in working memory. *Memory and Cognition*, *26*, 572–583.

Belleville, S., Rouleau, N., Van der Linden, M., and Collette, F. (2001). Inhibition and manipulation capacities of working memory: dissociations in patients with Alzheimer's disease. Submitted.

Bennet, K.M.B., Waterman, C., Scarpa, M., and Castiello, U. (1995). Covert visuospatial attentional mechanisms in Parkinson's disease. *Brain*, *118*, 153–166.

Bloxham, C.A., Dick, D.J., and Moore, M. (1987). Reaction times and attention in Parkinson's disease. *Journal of Neurology, Neurosurgery and Psychiatry*, *50*, 1178–1183.

Brandt, J. and Butters, N. (1996). Neuropsychological characteristics of Huntington's disease. In I. Grant and K. M. Adams (eds) *Neuropsychological Assessment of Neuropsychiatric Disorders*. New York: Oxford University Press, pp. 312–341.

Brazzelli, M., Cocchini, G., Della Sala, S., and Spinnler, H. (1994). Alzheimer patients show a sensitivity decrement over time on a tonic alertness task. *Journal of Clinical and Experimental Neuropsychology*, *16*, 851–860.

Brown, R.G. and Marsden, C.D. (1988). Internal versus external cues and the control of attention in Parkinson's disease. *Brain*, *111*, 323–345.

Burgess, P.W. and Shallice, T. (1996). Response suppression, initiation and strategy use following frontal lobe lesions. *Neuropsychologia*, *34*, 263–273.

Camicioli, R., Howieson, D., Lehman, S., and Kaye, J. (1997). Talking while walking: the effect of a dual task in aging and Alzheimer's disease. *Neurology*, *48*, 955–958.

Claus, J.J. and Mohr, E. (1996). Attentional deficits in Alzheimer's, Parkinson's and Huntington's diseases. *Acta Neurologica Scandinavia*, *93*, 346–351.

Collette, F., Van der Linden, M., Bechet, S., and Salmon, E. (1999). Phonological loop and central executive functioning in Alzheimer's disease. *Neuropsychologia*, *37*, 905–918.

Collette, F., Van der Linden, M., and Salmon, E. (2000). Relationships between cognitive performance and cerebral metabolism in Alzheimer's disease. *Current Psychology Letters: Brain, Behavior and Cognition*, *1*, 55–69.

Collette, F., Van der Linden, M., Delfiore, G., Degueldre, C., and Salmon, E. (2001b). The functional antomy of inhibition processes investigated with the Hayling task. *Neuroimage*, *13*, 258–267.

Collette, F., Van der Linden, M., and Salmon, E. (2001a). Executive dysfunction in Alzheimer's disease. *Cortex*, *35*, 57–72.

Dalrymple-Alford, J.C., Kalders, A.S., Jones, R.D., and Watson, R.W. (1994). A central executive deficit in patients with Parkinson's disease. *Journal of Neurology, Neurosurgery and Psychiatry*, *57*, 360–367.

Danckert, J., Maruff, P., Crowe, S., and Currie, J. (1998). Inhibitory processes in covert orienting in patients with Alzheimer's disease. *Neuropsychology*, *12*, 225–241.

D'Esposito, M., Detre, J.A., Alsop, C.D., Shin, R.K., Atlas, S., and Grossman, M. (1995). The neural basis of the central executive of working memory. *Nature*, *378*, 279–281.

Fabrigoule, C., Rouch, I., Taberly, A., Letenneur, L., Commenges, D., Mazaux, J.M., Orgogozo, J.M., and Dartigues, J.F. (1998). Cognitive process in preclinical phase of dementia. *Brain*, *121*, 135–141.

Faust, M.E. and Balota, D.A. (1997). Inhibition of return and visuospatial attention in healthy older adults and individuals with dementia of the Alzheimer type. *Neuropsychology*, *11*, 13–29.

Filoteo, J.V., Delis, D.C., Massman, P.J., Demadura, T., Butters, N., and Salmon, D.P. (1992). Directed and divided attention in Alzheimer's disease: impairments in shifting of attention to global and local stimuli. *Journal of Clinical and Experimental Neuropsychology*, *14*, 871–883.

Filoteo, J.V., Delis, D.C., Roman, M.J., Demadura, T., Ford, E., Butters, N., Salmon, D.P., Paulsen, J., Shults, C.W., Swenson, M., and Swerdlow, N. (1995). Visual attention and perception in patients with Huntington's disease: comparisons with other subcortical and cortical dementias. *Journal of Clinical and Experimental Neuropsychology*, *17*, 654–667.

Foster, J.K., Berhmann, M., and Stuss, D.T. (1999). Visual attention deficits in Alzheimer's disease: simple versus conjoined feature search. *Neuropsychology*, *13*, 223–245.

Fournet, N., Moreaud, O., Roulin, J.L., Naegele, B., and Pellat, J. (1996). Working memory in medicated patients with Parkinson's disease: the central executive seems to work. *Journal of Neurology, Neurosurgery and Psychiatry*, *60*, 313–317.

Fournet, N. Moreaud, O., Roulin, J.L., Naegele, B., and Pellat, J. (2000). Working memory functioning in medicated Parkinson's disease patients and the effect of withdrawal of dopaminergic medication. *Neuropsychology*, *14*, 247–253.

Fox, N.C., Warrington, E.K., Freeborough, P.A., Hartikainen, P., Kennedy, A.M., Stevens, J.M., and Rossor, M.N. (1996). Presymptomatic hippocampal atrophy in Alzheimer's disease. A longitudinal MRI study. *Brain*, *119*, 2001–2007.

Grady, C.L., Haxby, J.V., Horwitz, B., Sundaram, M., Berg, G., Schapiro, M.B., Friedland, R.P., and Rapoport, S.I. (1988). Longitudinal study of the early neuropsychological and cerebral metabolic changes in dementia of the Alzheimer type. *Journal of Clinical and Experimental Neuropsychology*, *10*, 576–596.

Grafman, J., Litvan, I., Gomez, C., and Chase, T.N. (1990). Frontal lobe function in progressive supranuclear palsy. *Archives of Neurology*, *47*, 553–558.

Grafman, J.G., Litvan, I., and Stark, M. (1995). Neuropsychological features of progressive supranuclear palsy. *Brain and Cognition*, *28*, 311–320.

Greene, J.D.W., Hodges, J.R., and Baddeley, A.D. (1995). Autobiographical memory and executive functions in early dementia of Alzheimer type. *Neuropsychologia, 33*, 1647–1670.

Haxby, J.V., Parasuraman, R., Gillette, J., and Raffaele, K. (1991). Selective and divided attention to visual features are impaired in patients with early dementia of the Alzheimer type [Abstract]. *Society for Neurosciences Abstracts, 17*, 696.

Jacoby, L.L. (1991). A process dissociation framework: Separating automatic from intentional uses of memory. *Journal of Memory and Language, 30*, 513–541.

Jahanshahi, M., Brown, R.G., and Marsden, C.D. (1992). Simple and choice reaction time and the use of advance information for motor preparation in Parkinson's disease. *Brain, 115*, 539–564.

Johannsen, P., Jakobsen, J., Bruhn, P., and Gjedde, A. (1999). Cortical responses to sustained and divided attention in Alzheimer's disease. *Neuroimage, 10*, 269–281.

Juillerat, A.C., Van der Linden, M., Seron, X., and Adam, S. (2000). La prise en charge des patients Alzheimer à un stade débutant. In X. Seron and M. Van der Linden (eds) *Traité de Neuropsychologie Clinique*. Marseilles: Solal, pp. 269–289 (Tome 2).

Kaye, J.A., Swihart, B.S., Howieson, D., Dame, A., Moore, M.M., Karnos, B.A., Camicioli, M.D., Ball, M., Oken, B., and Sexton, G. (1997). Volume loss of the hippocampus and temporal lobe in healthy elderly persons destined to develop dementia. *Neurology, 48*, 1297–1304.

Kertzman, C., Robinson, D.L., and Litvan, I. (1990). Effects of physotigmine on spatial attention in patients with progressive supranuclear palsy. *Archives of Neurology, 47*, 1346–1350.

Laakso, M.P., Soininen, H., Partanen, K., Lehtovirta, M., Hallikainen, M., Hanninen, T., Helkala, E.L., Vainio, P., and Riekkinen, P.J. (1998). MRI of the hippocampus in Alzheimer's disease: sensitivity, specificity, and analysis of the incorrectly classified subjects. *Neurobiological Aging, 19*, 23–31.

Lafleche, G. and Albert, M.S. (1995). Executive functions deficits in mild Alzheimer's disease. *Neuropsychology, 9*, 313–320.

Langley, L.K., Overmier, J.B., Knopman, D.S., and Prod'Homme, M.S. (1998). Inhibition and habituation: preserved mechanisms of attentional selection in aging and Alzheimer's disease. *Neuropsychology, 12*, 353–366.

Lawrence, A.D. and Sahakian, B.J. (1996). The neuropsychology of fronto-strial dementias. In R.T. Woods (ed.) *Handbook of the Clinical Psychology of Ageing*. Chichester: Wiley.

Lee, S.S., Wild, K., Hollnagel, C., and Grafman, J. (1999). Selective visual attention in patients with frontal lobe lesions or Parkinson's disease. *Neuropsychologia, 37*, 595–604.

Lines, C.R., Dawson, C., Preston, G.C., Reich, S., Foster, C., and Traub, M. (1991). Memory and attention in patients with senile dementia of the Alzheimer type and in normal elderly subjects. *Journal of Clinical and Experimental Neuropsychology, 13*, 691–702.

Martin, A. (1990). Neuropsychology of Alzheimer's disease: the case for sub-groups. In M.F. Schwartz (ed.) *Modular Deficits in Alzheimer-type Dementia*. Cambridge, MA: MIT Press.

Maruff, P., Malone, V., and Currie, J. (1995). Asymmetries in the covert orienting of visual spatial attention to spatial and non-spatial cues in Alzheimer's disease. *Brain, 118*, 1421–1435.

Massman, P.J., Delis, D.C., Filoteo, J.V., Butters, N., Salmon, D.P., and Demadura, T.L. (1993). Mechanisms of spatial impairment in Alzheimer's disease subgroups: Differential breakdown of directed attention to global–local stimuli. *Neuropsychology*, 7, 172–181.

Miller, B.L., Cummings, J.L., Villanueva-Meyer, J., Boone, K., Mehringer, C.M., Lesser, I.M., and Mena, I. (1991). Frontal lobe degeneration: clinical, neuropsychological, and SPECT characteristics. *Neurology*, *41*, 1374–1382.

Morris, R.G. (1992). Patterns of short term memory impairment in Alzheimer's disease. In L. Bäckman (ed.) *Memory Functioning in Dementia*. Amsterdam: North Holland, pp. 3–25.

Nebes, R.D. and Brady, C.B. (1989). Focused and divided attention in Alzheimer's disease. *Cortex*, *25*, 305–315.

Nebes, R.D. and Brady, C.B. (1992). Generalized cognitive slowing and severity of dementia in Alzheimer's disease: implication for the interpretation of response-time data. *Journal of Clinical and Experimental Neuropsychology*, *14*, 317–326.

Nebes, R.D. and Brady, C.B. (1993). Phasic and tonic alertness in Alzheimer's disease. *Cortex*, *29*, 77–90.

Nebes, R.D. and Madden, D.J. (1988). Different patterns of cognitive slowing produced by Alzheimer's disease and normal aging. *Psychology and Aging*, *3*, 102–104.

Neill, W.T. (1977). Inhibition and facilitation processes in selective attention. *Journal of Experimental Psychology: Human Perception and Performance*, *3*, 444–450.

Nestor, P.G., Parasuraman, R., Haxby, J.V., and Grady, C.L. (1991). Divided attention and metabolic brain dysfunction in mild dementia of the Alzheimer's type. *Neuropsychologia*, *29*, 379–387.

Norman, D.A. and Shallice, T. (1986). Attention to action: willed and automatic control of behavior. In R.J. Davidson, G.E. Schwarts, and D. Shapiro (eds) *Consciousness and Self-regulation. Advances in Research and Theory*. New York: Plenum Press, pp. 1–18.

Oken, B.S., Kishiyama, S.S., Kaye, J.A., and Howieson, D.B. (1994). Attention deficit in Alzheimer's disease is not simulated by an anticholinergic/antihistaminergic drug and is distinct from deficits in healthy aging. *Neurology*, *44*, 657–662.

Parasuraman, R. and Greenwood, P.M. (1998). Selective attention in aging and dementia. In R. Parasuraman (ed.) *The Attentive Brain*. Cambridge, MA: MIT Press, pp. 462–487.

Parasuraman, R., Greenwood, P.M., Haxby, J.V., and Grady, C.L. (1992). Visuospatial attention in dementia of the Alzheimer's type. *Brain*, *115*, 711–733.

Parasuraman, R., Greenwood, P.M., and Alexander, G.E. (1995). Selective impairment of spatial attention during visual search in Alzheimer's disease. *Neuroreport*, 6, 1861–1864.

Parasuraman, R., and Haxby, J.V. (1993). Attention and brain function in Alzheimer's disease: a review. *Neuropsychology*, 7, 242–272.

Pasquier, F. (1994). Troubles mnésiques et attentionnels dans la démence de type Alzheimer et la démence de type frontal. Université Charles de Gaulle, Lille III: Unpublished thesis.

Pasquier, F. and Lebert, F. (1995). Etude neuropsychologique. In F. Pasquier and F. Lebert (eds) *Les Démences fronto-temporales*. Paris: Masson, pp. 91–100.

Pate, D.S., Margolin, D.I., Friedrich, F.J., and Bentley, E.E. (1994). Decision-making and attentional processes in ageing and in dementia of the Alzheimer's type. *Cognitive Neuropsychology*, *11*, 321–329.

Perry, R.J. and Hodges, J.R. (1999). Attention and executive deficits in Alzheimer's disease. A critical review. *Brain*, *122*, 383–404.

Perry, R.J., Watson, P., and Hodges, J.R. (2000). The nature and staging of attentional dysfunction in early (minimal and mild) Alzheimer's disease: relationships to episodic and semantic memory impairment. *Neuropsychologia*, *38*, 252–271.

Petersen, S.E., Robinson, D.L., and Currie, J.L. (1989). Influences of lesion of parietal cortex on visual spatial attention in humans. *Experimental Brain Research*, *76*, 267–280.

Pillon, B., Dubois, B., Lhermitte, F., and Agid, Y. (1986). Heterogeneity of cognitive impairment in progressive supranuclear palsy, Parkinson's disease and Alzheimer's disease. *Neurology*, *36*, 1179–1185.

Posner, M.I. (1980). Orienting of attention. *Quarterly Journal of Experimental Psychology*, *32*, 325

Posner, M.I., Choate, L., Rafal, R.D., and Vaughan, J. (1985). Inhibition of return: Neural mechanisms and function. *Cognitive Neuropsychology*, *2*, 211–218.

Posner, M.I. and Cohen, Y. (1984). Components of visual orienting. In H. Bouma and D. G. Bouwhuis (eds) *Attention and Performance* X. London: Lawrence Erlbaum, pp. 531–556.

Posner, M.I. and Dehaene, S. (1994). Attentional networks. *Trends in Neurosciences*, *17*, 2, 75–79.

Posner, M.I. and Petersen, S.E. (1990). The attention system of the human brain. *Annual Review of Neurosciences*, *13*, 25–42.

Rafal, R. (1992). Visually guided behavior. In *Progressive Supranuclear Palsy: Clinical and Research Approaches*. New York: Oxford University Press, pp. 204–222.

Rafal, R.D. and Posner, M.I. (1988). Orienting of visual attention in progressive supranuclear palsy. *Brain*, *111*, 267–280.

Reid, W., Broe, G., Creasey, H., Grayson, D., McCusker, E., Bennet, H., Longley, W., and Sulway, M.R. (1996). Age at onset and pattern of neuropsychological impairment in mild early-stage Alzheimer disease. A study of community-based population. *Archives of Neurology*, *53*, 1056–1061.

Robertson, I.H., Ward, T., Ridgeway, V., and Nimmo-Smith, I. (1996). The structure of normal human attention: the test of everyday attention. *Journal of the International Neuropsychological Society*, *2*, 525–534.

Roman, M.J., Delis, D.C., Filoteo, J.V., Demadura, T.L., Paulsen, J., Swerdlow, N.R., Swenson, M.R., Salmon, D., Butters, N., and Shults, C. (1998). Is there a 'subcortical' profile of attentional dysfunction? A comparison of patients with Huntington's and Parkinson's diseases on a global–local focused attention task. *Journal of Clinical and Experimental Neuropsychology*, *20*, 873–874.

Rosvold, H.E., Mirsky, A.F., Sarason, I., Bransome, E.D., and Beck, L.H. (1956). A continuous performance test of brain damage. *Journal of Consulting Psychology*, *20*, 343–350.

Rouleau, N., Belleville, S., and Van der Linden, M. (2001). Exploration of multiple inhibitory systems and interference in dementia of the Alzheimer type. Submitted.

Sahakian, B.J., Downes, J.J., Eagger, S., Evenden, J.L., Levy, R., Philpot, M.P., Roberts, A.C., and Robbins, T.W. (1990). Sparing of attentional relative to mnemonic function in a subgroup of patients with dementia of the Alzheimer type. *Neuropsychologia*, 28, 1197–1213.

Salthouse, T.A. and Becker, J.T. (1998). Independent effects of Alzheimer's disease on neuropsychological functioning. *Neuropsychology*, *12*, 242–252.

Scinto, L.F.M., Daffner, K.R., Castro, L., Weintraub, S., Vavrik, M., and Mesulam, M. (1994). Impairment of spatially directed attention in patients with probable Alzheimer's disease as measured by eye movements. *Archives of Neurology*, *51*, 682–688.

Sharpe, M.H. (1990). Distractibility in early Parkinson's disease. *Cortex*, *26*, 239–246.

Simone, P.M. and Baylis, G.C. (1997). Selective attention in a reaching task: effects of normal aging and Alzheimer's disease. *Journal of Experimental Psychology: Human Perception and Performance*, *23*, 595–608.

Small, B.J., Herlitz, A., Fratiglioni, L., Almkvist, O., and Bäckman, L. (1997). Cognitive predictors of incident Alzheimer's disease: a prospective longitudinal study. *Neuropsychology*, *11*, 413–420.

Spieler, D.H., Balota, D.A., and Faust, M.E. (1996). Stroop performance in healthy younger and older adults and in individuals with dementia of the Alzheimer's type. *Journal of Experimental Psychology*, *22*, 461–479.

Spinnler, H. (1991). The role of attention disorders in the cognitive deficits of dementia. In F. Boller and J. Grafman (eds) *Handbook of Neuropsychology*. Amsterdam: Elsevier, pp. 79–122.

Sprengelmeyer, R., Lange, H., and Hömberg, V. (1995). The pattern of attentional deficits in Huntington's disease. *Brain*, *118*, 145–152.

Stroop, R.J. (1935). Studies of interference in serial verbal reactions. *Journal of Experimental Psychology*, *18*, 643–661.

Sturm, W., Willmes, K., Orgass, B., and Hartje, W. (1997). Do specific attention deficits need specific training? *Neuropsychological Rehabilitation*, 7, 81–103.

Sullivan, M.P., Faust, M.E., and Balota, D.A. (1995). Identity negative priming in older adults and individuals with dementia of the Alzheimer type. *Neuropsychology*, *9*, 537–555.

Taylor, A.E., Saint-Cyr, J.A., and Lang, A.E. (1990). Memory and learning in early Parkinson's disease: evidence for a frontal lobe syndrome. *Brain and Cognition*, *13*, 211–232.

Taylor, S.F., Kornblum, S., Lauber, E.J., Minoshima, S., and Koeppe, R.A. (1997). Isolation of specific interference processing in the Stroop task: PET activation studies. *Neuroimage*, 6, 81–92.

Tierney, M.C., Szalai, J.P., Snow, W.G., Fisher, R.H., Nores, A., Nadon, G., Dunn, E., and St.George-Hyslop, P.H. (1996). Prediction of probable Alzheimer's disease in memory-impaired patients: a prospective longitudinal study. *Neurology*, *46*, 661–665.

Tipper, S.P. (1985). The negative priming effect: inhibitory effects of ignored primes. *Quarterly Journal of Experimental Psychology*, *37A*, 571–590.

Treisman, A. and Gelade, G. (1980). A feature integration theory of attention. *Cognitive Psychology*, *12*, 97–136.

Van der Linden, M. (1994). Neuropsychologie des syndromes démentiels. In X. Seron and M. Jeannerod (eds) *Neuropsychologie humaine*. Bruxelles: Mardaga.

Venneri, A., Turnbull, O.H., and Della Sala, S. (1996). The taxonomic perspective: The neuropsychological diagnosis of dementia. *European Review of Applied Psychology*, *46*, 179–190.

Wright, M.J., Burns, R.J., Geffen, G.M., and Geffen, L.B. (1990). Covert orientation of visual attention in Parkinson's disease: an impairment in the maintenance of information. *Neuropsychologia*, *28*, 151–159.

Yamada, T., Izyuuinn, M., Schulzer, M., and Hirayama, K. (1990). Covert orienting of attention in Parkinson's disease. *Journal of Neurology, Neurosurgery and Psychiatry*, *53*, 593–596.

Zakzanis, K.K. (1998). The subcortical dementia of Huntington's disease. *Journal of Clinical and Experimental Neuropsychology*, *20*, 565–578.

Zimmermann, P. and Fimm, B. (1994). *The Test for Attentional Performance (TAP)*. Würselen: Psytest.

Part IV

Rehabilitation

Chapter 12

Rehabilitation of attention disorders: a literature review

Michel Leclercq and Walter Sturm

1 Introduction

Impairments of attentional functions are very frequent and can be expected to occur in 80% of all brain-damaged patients (van Zomeren, Brouwer and Deelman, 1984). Impairements give rise to a specific problem *per se* by slowing down the patient's reactions in everyday life, increasing irritability, and, especially after damage of the right cerebral hemisphere, by leading to a complete neglect of one intra- and/or extrapersonal lateral space. Attentional deficits may impair the efficacy of rehabilitation of other cognitive functions. Wood and Eames (1981) have pointed out that patients with severely impaired attentional functions profit least from rehabilitation programmes.

Following recent experimental and neuropsychological theorizing, attention has to be divided into separable domains. They are distributed according to two dimensions (van Zomeren and Brouwer, 1994): on the one hand, *intensity* which includes the tonic and phasic alertness, sustained attention and vigilance aspects; on the other hand, *selectivity* which comprises the selective or focused attention domains and divided attention (for more details on these specific attentional components see Chapter 1).

There is strong evidence now that differently localized brain lesions lead to different impairments concerning specific attentional mechanisms. Even if contemporary neuropsychological views of attention favour its implementation in widespread cortical and subcortical networks (Posner and Petersen, 1990; van Zomeren and Brouwer, 1994), numerous studies have shown that specific attention functions can be impaired selectively by focal brain damage. Impairments of both *alertness* and *vigilance* or *sustained attention* have been reported after lesions of the brainstem part of the reticular formation (Mesulam, 1985) and after lesions of the right hemisphere (Howes and Boller, 1975; Sturm and Büssing, 1986). Furthermore, studies with lateralized stimulus presentation in healthy subjects (Heilman and van den Abell, 1979; Sturm, Reul and Willmes, 1989) and in split-brain patients (Dimond, 1979) corroborate the assumption that the right hemisphere plays a crucial role in maintaining and controlling intensity aspects of attention. Additional evidence for right-hemisphere dominance in alertness and sustained attention comes from measurement of cerebral blood flow in PET or fMRI activation studies (Lewin *et al.*, 1996; Pardo *et al.*, 1991; Paus *et al.* 1997; Sturm *et al.* 1999).

Certain aspects of *attention selectivity* can be impaired in patients with left-hemisphere cortical lesions (Dee and van Allen, 1973; Sturm and Büssing, 1986), leading to a slowing down of response time and to increased error rates in choice reaction paradigms. Bisiach *et al.* (1982) and Jansen *et al.* (1992) also showed left-hemisphere dominance for choice reactions in studies with lateralized stimulus presentation in healthy subjects. In a PET scan study Corbetta *et al.* (1991) demonstrated the special role of the left lateral orbitofrontal cortex, of the basal ganglia (globus pallidus, caudate nucleus) and of the posterior thalamus during the performance of a selective attention task. In the same study, the authors also claimed a potentially important role for the dorsolateral prefrontal cortex of the right hemisphere in a *divided attention* task. Unfortunately, the task used by the authors did not strictly follow the commonly accepted divided attention paradigm, but closely resembled a *sustained attention* task. In the 'selective attention' condition of their experiment, subjects had to respond only to changes of *one* feature (colour, speed or shape) in a visual task, whereas in the 'divided attention' condition they were asked to respond to changes of *any* of these features. Since the latter task condition neither asks for any kind of selectivity nor shows any features of a dual- or multiple-task paradigm, the interpretation of the results in terms of a divided attention task becomes equivocal. There is, however, additional evidence from animal studies focusing on the important contribution of the dorsolateral frontal cortex in memory and attention control processes (Funahashi *et al.*, 1989; Goldman-Rakic, 1987). These findings agree with a frontal supervisory attentional system proposed by Shallice (1988) which is very similar to Baddeley's notion of a central executive in working memory (1986). The strong connection between these two processes is pointed out by Baddeley's recent notion (1993) that 'one is attending with one's working memory'.

2 Retraining of attention disorders

The number of publications concerning the retraining of attention disorders is relatively limited, and we will give an account of the main existing studies. We will subdivide these works into two categories. On the one hand, we will call some interventions 'unspecific' because the adopted training doesn't target one or several specifically impaired attentional mechanisms. Indeed, early attempts to retrain disorders of attentional processes after brain damage were quite global and did not take into account the distinctiveness of attention functions. In these types of studies the diagnoses before the intervention are not very differentiated and most of the time interventions consider attention as a unitary function. On the other hand, in the studies we call 'specific', a differentiation of the attentional components with clear identification of the impaired aspects has been made, and the rehabilitation plan takes into account the specific aspects of attention impairments. These studies have in common an approach which includes a comprehensive diagnosis of the attentional functioning, with the intervention targeting the components that are specifically disturbed.

2.1 Unspecific attention training

Blackburn (1958) and Shankweiler (1959) as well as Sturm and Büssing (1982) studied the influence of motivating instructions on the reaction performance of brain-damaged patients. Calming-down, reinforcing or instigating instructions were used and the performance in simple or choice reaction tasks following these instructions was compared with the baseline performance. Unequivocally the authors found a significant increase in performance after any kind of motivating instruction, although the patients never reached the performance level of normal control subjects.

Kallinger (1975; see also Hofer and Scherzer, 1977) tried to improve the reaction performance after brain damage by means of a complex choice reaction time apparatus, the Wiener Determinationsgerät (WDG; Vienna Determination Apparatus). Subjects have to respond as quickly and correctly as possible to differently coloured visual signals and/or to differently pitched tones, by depressing response keys with the hand or foot. Four control tests (simple reaction time task, cancellation test d2, tachistoscopic presentation of dot patterns, and a perseveration task by Mittenecker) were used before and after the training of the patients and of a normal control group to look for generalizing training effects. The brain-damaged group improved significantly in all four tasks, the normal group in only two. The author interpreted this result as a generalized effect of the training procedure. A verbal reinforcement did not show any additional beneficial effect. Unfortunately there was no baseline condition before the training period and so it is hard to disentangle spontaneous recovery and test repetition effects from the effects of the training.

Sturm *et al.* (1983) also made use of programmable versions of the Vienna Determination apparatus (WDG) plus the 'Vienna Cognitrone' – both manufactured by the Schuhfried company in Mödling, Austria – to retrain attention deficits in brain-damaged patients, mostly with traumatic etiology. With the cognitrone the subject has to indicate, by depressing a response key, whether a configuration formed by light-emitting diode bars is identical to one of a multiple choice set of four configurations presented for comparison. The set is changed after every ten items. Thus, both training devices follow choice reaction paradigms and represent trainings of selective attention. It is necessary to underline that all the subjects were submitted to the same selective attention training despite the fact that the deficits they presented probably related, at least for some of them, to other types of attentional processes. The efficacy of the training, including generalization to non-treated functions, was tested using a battery of sixteen standardized psychometric tests. This battery comprised tasks similar to the training procedure, and others which were related but which were not directly trained attention tasks, as well as tests of more general intellectual functions such as reasoning, word fluency, or spatial abilities. By means of a cross-over experimental design, two groups of patients and two normal control groups, matched for age, were studied to control for spontaneous recovery and test–retest effects. The results revealed training effects beyond spontaneous recovery and test repetition, which generalized to non-treated functions, although the largest improvements were related to tasks similar to the training procedure. The training effects remained stable at follow-up examination four weeks later.

Similar generalizing effects after the same unspecific training in traumatic brain injury (TBI) patients in the post-acute stage were reported by Poser *et al.* (1992).

Malec *et al.* (1984) studied the impact of two types of video games on sustained attention in a population of ten young subjects who were suffering from a severe TBI in the course of the six months (mean = 80 days) preceding the experimentation. The two games used moving targets presented on a screen; the most complex task included distractor stimuli moving in between the targets. Baseline testing comprised the Stroop paradigm, a symbols and letters cancellation task and a reaction time task with warning signal ('Ready?'). Subjects were randomly submitted to one of two sequences ABAB or BABA, where 'A' corresponds to playing games and 'B' to a period without training. The training on computer games was spread over periods of one week with two daily sessions of 30 minutes, each subject being submitted to re-evaluation on the different tests at the end of each four-week period. The authors point out that: 'Subjects in the study appeared to enjoy and to be engaged by the video games. The subjects actively participated in video game sessions even though many were highly uncooperative and distractible in other rehabilitation activities' (p. 22).

Data analysis showed no significant relation between the improvements on the dependent measurements during the study and age, sex, coma duration, GOAT score (Gavelston Orientation and Amnesia Test: Levin *et al.*, 1979) or brain lesions evaluated by CT scan. There was no significant difference between performance conditions: periods A or B. Only the data from the reaction time test approached the significance level after the training sessions.

The four patients in Wood's study (1986) were young victims (average age: 30) of very severe brain injury with a long post-traumatic amnesia (two months to one year) and in chronic phase (post-onset: 4 to 6 years) at the time of intervention. These subjects presented important attention difficulties in different activities which severely challenged the rehabilitation interventions. Two of these patients were first submitted to a behavioural approach with reinforcement procedures (token economy), with the aim of improving overt attention behaviour, namely head and gaze orientation towards the therapist during the training session. At the end of this first stage, which was fruitful, a similar procedure was implemented, this time including more cognitive aspects of attention. This procedure was applied daily for 28 days: each correct response was reinforced by a token which the patient could exchange for a reward; each error led to withdrawal of a token. The author pointed out that during a discrimination task of digits presented auditorily: 'this type of contingency avoided a high proportion of false-positive responses' (Wood, 1986, p. 48). The same reinforcements were delivered during a tracking task in which the subject had to control the movement of a light spot using a joystick in order to match it with specific symbols presented on the screen. Measurements used during baseline testing and after training were taken from video-recording the subjects' behaviour in different environmental settings, and three auditory memory tasks: a digit span test, the subtest of logical memory from Wechsler's memory scale and Rey's auditory memory test (Lezak, 1995).

At the end of the training, there was a statistically significant progressive improvement ($p<.01$) for the two tasks used. This improvement concerned the stability of attention during progressively longer periods, and an increase in information processing with concomitant reduction of errors. Analysis also showed a significant increase in attention behaviour (video recording) but, apart from a small improvement in Rey's test, no significant change in the three tasks of auditory memory.

It would have been interesting to evaluate the transfer of the training effects to some tasks requiring classical attentional selectivity (decision time, number of false alarms in multiple reaction time tasks, etc.) instead of assessing the impact of the training on memory tests. Indeed, it seems unrealistic to hope that this type of training may have some positive effects on memory functions which imply a set of much more elaborated processes than those solicited by tasks of visual and auditory discrimination. Futhermore, considering the lack of follow-up evaluation it is not possible to know if the observed improvements were stable over a prolonged period of time.

Ponsford and Kinsella (1988) assigned ten young (average age = 24) victims of a relatively recent (average interval between injury and study = 13.8 weeks) and severe brain injury to three experimental conditions: no treatment (phase A), followed by training without feedback (phase B), and finally treatment with feedback and reinforcements (phase C). The assessment of the information processing speed was carried out by a task of transcoding (one oral, one written), a multiple reaction time task and a cancellation task, which were submitted before, during and after the training. Attentional behaviour was assessed by means of a rating scale by occupational therapists and a video recording in the occupational setting.

'The training tasks were selected to provide repeated practice in responding rapidly, but selectively, to information presented visually on a computer screen. They allowed for measurement of change in accuracy as well as speed of response over time' (Ponsford and Kinsella, 1988, p. 698). Tasks included simple reaction time to stimuli presented in different parts of the visual field, a task of matching with visual material, and three multiple reaction time tasks: the subject had to react as quickly as possible to some specific coloured shapes, letters (letters vs. digits) or specific numbers.

All the subjects improved their performances with time, an observation probably linked to spontaneous recovery as the majority of them were still in acute phase (see above). However, analysis did not demonstrate significant impact of the training on the dependent variables. A lack of improvement was also observed for the comparison between phases B and C (treatment without and treatment with reinforcement), 'although there was a tendency for some subjects to respond to the feedback and reinforcement given' (p. 706). Results of the video-recording analysis were also disappointing: absence of any significant effect or of interaction between groups and experimental conditions. Ponsford and Kinsella argue that the difference between their results and the more favourable ones observed in other studies was possibly due to a more diversified approach to the deficits: the intensive training of several different attentional aspects instead of limiting the intervention to one of these aspects (processing speed). The authors also suggest examining the influence of such factors as subject's mood and motivation which might explain the lack of improvement.

Middleton, Lambert and Seggar (1991) compared the effects of two different trainings on two subgroups of patients. One treatment specifically targeted logical reasoning, the other attention and memory. Thirty-six subjects were distributed across two comparable groups. Patients were in a chronic state: the average time post-onset was one to three years. The majority of patients had suffered from a closed (82%) or an open (6%) head injury; the others had suffered from a cerebrovascular accident (6%) or an illness of a different etiology (6%). The training (total of 32 hours, spread over 8 weeks) was based on different computer tasks from Bracy's battery (1982, 1985), exercises targeting attention and memory for one group, and logical reasoning for the other one. The pre- and post-treatment evaluations of the attention/memory aspects were done by three tests: the digit span, the Knox cube subtest from the WAIS-R, and the Paired-associates subtest from the Wechsler Memory Scale.

The analysis demonstrated significant improvements for both groups: 12% for the group assigned to exercises of attention/memory, and 16% for the group assigned to the logical reasoning training. Inter-group comparisons did not show any specific effect attributable to each type of training. Middleton *et al.* also underlined the considerable variability among individual data. A multiple regression did not show significant effects of age, sex or length and severity of the illness.

Beyond the lack of specific impact of interventions, the absence of a control group in this study casts doubt on the assumption that the observed improvements were related to the training. This doubt is enhanced by the fact that all patients, in addition to the specific training, 'received 96 hours of educational training as part of the programme in which they were already enrolled. This focused on improving attention, concentration, perceptual skills, and problem solving' (Middleton *et al.*, 1991, p. 528). So, in addition to a lack of specificity in the approach, there were also severe methodological problems with this study.

In 1991, Sturm and Willmes repeated their study (Sturm *et al.* 1983, see above), but this time only in patients with vascular brain damage strictly confined to one cerebral hemisphere: 27 with a left-hemispheric lesion (LHL), and 8 with a right-hemispheric lesion (RHL). The time between the lesion onset and the beginning of the training was 4 to 36 weeks. In order to differentiate training effects for practice or spontaneous recovery, the authors constructed an experimental design including several sessions of control testing (Figure 12.1). Three subgroups were submitted to this design.

Two subgroups respectively comprised the RHL patients and half of the LHL patients; they were labelled 'late' because training started after two control test sessions separated by three weeks. The third subgroup was constituted from the other half of the LHL patients paired for age, sex and time post-onset with the first subgroup; treatment of this subgroup, labelled 'early', started immediately after the baseline testing. To look for stability of effects a follow-up session was conducted for each of the three subgroups. The evaluation sessions (± 90 minutes) consisted of applying a battery of 10 psychometric tasks with a total of 14 variables. This battery included specific versions of the tasks used during the training, differents tests of alertness, vigilance and selective attention, and several cognitive tasks without direct relation to the training tasks, for example, reasoning tasks or the WAIS Similarities subtest.

The three subgroups were assigned to a training for three weeks (14 sessions of 30 minutes) with a set of computerized tasks extracted from the Vienna Determination apparatus described above. These could be varied

Time course:	Day 1	3 weeks	6 weeks
'Early' group =	Testing 1 → Training	Testing 2	Follow-up
'Late' group =	Testing 1	Testing 2 → Training	Follow-up

Figure 12.1 Experimental design in the Sturm and Willmes study (1991)

with respect to several parameters: stimulus type (visual vs. auditory or combined), speed and mode of presentation, and specific stimulus–response combinations. By manipulating these parameters, the difficulty level of the training could be increased. Moving up to the next level was effective only when the subject showed 90% correct responses for the last trained level.

Statistical analysis demonstrated variable improvement according to the subgroup. General tendencies can be summarized as follows:

1 improvement was more marked in the subgroup of patients with LHL than for the RHL subjects, a difference which, as will be pointed out later, was probably induced by the types of tasks selected for the training;
2 the observed improvement in the LHL subgroup concerned more specifically some aspects of selective attention while for the RHL subgroup there was a general lack of improvement;
3 observed improvement was not attributable to spontaneous recovery nor to test repetition;
4 improvement remained stable at the end of 6 weeks for the 'late' subgroup and 9 weeks for the 'early' subgroup;
5 authors underlined the existence of a relatively constant relation between the amount of improvement and the initial level of performance, the most pronounced improvements being recorded in patients with lower initial level.

The generalization effects to other specific attentional functions were limited, and absent within other cognitive functions. In this study the generalizing effect of training was much more limited than in the first study with TBI patients after diffuse brain damage. It was confined to improvement in tests similar to the training procedure or to tests assessing the same attention function as the training, i.e. selective attention in choice reaction paradigms or in cancellation tests. Intensity aspects of attention, e.g. vigilance, did not improve nor was there any improvement in other cognitive tasks, e.g. verbal or non-verbal reasoning.

Sturm and Willmes explained the difference in results, as compared to their first study, by the fact that the more focal vascular lesions in the second study caused more distinct cognitive impairments beyond pure attention deficits, possibly masking the benefit of the training in some tests; for example, language for the aphasic patients or non-verbal reasoning for the RHL subjects. Furthermore, the fact that there was no transfer of training even to some attention tests, especially those representing intensity aspects, led the authors to the conclusion that distinct attention deficits might need specific training.

Gray and Robertson (1988) and Gray *et al.* (1992) studied a heterogeneous population of 31 patients including a majority of severe TBI subjects in the subacute phase. Patients were randomly divided into two subgroups: one composed of 17 subjects assigned to an attentional training with a set of computerized tasks; the other including 14 patients assigned to recreational activities. A *post hoc* analysis demonstrated that the two subgroups were correctly matched for age, sex, severity of attentional deficits assessed with the PASAT (Gronwall, 1977), duration of the disease and the subjects' scores for different questionnaires of anxiety, depression and social behaviour. A set of psychometric tests related to a broad range of cognitive functions (22 variables) was applied three times: before, during treatment, and in a follow-up session conducted six months after the end of training.

The experimental subgroup was confronted with five training programmes:

1 a set of simple and multiple reaction time tasks;
2 a detection task of digit sequences repeatedly presented with variable length and duration of presentation;
3 a digit/symbol matching task;
4 a version of the Stroop paradigm;
5 two tasks of divided attention, one of which required mental calculation.

The observed improvements were significantly more important in the experimental group. The benefits essentially concerned tasks requiring the processing of digits and manipulation in working memory: e.g. the global score in the PASAT ($p = .01$), the longest stretch without error in the PASAT ($p<.05$) and the score in the Arithmetic subtest ($p<.05$), of the WAIS. In fact, several tasks included in the training required maintenance and manipulation of information in working memory. Generally speaking there was no significant change for variables not targeted by the procedure. The performance of the experimental subgroup continued to improve after the end of the treatment, increasing the difference between the subgroups. Gray *et al.* interpreted this observation as the consequence of the learning of strategies acquired during the training phase, strategies which would become progressively automatic and finally should integrate into a broader behavioural range. In contrast, the improvement observed at the beginning in the control group was followed by a performance degradation in the follow-up session. This observation was interpreted in terms of non-specific treatment effect, i.e. the temporary increase of the level of attention and activation limited to the period of practice of recreational activities.

Finally, both subgroups showed some changes in their psychological well-being (Goldberg's, 1978, subscales of depression and anxiety) at the end of training and at follow-up as well. Considering the absence of any inter-group difference for the specific subscales at the end of the treatment and at follow-up, these changes were interpreted as unspecific effects, too.

In summary, this study demonstrated improvements for some attentional processes with favourable generalization to non-trained tasks assessing the same cognitive mechanisms. Effects of the observed improvements on the subjects' daily life activities were not investigated.

It is hard to understand why the favourable impact observed on working memory functioning had no beneficial effect on the evaluations of executive functions. Indeed, as underlined above, the notions of the central executive system described in Baddeley's model of working memory (1986) and the supervisory attentional system in Shallice's model (1982, 1988) very much resemble each other. Thus improvement in the different cognitive variables labelled as 'working memory functions' should also have shown up for the 'frontal functions' variables in which control of attention plays a crucial role. This lack of generalization to tasks addressing the 'central executive' might suggest that the central executive system itself has to be fractioned into several subcomponents.

As already pointed out earlier, all the studies we have described until now have in common that training procedures were not specific with respect to a certain aspect of attention. In particular, the choice of the training tasks was not directly influenced by the results of the pre-treatment assessment which should have permitted differentiation of the deficient aspects of attention from those that are preserved. Table 12.1 recapitulates the different procedures applied in these studies.

2.2 *Specific attention training*

More recently, different therapeutical approaches taking into account the specificity of attention dysfunctions have been tried. These approaches make

Table 12.1 Exercises used for the treatment in the non-specific studies

Blackburn (1958) Shankweiler (1959) Sturm and Büssing (1982)	Simple and multiple reaction time with reinforcements and motivating instructions
Kallinger (1975)	Complex multiple reaction time according to colours, pitched tones and response type
Sturm *et al.* (1983) Sturm and Willmes (1991)	Matching of visual configurations in multiple choice set
Malec *et al.* (1984)	Video games
Wood (1986)	Behavioural approach with reinforcements (token)
Ponsford and Kinsella (1988)	Simple, multiple reaction times and matching
Middleton *et al.* (1991)	Attention/memory computerized programs (Bracy 1982, 1985)
Gray and Robertson (1988) Gray *et al.* (1992)	Simple and multiple reaction time, auditory detection, matching, Stroop, divided attention

use of specific therapy programmes attributed to separable attention domains.

By means of an electronic device, called the 'Orientation Remediation Module' (ORM), Ben-Yishay, Piasetzky and Rattok (1987) treated 40 patients using five tasks of increasing complexity. Their population consisted of severely TBI subjects (young war victims) in the chronic phase of the disease: one to four years post-injury. They used this programme to address some of the most common attention impairments of these patients: (a) lack of alertness, (b) increased attentional variability paired with substantial lack of selectivity or focused attention, (c) problems with sustained focused attention over longer periods of time (vigilance), and (d) delayed, badly adapted responses and perseverations.

Both the theoretical approach and the practical handling of training closely followed Posner and Rafal's theory of attention (1987). Training addressed the attentional impairments in a hypothetically hierarchical order from (a) to (d). The training comprised five different exercises. The patient first learned to attend to signals from his surroundings and to respond quickly to them. This was accomplished by a simple visual reaction time task with feedback. The second exercise was aimed at reducing distractibility. A clock-like apparatus was used. By pressing a key, the pointer of the clock would start moving and the patient had to stop it at a distinct location by releasing the key. This location was changed several times within the same session.

The third exercise was aimed at an active scanning of the patient's surroundings including search for and identification of relevant signals. The training task comprised a board 80 cm in length on which two cubes could be arranged at different distances. The cube on the left-hand side contained a digital display, and the cube on the right five differently coloured lights. The signals in the two cubes could be presented either separately or simultaneously (divided attention) and showed a figure, a colour signal or both at the same time. The patient had to watch both sources and detect relevant signals in each one individually or in both simultaneously.

In the fourth exercise, patients were trained to rely on internal stimuli. They were instructed to estimate the length of time periods. At first, they were allowed to use a stop-watch and were asked to internalize the rhythm of the moving pointer. During later steps of training, the patients were asked to rely only on their internalized time estimation. They were encouraged to use strategies such as rhythmical movements of the body, silent counting or visual imagery.

The fifth task was aimed at modulating and sequencing responses. The patients had to imitate different rhythms on a Morse key. First, they were presented with a sequence of tones which they were asked to internalize. They then had to anticipate each tone of the sequence to achieve a synchronization between the given tonal rhythm and the rhythm of pressing the Morse key.

All of these tasks were designed in order to adapt the level of difficulty to the subject's performance and his/her development during training. The training was administered for six years (!). Finally, a computerized version was developed (Piasetzky *et al.*, 1983).

Before training, each patient was submitted to an assessment with a broad range of tasks including different cognitive, self- and hetero-evaluation measures, and several indices of functional adaptation: a total of 77 psychometric variables (Rattok *et al.*, 1982). Each selected patient presented a stable baseline for three months. Treatment efficacy was estimated from the tasks used during training (pre- and post-treatment comparison) and by a partial baseline retest which was administered to each subject at the end of training. A subgroup of 11 patients was also evaluated in each of the five tasks of the procedure at the end of each specific training; these patients were re-evaluated three months after the end of training, five being retested again three months later.

Data analysis showed a significant ($p<.001$) improvement in each trained task. The group data show an improvement from an initially deficient to a normal level or even higher for some tasks. There was also a statistically significant improvement for four of the measurements selected in the psychometric battery: a visual reaction time task, the digit span and picture completion subtests from the WAIS, and a task of picture description. The scores for the 11 patients assessed after each specific training showed a significant ($p<.005$) improvement which remained stable. The follow-up testing at six months further demonstrated the stability of the intervention effects. Lastly, observed improvement was associated with a significant increase (correlation analysis) in different measures of functional daily life adaptation: activity and initiative level, orientation in the family environment and social cooperation.

Since all five exercises for each patient were performed in the same order, in 11 patients the effect of each exercise on the baseline scores of the next exercise was investigated. Interestingly, there was no transfer from one exercise to the next one but only an improvement for the task just trained. This observation suggests that the training effects were extremely specific without any generalization to other attentional aspects. In this study, however, interpretation of the results remains problematic since training and control tasks were identical. Thus, the results might only reflect 'trivial' practice effects and not real therapy effects in the stricter sense.

In summary, this study demonstrated the existence of specific improvements in tasks selected for training, with limited generalization to some of the control tasks, and to the subjects' daily life. Considering the length of the treatment period one may have some doubt about the relation between the training and the functional adaptation improvement. One should emphasize that in this study for the first time the training tasks were constructed in terms of specific attentional mechanisms derived from Posner and

Rafal's model (1987). The organization of training tasks in a hierarchical way is also an interesting aspect of this study.

Strache's study (1987) concerned a heterogeneous group of 45 patients distributed over three parallel subgroups: two experimental and one non-treated control group.

Each of the two experimental groups was assigned to a different training procedure. For one of these groups (G1) the intervention was of increasing difficulty, regardless of the basic level of performance or the subjects' progress recorded during the training. For the other group (G2) the difficulty level was adapted according to the subjects' initial abilities and their progress during the training. The two groups were trained for four weeks by means of different tasks selected from the Vienna Test System according to the study by Sturm *et al.* (1983). Again, all training tasks mainly focused on sustained or selective aspects of attention. The author points out that 'generally, there was good acceptance of the training. Only about 15% experimental drop-outs occurred, the distribution of which indicates that the baseline and progress-dependent procedure was better accepted' (p. 4). Baseline and post-training assessments were conducted for the three groups from a set of tests comprised of 107 'intellectual, attentional and mnemonic variables'. The post-treatment evaluation was conducted four weeks after the end of the training.

Results may be summarized as follows: (a) the importance of improvement varied according to groups: 58, 56 and 47% of the dependent variables for groups G1, G2 and control respectively; (b) the difference between both experimental groups and the control group was statistically significant, suggesting that the progress in the experimental groups was related to training and cannot only be attributed to spontaneous recovery, practice effects or repeated evaluations; (d) improvements observed in group G1 – standard training – concerned functions very close to those targeted by the training, while in group G2 – training adapted to the subject's abilities – additional favourable consequences for other cognitive functions were observed: verbal fluency, short-term memory, free recall and recognition of verbal information. Qualitative analysis of improvements led Strache to point out the superiority of a procedure adapted to each subject's abilities. Transfer to daily life was not studied in this work but the period (one month) which elapsed between the end of training and the follow-up assessment testified to some stability of the intervention benefits.

The heterogeneity of the study population limits the possibility of replication. It would also have been of interest to know the number of single patients showing improvement or not after this intervention; moreover, the author gives no information about the specific outcome of some subjects according to the etiology of their disease.

Lamberti *et al.* (1988) constructed a computerized training to improve intra-individual response time variability and sustained attention in psychotic and brain-damaged patients of vascular origin. The training tried to optimize the patients' response time using a warning stimulus preceding the imperative stimulus in a phasic alertness procedure. For this, the trainees were offered a number of strategies, e.g. internal counting to predict the occurrence of the stimulus after the warning, or self-induced 'thought stop' to control for internal distractors. There were improvements in the variability of response times for different attention functions (e.g. alertness and selective attention) plus a generalization of the training effects to verbal memory tasks.

Sohlberg and Mateer (1987, 1989), using a multiple baseline across subjects single case design, also reported highly specific results after training either of attention or of visuo-cognitive functions in four patients: two closed head injury, one open brain injury and one patient suffering from a rupture of an aneurysm. Patients were rather young (25 to 30) with a similar educational (11–13 years) and intellectual (IQ = 80 to 87) level. The duration of their illness varied between 12 and 72 months; the time post-onset being sufficiently long to rule out the incidence of spontaneous recovery. The experimental design was based on a multiple baseline analysis across cases. In such a design, the treatment is applied sequentially to each of several target variables, and is considered to be effective when changes occur for the trained behaviour while untreated behaviours remain unchanged (Barlow and Hersen, 1984). Each subject in this study presented deficient performance in two tasks: the PASAT used to assess attention, and a test of spatial relations used to evaluate visuo-spatial control. To constitute the baseline before the treatment each subject was tested twice with these two tasks. The training comprised 7 to 9 individual sessions per week, and the duration of the intervention (4 to 8 weeks for each specific training of attention, visuo-spatial or memory) was determined by the severity of deficits. Training of attention targeted five components: focal and sustained attention, distractibility, attentional flexibility and divided attention. It included about fifteen exercises of increasing difficulty extracted from a module 'Attention Process Training' designed by the authors (Sohlberg and Mateer, 1986, 1989) or adapted from a set of published computer programs (among others: Gianutsos, 1983).

Once one subject had reached a certain level (predetermined according to his/her difficulties in the baseline) for each task of the specific attentional treatment, he/she was assigned to training of visuo-spatial control. At the end of this, three of the four subjects were additionally trained for memory functions. In order to control the possible impact of the order of the specific interventions, this order was reversed for one of the subjects. In order to estimate the impact of each type of intervention on the dependent variables, the baseline measures were applied several times before, during and after each specific training. Each specific intervention led to a significant improvement on the related measures. With regard to attention, each subject improved their performance in the PASAT during the attention training. The patient who first received the visuo-spatial training unexpectedly also showed an improvement in the PASAT, with continuation of improvement in this task during training of attention. These observations clearly demonstrate the existence of a specific effect of each type of intervention, an effect also present in the three other subjects. The increasing scores observed in the PASAT after training of attention remained stable: after 23, 23 and 12 weeks respectively for the three subjects who were first assigned to this type of training. The score for the visuo-spatial task remained stable during the attention training period while performances in the PASAT continued to increase; performances in the visuo-spatial task only improved with the specific training. As underlined by the authors: 'This double dissociation provides powerful support for independent improvements in specific cognitive areas' (Sohlberg and Mateer, 1987, p. 128).

Prior to the start of the training, none of the four subjects was living independently or successfully employed. At the end of the treatment, each of these subjects was living independently, two of them obtained sheltered employment and the two others could work in a normal environment. This increasing autonomy was still effective 5 to 8 months after the end of training. With justified caution, Sohlberg and Mateer (1987) point out: 'Although we cannot attribute these outcomes solely to cognitive training, observed functional gains correlated in time with improvements in cognitive performance' (p. 128).

Gray and Robertson (1989) presented three single cases also studied using a multiple baseline methodology. The three patients presented marked sustained attention deficits. For patient 1, a young man who was the victim of a severe TBI (post-traumatic amnesia >2 months), the target measure was a score combining a forward and backward digit span and a calculation task; a complex reaction time task was used as a control measure. Training (duration: two months) included two computerized tasks: the detection of the repeated occurrence of a digit, and a task of symbol/digit matching (from the Braun *et al.* battery, 1985). Statistical analysis showed the stability during the baseline of the targeted and the control functions, followed by a progressive and significant improvement of the targeted function during the training only.

Patient 2 was a 30-year-old man with bilateral frontal damage after an extremely severe brain injury he had suffered three years before. He was submitted to a computerized version of the Stroop test (Dyer, 1973), a version including three levels of cueing which are gradually faded out until the subject is able to decide which rule to use, to maintain the rule in working memory and to switch rules after error feedback. The target measure was the same as for patient 1. The control measure used during baseline and training periods was a score of recall from memory (Buschke paradigm); this score remained stable for the two periods. The target function, stable during the baseline, improved significantly during the training. The pre- and post-treatment comparisons of the performance in the PASAT and Wisconsin Card Sorting Test (Nelson, 1976) confirmed the existence of significant improvements.

The last patient was a 19-year-old man who six months earlier had suffered a severe brain injury. He underwent treatment for eight weeks, which included a combination of exercises of digit/symbol matching, tasks of the Stroop type, and exercises of psychomotor speed and visuo-motor coordination. Here again performance in the control task (Buschke) remained stable while, after treatment, there was a statistically significant improvement in the target measure, the Wisconsin Card Sorting Test and the PASAT.

To test the hypothesis whether specific attention deficits do need specific training, Sturm *et al.* (1997) developed computerized training programmes for the retraining of four attentional components: alertness, vigilance, selective attention and divided attention. All programmes have a game-like design but strictly reflect the four attention paradigms, converting them, however, into everyday-like situations. Alertness is trained by means of an animated car or motorcycle driving task, in which the patient has to control the speed of the vehicle in such a way that a high average speed is maintained, at the same time avoiding collisions with obstacles which suddenly appear on the road. One of the vigilance training tasks is a radar screen task, in which the subject has to watch flying objects which move extremely slowly across the screen. The patient has to respond either to sudden changes in the speed of the objects or to additional objects appearing on the screen for a short time. For the training of selective attention a choice reaction paradigm was adopted. In one training task a 'trap shooting' game is animated and the patient has to respond to a particular object or particular pairs of objects flying across the screen. A second training is called 'photo safari', in which the subject has to watch for relevant single or double objects popping up in front of a scenic background (e.g. a landscape). To retrain divided attention, a 'flight simulator' task was developed, in which the patient has to monitor up to three different stimulus sources (horizon, speedometer, motor sound) in combination.

To control for therapy effects, the respective subtests of the test battery for attention performance (TAP, Zimmermann and Fimm, 1994) were administered. These represent the same attention paradigms addressed in training, but they do it by completely different tasks. Thus, training and test procedures can clearly be separated from each other. Patients with vascular unilateral lesions, who showed attention deficits in at least two of the four attention domains, i.e. percentile ranks of <25 in the respective TAP subtests, at first were trained for fourteen training sessions in one of the impaired attention domains. After a second test session each patient was trained in one of the other impaired attention functions. At the end of this second phase a third test session was carried out (Figure 12.2). Since each patient showed deficits in at least two attention domains, with this type of study design in each of the two therapy periods there was one attention deficit which was trained specifically, and at least another one for which the training was not specific.

The results revealed that intensity aspects of attention (alertness and

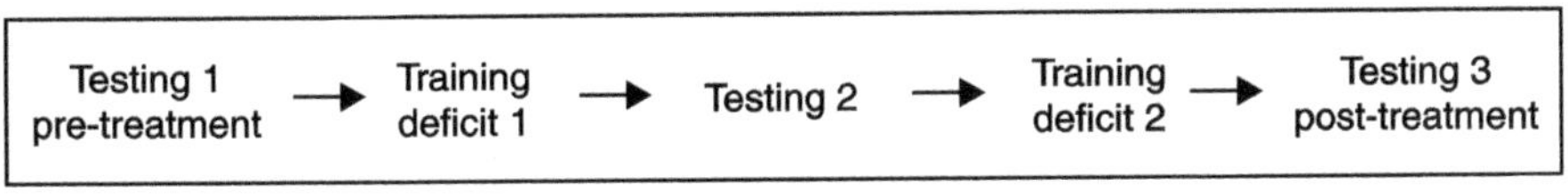

Figure 12.2 Study design of Sturm *et al.* (1997)

vigilance), especially, have to be trained specifically, i.e. significant improvement can only be achieved by the specific training procedure. For selectivity aspects of attention (selective and divided attention) too, the error rate could only be influenced positively by the specific training programmes; response time, however, for these attention domains could also be improved by training of attention intensity (Sturm *et al.*, 1997). These results were corroborated by a multicentric study including TBI patients (see Sturm *et al.*, Chapter 13 in this book) and by a study in patients suffering from multiple sclerosis (Plohmann *et al.*, 1998).

All in all these results showed (a) that it is very important to start an attention therapy with comprehensive diagnosis to work out the specific attention deficits the patient suffers from, and (b) that specific deficits have to be treated specifically. This is stressed by the fact that in patients with impairments of intensity aspects of attention, a 'wrong' training, e.g. focusing on selectivity aspects, may lead to a further deterioration of the already impaired function, probably due to overload of the system (Sturm *et al.*, 1997). In a PET activation study before and after training of alertness in patients with right-hemisphere vascular lesions, the authors (Longoni *et al.*, 1999, 2000) demonstrated a right-hemisphere prefrontal perilesional functional reorganization in patients who regained normal alerting function after the training.

To close this review we would like to mention the Robertson *et al.* study (1995) which found an interesting effect of a 'sustained attention training' in patients with right vascular lesions and left neglect. After the training there was not only an improvement of sustained attention but also a significant reduction of the neglect symptoms although no specific neglect training had been carried out. The authors interpret the effect as a spreading of attention activation from the frontal to the parietal areas of the right hemisphere.

Table 12.2 summarizes the targeted attentional deficits and the tasks used for the training in the studies using a specific approach.

3 Comments

As a whole and despite the fact of their relatively limited number, investigations of the efficacy of different types of training aiming at an improvement of attention lead to very divergent results. Indeed, the conclusions of these studies vary between the absence of any effect on attentional performance and

Table 12.2 Tasks and principal attentional functions targeted by the specific approaches

Ben-Yishay *et al.* (1987)	Visual reaction time with feedback Control of deplacements of a clock hand Detection of targets appearing on one screen or two screens Reproduction of sequences of tones	Alertness Sustained attention Selective attention Divided attention Attention and memory
Strache (1987)	Multiple reaction times: targets of different colours and tonalities	Sustained and selective attention
Lamberti *et al.* (1988)	Warning signal insertion, estimation of durations and self-suggestion	Lapses of attention and sustained attention
Sohlberg and Mateer (1989)	'Attention Processing Training' and published computerized software	Selective, divided, sustained attention
Gray and Robertson (1989)	Tasks of detection, matching and visuo-motor coordination	Sustained attention
Sturm *et al.* (1997)	Set of computerized tasks (AIXTENT) selected according to deficit types	Alertness, vigilance, selective and divided attention

significant improvements. Nevertheless, the existence of studies that have clearly demonstrated some progress is encouraging.

The diversity of the results obtained may be caused by the fact that, considered as a whole, these studies are disparate and sundry. The diversity relates to the populations, types and duration of intervention, and number and type of selected variables used to evaluate the impact of treatment. This renders comparisons difficult or even risky. Nevertheless and despite this diversity, it is possible to divide these works into three categories (see Table 12.3). The first is one for which no improvement could be demonstrated. In this category we also put the studies demonstrating some progress but for which doubts exist about the methodology used: absence of control group, absence of repeated baseline assessment or of clear differentiation between the tasks used for the training and those used to assess the impact of the intervention; for the latter indeed the improvements might only represent a practice effect.

To the second category belong the studies for which a non-trivial significant improvement was observed at the end of treatment. However, in these studies the improvement was limited to some tasks similar to those used during the intervention representing the same attentional functions as those addressed during the treatment, i.e. for these studies no generalization could be observed.

Finally, the last category includes the studies for which an improvement was observed for the targeted functions and where there was a generalization to other cognitive aspects, attentional or not. There are, however, very few

Table 12.3 Recapitulation of the reviewed studies (TBI = traumatic brain injury; CVA = cerebral vascular accident)

Studies	*Populations*	*Procedure*	*Treatment effects*	*Impact on daily life*
I. Absence of improvements and/or methodological problems:				
Kallinger, 1975	TBI	unspecific	+?	Not assessed
Malec et al., 1984	TBI	unspecific	—	Not assessed
Ponsford and Kinsella, 1988	TBI	unspecific	—	No
Middleton et al., 1991	Mainly TBI	unspecific	+?	Not assessed
II. Improvements limited to the trained functions:				
Sturm *et al.*, 1983	TBI & CVA	unspecific	+	Not assessed
Wood, 1986	TBI	unspecific	+	Not assessed
Gray and Robertson, 1989	TBI	specific	+	Not assessed
Sturm and Willmes, 1991	CVA	unspecific	+	Not assessed
Gray and Robertson, 1988, Gray *et al.*, 1992	Mainly TBI	unspecific	+	Not assessed
III. Improvements with transfer to other cognitive functions:				
Ben-Yishay *et al.*, 1987	TBI	specific	++	Yes
Strache, 1987	TBI & CVA	specific	++	Not assessed
Lamberti *et al.*, 1988	CVA & psychotics	specific	++	Not assessed
Sohlberg and Mateer, 1989	TBI & CVA	specific	++	Yes
Sturm *et al.*, 1997	CVA	specific	++	Not assessed

studies which have demonstrated a significant generalization of the attention improvements to other cognitive domains.

It is interesting to note that the majority of studies demonstrating favourable results explicitly refer to a theoretical model of attention. A theoretical frame of reference certainly helped to make a more precise diagnosis in terms of specific attentional impairments, to allow for a more precise choice of intervention and to help with the selection of measures to control the impact of treatment. In summary, the analysis based on a theoretical plan would seem to increase the precision of the approach both during the diagnosis and during the treatment phase.

Table 12.3 shows that the most favourable results were obtained in studies using a 'specific' training procedure (see also Park and Ingles, 2001), constructed in order to target as precisely as possible the deficient attentional components. Besides the fact that this type of approach turns out to be more efficient, it also allows us to refine the existing models of attentional functioning. Indeed, even if everyone agrees with the fact that the different attentional functions are interdependent, there is still very little agreement about relationships existing between these components. In particular, by the differential effects of specific approaches to the deficits a 'corner of the veil may be lifted'. Indeed, the functions of attention seem to be organized in a hierarchical manner. At the lowest level, one may expect to find aspects of an intensity dimension of attention. These aspects should constitute a necessary condition for an adequate functioning of the components of a higher attentional level, the selectivity dimension. For this dimension, the selection of the stimuli, characterizing the component of selective attention, should constitute the next level which, again, might be a necessary condition for the highest level, divided attention (Sturm *et al.*, 1997). Of course, this hypothesis will have to be confirmed by further works. If it is, it might have direct consequences for rehabilitation: the deficits existing for a certain level can only been treated with training aimed at the same level or a lower one.

Another point also emerges from this presentation: the existence of favourable effects of the treatment benefits on the subject's daily life still has to be demonstrated. Apart from a few exceptions, this aspect has not been investigated in the papers we have reviewed. The absence of assessment of these crucial aspects is partly due to the lack of reliable and validated tools in the domain of attention. As underlined by Robertson (1990), we need a more extensive range of sensible tools for evaluating attentional functions in real life, in order to exclude the possibility that the observed improvements are *exclusively* confined to the tests used for the neuropsychological assessment. Daily life situations are most frequently characterized by a broad range of attentional requirements which are, in the present state of knowledge, extremely difficult to evaluate and differentiate on a functional basis. The progressive refining of the available models might contribute to the elaboration of sensible and reliable tools allowing a more ecological evaluation of the impact of the deficits and the efficacy of treatments on the subject's adaptation to daily life situations.

Finally, the majority of the studies we have reviewed were based on direct stimulation of the deficient attentional functions. In other words, they are targeted at a restitution or restoration (Rothi and Horner, 1983) of the impaired processes. But recourse to other types of strategies might also be efficient and could constitute a complementary contribution to the restorative approach. Thus, for example, Wilson and Robertson (1992) used a technique of conditioning and self-suggestion in order to remediate the attentional fluctuations presented by a severely brain-injured patient during his reading activities. This subject was trained to use strategies of relaxation and breathing control which he had to practise before starting to read. He was also trained to define on his own a period of time during which he should try to read without lapses of attention; this duration was progressively lengthened. In a second phase of the treatment, the patient was trained to use the same strategies but this time in an environment with distractors, a situation closer to his usual employment setting. Thanks to these strategies, the patient became progressively able to read during longer and longer periods without lapses of attention. A generalization towards texts concerning his professional activities was also observed – texts which were not used during the treatment. Thus procedures or strategies supporting the subject's implication in the self-control or self-regulation of his/her attention may contribute to optimize the benefits resulting from a restorative approach.

References

Baddeley, A.D. (1986). *Working Memory*. London: Oxford University Press.

Baddeley, A.D. (1993). Working memory or working attention? In A.D. Baddeley and L. Weiskrantz (eds) *Attention: Selection, Awareness, and Control. A Tribute to Donald Broadbent*. Oxford: Oxford University Press.

Barlow, D.H. and Hersen, M. (1984). *Single Case Experimental Design* (2nd edn). New York: Pergamon Press.

Ben-Yishay, Y., Piasetzky, E.B. and Rattok, J. (1987). A systematic method for ameliorating disorders in basic attention. In M.J. Meier, A.L. Benton and L. Diller (eds) *Neuropsychological Rehabilitation*. Edinburgh: Churchill Livingstone.

Bisiach, E., Mini, M., Sterzi, R. and Vallar, G. (1982). Hemispheric lateralization of the decisional stage in choice reaction times to visual unstructured stimuli. *Cortex*, *18*, 191–198.

Blackburn, H.J. (1958). Effects of motivating instructions on reaction time in cerebral disease. *Journal of Abnormal and Social Psychology*, *56*, 359–366.

Bracy, O.L. (1982). *Cognitive Rehabilitation Programs for Brain Injured and Stroke Patients*. Indianapolis, IN: Psychological Software Service.

Bracy, O.L. (1985). *Foundation Skills II* (Computer programs). Indianapolis, IN: Psychological Software Service.

Braun, C., Bartolini, G. and Bouchard, A. (1985). *Cognitive Rehabilitation Software*. Quebec: Montreal University.

Corbetta, M., Miezin, F.M., Dobmeyer, S., Shulman, G.L. and Petersen, S.E. (1991). Selective and divided attention during visual discriminations of shape, color, and speed: functional anatomy by positron emission tomography. *Journal of Neuroscience*, *11*, 2383–2402.

Dee, H.L. and van Allen, M.W. (1973). Speed of decision making processes in patients with unilateral cerebral disease. *Archives of Neurology*, *28*, 163–166.

Dimond, S.J. (1979). Performance by split-brain humans on lateralized vigilance tasks. *Cortex*, *15*, 43–50.

Dyer, F.N. (1973). The Stroop phenomenon and its use in the study of perceptual, cognitive and response processes. *Memory and Cognition*, *1*, 106–120.

Funahashi, S., Bruce, C.J. and Goldman-Rakic, P.S. (1989). Mnemonic coding of visual space in the monkey's dorsolateral prefrontal cortex. *Journal of Neurophysiology*, *61*, 331–349.

Gianutsos, R. (1983). *Computer Programs for Cognitive Rehabilitation*. Bayport: Life Science Associates.

Goldberg, D. (1978). *General Health Questionnaire*. Windsor: NFER.

Goldman-Rakic, P.S. (1987). Circuitry of primate prefrontal cortex and regulation of behavior by representational memory. In F. Plum (ed.) *Handbook of Physiology, 5: Higher functions of the brain*. Bethesda: American Physiological Society.

Gray, J.M. and Robertson, I. (1988). Microcomputer-based attentional retraining after brain injury: a randomised group-controlled trial. *Journal of Clinical and Experimental Neuropsychology*, *10*, 332 (abstract).

Gray, J.M. and Robertson, I. (1989). Remediation of attentional difficulties following brain injury: three experimental single case studies. *Brain Injury*, *3*, 2, 163–170.

Gray, J.M., Robertson, I., Pentland, B. and Anderson, S. (1992). Microcomputer-based attentional retraining after brain damage: a randomized group controlled trial. *Neuropsychological Rehabilitation*, *2*, 97–115.

Gronwall, D.M. (1977). Paced Auditory Serial Addition Task: a measure of recovery from concussion. *Perceptual and Motor Skills*, *44*, 367–373.

Heilman, K.M. and van den Abell, T. (1979). Right hemispheric dominance for mediating cerebral activation. *Neuropsychologia*, *17*, 315–321.

Hofer, E. and Scherzer, E. (1977). Reaktionstraining in der Rehabilitation Hirnverletzter. *Zeitschrift für Krankengymnastik*, *29*, 661–666.

Howes, D. and Boller, F. (1975). Simple reaction time: evidence for focal impairments from lesions of the right hemisphere. *Brain*, *98*, 317–332.

Jansen, Ch., Sturm, W. and Willmes, K. (1992). Sex specific 'activation'-dominance of the left hemisphere for choice reactions: an experimental study regarding lateralization of attention functions. *Zeitschrift für Neuropsychologie*, *3*, 44–51.

Kallinger, S. (1975). Die Wirkungsweise eines Reaktionstrainings auf sensomotorische Leistungen von Hirnverletzten. Vienna: Unpublished medical dissertation.

Lamberti, G., Wieneke, K.H. and Franke, N. (1988). Der Computer als Hilfe beim Aufmerksamkeits-Training. Eine klinisch-experimentelle Studie. *Rehabilitation*, *27*, 190–198.

Levin, H.S., O'Donnell, U.M. and Grossman, R.G. (1979). The Galveston Orientation and Amnesia Test: a practical scale to assess cognition after head injury. *Journal of Nervous and Mental Disease*, *167*, 675–684.

Lewin, J.S., Friedman, L., Wu, D., Miller, D.A., Thompson, L.A., Klein, S.K., Wise, A.L., Hedera, P., Buckley, P., Metzer, H., Friedland, R.P. and Duerk, J.L. (1996). Cortical localization of human sustained attention: detection with functional MR using a visual vigilance paradigm. *Journal of Computer Assisted Tomography*, *20*, 695–701.

Lezak, M. (1995). *Neuropsychological Assessment* (3rd edn). New York: Oxford University Press.

Longoni, F., Sturm, W., Weis, S., Holtel, C., Specht, K., Herzog, H. and Willmes, K. (2000). Functional reorganization after training of alertness in two patients with right-hemisphere lesions. *Journal of Neuropsychology*, *11*, 250–261.

Longoni, F., Weis, S., Specht, K., Holtel, C., Herzog, H., Achten, B., Willmes, K. and Sturm, W. (1999). Functional reorganisation after training of alertness. *Neuroimage*, *9*, 6, S771. (Special issue on Human Brain Mapping conference in Düsseldorf, Germany.)

Malec, J., Jones, R., Rao, N. and Stubbs, K. (1984). Video game practice effects on sustained attention in patients with craniocerebral trauma. *Cognitive Rehabilitation*, *2*, 18–23.

Mesulam, M.-M. (1985). Attention, confusional states, and neglect. In M.-M. Mesulam (ed.) *Principles of Behavioral Neurology*. Philadelphia: Davis.

Middleton, D.K., Lambert, M.J. and Seggar, L.B. (1991). Neuropsychological rehabilitation: microcomputer-assisted treatment of brain-injured adults. *Perceptual and Motor Skills*, *72*, 527–530.

Nelson, H. (1976). A modified card sorting test sensitive to frontal lobe deficit. *Cortex*, *12*, 313–324.

Pardo, J.V., Fox, P.T. and Raichle, M.E. (1991). Localization of a human system for sustained attention by positron emission tomography. *Nature*, *349*, 61–64.

Park, N.W. and Ingles, J.L. (2001). Effectiveness of attention rehabilitation after an accident acquired brain injury: a meta-analysis. *Neuropsychology*, *15*, 199–210.

Paus, T., Zatorre, R.J., Hofle, N., Caramanos, Z., Gotman, J., Petrides, M. and Evans, A.C. (1997). Time-changes in neural systems underlying attention and arousal during the performance of an auditory vigilance task. *Journal of Cognitive Neuroscience*, *9*, 392–408.

Piasetzky, E.B., Rattok, J., Ben-Yishay, Y., Lakin, P., Ross, B. and Diller, L. (1983). Computerized ORM: a manual for clinical and research uses. In Y. Ben-Yishay, (ed.) *Working Approaches to Remediation of Cognitive Deficits in Brain Damaged Persons. Rehabiliation Monograph No. 66*. New York: NYU Medical Center.

Plohmann, A.M., Kappos, L., Ammann, W., Thordai, A., Wittwer, A., Huber, S., Bellaiche, Y. and Lechner-Scott, J. (1998). Computer assisted retraining of attentional impairments in patients with multiple sclerosis. *Journal of Neurology, Neurosurgery and Psychiatry*, *64*, 455–462.

Ponsford, J.L. and Kinsella, G. (1988). Evaluation of a remedial programme for attentional deficits following closed head injury. *Journal of Clinical and Experimental Neuropsychology*, *10*, 693–708.

Poser, U., Kohler, J., Sedlmeier, P. and Strätz, A. (1992). Evaluierung eines neuropsychologischen Funktionstrainings bei Patienten mit kognitiver Verlangsamung nach Schädelhirntrauma. *Zeitschrift für Neuropsychologie*, *3*, 3–24.

Posner, M.I. and Petersen, S.E. (1990). The attention system of the human brain. *Annual Review of Neurosciences*, *13*, 182–196.

Posner, M.I. and Rafal, R.D. (1987). Cognitive theories of attention and the rehabilitation of attentional deficits. In M.J., Meier, A.L. Benton and L. Diller (eds) *Neuropsychological Rehabilitation*. Edinburgh: Churchill Livingstone.

Rattok, J., Ben-Yishay, Y., Ross, B., Lakin, P., Silver, S., Thomas, L. and Diller, L. (1982). A diagnostic remedial system for basic attentional disorders in head trauma patients undergoing rehabilitation: a preliminary report. In Y. Ben-Yishay (ed.) *Working Approaches to Remediation of Cognitive Deficits in Brain Damaged Persons. Rehabilitation Monograph No. 64*, New York: NYU Medical Center.

Robertson, I. (1990). Does computerized cognitive rehabilitation work? A review. *Aphasiology*, *4*, 4, 381–405.

Robertson, I.H., Tegnér, R., Tham, K. and Nimmo-Smith, I. (1995). Sustained attention training for unilateral neglect: theoretical and rehabilitation implications. *Journal of Clinical and Experimental Neuropsychology*, *17*, 416–430.

Rothi, L.J. and Horner, J. (1983). Restitution and substitution: two theories of recovery with application to neurobehavioral treatment. *Journal of Clinical Neuropsychology*, *5*, 73–81.

Shallice, T. (1982). Specific impairments of planning. *Philosophical Transactions of the Royal Society of London*, *B*, *298*, 199–209.

Shallice, T. (1988). *From Neuropsychology to Mental Structure*. Cambridge: Cambridge University Press.

Shankweiler, D.P. (1959). Effects of success and failure instructions on reaction time in patients with brain damage. *Journal of Comparative and Physiological Psychology*, *52*, 546–549.

Sohlberg, M.M. and Mateer, C.A. (1986). *Attention Process Training (APT)*. Puyallup, WA: Association for Neuropsychological Research and Development.

Sohlberg, M.M. and Mateer, C.A. (1987). Effectiveness of an attention-training program. *Journal of Clinical and Experimental Neuropsychology*, 9, 117–130.

Sohlberg, M.M. and Mateer, C.A. (1989). *Introduction to Cognitive Rehabilitation: Theory and Practice*. New York: Guilford Press.

Strache, W. (1987). Effectiveness of two modes of training to overcome deficits of concentration. *International Journal of Rehabilitation Research*, Suppl. no. 5 to vol. 10, no. 4 (free papers).

Sturm, W. and Büssing, A. (1982). Zum Einfluß motivierender Testinstruktionen auf die Reaktionsleistung hirngeschädigter Patienten. *Nervenarzt*, *53*, 395–400.

Sturm, W. and Büssing, A. (1986). Einfluß der Aufgabenkomplexität auf hirnorganische Reaktionsbeeinträchtigungen – Hirnschädigungs – oder Patienteneffekt? *European Archives of Psychiatry and Neurological Sciences*, *235*, 214–220.

Sturm, W., Dahmen, W., Hartje, W. and Willmes, K. (1983). Ergebnisse eines Trainingsprogrammems zur Verbesserung der visuellen Auffassungsschnelligkeit und Konzentrationsfähigkeit bei Hirngeschädigten. *Archiv für Psychiatrie und Nervenkrankheiten*, *233*, 9–22.

Sturm, W., de Simone, A., Krause, B.J., Specht, K., Hesselmann, V., Radermacher, I., Herzog, H., Tellmann, L., Müller-Gärtner, H.-W. and Willmes, K. (1999). Functional neuroanatomy of intrinsic alertness: evidence for a fronto-parietal-thalamic-brainstem network in the right hemisphere. *Neuropsychologia*, *37*, 797–805.

Sturm, W., Reul, J. and Willmes, K. (1989). Is there a generalized right hemisphere dominance for mediating cerebral activation? Evidence from a choice reaction experiment with lateralized simple warning stimuli. *Neuropsychologia*, *27*, 747–751.

Sturm, W. and Willmes, K. (1991). Efficacy of a reaction training on various attentional and cognitive functions in stroke patients. *Neuropsychological Rehabilitation*, *1*, 259–280.

Sturm, W., Willmes, K., Orgass, B. and Hartje, W. (1997). Do specific attention deficits need specific training? *Neuropsychological Rehabilitation*, 7, 81–103.

van Zomeren, A.H. and Brouwer, W.H. (1994). *Clinical Neuropsychology of Attention*. New York: Oxford University Press.

van Zomeren, A.H., Brouwer, W.H. and Deelman, B.G. (1984). Attentional deficits: the riddles of selectivity, speed and alertness. In D.N. Brooks (ed.) *Psychological Deficits after Head Injury*. London: Oxford University Press.

Wilson, C. and Robertson, I.H. (1992). A home-based intervention for attentional slips during reading following head injury: a single case study. *Neuropsychological Rehabilitation*, *2*, 193–205.

Wood, R.L. (1986). Rehabilitation of patients with disorders of attention. *Journal of Head Trauma Rehabilitation*, *3*, 43–53.

Wood, R.L. and Eames, P.G. (1981). Application of behavioral modification in the rehabilitation of traumatically brain injured adults. In G. Davey (ed.) *Application of Conditioning Theory*. London: Methuen.

Zimmermann, P. and Fimm, B. (1994). *Test for Attention Performance (TAP)*. Würselen: Psytest.

Chapter 13

Computerized training of specific attention deficits in stroke and traumatic brain-injured patients

A multicentric efficacy study

W. Sturm, B. Fimm, A. Cantagallo, N. Cremel, P. North, A. Passadori, L. Pizzamiglio, M. Rousseaux, P. Zimmermann, G. Deloche and M. Leclercq

Early attempts of attention retraining did not take into account the distinctiveness of attention functions. A number of efficacy studies employing non-specific attention training programmes demonstrated a generalized improvement of attention and other cognitive functions in patients with diffuse traumatic lesions (Poser *et al.*, 1992; Sturm *et al.*, 1983; for a critical evaluation of study designs and results see also Robertson, 1990). There are, however, some studies which cast doubt on the generality of these training effects. Sohlberg and Mateer (1987) showed that an attention training did not generalize to a cognitive task requiring visual processing. Ben-Yishay *et al.* (1987) found no generalization effects at all for the different aspects of their ORM attention training procedure. In fact, there was only improvement for the specific attention domain being trained. Ponsford and Kinsella (1988) pointed out that when spontaneous recovery and practice effects are controlled for, little additional benefit due to training remained at all. Sturm and Willmes (1991) readministered their complex reaction training yielding generalized training effects in traumatic brain damage to a group of patients with focal unilateral vascular lesions. For this latter group there was considerably less generalization of the training effects. Contrary to the first study there were no effects on vigilance tasks and on verbal and non-verbal intelligence tests whether they were speeded or without time pressure. It is, however, difficult to interpret the results of these studies because either not all relevant aspects of attention were considered for training or testing, or the control tests were similar or even identical to the training tasks. Especially in the latter case it would be hard to argue that the training effects are more than mere drill or practice effects due to numerous task repetitions.

So the question arises, whether specific attention deficits call for specific training procedures. In order to test this hypothesis, specific computerized training programmes were developed (Sturm and co-workers 1994, 1997) for the two intensity aspects, alertness and vigilance, as well as for selective and divided attention representing selectivity aspects of attention. The training programmes have a game-like layout and represent the underlying attention paradigms in everyday-like scenarios. Another advantage of these training programmes is that they can be used in an adaptive mode, adjusting the task difficulty level to the individual patient's performance. Alertness is trained by means of an animated car or motorcycle driving task, in which the patient has to control the speed of the vehicle in such a way that a high average speed is maintained, at the same time avoiding collisions with obstacles which suddenly appear on the road. One of the vigilance training tasks is a radar screen task, in which the subject has to watch flying objects which move extremely slowly across the screen. The patient has to respond either to sudden changes in the speed of the objects or to additional objects appearing on the screen for a short time. For the training of selective attention a choice reaction paradigm was adopted. In one training task a 'trap shooting' game is animated and the patient has to respond to a particular object or particular pairs of objects flying across the screen. A second training is called 'photographic safari', in which the subject has to watch for relevant single or double objects popping up in front of a scenic background. To retrain divided attention, a 'flight simulator' task was developed, in which the patient has to monitor up to three different stimulus sources (horizon, speedometer, motor sound) in combination. To control for therapy effects, the respective subtests of the Test for Attentional Performance (TAP, Zimmermann and Fimm, 1994) were administered. They target the same attention components as the training, but they do it by completely different tasks. Thus, training and test procedures can clearly be separated from each other. Patients with vascular unilateral lesions, who showed attention deficits in at least two of the four attention domains, i.e. percentile ranks of <25 in the respective TAP subtests, at first were trained for fourteen training sessions in one of the impaired attention domains. After a second test session each patient was trained in one of the other impaired attention functions. At the end of this second therapy phase a third test session was carried out. Since each patient showed deficits in at least two attention domains, with this type of study design in each of the two therapy periods there was one attention deficit which was trained specifically, and at least another one for which the training was not specific. The results of these earlier studies revealed that intensity aspects of attention (alertness and vigilance), especially, have to be trained specifically, i.e. significant improvement can only be achieved by the specific training procedure. For selectivity aspects of attention (selective and divided attention), too, the error rate could only be influenced positively by the specific training programmes. Response time, however, for these attention domains could also be improved by training of attention intensity (Sturm and co-workers, 1997). These results were corroborated by a study in patients suffering from multiple sclerosis (Plohmann *et al.*, 1998).

Since the most prominent attention deficits can be expected after traumatic brain injury (TBI), in the present study the efficacy of the training programmes was also studied in a mixed group of TBI patients and patients with vascular brain damage. This was accomplished in a multicentric study within the scope of the European BIOMED-I- ESCAPE project (European Standardised Computerised Assessment Procedure for the Evaluation and Rehabilitation of Brain Damaged Patients). The following institutions participated in the project: Belgium: Centre Neurologique William Lennox, Ottignies. France: Service de Rééducation et de Convalescence Neurologiques, Lille; Service Rééducation Fonctionnelle, Centre de Réadaptation de Mulhouse, Mulhouse; Hôpital de la Salpêtrière, Paris; Service de Neuropsychologie, Clinique Neurologique, Strasbourg; Centre de Rééducation et d'Etude des Activités Mnésiques, Tassin-La-Demi-Lune. Germany: Neurological Clinic – Division of Neuropsychology, University Hospital RWTH Aachen, Aachen; Department of Psychology, Albert-Ludwig-University Freiburg, Freiburg. Italy: Ospedale S. Giorgio, Ferrara; Ospedale Misericordia, Grosseto; Istituto di ricovero e cura a carattere scientifico, Ospedale S. Lucia, Roma.

Methods

Training programmes

For this study, PC versions of the training programmes were developed (AIXTENT training programmes[1]). In order to minimize motor demands in the training procedure, the patient had to respond to the training tasks using only one or two large response keys. These keys were also used exclusively for the responses to the control tests. Patients with hemiparesis also had no difficulty in operating both keys with one hand. In the following sections, the four attention training programmes are described.

Alertness training

Animated driving tasks with a car or motorcycle displayed in a graphic design on the computer screen are used. The patient has to watch a car or a motorcycle driving on a winding track. The patient is not supposed to actually steer the car or the motorcycle. He/she only has to control the speed of the vehicle in such a way that a high average speed is maintained, at the same

1 The PC adaptation of the AIXTENT training programmes was financially supported by the German Kuratorium ZNS for TBI patients with lesions of the CNS.

time avoiding collisions with suddenly appearing obstacles. In order to accomplish this, the subject has to press either a 'gas' key to speed up the vehicle or a 'brake' key to reduce the vehicle's speed or to stop it. Forthcoming obstacles are indicated by graphic signs which serve as warning signals. In this way the training operationalizes the task paradigm of phasic alertness (reaction time task with warning signal). The difficulty level of the task can be changed by varying the maximum speed of the vehicle, the braking distance, the visibility of the warning signals – flashing, fixed and finally absent – and the position of the vehicle on the screen. Collisions with obstacles are indicated by optical and acoustic feedback.

Vigilance training

For the vigilance training a radar screen task was constructed. The subject has to watch several flying objects (planes, helicopters, balloons) on a radar screen. The objects move very slowly across the screen and the subject has to respond either to sudden changes of the speed of the objects or to additional objects appearing on the screen for a short time. Variation of task difficulty is introduced by changing the distinctiveness of the objects according to type and colour and the frequency of relevant events.

A second vigilance training programme simulates an assembly line. The patient has to watch objects moving on the assembly line and he/she has to sort out damaged objects by pressing a response key.

Selective attention training

For the training of selective attention two programmes were developed. In the first programme, a 'trap shooting' task is simulated, with objects flying across the screen in front of a scenic background. The patient is required to push a response key only if a particular object or particular pairs of objects defined at the beginning of the task appear on the screen. The second programme is a kind of 'photo safari', in which the subject has to watch for relevant single or double objects popping up in front of a scenic background. By pressing the response key he/she has to 'take a picture' of these everyday-life objects (e.g. telephone, birthday cake, hamburger). Irrelevant objects must not be responded to. For both programmes an increase in difficulty level can be effected by changing the overall number of objects and/or the number of relevant objects, as well as by varying the time interval for object presentation. For some variants of the trap shooting task the patient also has to watch for typical sounds associated with the objects. There is always an immediate optical or acoustic feedback for correct or false responses. The training procedure follows the paradigm of choice reaction tasks.

Divided attention training

For the PC version of the divided attention training, a 'flight simulator' task was developed, in which the subject has to monitor up to three different stimulus sources in combination. One source is the horizon, which moves up and down within certain limits. If the horizon passes one of these limits (the upper edge of the cockpit or the upper edge of the instrument panel), the subject has to respond. A second stimulus source is the speedometer which has to be monitored for passing an upper and lower speed limit. The third, auditory, source is the motor sound which has to be monitored for more than two successive interrupts. For the first training sessions, one auditory and one visual source are combined. During later sessions, to increase the difficulty level, either two visual stimuli are combined or all three stimulus sources can appear in combination.

All training programmes automatically adapt their difficulty level according to the performance of the patient. The adaptation criterion for increasing difficulty is a minimum of 90% correct responses across 50 responses, and for increasing it a minimum of 33% errors.

At the end of each training session or whenever the patient or the therapist wanted it, a numerical and graphical feedback of the mean reaction time, the kind and number of errors and the difficulty level of the different task parameters achieved could be presented. These parameters were stored under the individual patient's name and provided initial parameter values for the next training session.

Control tests

To examine the efficacy of the training programmes we used subtests of a computerized attention test battery (TAP; Zimmermann and Fimm, 1994; Zimmermann, North and Fimm, 1993). There was a test of phasic alertness requiring a response to a simple visual stimulus with or without a preceding auditory warning signal. Visual vigilance was tested over a period of 30 minutes at a rate of one critical stimulus per minute. Patients had to watch a horizontal light-bar moving up and down slowly within confined spatial limits. About once per minute the bar made a larger movement towards the top of the screen. This larger movement had to be detected and responded to. To assess selective attention we used a Go–nogo task in which the subject had to respond to only two critical visual patterns out of a total number of five. The divided attention test required monitoring a two-way array of visual stimuli for a specific square pattern as well as detecting the presence of two consecutive identically pitched tones in an otherwise alternating sequence of low- or high-pitched tone signals. For these subtests normative data from 200 healthy controls were available (Sturm and Willmes, 1993).

Subjects

A total of 33 patients were studied. Sample characteristics are given in Table 13.1. The number of patients per training varied considerably (6–11). Only a quarter of the patients were female. There was a clear predominance of traumatic etiology (n = 18) compared to eight vascular cases. Etiology was not known for seven cases. For eleven patients localization of lesion was not reported or was diffuse. Although the overall number of left- or right-sided lesions was similar, only right-sided, diffuse or bilateral (1) were found in the alertness training group. The situation was almost the reverse for the selective attention group. So, again, the data corroborate the theory of a different involvement of the right and left hemispheres in intensity or selectivity aspects of attention. Time post-onset varied from 3 months to 13 years. Median duration of illness was much lower for the alertness training group (9 months) compared to the other three groups (about 2 years or more).

Only patients without symptomatic epilepsy or any progressive neurological and internal disease were included. A second inclusion criterion was poor performance in at least two of the attention domains as assessed by the subtests of the attention test battery, i.e. for the reaction time measurements percentile ranks of ≤10, or more than three errors in the selective and divided attention tests, or less than 28 hits in the vigilance task. To avoid massive spontaneous recovery effects, only patients at least two months post-onset were admitted.

Study design

The study had the following design: after a baseline phase (four weeks) with two examinations by means of the Test for Attentional Performance (Zimmermann and Fimm, 1994) patients received one period of attention training for one of four attention domains (alertness, vigilance, selective attention, divided attention). Only patients who showed impairments in at least two attention domains were included in the study. Training for one of the most impaired functions was started only if the inclusion criteria held at the second pretest. For training, one of the subprogrammes of the AIXTENT attention training programme (Sturm *et al.*, 1983, 1994) aiming at only one of the impaired attention functions was used. As already pointed out in the introduction, since each patient showed deficits in at least two attention domains, with this type of study design there was one attention deficit which was trained specifically, and at least another one for which the training was not specific. Each patient was trained for fourteen training sessions. The difficulty level of the training adapted automatically to the patient's performance during the training. After the end of the training, the Attention Test Battery was administered again.

Table 13.1 Sample characteristics of the four training groups

Sample characteristics	*Training group*			
	Alertness ($n = 9$)	*Vigilance* ($n = 7$)	Selective attention ($n = 11$)	*Divided attention* ($n = 6$)
Female/male/not reported	1/7/1	3/4	3/8	1/4/1
Etiology (vascular/traumatic/other or unknown)	3/4/2	2/5	2/6/3	1/3/2
Localization (left/right/?/bilateral)	0/5/3/1	2/2/1/2	4/1/5/1	2/2/2/0
Age	34 (20–60)	26 (20–45)	34 (22–60)	43 (18–56)
Education (years)	9 (8–11)	12 (8–15)	10 (7–12)	12.5 (9–15)
Time post-onset (months)	9 (3–90)	38 (12–80)	21.5 (6–31)	28.5 (3–128)

Due to the low number of patients per training group, specific training effects could not be assessed separately either with respect to etiology or localization.

Results

Table 13.2 gives the descriptive statistical information on performance for the control test variables at the three test occasions. Looking at the medians in Table 13.2, performance after specific training for some of the variables has reached near-normal level except for the selective attention RT variable (although this is based on a subsample of only five individuals). Furthermore, it is interesting to note that the number of errors (false alarms) in the vigilance task is and stays high for patients with selective attention problems. This corroborates the notion that this parameter in the given vigilance task does not reflect vigilance performance but selectivity aspects of attention.

Inferential statistical analyses were carried out, first to test for stability of test performance at baseline, and second to look for specific training effects (comparison of second baseline and post-training test performance). Wilcoxon signed rank tests were used; p-values were two-tailed throughout for the baseline comparisons and for testing non-specific training effects. Specific training effects were tested in a one-tailed fashion since there were strong predictions from the first study with vascular patients (Sturm *et al.*, 1983, 1994). P-values are only reported if data from at least five patients were available. Table 13.3 containing the p-values for the baseline comparisons shows that only for the two most complex attention tasks (selective and divided attention) was significant or near-significant improvement in performance present. This could be due to test repetition effects, which are more likely with complex tasks for which a certain familiarity is necessary. Regression to the mean, i.e. the general tendency for a bigger relative improvement of more seriously impaired functions, could be another reason for the reduction in the number of errors or omissions after the baseline phase in the selective and divided attention groups respectively.

Table 13.4 shows the p-values for the comparison between the second baseline and the post-training test sessions. Except for the selective attention training, only improvements for the specific test variables matching the training procedure were present. The vigilance training also had a marginally ($p = 0.07$) beneficial effect for the reaction time parameter of the selective attention control test – a finding which was also present in the first efficacy study (Sturm *et al.*, 1997). Although not significant, there was a tendency for reaction time improvement in the selective attention task after selective attention training, but no effect for the error rate. Again, the pattern of changes in performance was similar to that found in the first study.

Table 13.2 Median of control test performance for baseline phase 1 (t_1) and 2 (t_2) and for the post training test (t_3). All response time data are given in T-scores based on a normative sample of n = 200 healthy subjects

Control tests		*Training*											
		Alertness (*n* = 9)			*Vigilance* (*n* = 7)			*Selective attention* (*n* = 11)			*Divided attention* (*n* = 6)		
		t_1	t_2	t_3	t_1	t_2	t_3	t_1	t_2	t_3	t_1	t_2	t_3
Alertness	Phasic alertness index	35.5	34	53	27.5	44	45	47	49	42	48.5	52	50
	RTwoW*	26	29	43	29.5	35	36	32	32	39	40	38.5	38.5
Vigilance	Errors	2	1	2	3	3	3	21.5	14	26	2.5	2	4
	Omissions	5	3	4	9	13	6	3	10.5	7.5	0.5	4	0
Selective attention	Errors	0	0	0	0	1	0	9	4	5	3	0.5	2
	RT	29	20	42	27	30	33	20	29	32	23	32.5	28
Divided attention	Omissions	5.5	6	6	7	4.5	6.5	5	11	5	17	13	5

Note: *RTwoW = Response time without warning

Table 13.3 P-values for change of performance (pretest 2 – pretest 1) in the four attention tasks after the baseline phase (Wilcoxon tests). Shaded areas correspond to the attentional aspects which will be targeted by the specific training during the training period after the baseline phase (see Table 13.4)

		Attention tasks								
		Alertness		*Vigilance*			*Selective attention*		*Divided attention*	
Training (not given during this phase)	*n*	*Phasic alertness index*	*RTwoW*	*Errors*	*Omiss.*	*RT*	*Errors*	*RT*	*Omiss.*	*RT*
Alertness training	9	.87 (n = 8)[1]	.31 (n = 8)	.50 (n = 7)	.89 (n = 7)	n = 4	1.00 (n = 7)	1.00 (n = 5)	.72 (n = 6)	n = 3
Vigilance training	7	.11 (n = 6) (3/0)[2]	.20 (n = 6) (3/1)	.22 (n = 5)	.89 (n = 5)	n = 4	.79 (n = 5)	1.00 (n = 5)	.07 (n = 5) (4/0)	n = 3
Selective attention training	11	.23	.61	.67 (n = 8)	.17 (n = 8) (1/5)	n = 4	.06 (9/2)	.47 (n = 5)	.45	n = 2
Divided attention training	6	.11 (4/1)	1.00	n = 4 (3/0)	n = 4	n = 2	.25 (5/1)	n = 2	.046 (5/1)	n = 1

Notes:
[1] n for the analyses (in case of incomplete sample); if n <5, no p-values are reported
[2] Proportion of improvements/deteriorations

Table 13.4 P-values for change of performance (post-test 1 – pretest 2) in the four attention tasks after the training phase (Wilcoxon tests). Shaded areas indicate specific training effects

		Attention tasks								
		Alertness		*Vigilance*			*Selective attention*		*Divided attention*	
Training	*n*	*Phasic alertness index*	*RTwoW*	*Errors*	*Omiss.*	*RT*	*Errors*	*RT*	*Omiss.*	*RT*
Alertness training	9	.0039 (9/0)[2]	.0173 (6/1)	.50 (n = 8)[1]	.24 (n = 8) (1/6)	n = 4	.75	.47 (n = 5)	.29 (n = 8) (6/2)	n = 3
Vigilance training	7	.79	.46	.17 (3/3)	.018 (6/1)	.022 n = 5 (5/0)	.29 (n = 6)	0.7 (n = 5) (4/0)	.40 (n = 6)	n = 3
Selective attention training	11	.80 (n = 10)	.33 (n = 9)	.53 (n = 8)	.93 (n = 8)	.22 (n = 5)	.38	.23 (n = 5) (3/1)	.22	n = 2
Divided attention training	6	.22	n = 4 (2/2)	.72 (n = 5)	.27 (n = 5)	(n = 2)	.50 (4/1)	n = 2	.014 (6/1)	n = 1

Notes:
[1] *n* for the analyses (in case of incomplete sample); if *n* <5, no p-values are reported
[2] Proportion of improvements/deteriorations

Evaluation of individual patients

Since for all reaction time parameters of the control tests, standard norms (T-scores) as well as reliability estimates are available, critical differences according to the methods of psychometric single-case analysis (Huber, 1973; Willmes, 1985, 1990) were computed. If the critical difference is surpassed by the observed difference between pre- and post-test, this change in performance cannot be attributed to measurement errors alone. For the non-standardized error scores, the numbers of errors in pre- and post-test were compared by Fisher's exact test. For single-case analysis a type-I error of 10% is generally recommended (Huber, 1973; Willmes, 1990).

Table 13.5 shows the critical differences for the subtest scores of the TAP used in this study.

Figures 13.1 and 13.2 show the performance of single cases after specific or unspecific attention training for the two test variables representing intensity aspects of attention (alertness, vigilance).

Figure 13.1 shows the T-scores for response times in the tonic alertness task before and after training in alertness, vigilance, selective attention or divided attention. The figure demonstrates that only the specific training for alertness did not lead to deterioration of performance, but in most cases the training led to an improvement in the alertness test of the TAP (a significant change is indicated by an asterisk).

Figure 13.2 presents similar effects for the number of omissions in the vigilance task. After the training, only for the vigilance training group is there a consistent decrease of omissions.

Conclusion

All in all, the results of this multicentric study corroborate the findings of the former studies by Sturm and co-workers (1997) and by Plohmann and co-workers (1998), showing again highly specific training effects especially for intensity aspects of attention performance (alertness and vigilance) but also for divided attention. This holds true not only for patients with vascular

Table 13.5 Reliabilities and critical differences (d_{crit}) for the T-scores of the TAP subtests

TAP subtests (reaction time)	r_{tt}	d_{crit} *(T-score)*
Alertness without warning	.981	4
Alertness with warning	.981	4
Divided attention	.798	12
Go/nogo	.922	8
Vigilance, visual	.947	6

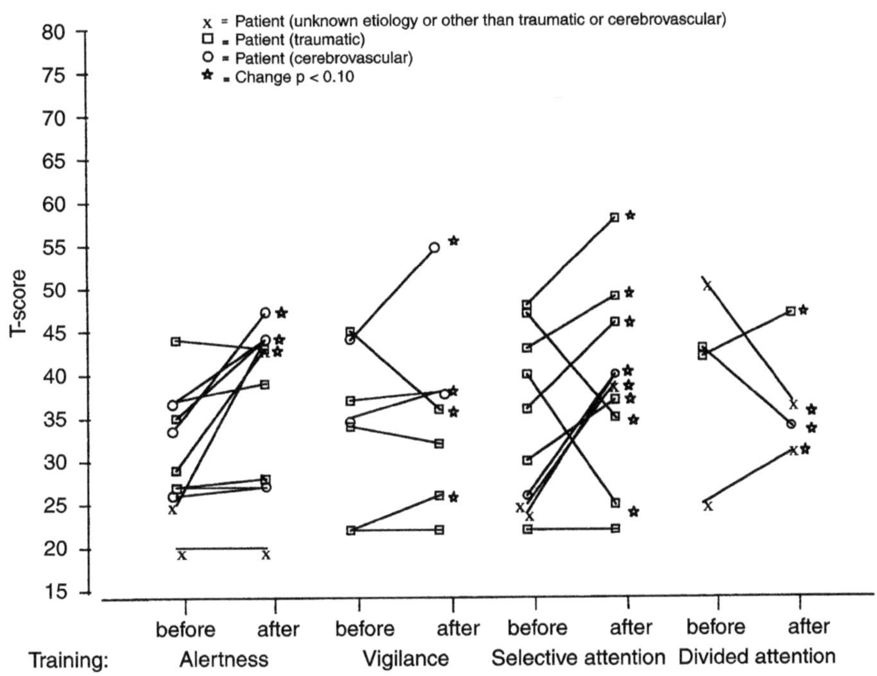

Figure 13.1 Individual changes in performance (T-scores) in the control test variable 'alertness without warning' after training of alertness, vigilance, selective or divided attention. Significant changes for single patients (p<.10) are indicated by an asterisk

etiology of brain damage but for traumatically brain-damaged patients as well. This can best be seen in Figures 13.1 and 13.2, where CVA and TBI patients are depicted as single cases. During the baseline phase, only slight improvements for selectivity aspects of attention – probably caused by practice effects during test repetition – occurred, but no changes for the intensity aspects, alertness and vigilance. Thus, especially the specific effects for intensity aspects of attention during the training phase cannot be interpreted as effects of test repetition or spontaneous recovery. Analysis of individual patients' changes in control test performance after the training showed that specific effects can be shown not only for the patient groups but for a considerable number of individual patients, too. On the other hand, this single-case analysis again reveals that in patients showing impairments of intensity aspects of attention a non-specific training may even cause further deterioration of performance, especially when the patient is trained by means of too complex training procedures focusing on selectivity aspects of attention. This

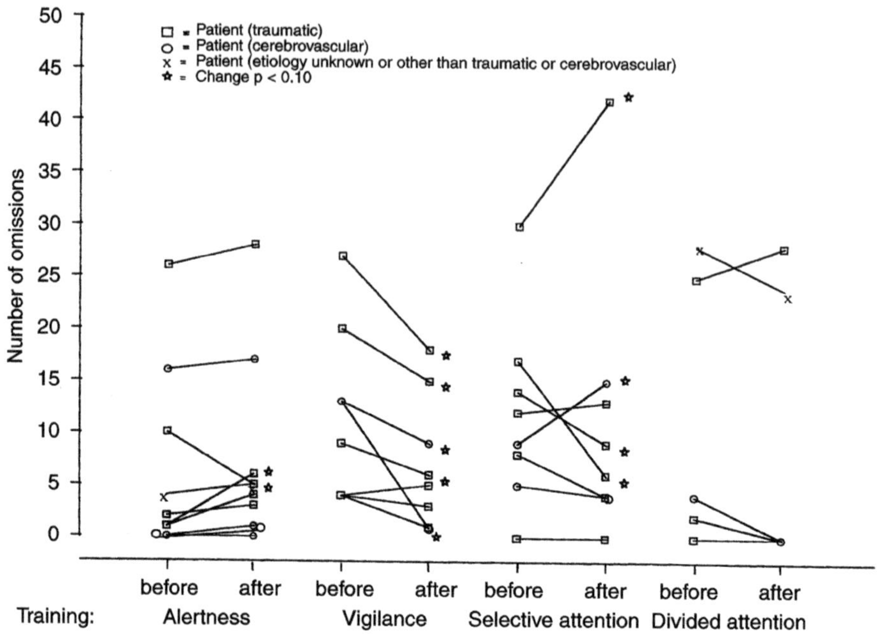

Figure 13.2 Individual changes in performance (number of omissions) in the control test 'visual vigilance' after training of alertness, vigilance, selective or divided attention. Significant changes for single patients ($p<.10$) are indicated by an asterisk

might be explained by the notion that intensity aspects of attention, such as alertness and the ability to maintain a certain level of activation over time, are prerequisites of more complex attention functions. If patients suffer from basic attention deficits, a training of selectivity aspects of attention does not focus on these attentional prerequisites and may lead to an 'overload' and further breakdown of the attentional system.

Similar to the results of the first study, the results show that it is very important to start an attention therapy by comprehensive diagnostics to work out the specific attention deficits the patient suffers from, and that specific deficits have to be treated specifically. This study did not look for ADL implications of attention. In the study by Plohmann and co-workers (1998), however, a questionnaire for everyday aspects of attention was given to MS patients before and after the training. The authors reported a significant improvement of self-estimated attention performance after the administration of the AIXTENT programmes. Unfortunately there was no baseline phase in the study, so the subjective improvement cannot be clearly attributed to the training procedure. Now that the principal and specific efficacy of computerized attention training procedures has been proved experimentally

Zimmermann, P., North, P., and Fimm, B. (1993). Diagnosis of attentional deficits: theoretical considerations and presentation of a test battery. In F. Stachowiak (ed.) *Developments in the Assessment and Rehabilitation of Brain-damaged Patients*. Tübingen: G. Narr-Verlag.

Author Index

Subject Index

For Product Safety Concerns and Information please contact our EU representative GPSR@taylorandfrancis.com
Taylor & Francis Verlag GmbH, Kaufingerstraße 24, 80331 München, Germany

www.ingramcontent.com/pod-product-compliance
Ingram Content Group UK Ltd.
Pitfield, Milton Keynes, MK11 3LW, UK
UKHW022007180926
475701UK00003B/235

* 9 7 8 0 4 1 5 6 5 3 5 6 5 *